D0292758

VIRGINIA & MARYLAND

9th Edition

**Where to Stay and Eat
for All Budgets**

**Must See Sights
and Local Secrets**

Ratings You Can Trust

Fodor's Travel Publications   New York, Toronto, London, Sydney, Auckland
www.fodors.com

FODOR'S VIRGINIA & MARYLAND
Editor: Caroline Trefler

Editorial Production: Evangelos Vasilakis
Editorial Contributors: Loretta Chilcoat, Andrew Collins, Matthew Cordell, Denise Leto, John Kelly, Kevin and Erica Myatt, Norman Renouf, Sam Sessa, CiCi Williamson
Maps: David Lindroth *cartographer;* Bob Blake and Rebecca Baer, *map editors*
Design: Fabrizio La Rocca, *creative director;* Guido Caroti, *art director;* Tina Maleney, *designer;* Moon Sun Kim, *cover designer;* Melanie Marin, *senior picture editor*
Cover Photo (Williamsburg): Henryk Kaiser/eStock Photo
Production/Manufacturing: Robert B. Shields

COPYRIGHT

Ninth Edition

ISBN 978-1-4000-1749-2

ISSN 1075-0711

SPECIAL SALES

This book is available for special discounts for bulk purchases for sales promotions or premiums. Special editions, including personalized covers, excerpts of existing books, and corporate imprints, can be created in large quantities for special needs. For more information, write to Special Markets/Premium Sales, 1745 Broadway, MD 6-2, New York, New York 10019, or e-mail specialmarkets@randomhouse.com.

AN IMPORTANT TIP & AN INVITATION

Although all prices, opening times, and other details in this book are based on information supplied to us at press time, changes occur all the time in the travel world, and Fodor's cannot accept responsibility for facts that become outdated or for inadvertent errors or omissions. So **always confirm information when it matters,** especially if you're making a detour to visit a specific place. Your experiences—positive and negative—matter to us. If we have missed or misstated something, **please write to us.** We follow up on all suggestions. Contact the Virginia & Maryland editor at editors@fodors.com or c/o Fodor's at 1745 Broadway, New York, New York 10019.

PRINTED IN THE UNITED STATES OF AMERICA

10 9 8 7 6 5 4 3 2 1

Be a Fodor's Correspondent

Your opinion matters. It matters to us. It matters to your fellow Fodor's travelers, too. And we'd like to hear it. In fact, we *need* to hear it.

When you share your experiences and opinions, you become an active member of the Fodor's community. That means we'll not only use your feedback to make our books better, but we'll publish your names and comments whenever possible. Throughout our guides, look for "Word of Mouth," excerpts of your unvarnished feedback.

Here's how you can help improve Fodor's for all of us.

Tell us when we're right. We rely on local writers to give you an insider's perspective. But our writers and staff editors—who are the best in the business—depend on you. Your positive feedback is a vote to renew our recommendations for the next edition.

Tell us when we're wrong. We're proud that we update most of our guides every year. But we're not perfect. Things change. Hotels cut services. Museums change hours. Charming cafés lose charm. If our writer didn't quite capture the essence of a place, tell us how you'd do it differently. If any of our descriptions are inaccurate or inadequate, we'll incorporate your changes in the next edition and will correct factual errors at fodors.com *immediately*.

Tell us what to include. You probably have had fantastic travel experiences that aren't yet in Fodor's. Why not share them with a community of like-minded travelers? Maybe you chanced upon a beach or bistro or B&B that you don't want to keep to yourself. Tell us why we should include it. And share your discoveries and experiences with everyone directly at fodors.com. Your input may lead us to add a new listing or highlight a place we cover with a "Highly Recommended" star or with our highest rating, "Fodor's Choice."

Give us your opinion instantly at our feedback center at www.fodors.com/feedback. You may also e-mail editors@fodors.com with the subject line "Virginia & Maryland Editor." Or send your nominations, comments, and complaints by mail to Virginia & Maryland Editor, Fodor's, 1745 Broadway, New York, NY 10019.

You and travelers like you are the heart of the Fodor's community. Make our community richer by sharing your experiences. Be a Fodor's correspondent.

Happy Traveling!

Tim Jarrell, Publisher

CONTENTS

ABOUT THIS BOOK

Our Ratings

Sometimes you find terrific travel experiences and sometimes they just find you. But usually the burden is on you to select the right combination of experiences. That's where our ratings come in.

As travelers we've all discovered a place so wonderful that its worthiness is obvious. And sometimes that place is so experiential that superlatives don't do it justice: you just have to be there to know. These sights, properties, and experiences get our highest rating, **Fodor's Choice**, indicated by orange stars throughout this book.

Black stars highlight sights and properties we deem **Highly Recommended**, places that our writers, editors, and readers praise again and again for consistency and excellence.

By default, there's another category: any place we include in this book is by definition worth your time, unless we say otherwise. And we will.

Disagree with any of our choices? Care to nominate a place or suggest that we rate one more highly? Visit our feedback center at www.fodors.com/feedback.

Budget Well

Hotel and restaurant price categories from ¢ to $$$$ are defined in the opening pages of each chapter. For attractions, we always give standard adult admission fees; reductions are usually available for children, students, and senior citizens. Want to pay with plastic? **AE, D, DC, MC, V** following restaurant and hotel listings indicate if American Express, Discover, Diners Club, MasterCard, and Visa are accepted.

Restaurants

Unless we state otherwise, restaurants are open for lunch and dinner daily. We mention dress only when there's a specific requirement and reservations only when they're essential or not accepted—it's always best to book ahead.

Hotels

Hotels have private bath, phone, TV, and air-conditioning and operate on the European Plan (aka EP, meaning without meals), unless we specify that they use the Continental Plan (CP, with a continental breakfast), Breakfast Plan (BP, with a full breakfast), or Modified American Plan (MAP, with breakfast and dinner) or are all-inclusive (including all meals and most activities). We always

list facilities but not whether you'll be charged an extra fee to use them, so when pricing accommodations, find out what's included.

Many Listings

- ★ Fodor's Choice
- ★ Highly recommended
- ⊠ Physical address
- ✛ Directions
- ⬠ Mailing address
- ☎ Telephone
- ⎙ Fax
- ⊕ On the Web
- ✉ E-mail
- 🎫 Admission fee
- ☉ Open/closed times
- ▶ Start of walk/itinerary
- Ⓜ Metro stations
- ▭ Credit cards

Hotels & Restaurants

- 🏨 Hotel
- ⮑ Number of rooms
- ⬧ Facilities
- ❍ Meal plans
- ✕ Restaurant
- ⬟ Reservations
- 🏛 Dress code
- ↘ Smoking
- ⛿ BYOB
- ✕🏨 Hotel with restaurant that warrants a visit

Outdoors

- 🏌 Golf
- ⛺ Camping

Other

- ☕ Family-friendly
- 🔢 Contact information
- ⇨ See also
- ⊠ Branch address
- ☞ Take note

WASHINGTON, D.C.	Although it's technically distinct from Virginia and Maryland, the District is the urban heart of the region, not to mention the political hub of the United States. The roughly 65-square-mi city contains many of the nation's seminal museums, political buildings, monuments, and cultural institutions, to say nothing of a sophisticated restaurant and nightlife scene and a bounty of luxury hotels and alluring historic inns. Despite its international vibe, D.C. can suffer a bit from a sense of political provincialism—it can seem like everyone in the city is obsessed with deal-making, lobbying, and hobnobbing. But it's also very much a city on the up, and a number of once-forlorn neighborhoods have experienced a rebirth in the past decade or so. You may want to plan your visit to avoid holidays and summer weekends, when the streets here teem with tourists, but it would be a shame to pass through without touring at least a few of the phenomenal attractions.
NORTHERN VIRGINIA	Much more than a mere satellite of Washington, D.C., northern Virginia is a repository of Colonial and Civil War history as well as a vibrant—if sprawling—clutch of corporate campuses, suburban neighborhoods, and mid- to upscale retail and dining centers. Fringed by the Potomac River and the Blue Ridge Mountains, the area offers plenty of opportunities for recreation, plus some fine wineries and the famed Wolf Trap Farm Performing Arts Center. Alexandria, with its urbane Old Town, holds a substantial number of historic buildings, churches, and museums as well as a bumper crop of great restaurants and hotels. Arlington, Fairfax, and Loudoun counties are sprinkled with vital historic sites and monuments, such as Mount Vernon, Arlington Cemetery, and Manassas battlefield (aka "Bull Run"). Loudoun County is also Virginia's quintessential horse country, anchored by such handsome towns as Middleburg and Leesburg.
D.C.'S MARYLAND SUBURBS	A sizeable, relatively affluent, tract of suburbia whose residents often identify more with nearby D.C. than with the rest of Maryland, Montgomery and Prince George's counties do have some notable draws, including the Washington Redskins, Six Flags America, the College Park Aviation Museum, and Strathmore Hall Arts Center. And the area isn't entirely built up—prominent great green spaces include the C&O Canal National Historical Park and Piscataway Park. Diners from both sides of the Potomac River head to Bethesda and

Silver Spring to sample cuisine from all over the world, especially the superb Asian fare.

CENTRAL & WESTERN VIRGINIA	Mountains rule the horizons in dramatic interior Virginia, a favorite getaway for urbanites and suburbanites seeking crisp and cool air, stunning scenery, old-fashioned mountain music, and outdoorsy activities. The dapper college town of Charlottesville is the area's cultural center, an excellent base from which to explore Thomas Jefferson's venerable Monticello estate, Shenandoah National Park, and George Washington National Forest. The Shenandoah Valley, once the home of early European settlers and later a Civil War thoroughfare, rests between the Blue Ridge and the Allegheny mountains and contains the up-and-coming artsy town of Staunton as well as the charming college community of Lexington. Farther south, inside a bowl-shape depression encircled by bluish ridgelines, is bustling Roanoke, with several fine museums. To the west and south of that bustling city are the New River Valley and the gorge-incised Appalachian Plateau, from whose hollows old-time mountain music still echoes.
RICHMOND, FREDERICKSBURG & THE NORTHERN NECK	Richmond, capital of the commonwealth and former capital of the Confederacy, is not only full of historic sites but also one of the South's preeminent art cities and a major industrial center. It's pierced by the James River, and you can white-water raft within view of downtown skyscrapers. Among its appealing restored neighborhoods is the turn-of-the-20th-century Fan District, the cobblestone Shockoe Bottom area with its many bars and restaurants, and offbeat Carytown, known for its boutiques and coffeehouses. At Petersburg, south of Richmond, the Confederacy made its last stand. In Fredericksburg, midway between Richmond and Washington, D.C., are historic 18th- and 19th-century homes, antiques shops, and Civil War battlefields. The rural peninsula of the Northern Neck extends east from Fredericksburg to the Chesapeake, rewarding visitors with sylvan vistas and such notable historic sites as George Washington's birthplace and Stratford Hall Plantation.
WILLIAMSBURG & HAMPTON ROADS	Colonial Williamsburg, a re-created 18th-century American city complete with historic buildings, working shops, and costumed interpreters, is Virginia's most-visited attraction and one of the world's most impressive living-history museums. But this is just the tip of the iceberg when it comes to exploring the area's rich heritage, which is also celebrated at Historic

Jamestowne, where the first permanent English settlers made their homes; Jamestown Settlement, a re-creation of the original ships and fort; and Yorktown, site of the final major battle in the American War of Independence. Even if your time in Virginia is limited, try to make it to this fascinating area. Hampton Roads—the channel where the James, Elizabeth, and Nansemond rivers meet—is surrounded by both small and larger towns that include the historic settlements of Hampton and Portsmouth, and Newport News, builder of the navy's biggest nuclear ships. The biggest communities in the area are the port city of Norfolk, which has enjoyed a laudable renaissance in recent years and contains a number of worthwhile cultural attractions, and the busy resort town of Virginia Beach, the state's largest city, which is home to dozens of seaside resorts and beach condos as well as an excellent aquarium.

BALTIMORE

An industrial powerhouse that received relatively little attention as a tourist destination for many years, Baltimore has been beautifully revitalized and now ranks among one of the Eastern Seaboard's best urban getaways, with attractions geared to families and sophisticated adults. Kids love the lively Inner Harbor, with its constellation of draws that include the National Aquarium, American Visionary Art Museum, Baltimore Maritime Museum, Maryland Science Center, Fort McHenry, and various sightseeing boat tours. The many restaurants and shops in this area are touristy, to be sure, but great fun, and don't miss nearby Camden Yards, home to baseball's Baltimore Orioles, when there's a game in town. Adults are drawn more to Baltimore's hipper areas, such as historic Fells Point, the center of shipbuilding in the 18th and 19th centuries, and Federal Hill, with its art galleries, antiques shops, coffeehouses, and cobblestone streets. If you're a fan of city life, don't miss this still up-and-coming metropolis.

FREDERICK & WESTERN MARYLAND

Rugged, scenic mountains dominate the landscape of western Maryland, which isn't as dramatic in appearance or as popular with tourists as interior Virginia—but this can be a good reason to spend time here, as there will be fewer crowds to compete with. The mountains frame such small cities as Frederick and Cumberland, which each have their share of attractions, parks, and—especially in the case of Frederick—swanky restaurants and quaint inns. The region is also marked by pastoral valleys, verdant state forests, and intriguing historic

WHAT'S WHERE

parks. One of the top attractions in western Maryland is the Western Maryland Scenic Railroad, whose scenic train excursions afford great views of all this impressive scenery. Once crossed by the nation's first pioneers on their westward journey, these mountains are rich with remnants of an earlier time; today you can still hike along what was once the towpath for the Chesapeake & Ohio (C&O) Canal—the region's main trade route in the mid-19th century.

ANNAPOLIS & SOUTHERN MARYLAND

Weekenders from D.C., Baltimore, and the surrounding 'burbs have long headed to regal Annapolis and the many charming towns that make up southern Maryland, drawn by some of the Mid-Atlantic's most inviting country inns and taverns. Maryland traces its origins to the Chesapeake Bay's Western Shore, where English Colonists arrived in the 1600s. Today, Annapolis, the state capital, is rich with Colonial architecture and history—it's home to the dashing buildings that make up the venerable U.S. Naval Academy, as well as William Paca House and Garden. Tobacco fields, once the livelihood of early Colonists, still blanket the gentle landscape of the southern part of the state, although more sparsely than before. Here in Calvert County you can visit quiet hamlets like Chesapeake Beach and Solomons. Farther south, St. Mary's County was settled in 1634 and is anchored by historic St. Mary's City.

THE EASTERN SHORE

Separated from mainland Maryland by the Chesapeake Bay and bounded on the east by the Atlantic Ocean, this peninsula is a land apart, ideal whether you love sandy ocean beaches or the offbeat, historic villages that dot eastern Chesapeake Bay. Marshy wildlife refuges, isolated islands, and rivers traversed by fishermen and sailors set the stage for a quieter way of life along the bay. Don't miss the enchanting town of St. Michaels, a former shipbuilding hub that's now rife with fine inns and restaurants. At the ocean, beware the intense summer crowds of Ocean City, a classic beach resort with a bit of a honky-tonk flavor and plenty of fun amusements. Virginia's Eastern Shore, which extends south from Maryland and is also accessible from Virginia Beach via the Chesapeake Bay Bridge-Tunnel, is a largely undisturbed area of tiny towns and abundant wildlife, including the wild "ponies" at Assateague Island and Chincoteague Island national seashores.

WHEN TO GO

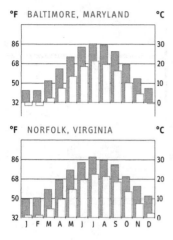

°F BALTIMORE, MARYLAND °C

86 — 30
68 — 20
50 — 10
32 — 0

°F NORFOLK, VIRGINIA °C

86 — 30
68 — 20
50 — 10
32 — 0
J F M A M J J A S O N D

Spring brings horse racing to Baltimore, northern Virginia, and the Virginia Piedmont; the Preakness Stakes is highly festive, but many point-to-points and steeplechases are more interesting to watch and visit. Public gardens are in full bloom; garden clubs conduct tours of private properties throughout both states. In Shenandoah National Park, Skyline Drive overlooks a blooming panorama. If you happen to travel to Baltimore in early May, don't miss Sherwood Gardens, known for hundreds of thousands of tulips, azaleas, pansies, and blossoming trees.

Summer draws the largest numbers of visitors, particularly at Virginia Beach, Ocean City, and other resorts on the bay and the ocean. Baltimore's Inner Harbor can be thronged with tourists and yachters. On warm days the promenade is filled with visitors from around the world.

Autumn brings spectacular colors in the foliage of the rolling Piedmont region of Virginia and the Catoctin Mountains west of Baltimore; the temperatures become more comfortable for hiking and biking. Equestrian events resume, and in Maryland the sailboat and powerboat shows in Annapolis and the Waterfowl Festival in Easton attract thousands of people in October and November.

Winter temperatures may make it too cold to swim, yet the major resorts continue to draw vacationers with seasonal peace and quiet at much lower off-season rates. Other travelers come for romantic seclusion at a B&B. Virginia was the first Southern state to develop skiing commercially, and now both downhill and cross-country skiing are popular activities at resorts in the Shenandoah Valley and western Maryland.

Climate

The best time to visit is in spring and fall, when the temperatures are cooler. The summers in both states are very hot and humid, though the mountainous regions tend to be 10 to 15 degrees cooler. Winters are rainy and damp, though the region does occasionally get blanketed with heavy snow.

🚩 **Weather Channel Connection** ☎ 900/932–8437 95¢ per minute from a Touch-Tone phone ⊕ www.weather.com.

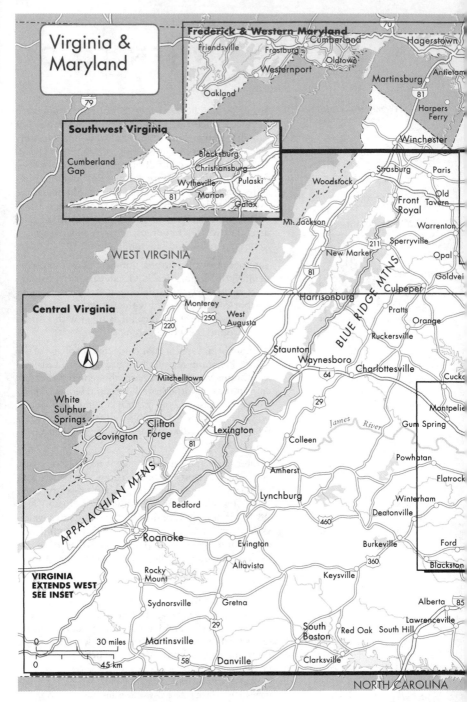

Virginia & Maryland

Frederick & Western Maryland

Friendsville • Frostburg • Cumberland • Hagerstown
Westernport • Oldtown
Oakland • Martinsburg • Antietam
81
Harpers Ferry
Winchester

79

Southwest Virginia

Cumberland Gap
Blacksburg
Christiansburg
Wytheville • Pulaski
Marion
81
Galax
Mt. Jackson

Strasburg • Paris
Old Tavern
Front Royal
Warrenton
Woodstock
211 Sperryville
New Market • Opal
Goldvei
81
Culpeper

WEST VIRGINIA

BLUE RIDGE MTNS

Central Virginia

Monterey • Harrisonburg
250 West Augusta • Pratts • Orange
220 Ruckersville
Staunton
Waynesboro • Charlottesville
Mitchelltown
64 Cucko
Montpelie
White Sulphur Springs
29
Clifton Forge • Lexington
Gum Spring
Covington
81 Colleen
Powhatan
James River
Amherst
Flatrock
APPALACHIAN MTNS
Bedford
Lynchburg • Winterham
460 Deatonville
Roanoke • Evington • Burkeville • Ford
Rocky Mount • Altavista
360 Blackston
VIRGINIA EXTENDS WEST SEE INSET
Keysville
Sydnorsville • Gretna
29 Alberta 85
0   30 miles
Martinsville
South Boston • Red Oak • South Hill • Lawrenceville
0   45 km
58 Danville • Clarksville

NORTH CAROLINA

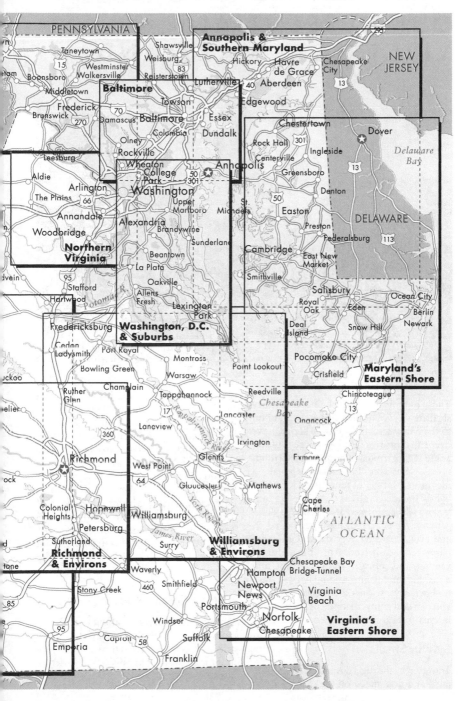

QUINTESSENTIAL VIRGINIA & MARYLAND

The Crab Craze

Those humble, bottom-feeding, predatory shellfish known as blue crabs, so common to the Maryland and Virginia shore, have over the centuries developed a reputation as the region's most famous—and scrumptious—delectable. Local crabs appear on menus in a variety of tantalizing forms: as lightly breaded crab cakes, sautéed in butter and garlic, steamed and dipped in a ginger-soy sauce, served over eggs Benedict, and even scattered over pizza. Crabs are harvested locally from April through November, and concerns of over-fishing and a steadily diminishing annual harvest have led lawmakers to pass strict regulations, but you can still enjoy all kinds of crabby fare in area restaurants throughout the year.

Sylvan Strolls

Traversed by the rugged Appalachian Mountains and dominated on the east by a verdant coastal plain, Virginia and Maryland offer some of the best hiking in the East. Along the shore, you may spy wild horses as you wander the terrain of Chincoteague and Assateague islands. But it's the mountainous west that so delights ardent outdoors enthusiasts: You can enjoy the scenery of Virginia and Maryland on a long and challenging hike through Shenandoah National Park or Catoctin Mountain Park, and nearly 600 mi of the famed Appalachian Trail pass through both states. And casual walkers will find dozens of easy but visually rewarding trails lacing the entire region.

History Comes Alive

Virginia and Maryland, along with Washington, D.C., have always played a crucial role in U.S. history. Even the smallest communities typically have historical societies, house-museums, and centuries-old inns

If you want to get a sense of culture in Virginia and Maryland and indulge in some of the region's pleasures, start by familiarizing yourself with the rituals of daily life. These are a few highlights—things you can take part in with relative ease.

and restaurants brimming with character but a number of more prominent attractions and sites truly shaped the ethic, spirit, and personality of the nation. In Virginia you can tour the homes of Presidents (William) Harrison, Jefferson, Madison, Monroe, Taylor, Tyler, Van Buren, Washington, and Wilson; the remains of America's earliest permanent settlement at Jamestown; the living-history experience that is Colonial Williamsburg; and such pivotal Civil War sites as Yorktown, Richmond, Appomattox Courthouse, and Manassas. In Washington, D.C., history abounds as you tour the National Mall with its monuments and political institutions, and Maryland is home to the venerable U.S. Naval Academy, Fort McHenry (of "Star-Spangled Banner" fame), and Antietam National Battlefield. Especially in recent decades, these key historic attractions have reinvented the way they interpret the past, with high-tech interactive exhibits, dynamic reenactments, and riveting multimedia presentations.

Vintage Virginia

Although more than a few East Coast states are now producing superb wine these days, Virginia stands out both for its volume (more than 100 wineries produce some 300,000 cases annually) and quality. You'll find plenty of excellent restaurants in Virginia and the neighboring areas serving vintages from some of the state's most-respected producers. The real joy in sampling Virginia wine, however, comes with actually visiting the vineyards and tasting rooms and chatting with the proprietors. Many of these facilities occupy scenic farms. You can also soak up the spirit of the viticulture at events and festivals, such as late April's James River Wine Festival in Richmond, and late May's Annual Virginia Wine & Craft Festival in Front Royal. (Check www.virginiawines.org for a full listing of the over 300 yearly wine events in Maryland).

IF YOU LIKE

Great Battlefields

Some of the fiercest and most pivotal battles ever staged on American soil took place in Maryland and Virginia, including campaigns during the American Revolution, the War of 1812, and—most famously (or infamously)—the Civil War. The U.S. National Park Service operates many of these battlefield sites as living-history museums, with carefully preserved or reconstructed fortifications, interpretive centers that show poignant films and exhibits, and a wide range of narrated walking and driving tours. There are also battle reenactments held at many of these sites. You don't have to be a history buff to appreciate the significance of these seminal venues—at several of them, the very course of U.S. history was determined.

- At Maryland's **Antietam National Battlefield**, the bloodiest fight of the Civil War occurred in 1862. When it was over, more than 23,000 soldiers had either died or been wounded.

- From Baltimore's brick-and-earthen **Fort McHenry** during the War of 1812, Francis Scott Key penned "The Star-Spangled Banner" while the British bombarded the beleaguered city.

- No tour of Civil War sites is complete without a stop at **Manassas National Battlefield Park** (aka "Bull Run") in Northern Virginia. This battlefield hosted two of the most important victories for Confederate troops.

- When French and American troops successfully compelled Lord Cornwallis to surrender at **Yorktown Battlefield**, near historic Williamsburg, the Revolutionary War drew to a dramatic close.

Swank Country Inns

The tranquil yet increasingly sophisticated mountain towns and bayside villages of Virginia and Maryland have some of the most sumptuous country inns in America: accommodations that are destinations in and of themselves. Many of these princely retreats boast talented chefs turning out innovative, regionally driven cuisine and it's not uncommon to find great fly-fishing, hiking, and golfing on-site or just down the road. Some inns even have posh spas. Here are a few places around the region where you're sure to experience over-the-top luxury, but in a laid-back, countrified setting.

- **Antrim 1844** appeals to fans of history and romance—the supremely elegant antebellum mansion has 29 plush rooms and suites and is 10 mi south of Gettysburg, near Frederick, Maryland.

- Since 1766 the **Homestead** has stood as one of the Mid-Atlantic's most distinguished addresses. This lavish 15,000-acre resort has every amenity and activity imaginable, from golfing to skiing to spa-going, and its several restaurants are top-notch.

- Acclaimed chef and co-owner Patrick O'Connell has helped make the **Inn at Little Washington,** in central Virginia, a favorite of top celebs and politicos, who appreciate this legendary inn as much for its fabulous seven-course dinners as for the lavish decor.

- Set on 226 sylvan acres on Maryland's Eastern Shore, the **Kent Manor Inn & Restaurant** earns kudos for its elegant rooms, as well as the fresh-caught seafood served in the romantic restaurant.

Taking to the Water

Given that Virginia and Maryland fringe the ocean, are traversed by countless rivers, and contain one of the nation's largest bays, it's no wonder that one of the best ways to appreciate it is from a boat, whether a charter fishing yacht or a nimble kayak. Companies renting all types of boats and offering a wide range of tours and excursions exist all around the region, and in the mountains you'll find exhilarating whitewater rafting. Even taking a ride on a tour boat in Baltimore's Inner Harbor along the Potomac River in Washington, D.C., offers a fabulous scenery. Here are a few great ways to take to the water in and around Virginia and Maryland.

- **American Rover Sailing Tours,** in Norfolk, offers fascinating tours of Virginia's Hampton Roads waterways on a 135-foot topsail schooner.

- In Maryland you can spend a full day boating around the Eastern Shore and admiring a dozen lighthouses during one of the excursions available through **Chesapeake Bay Lighthouse Tours.**

- Fans of deep-sea fishing need look no farther than Maryland's **Ocean City Fishing Center,** which has more than 30 vessels providing charter sportfishing trips to catch blue marlin, wahoo, and big-eye tuna.

- Right in Virginia's bustling capital city, **Richmond Raft** offers hair-raising whitewater trips along the frothy Class III and IV rapids of the James River.

- For an unusual view of Washington, D.C.'s monuments and prominent buildings, take one of the kayaking tours on the Potomac offered by the **Thompson Boat Center** in Georgetown.

National Parks & Forests

From the mountains to the seashore, a number of stunning—sometimes historic—national parks are found in Virginia and Maryland. The parks provide wonderful opportunities for scenic country drives and bike rides, overnight camping or stays in rustic park-service lodges, and up-close encounters with myriad wildlife, from black bears to bald eagles to wild horses. The famous Appalachian Trail cuts a rugged path through both states, and virtually every major park and forest in the region offers a wealth of rigorous hikes and shorter nature walks. Here are some must-sees.

- A 37-mi-long barrier island on the border of Virginia and Maryland, **Assateague Island National Seashore** is a good place to find pristine beaches, wild ponies, deer, and 300 species of birds.

- **Blackwater National Wildlife Refuge,** southeast of Annapolis, is one of the East Coast's premier spots for viewing migratory waterfowl, bald eagles, and ospreys.

- **Catoctin Mountain Park** in Maryland is one of the somewhat smaller gems of the national park system, the site of the secretly situated Camp David presidential retreat, and home to 20 mi of scenic hikes.

- The Potomac River, the waterway that divides Maryland and Virginia, is the route of the 185-mi linear park, the **C&O Canal National Historical Park.** It's a favorite with hikers and bicyclists.

- In Virginia's Shenandoah Mountains lies the stunning Skyline Drive, a celebrated 105-mi route through **Shenandoah National Park.**

GREAT ITINERARIES

THE BEST OF VIRGINIA, MARYLAND & WASHINGTON, D.C.

There's much to see in this geographically and socially diverse region, but in 10 days it's possible to get a genuine sense of Virginia, Maryland, and D.C., and see some of the best attractions in each region, from sea to city to mountains.

Days 1 & 2: Washington, D.C.

You could spend the entire 10 days of this itinerary poking around the nation's capital city without running out of things to see and do. With two days, try the following strategy: spend the first day exploring the National Mall and checking out a handful of the Smithsonian museums and the major monuments—another must in this neighborhood is the U.S. Holocaust Memorial Museum. Fans of political intrigue might want to tour the White House or the Capitol. On your second day, avoid the touristy areas and opt instead to venture about some of the city's several intriguing residential neighborhoods, such as Dupont Circle, U Street, Adams-Morgan, or Georgetown. Each abounds with chic shops, funky galleries, and handsome Victorian town houses. You'll also find many of the city's coolest hotels in these parts (the Hotel Rouge, for example) as well as restaurants serving everything from haute contemporary fare to authentic Ethiopian, Thai, and soul food. Culture-vultures shouldn't miss the Phillips Collection modern-art museum in Dupont Circle, and nature-lovers should spend a little time in 1,600 Rock Creek Park, which divides Georgetown and Dupont Circle.

Day 3: Baltimore

On Day 3 drive up I–95 or Route 295 to Baltimore, the geographical and cultural center of Maryland; it's a must-see for first-time visitors and is a striking contrast to Washington, D.C., which is somewhat more formal and tourism-driven. Take in some of the major sights that are clustered around the colorful Inner Harbor, such as the National Aquarium of Baltimore and the American Visionary Art Museum. And be sure to save at least a little time, perhaps in the evening, checking out the great shopping and dining in two historic neighborhoods, Mount Vernon and Fells Point.

Day 4: Annapolis & Solomons

On the morning of Day 4 head southeast from Baltimore via I–97 to experience Maryland's Colonial past in Annapolis, the state capital, which is also home to the impressive grounds of the vaunted U.S. Naval Academy. Harry Browne's, with its seasonal sidewalk seating, is a great bet for lunch. Mid-afternoon, follow Route 2 into rural and scenic southern Maryland, eventually winding your way to the lovely town of Solomons, a longtime favorite getaway for folks who love boating and Chesapeake Bay. The Back Creek Inn is a lovely place to spend the night.

Day 5: Alexandria

The morning of Day 5 head south to the historic village of St. Mary's County, where you can view the ongoing archaeological and reconstruction work related to this area's early English settlement from 1634. Then head north up Route 5 and west on I–495 to reach Alexandria, an excellent base for exploring northern Virginia's top sites, such as Arlington Cemetery, Mount

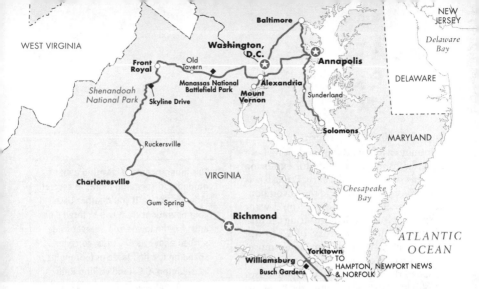

Vernon (George Washington's home), and Manassas National Battlefield Park. Alexandria contains a charming, historic Old Town district and numerous fine restaurants and inns. Try to visit Christ Church if you have a chance—both George Washington and Robert E. Lee were pewholders at this 1773 Georgian-inspired church. And if you're an art lover, don't miss the Torpedo Factory Art Center, where more than 160 artisans work and show their wares. For accommodations the Morrison House hotels offers the most stylish rooms in town.

Days 6 & 7: Charlottesville

From Alexandria head west on I–495 and then I–66, exiting at Front Royal and then driving along Skyline Drive through beautiful Shenandoah National Park. Keep in mind that it can take a while to drive along this meandering scenic road, with its 35 mph speed limit. At U.S. 33, travel east to U.S. 29, and then south to the lively and inviting university town of Charlottesville. Here you can find a number of hip restaurants as well as such appealing lodging options as Keswick Hall at Monticello and the more affordable Silver Thatch Inn. Use "C-ville" as a base to explore Thomas Jefferson's plantation home, Monticello; James Madison's estate, Montpelier; and

the regal campus of the University of Virginia. If you have time, consider checking out one of the fine wineries in the general vicinity, such as Barboursville, which offers excellent tours and has historic ties to Thomas Jefferson.

Day 8: Richmond

Drive east on I–64 from Charlottesville to reach Virginia's capital, Richmond, which is home to several fine museums, Civil War sites, and historic neighborhoods. An especially appealing section for a stroll is the Victorian Fan District, home to the excellent Virginia Museum of Fine Arts and close to the grand Jefferson Hotel. Richmond is a short drive from Petersburg and Pamplin Historical Park, where General Lee's defenses were routed during the Civil War—history buffs should budget time for an excursion to this area, while out doorsy types might want to plan a white-water rafting trip on the exciting James River, whose rapids pass right through downtown Richmond. In the evening, venture into the revitalized Shockoe Bottom and Shockoe Slip areas downtown, whose cobblestone streets are lined with cool restaurants and lively bars and lounges. Europa, a Mediterranean-inspired tapas bar, is one of the best.

GREAT ITINERARIES

Days 9 & 10: Williamsburg

Continue east from Richmond along I–64 to Williamsburg, your base for exploring such historic sites as the early English settlements of Jamestown and the Revolutionary battlefield at Yorktown. You'll want to spend at least a full day touring the museums and living history of Colonial Williamsburg, with its many house-museums staffed by costumed interpreters. Plan to spend the night in the Colonial Houses of Williamsburg, which offer the most authentically historic lodging experience. If you're traveling with kids, budget some time to enjoy the wild rides at nearby Busch Gardens. On your final day, if you still have energy and time, you might want to continue along I–64 east to the Hampton Roads area to spend a little time at the Mariners' Museum in Newport News or the Chrysler Museum of Art in the up-and-coming city of Norfolk. You could also continue directly to the resorts of Virginia Beach, or drive up U.S. 13, which affords you access to both Virginia's and Maryland's Eastern Shore regions.

TIPS

❶ This itinerary entails covering a lot of ground and spending nights at several different hotels. If you'd rather base your operations from two or three cities and visit the towns and attractions described above as day trips, consider spending the first three or four nights in Washington, D.C. (and visiting Baltimore, Annapolis, St. Mary's City, and Alexandria as daytime excursions), and then the final five or six nights hunkered down in Richmond or Williamsburg, from where you can easily explore the rest of central Virginia during your mornings and afternoons.

❷ This itinerary works anytime of year, but you'll battle significant crowds and possibly sultry weather in summer; you can take advantage of the most delightful scenery and weather in spring (when flowers bloom in radiant colors) and fall (when the foliage of Shenandoah Park is magnificent).

A CIVIL WAR TOUR

Civil War sites are among the most compelling reasons to visit Virginia and Maryland, and the Civil War itinerary below covers the standout attractions. When Virginia seceded from the Union in 1861, it doomed itself to becoming a major battleground; thus, much of this tour is in Virginia, with a brief foray into Maryland.

Day 1: Hampton
Start your tour at Hampton, on the Virginia Peninsula, where the Union general George McClellan launched his drive toward Richmond. The Hampton History Museum contains excellent exhibits on Civil War ironclad ships. Across the channel is Fort Monroe—the Union stronghold in which the president of the Confederacy, Jefferson Davis, was imprisoned.

Day 2: Richmond
On Day 2 drive northwest on I–64 up the peninsula to Richmond's Museum and White House of the Confederacy and the Richmond National Battlefield Park Visitor Center. Also see the Virginia Historical Society Museum of Virginia History, which has some 800 pieces of Confederate weaponry. Proceed 20 mi south on I–95 to Petersburg, the city that was under an extended siege by Grant's army. Visit 1,500-acre Petersburg National Battlefield, the Siege Museum, and Pamplin Historical Park—which commemorates an important Union attack on Lee's supposedly impenetrable defense line—before returning to spend the night in Richmond.

Days 3 & 4: Fredericksburg
For Days 3 and 4, proceed north from Richmond up I–95 to Fredericksburg, which has blocks of historic Civil War–era homes and a Confederate Cemetery with the remains of more than 2,000 soldiers. Detour to see the four battlefields at Fredericksburg/Spotsylvania National Military Park, then venture an hour outside of town to see Stratford Hall plantation, where Robert E. Lee was born.

Days 5 & 6: Northern Virginia
For Days 5 and 6, base yourself around Arlington or Fairfax, which puts you close to the key attractions in this area—from Fredericksburg, you reach the area by heading north up I–95. Spend one day touring Manassas National Battlefield Park (aka "Bull Run"), site of two important Confederate victories—it's here that Gen. Thomas Jonathan Jackson earned the nickname "Stonewall," when he and his brigade "stood like a stone wall." On your second day, head to Arlington National Cemetery and Arlington House (Lee's home for 30 years before the Union army confiscated it and turned the grounds into the cemetery).

Day 7: Frederick
From northern Virginia, head north on I–270 into Maryland. North of Frederick, catch Route 34 out of Boonsboro and follow it to the Antietam National Battlefield, site of the bloodiest single day of Civil War fighting (more than 23,000 troops were killed or wounded during the gruesome engagement). In Frederick, where you can spend the night, is the National Museum of Civil War Medicine with its 3,000 artifacts and 2 mi southeast of Frederick is Monocacy National Battlefield, where Union troops thwarted a Confederate invasion of Washington, D.C.

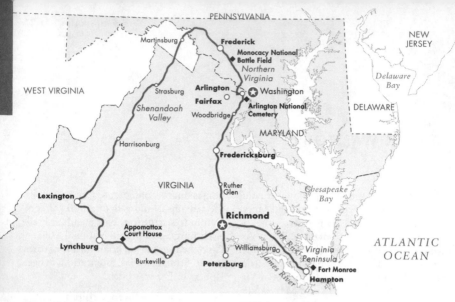

Days 8 & 9: Lexington

From western Maryland follow I-81 south back into Virginia and through the Shenandoah Valley to reach Lexington, a quaint and scenic college town (home to Washington and Lee University). Visit the Lee Chapel and Museum, where Lee is buried, and the Virginia Military Institute Museum, which has displays on Stonewall Jackson.

Day 10: Lynchburg

From Lexington, drive east on U.S. 60, then south on U.S. 29 to reach Lynchburg, a good place to spend the night and tour Monument Terrace, a poignant Civil War memorial that comprises 139 limestone and granite steps ascending to the Old City Courthouse.

Day 11: Richmond

On your final day return to Richmond to spend some additional time exploring any of the city's Civil War–related attractions. En route from Lynchburg stop at Appomattox Court House, which you reach from Lynchburg by driving east on U.S. 460. Here Lee formally surrendered to Grant, thus officially ending the Civil War. The park here consists of some 27 original structures, and the self-guided tour is exceptionally good. From here it's a leisurely and scenic drive east on U.S. 460 and then northeast on U.S. 360 back to the state capital.

TIPS

❶ One of the most compelling times to visit a Civil War battlefield is when volunteers are staging a battle reenactment. Thousands of Civil War history enthusiasts participate in these events, which often last for several days. For information on upcoming reenactments, log on to www.civilwarnews.com.

❷ This Civil War itinerary requires plenty of driving and entails a number of different overnight stops. If you prefer to limit the number of times you change accommodations, consider basing your trip out of Alexandria or Arlington for the northern Virginia and western Maryland attractions, and in Richmond for the central and eastern Virginia sites.

❸ Although it's not generally thought of as a major stop for Civil War buffs, Washington, D.C., does have a handful of relevant attractions, including the Capitol, whose expensive construction Lincoln defended by calling it a "sign we intend the Union shall go on." Also, Dupont Circle is named for Civil War hero Samuel F. Dupont.

ON THE CALENDAR

ONGOING Late April– early May	**Virginia Waterfront International Arts Festival** ☎ 757/282–2822 ⊕ www.vafest.com showcases performances by the Virginia Symphony, Virginia Opera, and out-of-state orchestras and artists.
Late July– early August	The two-week-long **Virginia Highlands Festival** ☎ 800/435–3440 or 276/676–2282 ⊕ www.vahighlandsfestival.org in Abingdon celebrates Appalachia with juried displays and demonstrations of arts and crafts, exhibitions of animals, sales of antiques, and performances of country music.
WINTER Early December	During the **The Grand Illuminations** ☎ 800/447–8679 ⊕ www.history.org in Williamsburg, Virginia, 18th-century entertainment is performed on several outdoor stages and fireworks are set off at several points through the evening.
	The **Historic Alexandria Candlelight Tour** ☎ 703/838–4242 ⊕ www.historicalexandria.org is a visit to historic houses for light refreshment and performances of period music of the season.
	The **Candlelight Tour of Historic Houses of Worship** ☎ 301/228–2888 or 800/999–3613 ⊕ www.visitfrederick.org, in downtown Frederick, is a self-guided tour of historic churches and a synagogue, most of them within walking distance of one another. The churches are decorated for the holidays, and Christmas music and refreshments add to the festivities.
	New Year's Eve ☎ 410/752–8632 ⊕ www.bop.org festivities in Baltimore include a concert at the Harborplace amphitheater and a midnight fireworks display over Inner Harbor. **First Night Annapolis** ☎ 410/268–8553 ⊕ www.firstnightannapolis.org is a family-oriented, alcohol-free, and affordable celebration of the lively arts. Live performances are held throughout the day and evening at 40 venues.
January	Maryland's three-day **Annapolis Heritage Antiques Show** ☎ 410/961–5121 ⊕ www.armacostantiquesshows.com is one of the major Mid-Atlantic events of its kind.
February	The **ACC Crafts Fair** ☎ 800/836–3470 in Baltimore draws more than 800 exhibitors for three days of artful displays and sales.
	George Washington's Birthday ☎ 703/549–7662 ⊕ www.washingtonbirthday.net is celebrated in Alexandria, Virginia, with a parade—175 floats and marching units—and a reenactment of a Revolutionary War skirmish at Fort Ward nearby.

ON THE CALENDAR

March	**Military Through the Ages** ☎ 757/253–4838 ⊕ www.historyisfun.org in Jamestown, Virginia, uses authentic weapons in a series of reenactments of battles from the Middle Ages through the 20th century.
SPRING April	Norfolk's **Azalea Festival** ☎ 757/282–2801 ⊕ www.azaleafestival.org salutes NATO through battleship tours, a parade, an air show, concerts, a ball, and the crowning of a queen from the year's honored NATO member nation.
	Historic Garden Week ☎ 804/644–7776 ⊕ www.vagardenweek.org throughout Virginia is a time when several hundred grand private homes, otherwise closed to the public, open their doors and grounds to visitors.
	The **Celtic Festival and Highland Gathering of Southern Maryland** ☎ 443/404–7319 ⊕ www.cssm.org, which takes place south of Annapolis in St. Leonard, includes piping and fiddling competitions, dancing, games, and the foods and crafts of the United Kingdom, Ireland, and Brittany.
May	**Virginia Gold Cup** ☎ 540/347–2612 ⊕ www.vagoldcup.com steeplechase horse races, held near Middleburg in Northern Virginia, have been among the most prominent social and sporting events of the state since the 1920s.
	Baltimore's **Maryland Preakness Celebration** ☎ 410/542–9400 ⊕ www.preakness.com is a weeklong festival that includes parades, street parties, fund-raisers, and hot-air-balloon races. The celebration culminates in the annual running of the Preakness Stakes at Pimlico Racetrack, on the third Saturday in May.
	The **Chestertown Tea Party** ☎ 410/778–0416 ⊕ www.chestertownteaparty.com on Maryland's Eastern Shore commemorates patriots' 1774 act of hurling British tea into the Chester River.
	Commissioning Week ☎ 410/293–2292 ⊕ www.usna.edu at the U.S. Naval Academy in Annapolis, Maryland, is a time of dress parades, traditional stunts such as the Herndon Monument Climb, and a spectacular aerobatics demonstration by the navy's famous Blue Angels precision flying team.
SUMMER June	The **Fiddlers' Convention at the Carroll County Farm Museum** ☎ 410/876–2667, an annual gathering in Westminster, Maryland, attracts some of the nation's finest bluegrass entertainers and fiddlers.
	The **Hampton Jazz Festival** ☎ 757/838–4203 ⊕ www.hamptoncoliseum.org in Hampton, Virginia, brings together top performers in different styles of jazz.

July	**Independence Day** celebrations in Baltimore culminate in a major show of fireworks over the Inner Harbor. The **Pony Swim and Auction** ☎ 757/336–6161 ⊕ www.chincoteague chamber.com in Chincoteague, Virginia, is the annual roundup of wild ponies from Assateague Island; the foals are auctioned off to support the volunteer fire department.
August	During the first three weekends of August, "Shakespeare at the Ruins" at **Barboursville Vineyards** ☎ 540/832–3824 ⊕ www.barbours villewine.com brings outdoor performances of the Bard's classics to these beautiful vineyards, between Charlottesville and Orange in Virginia. The **Maryland State Fair** ☎ 410/252–0200 ⊕ www.marylandstate fair.com, in Timonium, is 10 days of horse racing, livestock judging, live entertainment, agricultural displays, farm implements, and plenty of food. The **Maryland Renaissance Festival** ☎ 410/266–7304 or 800/296–7304 ⊕ www.rennfest.com celebrates 16th-century England with entertainment, food, and crafts shops. The grounds near Annapolis include a 5,000-seat jousting area and 10 stages. The event continues through late October.
FALL September	**Defenders' Day** ☎ 410/962–4290 ⊕ www.nps.gov/fomc celebrations at Fort McHenry in Baltimore commemorate with music, drilling, mock bombardment, and fireworks—the battle that led to the writing of the national anthem. Crisfield, Maryland's **National Hard Crab Derby** ☎ 410/968–2500 ⊕ www.crisfieldchamber.com/crabderby.htm celebrates—what else?—the Eastern Shore's crabs with a crab race, steamed crabs, and the crowning of Miss Crustacean. College Park Aviation Museum in Maryland hosts all sorts of airplanes at the **Annual Air Fair** ☎ 301/314–7777. Baltimore's Hampden neighborhood celebrates the spirit of "Hon" with music, food, and festivities at **Hampdenfest** ☎ 410/235–5800 ⊕ www.hampdenfest.com. The **Virginia State Fair** ☎ 804/228–3200 ⊕ www.statefair.com, in Richmond, is a classic conglomeration of carnival rides, livestock shows, displays of farm equipment, and lots of food for sale.

ON THE CALENDAR

	Ocean City, Maryland, celebrates the quest for endless summer with **Sunfest Kite Festival** ☎ 410/289–7855 ⊕ www.kiteloft.com, a four-day blowout with all sorts of entertainment, kite contests, and a crafts show.
	The **Baltimore Book Festival** ☎ 410/837–4636 or 800/282–6632 ⊕ www.bop.org, held in the historic Mount Vernon neighborhood, celebrates books and Baltimore's literary past.
October	The **Autumn Glory Festival** ☎ 301/387–4386 ⊕ www.garrettchamber. com, held in Oakland in Maryland's westernmost county, is a celebration of the peak fall foliage that includes state banjo and fiddle championships, Oktoberfest festivities, arts, crafts, and antiques.
	The **October Homes Tour and Crafts Exhibit** ☎ 540/882–3018 ⊕ www.waterfordva.org in Waterford, Virginia, draws tens of thousands to this historic community.
	The first Saturday of October, Bethesda restaurants sell samples of their fare at the food festival, **Taste of Bethesda** ☎ 301/215–6660 ⊕ www.bethesda.org.
	The **Chincoteague Oyster Festival** ☎ 757/336–6161 ⊕ www. chincoteaguechamber.com, on Virginia's Eastern Shore, typically sells out months in advance.
	Yorktown Day ☎ 757/898–2410 ⊕ www.nps.gov/colo observances in Yorktown, Virginia, celebrate the Colonial victory in the American War of Independence (October 19, 1781) with 18th-century tactical demonstrations, patriotic exercises, and a wreath-laying ceremony.
	The **Virginia Film Festival** ☎ 800/882–3378 ⊕ www.vafilm.com, in Charlottesville, Virginia, is becoming a major event in the motion picture industry, with screenings of important new movies and appearances by their stars.
November	The **Waterfowl Festival** ☎ 410/822–4567 ⊕ www.waterfowlfestival. org in Easton, Maryland, involves decoy exhibitions, carving demonstrations, duck-calling contests, and retriever exercises during a three-day weekend.
	Waterfowl Week ☎ 757/336–6122 ⊕ www.chincoteaguechamber. com in Chincoteague, Virginia, is when the National Wildlife Refuge opens to motor vehicles, allowing drivers to watch the Canada and snow geese on their southward migration.

Washington, D.C.

WORD OF MOUTH

"All of the memorials are impressive, but the Korean War Memorial is especially impressive if you see it in the moonlight. It is eerily realistic. You can almost feel what it would be like to be with a group of soldiers on a patrol at night. For a vet like me, it was quite moving   "

—Travelermebe

"The obvious is that you will want to do the Smithsonian museums, but in addition to that, I highly recommend the Spy museum. I've taken guests to it and both my guests and I have really enjoyed it."

—npurpleh2

Updated by
Matthew
Cordell

THE BYZANTINE WORKINGS of the federal government, the sound-bite–ready oratory of the well-groomed politicians, and the murky foreign policy pronouncements issued from Foggy Bottom cause many Americans to cast a skeptical eye on anything that happens "inside the Beltway." Washingtonians take it in stride—all in a day's work. Besides, such ribbing is a small price to pay for living in a city with charms that extend far beyond the bureaucratic. World-class museums and art galleries (nearly all of them free), tree-shaded and flower-filled parks and gardens, bars and restaurants that benefit from a large immigrant community and droves of young people, and nightlife that seems to get better with every passing year are as much a part of Washington as floor debates or filibusters.

The city that calls to mind politicking, back-scratching, and delicate diplomatic maneuvering is itself the result of a compromise. The deal was struck when Virginia's Thomas Jefferson agreed that the federal government would assume the war debts of the colonies if Alexander Hamilton and other Northern legislators would agree to locate the capital on the banks of the Potomac, near George Washington's estate at Mount Vernon. Soon after, in 1791, Pierre-Charles L'Enfant, a French engineer who had fought in the Revolution, designed a city with a "vast esplanade" now known as the "Mall," wide diagonal boulevards crossing a grid of streets, and a focal triangle formed by the Capitol, the president's house, and a statue where the Washington monument now sits. Although L'Enfant's plans seem grand now, for almost a century this city was little more than a sparsely populated swamp with empty dirt avenues. Cattle grazed on the Mall and America's famous early leaders worked in and inhabited dank, dilapidated buildings.

EXPLORING WASHINGTON, D.C.

There's no denying that Washington, the world's first planned capital, is also one of its most beautiful. And although the federal government dominates many of the city's activities and buildings, there are always places where you can leave politics behind. Washington is a city of vistas—pleasant views that shift and change from block to block, a marriage of geometry and art. Unlike other large cities, Washington isn't dominated by skyscrapers, largely because, in 1899, Congress passed a height-restrictions act to prevent federal monuments from being overshadowed by commercial construction. Its buildings stretch out gracefully and are never far from expanses of green. Like its main industry, politics, Washington's design is a constantly changing kaleidoscope that invites inspection from all angles.

Washington's centerpiece is the National Mall, a mile-long stretch of grass that reaches from the Capitol past the bulk of the Smithsonian's grand museums to the Washington Monument. The White House, due north of the Washington Monument, and the other major monuments, to the southwest, are not far away. In recent years, Downtown, north of Pennsylvania from the Capitol to the White House, has become the city's nerve center, quickly gentrifying with new bars, restaurants, world-class theaters, and a renovated Smithsonian Museum of American Art

1

FINDING YOUR WAY AROUND D.C.

The city is divided into the four quadrants of a compass (NW, NE, SE, SW), with the U.S. Capitol at the center. Because the Capitol doesn't sit in the exact center of the city (the Washington Monument does), Northwest is the largest quadrant.

If someone tells you to meet them at 6th and G, ask them to specify the quadrant, because there are actually four different 6th and G intersections (one per quadrant). Within each quadrant, numbered streets run north–south, and lettered streets run east–west (the letter J was omitted to avoid confusion with the letter I). The streets form a fairly simple grid—for instance, 900 G Street NW is the intersection of 9th and G streets in the NW quadrant of the city. Likewise, if you count the letters of the alphabet, skipping J, you can get a good approximation of an address for a numbered street. For instance, 1600 16th Street NW is close to Q Street, Q being the 16th letter of the alphabet if you skip J.

As if all this weren't confusing enough, Major Pierre L'Enfant, the Frenchman who originally designed the city, threw in diagonal avenues recalling those of Paris. Most of D.C.'s avenues are named after U.S. states. You can find addresses on avenues the same way you find those on numbered streets, so 1200 Connecticut Avenue NW is close to M Street, because M is the 12th letter of the alphabet when you skip J.

and National Portrait Gallery. Tony Georgetown, up Pennsylvania Avenue from the White House, sports tree-shaded streets lined with million-dollar row houses and the city's best upscale shopping. U Street, once Washington's Harlem, has regained its status as D.C.'s hippest neighborhood. The shaded areas along the Metro's red line—Dupont Circle, Woodley Park, and Cleveland Park—offer a pleasant respite from the federal bustle and some top-notch shops and art galleries.

THE MALL

The Mall is the heart of almost every visitor's trip to Washington. The front yard for nearly a dozen free museums, a picnicking park, a jogging path, and an outdoor stage for festivals, movies, musical performances, and fireworks, America's town green is the closest thing the capital has to a theme park.

Top 5 Experiences for Washington, D.C.

• **Shop in Georgetown:** Stroll the cobblestone streets and dip into shops offering cutting-edge fashion and priceless antiques.

• **Taste the Emerging Theater Scene:** Feast your eyes on brilliantly staged productions at the Kennedy Center, Shakespeare Theater, Arena Stage, and Woolly Mammoth.

• **Walk the Halls of Power:** At the White House, the Capitol, and the Supreme Court, take a peek behind the curtain.

Cleveland Park

Adams-Morgan

Dupont Circle &
Northwest D.C.

Georgetown
& Foggy Bottom

The White
House Area

Theodore
Roosevelt
Island

Vietnam
Veterans
Memorial

Washington
Monument

Lincoln
Memorial

National World
War II
Monument

Reflecting Pool

Kutz
Bridge

Tidal Basin

ARLINGTON

ARLINGTON
NATIONAL
CEMETERY

Columbia
Island

FDR
Memorial

Inlet
Bridge

Potomac River

VIRGINIA

To
Old Town
Alexandria

The Monuments

Exploring
Washington, D.C.

● **Explore the Smithsonian:** Spend days savoring a variety of brilliant exhibits in the Smithsonian's 13 museums, all free.

● **Get a Bird's Eye View:** At the Old Post Office, Washington Monument, and Hotel Washington terrace, enjoy a full view of this marble- and monument-laden city.

What to See

⟲ ❽ **Bureau of Engraving and Printing.** The powerful presses here turn out more than $38 million a day, in addition to stamps, military certificates, and presidential invitations. You can only enter the bureau on the official tours, which last about 45 minutes. From March through September, same-day timed-entry tour passes are issued starting at 8 AM at the Raoul Wallenberg Place SW entrance. ⊠ *14th and C Sts. SW, The Mall* ☎ *202/874–3019 or 202/874–2330, 866/874–2330 tour information* ⊕ *www.moneyfactory.com* ⌦ *Free* ☉ *Tours every 15 mins, Sept.–Apr., weekdays 9–10:45 and 12:30–2; May–Aug., weekdays 9–10:45, 12:30–2, and 5–7* Ⓜ *Smithsonian.*

> **CAPITAL FACTS**
>
> The Bureau of Engraving and Printing turns out some $38 million worth of currency a day.

❶ **Hirshhorn Museum and Sculpture Garden.** Conceived as the nation's museum of modern and contemporary art, the Hirshhorn is home to more than 12,000 top-notch works by masters ranging from Pablo Picasso, Joan Miró, and Piet Mondrian to Willem de Kooning, Andy Warhol, and Edward Hopper. Designed by Gordon Bunshaft, the striking round poured-concrete building was dubbed the "Doughnut on the Mall" when it was constructed in 1974. Inside, highlights of the Hirshhorn's sculpture collection include masterpieces by Henry Moore, Alberto Giacometti, Constantin Brancusi, and a roomful of giant, playful Alexander Calder mobiles. Outside, sculptures dot a sunken grass-and-granite garden, which makes an inspiring spot for an outdoor lunch. In addition to a 32-foot-tall sculpture of a cartoon brushstroke by pop-art iconographer Roy Lichtenstein, the garden boasts Henri Matisse's *Backs I–IV* and Auguste Rodin's *Burghers of Calais.* ⊠ *Independence Ave. and 7th St. SW, The Mall* ☎ *202/633–4674, 202/633–8043 TDD* ⊕ *www.hirshhorn.si.edu* ⌦ *Free* ☉ *Museum daily 10–5:30, sculpture garden 7:30–dusk* Ⓜ *Smithsonian or L'Enfant Plaza (Maryland Ave. exit).*

★ ⟲ ❷ **National Air and Space Museum.** The 23 galleries in this museum, thought to be the most-visited in the world, tell the story of aviation from the earliest human attempts at flight. As you walk through, look up to see the world's most famous aircraft, including the Wright 1903 Flyer, which Wilbur Wright piloted over the sands of Kitty Hawk, North Carolina; Charles Lindbergh's *Spirit of St. Louis;* the X-1 rocket plane in which Chuck Yeager broke the sound barrier; and an X-15, the first aircraft to exceed Mach 6. Other highlights include a 4-billion-year-old slice of moon rock and a backup model of the Skylab orbital workshop that you can walk through.

Recent Changes in Washington, D.C.

A SURGE OF NEW ADDITIONS are set for the District in 2007. The once down-at-the-heels neighborhood of Penn Quarter is now thoroughly revitalized and continues to explode with development. It's home to the most hotly anticipated reopening of 2006: the **National Portrait Gallery** and **Smithsonian American Art Museum,** which, after having been closed to the public for six years, reopened their doors under one roof.

On Capitol Hill, 2007 will see the opening of the vast new **Capitol Visitors' Center,** an underground behemoth whose expanse—and expense—continues to grow. Outside the dome, the gracious new **National Garden** opened on October 1st, 2006.

Sports fans will know that Washington has gained another exciting addition that has nothing to do with politics or marble museums: D.C. once again has its own major league baseball team, and hometown pride for the **Nationals** (aka the Nats) has swept the city.

Heightened security has been a tourist concern since the events of September 11, 2001. You'll encounter metal detectors and your bags will be searched at all government buildings and museums, and you may be asked for a photo ID. To make things easier, carry a small bag of essentials that can be easily opened by a security guard, and expect to wait at the more popular attractions such as the Air and Space Museum and the National Gallery of Art. Government buildings such as the Capitol and the Supreme Court Building do not allow loitering, and there's a list of prohibited items on the Court's Web site (⊕ www. supremecourtus.gov). Tours of the **Pentagon, Treasury Building,** and **Eisenhower Executive Building** have been suspended indefinitely.

The good news is that **White House** tours have been reinstated, as have those at the **Bureau of Engraving and Printing** and **U.S. Naval Observatory.**

Films shown on the five-story-high IMAX screen—including the now classic *To Fly!*—employ swooping aerial scenes that make you feel as if you've left the ground. Upstairs, the Albert Einstein Planetarium's "all-dome" digital technology creates a feeling of movement through space. A shuttle bus runs from the museum entrance on the Mall to the Na-tional Air and Space Museum Steven F. Udvar-Hazy Center (*see* Chapter 2). ⊠ *Independence Ave. and 6th St. SW, The Mall* ☎ *202/357–1729, 202/357–1686 movie information, 202/357–1729 TDD* ⊕ *www.nasm. si.edu* ⊠ *Free, IMAX $7.50, planetarium $7.50* ☉ *Daily 10–5:30* Ⓜ *Smithsonian.*

☾ ❹ **National Gallery of Art, East Building.** The I. M. Pei–designed East Building was conceived as a response to the changing needs of the National Gallery. The atrium is dominated by Alexander Calder's mobile *Untitled,* and the galleries display modern and contemporary art, although you'll also find major temporary exhibitions that span many years and artistic styles. Permanent works include Pablo Picasso's *The Lovers*

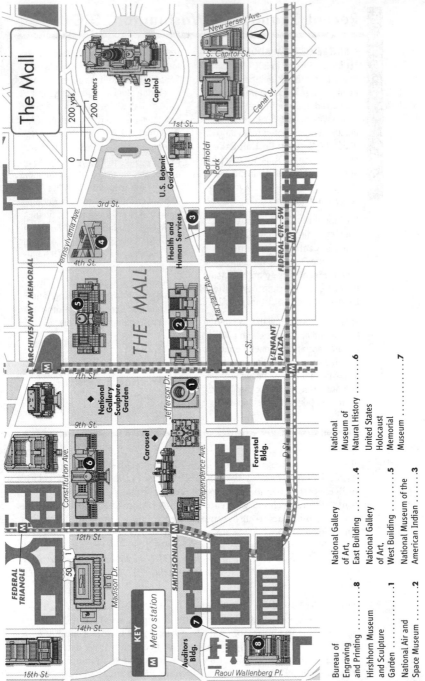

The Mall

US Capitol

New Jersey Ave.

S. Capitol St.

Canal St.

1st St.

Bartholdi Park

U.S. Botanic Garden

3rd St.

Pennsylvania Ave.

Health and Human Services

4th St.

THE MALL

Maryland Ave.

C. St.

L'ENFANT PLAZA

FEDERAL CTR.-SW

ARCHIVES/NAVY MEMORIAL

7th St.

National Gallery Sculpture Garden

9th St.

Jefferson Dr.

Carousel

Constitution Ave.

Independence Ave.

Forrestal Bldg.

D St.

FEDERAL TRIANGLE

12th St.

Madison Dr.

14th St.

SMITHSONIAN

KEY
M Metro station

Auditors Bldg.

15th St.

Raoul Wallenberg Pl.

200 yds
200 meters

Bureau of Engraving and Printing 8	National Museum of Natural History 6
Hirshhorn Museum and Sculpture Garden 1	United States Holocaust Memorial Museum 7
National Air and Space Museum 2	National Gallery of Art, East Building 4
	National Gallery of Art, West Building 5
	National Museum of the American Indian 3

and *Family of Saltimbanques,* four of Matisse's cutouts, Miró's *The Farm,* and Jackson Pollock's *Lavender Mist.* An underground concourse, lined with gift shops, a café, and a cafeteria, links to the West Building. ⊠ *Constitution Ave. between 3rd and 4th Sts. NW, The Mall* ☏ *202/ 737–4215, 202/842–6176 TDD* ⊕ *www.nga.gov* ☐ *Free* ☉ *Mon.–Sat. 10–5, Sun. 11–6* Ⓜ *Archives/Navy Memorial.*

❺ National Gallery of Art, West Building. The two buildings of the National
Fodor's Choice Gallery hold one of the world's foremost collections of paintings, sculp-
★ tures, and graphics. ■ **TIP→ If you want to view the museum's holdings in (more or less) chronological order, start your exploration in the West Building, a gift to the nation from wealthy financier, industrialist, and Secretary of the Treasury Andrew Mellon.** The rotunda, with 24 marble columns surrounding a fountain topped with a statue of Mercury, sets the stage for the masterpieces on display in more than 100 galleries. But don't get overwhelmed; two serene gardens punctuate the center of each wing. The permanent collection includes *The Adoration of the Magi* by Fra Angelico and Filippo Lippi, *Ginevra de' Benci* (the only painting by Leonardo da Vinci on display in the Western Hemisphere), *Daniel in the Lions' Den* by Peter Paul Rubens, a self-portrait by Rembrandt, Salvador Dalí's *Last Supper,* and works by Impressionists such as Edgar Degas, Claude Monet, Auguste Renoir, and Mary Cassatt.

The **National Gallery of Art Sculpture Garden** is between 7th and 9th streets along the Mall. Granite walkways take you through the garden, which is planted with shade trees, flowering trees, and perennials. Sculptures on display include Roy Lichtenstein's playful *House I;* Alexander Archipenko's *Woman Combing Her Hair;* Miró's *Personnage Gothique, Oiseau-Eclair;* and Isamu Noguchi's *Great Rock of Inner Seeking.* The huge central fountain becomes a skating rink in winter. ⊠ *Constitution Ave. between 4th and 7th Sts. NW, The Mall* ☏ *202/737–4215, 202/ 842–6176 TDD* ⊕ *www.nga.gov* ☐ *Free* ☉ *Mon.–Sat. 10–5, Sun. 11–6* Ⓜ *Archives/Navy Memorial.*

⟲ ❸ National Museum of the American Indian. The Smithsonian's newest addition to the Mall tells the 10,000-year-old story of the native groups living in the Western Hemisphere with multimedia displays that far exceed the traditional anthropolitical treatment of Native Americans. The exterior, fashioned out of Minnesota limestone, resembles a weather-worn rock mass, which sits on a serene 4¼-acre plot peppered with fountains and "grandfather rocks." Inside, a three-story atrium connects three floors that display wood and stone carvings, clothing and headgear, baskets and pottery, and nearly a million other crafts and works of art from the Americas. *1,000 Roads,* a film about the lives of contemporary Native Americans, is shown hourly in the museum's Lelawi Theater. ⊠ *4th St. and Independence Ave. SW* ☏ *202/633–1000* ⊕ *www.americanindian. si.edu* ☐ *Free* ☉ *Daily 10–5:30* Ⓜ *L'Enfant Plaza.*

⟲ ❻ National Museum of Natural History. This is one of the world's great natural history museums, filled with the largest African bull elephant ever found, dinosaur bones, fossils, and other natural delights—124 million specimens in all. The highlight of the second floor is the **Janet Annenberg Hooker Hall of Geology, Gems, and Minerals,** which includes a pair of Marie Antoinette's earrings, the Rosser Reeves ruby, and, of course, the Hope Diamond. There are tarantula feedings Tuesday through Friday at 10:30, 11:30, and 1:30. The Samuel C. Johnson IMAX theater shows two- and three-dimensional natural-history films, including the 3-D movie *T-REX*. ⊠ *Constitution Ave. and 10th St. NW, The Mall* ☎ *202/ 633–1000, 202/357–1729 TDD* ⊕ *www.mnh.si.edu* ⊠ *Free, IMAX $8* ⊙ *Museum daily 10–5:30; Discovery Room Labor Day–Memorial Day, Tues.–Fri. noon–2:30,* weekends 10:30–3:30 Ⓜ *Smithsonian or Federal Triangle.*

> **WORD OF MOUTH**
>
> "Kids LOVE the Natural History Simthsonian because that is where the dinosaur skeletons are! I still remember my visits there when I was a kid! I also loved seeing the gem collection, especially the Hope Diamond. If memory serves correctly, they also had an impressive insect collection (live) and that never ceases to amaze kids."
>
> –ChristieP

★ ❼ **United States Holocaust Memorial Museum.** A permanent exhibition tells the stories of the millions killed by the Nazis between 1933 and 1945, and it doesn't pull any punches. Upon arrival, you are issued an "identity card" that details the life of a holocaust victim. The museum recounts the Holocaust through documentary films, video- and audiotaped oral histories, and a collection that includes items such as a freight car like those used to transport Jews from Warsaw to the Treblinka death camp and the Star of David patches that Jews were made to wear. Like the history it covers, the museum can be profoundly disturbing; it's not recommended for children under 11, although Daniel's Story, a ground-floor exhibit not requiring tickets, is designed for children ages 8 and up. In addition to the permanent exhibition, the museum also has a multimedia learning center, a resource center for students and teachers, a registry of Holocaust survivors, and occasional special exhibitions. Timed-entry passes (distributed on a first-come, first-served basis at the 14th Street entrance starting at 10 AM or available in advance through tickets.com) are necessary for the permanent exhibition. ⊠ *100 Raoul Wallenberg Pl. SW, enter from Raoul Wallenberg Pl. or 14th St. SW, The Mall* ☎ *202/488–0400, 800/400–9373 tickets.com* ⊕ *www.ushmm. org* ⊠ *Free* ⊙ *Daily 10–5:30* Ⓜ *Smithsonian.*

THE MONUMENTS

Washington is a city of monuments. In the middle of traffic circles, on tiny slivers of park, and at street corners and intersections, statues, plaques, and simple blocks of marble honor the generals, politicians, poets, and statesmen who helped shape the nation. The monuments dedicated to the most famous Americans are west of the Mall on ground reclaimed from the marshy flats of the Potomac. This is also the location of Washington's greatest single display of cherry trees, gifts from Japan.

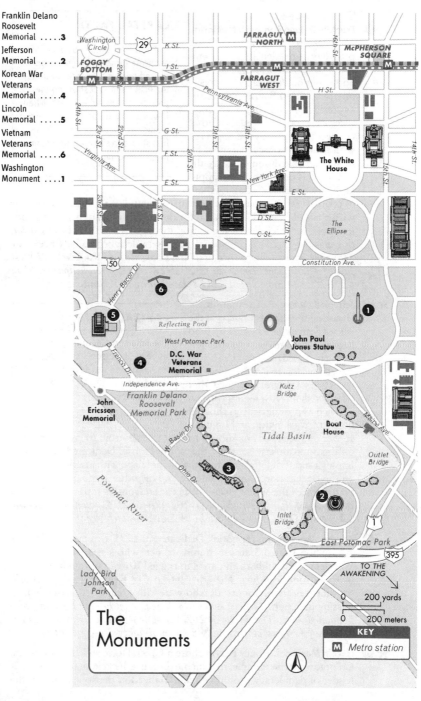

The
Monuments

What to See

⟲ ❸ **Franklin Delano Roosevelt Memorial.** This 7½-acre memorial to the 32nd president, unveiled in 1997, employs waterfalls and reflection pools, four outdoor gallery rooms—one for each of Roosevelt's terms as president—and 10 bronze sculptures. The granite megaliths that connect the galleries are engraved with some of Roosevelt's most famous quotes. Although today the memorial is one of the most popular in the District, it's had its share of controversy. When unveiled, the monument did not depict Roosevelt with a wheelchair, which he used for the last 24 years of his life, including those in which he led the nation through World War II. However, this was the first D.C. memorial purposely designed to be wheelchair accessible, and the first to honor a First Lady, Eleanor Roosevelt. ⊠ *West side of Tidal Basin, The Mall* ☎ *202/426–6841* ⊕ *www.nps.gov/fdrm* ⊠ *Free* ☉ *24 hrs; staffed daily 8 AM–midnight* Ⓜ *Smithsonian.*

> ### CAPITAL FACTS
>
> In 2001, after protest by disability advocate groups, Congress approved adding a bronze statue to the FDR memorial showing the president in his wheelchair. When it was added to the entrance of the memorial in 2001, it became the first statue to show a world leader in a wheelchair.

★ ❷ **Jefferson Memorial.** The monument honoring the third president of the United States was modeled by John Russell Pope after a style that Jefferson had used himself when he designed the University of Virginia. In the 1930s Congress decided that Jefferson deserved a monument positioned as prominently as those in honor of Washington and Lincoln, so workers scooped and moved tons of river bottom to create dry land on this spot directly south of the White House. Dedicated in 1943, it houses a statue of Jefferson, and its walls are lined with inscriptions based on the Declaration of Independence and his other writings. One of the best views of the White House can be seen from its top steps. ⊠ *Tidal Basin, south bank, The Mall* ☎ *202/426–6821* ⊕ *www.nps.gov/thje* ⊠ *Free* ☉ *Daily 8 AM–midnight* Ⓜ *Smithsonian.*

> ### CAPITAL FACTS
>
> The Jefferson Memorial was dubbed "Jefferson's muffin"; critics lambasted the design as outdated and too similar to that of the Lincoln Memorial.

❹ **Korean War Veterans Memorial.** Dedicated in 1995, this memorial to the 1.5 million United States men and women who served in the Korean War depicts 19 soldiers on patrol in rugged Korean terrain heading toward an American flag. The adjacent Pool of Remembrance, a choice spot for reflection, honors all who were killed, captured, wounded, or missing in action. ⊠ *West end of Mall at Daniel French Dr. and Independence Ave., The Mall* ☎ *202/426–6841* ⊕ *www.nps.gov/kwvm* ⊠ *Free* ☉ *24 hrs; staffed daily 8 AM–midnight* Ⓜ *Foggy Bottom.*

★ ❺ **Lincoln Memorial.** Henry Bacon chose a Greek Doric style for this white Colorado-marble temple to Lincoln because he felt that a great defender of democracy should be memorialized in the style found in the

A City of Statues

WASHINGTON, D.C., HAS MORE equestrian statues than any other city in the nation; stone-and-metal men atop steeds are everywhere, watching the city from traffic circles, squares, and parks. The statues proliferated in the 19th century, when Civil War generals who went into politics seemed virtually assured of this legacy—regardless of their success in either endeavor.

Standing in Lafayette Square across from the White House, the statue of President Andrew Jackson is by sculptor Clark Mills, who had never seen an equestrian statue, much less created one. To get the proportions of the rearing horse correct, Mills had a horse trained to remain in an upright position so he could study the anatomy of its muscles.

Directly up 16th Street from Lafayette Square at Massachusetts and Rhode Island avenues is a statue of Lt. Gen. Winfield Scott, in the circle bearing his name. He was to be shown atop his favorite mount, a lightweight mare, but right before the statue was cast, some of Scott's descendants decided that a stallion would be a more appropriate horse for him to ride into battle upon (regardless of historical accuracy). The sculptor, H. K. Brown, was forced to give the horse a last-minute sex change.

Farther up Massachusetts Avenue, at 23rd Street, is a statue of Civil War Gen. Philip Henry Sheridan, also in a circle bearing his name. The piece is by Gutzon Borglum, who completed more than 170 public statues, including the head of Abraham Lincoln in the Capitol Rotunda, and whose final work was Mount Rushmore's presidential faces. The statue of the leader riding Rienzi (who was later renamed Winchester for Sheridan's victory there) stands in the type of circle Pierre-Charles L'Enfant envisioned in his plan for Washington—a small, formal park where avenues come together surrounded by isolated houses and buildings.

The statue of Gen. William Tecumseh Sherman at 15th Street and Treasury Place is often overlooked—in summer, the general's head is obscured by trees, and all year long he presents his back and his mount's hindquarters to pedestrians. He's positioned where he is thought to have stood while reviewing the Union troops on their victorious return from Georgia. The bar at the Hotel Washington, which affords some of the best views of the city, is also the place for a good look at Sherman.

A long-held theory says that the number of raised legs on the mount of an equestrian statue reveals how the rider died: one leg raised means the rider died of wounds sustained in battle, two legs raised means the rider died in battle, and four feet on the ground means the rider died of natural causes. None of this is true, though, and of the more than 30 equestrian statues in Washington, only about a third (including Scott, Sheridan, and Sherman, but not Jackson) follow this "code."

—Lisa Greaves

birthplace of democracy. Although detractors thought it inappropriate that the humble president be honored with what amounts to a modified but grandiose Greek temple, this memorial has become one of the nation's most recognizable icons, used repeatedly as a backdrop in TV, film, and for one of the most famous speeches in American history, Martin Luther King Jr.'s "I Have a Dream" speech in 1963. Daniel Chester French's 19-foot-high somber statue of the seated president, in the center of the memorial, is composed of 28 interlocking pieces of Georgia marble. ■ TIP→ Although visiting the area around the Lincoln Memorial during the day allows you to take in an impressive view of the Mall to the east, the best time to see the memorial itself is at night, when spotlights illuminate the outside. ⊠ West end of Mall, The Mall ☎ 202/426–6895 ⊕ www. nps.gov/linc ☒ Free ⊙ 24 hrs; staffed daily 8 AM–midnight Ⓜ Foggy Bottom.

❻ Vietnam Veterans Memorial. Opinions on this stark monument, now one of the most visited sites in Washington, were once as divided as those on the conflict that it commemorates. The simple design by Maya Lin, a 21-year-old architecture student at Yale, was selected in a 1981 competition. Upon its completion in 1982, the memorial was decried by some veterans as a "black gash of shame." The names of more than 58,000 Americans are etched on the memorial's black granite panels, which reflect the sky, the trees, and the faces of those looking for the names of friends or relatives who died in the war. For help in finding a name, ask a ranger at the blue-and-white hut near the entrance. You can get paper and pencil from a park ranger if you'd like to make a rubbing. Thousands of offerings are left at the wall each year: letters, flowers, medals, uniforms, snapshots. The National Park Service stores these, and some are on display at the National Museum of American History. ⊠ Constitution Gardens, 23rd St. and Constitution Ave. NW, The Mall ☎ 202/ 634–1568 ⊕ www.nps.gov/vive ☒ Free ⊙ 24 hrs; staffed daily 8 AM–midnight Ⓜ Foggy Bottom.

⟨ᴥ⟩ ❶ Washington Monument. At the western end of the Mall, the 555-foot, 5-inch Washington Monument, the world's tallest masonry structure, punctuates the capital like a huge exclamation point. The cornerstone was laid in 1848, but building stopped in 1854 for 20 years, in part due to members of the anti-Catholic Know-Nothing party stealing and destroying a block donated by Pope Pius IX. During this period, herds of cattle grazed on the grounds of the half-finished monument. A clearly visible ring about a third of the way up the obelisk testifies to this unfortunate stage of the monument's history: the stone used for the second phase of construction came from a different stratum. The view from the top takes in most of the District and parts of Maryland and Virginia. ■ TIP→ The Washington Monument uses a free timed-ticket system. A limited number of tickets are available each day at the kiosk on 15th Street, beginning a half hour before the monument opens, though in spring and summer lines are likely to start well before then. ⊠ Constitution Ave. and 15th St. NW, The Mall ☎ 202/426–6841, 800/967–2283 for up to 6 advance tickets ⊕ www.nps.gov/wamo ☒ Free, advance tickets require a $2 service-and-handling fee per ticket ⊙ Daily 9–5 Ⓜ Smithsonian.

THE WHITE HOUSE AREA

In a world full of recognizable images, few are better known than the whitewashed, 132-room mansion at 1600 Pennsylvania Avenue. The residence of perhaps the single most powerful person on the planet, the White House has an awesome majesty, having been the home of every U.S. president but George Washington. The president's neighborhood includes some of the city's oldest houses.

What to See

6 Corcoran Gallery of Art. This beaux arts gallery's permanent collection of 14,000 works includes paintings by the greatest of the early American portraitists: John Copley, Gilbert Stuart, and Rembrandt Peale. The Hudson River School is represented by works such as *Mount Corcoran* by Albert Bierstadt and Frederic Church's *Niagara*. There are also portraits by John Singer Sargent, Thomas Eakins, and Mary Cassatt. The Walker Collection shows late-19th- and early-20th-century European paintings, including works by Gustave Courbet, Claude Monet, Camille Pissarro, and Pierre-Auguste Renoir. Dutch, Flemish, and French Romantic paintings are on display at the Clark Collection, as is the restored 18th-century Salon Doré that was once part of the Hotel de Clermont in Paris. Be sure to see Samuel Morse's *Old House of Representatives* and Hiram Powers's *Greek Slave,* which scandalized some parts of Victorian society but was seen by thousands. Photography and works by contemporary American artists are also among the Corcoran's strengths. ✉ *500 17th St. NW, White House area* ☎ *202/639–1700* ⊕ *www. corcoran.org* 🏷 *$8.00, free Thurs. after 5* ☼ *Wed. and Fri.–Sun. 10–5, Thurs. 10–9* Ⓜ *Farragut West or Farragut North.*

4 Decatur House. This redbrick Federal-style building designed by Benjamin Latrobe was the first private residence on Lafayette Square. Occupants of the house included Henry Clay, Martin Van Buren, and the Beales, a prominent western family. The house, now operated by the National Trust for Historic Preservation, has a first floor furnished as it was in Decatur's time and a second floor done in the Victorian style favored by the Beales. Many of the row houses along Jackson Place date from the pre–Civil War or Victorian period; even the more modern additions, though—such as those at 718 and 726—are designed to blend in with their more historic neighbors. ✉ *748 Jackson Pl. NW, White House area* ☎ *202/842–0920* ⊕ *www.decaturhouse.org* 🏷 *Free* ☼ *Tues.–Sat. 10–5, Sun. noon–4; tours every hr at quarter past the hr* Ⓜ *Farragut West.*

3 Lafayette Square. With such an important resident across the street, the National Capital Region's National Park Service gardeners lavish extra attention on this square's trees and flower beds. During the construction of the White House, workers' huts and a brick kiln were set up, and soon residences began popping up around the square, including the Blair House, which is now used by heads of state visiting Washington. Soldiers camped in the square during the War of 1812 and the Civil War, turning it both times into a muddy pit. Today, protesters set their placards up in Lafayette Square.

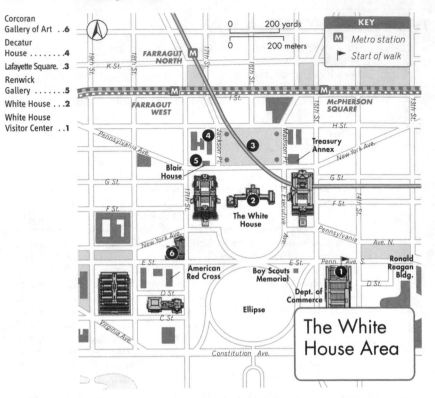

The White
House Area

In the center of the park is a large **statue of Andrew Jackson.** Erected in 1853 and cast from bronze cannons that Jackson captured during the War of 1812, this was the second equestrian statue made in America. The other statues in the park are of foreign-born soldiers who helped in America's fight for independence. In the southeast corner is the park's namesake, the **Marquis de Lafayette,** the young French nobleman who came to America to fight in the Revolution. ⊠ *Bounded by Pennsylvania Ave., Madison Pl., H St., and Jackson Pl., White House area* Ⓜ *McPherson Sq.*

NEED A BREAK? One block north of Pershing Park is the venerable **Hotel Washington** (⊠ 515 15th St. NW, White House area ☎ 202/638-5900 ⊕ www.hotelwashington.com), where the view from the Rooftop Terrace is one of the best in the city. From May to October, you can sit outside. (During cooler months, an extension shields you from the elements.) Drinks, coffee, and a light menu are available.

❺ **Renwick Gallery.** This French Second Empire–style gallery, designed by architect James Renwick in 1859, is part of the Smithsonian American Art Museum and features utilitarian items, as well as crafts made from traditional materials. Not everything in the museum is Shaker furniture and enamel jewelry, though. The second-floor Grand Salon is still furnished in the opulent Victorian style William Corcoran favored when his collection adorned the Renwick's walls. ⊠ *Pennsylvania Ave. at 17th St. NW, White House area* ☎ *202/633–2850, 202/357–1729 TDD* ⊕ *www.americanart.si.edu* ⌨ *Free* ⊙ *Daily 10–5:30* Ⓜ *Farragut West.*

> **CAPITAL FACTS**
>
> The White House wasn't ready for its first occupant, John Adams, the second U.S. president, until 1800: George Washington, who seems to have slept everywhere else, never stayed here.

☾ ❷ **White House.** Irishman James Hoban's plan, based on the Georgian design of Leinster Hall in Dublin and of other Irish country houses, was selected in a 1792 contest. The building has undergone many structural changes since then. Major renovations occurred after the British burned the House in 1814 and a piano almost broke through the second-story floor during President Truman's Administration because of the House's deteriorating condition. Truman had the entire structure gutted and restored, adding a second-story porch to the south portico.

■ **TIP→** Visitors wishing to tour the White House must make arrangements at least three months in advance through the office of their member of Congress. Non–U.S. citizens must make arrangements through their embassy. The self-guided tour includes several rooms on the ground floor and, on the State Floor, the large white-and-gold **East Room,** the site of presidential social events. In 1814 Dolley Madison saved the room's full-length portrait of George Washington from torch-carrying British soldiers by cutting it from its frame, rolling it up, and spiriting it out of the White House. The **State Dining Room,** second in size only to the East Room, is dominated by G. P. A. Healy's portrait of Abraham Lincoln, painted after the president's death.

❶ Since White House tours are self-guided, it's a good idea to come to the **White House Visitor Center** (⊠ Entrance: Department of Commerce's Baldrige Hall, E St. between 14th and 15th Sts. ☎ 202/208–1631, 202/456–7041 24-hr information line ⊕ www.nps.gov ⊙ Daily 7:30–4) first to catch the photographs, artifacts, and videos that relate to the White House's construction, decor, and residents. ⊠ *1600 Pennsylvania Ave. NW, Downtown* ☎ *202/208–1631, 202/456–7041 24-hr information line* ⊕ *www.whitehouse.gov* Ⓜ *Federal Triangle.*

CAPITOL HILL

The people who live and work on "the Hill" do so in the shadow of the edifice that lends the neighborhood its name: the gleaming white Capitol. More than just the center of government, however, the Hill also includes charming residential blocks lined with Victorian row houses and a fine assortment of restaurants, bars, and shops.

What to See

☾ ❷ **Capitol.** The Capitol's cornerstone was laid by George Washington in a
Fodor'sChoice Masonic ceremony on September 18, 1793. The "Congress House" grew
★ slowly and suffered a grave setback on August 24, 1814, when British

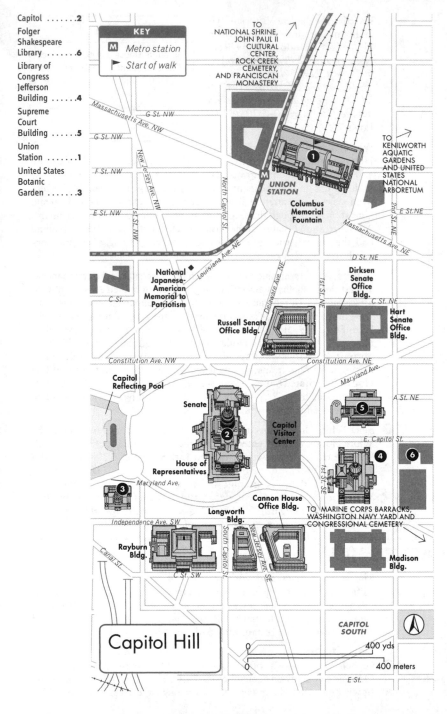

KEY

Ⓜ Metro station

▶ Start of walk

TO
NATIONAL SHRINE,
JOHN PAUL II
CULTURAL
CENTER,
ROCK CREEK
CEMETERY,
AND FRANCISCAN
MONASTERY

Massachusetts Ave. NW

G St. NW

G St. NW

F St. NW

New Jersey Ave. NW

North Capitol St.

1st St. NW

E St. NW

❶

Ⓜ
**UNION
STATION**

TO
KENILWORTH
AQUATIC
GARDENS
AND UNITED
STATES
NATIONAL
ARBORETUM

**Columbus
Memorial
Fountain**

2nd St. NE   E St. NE

Massachusetts Ave. NE

D St. NE

Louisiana Ave. NE

National
Japanese-
American
Memorial to
Patriotism

C St.

Delaware Ave. NE

1st St. NE

**Dirksen
Senate
Office
Bldg.**

C St. NE

**Hart
Senate
Office
Bldg.**

**Russell Senate
Office Bldg.**

Constitution Ave. NW

Constitution Ave. NE

Maryland Ave.

**Capitol
Reflecting Pool**

Senate

A St. NE

❺

❷

**Capitol
Visitor
Center**

E. Capitol St.

**House of
Representatives**

Maryland Ave.

1st St. SE

❹   ❻

❸

**Cannon House
Office Bldg.**

**Longworth
Bldg.**

Independence Ave. SW

South Capitol St.

New Jersey Ave. SE

TO MARINE CORPS BARRACKS,
WASHINGTON NAVY YARD AND
CONGRESSIONAL CEMETERY

**Rayburn
Bldg.**

Canal St.

C St. SW

**Madison
Bldg.**

**CAPITOL
SOUTH**

0   400 yds

0   400 meters

E St.

Capitol Hill

1

troops marched on Washington and set fire to the Capitol, the White House, and numerous other government buildings. In 1855, to keep the scale correct after the edifice was elongated to accommodate a growing government, work began on a taller, cast-iron dome. President Lincoln was criticized for continuing this expensive project while the country was in the throes of the Civil War, but he called the construction "a sign we intend the Union shall go on." This twin-shell dome, a marvel of 19th-century engineering, rises 285 feet above the ground and weighs 4,500 tons. It expands and contracts up to 4 inches a day, depending on the outside temperature.

Tours start under the center of the **Rotunda's** dome, at the center of which is Constantino Brumidi's 1865 fresco, *Apotheosis of Washington*. South of the Rotunda is **Statuary Hall,** once the legislative chamber of the House of Representatives. The room has an architectural quirk that maddened early legislators: a slight whisper uttered on one side of the hall can be heard on the other. To the north, on the Senate side, is the chamber once used by the Supreme Court and, above it, the splendid Old Senate Chamber, both of which have been restored.

The **Capitol Visitor Center,** a $550-million subterranean education and information area beneath the east side of the building, is tentatively scheduled to open in mid-2007, but the project has been plagued by delays. Tours will run from this site Monday through Saturday from 9:30 AM to 4:30 PM. Until then, free, timed-entry tickets will continue to be distributed, one per person, on a first-come, first-served basis, at the Capitol Guide Service kiosk located along the curving sidewalk southwest of the Capitol (near the intersection of 1st Street SW and Independence Avenue). Tickets are distributed starting at 9 AM. Free gallery passes to watch the House or Senate in session can be obtained only from your senator's or representative's office; both chambers are closed to the public when Congress is not in session. Note that there's a strict limit on the baggage and possessions that can be brought into the building, and there are no facilities for checking personal belongings. ✉ *East end of Mall, Capitol Hill* ☎ *202/224–3121 Capitol switchboard, 202/225–6827 guide service* ⊕ *www.aoc.gov* 🎟 *Free* Ⓜ *Capitol S or Union Station.*

❻ **Folger Shakespeare Library.** The Folger Library's collection of works by and about Shakespeare and his times is second to none. The white marble art deco building, designed by architect Paul Philippe Cret and dedicated in 1932, is decorated with scenes from the Bard's plays. Inside is a reproduction of a 16th-century inn-yard theater—the site for performances of chamber music, baroque opera, and Shakespearean plays—and a gallery, designed in the manner of an Elizabethan Great Hall, which holds rotating exhibits from the library's collection. Henry Clay Folger, the library's founder, was Standard Oil's president and chairman of the board. ✉ *201 E. Capitol St. SE, Capitol Hill* ☎ *202/544–4600* ⊕ *www. folger.edu* 🎟 *Free* ☉ *Mon.–Sat. 10–4* Ⓜ *Capitol S.*

❹ **Library of Congress.** Provisions for a library to serve members of Congress were originally made in 1800, when the government set aside $5,000 to purchase books that legislators might need to consult. This small collection was housed in the Capitol but was destroyed in 1814, when the

L'Enfant, the City's Architect

THE LIFE OF PIERRE-CHARLES L'ENFANT, architect of the city of Washington, has all the elements of a television miniseries: a handsome and idealistic 22-year-old Parisian volunteers in the American war for independence; he rises to the rank of major of engineers and is popular with fellow officers (and their wives); he becomes the toast-of-the-town architect in New York City and is selected by President George Washington to plan the new Federal City; he is fired amid controversy and dies bitter and broke; he is vindicated posthumously.

L'Enfant was educated as an architect and engineer in France and at least one of his teachers profoundly influenced his career and, ultimately, his plan for Washington: he studied landscape architecture with André LeNotre, who designed the gardens at Versailles. Congress voted in 1785 to create a permanent Federal City and, in 1789, L'Enfant wrote to George Washington with an offer to create a capital "magnificent enough to grace a great nation." He got the job, and arrived in Washington in 1791 to survey the land.

L'Enfant's 1791 plan borrowed much from Versailles, including ceremonial circles and squares, a grid pattern of streets, and broad, diagonal avenues. He described Jenkins Hill, the gentle rise on which he intended to erect the "Congress House," as "a pedestal waiting for a monument." He envisioned the area west of the Congress House (what we now know as the Mall) as a "Grand Avenue, 400 feet in breadth, and about a mile in length, bordered with gardens, ending in a slope from the houses on each side."

Pennsylvania Avenue was to be a broad, uninterrupted line running from the Capitol to the site chosen for the Executive Mansion, but the construction of the Treasury Building in 1836 ruined this straight sight line. The area just north of the White House (basically the president's front yard) was to be part of "President's Park," but Thomas Jefferson, concerned that large, landscaped White House grounds weren't befitting a democratic country, ordered that the area be turned into a public park (now Lafayette Park).

Though skilled at city planning, headstrong L'Enfant had trouble with the game of politics. Things went slightly awry early on when L'Enfant had difficulty with the engravers of the city plan, they got worse when he expressed his resentment at dealing with Secretary of State Thomas Jefferson rather than the president, and they hit rock bottom when he enraged the city commissioners by tearing down a manor house being constructed where he had planned a street. The house belonged to Daniel Carroll—one of the commissioners. Only 11 months after his hire, L'Enfant was let go. He continued to work as an architect, but when he died in 1825, he was poor and bitter, feeling he hadn't been recognized for his genius. His contributions to the city were finally recognized, though, when, in 1909, amid much ceremony, his body was moved from his original burial site in Maryland to Arlington Cemetery at the request of the Washington, D.C., board of commissioners.

British burned the city. Thomas Jefferson, then in retirement at Monticello, offered his personal library as a replacement, noting that "there is, in fact, no subject to which a Member of Congress may not have occasion to refer." Jefferson's collection of 6,487 books laid the foundation for the great national library. The largest library in the world now has almost 130 million items—2.7 million recordings, 12 million photographs, 4.8 million maps, and 58 million manuscripts—on approximately 530 mi of bookshelves.

Built in 1897, the copper-dome Thomas Jefferson Building, based on the Paris Opera House, is the oldest of the three that make up the library. The building's octagonal Main Reading Room contains a grand central desk surrounded by mahogany readers' tables under a 160-foot-high domed ceiling. Computer terminals have replaced card catalogs, but books are still retrieved and dispensed the same way: readers (18 years or older) hand request slips to librarians and wait patiently for their materials to be delivered. Items from the library's collection—which includes one of only three perfect Gutenberg Bibles in the world—are on display in the Jefferson Building's second-floor Southwest Gallery and Pavilion. Information about current and upcoming exhibitions, which can include oral history projects, presidential papers, photographs, and the like, is available by phone or on the Library's Web site. To even begin to come to grips with the magnitude of scope and grandeur of the library, taking one of the free hourly tours is strongly recommended. Well-informed docents can decode the dozens of quirky allegorical sculptures and paintings throughout the building, and can bring you into spaces—such as the glassed-in observation deck over the Main Reading Room—that are closed to solo visitors. ⊠ *Jefferson Bldg., 1st St. and Independence Ave. SE, Capitol Hill* ☎ *202/707–4604, 202/707–5000, or 202/707–6400* ⊕ *www.loc.gov* ✆ *Free* ☉ *Mon.–Sat. 10–5:30; reading room hrs may extend later. Free tours Mon.–Sat. at 10:30, 11:30, 1:30, and 2:30; also 3:30 on weekdays* Ⓜ *Capitol S.*

NEED A BREAK?

True to its name, **The Hawk 'n' Dove** (⊠ 329 Pennsylvania Ave. SE, Capitol Hill ☎ 202/543–3300) may well be the best place in town to overhear aides talk partisan politics over pints. The menu is long on the likes of pastrami sandwiches and old-fashioned chipped beef on toast.

❺ **Supreme Court Building.** It wasn't until 1935 that the Supreme Court got its own building: a white-marble temple with twin rows of Corinthian columns designed by Cass Gilbert. The Supreme Court convenes on the first Monday in October and remains in session until it has heard all of its cases and handed down all of its decisions (usually the end of June). On Monday through Wednesday of two weeks in each month, the justices hear oral arguments in the velvet-swathed court chamber. Visitors who want to listen can choose to wait in either of two lines. One, the "three- to five-minute" line, shuttles you through, giving you a quick impression of the court at work. If you choose the other, and you'd like to stay for the whole show, it's best to be in line by 8:30 AM. The *Washington Post* carries a daily listing of what cases the court will hear. ⊠ *1 1st St. NE, Capitol Hill* ☎ *202/479–3000* ⊕ *www.supremecourtus. gov* ✆ *Free* ☉ *Weekdays 9–4:30* Ⓜ *Union Station or Capitol S.*

❶ Union Station. Chicago architect and commission member Daniel H. Burnham patterned Washington's train depot after the Roman Baths of Diocletian (AD 305). In its heyday, during World War II, more than 200,000 people passed through the building daily. By the 1960s, however, the decline in train travel had turned the station into an expensive white-marble elephant, and by 1981 rain was pouring in through its neglected roof. The Union Station you see today is the result of a restoration, completed in 1988, intended to begin a revival of Washington's east end. Between train travelers and visitors to the shops, restaurants, and a nine-screen movie theater, 70,000 people a day pass through the beaux arts building. The jewel of the structure is the main waiting room, with a 96-foot-high coffered ceiling inlaid with 8 pounds of gold leaf. Forty-six statues of Roman legionnaires, one for each state in the Union when the station was completed, ring the grand room. ⊠ *50 Massachusetts Ave. NE, Capitol Hill* ☎ *202/289–1908* ⊕ *www.unionstationdc.com* Ⓜ *Union Station.*

┏━━ **On Union Station's lower level are more than 20 food stalls with everything from**
┃ NEED A   **pizza to sushi.**
  BREAK?

☕ **❸ United States Botanic Garden.** This glistening, plant-filled oasis was established by Congress in 1842 when surly sea captain Lieutenant Charles Wilkes, rumored to be a model for Captain Ahab, returned from a Congressionally sponsored cartography expedition with a collection of exotic plant species. With equal attention paid to science and aesthetics, the Botanic Garden still contains plants from all around the world, with an emphasis on tropical and economically useful plants, desert plants, and orchids. The adjacent Bartholdi Park, which highlights the art of home landscaping, contains a fountain created by Frédéric-Auguste Bartholdi, sculptor of the Statue of Liberty. On a 3-acre plot immediately to the west, the new **National Garden** is being constructed. It's scheduled to open in September 2006. ⊠ *1st St. and Maryland Ave. SW, Capitol Hill* ☎ *202/225–8333* ⊕ *www.usbg.gov* ⊠ *Free* ☉ *Daily 10–5* Ⓜ *Federal Center SW.*

EAST END

In recent years, developers have rediscovered the "East End," which had been a hole in the city since riots rocked the capital in 1968 after the assassination of Martin Luther King Jr. Buildings are now being torn down, built up, and remodeled at an amazing pace. **Penn Quarter,** the neighborhood immediately surrounding the once down-at-the-heels stretch of Pennsylvania Avenue, has blossomed into one of the hottest addresses in town for nightlife and culture. With its proximity to the venerable Ford's Theatre and the National Theater, a newly opened theater by the acclaimed progressive Woolly Mammoth company, and a major new expansion and arts center from the prestigious Shakespeare Theater due to open in 2007, the neighborhood can rightfully claim to be Washington's own theater district. Meanwhile, new galleries, restaurants, and other cultural hotspots are constantly appearing.

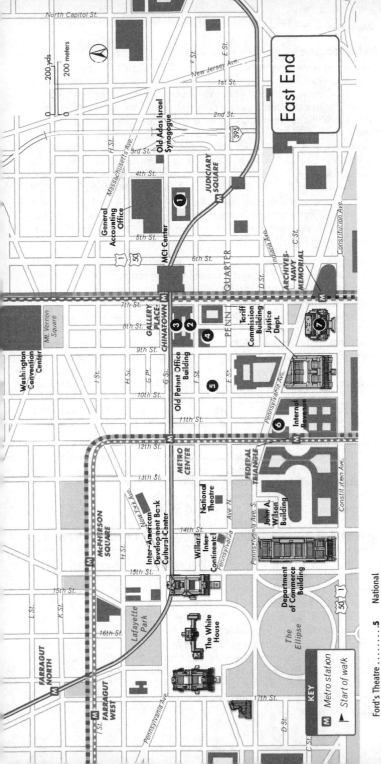

East End

North Capitol St.

200 yds
200 meters

New Jersey Ave.
F St.
E St.
1st St.
2nd St.
395

Old Adas Israel Synagogue
3rd St.
Massachusetts Ave.
H St.
4th St.
General Accounting Office
JUDICIARY SQUARE
M
5th St.
MCI Center
1
1 50
6th St.
PENN QUARTER
C St.
Constitution Ave.
Indiana Ave.
D St.
ARCHIVES-NAVY MEMORIAL
M

7th St.
GALLERY PLACE CHINATOWN
M
8th St.
3 **2**
4
Tariff Commission Building
Justice Dept.
7

Mt. Vernon Square
Washington Convention Center
9th St.
Old Patent Office Building
I St.
H St.
G Pl.
G St.
F St.
E St.
5
Pennsylvania Ave.
Internal Revenue

10th St.
11th St.
6

Metro Center
M
12th St.
13th St.
New York Ave.
National Theatre
FEDERAL TRIANGLE
John A. Wilson Building
Constitution Ave.

Inter-American Development Bank Cultural Center
Willard Inter-Continental
14th St.
Pennsylvania Ave. N
Pennsylvania Ave. S
Department of Commerce Building
50 1

McPHERSON SQUARE
M
H St.
15th St.
Lafayette Park
The White House
The Ellipse

FARRAGUT NORTH
M
FARRAGUT WEST
M
L St.
K St.
15th St.
16th St.
17th St.
Pennsylvania Ave.
D St.
C St.

KEY
M Metro station
▲ Start of walk

Ford's Theatre **5**
International
Spy Museum **4**
National Archives **7**
National
Building Museum **1**

National
Portrait Gallery **2**
Old Post Office **6**
Smithsonian American
Art Museum **3**

What to See

🐾 ❺ **Ford's Theatre.** On the night of April 14, 1865, during a performance of *Our American Cousin,* John Wilkes Booth entered the state box at this successful music hall and shot Abraham Lincoln in the back of the head. The stricken president was carried across the street to the house of tailor William Petersen and died the next morning. You can see the house's restored front and back parlors and the bedroom where the president died. The basement museum at the theater contains artifacts such as Booth's pistol and the clothes Lincoln was wearing when he was shot. The theater itself presents a complete schedule of plays; *A Christmas Carol* is an annual holiday favorite. ⊠ *511 10th St. NW, East End* ☏ *202/ 426–6924* ⊕ *www.nps.gov/foth* 🎟 *Free* ☉ *Daily 9–5; theater closed to visitors during rehearsals and matinees, generally Thurs. and weekends; Lincoln museum in basement remains open at these times* Ⓜ *Metro Center or Gallery Pl.*

🐾 ❹ **International Spy Museum.** Cryptologists, masters of disguise, and former officials of the CIA, FBI, and KGB are among the advisers of this museum, which displays the largest collection of spy artifacts anywhere in the world. Fans of novelist John Le Carré will revel in exhibits such as the School for Spies, which describes what makes a good spy and how they are trained; the Secret History of History, about spying from biblical times to the early 20th century; and 21st-Century Spying, in which espionage experts analyze the latest spy trends. Advance tickets are recommended, particularly in spring and summer. A large gift shop, a café, and the restaurant Zola are here as well. ⊠ *800 F St. NW, East End* ☏ *202/393–7798* ⊕ *www.spymuseum.org* 🎟 *$15, children $12* ☉ *Apr.–Oct., daily 9–8; Nov.–Mar., daily 10–6; hrs subject to change; check Web site before visiting* Ⓜ *Gallery Pl./Chinatown.*

🐾 ❼ **National Archives.** The National Archives and Records Administration is charged with preserving and archiving the United States' most historically important government records. Its 8 billion paper records and 4 billion electronic records date back to 1775, and cover a vast array of subjects. Its three most famous documents, the original Declaration of Independence, Constitution, and Bill of Rights, are housed in the Archives' cathedral-like rotunda, each on a marble platform, encased in bulletproof glass, and floating in pressurized argon, which protects the irreplaceable documents. Though these documents are the star attractions, the 10,000-square-foot Public Vaults—opened in 2004 to great acclaim—showcase the fascinating history and breadth of their holdings. Here you might see anything from the treaty of the Louisiana Purchase to the first edition of *Mad Magazine.* The exhibit also includes holdings from the Archives' 300,000 reels of motion picture film and 200,000 sound recordings. Many of the exhibits are interactive and kidfriendly. While this section operates as a museum, the Archives are also a research resource open to anyone. ⊠ *Constitution Ave. between 7th and 9th Sts. NW, The Mall* ☏ *202/501–5000, 202/501–5205 tours* ⊕ *www.nara.gov* 🎟 *Free* ☉ *Apr.–Labor Day, daily 10–9; Labor Day–Mar., daily 10–5:30; tours weekdays at 10:15 and 1:15* Ⓜ *Archives/ Navy Memorial.*

1

C B ❶ **National Building Museum.** The open interior of this mammoth redbrick edifice is one of the city's great spaces and has been the site of many an inaugural ball, the first of which was for Grover Cleveland in 1885. The eight central Corinthian columns, each made of brick covered with plaster, are among the largest in the world, rising to a height of 75 feet. The museum is devoted to architecture and the building arts: recent exhibits have covered home improvement in 20th-century America, the preservation of Mount Vernon, and tools as an art form. The hands-on displays here are great for kids. Tours are offered at 12:30 Monday through Wednesday; 11:30, 12:30, and 1:30 Thursday through Saturday; and 12:30 and 1:30 Sunday. Family programs are available at 2:30 on weekends. ✉ *401 F St. NW, between 4th and 5th Sts., East End* ☎ *202/ 272-2448* ⊕ *www.nbm.org* 🎫 *Free* ☉ *Mon.–Sat. 10–5, Sun. 11–5* Ⓜ *Judiciary Sq.*

Reynolds Center for American Art and Portraiture. Recently reopened after a six-year, $300 million renovation, the Old Patent Office Building, once the largest in the country, now contains the National Portrait Gallery and the Smithsonian American Art Museum.

❷ Dedicated to collecting images of those who have made "significant contributions" to America's "history, development and culture," the **National Portrait Gallery** has reopened with a new face that will likely make the museum more accessible. No longer is the collection bound by the stipulation that portraits must be of those dead 10 years or more. Along with the iconic "Lansdowne" portrait of George Washington by Gilbert Stuart, and Edgar Degas' portrait of Mary Cassatt, the gallery's 19,000 images now include visions of Tom Wolfe, Toni Morrison, and Shaquille O'Neal.

❸ The **Smithsonian American Art Museum**, considered to be the world's biggest and most diverse collection of American art, has five times more of its collection on display post-renovation. Its more than 41,000 holdings span three centuries, from Colonial portraits to 20th-century abstractionists. Among the 7,000 American artists represented are John Singleton Copley, Winslow Homer, Mary Cassatt, Georgia O'Keeffe, Edward Hopper, David Hockney, and Robert Rauschenberg. ✉ *G St. between 7th and 9th Sts., East End* ☎ *202/633-1000* ⊕ *www. reynoldscenter.org* 🎫 *Free* ☉ *Daily 11:30 7* Ⓜ *Gallery Pl./Chinatown.*

C B ❻ **Old Post Office.** Even better, it's usually not as crowded, the windows are bigger, and—unlike the monument's windows—they're open, allowing cool breezes to waft through. (For self-guided tours, use the entrance at 12th Street and Pennsylvania Avenue and take the glass elevator to the 9th floor.) ■ **TIP➔ Although not as tall as the Washington Monument, the Old Post Office offers nearly as impressive a view.**

✉ *12th St. and Pennsylvania Ave. NW, East End* ☎ *202/606–8691*

WORD OF MOUTH

"The view from the top of the Old Post Office building is almost as good as from the Washington monument and less crowded."

–BOB_KY

tower, 202/289–4224 pavilion ⊕ *www.oldpostofficedc.com* ⊠ *Free*
⊙ *Tower early May–early Sept., daily 8–10:45; mid-Sept.–early May,*
daily 10–5:45; pavilion Apr.–Labor Day, Mon.–Sat. 10–8, Sun. noon–7;
Labor Day–Apr., Mon.–Sat. 10–7, Sun. noon–6 Ⓜ *Federal Triangle.*

GEORGETOWN & FOGGY BOTTOM

Long before the District of Columbia was formed, Washington's oldest and wealthiest neighborhood was a separate city with a harbor full of ships and warehouses filled with tobacco. Washington has filled in around Georgetown over the years, but the former tobacco port retains an air of aloofness. Today some of Washington's most famous residents call Georgetown home, including former *Washington Post* executive editor Ben Bradlee, political pundit George Stephanopoulos, Senator (and 2004 presidential nominee) John Kerry, and *New York Times* op-ed doyenne Maureen Dowd. This is one of Washington's main areas for restaurants, bars, nightclubs, and boutiques.

Foggy Bottom, across the Potomac from Georgetown, has three main claims to fame: the State Department, the Kennedy Center, and George Washington University. Its name is derived from the wharves, breweries, lime kilns, and glassworks that were near the water. Smoke from these factories combined with the swampy air of the low-lying ground to produce a permanent fog along the waterfront.

What to See

Ⓒ **C&O Canal.** When it opened in 1850, this waterway's 74 locks linked Georgetown with Cumberland, Maryland, 184 mi to the northwest, and kept Georgetown open to shipping after its harbor had filled with silt. Lumber, coal, iron, wheat, and flour moved up and down the canal, but it was never as successful as its planners had hoped. Today the canal is part of the National Park System; walkers follow the towpath once used by mules while canoeists paddle the canal's calm waters. Between April and November you can go on a mule-drawn trip aboard the *Georgetown* canal boat. Tickets for the rides, which last about an hour, are available across the canal, next to the Foundry Building. ⊠ *Canal Visitor Center, 1057 Thomas Jefferson St. NW, Georgetown* ☎ *202/653–5190.*

Dumbarton Oaks. Don't confuse Dumbarton Oaks with the nearby Dumbarton House. In 1944 one of the most important events of the 20th century took place here, when representatives of the United States, Great Britain, China, and the Soviet Union met in the music room to lay the groundwork for the United Nations. Career diplomat Robert Woods Bliss and his wife, Mildred, bought the property in 1920, tamed the sprawling grounds, and removed later 19th-century additions that had obscured the Federal lines of the 1801 mansion. In 1940 the Blisses gave the estate to Harvard University, which maintains world-renowned collections of Byzantine and pre-Columbian art and artifacts here. Normally on view to the public are the lavishly decorated music room and selections from Mrs. Bliss's collection of rare illustrated garden books. Because of ongoing renovations at the estate, both art collections and the music room are closed until 2007. Planned by noted landscape ar-

1

chitect Beatrix Farrand, the gardens incorporate elements of traditional English, Italian, and French styles such as a formal rose garden, an English country garden, and an orangery (circa 1810). ✉ *1703 32nd St. NW, Georgetown* ☎ *202/339–6401 or 202/339–6400* 💲 *$7* ☉ *Gardens Apr.–Oct., daily 2–6; Nov.–Mar., daily 2–5.*

John F. Kennedy Center for the Performing Arts. The opening of the Kennedy Center in 1971 instantly established the capital as a locale for the performing arts on an international scale. The Grand Foyer, lighted by 18 1-ton Orrefors crystal chandeliers, is 630 feet long. Many of the center's furnishings were donated by foreign countries: the chandeliers came from Sweden; the tapestries on the walls came from Brazil, France, and Mexico; and the 3,700 tons of white Carrara marble for the interior and exterior of the building were a gift from Italy. Flags fly in the Hall of Nations and the Hall of States, and in the center of the foyer is a 7-foot-high, bronze bust of Kennedy by sculptor Robert Berks. ✉ *New Hampshire Ave. and Rock Creek Pkwy. NW, Foggy Bottom* ☎ *202/467–4600* ⊕ *www.kennedy-center.org* 💲 *Free* ☉ *Daily 10–until end of last show* Ⓜ *Foggy Bottom (free shuttle-bus service every 15 mins to and from Kennedy Center on performance days).*

DUPONT CIRCLE & NORTHWEST D.C.

The main thoroughfares of Connecticut, New Hampshire, and Massachusetts avenues all intersect at Dupont Circle with a small, handsome park and a splashing fountain in the center. Upscale restaurants, offbeat shops, coffeehouses, art galleries, and specialty bookstores give the neighborhood a distinctive, cosmopolitan air. Stores and clubs catering to the neighborhood's large gay community are abundant. Most of the sights in other sections of Northwest D.C. are immediately adjacent to Red Line Metro stops, but all can be easily reached by serious walkers, who will appreciate the leafy thoroughfares of these neighborhoods.

Dupont Circle. Originally known as Pacific Circle, this hub was the westernmost circle in Pierre-Charles L'Enfant's original design for the Federal City. The name was changed in 1884, when Congress authorized construction of a bronze statue honoring Civil War hero Admiral Samuel F. Dupont. The marble fountain in the Circle, with allegorical figures Sea, Stars, and Wind, was created by Daniel Chester French, the sculptor of Lincoln's statue in the Lincoln Memorial.

The Renaissance-style house at **15 Dupont Circle,** next to P Street, was built in 1903 for Robert W. Patterson, publisher of the *Washington Times-Herald,* whose daughter "Cissy" was known for giving parties that attracted notables such as William Randolph Hearst, Douglas MacArthur, and J. Edgar Hoover. Calvin Coolidge and his guest, aviator Charles Lindbergh, also stayed here; some of the most famous photographs of Lindy were taken as he stood on the house's balcony and smiled down at the crowds below. ✉ *Intersection of Connecticut, Massachusetts, and New Hampshire Aves.* Ⓜ *Dupont Circle.*

☾ **National Geographic Society.** Founded in 1888, the society is best known for its magazine. But it has also sponsored numerous expeditions throughout its history, including those of admirals Robert Peary and Richard Byrd and underwater explorer Jacques Cousteau. Explorers Hall, entered from 17th Street, invites you to learn about the world in a decidedly interactive way: you can experience a mini-tornado or use video touch screens that explain geographic concepts and then quiz you. The most dramatic events take place in Earth Station One Interactive Theatre, a 72-seat amphitheater that sends the audience on a journey around the world. The centerpiece is a hand-painted globe, 11 feet in diameter, that floats and spins on a cushion of air, showing off different features of the planet. ⊠ *17th and M Sts. NW, Dupont Circle* ☎ *202/857–7588, 202/857–7689 group tours* ⊕ *www.nationalgeographic.com* ⌨ *Free* ☉ *Mon.–Sat. 9–5, Sun. 10–5* Ⓜ *Farragut North.*

🐾 **National Zoo.** Created by an Act of Congress in 1889, the 163-acre park was designed by landscape architect Frederick Law Olmsted, who also designed the U.S. Capitol grounds. On July 9, 2005, the zoo welcomed its most famous resident, Tai Shan, a giant panda cub born to parents Tian Tian and Mei Xiang. Tai Shan is the first giant panda cub to survive from birth at the National Zoo, and only the third to survive in the United States. Visitors hoping to see the cub should make plans early. Free timed-entry tickets to see the pandas may be reserved weeks in advance, and Tai Shan won't be around for long—he is scheduled to be returned to China in early 2007. Elsewhere in the zoo, innovative compounds show many animals in naturalistic settings, including the Great Flight Cage—a walk-in aviary—open from May to October. Between 10 and 2 each day, you can catch the orangutan population traveling on the "O Line," a series of cables and towers near the Great Ape House that allows the primates to swing hand over hand about 35 feet over your head. The Reptile Discovery Center, the Bird Resource Center, and an exhibition called "How Do You Zoo?" all teach children about biology. The most ambitious addition to the zoo is Amazonia, a reproduction of a South American rain-forest ecosystem. Fish swim behind glass walls, while overhead, monkeys and birds flit from tree to tree. ⊠ *3001 Connecticut Ave. NW, Woodley Park* ☎ *202/673–4800 or 202/673–4717* ⊕ *www. si.edu/natzoo* ⌨ *Free, parking $16* ☉ *May–mid-Sept., daily 6 AM–8 PM; mid-Sept.–Apr., daily 6–6. Zoo buildings open at 10 and close before zoo closes* Ⓜ *Cleveland Park or Woodley Park/Zoo.*

★ **Phillips Collection.** In 1918 Duncan Phillips started to collect art for a museum in his Georgian Revival house that would become America's first permanent museum of modern art. The museum was intended as a memorial to his father and brother, who had died within 13 months of each other. Having no interest in a painting's market value or its faddishness, Phillips searched for pieces that impressed him as outstanding products of a particular artist's unique vision. Holdings include works by Georges Braque, Georgia O'Keeffe, Paul Cézanne, Paul Klee, Henri Matisse, John Henry Twachtman, and Pierre Bonnard. Tempo-

---

WORD OF MOUTH

"One of our very favorite museums that just reopened is the Phillips collection. It is right in Dupont, so would make a nice afternoon activity followed by dinner." –CherylP

rary exhibits frequently pay homage to Phillips's interest in illuminating aesthetic connections between artists. In 2006, the museum unveiled a major new 30,000-square-foot expansion, which includes exhibition spaces for large-scale contemporary art, a 180-seat auditorium, a sculpture garden, and a café.

On Thursday the museum stays open late for live jazz and gallery talks. From September to May, there's a Sunday afternoon concert series at 5 PM in the music room. It's free with museum admission. ✉ *1600 21st St. NW, Dupont Circle* ☎ *202/387-2151* ⊕ *www.phillipscollection.org* ✉ *Free for permanent collection on weekdays; admission varies on weekends and for special exhibitions* ⊙ *Oct.–May, Tues., Wed., Fri., and Sat. 10–5, Thurs. 10–8:30, Sun. noon–7; June–Sept., Tues., Wed., Fri., and Sat. 10–5, Thurs. 10–8:30, Sun. noon–5. Tours Sat. at 2 and Thurs. at 6 and 7. Gallery talk 1st and 3rd Thurs. at 12:30* Ⓜ *Dupont Circle.*

☾ **Rock Creek Park.** The 1,800 acres surrounding Rock Creek have provided a cool oasis for D.C. residents ever since Congress set them aside for recreational use in 1890. Bicycle routes and hiking and equestrian trails wind through the groves of dogwoods, beeches, oaks, and cedar, and 30 picnic areas are scattered about. Rangers at the **Nature Center and Planetarium** (✉ South of Military Rd., 5200 Glover Rd. NW, Northwest ☎ 202/426–6829) introduce visitors to the park and keep track of daily events; guided nature walks leave from the center weekends at 2. The center and planetarium are open Wednesday through Sunday from 9 to 5. ☎ *202/282–1063 park information.*

Washington National Cathedral. Construction of Washington National Cathedral—the sixth-largest cathedral in the world—started in 1907; it was finished and consecrated in 1990. Like its 14th-century Gothic counterparts, the stunning cathedral (officially the Cathedral Church of St. Peter and St. Paul) has a nave, flying buttresses, transepts, and vaults that were built stone by stone. The expansive view of the city from the Pilgrim Gallery is exceptional. The cathedral is Episcopalian but has held services of many denominations, as well as state events such as the funerals of presidents. Its grounds have been shaped into the compact, English-style **Bishop's Garden.** Boxwoods, ivy, tea roses, yew trees, and an assortment of arches, bas-reliefs, and stonework from European ruins provide a restful counterpoint to the cathedral's towers. ✉ *Wisconsin and Massachusetts Aves. NW, Upper Northwest* ☎ *202/537–6200, 202/537–6207 tour information* ⊕ *www.cathedral.org/cathedral* ✉ *Suggested tour donation $3* ⊙ *Early May–early Sept., weekdays 10–5, Sat. 10–4:30, Sun. 8–5; early Sept.–early May, daily 10–5. Sun. services at 8, 9, 10, 11, and 4; evening prayer daily at 4:30; tours every 15 mins Mon.–Sat. 10–11:30 and 12:45–3:15, Sun. 12:45–2:30* Ⓜ *Cleveland Park or Tenleytown.*

WHERE TO EAT

Wall-to-wall ethnic spots line 18th Street NW south from Columbia Road in Adams-Morgan. Parking can be impossible on weekends, but you can walk from the nearest Metro stop, Woodley Park/Zoo, in 10 to 15 minutes. In the East End, restaurants of all stripes (some casual and moderately priced, others upscale and trendy) have sprung up to serve the crowds that attend games at the MCI Center and that enjoy the increasingly chic bar scene. Chinatown, centered on G and H streets NW between 6th and 8th, hosts Chinese, Burmese, Thai, and other Asian restaurants. Capitol Hill has a number of bars that cater to congressional types who need to fortify themselves with food and drink after a day spent running the country, and Union Station houses a large food court offering quick bites that range from barbecue to sushi. Dupont Circle is dense with restaurants and cafés, many with outdoor seating. On Georgetown's main drags, Wisconsin Avenue and M Street, white-tablecloth establishments coexist easily with hole-in-the-wall joints. With some of the hippest bars in the District, quirky vintage stores, and small and lively nightclubs, the U Street neighborhood draws a young crowd day and night. Restaurants stay open late on weekend nights and serve everything from burgers to gourmet pizza and Ethiopian dishes at low prices.

Prices

One way to keep prices down at more upscale places is to go for pretheater menus, where choices may be limited and the tab lower. Many high-end restaurants have separate bar menus that showcase the creativity of the chef at gentler prices. Going to a heavy hitter for lunch rather than dinner is another option. All restaurants are open daily for lunch and dinner unless stated otherwise.

WHAT IT COSTS					
	$$$$	$$$	$$	$	¢
AT DINNER	over $35	$26–$35	$18–$25	$10–$17	under $10

Prices are per person for a main course at dinner.

Adams-Morgan & Woodley Park

African

$ ✕ **Meskerem.** At this bright, appealing Ethiopian restaurant, entrées like stews made with spicy *berbere* chili sauce are served family-style with injera (sourdough flatbread). ⊠ *2434 18th St. NW, Adams-Morgan* ☎ *202/462–4100* ⚹ *Reservations essential* ▤ *AE, DC, MC, V* Ⓜ *Woodley Park/Zoo.*

Latin

¢–$ ✕ **Lauriol Plaza.** Hill staffers flock to this noisy dining room and roof deck for its frozen margaritas and Latin American, Cuban, and Spanish dishes, especially the Cuban-style pork and *lomo saltado* (Peruvian-style strip steak). ■ **TIP➔ The free parking is especially enticing in this area.** ⊠ *1835 18th St. NW, Adams-Morgan* ☎ *202/387–0035* ⚹ *Reservations not accepted* ▤ *AE, D, DC, MC, V* Ⓜ *Dupont Circle.*

Mexican

☺ $ ✕ **Mixtec.** The food's the draw at this truly Mexican restaurant. Although the setting might at worst be described as dingy, the fajitas, enchiladas, and seafood, cooked in the regional styles of Veracruz, Mazatlán, and Acapulco might make you wonder why anybody ever created Tex-Mex. ⊠ *1792 Columbia Rd. NW, Adams-Morgan* ☎ *202/332–1011* ⌕ *Reservations not accepted* ▤ *MC, V* Ⓜ *Woodley Park/Zoo.*

Middle Eastern

$ ✕ **Lebanese Taverna.** The Arabesque ostentation at Taverna gives it a warm elegance. But what really satisfies is the food, including Arabic bread baked in a wood-burning oven and the lamb, beef, chicken, and seafood grilled on kebabs, slow roasted, or smothered with a garlicky yogurt sauce. ⊠ *2641 Connecticut Ave. NW, Woodley Park* ☎ *202/265–8681* ▤ *AE, MC, V* Ⓜ *Woodley Park/Zoo.*

Capitol Hill

American

$$–$$$$ ✕ **Charlie Palmer.** It's hard not to feel like a master of the universe when ensconced in this coolly elegant dining room with a drop-dead view of the Capitol. Oversize floral arrangements, senators making deals nearby, and a dramatic glass-enclosed wine cellar form a backdrop to the contemporary cuisine. The steaks are exquisite. ⊠ *101 Constitution Ave., Capitol Hill* ☎ *202/547–8100* ▤ *AE, D, DC, MC, V* ☉ *Closed Sun. No lunch Sat.* Ⓜ *Union Station.*

Belgian

$–$$ ✕ **Belga Café.** The "Euro-fusion" menu at this sleek café done up with dark wood and exposed brick also includes traditional items such as mussels and the crispiest of french fries. Refreshingly, Belga's expertly turned out brunch menu features items not available elsewhere in town, like the warm goat cheese waffle with red pepper coulis. The Belgian beer list is long and well conceived. ⊠ *514 8th St. SE, Capitol Hill* ☎ *202/544–0100* ▤ *AE, MC, V* ☉ *Closed Mon.*

French

$–✕ **Montmartre.** With its sidewalk café, cheerful yellow walls, and chic fare, Montmartre evokes the Left Bank of Paris. This unpretentious bistro (still a politicians' hangout) straddles classic and modern effortlessly with dishes like cream of chestnut soup, braised rabbit with olives and shiitake mushrooms, and cod with homemade spaetzle. ⊠ *327 7th St., Capitol Hill* ☎ *202/544–1244* ⌕ *Reservations essential* ▤ *AE, D, MC, V* ☉ *Closed Mon.* Ⓜ *Eastern Market.*

Downtown

African

$$$ ✕ **Marrakesh.** In a neighborhood better known for auto-supply shops, Marrakesh supplies a taste of Morocco in a fixed-price ($29 per person) five-course feast. Belly dancers perform nightly. ⊠ *617 New York Ave. NW, Downtown* ☎ *202/393–9393* ⌕ *Reservations essential* ▤ *No credit cards* Ⓜ *Mt. Vernon/UDC.*

American

★ $$$$ ✕ **CityZen.** In this glowing space with soaring ceilings, chef Eric Zeibold, formerly of Napa Valley's famed French Laundry, creates luxe fixed-price

Where to Eat in Washington, D.C.

meals from the finest ingredients. Unexpected little treasures, such as scrambled eggs with white truffles shaved at the table and buttery miniature Parker House rolls, accentuate the main courses, which include black bass over caramelized cauliflower and braised veal shank with potato gnocchi. ⊠ *Mandarin Oriental, 1330 Maryland Ave. SW, Downtown* ☎ *202/787–6868* ⚭ *Reservations essential* ▤ *AE, D, DC, MC, V* ☉ *Closed Mon. No lunch.*

Asian

¢–$ ✕ **Nooshi.** Always packed, with long lines waiting for tables and takeout, this attractive Pan-Asian noodle house has remarkably good Chinese, Thai, Indonesian, Malaysian, and Vietnamese dishes and sushi. Try the Thai drunken noodles soused in sake; gado-gado, a "cooked" Filipino salad; or the Vietnamese rice noodles with grilled chicken. ⊠ *1120 19th St. NW, Dupont Circle* ☎ *202/293–3138* ⚭ *Reservations essential* ▤ *AE, DC, MC, V* ☉ *No lunch Sun.* Ⓜ *Farragut North.*

☾ ¢ ✕ **Teaism.** This informal teahouse stocks more than 50 teas imported from India, Japan, and Africa, along with healthy and delicious Japanese, Indian, and Thai food. Small dishes include tandoori kebabs, tea-cured salmon, and Indian flat breads. The larger *palaak paneer,* a spinach-based Indian dish, and a juicy ostrich burger are particularly tasty. ⊠ *400 8th St. NW, Downtown* ☎ *202/638–7740* ▤ *AE, MC, V* Ⓜ *Navy/Archives* ⊠ *800 Connecticut Ave. NW, Downtown* ☎ *202/ 835–2233* Ⓜ *Farragut West.*

Contemporary

$–$$ ✕ **Poste.** Inside the trendy Hotel Monaco, Poste woos with a towering skylighted space that until 1901 was the General Post Office. Chef Robert Weland conjures up modern American brasserie fare such as foie gras terrine with cognac jelly and pan-roasted sirloin with truffled frites. In season, panfried softshell crabs are not to be missed. In warmer months, the neoclassical courtyard is a serene spot for cocktails and light fare. ⊠ *Hotel Monaco, 555 8th St. NW, Downtown* ☎ *202/783–6060* ▤ *AE, D, DC, MC, V* Ⓜ *Gallery Pl./Chinatown.*

☾ ¢ ✕ **Breadline.** Crowded, quirky, sometimes chaotic, this restaurant makes not only the city's best baguette but also some of its best sandwiches, including tuna salad with preserved lemons. Owner Mark Furstenberg makes everything on the premises. Arrive early or late to avoid the noontime rush. Outdoor seating is available in warmer months. ⊠ *1751 Pennsylvania Ave. NW, Downtown* ☎ *202/*

CHEAP, QUICK & TASTY: LUNCH

D.C. is a hardworking city, but it has more than its fair share of good-deal lunch spots. In Dupont, **Well-Dressed Burrito** (⊠ 1220 19th St. NW), **Nooshi** (⊠ 1120 19th St. NW), and **Julia's Empanadas** (⊠ 1221 Connecticut Ave.) shouldn't be missed. Near the White House, stop in for a sandwich at **Breadline** (⊠ 1751 Pennsylvania Ave. NW). Hitting the museums? Try the cafés at the Museum of the Native American, the Museum of Natural History, the National Gallery of Art, and the Reynolds Center for American Art and Portraiture.

822–8900 ⌘ *Reservations not accepted* ▭ *AE, MC, V* ☉ *Closed weekends. No dinner* Ⓜ *Farragut West.*

Indian

$–$$ ✕ **Bombay Club.** One block from the White House, the beautiful Bombay Club re-creates the refined aura of British private clubs in Colonial India. On the menu are unusual seafood specialties and a large number of vegetarian dishes, but the real standouts are the breads and the seafood appetizers. Most men wear jackets here. ⊠ *815 Connecticut Ave. NW, Downtown* ☎ *202/659–3727* ⌘ *Reservations essential* ▭ *AE, D, DC, MC, V* ☉ *No lunch Sat.* Ⓜ *Farragut West.*

Italian

$$–$$$
Fodor'sChoice
★
✕ **Galileo.** Sophisticated Piedmont-style cooking is served at what is really three restaurants under one roof by entrepreneur-chef Roberto Donna. These days, the main dining room is eclipsed by Laboratorio, Donna's 30-seat restaurant within a restaurant, where he cooks a 12-course meal in a glamorous open kitchen ($110 weekdays, $125 weekends), and the Osteria, where prices are low (¢–$) and the fare rustic. ⊠ *1110 21st St. NW, Downtown* ☎ *202/293–7191* ⌘ *Reservations essential* ▭ *AE, D, DC, MC, V* ☉ *No lunch weekends* Ⓜ *Foggy Bottom/GWU.*

Latin American

$–$$ ✕ **Café Atlántico.** At this inventive *nuevo Latino* restaurant guacamole is made table-side and scallops are served with coconut rice, ginger, squid, and squid-ink oil. On weekends, Atlántico offers tapas-size portions of dishes such as duck confit with passion-fruit oil, pineapple shavings, and plantain powder. At the six-stool Minibar, you can explore an $85 prix-fixe meal of 30 creative morsels, such as a foie gras "lollipop" coated with cotton candy, conjured up before your eyes. ⊠ *405 8th St. NW, Downtown* ☎ *202/393–0812* ⌘ *Reservations essential* ▭ *AE, DC, MC, V* Ⓜ *Archives/Navy Memorial.*

Middle Eastern

¢–$$ ✕ **Zaytinya.** This sophisticated urban dining room with soaring ceilings is a local favorite for meeting friends or dining with a group. Zaytinya devotes practically its entire menu to Turkish, Greek, and Lebanese small plates, including the popular braised lamb with eggplant puree and cheese and the baba ghanoush, made of mashed eggplant. ■ **TIP→ The multitude of options makes this a great choice for vegetarians and meat lovers alike.** Reservations for times after 6:30 are not accepted. ⊠ *701 9th St. NW, Downtown* ☎ *202/638–0800* ▭ *AE, DC, MC, V* Ⓜ *Gallery Pl./Chinatown.*

Southern

$–$$ ✕ **Georgia Brown's.** An elegant New South eatery with an airy dining room that's a favorite hangout of local politicians, Georgia Brown's serves shrimp Carolina-style (head intact, with steaming grits on the side), fried-green tomatoes filled with herb cream cheese, and a pecan pie made with bourbon and imported Belgian dark chocolate. ⊠ *950 15th St. NW, Downtown* ☎ *202/393–4499* ▭ *AE, D, DC, MC, V* ⌘ *Reservations essential* ☉ *No lunch Sat.* Ⓜ *McPherson Sq.*

Good Brews

CLOSE UP

SEVERAL NOTEWORTHY MICROBREWERIES and brewpubs call the Washington area home. The Olde Heurich Brewing Company, successor to the Christian Heurich Brewing Co. (founded 1873), makes Foggy Bottom ale and lager, available at select bars, restaurants, and stores in metro D.C., but they do not currently operate a brewpub.

At **Capitol City Brewing Company's** three locations—Capitol Hill near Union Station (✉ 2 Massachusetts Ave. NW ☎ 202/842–2337); Downtown (✉ 1100 New York Ave. NW ☎ 202/628–2222); Arlington, VA (✉ 2700 S. Quincy St. ☎ 703/578–3888)—you'll find ales, pilsners, and lagers along with beer-friendly eats such as bratwurst, burgers, fish-and-chips, and a root-beer float made with house-brewed root beer. Kolsch, made with ale and lager yeasts, is an unusual must-try.

In Virginia, Alexandria's **Shenandoah Brewing Company** (✉ 652 S. Pickett St. ☎ 703/823–9508) is an award

winner. Aficionados praise its stouts and ales, especially the Bourbon Stoney Stout, aged in oak casks previously used to make premium bourbon. Inside, the atmosphere is slightly industrial and the menu is limited to foods grown or made in Virginia: peanuts, potato chips, chili, and a delicious beer-queso dip.

Two national chains also have brewpubs in the D.C. area: California-based **Gordon Biersch** (✉ 900 F St. NW ☎ 202/783–5454) makes lagers like the crisp Golden Export in a converted downtown bank building, where you can accompany your beer with anything from pizza to meat loaf. The Colorado-based **Rock Bottom Brewery** has brewpubs in Arlington, Virginia (✉ 4238 Wilson Blvd., #1256 ☎ 703/516–7688) and Bethesda, Maryland (✉ 7900 Norfolk Ave. ☎ 301/652–1311), and pours ales, lagers, and porters alongside fixings such as fried chicken, barbecued ribs, pizza, and cheesecake made with the house stout.

Spanish

$$–$$$$ ✕ **Jaleo.** You are encouraged to make a meal of the long list of tapas at this lively Spanish bistro, although entrées such as paella are just as tasty. Tapas highlights include the *gambas al ajillo* (sautéed garlic shrimp), fried potatoes with spicy tomato sauce, and the grilled chorizo. Flamenco dancers heat up the restaurant on Wednesdays. ✉ *480 7th St. NW, Downtown* ☎ *202/628–7949* ▤ *AE, D, DC, MC, V* Ⓜ *Gallery Pl./Chinatown.*

Dupont Circle

Contemporary

★ **$$–$$$$**   ✕ **Komi.** Johnny Monis, the young, energetic chef–owner of this small, personal restaurant, offers one of the city's most adventurous dining experiences. Star plates from the Mediterranean-influenced menu (prix fixe on weekends) include fresh sardines with pickled lemons, suckling pig over apples and bacon with polenta, and mascarpone-filled dates with sea salt. ✉ *1509 17th St., Dupont Circle* ☎ *202/332–9200*

⚠️ *Reservations essential* 🍴 *AE, D, MC, V* ☺ *Closed Mon. No lunch* Ⓜ *Dupont Circle.*

$$–$$$ ✕ **Nora.** The organic food served here, like the quilt-decorated dining room, is sophisticated and attractive. Entrées such as seared rockfish with artichoke broth, grilled lamb chops with a white-bean sauce, and risotto with winter vegetables emphasize well-balanced, complex ingredients. ✉ *2132 Florida Ave. NW, Dupont Circle* ☎ *202/462–5143* ⚠️ *Reservations essential* 🍴 *AE, D, MC, V* ☺ *Closed Sun. No lunch* Ⓜ *Dupont Circle.*

French

¢–$$ ✕ **Bistrot du Coin.** This moderately priced French bistro with a monumental zinc bar is noisy, crowded, and fun. The comforting, traditional bistro fare includes starter portions of mussels in several different preparations, hangar steak garnished with a pile of crisp fries, and a duck-leg confit. ✉ *1738 Connecticut Ave. NW, Dupont Circle* ☎ *202/234–6969* 🍴 *AE, D, DC, MC, V* Ⓜ *Dupont Circle.*

Italian

☕ **$** ✕ **Pizzeria Paradiso.** A trompe-l'oeil ceiling adds space and light to a simple interior at the ever-popular Pizzeria Paradiso. Although the standard pizza is satisfying, you can enliven it with fresh buffalo mozzarella or unusual toppings such as potatoes, capers, and mussels. The intensely flavored gelato is a house specialty. A larger location with a beer cellar is in Georgetown. ✉ *2029 P St. NW, Dupont Circle* ☎ *202/223–1245* ⚠️ *Reservations not accepted* 🍴 *DC, MC, V* Ⓜ *Dupont Circle* ✉ *3282 M St. NW, Georgetown* ☎ *202/337–1245* ⚠️ *Reservations not accepted* 🍴 *DC, MC, V.*

Georgetown/West End/Glover Park

American

$$–$$$ ✕ **Palena.** Chef Frank Ruta and pastry chef Ann Amernick met while working in the White House kitchens. At their contemporary American restaurant, the French- and Italian-influenced menu changes seasonally, but includes earthy items like crisp puff pastry with fresh sardines and greens, chervil-and-morel soup, a veal chop with a barley-stuffed pepper, and a sprightly lemon caramel tart. Reservations are not accepted for the equally fabulous lounge, where the inexpensive menu ($) includes a cheeseburger with truffles and an extravagant platter of fries, fried onion rings, and paper-thin fried Meyer lemon slices. ✉ *3529 Connecticut Ave. NW, Cleveland Park* ☎ *202/537–9250* ⚠️ *Reservations essential* 🍴 *AE, D, DC, MC, V* ☺ *Restaurant and lounge closed Sun. Restaurant closed Mon. No lunch* Ⓜ *Cleveland Park.*

☕ ¢ ✕ **Five Guys.** This homegrown fast-food burger house gets just about everything right, from the grilled hot dogs and hand-patted burger patties to the fresh hand-cut fries with the skins on and the high-quality toppings such as sautéed onions and mushrooms. ✉ *1335 Wisconsin Ave. NW, Georgetown* ☎ *202/337–0400* 🍴 *MC, V.*

Asian

$–$$ ✕ **Sushi-Ko.** At one of the city's best Japanese restaurants, daily specials are always innovative: sesame oil–seasoned trout is layered with crisp wonton crackers, and a sushi special might be salmon topped with a touch of mango sauce and a sprig of dill. ⊠ *2309 Wisconsin Ave. NW, Georgetown* ☎ *202/333–4187* ⌔ *Reservations essential* ⊟ *AE, MC, V* ۞ *No lunch Sat.–Mon.*

Contemporary

$$$$ ✕ Citronelle. See all the action in the glass-front kitchen at chef Michel
Fodor'sChoice Richard's flagship California–French restaurant. Appetizers might in-
★ clude foie gras with lentils prepared three ways, and main courses include lobster medallions with lemongrass and saddle of lamb crusted with herbs. A chef's table in the kitchen gives you a ringside seat. The fixed-price menu ranges from $85 to $150; the bar menu ($–$$$) has morsels such as mushroom "cigars" and Serrano ham. ⊠ *Latham Hotel, 3000 M St. NW, Georgetown* ☎ *202/625–2150* ⌔ *Reservations essential* ⋒ *Jacket required* ⊟ *AE, D, DC, MC, V* ۞ *No lunch.*

$$–$$$$ ✕ 1789. This dining room with Early American paintings and a fireplace could easily be a room in the White House. But all the gentility of this 19th-centurytown-house–restaurant is offset by the down-to-earth food on the seasonal menu. Rack of lamb and fillet of beef are specialties, and the seafood dishes are excellent. ⊠ *1226 36th St. NW, Georgetown* ☎ *202/965–1789* ⌔ *Reservations essential* ⋒ *Jacket required* ⊟ *AE, D, DC, MC, V* ۞ *No lunch.*

Seafood

$$–$$$ ✕ Black Salt. Black Salt is part fish market, part gossipy neighborhood hangout, part modern restaurant. The pristine dishes vary from classics like oyster stew and fried Ipswich clams to more offbeat fixings like fluke with cider vinegar and a tiramisu martini for dessert. ⊠ *4883 MacArthur Blvd., Palisades* ☎ *202/342–9101* ⌔ *Reservations essential* ⊟ *AE, D, DC, MC, V* ۞ *Closed Mon.*

U Street

Italian

$–$$ ✕ Coppi's Organic Restaurant. An Italian bicycling motif permeates this restaurant, from the photographs on the walls to the monogrammed racing shirts worn by the staff. The wood oven–baked pizzas are always good, but the frequently changing menu also includes items such as asparagus, English peas, and favas gently sautéed with butter and mint, or pastas such as gnocchi with black-truffle pesto, and *trenette* with porcini and strip steak. For dessert, there's biscotti made in the brick oven and a sweet calzone filled with Nutella. ⊠ *1414 U St. NW, U St. corridor* ☎ *202/319–7773* ⊟ *AE, D, DC, MC, V* ۞ *No lunch* Ⓜ *U Street/ Cardozo.*

WHERE TO STAY

Forced to cater to all stripes, from lobbyists with expense accounts to those in town for the free museums, from bigwigs seeking attention to those flying under the radar, Washington's rooms suit everyone. The high-end and business-class hotels are located mainly near the halls of power, whether in Georgetown rowhouses, near the White House, or on Capitol Hill. Downtown, quickly becoming the city's nerve center, also has its fair share. There's a good chance that, if you stay in one of the pricier digs in these areas, you can sign a guest register touched by diplomats and then sleep in beds where royalty rested. The District's boutique hotels and cool guesthouses tend to congregate in the shadier areas of Northwest D.C.

Prices

	WHAT IT COSTS				
	$$$$	$$$	$$	$	¢
FOR 2 PEOPLE	over $400	$296–$399	$211–$295	$125–$210	under $125

Prices are for a standard double room in high season, excluding 14.5% room tax.

Capitol Hill

$–$$ ⊞ **Holiday Inn on the Hill.** Rooms here are unexpectedly stylish, with silky blue comforters, black granite countertops, and ergonomic chairs. Enjoy free high-speed Internet access and a rooftop swimming pool. Children under 12 eat free. ⊠ *415 New Jersey Ave. NW, Capitol Hill 20001* ☎ *202/ 638–1616 or 800/638–1116* 🖨 *202/638–0707* ⊕ *www.holiday-inn. com* ⟿ *343 rooms, 4 suites* ⚬ *Restaurant, room service, cable TV with movies and video games, in-room broadband, pool, exercise equipment, gym, bar, business services, meeting rooms, parking (fee)* ▤ *AE, D, DC, MC, V* Ⓜ *Union Station.*

Downtown

$$$–$$$$ ⊞ **Hotel Monaco.** The interior of the 1839 Tariff Building has been bril-
Fodor's Choice liantly restored to add a colorful, playful twist to the landmark edifice.
★ Rooms have 15-foot vaulted ceilings, eclectic furnishings, and martini kits. Poste Brasserie serves contemporary American cuisine. ⊠ *700 F St. NW, Penn Quarter 20004* ☎ *202/628–7177 or 800/649–1202* 🖨 *202/628–7277* ⊕ *www.monaco-dc.com* ⟿ *167 rooms, 16 suites* ⚬ *Restaurant, room service, in-room safes, in-room broadband, gym, laundry service, concierge, parking (fee), some pets allowed* ▤ *AE, D, DC, MC, V* Ⓜ *Gallery Pl./Chinatown.*

$$$–$$$$ ⊞ **Mandarin Oriental Washington, D.C.** This sophisticated hotel offers some-
what plain rooms—decorated with soft Asian touches and high-tech amenities—that overlook either the Mall or the nearby Jefferson Memo-
rial. The Mandarin has a stunning art collection, a gorgeous spa, and CityZen, one of Washington's hottest restaurants. ⊠ *1330 Maryland Ave. SW, Downtown 20024* ☎ *202/554–8588 or 888/888–1778* 🖨 *202/ 554–8999* ⊕ *www.mandarinoriental.com* ⟿ *347 rooms, 53 suites* ⚬ *2 restaurants, room service, in-room safes, minibars, in-room data ports, indoor pool, fitness classes, health club, hair salon, spa, bar, lobby lounge, dry cleaning, laundry service, concierge, concierge floor, busi-
ness services, meeting rooms, airport shuttle, parking (fee), no-smok-
ing floors* ▤ *AE, D, DC, MC, V* Ⓜ *Smithsonian.*

$$$–$$$$ ⊞ **Sofitel Lafayette Square Washington.** This boutique hotel has maintained its 1920s stylings, with a sophisticated lobby and chic, though slightly

Where to Stay in Washington, D.C.

D.C. HOTEL TIPS

■ If you can stand semitropical weather, come in August, during the congressional recess, when Washington is calm and less expensive. Rates also drop in late December and January, except around an inauguration.

■ Reservations: With more than 63,000 guest rooms, Washington can almost always provide a place to stay—though it's always prudent to reserve. Hotels often fill up with conventioneers, politicians in transit, families, and, in spring, school groups. Hotel rooms in D.C. can be hard to come by during the Cherry Blossom Festival in late March or early April, and also in May, when so many graduate from college. Late October's Marine Corps Marathon also increases demand for rooms. The **Washington, DC Convention and Tourism Corporation** (☎ 800/ 422–8644 ⊕ www.washington.org) runs a reservation service.

■ Parking: Hotel parking fees range from free (often in the suburbs) to $30 (plus tax) per night. This sometimes involves valet parking, with its implied additional gratuities. Street parking is free, but sparse, on Sunday and usually after 6:30 PM weekdays.

small, guest rooms with beautiful marble bathrooms. Cafe 15 serves artful French dishes under the consultation of a Michelin three-star chef. ⊠ *806 15th St. NW, Downtown 20005* ☎ *202/730–8800* 🖷 *202/730–8500* ⊕ *www.sofitel.com* 📞 *221 rooms, 16 suites* ♦ *Restaurant, room service, in-room safes, minibars, in-room broadband, gym, bar, dry cleaning, concierge, business services, meeting rooms, some pets allowed* ▤ *AE, D, DC, MC, V* Ⓜ *MacPherson Sq.*

★ $$$–$$$$ 🏨 **Willard InterContinental.** The historic beaux artslobby, long a favorite of American presidents, showcases great columns, sparkling chandeliers, and mosaic floors. Period detail is reflected in the rooms, which have elegant, Federal-style furniture, as well as sleek marble bathrooms. The Willard also has an outstanding spa and fitness center. ⊠ *1401 Pennsylvania Ave. NW, Downtown 20004* ☎ *202/628–9100* 🖷 *202/637–7326* ⊕ *www.washington.interconti.com* 📞 *301 rooms, 40 suites* ♦ *3 restaurants, room service, in-room safes, minibars, some microwaves, cable TV, in-room broadband, health club, bar, shops, babysitting, dry cleaning, laundry service, concierge, business services, meeting rooms, parking (fee), some pets allowed* ▤ *AE, D, DC, MC, V* Ⓜ *Metro Center.*

$$$ 🏨 **Hay-Adams Hotel.** Statesman John Hay and historian Henry Adams once owned homes on the site where this Italian Renaissance mansion now stands. The elegant hotel offers outstanding personalized service, and the White House views from the upper floors are stunning. The Lafayette Room serves exquisite American cuisine. ⊠ *1 Lafayette Sq. NW, Downtown 20006* ☎ *202/638–6600 or 800/853–6807* 🖷 *202/638–2716 or 202/638–3803* ⊕ *www.hayadams.com* 📞 *125 rooms, 20 suites* ♦ *Restaurant, room service, minibars, some refrigerators, cable TV with movies, Wi-Fi, bar, dry cleaning, laundry service, concierge, business services, parking (fee), some pets allowed* ▤ *AE, D, DC, MC, V* Ⓜ *McPherson Sq. or Farragut North.*

$$$ 🏨 **Renaissance Mayflower Hotel.** FDR wrote his first inaugural address in Suite 776 of this luxury hotel, built in 1925. The Mayflower's two-level lobby with its block-long parade of chandeliers is a magnificent neoclassic public space. Rooms are elegant, though on the small side. Café Promenade serves contemporary Mediterranean cuisine. ✉ *1127 Connecticut Ave. NW, Downtown 20036* 🕿 *202/347–3000 or 800/228–7697* 🖷 *202/776–9182* ⊕ *www.marriott.com* 🛏 *657 rooms, 74 suites* ⚐ *Restaurant, room service, minibars, cable TV with movies and video games, Wi-Fi, gym, bar, babysitting, dry cleaning, laundry service, concierge, concierge floor, business services, parking (fee)* ⊟ *AE, D, DC, MC, V* Ⓜ *Farragut North.*

$$–$$$ 🏨 **Morrison-Clark Inn.** This Victorian inn functioned as the Soldiers', Sailors', Marines', and Airmen's Club in the early 1900s. The antiques-filled public rooms have marble fireplaces, bay windows, and 14-foot pier mirrors. Rooms have antique furnishings, and six have fireplaces. ✉ *1015 L St. NW, Downtown 20001* 🕿 *202/898–1200 or 800/332–7898* 🖷 *202/289–8576* ⊕ *www.morrisonclark.com* 🛏 *42 rooms, 13 suites* ⚐ *Restaurant, room service, minibars, cable TV, Wi-Fi, gym, dry cleaning, laundry service, concierge, business services, parking (fee)* ⊟ *AE, D, DC, MC, V* ⦿l *CP* Ⓜ *Metro Center.*

$–$$ 🏨 **Lincoln Suites.** The "suites" are large efficiency rooms with full or partial kitchens and vanity areas. The hotel's location and low rates make it an excellent value. ✉ *1823 L St. NW, Downtown 20036* 🕿 *202/223–4320 or 800/424–2970* 🖷 *202/223–8546* 🛏 *99 rooms* ⚐ *2 restaurants, kitchenettes, cable TV with movies, laundry facilities, business services, parking (fee), some pets allowed* ⊟ *AE, D, DC, MC, V* ⦿l *CP* Ⓜ *Farragut North or Farragut West.*

Dupont Circle

$$–$$$ 🏨 **Westin Embassy Row.** This formal Westin has an English hunt-club theme and complimentary butler service. The intimate guest rooms are furnished with brocade draperies and reproduction antiques from late-1800s Washington. ✉ *2100 Massachusetts Ave. NW, Dupont Circle 20008* 🕿 *202/293–2100 or 888/625–5144* 🖷 *202/293–0641* ⊕ *www.starwoodhotels.com/westin* 🛏 *160 rooms, 46 suites* ⚐ *Restaurant, room service, in-room safes, minibars, cable TV, in-room broadband, gym, massage, sauna, bar, laundry service, concierge, business services, meeting rooms, parking (fee), some pets allowed (fee)* ⊟ *AE, D, DC, MC, V* Ⓜ *Dupont Circle.*

★ $–$$$ 🏨 **Hotel Rouge.** This gay-friendly postmodern hotel bathed in red exudes Florida's South Beach club scene. Guest rooms, decorated with swank eye-catching furniture, are an extension of the hip lobby lounge. ✉ *1315 16th St. NW, Dupont Circle 20036* 🕿 *202/232–8000 or 800/738–1202* 🖷 *202/667–9827* ⊕ *www.rougehotel.com* 🛏 *137 rooms* ⚐ *Restaurant, room service, in-room safes, some kitchenettes, minibars, refrigerators, cable TV with video games, Wi-Fi, health club, bar, concierge, business services, parking (fee), some pets allowed* ⊟ *AE, D, DC, MC, V* Ⓜ *Dupont Circle.*

★ ¢–$ 🏨 **Hotel Tabard Inn.** Although (or because) the wooden floorboards creak and room sizes vary considerably (some share bathrooms), this dimly lighted hotel feels like an old-world inn with alluring nooks and crannies and a brick-walled garden. The Tabard Inn's fireside bar is one of the city's coziest winter retreats. Passes are provided to the nearby YMCA. ⊠ *1739 N St. NW, Dupont Circle 20036* ☎ *202/785–1277* 🖷 *202/785–6173* ⊕ *www.tabardinn.com* ⇘ *40 rooms, 25 with bath* ⚖ *Restaurant, in-room data ports, Wi-Fi, bar, lobby lounge, laundry facilities, business services, some pets allowed; no TV in some rooms* ▤ *AE, D, DC, MC, V* ⦿❘ *CP* Ⓜ *Dupont Circle.*

Georgetown

$$$$ ⌾ **Ritz-Carlton Georgetown.** This Ritz, industrial but cozy, is built on the site of Georgetown's 1932 incinerator: the smokestack's still here. The upper-level rooms and suites facing south have amazing views of the Potomac; all have feather duvets, goose-down pillows, marble baths, and access to a personal concierge. ⊠ *3100 South St. NW, Georgetown 20037* ☎ *202/912–4200 or 800/241–3333* 🖷 *202/912–4199* ⊕ *www.ritzcarlton. com/hotels/georgetown* ⇘ *57 rooms, 29 suites* ⚖ *Restaurant, room service, in-room safes, minibars, cable TV, in-room data ports, health club, bar, lobby lounge, cinema, laundry service, concierge, meeting rooms, parking (fee)* ▤ *AE, D, DC, MC, V.*

Woodley Park

¢–$ ⌾ **Woodley Park Guest House.** This warm, peaceful B&B on a quiet residential street lies near the zoo, Adams-Morgan, and Rock Creek Park. Antiques-filled rooms are individually decorated, and some have private baths. A two-night minimum stay is required. ⊠ *2647 Woodley Rd. NW, Woodley Park 20008* ☎ *202/667–0218 or 866/667–0218* 🖷 *202/667–1080* ⊕ *www.woodleyparkguesthouse.com* ⇘ *18 rooms, 11 with bath* ⚖ *Laundry service, Wi-Fi, parking (fee); no room TVs, no kids under 12* ▤ *AE, MC, V* ⦿❘ *CP* Ⓜ *Woodley Park/Zoo.*

¢ ⌾ **Adam's Inn.** The Victorian-style rooms at this bed-and-breakfast are small but comfortable. Many share baths, but those that do also have a sink in the room. A communal kitchen and limited garage parking are available. There are pay phones, cable TV, and free Wi-Fi in the public areas. ⊠ *1744 Lanier Pl. NW, Woodley Park 20009* ☎ *202/745–3600 or 800/578–6807* 🖷 *202/319–7958* ⊕ *www.adamsinn.com* ⇘ *26 rooms, 15 with bath* ⚖ *Laundry facilities, business services, parking (fee); no room phones, no room TVs* ▤ *AE, D, DC, MC, V* ⦿❘ *CP* Ⓜ *Woodley Park/Zoo.*

NIGHTLIFE & THE ARTS

From buttoned-down political appointees to laid-back folks who were born here, Washingtonians have plenty of options when they head out for the night. Most bars are clustered in several key areas. Penn Quarter near the Verizon Center and U Street NW between 12th and 15th streets are quickly becom-

> **GOOD TO KNOW**
>
> Last call in D.C. is 2 AM, and most bars and clubs close by 3 AM on the weekends and between midnight and 2 AM during the week.

ing the hottest spots in town. Georgetown has dozens of bars, nightclubs, and restaurants at the intersection of Wisconsin and M streets. A host of small live-music venues and popular bars line the 18th Street strip in Adams-Morgan between Columbia Road and Kalorama Avenue. The stretch of Pennsylvania Avenue between 2nd and 4th streets SE has a half-dozen Capitol Hill bars. Hill staffers also hang out on Barrack's Row, 8th Street SE south of D Street. For a high-powered happy hour, head to the intersection of 19th and M streets NW, near lawyer- and lobbyist-filled downtown.

D.C. has also gone from being a cultural desert to a thriving arts center in the past 40 years. To satiate the educated young professionals who flock here for opportunities in government, the arts scene has exploded. To sift through the flurry of events, check out the daily "Guide to the Lively Arts," in the *Washington Post,* and the "Weekend" section on Friday. On Thursday, look for the free weekly *Washington CityPaper* (⊕ www.washingtoncitypaper.com). The *Washington Post* (⊕www.washingtonpost.com/cityguide) also publishes an Internet-based entertainment guide.

TICKETplace sells half-price, day-of-performance tickets for select shows. ⊠ *Old Post Office Pavilion, 406 7th St. NW, Downtown* ☎ *202/842–5387* ⊕ *www.ticketplace.org* Ⓜ *Archives/Navy Memorial.*

Live Music

Blues Alley. This legendary club, where jazz greats Dizzy Gillespie and Charlie Byrd once recorded live albums, still pulls well-known performers. ■ TIP➔ Buying a meal gets you better seats. ⊠ *1073 Wisconsin Ave. NW, near M St., Georgetown* ☎ *202/337–4141* Ⓜ *Foggy Bottom.*

HR-57. This warm, inviting club spotlights local musicians, some of whom have national followings. Fried chicken and collard greens are served; beer and wine are available, or bring your own bottle. ⊠ *1610 14th St. NW, Logan Circle* ☎ *202/667–3700* Ⓜ *U St./Cardozo.*

★ **9:30 Club.** The best of the nonstadium performers, and some of the bigger acts, play this large but cozy space. ⊠ *815 V St. NW, U Street corridor* ☎ *202/393–0930* Ⓜ *U St./Cardozo.*

Performance Venues

Fodor'sChoice **John F. Kennedy Center for the Performing Arts.** This complex on the bank
★ of the Potomac River is the gem of the D.C. arts scene and home to the **National Symphony Orchestra,** the **Washington Ballet,** and the **Washington National Opera.** The best out-of-town acts perform in its three striking spaces. On the Millennium Stage, you can catch free performances al-

most any day at 6 PM. ■ TIP→ On performance days, a free shuttle bus runs to the Foggy Bottom/GWU Metro stop. ✉ *New Hampshire Ave. and Rock Creek Pkwy. NW, Foggy Bottom* ☎ *202/467–4600 or 800/444–1324* Ⓜ *Foggy Bottom/GWU.*

Verizon Center. This 19,000-seat arena hosts the biggest musical acts. ✉ *601 F St. NW, Chinatown* ☎ *202/628–3200* Ⓜ *Gallery Pl./Chinatown.*

Theater

Arena Stage. One of the city's most-respected resident companies, this troupe performs mainly American theater with superb acting and dynamic staging. ✉ *1101 6th St. SW, Waterfront* ☎ *202/488–3300* Ⓜ *Waterfront.*

★ **Shakespeare Theatre.** This acclaimed company, known as one of the world's three great Shakespearean companies, crafts fantastic performances of works by Shakespeare and his contemporaries. ✉ *450 7th St. NW, Downtown* ☎ *202/547–1122* Ⓜ *Gallery Pl./Chinatown or Archives/ Navy Memorial.*

Woolly Mammoth. Unusual but brilliant avant-garde shows have earned Woolly Mammoth favorable comparisons to Chicago's Steppenwolf. In 2005 the company settled into a modern, 265-seat theater. ✉ *641 D St. NW, Downtown* ☎ *202/393–3939* Ⓜ *Gallery Pl./Chinatown or Archives/Navy Memorial.*

SPORTS & THE OUTDOORS

Washington's 69 square miles are in part a fantastic recreational backyard, with dozens of beautiful open spaces. Rock Creek Park has miles of wooded trails and paths for bikers, runners, and walkers that extend to almost every part of the city. The National Mall connects the Lincoln Memorial and the Capitol building. With the monuments as a backdrop, you can spike a volleyball, ride a bike, or take a jog. Into watching more than doing? Washington's myriad professional sports teams will sate your hunger for top level competition no matter what your favorite game.

Ice-Skating

The **National Gallery of Art Ice Rink** (✉ Constitution Ave. NW, between 7th and 9th Sts., Downtown ☎ 202/289–3361 Ⓜ Navy Memorial/ Archives) is surrounded by the gallery's Sculpture Garden.

The **Pershing Park Ice Rink** (✉ Pennsylvania Ave. and 14th St. NW, Downtown ☎ 202/737–6938 Ⓜ Metro Center) is a few blocks from the White House, major hotels, and a Metro station.

Professional Sports

D.C. United (✉ Robert F. Kennedy Stadium, 2400 E. Capitol St. SE, Capitol Hill ☎ 202/547–3134 Ⓜ Stadium) is one of the best Major League Soccer (U.S. pro soccer) teams. International matches, including some World Cup preliminaries, are often played on RFK Stadium's grass field. Games are April through September.

One of pro hockey's better teams, the **Washington Capitals** (⊠ Verizon Center, 6th and F Sts., Downtown ☎ 202/432–7328 Ⓜ Gallery Pl./Chinatown), play home games October through April.

The WNBA's **Washington Mystics** (⊠ Verizon Center, 6th and F Sts., Downtown ☎ 202/432–7328 Ⓜ Gallery Pl./Chinatown) play late May to August.

Fodor'sChoice
★
Major League Baseballhas returned to D.C., where the **Washington Nationals** (⊠ 2400 E. Capitol St. SE, Washington, DC ☎ 202/675–6287 Ⓜ Stadium-Armory) of the National League play in their temporary home, Robert F. Kennedy Stadium.

The **Washington Redskins** (☎ 301/276–6000 FedEx Field stadium) have the largest football stadium in the NFL, but all 80,000 seats are held by season-ticket holders. Occasionally you can find tickets advertised in the classifieds of the *Washington Post* or buy them from online ticket vendors and auction sites—at top dollar, of course. ■ TIP➜ **Fans can see the players up close and for free at training camp, held in August.**

★ The NBA's **Washington Wizards** (⊠ Verizon Center, 6th and F Sts., Downtown ☎ 202/432–7328 Ⓜ Gallery Pl./Chinatown) play from October to April.

Running & Biking

The numerous cycling trails in the District and its surrounding areas are well maintained and clearly marked. Running is one of the best ways to see the city. It can be dangerous to run at night on the trails, although the streets are fairly well lighted. Even in daylight, it's best to run in pairs when venturing beyond public areas or heavily used sections of trails.

The 89-mi-long **C&O Canal Towpath** is mostly gravel and dirt, making it easy on knees and feet.

The most popular running and cycling route in Washington is the 4½-mi loop on **The Mall** around the Capitol and past the Smithsonian museums and the major monuments.

Rock Creek Park has 15 mi of trails, a bicycle path, a bridle path, picnic groves, playgrounds, and the boulder-strewn rolling stream that gives it its name. Starting one block south of the corner of P and 22nd streets on the edge of Georgetown, Rock Creek Park runs all the way to Montgomery County, Maryland. The roadway is closed to traffic on weekends.

★ Cyclists interested in serious training might try the 3-mi loop around the golf course in **East Potomac Park** (☎ 202/485–9874 National Park Service) at Hains Point, the southern area of the park (entry is near the Jefferson Memorial). ■ TIP➜ **Going to the most southern point in the park, where the Anacostia and Potomac rivers merge, you'll come face to face with one of Washington's most unique and fun sculptures, *The Awakening*, a half-buried giant.**

Rentals & Tours

Thompson's Boat Center (⊠ 2900 Virginia Ave. NW, Foggy Bottom ☎ 202/333–4861) allows easy access to the Rock Creek Trail and the

C&O Towpath and is close to the monuments. All-terrain bikes are $8 per hour and $25 per day. Fixed-gear and children's bikes are $8 per hour and $15 per day. Children's trailers (attachments to adult bikes) rent for $4 per hour or $15 per day.

SHOPPING

For those who see Washington as a wonky, buttoned-down city, the abundance of D.C. shopping options, from high-end show rooms to funky boutiques, might come as a surprise. **Georgetown** is not on a subway line and parking is difficult at best, but people still flock here for tony antiques, elegant crafts, and high-style shoe and clothing boutiques, along with national chains. **Dupont Circle,** a younger, less staid version of Georgetown, has many art galleries, offbeat shops, and specialty book and record stores that give it a cosmopolitan air. Northeast of Dupont, **U Street,** once known for its classy theaters and jazz clubs and then its decline, has been revitalized with a string of chic clothing stores and homewares shops. As the **Capitol Hill** area has become gentrified, unique shops and boutiques have sprung up, many clustered around the redbrick **Eastern Market,** where a weekend flea market presents nostalgia and local crafts by the crateful. And don't forget the **museum shops**—especially at the National Gallery of Art, the National Museum of the American Indian, the National Building Museum, and the National Museum of Natural History—where you can pick up unique items like prints of masterpiece paintings, models of dinosaur skeletons, and period jewelry.

Capitol Hill/Eastern Market

CRAFTS & GIFTS   **Alvear Studio.** This popular design and imports store overflows with a ★ colorful bounty from the worldwide travels of its owners, including art, furniture, and jewelry. ⊠ *705 8th St. SE, Capitol Hill* ☎ *202/546–8484* Ⓜ *Eastern Market.*

MALL   **Union Station.** Inside this working train station, you'll find several familiar retailers, including Joseph A. Bank, Swatch, and Ann Taylor, as well as a bookstore, a multiplex movie theater and the east hall filled with vendors of expensive and ethnic wares who sell from open stalls. ⊠ *50 Massachusetts Ave. NE, Capitol Hill* ☎ *202/289–1908* Ⓜ *Union Station.*

Dupont Circle

ART GALLERIES   **Fusebox.** One of D.C.'s hottest galleries, Fusebox presents serious and stimulating contemporary art from a bright, Chelsea-esque space in Logan Circle. ⊠ *1412 14th St. NW, Logan Circle* ☎ *202/299–9220* ☉ *Closed Sun. and Mon.* Ⓜ *Dupont Circle.*

★   **Hemphill Fine Arts.** This spacious gem of a gallery shows established artists such as Jacob Kainen and William Christenberry as well as emerging artists, including Colby Caldwell. ⊠ *1515 14th St. NW, 3rd fl., Logan Circle* ☎ *202/234–5601* Ⓜ *Dupont Circle.*

BOOKS   **Kramerbooks & Afterwords.** One of Washington's best-loved independents, **Fodor's**Choice   this cozy shop has a small but choice selection of fiction and nonfiction. ★   Open 24 hours on weekends, Kramerbooks shares space with a café that has late-night dining and weekend entertainment. ⊠ *1517 Connecticut Ave. NW, Dupont Circle* ☎ *202/387–1400* Ⓜ *Dupont Circle.*

Lambda Rising. This famous bookstore is *the* source for information and literature for and about the gay, lesbian, bisexual, and transgendered communities. ⊠ *1625 Connecticut Ave. NW, Dupont Circle* ☎ *202/462–6969* Ⓜ *Dupont Circle.*

WOMEN'S CLOTHING ★ **Secondi.** One of the city's finest consignment shops, Secondi carries a well-chosen selection of women's designer and casual clothing, accessories, and shoes, including selections from Marc Jacobs, Louis Vuitton, and Prada. ⊠ *1702 Connecticut Ave. NW, 2nd fl., Dupont Circle* ☎ *202/667–1122* Ⓜ *Dupont Circle.*

Georgetown

ANTIQUES & COLLECTIBLES ★ **Jean Pierre Antiques.** Very Georgetown, this gorgeous shop sells antique furniture from France, Germany, and Italy. ⊠ *2601 P St. NW, Georgetown* ☎ *202/337–1731* Ⓜ *Dupont Circle.*

Old Print Gallery. Here you'll find the capital's largest collection of old prints, with a focus on maps and 19th-century decorative prints (including Washingtoniana). ⊠ *1220 31st St. NW, Georgetown* ☎ *202/965–1818* ⊘ *Closed Sun.* Ⓜ *Foggy Bottom/GWU.*

> **WORD OF MOUTH**
>
> "Breakfast. Wander. Shop. I think Georgetown would fit the bill nicely."   –obxgirl

HOME FURNISHINGS ★ **A Mano.** The store's name is Italian for "by hand," and it lives up to its name, stocking colorful hand-painted ceramics, hand-dyed tablecloths, blown glass stemware, and other home and garden accessories by Italian and French artisans. ⊠ *1677 Wisconsin Ave. NW, Georgetown* ☎ *202/298–7200.*

SHOES ★ **Hu's Shoes.** This cutting-edge shoe store features ballet flats, heels, and boots from designers like Chloé, Proenza Schouler, Sonia Rykiel, and Viktor&Rolf. ⊠ *3005 M St. NW, Georgetown* ☎ *202/342–0202* Ⓜ *Foggy Bottom/GWU.*

SPAS & BEAUTY SALONS ★ **Blue Mercury.** Hard-to-find skin-care lines—Laura Mercier, Eve Lom, and Paula Dorf are just a few—are what set this small national chain apart. At the "skin gym" you can treat yourself to facials, waxing, massage, and oxygen treatments. ⊠ *3059 M St. NW, Georgetown* ☎ *202/965–1300* Ⓜ *Foggy Bottom/GWU* ✉.

WOMEN'S CLOTHING FodorsChoice ★ **Urban Chic.** Gorgeous suits, jeans, cocktail dresses, and accessories from designers like Catherine Malandrino, Paul&Joe, Ella Moss, Rebecca Taylor, and Susana Monaco can be had for a price at this fashionista hangout. The handbags are a highlight. ⊠ *1626 Wisconsin Ave. NW, Georgetown* ☎ *202/338–5398.*

U Street

ANTIQUES & COLLECTIBLES ★ **Good Wood.** This friendly shop sells vintage and antique wood furniture, including wonderful 19th-century American pieces, along with stained glass and other decorative items. ⊠ *1428 U St. NW, U St. cor-*

ridor ☎ *202/986–3640* ☉ *Closed Mon.–Wed.* Ⓜ *U Street/Cardozo.*

HOME FURNISHINGS

FodorśChoice
★

Muléh. You'll find exquisite contemporary Balinese and Filipino home furnishings and trendy clothes from LA and New York at this expansive showroom. ✉ *1831 14th St. NW, U Street corridor* ☎ *202/667–3440* ☉ *Closed Mon.* Ⓜ *U St./Cardozo.*

WOMEN'S CLOTHING

Nana. The hip, friendly staff here is one of the reasons D.C. women love this store, which stocks both new and vintage women's clothes at affordable prices. You'll also find handmade jewelry and cool handbags. ✉ *1528 U St. NW, Upstairs, U St. corridor* ☎ *202/667–6955* Ⓜ *U Street/Cardozo.*

WASHINGTON, D.C., ESSENTIALS

To research prices, get advice from other travelers, and book travel arrangements, visit ⊕ *www.fodors.com.*

Transportation

BY AIR

The major gateways to D.C. are Ronald Reagan Washington National Airport in Virginia, 4 mi south of downtown Washington; Dulles International Airport, 26 mi west of Washington, D.C.; and Baltimore/Washington International-Thurgood Marshall (BWI) Airport in Maryland, about 30 mi to the northeast.

The Metro subway ride downtown from Ronald Reagan Washington National Airport takes about 20 minutes and costs about $1.85.

By bus: Washington Flyer links Dulles International Airport and the West Falls Church Metro station. The 25-minute ride is $9 for adults, free for children under six. Buses run every half hour from 5:45 AM to 10:15 PM. Fares may be paid with cash or credit card.

The Washington Metropolitan Area Transit Authority (WMATA) operates express bus service between Dulles and several stops in downtown D.C., including the L'Enfant Plaza Metro station. Bus 5A, which costs $3, runs every hour between 5:30 AM and 11:30 PM. Exact fare is required. WMATA also operates express bus service ($3) between BWI and the Greenbelt Metro station. Buses run between 6 AM and 10 PM.

National, Dulles, and BWI airports are served by SuperShuttle. The approximately 20-minute ride from Reagan National to downtown averages $10; the roughly 45-minute ride from Dulles runs $22; the ride from BWI, which takes about 60 minutes, averages $31. Each additional person traveling with a full-fare passenger is $10.

By taxi, expect to pay $9–$15 to get from National to downtown, $44–$55 from Dulles, and $60–$65 from BWI, plus $1.50 airport surcharge for all. A $1 surcharge is added 7–9:30 AM and 4–6:30 PM.

Free shuttle buses carry passengers between airline terminals and the train station at BWI. Amtrak and Maryland Rail Commuter Service (MARC) trains run between BWI and Washington, D.C.'s Union Station from around 6 AM to 10 PM. The cost of the 30-minute ride is $13–$36 on Amtrak and $6 on MARC, which runs only on weekdays.

⚡ Airports Baltimore/Washington International-Thurgood Marshall Airport ☎ 410/859-7100 ⊕ www.bwiairport.com. **Dulles International Airport** ☎ 703/572-2700 ⊕ www.metwashairports.com/Dulles. **Ronald Reagan Washington National Airport** ☎ 703/417-8000 ⊕ www.metwashairports.com/National.

⚡ Taxis & Shuttles Amtrak ☎ 800/872-7245 ⊕ www.amtrak.com. **D.C. Taxicab Commission** ☎ 202/645-6018 ⊕ www.dctaxi.dc.gov. **Maryland Rail Commuter Service** ☎ 410/767-3999, 410/539-3497 TDD, 800/325-7245 ⊕ www.mtamaryland.com. **Super-Shuttle** ☎ 800/258-3826 or 202/296-6662 ⊕ www.supershuttle.com. **Washington Flyer** ☎ 888/927-4359 ⊕ www.washfly.com. **Washington Metropolitan Area Transit Authority** ☎ 202/637-7000, 202/638-3780 TDD ⊕ www.wmata.com.

BY BUS

Washington's Greyhound bus terminal is in a desolate area four blocks north of Union Station. Taxis are often waiting at the terminal. You can purchase your ticket by phone, on the Internet, or at the station before you board the bus. Buses head to New York City around once an hour. Service south is less frequent and less convenient.

The red, white, and blue WMATA buses ($1.25, $3 on express buses) crisscross the city and the nearby suburbs. One-day bus passes for $3 and seven-day bus passes for $11 are available at the Metro Center sales office, open weekdays from 7:30 AM to 6:30 PM.

The D.C. Circulator offers $1 rides to cultural and entertainment destinations along three routes within the city's central core. The north–south route runs from the D.C. Convention Center at 6th and Massachusetts NW, to the Southwest Waterfront, at 6th Street and Maine Avenue. The east–west route runs from Union Station at Columbus Plaza NW, to Georgetown, at M Street and Wisconsin Avenue NW. A third loop circles the National Mall and includes stops at the National Gallery of Art and the Smithsonian. Passengers can pay cash when boarding (exact change only) or use metro Farecards, SmarTrip cards, all-day passes, and Metro bus transfers. Tickets also may be purchased at fare meters or multispace parking meters on the sidewalk near Circular stops. Machines accept change or credit cards and make change. Buses run every 5–10 minutes from 7 AM to 9 PM, seven days a week.

⚡ D.C. Circulator (District Department of Transportation) ☎ 202/962-1423 ⊕ www.dccirculator.com. **Greyhound** ✉ 1005 1st St. NE ☎ 202/289-5154, 800/229-9424 tickets, 800/229-9424 fares and schedules ⊕ www.greyhound.com. **Washington Metropolitan Area Transit Authority** ☎ 202/637-7000, 202/638-3780 TDD ⊕ www.wmata.com.

BY CAR

A car is often a drawback in Washington, D.C. Traffic is horrendous, especially at rush hour, and driving is often confusing, with many lanes and some entire streets changing direction suddenly during rush hour. Interstate 95 skirts D.C. as part of the Beltway (also known as I–495 in parts), the six- to eight-lane highway that encircles the city.

Parking here is an adventure; the police are quick to tow away or immobilize with a boot any vehicle parked illegally. Private parking lots downtown often charge around $5 an hour and $25 a day. There's free, three-hour parking around the Mall on Jefferson and Madison drives, though these spots are almost always filled. The closest free parking is in three lots in East Potomac Park, south of the 14th Street Bridge. Note that it's illegal to use a handheld phone while driving in Washington, D.C.

BY SUBWAY

The Washington Metro is one of the country's cleanest and safest subway systems. It begins operation at 5 AM on weekdays and 7 AM on weekends and closes on weekdays at midnight and weekends at 3 AM. During the weekday peak periods (5–9:30 AM and 3–7 PM), trains come along every three to six minutes. At other times trains run about every 12–15 minutes.

The Metro's base fare is $1.35; the actual price you pay depends on the time of day and the distance traveled. Up to two children under age five ride free with a paying passenger.

Buy your ticket at the Farecard machines, some of which accept credit cards. One-day passes are $6.50 and seven-day passes are $32.50. Locals use the SmarTrip card, a plastic card that can hold any fare amount and can be used throughout the subway system. Buy passes or Smar-Trip cards at the Metro Center sales office.

Make sure you **hang on to your Farecard**—you need it to exit at your destination.

Metro Center sales office ⊠ Metro Center Metro Station, 12th and F Sts. NW. **Washington Metropolitan Area Transit Authority (WMATA)** ☎ 202/637-7000, 202/638-3780 TTY, 202/962-1195 lost and found ⊕ www.wmata.com.

BY TAXI

You can hail a taxi on the street just about anywhere in the city, though they tend to congregate around major hotels. Drivers are allowed to pick up more than one fare at a time.

Taxis in the District are not metered; they operate on a zone system that can be confusing to newcomers. The basic rate for traveling within one zone is $6.50, and the fare increases when you cross into another zone. A zone map is posted in the rear of every taxi. **Before you set off, ask your cabdriver how much the fare will be.**

Diamond ☎ 202/387-4011. **Mayflower** ☎ 202/783-1111. **Yellow** ☎ 202/544-1212.

BY TRAIN

More than 80 trains a day arrive at Washington, D.C.'s, Union Station. Amtrak's regular service runs from D.C. to New York in 3¼–3¾ hours and from D.C. to Boston in 7¾–8 hours. Acela, Amtrak's high-speed service, travels from D.C. to New York in 2¾–3 hours and from D.C. to Boston in 6½ hours. Two commuter lines—Maryland Rail Commuter Service and Virginia Railway Express—run to the nearby suburbs. They're cheaper than Amtrak, but they don't run on weekends.

Amtrak ☎ 800/872-7245 ⊕ www.amtrak.com. **Maryland Rail Commuter Service (MARC)** ☎ 800/325-7245 ⊕ www.mtamaryland.com. **Union Station** ⊠ 50 Massachusetts Ave. NE ☎ 202/371-9441 ⊕ www.unionstationdc.com. **Virginia Railway Express (VRE)** ☎ 703/684-1001 ⊕ www.vre.org.

Contacts & Resources

EMERGENCIES

Dial 911 to report accidents on the road and to reach police, the highway patrol, or the fire department. For police nonemergencies, dial 311.

The hospital and emergency room closest to downtown is George Washington University Hospital. Howard University and Georgetown University also have hospitals and emergency rooms. 1-800-DOCTORS is a referral service that locates doctors, dentists, and urgent-care clinics. CVS operates 24-hour pharmacies.

7 **CVS** ✉ 6 Dupont Circle ☎ 202/785-1466 ✉ 2240 M St. NW ☎ 202/296-9876 ✉ 6514 Georgia Ave. ☎ 202/829-5234. **Georgetown University Hospital** ✉ 3800 Reservoir Rd. NW ☎ 202/444-2119 ⊕ www.georgetownuniversityhospital.org. **George Washington University Hospital** ✉ 900 23rd St. NW ☎ 202/715-4000 or 888/449-4677 ⊕ www.gwhospital.com. **Howard University Hospital** ✉ 2041 Georgia Ave. NW ☎ 202/865-1121 ⊕ www.huhosp.org. **1-800-DOCTORS** ☎ 800/362-8677. **U.S. Park Police** ☎ 202/619-7300.

INTERNET, MAIL & SHIPPING

The post office with the longest hours is National Capitol Station, across the street from Union Station. It is open 7 AM–midnight on weekdays and 7 AM–8 PM on weekends. Farragut Station and McPherson Station, both in downtown D.C., and Georgetown Station are open weekdays 9–5.

Dupont Circle has free 24-hour Wi-Fi service, as do the steps of the Supreme Court and Library of Congress. All D.C. public libraries offer free Internet access. Busboys and Poets, Love Cafe, Soho Tea & Coffee, and Tryst (on weekdays) offer free Wi-Fi to patrons.

7 Internet Resources **Busboys and Poets** ✉ 2021 14th St. NW ☎ 202/387-7638 ⊕ www.busboysandpoets.com. **Georgetown Neighborhood Library** ✉ 3260 R St. NW ☎ 202/282-0220 ⊕ www.dclibrary.org/branches/geo. **Love Cafe** ✉ 1501 U St. NW ☎ 202/265-9800. **Martin Luther King Jr. Memorial Library** ✉ 901 G St. NW ☎ 202/727-0321 ⊕ www.dclibrary.org/mlk. **Soho Tea & Coffee** ✉ 2150 P St. NW ☎ 202/463-7646. **Tryst Coffeehouse and Bar** ✉ 2459 18 St. NW ☎ 202/232-5500 ⊕ www.trystdc.com.

7 Post Offices **Farragut Station** ✉ 1800 M St. NW, 20036 ☎ 202/523-2024 ⊕ www.usps.gov. **Georgetown Station** ✉ 1215 31st St. NW, 20007 ☎ 202/523-2026 ⊕ www.usps.gov. **McPherson Station** ✉ 1750 Pennsylvania Ave. NW, 20006 ☎ 202/523-2394 ⊕ www.usps.gov. **National Capitol Station** ✉ 2 Massachusetts Ave. NE, 20002 ☎ 202/523-2368 ⊕ www.usps.gov.

TOUR OPTIONS

Old Town Trolley Tours ($28), orange-and-green motorized trolleys, take in the main downtown sights and also head into Georgetown and the upper Northwest in a speedy two hours if you ride straight through. However, you can hop on and off as many times as you like. Tourmobile buses, authorized by the National Park Service, operate in a similar fashion, making 25 stops at historical sites between the Capitol and Arlington National Cemetery. Tickets, available at kiosks at Union Station and Arlington National Cemetery, are $20 for adults.

Special tours of government buildings with heavy security, including the White House and the Capitol, can be arranged through your representative's or senator's office. Limited numbers of these so-called VIP tickets are available, so **plan up to six months in advance of your trip.** Governmental buildings close to visitors when the Department of Homeland Security issues a high alert, so call ahead.

Guided walks around Washington, D.C., and nearby communities are routinely offered by the Smithsonian Associates Program; advance tickets are required. Tour D.C. specializes in walking tours of Georgetown and Dupont Circle, covering topics such as the Civil War, the Underground Railroad, and Kennedy's Georgetown. Anecdotal History Tours leads tours in Georgetown, Adams-Morgan, and Capitol Hill, as well as tours of where Lincoln was shot and the homes of former presidents. Washington Walks has a wide range of tours, including a Tuesday series called "Washington Sleeps Here" about interesting neighborhoods.

The nonprofit group Cultural Tourism DC leads guided walking tours that cover the history and architecture of neighborhoods from the southwest waterfront to points much farther north. The self-guided "Civil War to Civil Rights: Downtown Heritage Trail" highlights historic sites with markers. The United States Capitol Historic Society leads two-hour tours of the exterior of the famous domed building Mondays at 10 AM from March to November.

🔢 **Anecdotal History Tours** ✉ 9009 Paddock La., Potomac, MD 20854 ☎ 301/294-9514 ⊕ www.dcsightseeing.com. **Cultural Tourism DC** ✉ 1250 H St. NW, 10th fl., Washington, DC 20005 ☎ 202/661-7581 ⊕ www.culturaltourismdc.org. **Department of State** ✉ 2201 C St. NW ☎ 202/647-3241, 202/736-4474 TDD ⊕ www.state.gov/m/drr. **Old Town Trolley Tours** ☎ 202/832-9800 ⊕ www.historictours.com. **Smithsonian Associates Program** ☎ 202/357-3030 ⊕ www.smithsonianassociates.org. **Tour D.C.** ✉ 1912 Glen Ross Rd., Silver Spring, MD 20910 ☎ 301/588-8999 ⊕ www.tourdc.com. **Tourmobile** ☎ 202/554-5100 or 888/868-7707 ⊕ www.tourmobile.com. **United States Capitol Historic Society** ☎ 202/543-8919. **Washington Walks** ☎ 202/484-1865 ⊕ www.washingtonwalks.com.

VISITOR INFORMATION

It's a good idea to gather information about the city before your trip, as the D.C. Visitor Information Center has a disinterested staff and a lackluster collection of brochures. The center is inconveniently located in the Ronald Reagan International Trade Center, a government office building that you can enter only after flashing your ID and passing through a metal detector.

The most popular sights in D.C. are run by the National Park Service or the Smithsonian; the "Dial-A-Park" and "Dial-a-Museum" lines have recorded information about locations and hours of operation.

🔢 **D.C. Visitor Information Center** ✉ 1300 Pennsylvania Ave. NW, Washington, DC 20004 ☎ 202/328-4748 ⊕ www.dcvisit.com. **National Park Service** ☎ 202/619-7275 "Dial-a-Park" park information ⊕ www.nps.gov. **Smithsonian** ☎ 202/357-2020 "Dial-a-Museum" ⊕ www.si.edu.

D.C.'s Maryland Suburbs

WORD OF MOUTH

"If you're looking for a cheap place to stay in the D.C. suburbs . . . the key is to stay not far from a metro stop. Anywhere in Bethesda around Wisconsin Ave is nice."

—Stephanie

Updated by
Matthew
Cordell

SUBURBAN MARYLAND IS D.C.'S BACKYARD. In 1791 Montgomery and Prince George's counties ceded 90 square mi to the new United States government to create the nation's capital, then called simply "The Federal City." Montgomery County is to the west and north of the capital's sharply drawn boundaries, and Prince George's County is to the east. Because of their proximity to D.C., the counties are the most densely populated in Maryland, and many residents consider themselves Washingtonians, though some Washingtonians think otherwise.

Traffic between the District and the Maryland suburbs goes both ways (each way slowly). Federal agencies that maintain offices in the area include the National Institutes of Health, the Internal Revenue Service, and the National Aeronautic Space Administration. Even the Washington Redskins play in Prince George's County.

One of the most affluent counties in the country, Montgomery County is host to Bethesda's bounty of restaurants and a breathtaking view of the Potomac River and Great Falls. Prince George's County holds the University of Maryland's College Park campus; historic houses, such as the Surratt House Museum; and great green spaces that include Fort Washington Park, the Colonial Farm, and the Merkle Wildlife Sanctuary.

Top 5 Experiences for D.C.'s Maryland Suburbs

- **Shopping in Friendship Heights:** Dive into this three-mall treasure trove of couture and discount shopping.

- **American Film Institute Silver Theatre & Cultural Center:** Watch beautifully maintained classics, along with new releases, in the AFI's art deco theaters.

- **Bethesda:** Satisfy your desire for nightlife, dining, art, and theater in Maryland's most happening suburb.

- **Glen Echo Park:** Rediscover (or enjoy) your childhood on the park's antique carousel.

- **Antique Row:** Rummage through Kensington's 80 antiques shops for hidden treasures.

Exploring Suburban Maryland

An automobile is a must to travel throughout the counties, but avoid the Capital Beltway (Interstate 495) during morning and afternoon rush hours. At those times the congestion is second only to Los Angeles. Most attractions, restaurants, and shops in Montgomery County are clustered "down-county" in areas closest to D.C. In Prince George's County, places to explore are sprinkled throughout the area.

About the Restaurants & Hotels

Like many suburbs, Bethesda has its share of big and bright restaurants that lack the character of those in the city, but the range of cuisine and depth of innovation here is starting to reflect the culinary sophistication and affluence of the residents. Many Washington restaurants have opened Bethesda branches, and alfresco dining is available during good weather at most places. Bethesda's largest concentration of restaurants (about 75) is within the Woodmont Triangle, bounded by Old George-town Road, Woodmont Avenue, and Rugby Avenue. Bright blue signs identify parking; on weekends you can park free in public garages.

For a Bethesda dining guide, *Taste of Bethesda,* contact the **Bethesda Urban Partnership** (☎ 301/215–6660 ⊕ www.bethesda.org).

It's best to book your hotel room in advance. Occupancy rates are high, and you're likely to pay only a little less than you would in Washington. Tourists coming to see Washington's cherry blossoms make spring the busiest season. December and January tend to be the slowest and least expensive months, except around a presidential inauguration.

WHAT IT COSTS					
	$$$$	$$$	$$	$	¢
RESTAURANTS	over $30	$22–$30	$14–$22	$7–$14	under $7
HOTELS	over $250	$175–$250	$130–$175	$80–$130	under $80

Restaurant prices are per person for a main course at dinner. Hotel prices are for a standard double room, excluding state and local taxes.

MONTGOMERY COUNTY

Numbers in the margin correspond to points of interest on the Montgomery County map.

In 1776 Montgomery County, named after Revolutionary War hero General Richard Montgomery, became the first Maryland county to drop the custom of naming jurisdictions after royalty. In between housing developments, strip malls, and office parks, the northern portion of the county retains traces of the area's agrarian beginnings.

Bethesda

● *2 mi north of Washington, D.C.*

Bethesda was named in 1871 after the Bethesda Meeting House, which was built by the Presbyterians. The name alludes to a biblical pool that had great healing power. Today people seek healing in Bethesda at the National Institutes of Health and the soothing aqua vitae available in the suburb's relatively tame restaurants and bars. Bethesda has changed from a small community into an urban destination, but in certain ways time has stood still east of Bethesda in Chevy Chase, a tony town of country clubs, stately houses, and huge trees.

A self-guided nature trail winds through a verdant 40-acre estate and around the **Audubon Naturalist Society.** The estate is known as Wood-end, as is the mansion, which was designed in the 1920s by Jefferson Memorial architect John Russell Pope. The society leads wildlife identification walks, environmental education programs, and—September through June—a weekly Saturday bird walk at its headquarters. The bookstore stocks titles on conservation, ecology, and birding, as well as nature-related gifts such as jewelry and toys. ⊠ *8940 Jones Mill Rd.,*

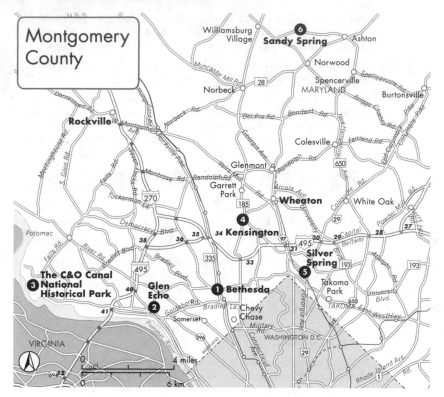

Chevy Chase ☎ *301/652–9188, 301/652–1088 for naturalist tape* ⊕ *www.audubonnaturalist.org* ✉ *Free* ☉ *Grounds daily sunrise–sunset, bookstore weekdays 10–5, Sat. 9–5, Sun. noon–5.*

More than 750 varieties of azaleas bloom at **McCrillis Gardens and Gallery** from late March through July, and usually peak around May 1. Ornamental trees and shrubs, including a remarkable collection of rhododendrons, bloom in the warm months. A small art gallery hosts monthly exhibitions by local artists. ✉ *6910 Greentree Rd.* ☎ *301/962–1455* ⊕ *www.mc-mncppc.org/parks/brookside/mccrilli.shtm* ✉ *Free* ☉ *Gardens daily 10–sunset; gallery Feb.–Nov., Tues.–Sun. noon–4.*

National Institutes of Health (NIH). One of the world's foremost biomedical research centers, with a sprawling 300-acre campus, the NIH offers tours for the public, including an orientation tour at the NIH Visitor Information Center and one at the National Library of Medicine, that will likely be quite interesting to those interested in medicine and a little dry to everyone else. Although best known for its books and journals—there are more than 5 million—the National Library of Medicine also houses historical medical references dating from the 11th century. A library tour includes a look at historical documents, the library's databases, and "visible human," which provides a view of everything from how the kneecap works to how physicians use surgical simulators. ⊠ *Visitor Information Center, 9000 Rockville Pike, Bldg. 10* ☎*301/ 496–1776* ✉ *National Library of Medicine, 8600 Rockville Pike, Bldg. 38A* ☎ *301/496–6308* ⊕ *www.nih.gov* ✉ *Free* ☉ *Call for tour times, library hrs, and information on forms of ID to bring, plus other security measures* Ⓜ *Medical Center.*

Where to Eat

$–$$$ ✕ **Thyme Square.** The menu is predominantly vegetarian at this hip-and-healthy joint, but the meaty options also wow. Although the selection changes seasonally, Brazilian shellfish stew—shrimp, mussels, and fish in a spicy tomato and coconut broth—remains a constant favorite. Individually crafted entrées sometimes take a while. ⊠ *4735 Bethesda Ave.* ☎ *301/657–9077* ▤ *AE, D, MC, V.*

$$ ✕ **Bacchus.** The lamb dishes and appetizers ("mezze") are excellent at this Lebanese restaurant, which is much bigger—and some say better—than its location in Washington, D.C. Outdoor seating is available, and both vegetarians and meat eaters will find good options on the creative menu. ⊠ *7945 Norfolk Ave.* ☎ *301/657–1722* ▤ *AE, D, MC, V.*

$–$$ ✕ **Passage to India.** Although the delivery is sometimes stiff, the regional Indian dishes in this stately, quiet dining room are delicious. Anything tandoori is not to be missed, as are the goat curry and the *kamal-kakri masala,* a lotus-stem and pea stew. ⊠ *4931 Cordell Ave.* ☎ *301/656–3373* ▤ *AE, D, MC, V.*

$–$$ ✕ **Tara Thai.** Blue walls and paintings of sea life reflect the owner's childhood home in Thailand; so does the extensive menu at this branch of a busy chain, whose many seafood dishes include fresh flounder and rockfish. Favorites include the mild and traditional pad thai and the spicy *Goong Phuket,* grilled black tiger shrimp topped with crabmeat and chicken sauce. ⊠ *4828 Bethesda Ave.* ☎ *301/657–0488* ✉ *12071 Rockville Pike, Rockville* ☎ *301/231–9899* ▤ *AE, D, DC, MC, V.*

¢–$ ✕ **Tastee Diner.** The Tastees are part of the culinary past in the Washington area, with a handful still left in Silver Spring, Laurel, and Bethesda, the flagship location. These 24-hour diners are sentimental favorites among many area residents, who value them for their hand-formed hamburgers, the tastiness of which is subjective. Students and others on low budgets (or little sleep) ignore the dust and relish the coffee, which flows endlessly. Breakfast is served around the clock. ⊠ *7931 Woodmont Ave.* ☎ *301/652–3970* ♣ *Reservations not accepted* ▤ *MC, V.*

¢ ✕ **California Tortilla.** Friendly, quick service helps make this counter-service restaurant a local favorite. The blackened chicken Caesar burrito outsells other items three to one. Add spice to your meal with a dash or two from 75 hot sauces lined up on the wall, and grab a seat inside or out. On Monday nights, spin the Burrito Wheel for discounts and freebies. ⊠ *4862 Cordell Ave.* ☎ *301/654–8226* ✉ *7727 Tuckerman La., Potomac* ☎ *301/765–3600* ▤ *MC, V.*

Where to Stay

★ $$$$ ☷ **Embassy Suites.** Shopping and sightseeing couldn't be more convenient at this all-suites hotel, which is adjacent to the upscale Chevy Chase Pavilion and an elevator ride up from the Friendship Heights Metro Station. Each suite includes a bedroom and separate living room with a sleeper sofa, kitchen space, and a table suitable for dining and working. The fitness center has more than 20 exercise stations and a personal trainer available at no charge. Complimentary breakfast and evening cocktails are offered daily in the sun-filled atrium. A dozen restaurants and no fewer than three large shopping malls are within walking distance. ✉ *4300 Military Rd., Washington, DC 20015* ☎ *202/362–9300 or 800/ 362–2779* 🖷 *202/686–3405* ⊕ *www.embassysuites.com* ⟿ *198 suites* ⚐ *Restaurant, room service, cable TV, in-room data ports, microwaves, indoor pool, health club, laundry service, parking (fee), no-smoking rooms* ▭ *AE, D, DC, MC, V* Ⓜ *Friendship Heights* ⦿Ⓘ *BP.*

$$$$ 🖫 **Hyatt Regency Bethesda.** Part of a busy nexus of restaurants, world-class shops, and movie theaters, this hotel, next to the Metro entrance, is a convenient refuge for weary travelers. For those with energy to spare, an adjacent plaza has a small ice rink, open in winter. The room rates drop considerably on the weekend. ✉ *1 Bethesda Metro Center, on 7400 block of Wisconsin Ave., 20814* ☎ *301/657–1234 or 800/233–1234* 🖷 *301/657–6453* ⊕ *www.hyatt.com* ⟿ *390 rooms, 5 suites* ⚐ *Restaurant, café, room service, cable TV, in-room data ports, indoor pool, health club, bar, lobby lounge, laundry service, business services, convention center, meeting rooms, parking (fee)* ▭ *AE, D, DC, MC, V* Ⓜ *Bethesda.*

$–$$$ 🖫 **Holiday Inn Washington-Chevy Chase.** A short walk from the Friendship Heights Metro on the D.C. border, this comfortable hotel is inside one of the area's most upscale shopping districts. The Avenue Deli and an Italian restaurant, Julian's, are in the hotel. A large outdoor swimming pool is set near the hotel's beautiful rose garden terrace. ✉ *5520 Wisconsin Ave., Chevy Chase 20815* ☎ *301/656–1500 or 800/465–4329* 🖷 *301/656–5045* ⊕ *www.sixcontinentshotels.com* ⟿ *214 rooms, 10 suites* ⚐ *Restaurant, snack bar, room service, cable TV, in-room data ports, pool, gym, hair salon, bar, laundry facilities, business services, meeting rooms, parking (fee), some pets allowed* ▭ *AE, D, DC, MC, V* Ⓜ *Friendship Heights* ⦿Ⓘ *CP.*

$–$$ 🖫 **American Inn of Bethesda.** At the north end of downtown Bethesda, the American Inn breaks no new fashion frontiers for motel decor, but the rooms are clean, generally bright, and affordable. The hotel houses Guapo's restaurant, serving moderately priced Tex-Mex fare. Many other restaurants and nightclubs are within walking distance; the Bethesda Metro is a 10-minute walk away. Use of the business center—including access to the Internet and e-mail service—is free. The hotel also provides a free shuttle to the National Institutes of Health and the Naval Hospital. ✉ *8130 Wisconsin Ave., 20814* ☎ *301/656–9300 or 800/323–7081* 🖷 *301/656–2907* ⊕ *www.american-inn.com* ⟿ *75 rooms, 1 suite* ⚐ *Restaurant, refrigerators, cable TV, pool, bar, laundry facilities, laundry service, Internet room, business services, free parking, no-smoking floors* ▭ *AE, D, DC, MC, V* ⦿Ⓘ *CP* Ⓜ *Bethesda.*

Nightlife & the Arts

On weekends from Memorial Day through Labor Day, you can dance to the beat of live bands at free concerts held at the intersection of Wisconsin Avenue, Old Georgetown Road, and East West Highway.

THE ARTS ★ A sharp, state-of-the-art facility, the 347-seat **Round House Theatre** (✉ 7501 Wisconsin Ave. ☎ 240/644–1100 Ⓜ Bethesda) primarily produces local premieres of quirky, contemporary, off-Broadway plays. The season usually also includes at least one world premiere, a traditional favorite, and a holiday musical.

> **FREE CONCERTS**
>
> On Tuesday and Thursday in summer, concertgoers spread out on the expansive lawn of the Strathmore Hall Arts Center to listen to free concerts—everything from classical to Cajun and Brit pop.

2

Strathmore Hall Arts Center. Local and national artists exhibit in the galleries and jazz, chamber, folk, and popular musicians perform year-round at this mansion built around 1900. Whimsical pieces, part of the permanent collection, are on display in the sculpture garden. A free series that includes poetry, music, art talks, and demonstrations takes place on Wednesday evening and Thursday morning (call ahead for hours). The 2,000-seat Music Hall, home to the Baltimore Symphony Orchestra in Montgomery County, opened in 2005. Strathmore's Tea is served in a well-lighted wood-panel salon, Tuesday and Wednesday at 1 (reservations essential). ✉ *10701 Rockville Pike* ☎ *301/530–0540* ✉ *Free, Backyard Theater $6, tea $17* ⊙ *Mon., Tues., Thurs., and Fri. 10–4, Wed. 10–9, Sat. 10–3* Ⓜ *Grosvenor/Strathmore.*

NIGHTLIFE Arcade games provide the most action at **Dave & Buster's** (✉ White Flint Mall, 11301 Rockville Pike ☎ 301/230–5151), but this 60,000-square-foot entertainment complex also includes billiard tables, shuffleboards, interactive video games and simulators, a casual restaurant, and two bars. Every other Saturday at 8 PM, a murder mystery dinner adds to the usual choices. Patrons under 21 must leave by 10 PM.

With a space large enough to accommodate loungers and dancers, karaoke (on Thursday), DJs spinning hip-hop and reggae, live music, and dance lessons, swanky **Juste Lounge** (✉ 6821 Reed St. ☎ 202/393–0939) draws an eclectic crowd.

Sports & the Outdoors

★ ☾ One of the best playgrounds in the Washington area, **Cabin John Regional Park** (✉ 7400 Tuckerman La. ☎ 301/299–4160) has plastic slides, bouncing wooden bridges, swings, and mazes to delight both toddlers and preteens. On the park grounds there's also an ice rink, indoor and outdoor tennis courts, a nature center, hiking trails, and trains that operate seasonally. Free military concerts join the chorus of cicadas every summer.

The paved **Capital Crescent Trail** runs along the old Georgetown Branch, a B&O Railroad line completed in 1910 that saw its last train in 1985. Bicyclists, walkers, rollerbladers, and strollers take the 7½-mi route from near Key Bridge in Washington's Georgetown to Bethesda and Woodmont avenues in central Bethesda. The trail picks up again at a well-lighted tunnel near the Thyme Square Restaurant (4735 Bethesda Ave.) and continues into Silver Spring. From Bethesda to the outskirts of Silver Spring, the 3½-mi trail is gravel. The Georgetown Branch Trail, as this section is officially named, connects with the Rock Creek Trail, which goes to Rockville in the north and Memorial Bridge past the Washington Monument in the south. For more information, contact the **Coalition for the Capital Crescent Trail** (☎ 202/234–4874).You can rent bikes at **Big Wheel Bikes** (✉ 6917 Arlington Rd., Bethesda ☎ 301/652–0192).

Shopping

Bethesda isn't known for bargains, although one of its best-known malls contains a Filene's Basement. Shoppers who love discounts should head north on Wisconsin Avenue to Rockville Pike (Route 355). Four of the area's seven regional malls are in Bethesda and the Chevy Chase section of Washington, D.C. Downtown Bethesda has no fewer than 13 bookstores, including a huge Barnes & Noble.

CLOTHING **Lemon Twist.** Inside this boutique are classic women's wear and children's clothes, gifts, and more from designers such as Lilly, C. J. Lang, Susan Bristol, and CanvasBack. But most of all Lemon Twist has been known for its customer service since 1977. ✉ *8534 Connecticut Ave., Chevy Chase* ☎ *301/986–0271.*

Wear It Well. From funky jackets and slacks to tailored business suits, this local shop specializes in items that wear and travel well. ✉ *4816 Bethesda Ave., Bethesda* ☎ *301/652–3713.*

DEPARTMENT **Filene's Basement.** The Boston-based upscale fashion discounter attracts
STORES bargain hunters looking for steep discounts on designer clothing—if you find something that suits you, it'll be the best deal in town by far. Off-price shoes, children's clothing, household goods, perfume, and accessories are sold as well. ✉ *5300 Wisconsin Ave. NW, Washington, DC* ☎ *202/966–0208* Ⓜ *Friendship Heights.*

Saks Fifth Avenue. Despite its New York origin and name, Saks is a Washington institution. It has a wide selection of European and American couture clothing; other attractions include the shoe, jewelry, fur, and lingerie departments. ✉ *5555 Wisconsin Ave., Chevy Chase* ☎ *301/657–9000* Ⓜ *Friendship Heights.*

MALLS **Chevy Chase Pavilion.** Across from Mazza Gallerie is the newer, similarly upmarket Chevy Chase Pavilion. Its women's clothing stores range from Alpaca International to Ann Taylor Loft and Talbots. ✉ *5335 Wisconsin Ave. NW, Washington, DC* ☎ *202/686–5335* Ⓜ *Friendship Heights.*

The Collection at Chevy Chase. This mall is the latest addition to the luxurification of Friendship Heights, which now can claim Bulgari, Dior, Ralph Lauren, Louis Vuitton, Jimmy Choo, and Barney's Co-op. ✉ *5471–5481 Wisconsin Ave. NW, Washington, DC* ☎ *No phone* Ⓜ *Friendship Heights.*

Mazza Gallerie. This four-level mall is anchored by the ritzy Neiman Marcus department store and the discounter Filene's Basement. Other draws include Williams-Sonoma's kitchenware and a seven-screen movie theater. ✉ *5300 Wisconsin Ave. NW, Washington, DC* ☎ *202/966–6114* Ⓜ *Friendship Heights.*

Montgomery Mall. Stores in the county's largest mall include Crate & Barrel, Sears, Hecht's, and Nordstrom. Just off I–270 and I–495, it's not close to any metro stops. ⊠ *7101 Democracy Blvd.* ☎ *301/469–6025.*

White Flint Mall. Bloomingdale's, Lord & Taylor, and Borders Books & Music, plus 125 other stores, pull in the serious shoppers. ⊠ *11301 Rockville Pike, North Bethesda* ☎ *301/231–7467* Ⓜ *White Flint.*

Glen Echo

❷ *4 mi west of downtown Bethesda, 2½ mi from the Capital Beltway.*

Glen Echo, now a charming village of Victorian houses, was founded in 1891 by Edwin and Edward Baltzley, inventors of a type of mechanical eggbeater. The brothers fell under the spell of the Chautauqua movement, an organization that ran what can best be described as an educational summer camp with prominent lecturers and performers. To further their dream, the brothers sold land and houses, but the Glen Echo Chautauqua lasted only one season.

The **Clara Barton National Historic Site** is a monument to the founder of the American Red Cross. Known as the "angel of the battlefield" for nursing wounded soldiers during the Civil War, Barton used the striking Victorian structure at first to store Red Cross supplies (it was built for her by the town's founders). It later became both her home and the organization's headquarters. Today the building is furnished with many of her possessions and period artifacts. Access is by guided tours, which last approximately 35 minutes. ⊠ *5801 Oxford Rd., next to Glen Echo Park parking lot, Glen Echo* ☎ *301/492–6245* ⊕ *www.nps.gov/clba* ☞ *Free* ☉ *Daily 10–5; tours on the hr 10–4.*

A few miles east of Glen Echo Park in Georgetown, **Fletcher's Cove** rents rowboats, canoes, and bicycles and sells tackle, snack foods, and D.C. fishing licenses. Here you can catch shad, perch, catfish, striped bass, and other freshwater species. Canoeing is allowed in the canal and, weather permitting, in the Potomac. Bicycles are for rent here; the C&O Canal path connects to Virginia bike paths via Key Bridge. There's a large picnic area along the riverbank. ⊠ *4940 Canal Rd., at Reservoir Rd., Georgetown* ☎ *202/244–0461* ☉ *Late Mar.–May, daily 7:30–7; June–Aug., daily 9–7; Sept.–Nov., daily 9–6.*

ⓒ The Baltzley brothers' 10-acre compound, **Glen Echo Park**, was once known FodorśChoice for its whimsical architecture, including a stone tower, from the Chau-★ tauqua period. The area was later the site of an amusement park, and you can still see the skeletons of the once thriving rides. Only the splendid 1921 Dentzel **carousel** still runs (May–September, Wednesday and Thursday 10–2, weekends 10–6; July and August also Friday 10–2), with musical accompaniment from a rare Wurlitzer military band organ. The National Park Service now administers the property, which is the site of folk festivals as well as a puppet company and a children's theater that operate nights and Sunday afternoons in the 1933 Spanish Ballroom. Two art galleries have ongoing exhibits and demonstrations. ⊠ *7300 MacArthur Blvd.* ☎ *301/492–6229* ⊕ *www.glenechopark.org*

🎠 *Carousel rides $1, puppet shows $7, plays $7, cost of dances vary* ☉ *Daily dawn–dusk.*

Where to Eat

★ $–$$$ ✕**Irish Inn at Glen Echo.** This turn-of-the-20th-century inn used to be a biker bar and a brothel. Now it's a cozy, popular destination with a pub and a restaurant, each serving excellent Irish comfort food. If you're feeling more adventurous than upscale corned beef and cabbage or shepherd's pie, try the salt-crusted salmon or braised lamb shank with roasted root vegetables. The pub, which has an attractive selection of Irish whiskey and a relatively affordable menu, stays open until 2 AM. Just don't expect to hear "Danny Boy." ✉ *6119 Tulane Ave.* ☎ *301/ 229–6600* ⊟ *AE, D, DC, MC, V.*

Potomac

8 mi north of Glen Echo, 7 mi northwest of Bethesda.

The popular translation of the Native American name "Patawomeck" is "they are coming by water." Although today's visitors are likely to drive, it is still possible to view the mighty Potomac River by hiking along the towpath of the C&O canal and climbing the rocks at Great Falls, which Maryland and Virginia share a view of opposite banks. Potomac is also known for its elegant estates and houses.

❸ **The C&O Canal National Historical Park** extends along the Potomac River 184.5 mi from Washington, D.C., to Cumberland, Maryland. Three miles south of the town of Potomac, the **Great Falls Tavern,** a museum and visitor center, serves as the park's local anchor. Barge trips and a vista on the powerful Great Falls are the draws here. A ½-mi, wheelchair-accessible walkway to the platform on Olmsted Island provides a spectacular view of the churning waters. Swimming and wading are prohibited, but you can fish (a Maryland license is required for anglers 16 and older) or climb rocks; only experienced boaters can go white-water kayaking below the falls—all along this stretch of the river, the currents are deadly. ■ TIP→ **The tavern ceased food service long ago, so if you're hungry, head for the snack bar a few paces north or bring your own picnic.** ✉ *11710 MacArthur Blvd.* ☎ *301/767–3714* ⊕ *www.nps.gov/choh* 🎫 *$5 per vehicle, $3 per person without vehicle, good for 3 days on MD and VA sides of park* ☉ *Park, daily sunrise–sunset; tavern and museum, daily 9–4:45; barge trips Apr.–Oct., call for hrs.*

Where to Stay & Eat

★ $$$–$$$$ ✕**Old Angler's Inn.** The inn, where Civil War soldiers from the North and South found respite and Teddy Roosevelt stopped after hunting and fishing, was restored in 1957 and began its foray into fine dining. Diners like the cozy fireplace and menu favorites like crispy-skin Scottish salmon and cocoa-dusted venison with a black truffle sauce. ✉ *10801 MacArthur Blvd.* ☎ *301/299–9097* ⊟ *AE, D, MC, V* ☉ *Closed Mon.*

$$–$$$ ✕**Normandie Farm.** Built on top of a half-finished country club that was foreclosed on during the Great Depression, Normandie Farm maintains the French provincial cuisine and romantic, rustic surroundings that the original owner grew to love during her time at cooking school in Normandy,

France. The classic menu has likewise remained nearly unchanged; the most popular dishes are beef Wellington, poached salmon, and lamb chops accompanied by fabulous popovers. Although French flavor imbues the farm, famous locals—like Maryland crab—also have a starring role. ⊠ *10710 Falls Rd.* ☎ *301/983–8838* ☐ *AE, DC, MC, V* ☉ *Closed Mon.*

Kensington

❹ *4 mi northeast of Bethesda.*

Established in 1890, Kensington was one of Montgomery County's first villages. Borrowing both its name and architecture from the tony London neighborhood, Kensington was a planned Victorian community from the start. Its neighbor Garrett Park even has a few "Chevy houses": built in 1930, these smallish houses came with a mortgage that financed a Chevrolet in the driveway and an RCA radio inside. Start on Armory Avenue and wander through the Historic District to see the entire spectrum of domestic architecture here.

The **Temple of the Church of Jesus Christ of Latter-day Saints** is impossible to miss from the Beltway near Silver Spring. One of its white towers is topped with a golden statue of the Mormon angel Moroni. It's closed to non-Mormons, but a visitor center provides a lovely view of the mammoth white-marble temple and runs a film about the temple and what takes place inside. Tulips, dogwoods, and azaleas bloom in the 57-acre grounds each spring. In December locals of all faiths enjoy the Festival of Lights—400,000 of them—and a live Nativity scene. ⊠ *9900 Stoneybrook Dr.* ☎ *301/587–0144* ☉ *Grounds and visitor center daily 10–9.*

Where to Eat

¢ ✕ **Café Monet.** Yellow walls and impressionist paintings lend charm to this little counter-service café, a favorite of local ladies of all ages who linger over espresso, scones, and muffins. You can order a panini named after your favorite Impressionist artist or a Turkish *borek*, phyllo filled with spinach and feta. Outdoor seating is available. ⊠ *10417 Armory Ave.* ☎ *301/946–9404* ☐ *AE, D, MC, V* ☉ *No dinner.*

Shopping

Fodor'sChoice ★ At Kensington's **Antique Row** (⊠ Howard Ave. ☎ 301/949–5333), east of bustling Connecticut Avenue, more than 80 shops sell jewelry, china, art, toys, silver, and furniture in buildings as old as some of the items. On the west side of Connecticut Avenue, Howard Avenue alternates auto body repair shops with 100,000 square feet of antiques warehouses that specialize in furniture from Belgium, England, Italy, France, and the United States. For a full listing of the **Antique Dealers of West Howard Avenue,** visit www.westhowardantiques.com. At **Antiques-Uniques** (⊠ 3762 Howard Ave. ☎ 301/942–3324) you can find porcelain dolls, Tiffany lamps, and china. **Banning** + Low (⊠ 3730 Howard Ave. ☎ 301/933–0700) sells vintage posters and campaign memorabilia. **Hunters and Gatherers** (⊠ 4229 Howard Ave. ☎ 301/896–0348) stocks fabrics from Brunschwig and Fils, Fortuny lighting, and Carlo Moretti glassware. The **Prevention of Blindness Antiques Shop** (⊠ 3716 Howard Ave. ☎ 301/942–4707) sells furniture, linens, and vintage clothing.

Silver Spring

⑤ *5 mi southeast of Kensington via Rte. 97.*

With a population of some 220,000, the greater Silver Spring area is one of Washington, D.C.'s largest suburbs and is currently undergoing something of a rebirth, with businesses and entertainment venues staking their claims in the original downtown area. Silver Spring was named when Francis Preston Blair, editor of the *Washington Globe,* friend to President Andrew Jackson, and owner of the Blair House (now the nation's official guest quarters for foreign dignitaries), was riding his horse through the countryside, looking for a pastoral retreat from Washington. His horse threw him, and, as he looked for his mount, he noticed a spring in which sand and mica shone like silver. Wheaton, a more suburban locale 4 mi to the north, is home to the popular National Capitol Trolley Museum.

Fodor'sChoice
★

American Film Institute Silver Theatre & Cultural Center. This three-screen, state-of-the-art center for film is a restoration of architect John Eberson's art deco Silver Theatre, built in 1938. The AFI hosts film retrospectives, new releases, on-stage appearances, and tributes to stars that have included Jeanne Moreau and Russell Crowe. Each June, in partnership with the Discovery Channel, the AFI hosts the glitzy SILVERDOCS documentary film festival, one of the world's best. ⊠ *8633 Colesville Rd.* ☎ *301/495–6700* ⊕ *www.afi.com/silver* Ⓜ *Silver Spring.*

At the rolling 50-acre **Brookside Gardens,** the series of theme areas highlight roses, azaleas, flowers with particularly potent fragrance, and plants that attract butterflies, among many others. Inside, two conservatories house seasonal displays and exotic tropicals throughout the year. The visitor center has an auditorium, classrooms for adults and children, a 3,000-volume horticulture library, a gift shop, and an information booth. ⊠ *1800 Glenallan Ave., Wheaton MD* ☎ *301/962–1400* ⊕ *www.brooksidegardens.org* ✉ *Free, class fees $7–$35* ☉ *Daily; conservatories 10–5, visitor center 9–5, gift shop Mon.–Sat. 10–4 and Sun. noon–4, horticulture library 10–3.*

Permanent and changing exhibits at the **George Meany Memorial Archives** document work life and United States labor history. The archives preserve the historical record of the American Federation of Labor and Congress of Industrial Organizations (AFL-CIO). ⊠ *10000 New Hampshire Ave.* ☎ *301/431–5451* ⊕ *www.georgemeany.org/archives* ✉ *Free* ☉ *Weekdays 9–4:30.*

A selection of the capital's historic trolleys has been rescued and restored at the **National Capital Trolley Museum,** along with streetcars from Europe, Canada, and elsewhere in America. The museum is run by volunteers whose childhood fascination with trains never left them at the station. For a nominal fare you can go on a 2-mi ride through the countryside. ⊠ *1313 Bonifant Rd., Wheaton MD* ☎ *301/384–6088* ⊕ *www.dctrolley. org* ✉ *Museum free, trolley ride $3* ☉ *Jan. 2–Mar. 14, May 16–June 14, Aug. 16–Sept. 30, and Nov. 16–Nov. 30, weekends noon–5; Mar. 15–May 15 and Oct. 1–Nov. 15, Thurs. and Fri. 10–2, weekends* *noon–5; June 15–Aug. 15, Thurs. and Fri. 11–3, weekends noon–5; Dec., weekends 5 PM–9 PM. Last train leaves station ½ hr before closing time.*

National Museum of Health and Medicine. Opened in 1862 to train doctors during the Civil War, this medical museum now features displays on the Lincoln and Garfield assassinations and one of the world's largest collections of microscopes. Because some exhibits are fairly graphic (the wax surgical models and the preserved organs in particular), the museum may not be suitable for young children or the squeamish. Adult visitors must present a photo ID to enter. ⊠ *6900 Georgia Ave. NW* ☎ *202/782–2200* ⊕ *nmhm.washingtondc.museum* ⊠ *Free* ☉ *Daily 10–5:30; tours 2nd and 4th Sat. at 1* Ⓜ *Silver Spring.*

Where to Stay & Eat

$$$–$$$$ ✕ **Mrs. K's Toll House.** In one of the last tollhouses in Montgomery County, Mrs. K's has welcomed diners since 1930 and continues to please both those in search of comfort food and those with adventurous palates. Designed to resemble a country inn, the restaurant is filled with antique furniture, "Historic Old Blue" Staffordshire plates, and Nicholas Lutz glass. Both the menu (prix fixe only) and the decorations change seasonally. A live jazz band plays on Thursday night. ⊠ *9201 Colesville Rd.* ☎ *301/589–3500* ⊟ *AE, D, DC, MC, V.*

$–$$$$ ✕ **The Original Crisfield Seafood Restaurant.** With not much more elegance than a neighborhood barbershop, the prices here might seem absurd. But you get your money's worth: no-nonsense seafood and an eyeful of Old Maryland arrested in time. Crab cakes don't get any more authentic than these, presented with just enough structural imperfection to guarantee they're made by hand; the clam chowder—creamy, chunky, and served with a bottomless bowl of oyster crackers—is rendered with similar, down-home care. The fancier (and pricier) location in Lee Plaza has an art deco style and also serves chicken and steak. It's under separate management. ⊠ *8012 Georgia Ave.* ☎ *301/589–1306* ⊠ *Lee Plaza, 8606 Colesville Rd.* ☎ *301/588–1572* ⊟ *AE, MC, V* ☉ *Original closed Mon. No lunch weekends at Lee Plaza.*

★ $$–$$$ ✕ **Ceviche.** This hip Andean restaurant offers a selection of creative dishes in its modern dining room, which buzzes with the chatter of lounging twentysomethings. Try the chile relleno, the slow roasted chicken in a yellow pepper sauce, and, of course, the various takes on Ceviche's citrus and raw seafood namesake. ⊠ *921–J Ellsworth Dr.* ☎ *301/608–0081* ⊟ *AE, D, DC, MC, V.*

$–$$ ☷ **Crowne Plaza Hotel.** Four blocks from the Silver Spring Metro, this chain hotel doesn't offer many of luxuries, but is a dependable, pleasant place to stay. Some rooms have refrigerators, double sinks, couches, or recliners. A shuttle bus runs within a 4-mi radius on weekdays. ⊠ *8777 Georgia Ave., 20910* ☎ *301/589–0800* 🖷 *301/587–4791* ⊅ *221 rooms, 10 suites* ⌂ *Restaurant, room service, indoor pool, gym, bar, free parking* ⊟ *AE, D, DC, MC, V* Ⓜ *Silver Spring.*

$ ☷ **Ramada Inn.** This unpretentious hotel is close to Silver Spring's growing entertainment and dining hub on Colesville Road, as well as to the Silver Spring Metro. Rooms are comfortable, if unremarkable. There isn't any room service, but many local restaurants will deliver. ⊠ *7990*

Georgia Ave., 20910 ☎ *301/565–3444* 🖷 *301/588–2207* ⊕ *www. ramada.com* ⇨ *125 rooms* ⚿ *In-room data ports, laundry facilities, free parking* ▭ *AE, D, MC, V* ⦺ *CP* Ⓜ *Silver Spring.*

Sandy Spring

❻ *14 mi north of Silver Spring.*

Best known for the refuge that the Society of Friends gave slaves here as part of the Underground Railroad, Sandy Spring is still the home of an active Quaker community. Design your own tour of the town with maps available at the Sandy Spring Museum. Of the town's dozens of buildings, five homes were associated with the Underground Railroad. Unfortunately, only one, Woodlawn (16501 Norwood Road), is accessible to visitors, and that's only to see the grounds.

Sandy Spring Museum houses a hodgepodge of items including Native American arrowheads and early-20th-century town-store memorabilia. A carriage museum displaying various antique farming implements and buggies and a blacksmith shop are also on the grounds. ⊠ *17901 Bentley Rd.* ☎ *301/774–0022* ⊕ *www.sandyspringmuseum.org* 🎫 *$3* ⊙ *Mon., Wed., and Thurs. 9–4, weekends noon–4.*

PRINCE GEORGE'S COUNTY

Named in 1695 for Denmark and Norway's prince (the husband of the heir to the throne of England, Princess Anne), the county was once famous for its tobacco auctions, which are still held in its southern end. Tobacco created a wealthy leisure class that enjoyed cricket, fox hunting, and horse racing, a sport still popular in the area. Much of the county today, where nearly 60% of the population is African-American, remains affluent.

Nature lovers should try to make a visit to the National Wildlife Visitor Center and the Merkle Wildlife Sanctuary. Flight fans can check out the world's oldest airport in College Park. For those who prefer 60-second thrills, Six Flags is full of roller coasters, water slides, and kiddie rides. Sports fans may not be able to see the Redskins, but they can get a fix at a Maryland Terrapins game or at a Bowie Baysox minor-league baseball game. Historic sites, including the Surratt House Museum, are scattered throughout the county.

To tour the county, start in College Park and work your way up to Laurel. Then head south to the heart of the county before visiting sites along the Patuxent and Potomac rivers.

College Park

❼ *6 mi east of Silver Spring via I–495, 9 mi north of Washington, D.C.*

As its name implies, College Park is primarily a university town on gently rolling terrain. One of the largest campuses in the country, the **University of Maryland at College Park** has an enrollment of 34,000. The College Park campus began as an agricultural college in 1856, and became part of the University of Maryland in 1920. The university's ath-

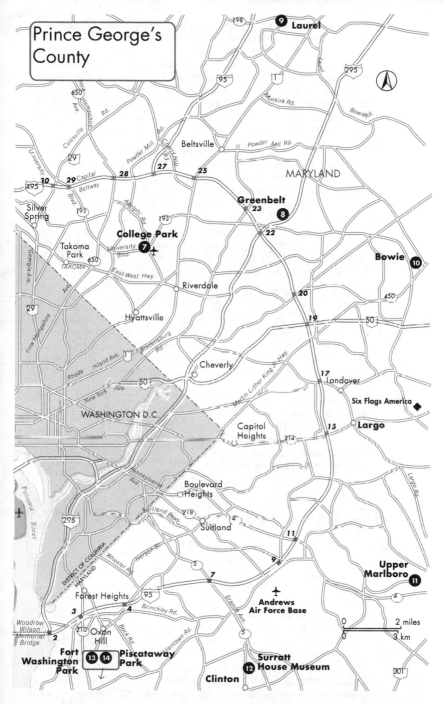

Prince George's County

letic teams (the Terrapins) participate in the highly competitive Atlantic Coast Conference and draw large crowds to Byrd Stadium and the 17,100-seat Comcast Center. In Turner Hall, visitor-center staff provide information about the university and maps for getting around the sprawling campus of 1,580 acres and 270 buildings. At the dairy, ice cream made from campus cows' milk is available by the cone or carton. ⊠ *Turner Hall, U.S. Rte. 1 and Rossborough La.* ☎ *301/314–7777* ⊕*www.umd.edu* ☉ *Turner Hall weekdays 8–5, Sat. 9–3. Dairy Oct.–Apr., weekdays 8–5; May–Sept., weekdays 8–5, Sat. noon–3.*

The Wright Brothers once trained military officers to fly at College Park Airport, the world's oldest continuously operating airport, which is now affiliated with the Smithsonian Institution. The **College Park Aviation Museum** is a tribute to the Wright Brothers and early aviation. Children can spin propellers and dress up like aviators. A "Speaking of Flight" lecture series is held in spring and fall. At the Peter Pan program, preschoolers make airplanes and hear stories on the second and fourth Thursday of the month (10:30 to noon). ⊠ *College Park Airport, 1985 Corporal Frank Scott Dr.* ☎ *301/864–6029, 301/861–4765 TDD* ⊕ *www.collegeparkaviationmuseum.com* ✉ *$4* ☉ *Daily 10–5.*

Where to Stay & Eat

¢–$$ ✕ **Ledo's.** Students, alumni, and locals have made Ledo's pizza popular throughout the state. There are dozens of Ledo's franchises in Maryland, but many insist that the best pizza—with smoked provolone so gooey you need a knife and fork—comes from the original restaurant, which opened in 1955 and is still family run. Adelphi is just outside of College Park city limits. ⊠ *2420 University Blvd., Adelphi* ☎ *301/ 422–8622* ▭ *MC, V.*

¢–$$ ✕ **R. J. Bentley's.** The walls are covered with license plates and gas-pump memorabilia, except the "wall of fame," hung with jerseys from the university's past athletes. Students and alumni head to this hangout for beer, chili, wings, and sandwiches; the bar packs in fans after home games. ⊠ *7323 Baltimore Ave.* ☎*301/277–8898* ▭*AE, MC, V.*

$$ ▥ **The Inn and Conference Center/ University of Maryland and University College.** Renovated in 2004, the center is a certified "green" building, with an air-conditioning system that is chlorofluorocarbon free. Those staying here can use the campus recreation center and indoor pool for free. Late May and early June are especially busy; parents start booking rooms months before graduation. A complimentary shuttle links the hotel with both the College Park and Prince George's Plaza Metro stops. ⊠ *3501 University Blvd. E, at Adelphi Rd., 20783* ☎ *301/985–7300 or 800/727–8622* 🖨 *301/985–7517* ⊕ *marriott.com/property/propertypage/wasum* ⇄ *127 rooms, 15 suites*

> ## TIPS ON FINDING LOCAL FARE
>
> Greenbelt has a smattering of Thai and Indian restaurants as well as hamburger joints, most of them on Greenbelt Road in or near the Beltway Plaza Mall. Diners looking for the best of local fare should head a few miles south to Kenilworth Avenue in Bladensburg, where taquerias serve up delicious Mexican food.

⚮ 2 restaurants, cable TV, in-room data ports, indoor pool, gym, bar, business services, parking (fee) ⊟ AE, D, MC, V.

Greenbelt

8 *4 mi northeast of College Park.*

Planned as part of a New Deal program during the Great Depression, Greenbelt was one of three cooperative communities built for low- and middle-income families (the others are outside of Milwaukee and in Ohio). These quasi-utopian "greenbelt" communities, constructed and planned by the U.S. Department of Agriculture, were meant to be self-sufficient areas, with the side benefit that they would relieve some of the housing pressure in nearby metropolitan areas. The town is now a National Historic Landmark. Walk down Crescent Road to the Greenbelt Museum (15 Crescent Road) for a glimpse at some representative houses, including one International Style house (10b Crescent Road) filled with artifacts from the 1930s such as Fiestaware and children's toys.

Backyard fly zappers, orange juice from concentrate, and seedless grapes are just three examples of some of the everyday innovations that were developed at the Agricultural Research Service's (ARS) **Beltsville Agricultural Research Center.** Even penicillin was discovered here, developed during World War II. Today the emphasis is on charting environmental stress, such as the depletion of the ozone layer, but you can also catch up on the latest in food technology. After a brief orientation at the visitor center, inside a log lodge built in 1937 by the Civilian Conservation Corps, you tour the farm by van or bus. Tours, which can be tailored to interests such as nutrition and genetic engineering, take at least two hours. Because of their length and technical nature, tours are not recommended for children below middle-school age. ■ TIP→ **The researchers work to develop heartier, safer, and sometimes tastier foods, but you won't get to try them here: there are neither free samples nor cafeterias on-site.** Reservations are essential; call two weeks in advance. ✉ *Bldg. 302, 10300 Baltimore Ave., 3 mi northeast of Greenbelt, Beltsville* ☎ *301/504–9403* ⊕ *www.ars.usda.gov* ⬚ *Free* ☉ *Weekdays 8–4:30.*

Where to Stay

$–$$$ 🏨 **Greenbelt Marriott.** This full-service hotel is a 10-minute walk from the Greenbelt Metro and a 15-minute drive to College Park. Shuttle service to the Metro runs every half hour from 7 AM to 9 PM. The hotel works with four tour companies to arrange sightseeing excursions to both Baltimore and Washington. ✉ *6400 Ivy La., 20770* ☎ *301/441–3700 or 800/228–9290* 🖷 *301/441–3995* ⊕ *marriott.com/property/propertypage/WASGB* ⬚ *283 rooms, 4 suites* ⚮ *Restaurant, room service, in-room data ports, 2 pools (1 indoor), health club, bar, travel services, free parking* ⊟ *AE, D, DC, MC, V.*

Laurel

9 *7 mi north of Greenbelt.*

Three other Maryland counties claim a section of this town (Anne Arundel, Howard, and Montgomery) but most of the suburb is in Prince George's.

On 75 acres of parkland, **Montpelier Mansion** is a masterpiece of Georgian architecture that George Washington used as a guesthouse on the way to and from the Constitutional Convention. It was built and owned by the Snowdens, who earned their wealth through tobacco and an iron foundry. Interesting features include a 35- by 16-foot reproduction of a hand-painted floor cloth and an offset central hall staircase. Also on the property is an 18th-century summerhouse where ladies took their tea, boxwood gardens, an herb-and-flower garden with plants grown in the 1800s, and a cultural arts center with three galleries and artists' studios. ⊠ *Rte. 197 and Muirkirk Rd.* ☎ *301/953–1376, 301/953–1993 arts center* ☒ *$3* ☉ *Dec.–Feb., Sun. tours at 1 and 2; Mar.–Nov., Sun.–Thurs. noon–3, tours on the hr. Art center daily 10–5.*

One of the Department of the Interior's largest science and environmental education centers, the **Patuxent National Wildlife Visitor Center,** between Laurel and Bowie, showcases interactive exhibits on global environmental issues, migratory bird routes, wildlife habitats, and endangered species. A viewing station overlooks a lake area that beavers, bald eagles, and Canada geese use as a habitat. Weather permitting, you can take a 30-minute tram tour through meadows, forests, and wetlands and then explore the trails on your own. The paved Loop Trail runs ⅓ mi; another 4 mi of trails crisscrosses the property. ⊠ *10901 Scarlet Tanager Loop, off Powder Mill Rd.* ☎ *301/497–5760* ⊕ *patuxent.fws.gov* ☒ *Free, tram ride $3* ☉ *Daily 10–5:30; tram weekends 11:30, 1, 2:30, and 3:30; late June–Aug., weekdays 11:30, 1, and 2:30.*

Sports & the Outdoors

FISHING & HUNTING The mission of **Patuxent Research Refuge** is to conserve and protect wildlife through research and to educate the public. The north tract of the refuge is available for fishing. Educational programs are also available here. To enter you must check in and receive an access pass. A Maryland nontidal fishing license is also required. Hunting (to cull certain species) is allowed from September through January. ⊠ *230 Bald Eagle Dr.* ☎ *410/674–3304, 410/674–4625 TDD* ⊕ *patuxent.fws.gov* ☒ *Free* ☉ *Nov.–Feb., daily 8–4:30; Mar., daily 8–6; Apr.–Aug., daily 8–8; Sept. and Oct., daily 8–6:30.*

HORSE RACING Maryland has a long-standing love for the ponies. You can watch and wager on thoroughbreds at **Laurel Park** (⊠ Rte. 198 and Race Track Rd. ☎ 301/725–0400) from January to March, mid-June to August, and mid-October to December. Horses usually run from Wednesday through Sunday, but races are simulcast seven days a week.

Bowie

❿ *13 mi southeast of Laurel, 15 mi east of College Park.*

Bowie started as a few buildings around a railroad junction in 1870, but has grown into the largest municipality in Prince George's County and the home of Bowie State University, a historically black college within the University of Maryland system.

Built in the mid-1700s as a country retreat for provincial Maryland governor Samuel Ogle, the Georgian-style **Belair Mansion** was subsequently owned in the early 1900s by William Woodward, one of the first people to bring thoroughbred horses to the U.S. from England. The house displays British and Early American paintings, silver, and furniture. In 1914 Woodward built additions to the house, including the **Belair Stable**, which began the legacy of the Belair Stud, the line responsible for Omaha and his sire Gallant Fox, each of whom won the Triple Crown in the mid 1900s. One-hour tours of the mansion and stable emphasize the contributions of the families and their horses to racing history. ⊠ *12207 Tulip Grove Dr.* ☎ *301/809–3089* ⬚ *Free* ⊙ *Wed.–Sun. noon–4.*

Sports & the Outdoors

FedEx Stadium (⊠ 1600 FedEx Way, Landover ☎ 301/276–6000) is where the Washington Redskins play, but all the tickets are owned by season pass holders. Football fans who don't have megabucks to buy a ticket (they're often sold through the classifieds or through online auction sites) may be able to get tickets for other events. The Rolling Stones, George Strait, and other superstars have all performed at this 86,000-seat stadium. **Bowie Baysox** (⊠ 4101 N.E. Crain Hwy. ☎ 301/805–6000), the AA affiliate of the Baltimore Orioles, play at the 10,500-seat Prince George's Stadium. Children have major-league fun off the field at a carousel, child-oriented concession stands, and a playground. Fireworks light up the sky at every home game held on Saturday evening between April and Labor Day, as well as at Thursday night games in July and August. Tickets cost $9.

Largo

9 mi south of Bowie.

Maryland's only amusement park, **Six Flags America** combines a theme park with Paradise Island, a water park. On the "dry" side, high-speed revelers enjoy eight old-fashioned wood or modern steel coasters. "Batwing" puts riders headfirst, face and belly down, with nothing between them and the ground but a safety strap. Children under 48 inches can coast on a minimodel, "drive" an 18-wheeler, and earn their wings flying minijets. On the "wet" side, children of all ages beat the heat whizzing down water slides and swimming in pools. A barrel over Crocodile Cal's (named for Cal Ripkin, legendary star of the Baltimore Orioles) Outback Beach House dumps 1,000 gallons of water on unsuspecting passersby every few minutes. When your body has been through enough, sit back for the stage and musical entertainments. ⊠ *13710 Central Ave., Largo* ☎ *301/249–1500* ⊕ *www.sixflags.com/America* ⬚ *$37, kids under 48" $26, kids 3 and under free; parking $9* ⊙ *Mid-Apr.–Memorial Day, weekends 10:30–6; Memorial Day–Labor Day, daily 10:30–9; Fright Fest, Oct., Fri. 5–10, weekends noon–10.*

Where to Stay & Eat

$–$$ ✕ **Jasper's.** People come here as much to be seen as to eat. The Largo location is one of four in the state. On the American menu, she-crab soup, the stuffed fish of the day, and the grilled-chicken Caesar salad are among the favorites; all desserts are made in-house. Jazz and rhythm and blues can be heard every night. ⊠ *9640 Lottsford Ct., near US Airways Arena, Largo* ☎ *301/883–2199* ⊟ *AE, D, DC, MC, V.*

$$ ▦ **New Carrollton Landover Courtyard by Marriott.** This business-district hotel caters to a corporate crowd, but it's also a convenient roosting spot for visitors to Six Flags and other sights. Free shuttle service runs to the D.C. Metro and to Amtrak's New Carrollton station, about three minutes away. Prices drop below $100 on weekends. ⊠ *8330 Corporate Dr., Landover 20785* ☎ *301/577–3373* 🖷 *301/577–1780* ⊕ *marriott.com/property/propertypage/WASLD* ⇆ *136 rooms, 14 suites* ♿ *Restaurant, room service, in-room data ports, pool, gym, bar, free parking* ☰ *AE, D, DC, MC, V.*

Upper Marlboro

⓫ *14 mi south of Bowie, 11 mi east of Suitland.*

The county seat of Prince George's County was once famous for its tobacco auctions. Although tobacco is still bought and sold here, business today mostly revolves around the local government.

Ⓒ **Merkle Wildlife Sanctuary** is named after the conservationist Edgar A. Merkle, who began a breeding and habitat improvement program to bring Canada geese to Maryland's Patuxent River. Thousands of geese return here each September and remain through late February or early March; another 80–100 stay year-round. You can take a gander by hiking the nature trails or from observation decks at the visitor center, which has a discovery room where children can make crafts and observe turtles and snakes. On Sunday, from 10 to 3, the sanctuary sponsors self-guided driving tours of the marshlands, woodlands, farm ponds, and creeks. To reach the sanctuary take Route 301 south to Route 382 and turn left on St. Thomas Church Road. ⊠ *11704 Fenno Rd.* ☎ *301/888–1377* 💲 *$2 per vehicle* ☉ *Daily dawn–dusk; weekends 10–5, hrs subject to change.*

The **Show Place Arena** hosts consumer shows on everything from dolls to dogs as well as major equestrian events. The Prince George's County Equestrian Center is also here. ⊠ *14900 Pennsylvania Ave.* ☎ *301/952–7900, 301/952–7999 special events line.*

Clinton

10 mi southwest of Upper Marlboro.

The origin of the name Clinton is unclear—the town used to be called Surrattsville for Mary Surratt's husband, the postmaster John Surratt.

Ⓒ **Oxon Cove Park** preserves 19th-century farm life on a site where the Piscataway Native Americans once lived. Children can feed chickens, milk cows, and take a hayride. There's a fine view of Washington over the Potomac River. Throughout the year, the National Park Service offers programs such as sheep shearing (May), cider making (September), and "Talking Turkey," when kids can learn about and feed domestic and wild turkeys (November). ⊠ *6411 Oxon Hill Rd., 5 mi northwest of Clinton* ☎ *301/839–1176* ⊕ *www.nps.gov/nace/oxhi* 💲 *Free* ☉ *Daily 8–4:30.*

★ **⓬** The **Surratt House Museum,** once a house and tavern, is where John Wilkes Booth sought refuge after assassinating President Lincoln. For her role in the conspiracy, Mary Surratt became the first woman to be executed by the federal government. She was said to have told one of her tenants to get the "shooting irons ready" for Booth as he was fleeing after the assassination. You can trace Booth's escape route on an electronic map at the visitor center. Costumed docents give tours of the house, talk about 19th-century life in Prince George's County, and discuss the Civil War, but they won't get into debates about Surratt's innocence or guilt. The Surratt Society sponsors a 12-hour John Wilkes Booth escape route tour in April and September that covers the 12 days Booth spent on the run in Maryland, Virginia, and Washington, D.C. ⊠ *9118 Brandywine Rd.* ☎ *301/868–1121* ⊕ *www.surratt.org* ⊠ *$3* ⊙ *Thurs. and Fri. 11–3, weekends noon–4; tours every ½ hr.*

Fort Washington Park

⓭ *5 mi southwest of Clinton, 7 mi south of Oxon Hill.*

George Washington chose this site on a narrow portion of the Potomac River for the first fort to protect the nation's capital. It was destroyed during the War of 1812, only five years after its completion; the current fort was completed in 1824. Half-hour tours of the fort are given on weekend afternoons and on request on weekdays. One Sunday per month, costumed volunteers fire the fort's cannons. If you cross the drawbridge over the moat, you can see the 7-foot-thick stone and masonry walls, gun positions, and other defenses. Although the fort is impressive, most people visit the park to picnic along the river. ⊠ *13551 Fort Washington Rd.* ☎ *301/763–4600* ⊠ *$5 per vehicle, early Apr.–late Sept.; free weekdays early Oct.–early Apr., $5 on weekends* ⊙ *Early Apr.–late Sept., daily 9–5; early Oct.–early Apr., daily 9–4:30.*

Accokeek

10 mi south of Fort Washington.

By fighting off developers in the 1950s, the Accokeek Foundation helped keep the view from Mount Vernon as George Washington would have seen it. Today, the once rural area is being developed into a suburban community. Locals call Piscataway Park, tucked away at the end of the road by the river, a hidden treasure.

⓮ On 4,000 acres of land bought to protect the view from Mount Vernon across the river, **Piscataway Park** attracts history buffs, horticulturists, naturalists, hikers, and families. At **National Colonial Farm**, you can walk through a middle-class 18th-century farm dwelling and tobacco barn and reproductions of a smokehouse and out-kitchen used by farmers not quite as prosperous as the Washingtons on the other side of the Potomac. Guides point out the farmhouse's most valuable materials: the glass in the windows and its nails.

NATIONAL COLONIAL FARM VS. MOUNT VERNON

If you want to compare and contrast National Colonial Farm with Mount Vernon, board the *Potomac*, a dory boat that runs every weekend between mid-June and mid-September.

Whenever a house burned down in the 18th century, the owners would rummage through the remains for the nails. Old-time animal breeds and heirloom crop varieties are both raised here. Also on hand is an herb garden as well as bluebirds, great blue herons, and bald eagles. ⊠ *3400 Bryan Point Rd., 5 mi south of Fort Washington Park* ☎ *301/283–2113 Accokeek Foundation, 301/283–0112 National Park Service* ⊕ *www.nps.gov/ pisc* ⊠ *$2, families $5; $7 ferry rides; $16 ferry ride includes admission to Mount Vernon* ⊙ *Park, daily dawn–dusk; National Colonial Farm mid-Mar.–mid-Dec., Tues.–Sun. 10–4, tours weekends at 11, 1, and 3; ferry rides mid-June–mid-Sept., weekends at 10, noon, 2, and 4; ferry tickets must be picked up 15 mins before boarding. Reservations recommended.*

SUBURBAN MARYLAND ESSENTIALS

To research prices, get advice from other travelers, and book travel arrangements, visit www.fodors.com.

Transportation

BY AIR

Three major airports serve both suburban Maryland and the Washington, D.C., area. Baltimore-Washington International (BWI) Airport, 10 mi south of Baltimore off I–95 and Route 295, is closer to Montgomery and Prince George's counties than Ronald Reagan National Airport or Washington Dulles International Airport.

The Washington Metropolitan Area Transit Authority (WMATA) operates express bus service between BWI and the Greenbelt Metro station. Buses run between 6 AM and 10 PM. Exact fare ($3) is required. BWI is also served by SuperShuttle. By taxi, expect to pay around $32 to Laurel, $57 to Silver Spring, and $68 to Bethesda. Free shuttle buses carry passengers between airline terminals and the train station at BWI. Amtrak and Maryland Rail Commuter Service (MARC) trains run between BWI and Washington, D.C.'s Union Station and Prince George's County from around 6 AM to 10 PM. The cost of the 30-minute ride to Union Station is $13–$36 on Amtrak and $6 on MARC, which runs only on weekdays.

🚄 Amtrak ☎ 800/872-7245 ⊕ www.amtrak.com. Baltimore-Washington International (BWI) Airport ☎ 410/859-7111. MARC ☎ 410/767-3999 or 800/325-7245, 410/ 539-3497 TDD ⊕ www.mtamaryland.com. SuperShuttle ☎ 800/258-3826 or 202/ 296-6662 ⊕ www.supershuttle.com. WMATA ☎ 202/637-7000, 202/638-3780 TDD ⊕ www.wmata.com.

BY BUS

Greyhound Lines provides scheduled service to Silver Spring Station only. Metrobus makes local stops in both counties and in Washington, D.C. Ride-On, Montgomery County's own bus service, has service on more than 70 roads. Look for the blue-and-white bus stop signs throughout the county.

🚌 Greyhound Lines ☎ 800/231-2222. Metrobus ☎ 202/637-7000. Ride-On ☎ 240/ 777-7433. Silver Spring Station ⊠ 8100 Fenton St. ☎ 301/585-8700.

2

BY CAR

The primary transportation link throughout suburban Maryland is the Capital Beltway (I–495), which runs east–west. Interstate 95 runs north–south. Interstate 270, which intersects with I–495 in Montgomery County, reaches destinations north of Rockville in Montgomery County. Roads that run through the region and into downtown Washington include Wisconsin, Connecticut, Georgia, New Hampshire, and Pennsylvania avenues; routes 1 and 50 (the latter turns into New York Avenue upon entering the District); Baltimore Washington Parkway; and I–295, all of which get busy 7:30–9 AM and 5–6:30 PM.

BY SUBWAY

Suburban Maryland connects to Washington, D.C., through the Washington Metro, one of the country's cleanest and safest subway systems. Montgomery County is served by the system's busiest route, the Red Line. Prince George's County is served by the Blue, Orange, and Green lines. To travel from one county on the subway to another involves going through downtown Washington and transferring trains.

The Metro begins operation at 5 AM on weekdays and 7 AM on weekends. It closes on weekdays at midnight and weekends at 3 AM. During the weekday peak periods (5–9:30 AM and 3–7 PM), trains come along every three to six minutes. At other times and on weekends and holidays, trains run about every 12–15 minutes.

The Metro's base fare is $1.35; the actual price depends on the time of day and the distance traveled, which means you might end up paying $3.90 if you're traveling to a distant station at rush hour. Up to two children under age five ride free when accompanied by a paying passenger.

Buy your ticket at the Farecard machines; they accept coins and crisp $1, $5, $10, or $20 bills. Some newer machines will also accept credit cards. You can buy one day passes for $6.50 and seven-day passes for $32.50. Locals use the SmarTrip card, a plastic card that can hold any fare amount and can be used throughout the subway system. Buy passes or SmarTrip cards at the Metro Center sales office.

Insert your Farecard into the turnstile to enter the platform. Make sure you hang on to the card—you need it to exit.
Metrorail ☎ 202/637-7000 ⊕ www.wmata.com.

BY TAXI

You can hail a taxi on the street just about anywhere in Bethesda or Silver Spring. Taxis are metered. It costs $4 to drop the flag, plus 40¢ for each quarter mile. Extra charges include $1 for each additional passenger, $1 when you phone for a cab, and $2 during snow emergencies.
Taxi Companies Checker Cab ☎ 301/816-0066. **Montgomery Taxi Cab** ☎ 301/926-9300.

BY TRAIN

Amtrak has scheduled stops in New Carrollton and at BWI Airport as part of its East Coast service. The MARC commuter train has two lines that go through Montgomery and Prince George's counties, and it also goes into Washington's Union Station.

Amtrak ☎ 800/872-7245 ⊕ www.amtrak.com. **MARC** ☎ 800/325-7245 ⊕ www. mtamaryland.com. **New Carrollton Train Station** ✉ 4300 Garden City Dr. ☎ 202/906-3764.

Contacts & Resources

EMERGENCIES

Suburban Hospital is the designated trauma center for Montgomery County.

CVS's hotline can tell you which of its 24-hour pharmacies are near you.

Police, Fire, Ambulance ☎ 911.

Hospitals Holy Cross Hospital ✉ 1500 Forest Glen Rd., Silver Spring ☎ 301/754-7000. **Suburban Hospital** ✉ 8600 Old Georgetown Rd., Bethesda ☎ 301/896-3100. **Washington Adventist Hospital** ✉ 7600 Carroll Ave., Takoma Park ☎ 301/891-7600.

24-Hour Pharmacies CVS Pharmacy ☎ 800/746-7287.

INTERNET, MAIL & SHIPPING

Downtown Silver Spring has free 24-hour Wi-Fi service. Libraries in Montgomery County (in Bethesda, Chevy Chase, Potomac, Silver Spring, and Wheaton) and Prince George's County (in Laurel, Bowie, Upper Marlboro, and Accokeek) also have free Wi-Fi and Internet access.

The post office with the longest hours is National Capitol Station, across the street from Union Station. It is open 7 AM–midnight on weekdays and 7 AM–8 PM on weekends. Farragut Station and McPherson Station, both in downtown D.C., and Georgetown Station are open weekdays 9–5.

Post Offices Farragut Station ✉ 1800 M St. NW, 20036 ☎ 202/523-2024 ⊕ www. usps.gov. **Georgetown Station** ✉ 1215 31st St. NW, 20007 ☎ 202/523-2026 ⊕ www. usps.gov. **McPherson Station** ✉ 1750 Pennsylvania Ave. NW, 20006 ☎ 202/523-2394 ⊕ www.usps.gov. **National Capitol Station** ✉ 2 Massachusetts Ave. NE, 20002 ☎ 202/523-2368 ⊕ www.usps.gov.

Internet Bethesda Public Library ✉ 7400 Arlington Rd. ☎ 240/777-0970. **Silver Spring Public Library** ✉ 8901 Colesville Rd. ☎ 240/773-9420.

VISITOR INFORMATION

Bethesda Urban Partnership offers a comprehensive list of shopping, dining, and entertainment opportunities and special events in Bethesda. Both the Montgomery County and Prince George's County Conference & Visitors Bureaus offer the same information—although less complete—about their respective counties.

Tourist Information Bethesda Urban Partnership ✉ 7700 Old Georgetown Rd., Bethesda 20814 ☎ 301/215-6660 🖶 301/215-6664 ⊕ www.bethesda.org. **Montgomery County Conference & Visitors Bureau** ✉ 11820 Parklawn Dr., Suite 380, Rockville 20852 ☎ 301/428-9702 or 800/925-0880 🖶 301/428-9705 ⊕ www.cvbmontco.com. **Prince George's County Conference & Visitors Bureau** ✉ 9200 Basil Ct., Suite 101, Largo 20774 ☎ 301/925-8300 or 888/925-8300 🖶 301/925-2053 ⊕ www. goprincegeorgescounty.com.

Northern Virginia

WORD OF MOUTH

" . . . The drive to Mt. Vernon is breathtaking! It was all I could do to keep my eyes on the road on that drive."

—KatieL

" . . . Besides Mount Vernon we very much liked the nearby Woodlawn Plantation and, a little farther along, Cunston Hall, a fine 18th century estate with lovely gardens. The whole trip is about 2 hours of driving time."

—Underhill

Updated by
John A. Kelly

CLOSE TO D.C. IN MORE WAYS THAN ONE, Northern Virginia extends westward from the Potomac River to the Blue Ridge Mountains. Although its name echoes that of Confederate General Robert E. Lee's Army of Northern Virginia, today the prosperous area's business and residential life takes its cue from the national capital, to the east. What seems to be the missing bite from the otherwise regular diamond-shape of D.C. was Virginia's contribution. After many years without any federal construction, in 1846 this Virginia portion was returned and became Arlington—named for General Lee's family home—and Alexandria. Both cities have the Potomac as their irregular eastern boundary.

Buildings in Alexandria's old downtown, referred to often as "Old Town," are reminiscent of the Federal period (1790–1820); more than 2,000 of the area's 18th- and 19th-century buildings are listed on the National Register of Historic Places. Nearby areas have grown significantly in the recent past and have modern housing, government, and office buildings. Tysons Corner in Fairfax County has major retail outlets clustered close to the I–495 Beltway and has office buildings serving more than 400 corporations employing about 57,000 people, 95% of them commuters. Expansion toward Dulles International Airport has been particularly massive, especially along the toll road to the airport. Northern Virginia contains some of America's most precious acreage, including Mount Vernon and Arlington National Cemetery. Manassas (Bull Run), 26 mi from Washington, was the site of two of the most significant battles of the Civil War. Although Manassas is still predominantly rural, Washington sprawl has spilled over, and Bull Run has been the site of modern battles between the forces of development and those of preservation. In Loudoun County, horse lovers and spectators still practice the 18th-century diversions of fox hunting and the steeplechase.

Top 5 Experiences for Northern Virginia

- **Take a moment to reflect at Arlington National Cemetery:** See Arlington House and its Washington view; learn about prominent early Virginia families: Washington, Custis, Randolph and Lee. Visit the Tomb of the Unknowns, the Kennedy graves, and those of other famous Americans, all within these sacred grounds.

- **Get to know the first president at Mount Vernon:** Visit the historic plantation and learn about George Washington's many contributions as a farmer, patriot, general, and president. See his threshing barn, gristmill, distillery, and personal artifacts, and experience the new interactive displays.

- **Return to the first shot of the Civil War:** Explore the site of the first Civil War battle at Manassas National Battlefield Park in the peaceful Virginia countryside. A second Battle of Manassas lasted three days and resulted in 3,300 killed. (The Confederacy won both battles.)

- **Explore historic air- and spacecraft:** At the National Air and Space Museum Steven F. Udvar-Hazy Center, near Dulles Airport, see many important historic and modern aircraft, including the *Enola Gay* and space shuttle Enterprise. Fly simulators, watch an IMAX movie, and see Dulles flight operations from the center's observation tower.

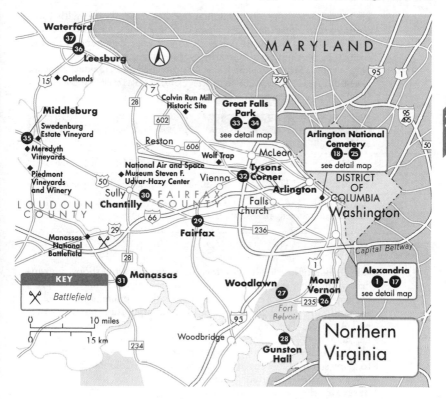

- **Wonder at the fall line in Great Falls Park:** Visit the scenic fall line of the Potomac River, a barrier to upriver navigation that necessitated settlements at Georgetown and Alexandria and the Potowmack Canal, remnants of which are in the park, and later the C&O Canal.

Exploring Northern Virginia

Northern Virginia is generally defined as the area close to and south and west of the Potomac River, including Arlington and Alexandria, Fairfax County, Loudoun County, and Prince William County, to the south.

About the Restaurants & Hotels

There is no need to go into the District to find a decent restaurant. Alexandria and Arlington have a wide variety of ethnic and American restaurants at reasonable prices. Alexandria has several good restaurants near the river on and around King Street, but parking is tough and the Metrorail station is far away. In Arlington, there is a good variety of dining between the neighborhoods of Ballston and Rosslyn around five closely spaced Metrorail stations. The Shirlington area, just off Shirley Highway south of the Pentagon and with loads of free parking, has become a convenient and reasonable dining destination for both Arlington and Alexandria.

Lodging choices range from familiar hotel chains to homes with 18th-century architecture blended with modern amenities. Alexandria & Arlington Bed and Breakfast Network can arrange accommodations in Arlington, Alexandria, and nearby Northern Virginia.

? Reservations Services **Alexandria & Arlington Bed and Breakfast Network** ⊠4938 Hampden La., Suite 164, Bethesda 20814 ☎703/549-3415 or 888/549-3415 🖷202/517-9179 ⊕ www.aabbn.com.

WHAT IT COSTS					
	$$$$	**$$$**	**$$**	**$**	**¢**
RESTAURANTS	over $30	$22–$30	$14–$22	$7–$14	under $7
HOTELS	over $250	$175–$250	$130–$175	$80–$130	under $80

Restaurant prices are per person for a main course at dinner. Hotel prices are for a standard double room, excluding state and local taxes.

ALEXANDRIA

A lively mix of historic homes, taverns, restaurants and shops, Alexandria seems to exist in two or three centuries at once. Founded in 1749 by Scottish merchants eager to capitalize on the booming tobacco trade, Alexandria first emerged as one of the most important ports in Colonial America. The city dwarfed Georgetown—Washington's oldest neighborhood—in the days before the Revolution, and, through the Civil War, had one of the country's largest slave markets. Alexandria is linked to many significant events and personages of the Colonial, Revolutionary, and Civil War periods. Members of the Lee family of Revolutionary and Civil War fame lived here, and George Washington had a town house and attended church here, though he lived a few miles south in Mount Vernon.

For many African-Americans fleeing slavery, part of their journey on the Underground Railroad included a stop in Alexandria. This was true of one of the largest and most celebrated slave escapes, in which 77 individuals, many of whom labored in homes in Alexandria, took refuge on the *Pearl,* a ship bound for New Jersey, which left from Washington's 7th Street Wharf in April 1848. Unfortunately the ship was captured in Maryland and most of its passengers were returned to Bruin's Slave Jail.

ALEXANDRIA VS. FAIRFAX

Founded as a Colonial port city, Alexandria was settled along the Potomac River, below the fall line at Great Falls. Old Town used to refer to this oldest area, but its boundaries have slipped considerably to the south and west. Jones Point Park, below the Woodrow Wilson Bridge, contains the southern boundary stone of the original District of Columbia, which included Alexandria and Arlington. Many of the homes and businesses south of the Beltway have an Alexandria address, although they are legally in Fairfax County.

5 INTERESTING THINGS ABOUT GENERAL LEE

- Richard Lee, General Lee's cousin once removed, and Francis Lightfoot Lee, the general's uncle, signed the Declaration of Independence.

- His father, Henry Lee, was a cavalry leader known as "Light Horse Harry" Lee during the Revolution and later was governor of Virginia.

- During John Brown's raid at Harpers Ferry, Lee was dispatched from his home at Arlington and put in charge of a makeshift group of troops built around the Marine Barracks of Washington, reinforcing Maryland militia, which retook the armory and captured the raiders. Lee's second in command was J. E. B. Stuart.

- Lee served as superintendent of West Point, and had both a son and nephew as cadets during his tenure. As superintendent, he reported to U.S. Secretary of War Jefferson Davis, who graduated from West Point a year ahead of him.

- Following the surrender at Appomattox, Lee became president of Washington College (originally Augusta Academy) and served there until his death in 1870. Following his death, the school was renamed Washington and Lee in his honor. His horse, Traveler, is buried outside the museum there.

This vibrant past remains alive in the historic district of **Old Town Alexandria**—an area of cobbled streets, restored 18th- and 19th-century homes, churches, and taverns close to the water. The main arteries of this district are Washington Street (the G. W. Parkway as it passes through town) and King Street. Most points of interest are on the east (Potomac) side of Washington Street. Visit them on foot if you're prepared to walk 20 blocks or so; parking is usually scarce, especially close to the river, and the parking police seem to catch every violation (especially in alleys). ■ TIP→ The visitor center at Ramsay House will give you a 24-hour permit for free parking at any two-hour metered spot.

Numbers in the text correspond to numbers in the margin and on the Old Town Alexandria map.

Main Attractions

🔟 **Boyhood Home of Robert E. Lee.** The childhood home in Alexandria of the commander of the Confederate forces of Virginia is a fine example of a 19th-century Federal town house. The house is privately owned and not open to visitors, but some of the home's furnishings are displayed at the Lyceum. ⊠ *607 Oronoco St., Old Town.*

7 **Carlyle House.** Alexandria forefather and Scottish merchant John Carlyle built a grand house here, completed in 1753 and modeled on a country manor house in the old country. Students of the French and Indian War will want to know that the dwelling served as General Braddock's headquarters. The house retains its original 18th-century woodwork and is furnished with Chippendale furniture and Chinese porcelain. An architectural exhibit on the second floor explains how the house was built; outside there's an attractive garden of Colonial-era plants. ⊠ *121*

N. Fairfax St., Old Town ☎ *703/ 549-2997* ⊕ *www.carlylehouse. org* 🖾 *$4* 🕐 *Tues.–Sat. 10–4, Sun. noon–4, guided tour every ½ hr.*

⑬ Christ Church. Both Washington and Robert E. Lee were pewholders in this Episcopal church, which remains in nearly original condition. (Washington paid £36 and 10 shillings—a lot of money in those days—for Pew 60.) Built in 1773, this fine example of an English Georgian country-style church has a Palladian window, an interior balcony, and an English wrought-brass-and-crystal chandelier. Docents give tours during visiting hours. ✉ *118 N. Washington St., Old Town* ☎ *703/549-1450* ⊕ *www. historicchristchurch.org* 🖾 *$5 donation suggested* 🕐 *Mon.–Sat. 9–4, Sun. 2–4:30.*

POTOMAC PASS
Alexandria's Potomac Pass includes a boat round-trip from Alexandria and admission to Mount Vernon, Carlyle House, and Gadsby's Tavern. The pass, valid April–October (in September and October, weekends only), costs $31 for adults. The Alexandria Very Important Patriot (VIP) Pass includes a walking history or ghost tour of Old Town, Alexandria, Gadsby's Tavern Museum, Carlyle House, and Lee-Fendall House Museum and Garden. Valid April–September, it's $22 for adults. Both passes, and others, are available from the Alexandria Convention and Visitors Association.

Confederate Statue. In 1861, when Alexandria was occupied by Union forces, the 800 soldiers of the city's garrison marched out of town to join the Confederate Army. In the middle of Washington and Prince streets stands a statue marking the point where they assembled. In 1885 Confederate veterans proposed a memorial to honor their fallen comrades. This statue, based on John A. Elder's painting *Appomattox*, is of a lone soldier glumly surveying the battlefields after General Robert E. Lee's surrender. The names of 100 Alexandria Confederate dead are carved on the base. ✉ *Washington and Prince Sts., Old Town.*

★ ☾ ❽ **Gadsby's Tavern Museum.** The two concerns that now comprise this museum—a circa-1785 tavern and the 1792 City Tavern and Hotel—were centers of political and social life. George Washington celebrated his birthdays in the ballroom. Other noted patrons included Thomas Jefferson, John Adams, and the Marquis de Lafayette. The taproom, dining room, assembly room, ballroom, and communal bedrooms have been restored to their original appearance. The tours on Friday evenings are led by a costumed guide carrying a lantern. ✉ *134 N. Royal St., Old Town* ☎ *703/ 838-4242* ⊕ *www.gadsbystavern.org* 🖾 *$4, lantern tour $5* 🕐 *Nov.–Mar., Tues.–Sat. 11–4, Sun. 1–4, last tour at 3:15; Apr.–Oct., Tues.–Sat. 10–5, Sun. and Mon. 1–5, last tour at 4:45; tours 15 mins before and after the hour. Half-hour lantern tours Mar.–Nov., Fri. 7–9:30.*

★ ⑯ **George Washington Masonic National Memorial.** Because Alexandria, like Washington, D.C., has no really tall buildings, the spire of this memorial dominates the surroundings and is visible for miles. The building overlooks King and Duke streets, Alexandria's major east–west arteries. It's a respectable uphill climb from the King St. Metrorail and bus

stations. From the ninth-floor observation deck (reached █
you get a spectacular view of Alexandria and Washington, D
cess above the first and mezzanine floors is by guided tou█
building contains furnishings from the first Masonic lodge █ Alexandria. George Washington became a Mason in 1753 in Fredericksburg,
and became Charter Master of the Alexandria lodge when it was chartered in 1788, remaining active in Masonic affairs during his tenure as
president, 1789–97. ⊠ *101 Callahan Dr., Old Town* ☎ *703/683–2007*
⊕ *www.gwmemorial.org* ▣ *Free* ☉ *Daily 9:30–5; 1-hr guided tour of
building and observation deck daily at 9:30, 11, 1, 2:15 and 3:30.*

❾ Lee-Fendall House. The Lee-Fendall House, at historic Lee Corner at North
Washington and Oronoco streets, was built in 1785; over the course of
the next 118 years it was home to 37 members of the Lee family and
served as a Union hospital. The house and its furnishings, of the 1850–70
period, present an intimate study of 19th-century family life. Highlights include a splendid collection of Lee heirlooms, period pieces produced by Alexandria manufacturers, and the beautifully restored,
award-winning garden. ⊠ *614 Oronoco St., Old Town* ☎ *703/548–
1789* ▣ *$4* ☉ *Feb.–mid-Dec., Tues., Thurs., Fri., and Sat. 10–4, Wed.
and Sun. 1–4; sometimes closed weekends.*

⓮ Lyceum. Built in 1839 and one of Alexandria's best examples of Greek
Revival design, the Lyceum is also the city's official history museum.
Over the years, the building has served as the Alexandria Library, a Civil
War hospital, a residence, and offices. Restored in the 1970s for the Bi-
centennial, it has an impressive collection including examples of 18th-
century silver, tools, stoneware, and Civil War photographs taken by
Mathew Brady. ⊠ *201 S. Washington St., Old Town* ☎ *703/838–4994*
⊕ *www.alexandriahistory.org* ▣ *Free* ☉ *Mon.–Sat. 10–5, Sun. 1–5.*

❶ Ramsay House. The best place to start a tour of Alexandria's Old Town
is at the **Alexandria Convention & Visitors Association,** in Ramsay House,
the home of the town's first postmaster and lord mayor, William Ramsay. The structure is believed to be at the site of the first house in Alexandria. The unusually helpful staff hands out brochures, maps for self-guided
walking tours, and 24-hour permits for free parking at any two-hour metered spot. ⊠*221 King St., Old Town* ☎*703/838–4200 or 800/388–9119,
703/838–6494 TDD* ⊕ *www.funside.com* ▣ *Guided tours $10–$15*
☉ *Daily 9–5; tours Mon.–Sat. 10:30 and 11:30, Sun. 10:30 and 2.*

★ ☾ ❻ Torpedo Factory Art Center. Torpedoes were manufactured here by the U.S.
Navy during both world wars. Now the building, housing the studios
and workshops of about 160 artists and artisans, has become one of
Alexandria's most popular attractions. You can observe printmakers,
jewelry makers, sculptors, painters, and potters as they create original
work in their studios. The Torpedo Factory also houses the Alexandria
Archaeology Museum, which displays artifacts such as plates, cups, pipes,
and coins from an early tavern, and Civil War soldiers' equipment. If
digging interests you, call to sign up for the well-attended public digs
(most Saturdays in June and September, 1:30–3; ☎ *703/838–4399; $5).*
Reservations are required. ⊠ *105 N. Union St., Old Town* ☎ *703/838–
4565* ⊕ *www.torpedofactory.org* ▣ *Free* ☉ *Daily 10–5.*

Old Town
Alexandria,
Virginia

KEY

Ⓜ Metro station

Also Worth Seeing

⑪ Alexandria Black History Museum. This museum, devoted to the history of African-Americans in Alexandria and Virginia from 1749 to the present, is at the site of the Robert H. Robinson Library, a building constructed in the wake of a landmark 1939 sit-in protesting the segregation of Alexandria libraries. The federal census of 1790 recorded 52 free African-Americans living in the city, and the port town was one of the largest slave exportation points in the South, with at least two bustling slave markets. ⊠ *902 Wythe St., Old Town* ☎ *703/838–4356* ⊕ *oha. ci.alexandria.va.us/bhrc* ⊠ *Free* ☉ *Tues.–Sat. 10–4.*

❹ Athenaeum. One of the most noteworthy structures in Alexandria, this striking, reddish-brown Greek Revival edifice at the corner of Prince and Lee streets stands out from its many redbrick Federal neighbors. Built in 1851 as a bank (Robert E. Lee had an account here) and later used as a Union Army hospital, then as a talcum powder factory for the Stabler-Leadbeater Apothecary, the Athenaeum now houses the gallery of the Northern Virginia Fine Arts Association and Alexandria Ballet. This block of Prince Street between Fairfax and Lee streets is known as **Gentry Row,** after the 18th- and 19th-century inhabitants of its imposing three-story houses. ⊠ *201 Prince St., Old Town* ☎ *703/548–0035* ⊠ *Free* ☉ *Wed.–Fri. 11–3, weekends 1–5.*

⑰ Bruin's Slave Jail. On this site, Joseph Bruin ran much of Alexandria's substantial slave trade, imprisoning in this Federal-style house African-Americans due to be sold. Harriett Beecher Stowe modeled her account of the slave trade in *Uncle Tom's Cabin* on this establishment. The building, now used as private offices, is closed to the public. ⊠ *1707 Duke St., Old Town.*

❺ Captain's Row. Many of Alexandria's sea captains once lived on this block. The cobblestones in the street were supposedly laid by Hessian mercenaries who had fought for the British during the Revolution and were held in Alexandria as prisoners of war. ⊠ *Prince St. between Lee and Union Sts., Old Town.*

⑮ Friendship Fire House. Alexandria's showcase firehouse dates from 1855 and has the appearance and implements of a typical 19th-century firehouse. According to local lore, George Washington helped found the volunteer fire company in 1774. Among early fire engines on display are a hand pumper built in Baltimore in 1851 and an Amoskeag steam pumper built in Manchester, New Hampshire, in 1860. Most everything can be seen through the windows even when the firehouse is closed. ⊠ *107 S. Alfred St., Old Town* ☎ *703/838–3891* ⊕ *oha.ci.alexandria.va.us* ▣ *Free* ☽ *Fri. and Sat. 10–4, Sun. 1–4.*

⑫ Lloyd House. A fine example of Georgian architecture, Lloyd House was built in 1797 and is owned by the City of Alexandria and used for offices. The interior has nothing on display so it is best admired from outside. ⊠ *220 N. Washington St., Old Town.*

❸ Old Presbyterian Meetinghouse. Except during 1899 through 1949, the Old Presbyterian Meetinghouse has been the site of an active Presbyterian congregation since 1775. Scottish pioneers founded the church, and Scottish patriots used it as a gathering place during the Revolution. Four memorial services were held for George Washington here. The tomb of an unknown soldier of the American Revolution lies in a corner of the small churchyard, where many prominent Alexandrians—including Dr. James Craik, physician to Washington, Lafayette, and John Carlyle—are interred. The original sanctuary was rebuilt after a lightning strike and fire in 1835. The interior is appropriately plain; if you'd like to visit the sanctuary you can borrow a key in the church office, or just peek through the many wide windows along both sides. ⊠ *321 S. Fairfax St., Old Town* ☎ *703/549–6670* ⊕ *www.opmh.org* ▣ *Free* ☽ *Weekdays 9–3.*

❷ Stabler-Leadbeater Apothecary. Once patronized by George Washington and the Lee family, the Stabler-Leadbeater Apothecary is the second-oldest apothecary in the country (the reputed oldest is in Bethlehem, Pennsylvania). Some believe that it was here, on October 17, 1859, that Lt. Col. Robert E. Lee received orders to lead Marines sent from the Washington Barracks to help suppress John Brown's insurrection at Harpers Ferry(then part of Virginia). The shop now houses a small museum of 18th- and 19th-century apothecary memorabilia, including one of the finest collections of apothecary bottles in the country (some 800 bottles in all). ■ TIP➔ **Tours include discussions of such early healing techniques as bloodletting, and pill-rolling demonstrations.** Tours designed especially for children are available. ⊠ *105–107 S. Fairfax St., Old Town* ☏ *703/836-3713* ⊕ *www.apothecarymuseum.org* ⬚ *$2.50* ⊘ *Mon.–Sat. 10–4, Sun. 1–5.*

NEED A BREAK? Grab a seat on the deck beside the Potomac River at the **Quarterdeck Snack Bar at Washington Sailing Marina** (⊠ 1 Marina Dr. ☏ 703/548-9027), beside the Potomac, where you can watch sailboats and airport operations and enjoy soups, salads, sandwiches, several reasonable draft beers, soft drinks, and coffee. It's a ½-mi south of Ronald Reagan National Airport just off the George Washington Memorial Parkway.

Where to Eat

$$$–$$$$ ✕ **La Bergerie.** Provençale and Basque cooking are served at this second-floor restaurant a couple of blocks from busy King Street. Look for dishes like quail, elk, and duck breast stuffed with apples and bacon. The $20 lunch menu offers several choices. ⊠ *218 N. Lee St.* ☏ *703/683-1007* ⊟ *AE, D, DC, MC, V* ⊘ *No lunch Sun.*

$$$ ✕ **Gadsby's Tavern.** In the heart of the historic district, this circa-1792 tavern provides a taste of the interior decoration, cuisine, and entertainment of Colonial days. A strolling balladeer makes the rounds on Friday and Saturday nights. The tavern was a favorite of George Washington, who is commemorated on the menu: George Washington's Favorite Duck is half a duck roasted with peach-apricot dressing and served with Madeira sauce. Other period offerings are Gentlemen's Pye (made with game), Sally Lunn bread, and a rich English trifle. Brunch is served on Sunday. ⊠ *138 N. Royal St.* ☏ *703/548-1288* ⊟ *AE, D, DC, MC, V.*

$$$ ✕ **The Grille at the Morrison House.** On a quiet street in central Alexandria, this hotel dining room serves breakfast and dinner only. Entrées include two or three seafood, veal, lamb, and pork dishes, all accompanied by vegetables, or splurge on the Summerfield Farm's Dry Aged New York Strip ($42). A pianist entertains in the intimate dining room Thursday through Saturday. ⊠ *Morrison House, 116 S. Alfred St.* ☏ *703/838-8000 or 866/834-6628* ⊟ *AE, DC, MC, V* ⊘ *No lunch.*

$$–$$$ ✕ **Majestic Café.** A 1930s-era landmark that had been closed since 1978, the Majestic Café reopened in 2002. The art deco facade remains; inside, the café brings a modern sensibility to its 1930s origins. The cooking style moves between trendy American dishes and traditional Southern fare. Some of the best plates are the sides, such as hush puppies with *remoulade* (a mayo-based sauce that includes shallots, garlic, tarragon, and chives), fluffy spoonbread, and stewed tomatoes. Main courses might include salmon or rabbit. The restaurant is about eight blocks from the Metrorail. ⊠ *911 King St.* ☏ *703/837-9117* ⊟ *AE, D, DC, MC, V* ⊘ *Closed Mon.* Ⓜ *King St.*

★ **$$–$$$** ✕ **La Porta's.** At the west end of Old Town and about three blocks from the King St. Metrorail station, La Porta's combines great food with a variety of gentle, good music nightly in an intimate setting. Fresh seafood is the strong suit here, especially the crab cakes. Monday and Tuesday you can choose two entrée specials plus a bottle of wine for $28 per couple—a great deal. Park free in their enclosed lot beside the restaurant. ⊠ *1600 Duke St.* ☎ *703/837–9117* ⊟ *AE, D, DC, MC, V* ⊗ *No lunch weekends* Ⓜ *King St.*

$$–$$$ ✕ **Las Tapas.** A big, bright, authentic Spanish restaurant, Las Tapas specializes in, what else? There are 59 tapas on the menu, besides substantial entrées, including six kinds of paella. Flamenco dancers perform Tuesday–Thursday nights; Friday and Saturday nights bring Spanish guitar music. ⊠ *710 King St.* ☎ *703/836–4000* ⊟ *AE, D, DC, MC, V.*

$$–$$$ ✕ **Le Refuge.** This petite French restaurant one block from Alexandria's busiest intersection has been a local favorite for 22 years. Enjoy lovingly prepared, authentic French country fare with beaucoup flavor; popular selections include trout, bouillabaisse, garlicky leg of lamb, frogs' legs, and beef Wellington. Personal service makes this cozy restaurant a gem. ⊠ *127 N. Washington St.* ☎ *703/548–4661* ⊟ *AE, DC, MC, V* ⊗ *Closed Sun.*

$$–$$$ ✕ **Stella's.** Across Diagonal Road from the King Street Metrorail, Metrobus, DASH, VRE and Amtrak station, Stella's is set back in a pleasant courtyard with outdoor dining in good weather. The cuisine runs to steak and seafood, and the old-fashioned bar, with several domestic and European beers on tap, is just the place to relax and wait for the end of rush hour. ⊠ *1725 Duke St.* ☎ *703/519–1946* ⊟ *AE, D, DC, MC, V* ⊗ *No lunch Mon.* Ⓜ *King St.*

$$–$$$ ✕ **Taverna Cretekou.** Whitewashed stucco walls and colorful macramé tapestries bring a bit of the Mediterranean to the center of Old Town. On the menu are *exohikon* (lamb baked in a pastry shell) and swordfish *xiphoias* (kebab), and the extensive wine list includes many Greek choices. In warm weather you can dine in the canopied garden. ■ **TIP➔ Thursday evenings bring live music, and if you are so moved, plates for breaking are $5 each–opa!** A buffet brunch is served on Sunday. ⊠ *818 King St.* ☎ *703/548–8688* ⊟ *AE, MC, V* ⊗ *Closed Mon.*

$–$$ ✕ **Bugsy's Pizza Restaurant and Sports Bar.** With a huge salad bar and a large, ever-changing assortment of good, hot pizzas, this is a great place to stop for weekday lunch or for late dinner Friday or Saturday. Upstairs, the authentic sports bar is loaded with interesting memorabilia, heavy on hockey—the personable owner used to play in the NHL. ⊠ *111 King St.* ☎ *703/683–0313* ⩘ *Reservations not accepted* ⊟ *AE, MC, V* ⊗ *No lunch Sun.*

$–$$ ✕ **King Street Blues.** Not a place for power-lunching, this informal, relaxed café just off King Street is popular for its hearty, quirky Southern menu. Whimsical neon and papier-mâché constructions surround diners here for the baked pecan-crusted catfish, po' boy sandwiches, gumbo, glazed pork chops, BBQ, and other New Orleans specialties. Wash your choice down with the excellent house beer. ⊠ *112 N. St. Asaph St.* ☎ *703/836–8800* ⊟ *AE, D, DC, MC, V.*

$–$$ ✕ **Il Porto.** Inside an old building two blocks from the Potomac, Il Porto's interior is reminiscent of Italy, with plaster walls, exposed wooden beams, and checkered tablecloths. The menu includes traditional Italian versions of veal, seafood, pasta, and chicken, and creative interpretations such as *Paradiso Terra e Mare* (chicken, shrimp, scallops, and chopped clams in white wine and lemon sauce). ⊠ *121 King St.* ☎ *703/836–8833* ⊟ *AE, D, MC, V.*

¢–$$ ✕ **Hard Times Café.** Piped-in country-and-western music and framed photographs of Depression-era Oklahoma set the tone at this casual, crowded hangout. Four kinds of chili—Texas (spicy), Cincinnati (sweeter), Terlingua (spicy) and vegetarian—are served. Texas chili is typically served over spaghetti; a "chili-mac" Cincinnati comes with cheese, onions, beans, or all three. Chicken and chicken salad sandwiches are offered. About 25 domestic and Mexican beers are available. ⊠ *1404 King St.* ☎ *703/ 837–0050* ⚑ *Reservations not accepted* ▤ *AE, MC, V* ⊗ *No lunch Sun.*

Where to Stay

☺ **$$–$$$**   ⊞ **Embassy Suites Old Town Alexandria.** The relaxing sound of rushing water from the atrium fountain adjacent to the restaurant greets you inside this modern all-suites hotel three blocks from Alexandria's landmark George Washington Masonic Temple. Train buffs should request a suite facing the Amtrak and Metrorail stations across the street. Each suite has a living room with overstuffed sofa and chairs and a work desk; beds have an abundance of fluffy pillows. A free shuttle is available to transport you to the scenic Alexandria riverfront, which has shops and restaurants. The cooked-to-order breakfast is complimentary, as is the cocktail reception every evening. Kids can romp in the playroom. ⊠ *1900 Diagonal Rd., 22314* ☎ *703/684–5900 or 800/362–2779* 🖷 *703/684–1403* ⊕ *www.embassysuites.com* ⇄ *268 suites* ⚭ *Restaurant, kitchenettes, refrigerators, cable TV, in-room broadband, in-room data ports, indoor pool, gym, hot tub, recreation room, laundry facilities, laundry service, business services, meeting rooms, parking (fee)* ▤ *AE, D, DC, MC, V* ⎥⎤⎢ *BP* Ⓜ *King St.*

★ **$$–$$$**   ⊞ **Holiday Inn Select Old Town.** The distinctive mahogany-panel lobby suggests a club room, and the guest rooms follow this motif, with hunting-and-horse prints on the walls. Service is extraordinary here: staff will bring exercise bicycles to rooms on request and lend free bicycles for use in the area. Some rooms on the fifth and sixth floors have views of the roofs of 18th- and 19th-century buildings and the river beyond— but only after the trees have shed their leaves. A free shuttle goes to the King Street Metrorail station and Washington Reagan National Airport. ⊠ *480 King St., 22314* ☎ *703/549–6080 or 800/368–5047* 🖷 *703/684– 6508* ⊕ *www.hiselect.com* ⇄ *227 rooms, 4 suites* ⚭ *Restaurant, in- room broadband, in-room data ports, Wi-Fi, indoor pool, sauna, bicycles, lobby lounge, airport shuttle* ▤ *AE, D, DC, MC, V.*

★ **$$–$$$**   ⊞ **Morrison House.** The architecture, parquet floors, crystal chandeliers, decorative fireplaces, and furnishings here are so faithful to the Federal period (1790–1820) that it's often mistaken for a renovation rather than what it is: a structure built from scratch in 1985. The hotel blends Early American charm with modern conveniences. Some rooms have fireplaces, and all have four-poster beds, hair dryers, and bathrobes. The highly regarded Grille restaurant serves American contemporary cuisine. Morrison House is in the heart of Old Town, about a 15-minute walk from the train and Metrorail stations. ⊠ *116 S. Alfred St., 22314* ☎ *703/ 838–8000 or 800/367–0800* 🖷 *703/684–6283* ⊕ *www.morrisonhouse. com* ⇄ *42 rooms, 3 suites* ⚭ *2 restaurants, room service, cable TV, in-*

room VCRs, in-room data ports, Wi-Fi, bar, piano bar, business services, parking (fee) ☲ *AE, DC, MC, V* Ⓜ *King St.*

$–$$ 🏨 **Best Western Old Colony Inn.** Just north of Old Town in a peaceful location within walking distance of most local attractions, this redbrick two-story hotel offers free shuttle service to the Braddock Road Metrorail stop, Old Town, and Washington Reagan National Airport. Rooms have Federal-style cherry furnishings with a work desk, upholstered lounge chair, quilted floral spreads, hair dryer, iron, ironing board, and coffeemaker. Rates include a full hot breakfast, free local calls, and a *USA Today* newspaper. ⊠ *1101 N. Washington St., 22314* ☎ *703/739–2222 or 800/937–8376* 🖷 *703/549–2568* ⊕ *www.bestwestern.com* 🛏 *49 rooms* ⊘ *Dining room, refrigerators, cable TV with movies, in-room DVDs, in-room broadband, in-room data ports, gym, sauna, hot tub, laundry facilities, laundry service, business services, meeting rooms, airport shuttle, free parking, no-smoking rooms* ☲ *AE, D, DC, MC, V* ❍ *BP.*

Nightlife & the Arts

Bars & Pubs

Murphy's Irish Pub (⊠ 713 King St., Old Town ☎ 703/548–1717) has authentic Irish entertainment nightly and a blazing fire when winter comes.

Live Music

The **Birchmere** is one of the best places outside the Blue Ridge Mountains to hear acoustic folk and bluegrass. It also gets more than its share of headliners, including frequent visitors Mary Chapin Carpenter, Lyle Lovett, and Dave Matthews. Tickets are on the expensive side, with big names fetching up to $95. ⊠ 3701 Mt. Vernon Ave., ☎ 703/549–7500.

La Porta's (⊠ 1600 Duke St. ☎ 703/683–6313) has jazz combos nightly.

Las Tapas (⊠ 710 King St., Old Town ☎ 703/836–4000) has flamenco dancing Tuesday–Thursday nights and Spanish guitar music Friday and Saturday nights, without cover charge.

Sports & the Outdoors

Boating

If you can't snag one of the 10 boats at the Washington Sailing Marina, try **Belle Haven Marina** (⊠ George Washington Pkwy. ☎ 703/768–0018), south of Wilson Bridge just off George Washington Memorial Parkway. This rustic outfit rents Sunfish ($30 for two hours weekdays, $35 weekends), Hobie Cats and Flying Scots ($46 for two hours weekdays, $54 weekends), and canoes and kayaks ($20 for two hours), from April to October. All-day rates are available.

The **Washington Sailing Marina** (⊠ 1 Marina Dr. ☎ 703/548–9027), on the George Washington Memorial Parkway just south of the airport, rents sailboats from around mid-May to September. Sunfish are $10 per hour, the larger Flying Scots are $19 per hour. There's a two-hour minimum, and reservations are required (along with certification from a sailing school or passing a written test). Phone early; boats are limited.

Hiking

Huntley Meadows Park (✉ 3701 Lockheed Blvd. ☎ 703/768–2525 🖻 Free ⊙ Park daily dawn–dusk; visitor center closed Tues.; call for hrs other days), a 1,460-acre refuge, is made for birders. You can spot more than 200 species—from ospreys to owls, egrets, and ibis. Much of the park is wetlands, home to a variety of aquatic species. A boardwalk circles through a marsh, enabling you to spot beaver lodges, and 4 mi of trails wind through the park, making it possible that you'll see deer, muskrats, and river otters as well.

The **Mount Vernon Trail** is a favorite with Washington runners and bikers. You can access it from the north just short of Key Bridge in Rosslyn, beside the I–66 off-ramp. The path crosses the George Washington Parkway, going to Theodore Roosevelt Island (directly across the river from the Kennedy Center), past Ronald Reagan Washington National Airport, and on to the Alexandria waterfront. This stretch is approximately 9½ mi one-way. South of National Airport, the trail runs beside the Washington Sailing Marina. The southern section of the trail (approximately 9 mi) takes you along the banks of the Potomac from Alexandria all the way to Mount Vernon. It passes Jones Point (under the Wilson Bridge), the southern apex of the original District of Columbia, just before entering protected wetlands for about 2 mi beginning at Hunting Creek.

> ### RENT A BIKE
>
> Rent a bike at the idyllic Washington Sailing Marina, on the Mount Vernon Bike Trail. A 12-mi ride south will take you to the front doors of Mount Vernon, and a 6-mi ride north across the Memorial Bridge will put you at the foot of the Washington Monument. All-terrain bikes rent for $6 per hour or $22 per day; cruisers cost $4 per hour or $16.50 per day. The marina is open 9–5 daily.

Washington Sailing Marina (✉ 1 Marina Dr., George Washington Memorial Pkwy. ☎ 703/548–9027).

Shopping

Old Town Alexandria is dense with antiques shops—many of them quite expensive—that are particularly strong in the Federal and Victorian periods. The Alexandria Convention and Visitors Association has maps and lists of the dozens of stores (available at Ramsay House).

The **Antique Guild** (✉ 113 N. Fairfax St., Old Town ☎ 703/836–1048 or 800/518–7322) is where silver flatware and estate jewelry goes when it's ready for a new home.

Sumpter Priddy III, Inc. (✉ 323 S. Washington St., Old Town ☎ 703/299–0800) specializes in American furniture from the early 19th century and folk art in different media.

★ Dating to 1753, the **Saturday Morning Market at Market Square** (✉ City Hall, 301 King St.) may be the country's oldest operating farmers' market. Vendors sell baked goods, fresh produce, plants, flowers, and high-quality crafts. Come early; the market opens at 5:30 AM, and by 10:30 AM it's all over.

ARLINGTON

Arlington has evolved since the end of World War I from a farming community into one of sprawling homes, large-scale retailing, and office buildings small to colossal. Connected to Washington by four bridges and three subway lines, the county is vital to the capital, providing office space to the Federal government and housing to its employees. First the War Department, then Department of Defense and all military service headquarters were moved to the Pentagon, then numerous other government offices and bureaus moved to Arlington and nearby Virginia communities like Langley (home of the C.I.A.) as they required larger quarters than were available in Washington. This trend continues. For the visitor, Arlington offers somber reflection at the nation's cemetery, a plethora of dining and lodging options, and easy access to the attractions of Washington.

Carved out of Fairfax County when the District of Columbia was created, Arlington was returned to Virginia along with the rest of the state's contribution in 1845 and until 1920 was the County of Alexandria. In the 18th century, members of the Custis family, including Martha Washington's first husband, had extensive land holdings in the area. Arlington was the name of the Custis family home that became the home of Robert E. Lee, now the Custis-Lee Mansion in Arlington Cemetery.

Numbers in the text correspond to numbers in the margin and on the Arlington National Cemetery map.

Main Attractions

㉟ Arlington House. It was in Arlington that the two most famous names in Virginia history—Washington and Lee—became intertwined. George Washington Parke Custis, raised by Martha and George Washington, his grandmother and step-grandfather, built Arlington House (also known as the Custis-Lee Mansion) between 1802 and 1817 on his 1,100-acre estate overlooking the Potomac. After Custis's death, the property went to his daughter, Mary Anna Randolph Custis. In 1831 Mary married Robert E. Lee, a graduate of West Point. For the next 30 years she lived at Arlington House while Lee went wherever the Army sent him, including the superintendency of West Point.

In 1861 Lee was offered command of the Union forces in Washington. It was understood that the first order of business would be a troop movement into nearby Virginia. He declined and resigned from the U.S. Army, deciding that he could never

> ### WORD OF MOUTH
>
> "The [bus tour of the Arlington National Cemetery] single-handedly made this experience the rich one it ought to be. Besides the fact that the cemetery is *huge* and difficult to thoroughly cover on foot, this tour was worth it for the wonderful details about the park which we would never have discovered on our own."   –Cheryl

take up arms against his native Virginia. The Lees left Arlington House that spring, never to return. Federal troops crossed the Potomac not long after that, fortified the estate's ridges, and turned the home into the Army of the Potomac's headquarters. Arlington House and the estate were confiscated in May 1864 when the Lees failed to pay $92.07 in property taxes in person. (General Lee's eldest son sued the U.S. government and after a 5–4 decision by the U.S. Supreme Court, was eventually compensated for the land.) Two hundred nearby acres were set aside as a national cemetery. Sixty-five soldiers were buried there on June 15, 1864, and by the end of the Civil War more than 16,000 headstones dotted Arlington's hills. Soldiers from the Revolutionary War and the War of 1812 were reinterred at Arlington as their bodies were discovered in other resting places.

The building's heavy Doric columns and severe pediment make Arlington House one of the area's best examples of Greek Revival architecture. The plantation home was designed by George Hadfield, a young English architect who, for a while, supervised construction of the Capitol. The view of Washington from the front of the house is superb. In 1934 the National Park Service acquired Arlington House and continued the restoration that the War Department had begun, and in 1972 Congress designated Custis-Lee Mansion as Arlington House, the Robert E. Lee Memorial. It looks much as it did in the 19th century, and a quick tour takes you past objects once owned by the Custises and the Lees.

In front of Arlington House, next to a flag that flies at half staff whenever there's a funeral in the cemetery, is the flat-top **grave of Pierre Charles L'Enfant,** designer of Washington, D.C. ⊠ *Between Lee and Sherman Drs.* ☎ *703/235–1530* ▦ *Free* ☉ *Daily 9:30–4:30.*

⑱ **Arlington National Cemetery.** More than 250,000 American war dead,
Fodor's Choice as well as many notable Americans (among them Presidents William
★ Howard Taft and John F. Kennedy, General John Pershing, and Admiral Robert E. Peary), are interred in these 612 acres across the Potomac River from Washington, established as the nation's cemetery in 1864. While you're at Arlington there's a good chance you'll hear a bugler playing taps, or the sharp reports of a gun salute. ■ TIP→ Approximately 20 funerals are held daily (it's projected that the cemetery will be filled in 2020).

To get here, you can take the Metrorail to either the Rosslyn or Arlington Cemetery station and then walk about ½ mi, arrive by Tourmobile tour bus, walk across Arlington Memorial Bridge (southwest of the Lincoln Memorial), or drive to the large paid parking lot at the skylighted visitor center on Memorial Drive ($1.25 per hour for the first three hours, then $2 per hour). Stop at the center for a free brochure with a detailed map of the cemetery. If you're looking for a specific grave, the staff can consult microfilm records and give you directions to it. You should know the deceased's full name and, if possible, his or her branch of service and year of death. You may phone ahead for this information, too.

Tourmobiles leave daily 8:30–4:30 (in fall and winter, daily 9:30–4:30) from just outside the visitor center, where you can buy tickets ($6) good all day for unlimited reboarding in the cemetery. The Tourmobile stops

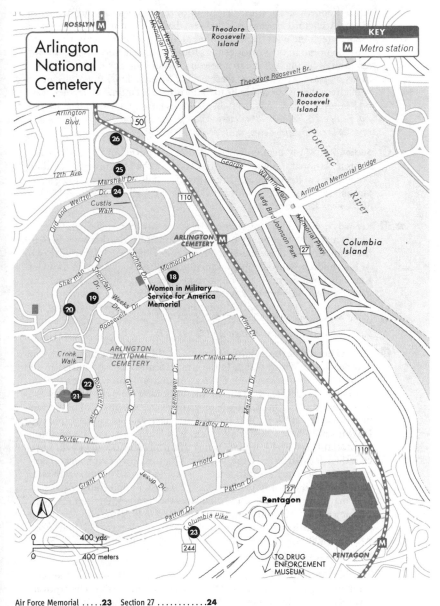

at the Kennedy grave sites, the Tomb of the Unknowns, and Arlington House. Arlington Cemetery is included in the Washington Tourmobile ticket ($20), which includes transportation across the Potomac from the Lincoln Memorial to the visitor center. Touring the cemetery on foot means a fair bit of hiking, but it can give you a closer look at some of the thousands of graves spread over these rolling Virginia hills. If you decide to walk, from the visitor center head to the ornate Memorial Gate, then west on Roosevelt Drive, and turn right on Weeks Drive. ⊠ *West end of Memorial Bridge* ☎ *703/607–8000 to locate a grave* ⊕ *www.arlingtoncemetery. org* ✉ *Free* ☉ *Apr.–Sept., daily 8–7; Oct.–Mar., daily 8–5.*

㉒ **Section 7A.** Many distinguished veterans are buried in this area of Arlington National Cemetery near the **Tomb of the Unknowns,** including boxing champ Joe Louis, ABC newsman Frank Reynolds, actor Lee Marvin, and World War II fighter pilot Colonel "Pappy" Boyington. ⊠ *Crook Walk near Roosevelt Dr.*

★ ⑲ **Kennedy graves.** A moving part of any visit to Arlington National Cemetery is a visit to the graves of John F. Kennedy and other members of his family. President Kennedy is buried under an eternal flame near two of his children, who died in infancy, and his wife, Jacqueline Bouvier Kennedy Onassis; his is the most-visited grave site in the country. The graves are a moderate walk west of the visitor center. Across from them is a low wall engraved with quotations from Kennedy's inaugural address. Nearby, marked by a simple white cross, is the grave of his brother Robert Kennedy. ⊠ *Sheridan and Weeks Drs.*

㉑ **Tomb of the Unknowns.** Many countries established a memorial to their war dead after World War I. In the United States, the first burial at the Tomb of the Unknowns took place at Arlington National Cemetery on November 11, 1921, when the Unknown Soldier from the "Great War" was interred under the large white-marble sarcophagus. Unknown servicemen killed in World War II and Korea were buried in 1958. The unknown serviceman killed in Vietnam was laid to rest on the plaza on Memorial Day 1984 but was disinterred and identified in 1998. Officials then decided to leave the Vietnam War unknown crypt vacant. Soldiers from the Army's 3rd Infantry ("The Old Guard") keep watch over the tomb 24 hours a day, regardless of weather conditions. Each sentinel marches exactly 21 steps, then faces the tomb for 21 seconds, symbolizing the 21-gun salute, America's highest military honor. The guard is changed with a precise ceremony during the day—every half hour from April through September and every hour the rest of the year. At night the guard is changed every hour.

The Memorial Amphitheater west of the tomb is the scene of special ceremonies on Veterans Day, Memorial Day, and Easter. Decorations awarded to the unknowns by foreign governments and United States and foreign organizations are displayed in an indoor trophy room. Across from the amphitheater are memorials to the astronauts killed in the *Challenger* space shuttle explosion and to the servicemen killed in 1980 trying to rescue American hostages in Iran. Rising beyond that is the mainmast of the USS *Maine,* the American ship sunk in Havana Harbor in 1898, killing 299 men and sparking the Spanish-American War. ⊠ *End of Crook Walk.*

Also Worth Seeing

㉓ **Air Force Memorial.** Dedicated in 2006, this memorial honors the service and sacrifices of the men and women of the U.S. Air Force and its predecessor organizations of the U.S. Army. Three curved spires—up to 270 feet tall—represent the transition to air. The memorial is just uphill from the Pentagon, beside the Navy Annex on Columbia Pike, and easy to see from a distance. ⊠ *Columbia Pike at Joyce St.*

OFF THE BEATEN PATH

DRUG ENFORCEMENT ADMINISTRATION MUSEUM – The very compact DEA Museum, inside one entrance to DEA headquarters, is across the street from the Fashion Centre at Pentagon City. It displays the methods and effects of dangerous drugs on America, starting with quaint 19th-century ads for opium-laced patent medicines and cocaine tooth drops (opiates, cannabis, and cocaine were unregulated then). Displays show current methods of illegal drug production, international drug smuggling, and the means of intercepting illegal drug shipments. Some displays are too stark for children. ⊠ *700 Army Navy Dr., at Hayes St.* ☎ *202/307–3463* ⊕ *www.deamuseum.org* ⊠ *Free* ☉ *Tues.–Fri. 10–4* Ⓜ *Pentagon City.*

㉕ **Netherlands Carillon.** Outside the Arlington National Cemetery is the lovely and unusual 49-bell musical carillon presented to the United States by the Dutch people in 1960 in gratitude for aid received during World War II. There are occasional performances on the carillon, usually around noon. For a good view of Washington, look to the east across the Potomac. From this vantage point, the Lincoln Memorial, the Washington Monument, and the Capitol appear side by side. ⊠ *Meade and Marshall Drs.*

Pentagon. This office building, the headquarters of the U.S. Department of Defense, is the largest in the world. The Capitol could fit into any one of its five wedge-shape sections. Approximately 23,000 military and civilian people work here. Astonishingly, this mammoth office building, completed in 1943, took less than two years to construct. Construction was overseen by General Leslie Grove, then a colonel, who later led the Manhattan Project to develop the atom bomb.

Parts of the structure were rebuilt following the September 2001 crash of hijacked American Airlines Flight 77 into the northwest side of the building. The damaged area was removed in just more than a month, and rebuilding proceeded rapidly (in keeping with the speed of the original construction). Renovations on all areas damaged by the terrorist attack were completed by spring 2003.

Tours of the building are given on a limited basis to educational groups by advance reservation; tours for the general public have been suspended indefinitely but you can drive right by, fairly close, with unobstructed views of all sides. ⊠ *I–395 at Columbia Pike and Rte. 27* ☎ *703/695–1776* ⊕ *pentagon.afis.osd.mil.*

㉔ **Section 27.** More than 3,800 former slaves are buried in this part of Arlington National Cemetery. They're all former residents of Freedman's

Village, which operated at the Custis-Lee estate for more than 30 years beginning in 1863 to provide housing, education, and employment training for ex-slaves who had traveled to the capital. In the cemetery the headstones are marked with their names and the word "Civilian" or "Citizen." Buried at Grave 19 in the first row of Section 27 is William Christman, a Union private who died of peritonitis in Washington on May 13, 1864. He was the first soldier (but not the first person) interred at Arlington. ⊠ *Ord and Weitzel Dr. near Custis Walk.*

OFF THE BEATEN PATH

THEODORE ROOSEVELT ISLAND – The island wilderness preserve in the Potomac River has 2½ mi of nature trails through marsh, swampland, and upland forest. It's an 88-acre tribute to the conservation-minded 26th president. Cattails, arrowarum, pickerelweed, willow, ash, maple, and oak grow on the island, which is also a habitat for frogs, raccoons, birds, lizards, and the occasional red or gray fox. The 17-foot bronze statue of Roosevelt, toward the center of the woods, was done by Paul Manship. A pedestrian bridge connects the island to a parking lot on the Virginia shore, which is accessible by car only from the northbound lanes of the George Washington Memorial Parkway. ⊠ *From downtown D.C., take Constitution Ave. west across Theodore Roosevelt Bridge to George Washington Memorial Pkwy. north; follow signs or walk or bike across Bridge beginning at Kennedy Center* ☎ *703/289–2500 for park information* ⊠ *Free* ☉ *Island daily dawn–dusk* Ⓜ *Rosslyn.*

㉖ United States Marine Corps War Memorial. Better known simply as "the Iwo Jima," this memorial, despite its familiarity, has lost none of its power to stir the emotions. Honoring Marines who gave their lives since the Corps was formed in 1775, the statue, sculpted by Felix W. de Weldon, is based on Joe Rosenthal's Pulitzer Prize–winning photograph of five Marines and a Navy corpsman raising a flag atop Mt. Suribachi on the Japanese island of Iwo Jima on February 19, 1945. By executive order the U.S. flag flies day and night from the 78-foot-high memorial. On Tuesday evenings from early June to mid August there's a Marine Corps sunset parade on the grounds of the memorial. Call ☎ 202/433–6060 for start times. On parade nights a free shuttle bus runs from the Arlington Cemetery visitors parking lot.

Women in Military Service for America Memorial. What is now this memorial next to the visitor center was once the Hemicycle, a huge carved retaining wall faced with granite at the entrance to Arlington National Cemetery. Built in 1932, the wall was restored, with stairways added leading to a rooftop terrace. Inside are 16 exhibit alcoves showing the contributions that women have made to the military—from the Revolutionary War to the present—as well as the history of the memorial itself. A 196-seat theater shows films and is used for lectures and conferences. A computer database has pictures, military histories, and stories of thousands of women veterans. A fountain and reflecting pool front the classical-style Hemicycle and entry gates.

Where to Eat

$$–$$$ ✕ Carlyle Grand Café. Whether you eat at the bustling bar or in the dining room upstairs, you'll find an imaginative, generous interpretation of modern American cooking. Start with the blue crab fritter, then move on to entrées such as pecan-crusted trout. The warm flourless chocolate-macadamia nut waffle with vanilla ice cream is classic. You can even buy a loaf of bread at the restaurant's own bakery, the Best Buns Bread Company, next door. ⊠ *4000 S. 28th St., Shirlington* ☎ *703/931–0777* ▤ *AE, D, DC, MC, V.*

$$–$$$ ✕ **Willow Restaurant.** This handsome restaurant and bar in mahogany and jewel tones with 1930s-style photographs has a jazz-era feel. The cuisine combines the freshest ingredients with classic French and Italian influences. Featured are grilled flatbreads with innovative toppings, vegetarian French green lentil ragu, rack of pork *Milanese,* and whole baked Carolina red snapper. Park free in the building's garage to avoid the conscientious parking enforcement. ⊠ *4301 N. Fairfax Dr., Ballston* ☎ *703/465–8800* ▤ *AE, D, DC, MC, V* Ⓜ *Ballston.*

$–$$ ✕ **Nam Viet.** Arlington has several Vietnamese restaurants, most on Wilson Boulevard, and this one a block off Wilson probably has the best food. Autographed photos of U.S. military and political leaders gaze down from the walls. The sweet-and-spicy salmon soup has many fans, as do the *cha gio* (spring rolls) and the green-papaya salad (with shrimp or beef jerky). Dine outside in good weather. ⊠ *1127 Hudson St., Clarendon* ☎ *703/522–7119* ▤ *AE, D, DC, MC, V* Ⓜ *Clarendon.*

Ⓒ **$–$$** ✕ **Rio Grande Café.** This Mexican café is always packed with enthusiastic crowds. While you're waiting for a table, order a "swirl," a mix of frozen sangria and frozen margarita in a frosted beer mug, or check out the tortilla-making machine. The menu sticks mostly to familiar Mexican fare, with grilled offerings that include sizzling fajitas and shrimp brochettes (shrimp stuffed with cheese and peppers wrapped in bacon), and a handful of more exotic entrées like quail and the more expensive Fajitas al Carbon ($29). ⊠ *4301 N. Fairfax Dr., Ballston* ☎ *703/528–3131* ⚖ *Reservations not accepted* ▤ *AE, D, DC, MC, V* Ⓜ *Ballston.*

Where to Stay

$$–$$$$ 🏨 **Marriott Crystal Gateway.** This elegant, modern Marriott caters to the business traveler and those who want to be pampered. Its two towers rise 17 stories above the highway; inside is mahogany, marble, and lots of greenery. Rooms have contemporary styling with fabrics in hues of white and cream with blue carpeting. Amenities include hair dryers, irons, ironing boards, and coffeemakers. Concierge Lounge serves continental breakfast, evening hors d'oeuvres, and all-day beverages to concierge floor guests. Unlimited in-room high-speed Internet access and long-distance phone calls in the 48 contiguous states cost $9.95 per day. ⊠ *1700 Jefferson Davis Hwy., Crystal City, 22202* ☎ *703/920–3230 or 800/228–9290* 🖷 *703/271–5212* ⊕ *www.marriott.com/wasgw* 🛏 *615 rooms, 82 suites* ⚖ *3 restaurants, cable TV with movies and video games, in-room broadband, in-room data ports, some Wi-Fi, indoor pool, gym, hot tub, 2 bars, lobby lounge, laundry facilities, laundry service, concierge, concierge floor, business services, meeting rooms, airport shuttle parking (fee)* ▤ *AE, DC, MC, V* Ⓜ *Crystal City.*

$$–$$$ 🏨 **Key Bridge Marriott.** A short walk across the Key Bridge from Georgetown, this family-friendly Marriott is three blocks from the Rosslyn Metrorail station, allowing easy access to sights in Washington. The hotel provides a shuttle to the station. Rooms on the Potomac side offer excellent Washington views, as does the rooftop restaurant. Rooms are comfortably appointed with Colonial reproduction furniture, luxury bedding, hair dryers, irons, ironing boards, coffeemakers; the hotel has an updated fitness center and expanded business amenities. For $9.95 daily, you get unlimited in-room high-speed Internet access and long-distance phone calls. ⊠ *1401 Lee Hwy., Rosslyn, 22209* ☎ *703/524–6400 or 800/228–9290* 🖷 *703/524–8964* 🖘 *582 rooms, 20 suites* ♨ *2 restaurants, room service, cable TV with movies and video games, in-room broadband, in-room data ports, indoor pool, health club, hair salon, 2 bars, lobby lounge, laundry facilities, laundry service, concierge, 3 concierge floors, business services, meeting rooms, parking (fee)* ☰ *AE, D, DC, MC, V* Ⓜ *Rosslyn.*

$–$$ 🏨 **Hilton Arlington and Towers.** Traveling to Arlington Cemetery, Washington, and Alexandria sights is easy from this hotel, just above the Ballston Metrorail stop. Rooms make use of neutral colors and traditional mahogany furniture, and all the suites have hot tubs. Entry to a nearby fitness club is available for a fee. The hotel has direct access via a skywalk to an adjacent shopping mall. ⊠ *950 N. Stafford St., Ballston, 22203* ☎ *703/528–6000 or 800/445–8667* 🖷 *703/812–5127* 🖘 *204 rooms, 5 suites* ♨ *Restaurant, room service, cable TV, in-room broadband, in-room data ports, hair salon, bar, shop, laundry service, business services, meeting rooms, parking (fee), no-smoking floors* ☰ *AE, D, DC, MC, V* Ⓜ *Ballston.*

$–$$ 🏨 **Holiday Inn Arlington at Ballston.** You can get to the major sights of Northern Virginia and D.C. quickly from this hotel, two blocks (or a free shuttle ride) from the Ballston Metrorail station. Guest rooms have a navy and burgundy color scheme with quilted spreads, overstuffed chair with ottoman, and mahogany dresser and work desk. Kids love the suspended model railroad at Lacey Station Dining Car Restaurant (named for the railroad station that was once 200 feet away); hotel guests 12 and under eat free from the kids' menu. Parking is free Friday and Saturday nights. ⊠ *4610 N. Fairfax Dr., Ballston, 22203* ☎ *703/243–9800* 🖷 *703/527–2677* ⊕ *www.hiarlington.com* 🖘 *211 rooms, 2 suites* ♨ *Restaurant, room service, cable TV with video games, in-room data ports, in-room broadband, pool, gym, lounge, laundry facilities, business services, parking (fee)* ☰ *AE, D, DC, MC, V* Ⓜ *Ballston.*

$ 🏨 **Best Western Pentagon.** This no-frills hotel has free shuttle service to three nearby Metrorail stops. Three two-story buildings have outside entrances and conventional motel rooms with pink-and-white-stripe wallpaper; a swivel desk chair makes working more comfortable. ⊠ *2480 S. Glebe Rd., South Arlington, 22206* ☎ *703/979–4400 or 800/937–8376* 🖷 *703/685–0051* ⊕ *www.bestwestern.com* 🖘 *205 rooms* ♨ *Restaurant, in-room safes, refrigerators, cable TV, in-room data ports, pool, gym, bar, laundry service, business services, airport shuttle, free parking; no smoking* ☰ *AE, D, DC, MC, V.*

$ 🏨 **Day's Inn Arlington.** Easy to find, on U.S. Route 50 across from Fort Myer, this Day's Inn isn't fancy, but is reasonable and accommodating. Rooms have hair dryers and a free *USA Today* newspaper, and a free shuttle takes you to the Rosslyn Metrorail station (or you can walk six blocks to another station). Coffee is complimentary in Rudy's Restaurant, open for breakfast and dinner. ⊠ *2201 Arlington Blvd., 22201* ☎ *703/525–0300 or 800/329–7466* 🖷 *703/525–5671* ⊕ *arlingtondaysinn.com* ⇥ *128 rooms* ⚬ *Restaurant, in-room data ports, cable TV with movies, pool, bar, meeting rooms, no-smoking rooms* ⊟ *AE, D, DC, MC, V.*

Nightlife & the Arts

MUSIC **Galaxy Hut.** This tiny storefront hosts local and out-of-town indie and alternative bands before they get famous. There's live music with a $5 cover charge on weekend nights. Monday is movie night, Wednesday is amateur DJ night, and Thursday is karaoke night. You can probably sample the entertainers before you go in by standing outside on the sidewalk. ⊠ *2711 Wilson Blvd., Clarendon* ☎ *703/525–8646* Ⓜ *Clarendo.*

Iota. The bands at Iota play alt-country or rock to unpretentious, attentive crowds. Expect to fight your way to the bar—it gets crowded quickly. There's music for a cover charge of $10 to $15 almost every night, except in the café, which serves food and charges no cover. ⊠ *2832 Wilson Blvd., Clarendon* ☎ *703/522–8340* Ⓜ *Clarendon.*

THEATER **Signature Theatre.** Presenting world and area premieres, Broadway revivals, and provocative contemporary works, this theater moved in 2006 to its new, larger space in Shirlington. ⊠ *2800 S. Stafford St., Shirlington* ☎ *703/218–6500.*

Washington Shakespeare Company. Often confused with the Shakespeare Theatre in D.C., this company stages the works of Shakespeare, the Greeks, and other important playwrights up through modern times. It performs in the Clark Street Playhouse, which can be hard to find—check directions carefully! ⊠ *601 S. Clark St., Crystal City* ☎ *703/418–4808* Ⓜ *Crystal City.*

Shopping

Fashion Centre at Pentagon City. Anchored by Macy's and Nordstrom, this four-story mall includes such shops as the Coach Store, Swatch, babyGap, Sephora, Williams-Sonoma, and a Discovery Channel store, as well as a six-screen cinema and day spas. In addition to a skylighted food court, there are four full-service restaurants to choose from. ⊠ *1100 S. Hayes St., Pentagon City* ☎ *703/415–2400* Ⓜ *Pentagon City.*

Crystal City Shops (☎ *703/922–4636*) is comprised of 130 street-level and underground stores and restaurants are connected to the Crystal City Metrorail station and near a Virginia Rail Express (VRE) station.

MOUNT VERNON, WOODLAWN & GUNSTON HALL

Long before Washington was planned, the shores of the Potomac had been divided into plantations by wealthy traders and gentlemen farmers. Most traces of the Colonial era were obliterated as the capital grew in the 19th century, but several splendid examples of plantation architecture remain on the Virginia side of the Potomac, 15 mi or so south

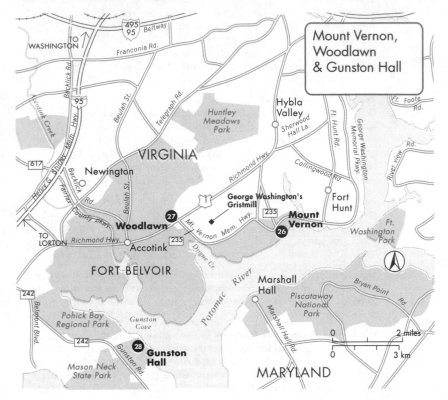

Mount Vernon,
Woodlawn
& Gunston Hall

of D.C. In one day you can easily visit three such mansions: Mount Vernon, the home of George Washington and one of the most popular sites in the area; Woodlawn, the estate of Washington's step-granddaughter; and Gunston Hall, the home of George Mason, author of the document on which the Bill of Rights was based. (Expect the longest wait times at Mount Vernon, particularly in spring and summer.) Set on hillsides overlooking the river, these estates offer magnificent vistas and bring back to vivid life the more palatable aspects of the 18th century.

Numbers in the margin correspond to points of interest on the Mount Vernon, Woodlawn, and Gunston Hall map.

Mount Vernon

16 mi south of Washington, D.C., 8 mi south of Alexandria, VA.

Fodor'sChoice
★

Mount Vernon and the surrounding lands had been in the Washington family for nearly 90 years by the time George inherited it all in 1761. Before taking over command of the Continental Army, Washington was an accomplished farmer managing the 8,000-acre plantation, of which more than 3,000 acres were under cultivation. He oversaw the transformation of the main house from an ordinary farm dwelling into what was, for the time, a grand mansion. The inheritance of his widowed bride, Martha, is largely what made that transformation possible.

The red-roof main house is elegant though understated, with a yellow pine exterior that's been painted and coated with layers of sand to resemble white-stone blocks. The first-floor rooms are quite ornate, especially the formal large dining room, with a molded ceiling decorated with agricultural motifs. The bright colors of the walls, which match the original paint, may surprise those who associate the period with pastels. Throughout the house are smaller symbols of the owner's eminence, such as a key to the main portal of the Bastille—presented to Washington by the Marquis de Lafayette—and Washington's presidential chair. As you tour the mansion, guides are stationed throughout the house to describe the furnishings and answer questions.

The real treasure of Mount Vernon is the view from around back: beneath a 90-foot portico, the home's dramatic riverside porch overlooks an expanse of lawn that slopes down to the Potomac. In springtime the view of the river (a mile wide where it passes the plantation) is framed by dogwood blossoms. U.S. Navy and Coast Guard ships render honors when passing the house during daylight hours. Although not required, foreign naval vessels often salute, too.

You can stroll around the estate's 500 acres and three gardens, visiting the workshops, kitchen, carriage house, greenhouse, slave quarters, and—down the hill toward the boat landing—the tomb of George and Martha Washington. There's also a pioneer farmer site: a 4-acre hands-on exhibit with a reconstruction of George Washington's 16-side treading barn as its centerpiece. Among the souvenirs sold at the plantation are stripling boxwoods that began life as clippings from bushes planted in 1798, the year before Washington died. A tour of house and grounds takes about two hours. A limited number of wheelchairs is available at the main gate. Evening candlelight tours are offered Friday–Sunday evenings in late November and early December.

Two new facilities just inside the main entrance on either side elucidate George Washington's life and contributions with interactive displays, movies, life-size models, and objects such as furnishings, Revolutionary War artifacts, books, and personal effects.

George Washington's Gristmill—a reproduction—operates on the site of his original mill and distillery. During the guided tours, led by costumed interpreters, you meet an 18th-century miller and watch the water-powered wheel grind grain into flour just as it did 200 years ago. The mill is 3 mi from Mount Vernon on Route 235 between Mount Vernon and U.S. Route 1, almost to Woodlawn. Tickets can be purchased either at the gristmill itself or at Mount Vernon's Main Gate. ⊠ *Southern end of George Washington Pkwy., Mount Vernon* ☎ *703/780–2000* ⊕ *www.mountvernon.org* ⊠ *$13, $4 gristmill, $15 combination ticket* ☉ *Mar., Sept., and Oct., daily 9–5; Apr.–Aug., daily 8–5; Nov.–Feb., daily 9–4.*

Woodlawn

🐾 ㉗ *3 mi west of Mount Vernon, 15 mi south of Washington, D.C.*

Woodlawn was once part of the Mount Vernon estate. From here you can still see traces of the bowling green that fronted Washington's home. The house was built for Washington's step-granddaughter, Nelly Custis, who married his favorite nephew, Lawrence Lewis. (Lewis had come to Mount Vernon from Fredericksburg to help Uncle George manage his five farms.)

The Lewises' home, completed in 1805, was designed by William Thornton, a physician and amateur architect from the West Indies who drew up the original plans for the U.S. Capitol. Like Mount Vernon, the Woodlawn house is constructed wholly of native materials, including the clay for its bricks and the yellow pine used throughout its interior. Built on a site selected by George Washington, the house has commanding views of the surrounding countryside and the Potomac River beyond. In the tradition of Southern riverfront mansions, Woodlawn has a central hallway that provides a cool refuge in summer. At one corner of the passage is a bust of George Washington set on a pedestal so the crown of the head is at 6 feet, 2 inches—Washington's actual height.

Woodlawn was once a plantation where more than 100 people, most of them slaves, lived and worked. As plantation owners, the Lewises lived in luxury. Docents talk about how the family entertained and how the slaves grew produce and prepared these lavish meals as well as their own. As intimates of the Washingtons' household, the Lewises displayed a collection of objects in honor of their illustrious benefactor. Many Washington family items are on display today. In 1957 the property was acquired by the National Trust for Historic Preservation, which had been operating it as a museum since 1951.

Also on the grounds of Woodlawn is the **Pope-Leighey House.** One of Frank Lloyd Wright's "Usonian" homes, the structure was built in 1940 as part of the architect's mission to create affordable housing. It was moved here from Falls Church, Virginia, in 1964, to save it from destruction during the building of Route 66. By design a very small, sparsely furnished home, it features many of Wright's trademark elements, including the use of local materials. Visitors are mostly students of architecture or of Wright. An in-depth tour is given on the first Sunday of the month. ⊠ *9000 Richmond Hwy., Alexandria* ☎ *703/780–4000* ⊕ *www.woodlawn1805.org* ⊠ *$7.50 for either Woodlawn or Pope-Leighey House, $13 combination ticket* ☉ *Mar.–Dec., daily 10–5; limited guided tours in Mar.; tours leave every ½ hr; last tour at 4:30.*

Gunston Hall

🐾 ㉘ *9 mi south of Woodlawn, 24 mi south of Washington, D.C.*

Fodor'sChoice
★
Gunston Hall Plantation, down the Potomac from Mount Vernon, was the home of another important George. Gentleman farmer George Mason was a colonel of the Fairfax militia and author of the Virginia

Declaration of Rights, the model for the U.S. Bill of Rights, which called for freedom of the press, tolerance of religion, and other fundamental democratic principles. Mason was a framer of the Constitution but refused to sign the final document because it didn't stop the importation of slaves, adequately restrain the powers of the federal government, or include a bill of rights. Mason's objections spurred the movement for the inclusion of the Bill of Rights into the Constitution.

Mason's home was begun about 1755. The Georgian-style mansion has some of the finest hand-carved ornamented interiors in the country. It's the handiwork of the 18th century's foremost architect, William Buckland, who also designed the Hammond-Harwood and Chase-Lloyd houses in Annapolis, but was at the time an indentured servant carpenter/joiner. Gunston Hall is built of native brick, black walnut, and yellow pine. The style of the time demanded absolute symmetry in all structures, which explains the false door set into one side of the center hallway and the "robber" window on a second-floor storage room. The house's interior, with carved woodwork in styles from Chinese to Gothic, has been meticulously restored, with paints made from the original formulas and carefully carved replacements for the intricate mahogany medallions in the moldings. Restored outbuildings include a kitchen, dairy, laundry, and smokehouse, and a schoolhouse has also been reconstructed.

The formal gardens, under excavation by a team of archaeologists, are famous for their boxwoods—some are thought to have been planted during George Mason's time, making them among the oldest in the country. The Potomac is visible past the expansive deer park, and Mason's landing road to the river was recently found and re-created using the same Aquia stone as the original. Also on the grounds is an active farmyard with livestock and an herb garden like those of Mason's era. Special programs, such as history lectures and hearth cooking demonstrations, are available throughout the year. A tour of Gunston Hall takes at least 45 minutes; tours begin at the visitor center, which includes a museum and gift shop. ⊠ *10709 Gunston Rd., Mason Neck* ☎ *703/550–9220* ⊕ *www.gunstonhall.org* ✉ *$8* ☉ *Daily 9:30–5; 1st tour at 10, last tour at 4:30.*

FAIRFAX COUNTY

In 1694 King Charles II of England gave the land that would become Fairfax County to seven English noblemen. It became a county in 1741 and was named after Thomas, sixth Lord Fairfax. Widespread tobacco farming, the dominant industry in the 18th century, eventually depleted the land. After tobacco, dairy farming became the major agricultural activity, and by 1925 Fairfax was first among all Virginia counties in dairy production. Today the economy depends upon business and government, and Fairfax County has one of the highest per capita incomes in the country. Wolf Trap, the only national park dedicated to the performing arts, is here, and throughout the year it draws concertgoers from miles around.

Fairfax

㉙ *10 mi west of Arlington.*

Fairfax is an independent city, not part of the county of the same name that surrounds it and whose courthouse and central administration building are within its limits.

The National Rifle Association's **National Firearms Museum** has exhibits on the role guns have played in the history of America. The permanent collection includes muzzle-loading flintlocks used in the Revolutionary War, high-tech pistols used by Olympic shooting teams, and weapons that once belonged to American presidents, including Teddy Roosevelt's 0.32-caliber Browning pistol and a Winchester shotgun used by Dwight Eisenhower. ✉ *National Rifle Association, 11250 Waples Mill Rd.* 🕾 *703/267–1600* ⊕ *www.nrahq.org/museum* 🖭 *Free* ☉ *Daily 10–4.*

Where to Stay

$$–$$$ ✗🖃**Bailiwick Inn.** Redbrick and green shutters distinguish this small luxury hotel in an 1812 building opposite the historic Fairfax County Courthouse. Named for prominent Virginians, guest rooms have antique and reproduction furniture, period detail, and luxurious, modern bathrooms. Four rooms have fireplaces; two have whirlpool baths. Rates include hair dryers, a four-course breakfast, afternoon tea, chocolate chip cookies to nibble throughout the day, and turn-down service. Even if you're not sleeping here, Christina's restaurant ($$$–$$$$) is a special dining destination with French-American cuisine including duck breast, lamb loin, salmon, braised short ribs, and sea scallops. Tea is open to the public on Tuesday, Thursday, and Sunday ($28–$31). ✉ *4023 Chain Bridge Rd., 22030* 🕾 *703/691–2266* 🖷 *703/934–2112* ⊕ *www. bailiwickinn.com* ⮑ *10 rooms, 1 suite* ₼ *Restaurant, minibars, bar, Wi-Fi* ⊟ *AE, MC, V* ⧖ *BP.*

$–$$$ 🖃**Hyatt Fair Lakes.** The pink granite, ultramodern Hyatt has an airy atrium lobby with the Houndstooth Grill and an inviting lounge. Large guest rooms (560 square feet) in pastel colors with modern decor have a separate seating area with work desk, hair dryer, iron, ironing board, and coffeemaker; a free newspaper is delivered daily (but Wi-Fi will cost you $9.95 per day). Lounge on the sun deck or explore the property's jogging trails. There's courtesy transportation to Fair Oaks Mall and nearby business parks. The location is convenient to the National Air and Space Museum Steven F. Udvar-Hazy Center, Wolf Trap, George Mason Center for the Arts, and Nissan Pavilion. ✉ *12777 Fair Lakes Circle, 22033* 🕾 *703/818–1234* 🖷 *703/653–6190* ⊕ *www.fairlakes.hyatt. com* ⮑ *316 rooms* ₼ *Coffee shop, grill, room service, cable TV, in-room broadband, in-room data ports, indoor pool, gym, hot tub, sauna, billiards, lobby lounge, shop, dry cleaning, laundry service, concierge, business services, meeting rooms, convention center, free parking, nosmoking rooms* ⊟ *AE, D, DC, MC, V.*

Nightlife & the Arts

Center for the Arts. This state-of-the-art performance complex on the Fairfax campus of George Mason University satisfies music, ballet, and drama patrons with regular performances in its 1,900-seat concert hall, the 500-

seat proscenium Harris Theater, and the intimate 150-seat flexible TheaterSpace, home to its professional company in residence, Theater of the First Amendment. The 9,500-seat Patriot Center, site of pop acts and sporting events, is also on campus. ⊠ *Rte. 123 and Braddock Rd.* ☎ *703/993–8888 or 888/945–2468.*

Sports & the Outdoors

Courses with reasonable greens fees are spread all over the region, mainly south and west of Arlington and Alexandria. A few miles south of Mount Vernon and near Gunston Hall is **Pohick Bay Regional Golf Course** (⊠ 10301 Gunston Rd., Lorton ☎ 703/339–8585). Eighteen holes cost $29–$41, depending on the day.

Chantilly

➌⓪ *8 mi northwest of Fairfax.*

★ Opened in 2003 to commemorate the 100th anniversary of the Wright brothers' flight, the **National Air and Space Museum Steven F. Udvar-Hazy Center** is beside Washington Dulles International Airport. The gargantuan facility displays 123 aircraft and 141 large space artifacts, including rockets, satellites, experimental flying machines, a Concorde, the Space Shuttle *Enterprise,* the *Enola Gay,* and a Lockheed SR-71 Blackbird, which in 1990 flew from Los Angeles to Washington, D.C. in just over an hour. An IMAX theater here shows films about flight. Parking is free after 4 PM. ⊠ *14390 Air and Space Museum Pkwy.* ☎ *202/633–1000* ⊕ *www. nasm.si.edu/udvarhazy* ☑ *Free, IMAX $8.50, parking $12* ⊙ *Daily 10:30–5:30.*

The main attraction for those who come to Chantilly is a Federal-period home called **Sully.** The house has changed hands many times since it was built in 1794 by Richard Bland Lee, Northern Virginia's first representative to congress. Citizen action in the 20th century saved it from destruction during construction of nearby Dulles Airport. In the 1970s the house and its outbuilding were restored to their original appearance, with a representative kitchen and flower gardens. A 45 minute tour is offered every hour on the hour, and tours of the outbuildings and slave quarters are available daily at 2 PM. Educational programs, special events, and living history programs are held here throughout the year. ⊠ *Rte. 28, 3601 Sully Rd.* ☎ *703/437–1794* ⊕ *www.fairfaxcounty.gov/ parks/sully* ☑ *$5* ⊙ *Wed.–Mon. 11–4.*

Manassas

➌➀ *16 mi southwest of Fairfax.*

↺ The Confederacy won two important victories—in July 1861 and August 1862—at **Manassas National Battlefield Park,** or Bull Run. General
Fodor'sChoice
★ Thomas Jonathan Jackson earned his nickname Stonewall here, when he and his brigade "stood like a stone wall." When the second battle ended, the Confederacy was at the zenith of its power. Originally farmland, the battlefield bore witness to the deaths of nearly 30,000 troops. The Stone House, used as a hospital during the war, still stands. Presi-

dent Taft led a peaceful reunion of thousands of veterans here in 1911—50 years after the first battle. The "Peace Jubilee" continues to be celebrated in Manassas every summer. A self-guided walking or driving tour of the park begins at the visitor center, whose exhibits and audiovisual presentations greatly enhance a visit. Bull Run is a 26-mi drive from Washington; from Arlington and Fairfax take I–66 west (use I–495 to get to I–66 from Alexandria) to Exit 47B (Sudley Road/Route 234 North). (Don't be fooled by the earlier Manassas exit for Route 28.) The visitor center is ½ mi north on the right. ✉ *6511 Sudley Rd.* ☎ *703/361–1339* ⊕ *www.nps.gov/mana* ☜ *$3 for 3 days* ☽ *Park daily dawn–dusk, visitor center daily 8:30–5.*

WORD OF MOUTH

"If you're going to Manassas I highly recommend spending at least a couple hours walking around . . .The Brawner Farm site is worth it to see right where the two sides lined up at about 50 yards and began blasting away. Also the spot where the Maine cannon on Chinn Ridge tried to hold off the charging mass of Confeds. On a final note on Manassas–go on Sunday: there are two heavily travelled roads running right through and the traffic noise in the week, particularly rush hour, can be heard from many areas."
–HooDrew

Where to Stay

$–$$ ▥ **Courtyard Manassas Battlefield Park.** You can't get any closer to the Manassas Battlefield than this—it's across the street from the main entrance. Business travelers appreciate the hostelry's location near the Dulles High Tech Corridor, with plenty of dining and shopping nearby. This beautifully landscaped, three-story hotel has comfy guest rooms that feature luxurious linens, paisley comforters, thick mattresses, and fluffy pillows. Included are a coffeemaker, hair dryer, iron and ironing board, and a free newspaper delivered to your room. ✉ *10701 Battleview Pkwy., 20109* ☎ *703/335–1300* 🖶 *703/335–9442* ➪ *137 rooms, 12 suites* ⅗ *Dining room, in-room data ports, refrigerators, cable TV with movies, Web TV, indoor pool, gym, laundry facilities, business services, meeting rooms, free parking, no-smoking rooms* ▤ *MC, V.*

Tysons Corner

㉜ *11 mi northwest of Alexandria.*

A highly developed commercial area of office buildings, hotels, restaurants, and two major shopping centers, Tysons Corner is a fashionable address in the Washington, D.C., area. Beware of the grating traffic jam on every road, side street, and parking lot at rush hour. Routes 123 and 7 and International Drive are the worst; I–495, the Beltway, is less affected.

Where to Eat

★ $$$$ ✕ **Maestro.** This award-winning, five-star dining room in the Ritz-Carlton is one of the best in D.C.'s metro area. Inside the state-of-the-art open kitchen, Chef Fabio Trabocchi emphasizes both traditional Italian cooking and what he calls *l'evoluzione,* his creative takes on the classics. The menu changes often, but you might find potato ravioli in black-truffle sauce, pan-fried scallops wrapped in focaccia, oxtail tortellini, sea bass with fennel confit, and grappa risotto. Desserts run to sweets like peppermint chocolate soufflé and bonbons filled with rose, lavender, and peach ice cream. Five courses (any combination) are $125, and a seven-course tasting menu is $150. Brunch is served on Sunday. ⊠ *Ritz-Carlton, Tysons Corner, 1700 Tysons Blvd., Tysons Corner, VA* ☎ *703/821–1515 or 703/917–5498* ⚱ *Reservations essential* ▤ *AE, D, DC, MC, V* ☻ *Closed Mon.*

$$$–$$$$ ✕**Capital Grille.** A small group of urban restaurants are tucked in a pocket of high-end stores in the suburb of Tysons Corner. Among them is the Capital Grille, where meat and potatoes means fine dry-aged porterhouse cuts and delicious cream-based potatoes. Another don't-miss is the pan-fried calamari with hot cherry peppers. ⊠ *1861 International Dr., at Rte. 7, McLean* ☎ *703/448–3900* ▤ *AE, D, DC, MC, V* ☻ *No lunch weekends.*

$–$$$ ✕**Clyde's of Tysons Corner.** A branch of a popular Georgetown pub, Clyde's has four art deco dining rooms, one or more of which may be devoted to private parties. The Palm Terrace has high ceilings and lots of faux greenery; less formal dining rooms adjoin each other and a couple of bars. Clyde's mostly attracts workers from the nearby corporate buildings, who appreciate the attentive service and high-quality fare. The lengthy, eclectic menu always includes fresh fish dishes, such as trout Parmesan. The wine list is equally long. ⊠ *8332 Leesburg Pike, Tysons Corner* ☎ *703/734–1900* ▤ *AE, D, DC, MC, V.*

Where to Stay

$–$$$$ ▥**Hilton McLean/Tysons Corner.** The staff has a reputation for friendliness at this upscale hotel, where rooms are decorated in an autumn color scheme with restful green carpeting and upholstered furniture. The large guest rooms have two overstuffed lounge chairs and a desk; many also have a matching sofa, work desk, hair dryer, iron, ironing board, coffeemaker, and free *USA Today* newspaper. The Cafe Restaurant serves American cuisine from 6:30 AM to 11 PM daily, and the hotel provides free shuttle service to the two vast shopping malls at Tysons Corner. ⊠ *7920 Jones Branch Dr., McLean 22102* ☎ *703/847–5000* ⊞ *703/761–5100* ⊕ *www.mclean.hilton.com* ⚐ *458 rooms, 18 suites* ⚑ *2 restaurants, room service, in-room data ports, minibars, indoor pool, gym, spa, shop, bar, business center, meeting rooms* ▤ *AE, D, DC, MC, V.*

$$$ ▥**Ritz-Carlton, Tysons Corner.** One of the most elegant hotels in the D.C. area has large guest rooms with antique furniture and 19th-century lithographs. Booking a concierge room gives you access to an exclusive club with five complimentary minimeals and appetizer services throughout the day and sweeping views of the Virginia countryside. On the third floor is the expansive Eden Spa. The lobby lounge's dark-panel walls and safari animal bronzes make it feel like a 19th-century club room. The hotel has a steak house and the outstanding Maestro restaurant, among the best in the D.C. area. The hotel adjoins the exclusive Tysons Galleria mall. ⊠ *1700 Tysons Blvd., McLean 22102* ☎ *703/506–4300* ⊞ *703/506–4305* ⊕ *www.ritzcarlton.com* ⚐ *348 rooms, 50 suites* ⚑ *2 restaurants, minibars, in-room data ports, in-room broadband, indoor pool, health club, spa, bar, shop, dry cleaning, laundry service,* *concierge, concierge floor, business services, convention center, parking (fee), no-smoking rooms* ⊟ *AE, D, MC, V.*

Shopping

The **Galleria at Tysons II.** Across a busy highway from Tysons Corner Center, the Galleria has about 100 generally upscale retailers, including Saks Fifth Avenue, Versace, and Neiman Marcus, and a variety of average to good restaurants (like Maggiano's) and fast-food outlets. ⊠ *2001 International Dr., McLean* ☎ *703/827–7700.*

Tysons Corner Center. Anchored by Bloomingdale's and Nordstrom, Tysons Corner Center houses more than 300 stores and restaurants and a 16-screen AMC Theatre. Traffic is extremely heavy around the evening rush. ⊠ *1961 Chain Bridge Rd., McLean* ☎ *703/893–9400.*

Wolf Trap

13 mi west of Alexandria.

★ A major venue in the greater D.C. area, **Wolf Trap National Park for the Performing Arts** hosts a wide variety of performances throughout the year. In warmer months popular and classical music, opera, dance, and comedy performances are given in a partially covered pavilion, the Filene Center, and in the Barns at Wolf Trap—two 18th-century barns transported from upstate New York—the rest of the year. Many food concessions are available; picnicking is permitted on the lawn, but not in the fixed seating under the pavilion.

Children's programs are emphasized at the outdoor Theater in the Woods, including mime, puppetry, animal shows, music, drama, and storytelling. (No food or drink other than water is allowed in the theater.) A major event in September is the International Children's Festival. At any event, allow extra time for parking, and expect a traffic jam after the performance. The 100-odd acres of hills, meadows, and forests here are closed to general use from two hours before to one hour after performances. Parking is free, and on performance nights, Metrorail operates a $5 round-trip shuttle bus between the West Falls Church Metrorail station and the Filene Center. The fare is exact change only, and the bus leaves 20 minutes after the show, or no later than 11 PM, whether the show is over or not. ⊠ *1551 Trap Rd., Vienna* ☎ *703/255–1900, 703/938–2404 Barns at Wolf Trap* ⊕ *www.wolf-trap.org* ☉ *Daily 7 AM–dusk* Ⓜ *West Falls Church, then bus to Filene Center only.*

Ⓒ **Colvin Run Mill Historic Site,** about 3 mi southeast of Wolf Trap, dates from the first decade of the 19th century, although the country store was added in the early 20th century. In addition to the restored grist mill, there's a small museum inside the miller's home. It offers hourly tours, educational programs, special events, and occasional outdoor concerts. You can picnic on the grounds, feed the ducks, and learn about America's technological roots. The Colvin Run Mill General Store originally served the local community and today offers penny candy, freshly ground cornmeal and wheat flour, popcorn, and various old-fashioned goods. The mill itself usually operates Sunday afternoons from March to November. ⊠ *Rte. 7 and 10017 Colvin Run Rd., Great Falls* ☎ *703/759–2771*

⊕ *www.co.fairfax.va.us/parks/crm* ⊠ *$5* ⊙ *Mar.–Dec., Wed.–Mon. 11–5; Jan. and Feb., Wed.–Mon. 11–4.*

Great Falls Park

20 mi northwest of Alexandria.

Numbers in the margin correspond to points of interest on the Great Falls Park map.

★ ㉝ Facing the C&O Canal National Historic Park (*see* Chapter 3) across the Potomac River on the Maryland side is **Great Falls Park,** where the steep, jagged falls of the Potomac roar into the narrow Mather Gorge, the rocky narrows that make the Potomac churn.

The 800-acre park is a favorite for outings; here you can follow trails past the old Patowmack Canal and among the boulders and forests lining the edge of the falls. Horseback riding is permitted—maps are available at the visitor center—but you can't rent horses in the park. Swimming, wading, overnight camping, and alcoholic beverages are not allowed, but you can fish (a Virginia, Maryland, or D.C. license is required for anglers 16 and older), climb rocks (climbers must register at the visitor center beforehand), or—if you're an experienced boater with your own equipment—go white-water kayaking (*below* the falls only). As is true all along this stretch of the river, the currents are deadly. Despite frequent signs and warnings, there are those who occasionally dare the water and drown.

A tour of the visitor center and museum takes 30 minutes. Staff members conduct special tours and walks year-round. ⊠ *Rte. 193/Old Georgetown Pike; Exit 44 off Rte. 495, the Capitol Beltway to Rte. 738, follow signs* 🕿 *703/285–2966* ⊕ *www.nps.gov/grfa* ⊠ *$5 per vehicle, good for 3 days, $3 for entry on foot, horse, motorcycle, or bicycle, good for 3 days* ⊙ *Year round, daily 7–dusk. Visitor center Apr.–Oct., daily 10–5; Nov.–Mar., daily 10–4.*

㉞ Downriver about 8 mi from Great Falls Park, the **Chain Bridge** links the District of Columbia with Virginia. Named for the chains that held up the original structure, the bridge was built to enable cattlemen to bring Virginia herds to the slaughterhouses on the Maryland side of the Potomac. The Virginia side of the river in the area around Chain Bridge is known for its good fishing and narrow, treacherous channel.

Where to Eat

★ $$$$ ✕ **L'Auberge Chez François.** Set in the Virginia countryside, this sprawling restaurant serves the German-influenced cuisine of Alsace. The decor is romantic and kitschy—a fireplace dominates the main dining room, German knickknacks line the walls, and red-jacketed waiters courteously guide you through the meal. *Choucroute* (sausage, duck, smoked pork, and foie gras served atop sauerkraut), Dover sole with lobster, and *Le sauté gourmandise Papa Ernest*—medallions of filet of beef and veal, a grilled lamb chop, and half a roasted Maine lobster tail—are a few of the generously portioned, outstanding entrées. You are asked in advance whether you'd like a soufflé. Say yes, unless it's the Alsatian

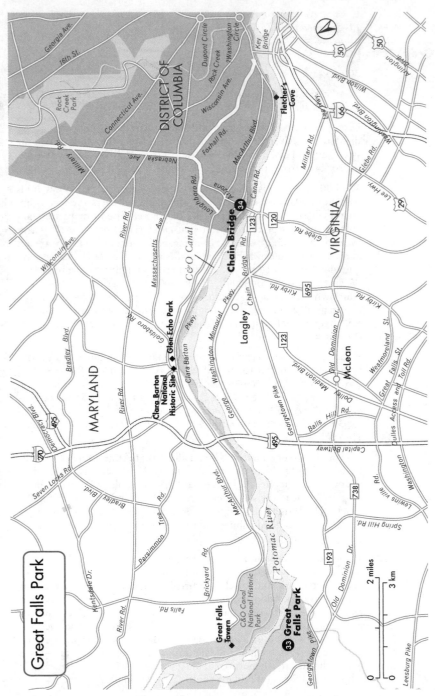

Great Falls Park

MARYLAND

DISTRICT OF COLUMBIA

VIRGINIA

Potomac River

C&O Canal

Rock Creek Park

Georgia Ave.
16th St.
Military Rd.
Rock Creek Park
Connecticut Ave.
Nebraska Ave.
Wisconsin Ave.
Wisconsin Rd.
Wisconsin Ave.
Bradley Blvd.
River Rd.
Massachusetts Ave.
Goldsboro Rd.
Dupont Circle
Washington Circle
Georgia Ave.
Arizona
Loughboro Rd.
Foxhall Rd.
MacArthur Blvd.
Canal Rd.
Key Bridge
Fletcher's Cove
Chain Bridge
Glen Echo Park
Clara Barton National Historic Site
Clara Barton Pkwy.
Washington Memorial Pkwy.
George Washington Memorial Pkwy.
Langley
Chain Bridge Rd.
123
120
34
695
123
Kirby Rd.
Kirby Rd.
McLean
Old Dominion Dr.
Dolley Madison Blvd.
Great Falls St.
Westmoreland St.
Balls Hill Rd.
Georgetown Pike
Lee Hwy.
Glebe Rd.
Glebe Rd.
Wilson Blvd.
Arlington Blvd.
Washington Blvd.
50
50
29
66
Bradley Blvd.
Democracy Blvd.
270
495
Seven Locks Rd.
Bradley Blvd.
Persimmon Tree Rd.
Kentsdale Dr.
River Rd.
Falls Rd.
Brickyard Rd.
MacArthur Blvd.
Capital Beltway
495
738
193
Lewinsville Rd.
Spring Hill Rd.
Washington
Dulles Access and Toll Rd.
Old Dominion Dr.
Georgetown Pike
Leesburg Pike
Great Falls Tavern
C&O Canal National Historic Park
Great Falls Park
33
2 miles
3 km
0
0

plum tart that's calling you instead. Make reservations up to a month in advance. ⊠ *332 Springvale Rd.*, *Great Falls* ☎ *703/759–3800* ⚓ *Reservations essential* 🎩 *Jacket required* ⊟ *AE, D, DC, MC, V* ☉ *Closed Mon. No lunch Tues.–Sat.*

LOUDOUN COUNTY

Loudoun County, capital of Virginia's horse country and an hour away from D.C., abounds with historic villages and towns, antiques shops, wineries, farms, and heritage sites; the countryside is littered with stables, barns, and stacked-stone fences. The Potomac River borders the county on the north. In the major towns in Loudoun, such as Leesburg, Middleburg, and Waterford, residents keep alive traditional rural Virginia pursuits like fox hunts, steeplechases, and high-profile entertaining.

Numbers in the margin correspond to points of interest on the Northern Virginia map.

Middleburg

㉟ *40 mi west of Alexandria.*

The area around here was surveyed by George Washington in 1763, when it was known as Chinn's Crossroads. It was considered strategic because of its location midway on the Winchester–Alexandria route (roughly what is now U.S. 50). Many of Middleburg's homes include horse farms, and the town is known for its steeplechases and fox hunts in spring and fall. Attractive boutiques and stores line U.S. 50 (the main street). Two miles east of town is the **Chrysalis Vineyard**, dedicated to producing both old- and new-world varieties of wine and hoping to revive interest in the fabled Norton, a grape native to Virginia. ⊠ *23876 Champe Ford Rd.* ☎ *540/687–8222 or 800/235–8804* ⊕ *www.chrysaliswine.com* ☉ *Daily 11–5.*

The vineyards in the Middleburg area often have tastings and tours. Three miles south of Middleburg, **Piedmont Vineyards and Winery** has 25 acres of vines, as well as an early-18th-century manor house. Piedmont specializes in white wines such as chardonnay and semillon, but also makes some reds. ⊠ *Rte. 626* ☎ *540/687–5528* ⊕ *www.piedmontwines.com* ☉ *Tours Sat. 11:30; tasting room Mon.–Sat. 11–6, Sun. noon–6.*

One mile east of Middleburg is the **Swedenburg Estate Vineyard**. The winery's modern building sits on a working farm, which raises Angus beef cattle. The Bull Run mountains form a backdrop for the vineyards. Swedenburg vineyard grows chardonnay, cabernet sauvignon, pinot noir, and Riesling. Juanita Swedenburg successfully petitioned the Supreme Court to repeal the ban on interstate wine shipments. ⊠ *Valley View Farm, Rte. 50/23959 Winery La.* ☎ *540/687–5219* ⊕ *www.swedenburgwines.com* ☉ *Daily 10–4.*

Where to Stay

\$\$–\$\$\$ ☲ **Middleburg Country Inn.** This three-story structure, built in 1820 and enlarged in 1858, was the rectory of St. John's Parish Episcopal Church until 1907. Its medium-size rooms are furnished with antiques and pe-

Virginia's Wine-Making Roots

IN 1609 ENGLISH SETTLERS in Jamestown, Virginia, produced the first wine—however humble—in America. In the nearly 400 years since, it has been sink or swim for the state's wine industry—mostly sink. But after numerous tries, Virginia can claim some 100-odd wineries.

In 1611 the Virginia Company, eager to establish wine making in the Colonies, brought over French winegrowers along with slips and seeds of European vine stocks. For the next two centuries, French viticulturists attempted but failed to transplant European rootstock to the New World. In 1769 the Virginia Assembly appointed the Frenchman Andrew Estave as wine maker and viticulturist. He couldn't get the European stock to take either but realized that the problem lay with Virginia's harsher climate of cold winters and hot, humid summers. Estave believed that growers should therefore use native American grapes, which were more likely to flourish.

Thomas Jefferson was anxious to promote grape growing, to encourage wine drinking for itself and to create a cash-crop alternative to tobacco. Although he appreciated European wines, Jefferson believed that successful wine making in America would depend on native varietals. By 1800 he and other Virginians had begun developing hybrids of American and European varieties, resulting in grapes that combined American hardiness with European finesse and complexity. The most popular are still grown today.

A strong wine-making industry developed in Virginia between 1800 and the Civil War. The war's fierce battles destroyed many vineyards but as recently as 1950, only 15 acres of grapes were being grown. In the 1960s the Virginia grape industry began a revival that has made it the sixth-largest wine-producing state. The revival began with American hybrids but has shifted to French hybrids.

Today Virginia's wines are winning national and international acclaim. The state produces more than 300,000 cases of wine yearly from 2,100 acres of wine grapes. The most popular variety, chardonnay, comes as a medium- to full-bodied dry white. It may be fruity, with a hint of apples or citrus. Other whites include vidal blanc, Viognier, Riesling, gewürztraminer, sauvignon blanc, and seyval blanc. Virginia's reds include cabernet franc, cabernet sauvignon, merlot, pinot noir, and chambourcin.

Virginia's wineries are spread around the state in six viticultural areas. The wine industry begun by Jefferson is in the Monticello region in central Virginia. Other areas are the Shenandoah, Northern Neck George Washington Birthplace, North Fork of Roanoke, Rocky Knob, and Virginia's Eastern Shore. Each area has been designated for its unique wine-growing conditions.

A free 90-page booklet, "Virginia Wineries Festival & Tour Guide" lists each of the state's wineries (many offer tours and tastings) and describes the 400 wine festivals and events that take place each year, attracting half a million visitors. It can be picked up at visitor information centers in the state or by contacting the **Virginia Wineries Association** (☎ 800/828-4637 ⊕ www.virginiawines.org).

riod reproductions. Unusual for a small inn, each guest room has its own phone and free wireless Internet. A full country breakfast includes your choice of three entrées, and, when weather permits, you can eat your meal alfresco. The inn is within walking distance of the historic downtown. ✉ *209 E. Washington St., Box 2065, 20117* ☎ *540/687–6082 or 800/262–6082* 🖷 *540/687–5603* 🌐 *www.middleburgcountryinn.com* *5 rooms, 3 suites* *Dining room, cable TV with movies, in-room broadband, Wi-Fi* 💳 *AE, D, MC, V* 🍽 *BP.*

3

$$–$$$ **The Red Fox Inn and Tavern.** Built in 1728 of local fieldstone, Mr. Chinn's Ordinary (tavern) was sited on the vast estate of Thomas, sixth Lord Fairfax. George Washington visited the popular tavern in 1748. During the Civil War, the inn served as a headquarters and hospital for Confederates. Today fresh flowers, bathrobes, and the *Washington Post* delivered to your four-poster bedroom are extras that make for a special stay in this romantic inn in the center of town. ✉ *2 E. Washington St., Box 385, 20118* ☎ *540/687–6301 or 800/223–1728* 🖷 *540/687–6053* 🌐 *www.redfox.com* *23 rooms* *Restaurant, in-room data ports, cable TV with movies, pub* 💳 *AE, D, MC, V* 🍽 *BP.*

EN ROUTE

Fodor'sChoice ★

Five miles south of Leesburg on Route 15, **Oatlands** is a former 5,000-acre plantation built by a great-grandson of Robert "King" Carter, one of the wealthiest pre-Revolution planters in Virginia. The Greek Revival manor house was begun in 1804 and a stately portico and half-octagonal stair wings were added in 1827. The house, a National Trust Historic Site, has been meticulously restored, and the manicured fields that remain host public and private equestrian events from spring to fall. Among these is the Loudoun Hunt Point-to-Point in April, a race that brings out the entire community for tailgates and picnics on blankets. The terraced walls here border a restored English garden of 4½ acres. ✉ *20850 Oatlands Plantation La., (Rte. 15)* ☎ *703/777–3174* 🌐 *www.oatlands.org* *$10; additional fee for special events* ⏲ *Mar. 30–Dec. 30., Mon.–Sat. 10–5, Sun. 1–5.*

Leesburg

36 *36 mi northwest of Alexandria.*

A staging area for George Washington's push to the Ohio Valley during the French and Indian War (1754–60), Leesburg is one of the oldest towns in northern Virginia. Its numerous fine Georgian and Federal buildings now house offices, shops, restaurants, and homes. In an early sign of changing allegiances, "George Town" changed its name to Leesburg in 1758 to honor Virginia's illustrious Lee family. When the British burned Washington during the War of 1812, James and Dolley Madison fled to Leesburg with many government records, including originals of the Declaration of Independence and the U.S. Constitution.

The 250-year history of the Loudoun County area is detailed in the **Loudoun Museum,** which displays art and artifacts of daily life from the time preceding the town's existence on through the present. ✉ *16 W. Loudoun St. SW* ☎ *703/777–7427* 🌐 *www.loudounmuseum.org* *$3* ⏲ *Mon. and Wed.–Sat. 10–5, Sun. 1–5, Tues. by appt.*

Within the 1,200 acres that make up **Morven Park** is the Morven Park International Equestrian Institute (a private riding school) and two museums: Winmill Carriage Museum and the Museum of Hounds and Hunting. The elegant mansion was originally a fieldstone farm house built in 1781. It evolved into a Greek Revival building that bears a striking resemblance to the White House (completed in 1800), so much so that it's been used as a stand-in for it in films. Two governors have lived here. The mansion and the Museum of Hounds and Hunting are closed for extensive renovation until 2008; however, the Winmill Carriage Museum, housing 25 historic vehicles, is open to those taking the tours. Most Saturdays a Civil War tour especially suited to children is offered. In the fall, a Civil War camp allows visitors to see huts used for winter quarters and clothing and other artifacts. Call for the latest info. ⊠ *Old Waterford Rd., 1 mi north of Leesburg* ☎ *703/777–2414* ⊕ *www. morvenpark.org* ☏ *$5* ☉ *Tours Apr.–Nov., Sat. at 1, Sun. at 1 and 3.*

Where to Stay & Eat

$$$ ╳ **Lightfoot Restaurant.** Housed in a Romanesque-Revival building (1888), this restaurant was the Peoples National Bank for more than half a century. Restored to its original grandeur, the restaurant was named in honor of Francis Lightfoot Lee, a signer of the Declaration of Independence. The wine "cellar" is actually the bank's vault. The seasonal American cuisine, based on local ingredients, includes Blue Ridge spinach salad, a variation on oysters Rockefeller, seared salmon topped with artichoke gratin and crab over apricot couscous, balsamic vinegar-and-sage-glazed pork chop with Asiago-potato soufflé, and many kinds of seafood. ⊠ *11 N. King St.* ☎ *703/771–2233* ☐ *AE, D, DC, MC, V.*

$$$–$$$$ ╳▣ **Lansdowne Conference Resort.** With 205 acres of hills and tall trees bordered by the Potomac River, Lansdowne specializes in outdoor activities and has miles of hiking and jogging trails. Polished wood furniture, handsome wall decorations, and marble-accented bathrooms help make the property elegant. Tall windows in the Lansdowne Grille ($$$–$$$$) look out on Sugarloaf Mountain. Main dishes include black sesame tuna, crab cakes, blackened swordfish, Chateaubriand and other steaks, and rosemary chicken. The Riverside Hearth ($$), a café overlooking an 18-hole golf course, serves American cuisine breakfast through dinner; its Sunday brunch buffet is renowned. ⊠ *44050 Woodridge Pkwy., off Rte. 7, 22075* ☎ *703/729–8400 or 800/541–4801* ☏ *703/729–4096* ⊕ *www.lansdowneresort.com* ⇨ *282 rooms, 14 suites* ₷ *2 Restaurants, 3 cafés, snack bar, cable TV with movies, in-room broadband, in-room data ports, 2 18-hole golf courses, 2 tennis courts, 5 pools (1 indoor), gym, billiards, racquetball, volleyball, 2 bars, dry cleaning, laundry service, concierge, convention center, meeting rooms, free parking, no-smoking rooms* ☐ *AE, D, DC, MC, V.*

Waterford

③⑦ *5 mi northwest of Leesburg, 45 mi northwest of Alexandria.*

The historic community of Waterford was founded by a Quaker miller and for many decades has been synonymous with fine crafts; its annual Homes Tour and Crafts Exhibit, held the first weekend of October, includes visits to 19th-century buildings. Waterford and more than 1,400 acres around it were declared a National Historic Landmark in 1970 in recognition of its authenticity as an almost original, ordinary 19th-century village. Information about Waterford is at ⊕ www.waterfordva-wca.org.

NORTHERN VIRGINIA ESSENTIALS

To research prices, get advice from other travelers, and book travel arrangements, visit www.fodors.com.

Transportation

BY AIR

Three major airports serve northern Virginia and Washington, D.C. The busy Ronald Reagan Washington National Airport, 3 mi south of downtown Washington in Virginia, has scheduled daily flights by all major U.S. carriers. Washington Dulles International Airport, 26 mi northwest of Washington, and Baltimore-Washington Thurgood Marshall International Airport (BWI), 37 mi northeast of the capital, are served by the major U.S. airlines and many international carriers.

Alexandria is only a few miles from Ronald Reagan Washington National Airport. It's easy to get there by Metrorail, taxi, or Metrobus. A taxi to Dulles or BWI airport is expensive, but BWI is well-served by reasonable ground transportation. Washington Metropolitan Transit Authority (WMATA) has an express bus there from its Greenbelt, Maryland, Metrorail station. All north-bound Amtrak and Maryland State Penn Line trains from Washington's Union Station make a BWI stop, where a free shuttle bus takes you to the terminal. Dulles is served by Washington Flyer bus every 30 minutes from the West Falls Church Metrorail station ($9), by Metrobus Route 5A express service ($3), and by limousine services like Super Shuttle.

⊡ Airport Contacts **Baltimore-Washington International Airport (BWI)** ☎ 410/859–7111 or 800/435–9294 ⊕ www.bwiairport.com. **Ronald Reagan Washington National Airport (DCA)** ☎ 703/417–8000 ⊕ www.metwashairports.com/National. **Washington Dulles International Airport (IAD)** ☎ 703/572–2700 ⊕ www.metwashairports.com/Dulles.

⊡ Transfer Contacts **Amtrak** ☎ 800/872–7245 ⊕ www.amtrak.com. **Maryland Transportation Authority (for Penn Line)** ☎ 410/539–5000 or 866/743–3682 ⊕ www.mtamaryland.com. **SuperShuttle** ☎ 800/258–3826 ⊕ www.supershuttle.com. **Virginia Railway Express (VRE)** ☎ 800/743–3873 ⊕ www.vre.org. **Washington Flyer** ☎ 703/685–1400 ⊕ www.washfly.com. **WMATA** ☎ 202/637–7000 ⊕ www.wmata.com.

BY BUS

The only practical bus station to use for visiting Northern Virginia is in downtown Washington, about three blocks from Union Station, from which commuter trains and WMATA subways (Metrorail) to suburban Virginia are available.

All in all, it's reasonable to visit Northern Virginia without a car. (Leesburg and Middleburg are exceptions: there's no bus or train service at all here.) WMATA operates a coordinated system here that links local buses (Metrobus) and the Metrorail system. Service in Alexandria and Arlington is quite comprehensive, and city- and county-operated bus lines connect with WMATA services; all the local bus systems accept WMATA's rail-to-bus transfers.

⊠ Arlington depot ⊠ Pentagon. **Ballston Metrorail station** ⊠ 4230 Fairfax Dr. **Fairfax Metrorail station** ⊠ I-66 and Nutley St. **Greyhound Lines** ☎ 800/231-2222. **King St. Metrorail station, Alexandria** ⊠ King St. at Commonwealth Ave. **Springfield Greyhound Station** ⊠ 6770 Frontier Dr., off I-395 ☎ 703/971-7598. **Tyson's Westpark Transit Station** ⊠ Tyco Rd. and International Dr., off the Dulles Toll Rd. **WMATA/ Metrobus** ☎ 202/637-7000 ⊕ www.wmata.com.

BY CAR
The Capital Beltway, I-495, circles the District of Columbia through Virginia and Maryland (and enters the District very briefly, as it crosses the Wilson Bridge), providing a circular bypass for I-95 around Washington. During commute hours it becomes congested—toward Tyson's Corner in the morning, and away in the evening—so if you plan to spend most of your time in downtown Washington or within the Beltway, it would be prudent to select lodging north of the I-95/I-495 interchange. The outer loop in Maryland around the intersection with I-270 is congested in the morning rush, as is the inner loop in the evening rush.

The Custis Memorial Parkway, I-66, runs east–west between Washington, D.C., and I-81 near Front Royal, which takes you south through the Shenandoah or north to West Virginia. Note that HOV restrictions prohibit single-person vehicles on I-66 inside the Beltway eastbound during morning rush hour and westbound during evening rush hour, unless the car is en route to Dulles Airport. For Dulles, exit to the right to the Dulles Access Road just before Falls Church, inside the Beltway.

Once you have reached Northern Virginia, it's convenient to use the area's excellent, clean, and safe Washington Metropolitan Area Transit Authority (WMATA) system (buses and subway) or local jurisdictions' bus systems, or travel by biking or walking. Biking was just made easier by the addition of bike racks to all WMATA Metrobuses (they've been allowed on the subways for many years). In the farther-out suburbs, a car is necessary.

At the Alexandria Convention and Visitors Association, you can obtain a free 24-hour parking permit for the two-hour metered zones (you must furnish your license plate number). Giving parking tickets is one of the things Capital-area jurisdictions do best, so if you park at meters, be careful and keep the meter fed. Also read parking signs carefully. There are many variations, and they are often quite confusing.

BY SUBWAY
Washington Metropolitan Transit Authority (WMATA) provides subway service (Metrorail) in the District and in the Maryland and Virginia suburbs. The Orange, Blue, and Yellow lines serve Northern Virginia. Other than morning and evening rush hours train intervals are about 12 minutes weekdays, 20 minutes weekday evenings, 15 minutes week-

end days, and 20 minutes weekend evenings. Stations open and trains begin at 5 on weekdays, 7 on weekends. Last trains and station closings begin before midnight on weekdays, and between 2:30 and 3:30 AM weekend nights. Rush-hour service is more frequent. Bikes are permitted on the Metrorail, except weekdays 7 AM–10 AM and 4 PM–7 PM, and most stations have racks.

The base fare is $1.35 and the maximum is $3.90; the actual fare depends upon the time of day and the distance traveled (and seniors over 65 pay half price). You may buy your ticket with coins and bills or credit cards at Farecard machines within station entrances. Hang on to the ticket; you need it to exit. You can add value to a Farecard in the vending machines at station entrances. A one-day pass ($6.50) is available at many hotels, banks, and Safeway and Giant grocery stores, and can be ordered at WMATA's Web site.

If you're transferring from Metrorail to a bus, pick up a rail-to-bus transfer from a machine at the originating Metrorail station; it lowers the bus fare to 35¢.

🚇 WMATA ☎ 202/637-7000 ⊕ www.wmata.com.

BY TAXI

Taxicabs are free to operate in adjoining jurisdictions and this is vital, considering that there are two states plus the District and several counties and cities in a small area. Virginia taxis are metered with rates set by the jurisdiction (about $2.75 to board and for the first ¼ mi and 20¢ per additional ⅛ mi), and many accept credit cards. Note that D.C. uses a complicated zone system that is displayed on a map visible to the passenger. Taxi stands are designated and numerous, and cruising (and hailing) is allowed. Taxis are usually waiting near the busier Metrorail stations like Ballston, King Street, and Rosslyn, and the bigger hotels.

Taxis at the Virginia airports are very tightly regulated. Washington Flyer cabs serve Dulles International Airport exclusively from the airport but any taxi can deliver there. A starter outside the arrivals area at Reagan National loads taxicabs from a regulated line of incoming taxis and will provide a fare sheet if desired. An airport fee of $1.75 is added to your fare to pay for this service. Taxis from both airports are required to accept credit cards, but at Reagan National you'd better remind the driver of that if you intend to use one.

🚕 Alexandria Diamond Cab ☎ 703/548-7505. Arlington Blue Top Cab ☎ 703/243-8294. Fairfax White Top Cab ☎ 703/644-4500.

BY TRAIN

Amtrak serves the region with nine trains to Alexandria and one to Manassas in each direction daily. Amtrak's Autotrain terminal is in Lorton, between Springfield and Woodbridge and just off I–95. The Alexandria station is colocated with a major bus hub and a Metrorail station. Virginia Rail Express (VRE) provides cheap workday service between Union Station in Washington, D.C., and Fredericksburg and Manassas, with 17 stops, including all Amtrak stations along the route. VRE offers discounted multiride, five-day, monthly, and senior ticket fares. Free parking is available at most suburban VRE stations.

🚻 **Alexandria Amtrak station** ✉ 110 Callahan Dr. ☎ 703/836-4339. **Amtrak** ☎ 800/ 872-7245 ⊕ www.amtrak.com. **Virginia Railway Express (VRE)** ☎ 800/743-3873 ⊕ www.vre.org.

Contacts & Resources

EMERGENCIES

🚻 **Emergency** ☎ 911.

🚻 **Hospitals Inova Alexandria Hospital** ✉ 4320 Seminary Rd., Alexandria ☎ 703/ 504-3000 ⊕ www.inova.com/inovapublic.srt/iah/index.jsp. **Inova Fairfax Hospital and Inova Fairfax Hospital for Children** ✉ 3300 Gallows Rd., Falls Church ☎ 703/ 776-4001 ⊕ www.inova.com/inovapublic.srt/ifh/index.jsp and www.inova.com/ inovapublic.srt/ifhc/index.jsp for children. **Inova Fair Oaks Hospital** ✉ 3600 Joseph Siewick Dr., Fairfax ☎ 703/391-3600 ⊕ www.inova.com/inovapublic.srt/ifoh/index. jsp. **Inova Mount Vernon Hospital** ✉ 2501 Parker's La., Alexandria ☎ 703/664-7000 ⊕ www.inova.com/inovapublic.srt/imvh/index.jsp. **Virginia Hospital Center** ✉ 1701 N. George Mason Dr., Arlington ☎ 703/558-5000 ⊕ www.virginiahospitalcenter.com. 🚻 **24-Hour Pharmacies CVS** ✉ 415 Monroe Ave., Alexandria ☎ 703/683-4433. **CVS** ✉ 3535 S. Jefferson St., Baileys Crossroads ☎ 703/820-6360. **CVS** ✉ 3133 Lee Hwy. Arlington ☎ 703/522-0260. **Rite Aid** ✉ 6711 Richmond Hwy., Alexandria ☎ 703/768-7233.

INTERNET, MAIL & SHIPPING

Free Internet access is easy to find in Northern Virginia. Besides the usual coffee and pastry shops, the four branches of the Alexandria public library have 57 terminals with free Internet access. Those most likely to be used by visitors are the Barrett Branch downtown and the Burke Branch, just off I-395. All of Arlington County's libraries offer free Internet access, and the Central, Aurora Hills, and Columbia Pike branches provide free Wi-Fi as well. A staff person can set up out-of-town visitors at a work station.

Alexandria's main post office is open weekdays 8–6:30 and Saturday 9–4.

🚻 **Post Office Alexandria Main Post Office** ✉ 1100 Wythe St. ☎ 703/684-7168 ⊕ www.usps.gov.

🚻 **Internet Resources Alexandria Public Library, Barrett Branch** ✉ 717 Queen St. ☎ 703/838-4555 ⊕ www.alexandria.lib.va.us. **Alexandria Public Library, Burke Branch** ✉ 4701 Seminary Rd. ☎ 703/519-6000 ⊕ www.alexandria.lib.va.us. **Arlington County Public Library, Central** ✉ 1015 N. Quincy St. ☎ 703/228-5990 ⊕ www. arlingtonva.us/Departments/Libraries/LibrariesMain.aspx. **Arlington County Public Library, Aurora Hills** ✉ 735 S. 18th St. ☎ 703/228-5715 ⊕ www.arlingtonva.us/ Departments/Libraries/LibrariesMain.aspx. **Arlington County Public Library, Columbia Pike** ✉ 816 S. Walter Reed Dr. ☎ 703/228-5710 ⊕ www.arlingtonva.us/Departments/ Libraries/LibrariesMain.aspx.

TOUR OPTIONS

The Alexandria Convention and Visitors Association runs walking tours that leave from its office 10:30 AM Monday through Saturday and 2 PM Sunday; tickets are $10. Alexandria Colonial Tours leads guided walk-

ing tours of historic Alexandria by reservation. Ghost-and-graveyard
(reservations not required) are conducted Friday, Saturday, and Sun
nights.

🏃 Walking Tours **Alexandria Colonial Tours** ☎ 703/519-1749.

VISITOR INFORMATION
Most visitor centers are open 9–5 daily.

🏃 Tourist Information **Alexandria Convention and Visitors Association** ✉ Ramsay
House, 221 King St., Alexandria 22314 ☎ 703/838-4200 or 800/388-9119 ⊕ www.
funside.com. **Arlington County Visitor Center** ✉1301 S. Joyce St., Arlington 22202 ☎703/
228-5720 or 800/677-6267 ⊕ www.stayarlington.com. **Fairfax County Visitors Center** ✉ 8180A Silverbrook Rd., Lorton 22079 ☎ 800/732-4732 ⊕ www.visitfairfax.org.
Loudoun Tourism Council ✉ 222 Catoctin Circle SE, Suite 100, Leesburg 20175 ☎ 703/
771-2617 or 800/752-6118 ⊕ www.visitloudoun.org. **Manassas Visitor Center** ✉ 9431
West St., Manassas ☎ 703/361-6599 ⊕ www.visitpwc.com. **Prince William Visitor Center** ✉ 200 Mill St., Occoquan ☎ 703/491-4045 ⊕ www.visitpwc.com. **Waterford Foundation** ✉ High St. ☎ 540/882-3018 ⊕ www.waterfordva.org.

ntral &
Western
Virginia

WORD OF MOUTH

"Go to Shenandoah National Park, it is very scenic and I love it . . . consider going in fall, in October or so, but even when the leaves are not changing it is still pretty."

—asdaven

"If you decide to head in the direction of the Shenandoah Valley, I'd recommend a stop in Lexington, Virginia . . . it's a beautiful, historic small town. You can visit Lee Chapel, where Lee and his family are buried, and see his residence when he was president of the University. You can also visit Stonewall Jackson's house. No battlefields in the immediate area but lots of history. Good place to spend half a day and grab a good meal."

—Virginia6

www.fodors.com/forums

Revised by
Kevin and
Erica Myatt

REFINED ELEGANCE. RUGGED COUNTRY. Much like the contrast between two of the region's Revolutionary War–era giants—Thomas Jefferson, the renowned statesman who steered the early United States into existence, and Patrick Henry, a rough-and-tumble rebel who demanded liberty or death—central and western Virginia presents both of these experiences to the traveler, often simultaneously.

Eastern Virginia's coastal plains start rolling into the gently undulating Piedmont west of Interstate 95. Charlottesville, 71 mi northwest of Richmond, epitomizes the refined elegance of this region, a center of culture amid vineyards and the homes of early American presidents. Jefferson, our nation's third president and a principal writer of the Declaration of Independence, left an indelible imprint on the region through his neoclassical Monticello homesite, the University of Virginia, and his summer retreat, Poplar Forest, farther south near Lynchburg.

4

Farther west the Blue Ridge juts suddenly out of the landscape, on Charlottesville's and Lynchburg's western horizon. Skyline Drive and the Blue Ridge Parkway ride the spine of the Blue Ridge. Shenandoah National Park's 200,000 acres snake along 80 mi of the ridge's crest, and Mount Rogers, Virginia's tallest peak at 5,729 feet, stands sentinel above the Virginia–North Carolina border. It's not the frontier of Patrick Henry's days, but a traveler can delve into Virginia's wild side on these scenic roads.

Beyond the Blue Ridge is the famed Shenandoah Valley, a 150-mi stretch of picturesque meadows and farms framed by mountains on either side. This region takes its Civil War history seriously: Confederate generals Robert E. Lee and Stonewall Jackson are revered at Lexington, the home of the Virginia Military Institute.

The bowl-shape Roanoke Valley lies just to the south of the Shenandoah Valley on Interstate 81. It is home to the sprawling Roanoke metropolitan area, a historic railroad center that has become the commercial and medical capital of southwest Virginia. A bit farther south on I–81 is the New River Valley, a region that takes pride in its inhabitants' vigorous outdoor lifestyle, its rapid growth, and Virginia Tech, the state's largest university.

West of these valleys, the country becomes its most rugged, in the Allegheny Mountains along the Virginia–West Virginia border, and the deeply gorged Appalachian Plateau coal country in the state's far southwest tip. This region is as varied as its elevation changes, ranging from poverty-stricken hollows where the soulful strains of bluegrass music cry, to the urbane elegance of a famed resort hotel and spa at the Homestead.

Top 5 Experiences for Central & Western Virginia

- **Thomas Jefferson:** Explore the contours of his mind at Monticello, the University of Virginia, and Poplar Forest.

- **Presidential history:** Get up close and personal not only with Jefferson, but also James Madison, James Monroe, and Woodrow Wilson at their restored homes.

- **Proud in defeat:** Relive the final days of the Civil War at Appomattox and honor the revered Southern general who surrendered there at Lee Chapel in Lexington.

- **Mountain sights:** Ride the Appalachian crests along the Blue Ridge Parkway and Skyline Drive. See a city beneath your feet from Roanoke's Mill Mountain, and soak in the scenery and healing springs at the luxurious Homestead resort.

- **Mountain sounds:** Dance to the twang of fiddles and banjoes outside the Floyd Country Store and all along the Crooked Road.

Exploring Central & Western Virginia

Charlottesville, just east of the Blue Ridge, centers around Thomas Jefferson's architectural genius—Monticello and the University of Virginia. To the south, the restored Civil War–era village of Appomattox Court House is a peek back in time. Along the western rim of Virginia in the Shenandoah Valley is Winchester, which changed hands no fewer than 72 times during the Civil War. Farther south is Lexington, known for its ties to Confederate generals Robert E. Lee and Stonewall Jackson. In Roanoke, Virginia's largest city west of Richmond, Market Square is a cultural anchor for Southwest Virginia. In this area you can hike and camp in the George Washington and Jefferson national forests, float along on the New River, and photograph wild ponies near the state's highest mountain.

About the Restaurants & Hotels

Both locally owned and major chain motels and hotels are plentiful along the interstate highways (I–81, I–64, I–77, I–66), with a particularly heavy concentration in the Charlottesville and Roanoke areas. Accommodations in private homes and converted inns are available through Blue Ridge Bed & Breakfast Reservation Service and various accommodations in and near Charlottesville can be found through Guesthouses.
🏠 Reservation Services **Blue Ridge Bed & Breakfast Reservation Service** ✉ 2458 Castleman Rd., Berryville 22611 ☎ 540/955-1246 or 800/296-1246 🖷 540/955-4240 ⊕ www.blueridgebb.com. **Guesthouses** 🖂 Box 5737, Charlottesville 22905 ☎ 434/979-7264 ⊕ www.va-guesthouses.com. W

WHAT IT COSTS				
$$$$	**$$$**	**$$**	**$**	**¢**
RESTAURANTS over $30	$22–$30	$14–$22	$7–$14	under $7
HOTELS over $250	$175–$250	$130–$175	$80–$130	under $80

Restaurant prices are per person for a main course at dinner. Hotel prices are for a standard double room, excluding state and local taxes.

CHARLOTTESVILLE & THE BLUE RIDGE

Surrounded by a lush countryside, Charlottesville is the most prominent city in the foothills of the Blue Ridge Mountains. Thomas Jefferson's hilltop home and the University of Virginia, the enterprise of his last years, draw appreciators of architecture. Twenty-five miles northeast, Orange County is where you find the estate of Jefferson's friend and compatriot James Madison. The tiny town of Washington, 30 mi beyond Orange, bears the stamp of another president: George Washington surveyed and plotted out this slice of wilderness in 1749. Lynchburg, to Charlottesville's south, is near the site of Jefferson's retreat home, the

> **PRESIDENTIAL SAVINGS**
>
> A Presidential Pass, purchased for $26 at the Monticello Visitors Center (U.S. 20 immediately off I–64 at Exit 121), grants access to Monticello, Ash Lawn-Highland, and Michie Tavern with a $5 combined savings.

octagonal Poplar Forest, and the ending battle of the Civil War, Appomattox. On the Blue Ridge itself is popular Shenandoah National Park, the park's spectacular but often-crowded Skyline Drive, and Wintergreen Resort, a haven for outdoor sports.

Numbers in the margin correspond to points of interest on the Charlottesville, the Blue Ridge, the Shenandoah Valley, and the Southwest Virginia map.

Charlottesville

❶ *71 mi northwest of Richmond via I–64.*

Charlottesville is still Mr. Jefferson's city, focused on Monticello and the University of Virginia. The downtown pedestrian mall, a brick-paved street of restored buildings that stretches along six blocks of Main Street, is frequented by humans and canines. Outdoor restaurants and cafés, concerts, and impromptu theatrical events keep things lively.

Standing in contrast to the grandiose Monticello is the modest **Ash Lawn-Highland.** James Monroe, who held more major political offices than any other U.S. president, intentionally kept it a simple farmhouse, building the home in 1799 2 mi from his friend Jefferson's estate. A later owner added on a more prominent two-story section where two original Monroe rooms burned down. Though it definitely has a more common feel than Monticello, the small rooms in Ash Lawn–Highland are similarly crowded with gifts from notables and souvenirs from Monroe's time as envoy to France. Allow a couple of hours to visit Monroe's estate, a perfect way to complete a day that begins at Monticello. The outdoor Ash Lawn Opera Festival draws music aficionados in July and August. ⊠ *1000 James Monroe Pkwy., Rte. 795 southwest of Monticello* ☎ *434/293–9539* ⊕ *www.ashlawnhighland.org* ⊠ *$9* ☉ *Apr.–Oct., daily 9–6; Nov.–Mar., daily 11–5.*

Housed in a converted 1916 school building, **McGuffey Art Center** contains the 2nd Street Gallery and the studios of painters, printmakers, metalworkers, and sculptors, all of which are open to the public. Dance performances are occasionally put on here. ⊠ *201 2nd St. NW, Downtown* ☎ *434/295–7973* ⊕ *www.mcguffeyartcenter.com* ⊠ *Free* ☉ *Tues.–Sat. 10–6, Sun. 1–5.*

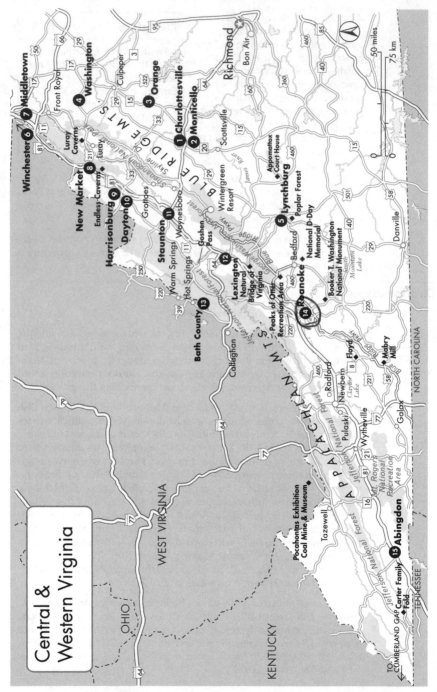

Central &
Western Virginia

Michie Tavern has become a popular attraction simply because of its location near Monticello. It is an interesting family stop to give children a sense of what life was like two centuries ago. Most of the complex was built 17 mi away at Earlysville in 1784 and moved here piece by piece in 1927. Costumed hostesses lead visitors into a series of rooms to watch historically based skits and hear recorded historical narrations. The Ordinary's lunch buffet is a bit pricey at $14.50, more than the tour of Monticello; you can skip the tavern tour and visit the general store, gift shop, and clothier shop for free. ⊠ *683 Thomas Jefferson Pkwy., Rte. 53* ☎ *434/977-1234* ⌨ *$8* ◷ *Daily 9–5.*

> ### WORD OF MOUTH
>
> "There are often huge lines on holidays and weekends, but Monticello (Thomas Jefferson's home near Charlottesville, VA) is totally fascinating. It is so much more than just a beautiful home with cool antique furnishings. The engineering and architectural brilliance displayed are amazing for (think of it) over 200 years ago!"
> –Diane

4

❷

Fodor'sChoice

★

Monticello, long featured on the back of the U.S. nickel, is well worth the admission and the almost inevitable wait. Arrive early, ideally on a weekday, and allow at least three hours to explore the nuances of Jefferson's life as exemplified by the architecture, inventions, and layout throughout his grand, hilltop estate. Monticello (which means "little mountain") is the most famous of Jefferson's homes, constructed from 1769 to 1809. Note the narrow staircases—hidden because he considered them unsightly and a waste of space—and his inventions, such as a seven-day clock and a two-pen contraption that allowed him to make a copy of his correspondence as he wrote it without having to show it to a copyist. On-site are re-created gardens (including huge poplar trees that date to Jefferson's life), the plantation street where his slaves lived, and a gift shop. ⊠ *Rte. 53* ☎ *434/984–9800* ⊕ *www.monticello.org* ⌨ *$14* ◷ *Mar.–Oct., daily 8–5; Nov.–Feb., daily 9–4:30.*

★ The **University of Virginia** is simply called "The University" by many associated with it, annoying its rivals. Unquestionably, though, it is one of the nation's most notable public universities, founded and designed by a 76-year-old Thomas Jefferson, who called himself its "father" in his own epitaph. Even if you're not an architecture or history buff, the green terraced expanse called the Lawn, surrounded by redbrick, columned buildings, is inviting. The Rotunda is a half-scale replica of Rome's Pantheon, suggesting Jefferson's Monticello and the U.S. Capitol. Behind the Pavilions, where senior faculty live, serpentine walls surround small, flowering gardens. Edgar Allan Poe's room—where he spent one year as a student until debt forced him to leave—is preserved on the West Range at No. 13. Campus tours (daily at 10, 11, 2, 3, and 4) begin indoors in the Rotunda, whose entrance is on the Lawn side, lower level. The **University of Virginia Art Museum** (⊠ Bayly Bldg., 155 Rugby Rd. ☎434/924–7458 ⌨Free ◷Tues.–Sun. 1–5), one block north of the Rotunda, exhibits art from around the world from ancient times to the present day. ⊠ *University* ☎ *434/924–3239* ⊕ *www.virginia.edu*

CLOSE UP

Thomas Jefferson

ONE OF THE NATION'S FOREMOST STATESMEN, Jefferson is best known for his first contribution to the country: drafting the Declaration of Independence in 1776. The sum of the 33-year political career that followed is better remembered than its milestones, which do, however, bear repeating.

His first office of weight was that of governor of his beloved Virginia, beginning in 1779. In 1790 he served as secretary of state under his friend George Washington, and resigned in 1793. A Republican presidential candidate in 1796, he lost by just three electoral votes to Federalist John Adams, and as rules then dictated, Jefferson became vice president. By the 1800 race, tensions between the Federalist and Republican parties were high and debilitating to a nation still finding its way. Jefferson won the nation's third presidency at this critical juncture and served two terms, after which he retired to Monticello.

The breadth of Jefferson's skills is astounding. He was a statesman, farmer and zealous gardener, writer, scientist, musician, and philosopher. One admiring contemporary described Jefferson as a man who could "calculate an eclipse, survey an estate, tie an artery, plan an edifice, try a cause, break a horse, dance a minuet, and play a violin." And as a lover of great wine, Jefferson introduced European vinifera grapes to Virginia. He has even been hailed as the father of the American gastronomic revolution, importing from France olive oil, Parmesan cheese, raisins, and pistachios. The

Garden Book, which he kept for upward of half a century, contains a wealth of minutiae, from planting times to the preferred method of grafting peach trees.

It's often noted that this architect of democracy was also a slave owner (he owned about 200 slaves at any given time, and freed only seven after his death, and one of the most enduring mysteries surrounding Jefferson has been whether he had a liaison with Sally Hemings, one of his slaves. DNA tests from 1998 showed that a member of the Jefferson family—many believe Thomas Jefferson himself—fathered her youngest son. Jefferson went through an inquiry into his conduct during his last year as governor of Virginia, and while president, Federalists accused him of improper relations with a white woman and with Hemings.

Virginians love Jefferson because he loved Virginia. Monticello, his experiment in architecture that had him making changes until the day before he died, attracts 500,000 people every year. The University of Virginia, which Jefferson called "the hobby of my old age," is now one of the nation's elite public universities. Charlottesville honors its most famous resident in a number of ways. On April 13—Jefferson's birthday—the Thomas Jefferson Center for the Protection of Free Expression presents the Muzzle Award to those guilty of trying to quash free speech. On the anniversary of his death, Independence Day, Monticello is the site of a naturalization ceremony for new Americans.

☞ *Free* ☉ *Rotunda open daily 9–4:45. University closed during winter break in Dec. and Jan. and spring exams 1st 3 wks of May.*

At the **Virginia Discovery Museum** children can step inside a giant kaleidoscope, explore a reconstructed log cabin, or watch bees in action in a working hive. The hands-on exhibits are meant to interest children (and their parents) in science, the arts, history, and the humanities. Exhibits in the Back Gallery change every few months. ✉ *524 E. Main St., Downtown* ☎ *434/977–1025* ⊕ *www.vadm.org* ☞ *$4* ☉ *Tues.–Sat. 10–5, Sun. 1–5.*

Where to Stay & Eat

$$$–$$$$ ✗**OXO.** Chef-owner John Haywood puts a modern twist on classic French cuisine and changes the menu every few weeks. Notable entrées include oven-roasted beef tenderloin with truffles, mashed potatoes, and sautéed spinach, and pan-seared snapper wrapped in potato crepes. The extensive wine list is mostly Californian. ✉ *215 W. Water St., Downtown* ☎ *434/977–8111* ⊟ *AE, D, MC, V* ☉ *No lunch Sun. and Mon.*

★ $$–$$$ ✗**C&O Restaurant.** Don't let the exterior fool you: behind the boarded-up storefront hung with an illuminated Pepsi sign is an exemplary restaurant. The formal dining room upstairs, the lively bistro downstairs, and the cozy mezzanine in between share a French-influenced menu that has Pacific Rim and American Southwest touches. For a starter try the pan-fried sweetbread medallions; the entrées include steak *chinoise* with fresh ginger, tamari, and scallion cream sauce. The wine list is 300 strong. ✉ *515 E. Water St., Downtown* ☎ *434/971–7044* ⊟ *AE, MC, V.*

$$ $$$ ✗**Duner's.** This former motel diner 5 mi west of Charlottesville fills up early. The fanciful menu, which changes daily, emphasizes fresh, seasonal fare in its seafood and pasta dishes. Appetizers may include lamb and green peppercorn pâté with grilled bread. For an entrée, try morel-mushroom risotto cakes or shrimp in lemongrass and coconut milk over linguine. The red-tile floor and decorative copper pots on the walls keep things bright and warm. ✉ *Rte. 250 W, Ivy* ☎ *434/293–8352* ☞ *Reservations not accepted* ⊟ *MC, V* ☉ *No lunch.*

$–$$$ ✗**Continental Divide.** A neon sign in the window of this locals' favorite says "Get in here"—you might miss the small storefront restaurant otherwise. The food is Southwestern cuisine, with quesadillas, burritos, spicy pork tacos, and enchiladas. The margaritas are potent. Cactus plants decorate the front window, and the booths have funky lights. It can get crowded and convivial, but customers like it that way. ✉ *811 W. Main St., Downtown* ☎ *434/984–0143* ☞ *Reservations not accepted* ⊟ *D, DC, MC, V* ☉ *No lunch.*

$–$$ ✗**Hardware Store.** This is simply a fun, inexpensive restaurant in the Downtown Mall. Deli sandwiches, burgers, crepes, salads, seafood, and ice cream from the soda fountain are what's on sale today in this former Victorian

WORD OF MOUTH

"Charlottesville is lovely. Monticello and UVA have wonderful history. There is cute shopping and dining on the downtown pedestrian mall and you are only a short drive from some beautiful hiking or scenic driving"   –Schlegal1

hardware store. Your condiments will be delivered in a toolbox, and make sure to help yourself at the pickle bar. Some of the wood paneling and brick walls have been here since 1890. ⊠ *316 E. Main St., Downtown* ☎ *434/977–1518 or 800/426–6001* ⊟ *AE, DC, MC, V* ☺ *Closed Sun.*

★ ¢–$ ✕ **Crozet Pizza.** It may look like a shack, but this red clapboard restaurant 12 mi west of Charlottesville serves up what is renowned as some of Virginia's best pizza. You have about three dozen toppings to choose from, including seasonal items such as snow peas and asparagus spears. Like its outside, the interior is rustic, with portraits of the owners' forebears and one wall covered with business cards from around the world. On the weekend, takeout must be ordered hours in advance. ⊠ *Rte. 240, Crozet* ☎ *434/823–2132* ⊟ *No credit cards.*

$$$–$$$$ ✕▣ **Boar's Head Inn.** Set on 55 acres in west Charlottesville, this local landmark resembles an English country inn, with flower gardens, ponds, and a gristmill from 1834. The rooms have king-size four-poster beds and Italian Anichini linens; many have balconies. Some suites have fireplaces. There are lots of activities here—even hot-air ballooning, through a nearby outfitter. The Old Mill Room restaurant ($$$–$$$$) serves new American cuisine and includes venison and seafood; the grilled filet mignon is a savory favorite. The $16 luncheon buffet includes an exceptional selection of salads, soups, meats, and desserts. ⊠ *U.S. 250 W, Ednam Forest, Box 5307, 22905* ☎ *434/296–2181 or 800/476–1988* 🖷 *434/ 972–6019* ⊕ *www.boarsheadinn.com* ↵ *160 rooms, 11 suites* ♨ *3 restaurants, cable TV with movies and video games, in-room data ports, 18-hole golf course, 20 tennis courts, 4 pools, health club, spa, fishing, racquetball, squash, shop, meeting rooms* ⊟ *AE, D, DC, MC, V.*

★ $$–$$$ ✕▣ **Silver Thatch Inn.** Four-poster beds and period antiques are just part of the charm of this 1780 white-clapboard Colonial farmhouse, 8 mi north of town. The friendly hosts help their guests arrange outdoor activities at nearby locations. The popular restaurant ($$–$$$) serves contemporary cuisine—the grilled beef tenderloin is renowned—and has a very fine wine cellar. ⊠ *3001 Hollymead Dr., 22911* ☎ *434/978–4686 or 800/261–0720* 🖷 *434/973–6156* ⊕ *www.silverthatch.com* ↵ *7 rooms* ♨ *Restaurant, pool; no room phones, no room TVs, no kids under 14, no smoking* ⊟ *AE, DC, MC, V* ⦿ *BP.*

★ $$$$ ▣ **Keswick Hall at Monticello.** If you've got the money for it, this 1912 Tuscan villa on 600 lush acres 5 mi east of Charlottesville is a luxurious, cosmopolitan retreat. Guest rooms and common areas are decorated in Laura Ashley fabrics and wallpapers, and each room is furnished with English and American antiques. Some have whirlpool baths and balconies. The 18-hole golf course, designed by Arnold Palmer, spreads across the rear of the estate. There's no check-in desk here; you are welcomed inside as if you are entering someone's home. The facilities of the private Keswick Club are open to those staying overnight. ⊠ *701 Club Dr., Keswick 22947* ☎ *434/979–3440 or 800/274–5391* 🖷 *434/ 977–4171* ⊕ *www.keswick.com* ↵ *40 rooms, 8 suites* ♨ *2 restaurants, dining room, cable TV with movies, in-room broadband,18-hole golf course, 5 tennis courts, 3 pools (1 indoor), health club, spa, fishing, bicycles, croquet, meeting rooms, some pets allowed (fee)* ⊟ *AE, D, DC, MC, V.*

$$$–$$$$ ⊞ **High Meadows Vineyard Inn.** Two styles of architecture are joined by a hall in this bed-and-breakfast (and working vineyard). Listed on the National Register of Historic Places, the inn is 15 mi south of Monticello. Rooms have curtains and bed hangings with a handcrafted look. Dinner is served in the dining room by reservation Wednesday through Saturday. Hors d'oeuvres and samples of Virginia wines are available on the weekend. ⊠ *55 High Meadows La., Scottsville 24590* ☎ *434/ 286–2218 or 800/232–1832* 🖷 *434/286–2124* ⊕ *www.highmeadows. com* ⇔ *9 rooms, 2 cottages* ⚲ *Dining room; no room TVs, no pets* ⊟ *MC, V* ⦿⎮ *BP.*

$$–$$$$ ⊞ **200 South Street Inn.** Two houses, one of them a former brothel, have been combined and restored to create this old-fashioned inn in the historic district, one block from the Downtown Mall. Furnishings throughout are English and Belgian antiques. Several rooms come with a canopy bed, sitting room, fireplace, and whirlpool. ⊠ *200 South St., Downtown, 22902* ☎ *434/979–0200 or 800/964–7008* 🖷 *434/979–4403* ⊕ *www.southstreetinn.com* ⇔ *16 rooms, 3 suites* ⚲ *Cable TV; no smoking* ⊟ *AE, DC, MC, V* ⦿⎮ *CP.*

$$–$$$ ⊞ **Omni Charlottesville.** This attractive member of the luxury chain looms over one end of the Downtown Mall. The triangular rooms at the point of the wedge-shape building get light from two sides. Cherry-color furnishings and sage fabrics decorate the guest quarters, and potted plants soften the bright seven-story atrium lobby. ⊠ *235 W. Main St., Downtown, 22902* ☎ *434/971–5500 or 800/843–6664* 🖷 *434/ 979–4456* ⊕ *www.omnihotels.com* ⇔ *204 rooms, 7 suites* ⚲ *Restaurant, lounge, cable TV with movies and video games, 2 pools (1 indoor), gym, hot tub, sauna, bar, Wi-Fi* ⊟ *AE, D, DC, MC, V.*

$–$$$ ⊞ **Wintergreen Resort.** This is a great place to get away any time of year and still have access to cultural attractions, 25 mi southwest of Charlottesville (via I–64, U.S. 250 and Rte. 151). With 6,700 acres of forest, six restaurants, and three golf courses, Wintergreen is more like a community in itself than just a resort. Skiing and snowboarding are the central attractions, with 20 downhill slopes and five chairlifts. In summer the stunning Blue Ridge location means that hiking, mountain biking, horseback riding, golf, tennis, and swimming can all be done in the cool that comes with a high elevation. One of the golf courses, at nearly 4,000 feet, is the highest in Virginia. Accommodations at the resort include everything from studio apartments to seven-bedroom houses. Most rooms have fireplaces and full kitchens; the housing units' wood exteriors blend into the surrounding forest. ⊠ *Rte. 664, Wintergreen 22958* ☎ *434/325–2200 or 800/266–2444* 🖷 *434/325–8003* ⊕ *www. wintergreenresort.com* ⇔ *305 units* ⚲ *6 restaurants, some kitchens, some kitchenettes, Wi-Fi, 9-hole golf course, 2 18-hole golf courses, 24 tennis courts, 2 pools (1 indoor), lake, gym, spa, boating, bicycles, hiking, horseback riding, downhill skiing, bar, laundry facilities, laundry service, convention center* ⊟ *AE, D, MC, V.*

$ ⊞ **Best Western Cavalier Inn.** This facility's best feature is its location, directly across the street from the grounds of the University of Virginia and one block from the sports arena. Rates include a deluxe continental breakfast. ⊠ *105 Emmet St., University, 22903* ☎ *434/296–8111*

4

☏ *434/290–3523* ⊕ *www.bestwestern.com* ⇗ *118 rooms* ⚭ *Cable TV, pool, lounge, in-room data ports, meeting rooms, airport shuttle* 🖃 *AE, D, DC, MC, V* ¡⊙¡ *CP.*

¢ 🖵 **English Inn.** A model treatment of the B&B theme on a large but comfortable scale, the English Inn has a three-story atrium lobby with cascading plants. The suites have a sitting room, wet bar, king-size bed, and reproduction antiques; other rooms have modern furnishings. ⊠ *2000 Morton Dr., Barracks/Rugby 22901* ☏ *434/971–9900 or 800/786–5400* ☏ *434/977–8008* ⊕ *www.englishinncharlottesville.com* ⇗ *67 rooms, 21 suites* ⚭ *Cable TV, Wi-Fi, indoor pool, gym, sauna, dry cleaning, airport shuttle* 🖃 *AE, D, DC, MC, V* ¡⊙¡ *BP.*

Nightlife & the Arts

For listings of cultural events, music, and movies, and a guide to restaurants, pick up a free copy of the *C-Ville Weekly* (www.c-ville.com), an arts and entertainment newspaper available in restaurants and hotels throughout the city. If you're near the University of Virginia campus, grab a free copy of the student newspaper, the *Cavalier Daily* (www.cavalierdaily.com), for the latest on college sports and events.

BARS & CLUBS **Miller's** (⊠ 109 W. Main St., Downtown Mall, Downtown ☏ 434/971–8511), a large and comfortable bar, hosts blues, folk, and jazz musicians. Rock musician Dave Matthews used to tend bar here. **Tokyo Rose** (⊠ 2171 Ivy Rd., University ☏ 434/295–7673) is a sushi bar that doubles as a performance space for up-and-coming independent rock bands.

COFFEEHOUSES **Prism Coffeehouse** (⊠ 214 Rugby Rd., University ☏ 434/977–7476) has been a venue for folk music since a group of university students opened it in 1966. National acoustic acts have included an Appalachian string band as well as bluegrass and Irish-music performers. No smoking or alcohol is allowed. It's closed July and August.

FESTIVALS In March, **Virginia Festival of the Book** (☏ 434/924–6890) draws authors that have included Garrison Keillor and Michael Ondaatje. Thousands attend the festival, which is open to the public and promotes literacy while celebrating the book.

Every autumn, Charlottesville hosts the **Virginia Film Festival** (☏ 800/882–3378), with screenings of important new movies, panel discussions, and appearances by stars of the cinema. The movies are shown at four sites around the university and downtown.

Sports & the Outdoors

CANOEING & **James River Runners Inc.** (⊠ 10082 Hatton Ferry Rd., Scottsville ☏ 434/
KAYAKING 286–2338), about 35 minutes south of Charlottesville, offers canoe, kayak, tubing, and rafting trips down the James.

Shopping

Charlottesville, at heart an academic community, supports a large number of independent bookstores, especially those that specialize in used and antiquarian books. Whether it's a rare first edition you are seeking or just some unique bargains, try **Blue Whale Books** (⊠ 115 W. Main St., Downtown ☏ 434/296–4646). Run by an antiquarian book dealer, the shop has thousands of books in all categories and price ranges, from one dollar to several hundred. **Daedalus Bookshop** (✉ 123 4th St. NE, Downtown ☎ 434/293–7595) has three floors of books crammed into every nook and cranny. **Heartwood Books** (✉ 5 Elliewood Ave., University ☎ 434/295–7083), close to the university campus, stocks scholarly works, including a good collection of theology and philosophy. Legal-thriller master John Grisham kicks off book tours at **New Dominion Bookshop** (✉ 404 E. Main St. Downtown ☎ 434/295–2552).

■ TIP→ **For a complete list of bookstores in Charlottesville, look on the Web at www.vabook.org/lit_links/bookstores.html.**

The **Downtown Mall** (✉ Main St., Downtown) is a six-block brick pedestrian mall with specialty stores, cinemas, art galleries, restaurants, and coffeehouses in restored 19th- and early 20th-century buildings.

Orange

❸ *25 mi northeast of Charlottesville via Rte. 20, 60 mi northwest of Richmond.*

Orange is a fertile agricultural area bearing reminders of the Civil War. Among the many estates dotting the countryside is the home of our nation's fourth president.

During the Civil War, a handsome Greek revival hotel, now the **Exchange Hotel Civil War Museum,** was transformed into a Confederate receiving hospital for wounded and dying soldiers. In addition to weapons, uniforms, and the personal effects of Union and Confederate soldiers, the museum displays the often crude medical equipment used for amputations, tooth extractions, and bloodletting. One room re-creates a hospital ward; an estimated 70,000 soldiers were treated here between 1862 and 1865. ✉ *400 S. Main St., Gordonsville* ☎ *540/832–2944* 💲*$6* ☉ *Mar.–Nov., Mon.–Sat. 10–4, Sun. 1–4.*

The **James Madison Museum** presents a comprehensive exhibition on the Founding Father most responsible for the Constitution (Madison became president in 1809). The collection includes some of the china and glassware recovered from the White House before the British torched it during the War of 1812. The fourth president's tiny Campeachy chair, an 18th-century piece made for him by his friend Thomas Jefferson, shows how short he was. ✉ *129 Caroline St.* ☎ *540/672–1776* 💲*$4* ☉ *Weekdays 9–5, Sat. 10–5, Sun. 1–5.*

Just outside of Orange is **Montpelier,** the former residence of James Madison (1751–1836), the fourth president of the United States. A massive renovation is under way to remove parts of the mansion added by its 20th-century owners, the duPont family. It's fascinating to watch the mansion being restored to its early-19th-century Madisonian state; a house tour allows access to many areas being revamped, a project slated to last until 2008 at least. Some of the Madisons' possessions, as well as a tribute to the "Father of the Constitution," have been set up in an Education Center on the grounds. The walking tour includes a stop at the cemetery where James and his wife, Dolley, are buried. Exotic conifers planted by the duPonts dot the meadowlike grounds, and a walk-

CLOSE UP

Virginia Wineries

JAMESTOWN'S COLONIAL SETTLERS are believed to have made the first wine in Virginia, but only in the past 25 years has the Commonwealth's wine industry truly come into its own. The number of wineries here has grown from fewer than 10 in the 1970s to more than 70 today. As you drive through the state, keep an eye out for grape-cluster signs on the highway, which identify nearby wineries. For more information on Virginia vineyards and wineries, contact the Virginia Wineries Association (☎ 800/828-4637 ⊕ www.virginiawines.org) or the Jeffersonian Wine Grape Growers Society (☎ 434/296-4188 ⊕ www. monticellowinetrail.org), sponsor of the Monticello Wine Trail.

Among Central and Western Virginia's more popular wineries are Barboursville Vineyards, near Charlottesville, and Château Morrisette Winery, on the Blue Ridge Parkway in the southern part of the state.

Barboursville Vineyards. This vineyard between Charlottesville and Orange was the first in the state to grow only vinifera (old-world) grapes. The grapes were planted in 1976 on the former plantation of James Barbour, governor from 1812 to 1814. His house, designed by Thomas Jefferson, was gutted by fire in 1884; the ruins remain. ✉ *17655 Winery Rd., near intersection of Rtes. 20 and 23, Barboursville* ☎ *540/832-3824* ⊕ *www.barboursvillewine.com* ☜ *Tours free; tastings $4* ⊗ *Tastings Mon.-Sat. 10-5, Sun. 11-5.*

Château Morrisette Winery. With the Rock Castle Gorge nearby, this winery has spectacular surroundings. Tastings allow you to sample the dozen different wines produced here. ✉ *Winery Rd., off Rte. 726, west of Blue Ridge Pkwy. at milepost 171.5, Meadows of Dan* ☎ *540/593-2865* ⊕ *www.thedogs.com* ☜ *Tour and tasting $5* ⊗ *Mon.-Thurs. 10-5, Fri. and Sat. 10-6, Sun. 11-5.*

---

ing path wanders amid an old-growth forest. The annual Montpelier Hunt Races, a steeplechase, have been held since 1934. When they run, on the first Saturday in November, the house tour is canceled. Admission to the races is $15. ✉ *Rte. 20, 4 mi southwest of Orange* ☎ *540/ 672-2728* ⊕ *www.montpelier.org* ☜ *$11* ⊗ *Apr.–Oct., daily 9:30–5; Nov.–Mar., daily 9:30–4:30.*

St. Thomas's Episcopal Church (1833), the one surviving example of Jeffersonian church architecture, is a replica of Charlottesville's demolished Christ Church, which Jefferson designed. It's here that Robert E. Lee worshipped during the winter of 1863–64. The church's biggest decorative asset is its Tiffany window. ✉ *119 Caroline St.* ☎ *540/672-3761* ☜ *Donations accepted* ⊗ *Tours by appt.*

WORD OF MOUTH

"We loved visiting Orange on our 'wine weekends' in Virginia. It is a lovely little town in beautiful country with some stunning old farms and homes. Also some excellent restaurants and, of course, the wineries in close proximity!"

–LadyofLesire

Where to Stay & Eat

★ **$$$$** ✕▣ **Willow Grove Inn.** This carefully preserved 1778 Virginia plantation house, an example of Jeffersonian classical revival architecture, served
as an encampment during the Revolutionary War and lay under siege
during the Civil War. On 37 acres a mile north of Orange, the inn has
furnishings from the 18th and 19th centuries. Rooms in the weaver's
cottage and two-room schoolhouse have fireplaces and private veran-
das. A baby grand piano accompanies the candlelight dining in the formal dining room (**$$$$**), where prix-fixe dinners are served. The menu's
regional Southern dishes may include smoked Rappahannock trout
cakes, toasted peanut- and pecan-crusted rack of lamb, or grilled quail
with corn pudding. Clark's Tavern (**$$–$$$**) is more casual, with items
such as panfried catfish and crayfish étouffée. ✉ *14079 Plantation
Way, 22960* ☎ *540/672–5982 or 800/949–1778* 🖷 *540/672–3674*
⊕ *www.willowgroveinn.com* ⇨ *5 rooms, 6 cottages* ♧ *Restaurant,
bar, pub, Internet room, some pets allowed; no room TVs* 🖃 *AE, D,
DC, MC, V* ⌑ *MAP.*

$$–$$$ ▣ **Mayhurst Inn.** An architectural rarity in the South, this Italianate Vic-
torian mansion was built in 1859 by a grandnephew of James Madison,
and generals Stonewall Jackson and Robert E. Lee were early guests. Now
Mayhurst is a cozy and comfortable B&B surrounded by 37 acres of woods
with hiking trails. Its rooms have floor-to-ceiling windows, marble fireplaces, and antique furnishings; some have whirlpool baths. ✉ *12460
Mayhurst La., 22960* ☎ *540/672–5597 or 888/672–5597* 🖷 *540/672–
7447* ⊕ *www.mayhurstinn.com* ⇨ *8 rooms, 2 suites* ♧ *Fishing, hiking;
no TV in some rooms, no smoking* 🖃 *AE, MC, V* ⌑ *BP.*

Washington

❹ *63 mi north of Charlottesville.*

Known as Little Washington to differentiate it from its big sister, this
tiny town packs in antiques shops, galleries, custom jewelry shops, and
two theaters in roughly five blocks—perfect for an afternoon stroll.

Where to Stay & Eat

$$$$ ✕▣ **The Inn at Little Washington.** What began as a small-town eatery in
Fodor's Choice 1978 has grown into a legend. The rich interior of the three-story white-
★ frame inn is the work of Joyce Conway-Evans, who has designed theatrical sets and rooms in English royal houses. Plush canopy beds,
marble bathrooms, and fresh flowers make the rooms sumptuous. Chef
Patrick O'Connell's much-loved New American food is served in a
slate-floor dining room with William Morris wallpaper. The seven-
course dinner costs $168 per person on Saturday, $148 on Friday, and
$138 Sunday through Thursday, not including wine and drinks; rooms
are equally pricey. ✉ *Middle and Main Sts., 22747* ☎ *540/675–3800*
🖷 *540/675–3100* ⊕ *www.theinnatlittlewashington.com* ⇨ *11 rooms,
3 suites* ♧ *Restaurant, in-room safes, bicycles* 🖃 *MC, V* ☺ *Hotel and
restaurant closed Tues. except in May and Oct.* ⌑ *CP.*

$$–$$$ ✕▣ **The Blue Rock Inn.** This former farmhouse is on 80 bucolic acres against
a backdrop of the Blue Ridge Mountains, with a fishing pond, rolling

pastures, and 7½ acres of vineyards spread across the foreground. An equestrian center on-site boards horses (you may bring your own) and trains them for riders; there's also a polo ring and steeplechase course. The guest rooms, simply furnished with light woods and lace curtains, are pleasing; the four upstairs have private balconies. The restaurant ($$$) uses many local ingredients for a menu that includes catfish and various Mediterranean dishes; it's closed Monday and Tuesday. ⊠ *12567 Lee Hwy., 22747* ☎ *540/987–3190* 🖶 *540/987–3193* ⊕ *www.thebluerockinn.com* ➦ *5 rooms* 🛁 *Restaurant, fishing, hiking, horseback riding, pub, some pets allowed; no room phones, no room TVs* 🚭 *AE, D, DC, MC, V* 🍴 *BP.*

Lynchburg

❺ *66 mi southeast of Charlottesville via Rte. 29, 110 mi west of Richmond.*

Lynchburg is best known today as the home of the Rev. Jerry Falwell, the evangelist who founded the politically and socially conservative "Moral Majority" in the 1980s. Falwell's rapidly growing Liberty University and Thomas Road Baptist Church are indeed centerpiece elements of Lynchburg, but do not define the entire city. Lynchburg was founded by John Lynch, a Quaker pacifist, but its most prominent landmark is Monument Terrace, a war memorial: at the foot and head of the 139 limestone and granite steps that ascend to the Old City Courthouse are statues honoring a World War I doughboy and a Confederate soldier.

At the **Anne Spencer House and Gardens** you can step into "Edankraal," the studio of this late poet of the Harlem Renaissance. Hers is the only work of a Virginian to appear in the *Norton Anthology of Modern American and English Poetry.* A librarian at one of Lynchburg's segregated black schools, Spencer (1882–1975) penned most of her work in this back-garden sanctuary, which has been left completely intact with her writing desk, bookcases, mementos, and walls tacked with photos and news clippings. ⊠*1313 Pierce St.* ☎*434/845–1313* ⊕*www.lynchburgbiz.com/anne_spencer/tours.html* 🎟 *$5* 🕙 *Tours by appt.*

At the **Legacy Museum of African-American History,** the rotating exhibits focus on such themes as health and medicine, education, business, the civil rights struggle, and the contributions African-Americans have made to society, the arts, and politics. ⊠ *403 Monroe St.* ☎ *434/845–3455* ⊕ *www.legacymuseum.org* 🎟 *$2* 🕙 *Thurs.–Sat. noon–4, Sun. 2–4, and by appt.*

The mansion on Daniel's Hill, **Point of Honor,** was built in 1815 on the site of a duel. Once part of a 900-acre estate, this redbrick house surrounded by lawns retains a commanding view of the James River. The facade is elegantly symmetrical, with two octagonal bays joined by a balustrade on each of the building's two stories. The interiors have been restored and furnished with pieces authentic to the early-19th-century Federal period. ⊠ *112 Cabell St.* ☎ *434/847–1459* ⊕ *www.pointofhonor.org* 🎟 *$6* 🕙 *Mon.–Sat. 10–4, Sun. noon–4.*

★ A must-see on the Thomas Jefferson tour of Virginia is his "occasional retreat," **Poplar Forest.** The octagonal architecture, now standing in a residential neighborhood and surrounded by only a few remaining poplars, was conceived and built by Jefferson, and he sometimes stayed here between 1806 and 1813. This Palladian hermitage exemplifies the architect's sublime sense of order that is so evident at Monticello.

Erected on a slope, the house has a front that's one story high, with a two-story rear elevation. The octagon's center is a square, skylighted dining room flanked by two smaller octagons. The restoration to its Jefferson-era state is ongoing, and likely to continue for years to come. Every July 4, there's a free celebration that includes a reading of the Declaration of Independence and living-history exhibits. ⊠ *Rte. 661, Forest* ☎ *434/525–1806* ⊕ *www.poplarforest.org* ⊠ *$8* ☉ *Apr.–Nov., Wed.–Mon. 10–4.*

OFF THE
BEATEN
PATH
Fodor'sChoice
★

APPOMATTOX COURT HOUSE – To many in Virginia, the Civil War has never ended, but the history books say it ended here, 25 mi east of Lynchburg, on April 9, 1865, when Confederate General Lee surrendered the Army of Northern Virginia to General Grant, leader of pursuing Union forces. There are 27 structures in the national historical park, restored to its 1865 appearance; most can be entered. A highlight is the reconstructed McLean House, in whose parlor the articles of surrender were signed. ⊠ *3 mi north of Appomattox, on State Rte. 24* ☎ *434/352–8987* ⊕ *www.nps.gov/apco/* ⊠ *June–Aug., $4; Sept.–May, $3* ☉ *Daily 8:30–5.*

RED HILL–PATRICK HENRY NATIONAL MEMORIAL – In the town of Brookneal is the final home of Revolutionary War patriot Patrick Henry, whose "Give me liberty or give me death" speech inspired a generation. The 1770s house has been reconstructed on its original site and contains numerous furnishings owned by the Henry family. Henry's grave is on the property. ⊠ *35 mi southeast of Lynchburg, off Rte. 619, Brookneal* ☎ *434/376–2044* ⊠ *$6* ☉ *Apr.–Oct., daily 9–5; Nov.–Mar., daily 9–4.*

Where to Eat

$–$$ ✕ **Meriwether's Market Restaurant.** Dubbing itself a "casual gourmet restaurant," Meriwether's offers American dishes generally made with local and regional ingredients, from game to seafood. For an entrée, try the spicy shrimp and grits or a specialty pizza. A lighter "intermezzo" menu is available to carry you through the lull between lunch and dinner (2:30–5:30). ⊠ *4925 Boonsboro Rd.* ☎ *434/384–3311* ▤ *AE, D, MC, V* ☉ *Closed Sun.*

Sports & the Outdoors

BIKING Lynchburg's fine municipal "greenway" system of trails is open to both bicyclists and hikers. The **Blackwater Creek Natural Area** (☎ 434/847–1640, City of Lynchburg Parks and Recreation Dept.) has more than 12 mi of trails, most of them level and asphalt, which wind through a pleasant tree-shaded natural area within the city limits. One trail goes through a 500-foot tunnel. The **Percival's Island Trail**, three blocks from one edge of the natural area and in the shadow of the downtown skyline, extends for more than a mile along a narrow strip of land in the middle of the James River.

To rent a bike, contact **Blackwater Creek Bike Rental** (✉ 1611 Concord Tpke. ☎ 434/845–4030), which is open weekdays 1 to 5 and weekends from 9 to sunset.

Shenandoah National Park

Southern entrance 18 mi west of Charlottesville via I–81; northern entrance at Front Royal.

Though Shenandoah National Park is only a narrow ribbon on the map, stretching 80 mi along the Blue Ridge but rarely more than 5 mi wide, it is easy to imagine being much deeper in the wilderness as you travel through it or spend a night camping here. Steep, wooded ridges with rocky slopes stand out in the foreground of vistas taking in the Shenandoah Valley to the west and the Piedmont to the east. Skyline Drive traverses the park end to end from Waynesboro to Front Royal and is the most common way to see the park. But hikers can find beautiful terrain just yards from the drive on some of the park's 500 mi of trails, trout fishers may wade into more than 25 streams, and riders can rent horses for wilderness trail rides. Those who want to know more about the area's flora and fauna may want to take a guided hike, which naturalists lead daily throughout the summer. The seasonal activities of the park are outlined in the *Shenandoah Overlook,* a free newspaper you can pick up on entering the park. The park parallels I–81; the northern limit at Front Royal is close to I–66, and the southern end at Waynesboro is close to I–64. ⓓ *Park Superintendent, Box 348, Rte. 4, Luray 22835* ☎ *540/999–3500* ⊕ *www.nps. gov/shen* ☞ *Park and Skyline Dr. $15 car ($10 car Dec.–Feb.), $10 motorcycle, $8 bicycle or pedestrian; tickets are valid 7 days.*

>
> **WORD OF MOUTH**
>
> "Skyline Drive . . . is literally like driving at the edge of the sky. Absolutely breathtaking."
>
> –Charlottesmom

Fodor'sChoice **Skyline Drive** runs 105 mi, alternating between open vistas and forest-
★ hemmed stretches and offering easily accessible wilderness. During weekends and holidays it can seem a little too much like city driving— a 35-mph speed limit, rubber-necking leaf-lookers, narrow overlook turnouts, and the occasional black bear sighting can back traffic up uncomfortably. It's best to choose a weekday and allow the entire day; you may want to spend an hour or two resting on one roadside boulder. Winter is a wonderful time to experience the park's rugged beauty with few crowds, but many facilities are closed and bouts of ice and snow bring out barricades on parts of the drive.

■ TIP→ Continue south on Skyline Drive past the park gates and over Interstate 64, and the road becomes the Blue Ridge Parkway, which continues 471 mi south to Cherokee, N.C. Unlike Skyline Drive, the parkway is free, and the speed limit is 45 mph.

Luray Caverns, 9 mi west of Skyline Drive on U.S. 211, are the largest caverns in the state. The world's only "stalacpipe organ" is composed of stalactites (calcite formations hanging from the ceilings of the caverns) that have been tuned to concert pitch and are tapped by rubber-tip plungers. The organ is played electronically for every tour and may be played manually on special occasions. A one-hour tour begins every 20 minutes. ⊠ *U.S. 211, Luray* ☎ *540/743–6551* ⊕ *www.luraycaverns.com*

> ### CAVE TOURS
>
> Want to make a caverns tour of Virginia? Other cave tours include Skyline Caverns near Front Royal, Shenandoah Caverns and Endless Caverns near New Market, Grand Caverns at Grottoes, and Dixie Caverns near Roanoke. For a complete listing of Virginia cave tours, go to www.virginia.org and search "Caverns."

4

$18 ⊙ *Mid-Mar.–mid-June, daily 9–6; mid-June–Labor Day, daily 9–7; Labor Day–Nov., daily 9–6, Nov.–mid-Mar., weekdays 9–4, weekends 9–5.*

Where to Stay

$$$ ⌂ **Jordan Hollow Farm.** The oldest of the four buildings here is a 1790 farmhouse, now a restaurant serving American regional cuisine. The youngest structure, built of hand-hewn logs almost 200 years later, contains four of the inn's most luxurious rooms, which include a fireplace, whirlpool, and TV. The 150-acre horse farm is near the tiny town of Stanley, 6 mi from Luray and 15 mi from Shenandoah National Park. From here you can gaze out over pastures full of horses and playful llamas toward a backdrop of the Blue Ridge Mountains. The only "pets" allowed are horses, which can be boarded here. Nearby trails are good for hiking and mountain biking. ⊠ *326 Hawksbill Park Rd., Stanley 22851* ☎ *540/778–2285 or 888/418–7000* 🖶 *540/778–1759* ⊕ *www.jordanhollow.com* ➟ *8 rooms, 7 suites* ◊ *Restaurant, refrigerators, cable TV, in-room DVDs, bicycles, hiking, bar, meeting rooms; no smoking, no kids* ☰ *AE, D, DC, MC, V* ⦿ *BP.*

$ ⌂ **Skyland Resort.** At the highest point on Skyline Drive (3,680 feet), with views across the Shenandoah Valley, this facility has lodging that ranges from rustic cabins and motel-style rooms to suites. There's no air-conditioning, but days above 80°F are rare at this altitude. ⊠ *Milepost 41.7 on Skyline Dr., 22835* ☎ *800/778–2851* ⊕ *www.visitshenandoah.com/lodging.shtml* ➟ *177 rooms* ◊ *Restaurant, bar, meeting rooms; no a/c, no room phones, no TV in some rooms* ☰ *AE, D, DC, MC, V* ⊙ *Closed Dec.–mid-Mar.*

△ **Shenandoah National Park.** Shenandoah has more than 600 campsites in four campgrounds, plus a fifth primitive campground (Dundo) for large educational groups. The Big Meadows Campground, at the approximate midpoint of the park, accepts reservations; other campsites are available on a first-come, first-served basis. ⊡ *Shenandoah National Park, Box 727, Luray 22835* ☎ *540/999–3231, 800/365–2267 for Big Meadows reservations* 🖶 *540/999–3601* ⊕ *www.nps.gov/shen* ➟ *53 tent-only sites, 164 RV or tent sites, 7 sites for educational groups* ◊ *Laundry facilities, flush toilets, dump station, drinking water, show-*

ers ✍ *Tent or RV sites $16–$19 per night, group sites $30* ▤ *AE, D, MC, V* ⊙ *Spring through Nov.*

Sports & the Outdoors

CANOEING   At **Downriver Canoe** (✉ Rte. 613, near Front Royal ☎ 540/635–5526), day and overnight trips start at $39 per canoe (or $28 per kayak, $14 per tube, and $65 per raft). **Front Royal Canoe** (✉ U.S. 340, near Front Royal ☎ 540/635–5440 or 800/270–8808) offers a $16 tube trip as well as canoe, kayak, and raft trips of one hour up to three days for $35–$120. The company also rents boats and sells fishing accessories. **Shenandoah River Outfitters** (✉ Rte. 684, 6502 S. Page Valley Rd., Luray 22835 ☎ 540/743–4159) rents canoes and kayaks for $20 to $50.

FISHING   To take advantage of the trout that abound in the 50 streams of Shenandoah National Park, you need a Virginia fishing license; a five-day license costs $5 ($12 for a year) and it's available in season (early April to mid-October) at concession stands along Skyline Drive.

HIKING   The **Appalachian Trail** is more than 2,000 mi long, but you don't have to go that far, or even 2,000 feet, along it to see glorious foliage, rock formations, and wildlife. The trail zigzags across Skyline Drive through the park, offering easy access by car, variable hike lengths from a few feet to many miles, and connections with the more than 500 mi of the park's own trail network.

HORSEBACK   **Trail rides** leave from the park's Skyland Stables several times daily from
RIDING   April through October, and on weekends in November. The route follows White Oak Canyon trail, which passes several waterfalls; you can choose a one-hour ride or a 2½-hour ride. You must book 24 hours in advance. ✉ *Skyland Lodge, milepost 41.7, near Luray* ☎ *540/999–2210* ⊙ *Apr.–Oct., daily 8–5; Nov., weekends 8–5.*

SHENANDOAH VALLEY

The fertile hills of the Shenandoah Valley reminded Colonial settlers from Germany, Ireland, and Britain of the homelands they left behind. They brought an agrarian lifestyle and Protestant beliefs that eventually spread across much of the Midwest. Today, the valley is full of historic, cultural, and geological places of interest, including Civil War sites; Woodrow Wilson's birthplace and a reproduction of Shakespeare's Globe Theatre, both at Staunton; many beautifully adorned caverns; and the famous hot mineral springs in aptly named Bath County.

Winchester

❻ *129 mi north of Charlottesville, 136 mi northwest of Richmond.*

Winchester served as a headquarters for Colonel George Washington during the French and Indian War. During the Civil War it was an important crossroads near the front line. It changed hands 72 times during the war, and was General Stonewall Jackson's headquarters for nearly two years. Things are more peaceful today; the biggest attraction is the Shenandoah Apple Blossom Festival in May. Specialty boutiques, regional art galleries, and antiques stores are throughout the town's 45-block historic district, especially on the six-block pedestrian mall. Winchester's biggest claim to 20th-century fame is as the birthplace of country music legend Patsy Cline; thousands visit her gravesite each year at the Shenandoah Memorial Park cemetery, where a bell tower memorializes her.

The **Museum of the Shenandoah Valley** brings together fine and decorative art collections and multimedia presentations that reflect the region's cultural history. The museum complex includes the Glen Burnie Historic House and Gardens, a 1736 Georgian country estate surrounded by 25 acres of formal gardens that was the home of Winchester's founder, Colonel James Wood. The collections include a gallery with 18th- and 19th-century furniture, fine arts, and decorative objects gathered by the last family member to live in the house, Julian Wood Glass Jr., who died in 1992. Another gallery assembles shadow box rooms and miniature furnished houses. ⊠ *901 Amherst St.* ☎ *540/662–1473 or 888/556– 5799* ⊕ *www.shenandoahmuseum.org* ⊠ *$12 for museum, house, and gardens; $6–$10 for other combinations* ⊙ *Museum Tues.–Sun. 10–4, house and gardens Mar.–Nov., daily 10–4.*

Stonewall Jackson's Headquarters Museum is a restored 1854 home. Jackson used this as his base of operations during the Valley Campaign in 1861–62. Among the artifacts on display are his prayer book and camp table. The reproduction wallpaper was a gift from the actress Mary Tyler Moore; it was her great-grandfather Lt. Col. Lewis T. Moore who lent Jackson the use of the house. A $7.50 block ticket purchased at the museum also includes entry to two nearby historical attractions: **George Washington's Office Museum,** a preserved log cabin where Washington briefly lived during the French and Indian War, and **Abram's Delight Museum,** the oldest residence in Winchester. The stone house was owned by Isaac Hollingsworth, a prominent Quaker. ⊠ *415 N. Braddock St.* ☎ *540/ 667–3242* ⊕ *www.winchesterhistory.org* ⊠ *$3.50* ⊙ *Apr.–Oct., Mon.–Sat. 10–4, Sun. noon–4; Nov.–Mar., Fri. and Sat. 10–4, Sun. noon–4.*

Where to Stay & Eat

$$–$$$$ ✕ **Violino Ristorante Italiano.** Homemade pasta—about 20 different kinds—fills the menu in this cheery, yellow-stucco restaurant in the city's Old Town. Owners Franco and Marcella Stocco and their son Riccardo (the men are chefs; Marcella manages the dining room) serve up their native northern Italian cuisine, including lobster *pansotti* (lobster-filled ravioli in a sauce of white wine and lemon). A strolling violinist entertains diners on the weekends. The outdoor patio, enclosed by potted plants, is a quiet spot in the midst of street bustle. ⊠ *181 N. Loudoun St.* ☎ *540/667–8006* ⊟ *AE, D, DC, MC, V* ⊙ *Closed Sun.*

$$–$$$ ✕ **L'Auberge Provencale.** Chef-owner Alain Borel and his wife, Celeste,
Fodor'sChoice   of Avignon, France, bring the warm elegance of the south of France to
★   this 1750s country inn, originally a sheep farm owned by Lord Fairfax. Rooms are eclectically decorated with French art and fabrics, and Victorian wicker and antiques; some have fireplaces. Breakfast includes fresh homemade croissants and apple crepes with maple syrup. The acclaimed prix-fixe restaurant serves authentic Provençale cuisine ($82 per person; reservations essential on weekends), dinner only, and is closed Monday

and Tuesday. ⊠ *Rte. 340, White Post 22663* ☏ *540/837–1375 or 800/ 638–1702* 🖷 *540/837–2004* ⊕ *www.laubergeprovencale.com* ⋤ *10 rooms, 4 suites* ᕃ *Restaurant, pool; no room phones, no room TVs, no kids under 10, no smoking* ⊟ *AE, D, MC, V* ☉ *Closed Jan.* ¶◎¶ *BP.*

Middletown

❼ *6 mi south of Winchester.*

Middletown has one of the area's loveliest historic homes. **Belle Grove,** an elegant farmhouse and 100-acre working farm, is a monument to the rural and the refined, two qualities that exist in harmony in the architecture here and throughout the region. Constructed in 1797 out of limestone quarried on the property, the building reflects the influence of Thomas Jefferson, said to have been a consultant. Originally built for Major Isaac Hite and his wife, Nelly (President James Madison's sister), this was the headquarters of the Union general Philip Sheridan during the Battle of Cedar Creek (1864), a crucial defeat for the Confederacy. Part of the battle was fought on the farm. ⊠ *Rte. 11* ☏ *540/869–2028* ⊕ *www.bellegrove.org* ⊠ *$7* ☉ *Apr.–Oct., Mon.–Sat. 10–3:15, Sun. 1–4:15; Nov., Sat. 10–4, Sun. noon–5.*

Where to Stay

$ ▦ **Wayside Inn.** This inn has been welcoming travelers since 1797, when it was a popular stagecoach stop. The 18th century is preserved through the extensive collection of antiques and fine art, which serve to make each room distinct. Some rooms have small bathrooms and lack a view, but all are pleasingly decorated. Rates include a continental breakfast on weekdays. The dining room serves regional cuisine, such as spoon bread, peanut soup, and country ham. ⊠ *7783 Main St., 22645* ☏ *540/869–1797* 🖷 *540/869–6038* ⊕ *www.alongthewayside.com* ⋤ *21 rooms, 2 suites* ᕃ *Restaurant, cable TV, bar, Wi-Fi, meeting rooms; no smoking* ⊟ *AE, D, DC, MC, V.*

▌EN
ROUTE

The **Strasburg Antique Emporium** (⊠ 150 N. Massanutten St., Strasburg ☏ 540/465–3711 ☉ Fri. and Sat. 10–7, Sun.–Thurs. 10–5), 5 mi south of Middletown, covers 1.4 acres. It's in the quirky and historic downtown of Strasburg, which was settled by Germans. Inside the emporium, more than 100 dealers and artisans sell everything from furniture to jewelry to vintage clothing.

Shopping

Route 11 Potato Chips (⊠ 2325 1st St. ☏ 540/869–0104 or 800/294–7783) makes chips: lightly salted, flavored with dill or barbecue, and the extremely hot "death rain," spiced with habanero and chipotle powder. On Friday (10–6) and Saturday (9–5), the factory is open to the public, who can watch its potato chips take shape.

New Market

❽ *35 mi southwest of Middletown via I–81.*

At New Market the Confederates had a victory at the late date of 1864. Inside the Hall of Valor, in the 260-acre **New Market Battlefield Historical Park,** a stained-glass window mosaic commemorates the battle, in which 257 Virginia Military Institute cadets, some as young as 15, were mobilized to improve the odds against superior Union numbers; 10 were killed. This circular building contains a chronology of the war, and a short film deals with Stonewall Jackson's legendary campaign in the Shenandoah Valley. A farmhouse that figured in the fighting still stands on the premises. The battle is reenacted at the park each May. ⊠ *I–81, Exit 264* ☏ *540/740–3101* ⌨ *$8* ⊙ *Daily 9–5.*

Nightlife & the Arts

The **Shenandoah Valley Music Festival** brings classical, jazz, and folk music to the Allegheny Mountains on weekends from May to September. The events are held at the Orkney Springs Hotel, an early-19th-century spa that's now an Episcopal retreat. Arts and crafts displays and an ice-cream social precede each concert. Concertgoers can sit on the lawn for $14 or in one of two pavilions for around $21; call ahead to reserve tickets. A bus to the festival from Woodstock (Exit 283 on I–81) costs $5. ⊠ *Rte. 263, 2 mi south of Bryce Resort* ☏ *540/459–3396.*

Sports & the Outdoors

FISHING **Murray's Fly Shop** (⊠ 121 Main St., Edinburg ☏ 540/984–4212), 15 mi north of New Market, is the place for advice on fishing the Shenandoah River or local trout streams. The store sells more than 30,000 flies and has hundreds of rods and reels available. A stream report, updated weekly, is available on the store's Web site.

Harrisonburg

❾ *18 mi southwest of New Market via Exit 251 from I–81.*

Harrisonburg is a workaday market town surrounded by rich farmlands. Settled in 1739, it's a stronghold of Mennonites, who wear plain clothes and drive horse-drawn buggies. The city is also a center of higher education, with James Madison University and Eastern Mennonite College in town and Bridgewater College nearby.

At the **Virginia Quilt Museum,** you can see examples of quilts made throughout the mid-Atlantic region and learn about the international heritage of quilting. ⊠ *301 S. Main St.* ☏ *540/433–3818* ⊕ *www.vaquiltmuseum.org* ⌨ *$5* ⊙ *Mon. and Thurs.–Sat. 10–4, Sun. 1–4.*

Where to Stay & Eat

★ $ ✕⊞ **Joshua Wilton House.** A row of trees guards the privacy of this circa 1888 B&B, decorated in the Victorian style and set on a large yard at the edge of the "Old Town" district. The sunroom and back patio are built for relaxation. Ask for Room 4; it has a lace-draped canopy bed and a turret sitting area with a view of the Blue Ridge Mountains looming over Main Street. Room 2 has a fireplace. The restaurant's menu changes daily, its components supplied by many

WORD OF MOUTH

"Harrisonburg is a lovely college town. Nearby is the Skyline Drive if mountains are your thing. There are civil war battles commemorated all over the valley . . . My favorite place to visit near Harrisonburg is the Dayton Farmers Market."   –Carla

small, local organic farmers. As an appetizer, try the smoked salmon on apple potato cake with dill crème fraîche; for a main dish, try the grilled stuffed pork tenderloin. ✉412 S. Main St., 22801 ☎888/294–5866 or 540/434–4464 ⊞540/432–9525 ⊕ www.joshuawilton.com ⊃5 rooms ♦ Restaurant, Wi-Fi; no room TVs, no kids under 8, no smoking ⊟AE, MC, V ⦿BP.

Shopping

The dozens of **antiques shops** in the Harrisonburg area are generally on or near Route 11. Contact the Harrisonburg-Rockingham Convention and Visitors Bureau for a list, or just keep an eye open while driving through communities such as Bridgewater, Dayton, Elkton, Mount Crawford, Mount Sydney, Verona, and Weyer's Cave.

OFF THE BEATEN PATH

NATURAL CHIMNEYS REGIONAL PARK – In Mount Solon, 23 mi south of Harrisonburg, these seven freestanding limestone pylons stand from 65 to 120 feet tall and are slender like the pillars of an Egyptian temple ruin. Facilities include connecting nature trails and a swimming pool. Every June and August a jousting tournament is held at the site. ✉ I–81, Exit 240 W, Mount Solon 22843 ☎ 540/350–2510 ✉ $4 per person; $8 maximum fee per car ⊙ Daily 9–dusk.

Dayton

🔟 2 mi west of Harrisonburg via Rte. 33 off I–81.

Dayton is best known for its large Mennonite population, whose black horse-drawn buggies share the road with latter-day SUVs. At the **Harrisonburg–Rockingham Historical Society,** multimedia folk art reflects the largely German and Scotch-Irish culture of the valley. One Civil War exhibit includes an electric map that traces Stonewall Jackson's famous 1862 Valley Campaign. ✉ 382 High St. ☎ 540/879–2616 or 540/879–2681 ⊕ www.heritagecenter.com ✉ $5 ⊙ Mon.–Sat. 10–4.

Also known as the Daniel Harrison House, **Fort Harrison** (from circa 1749) is of fortified stone and decorated in prosperous frontier style. Costumed interpreters discuss how the furnishings—beds with ropes as slats and hand-quilted comforters—were made. Artifacts on display come from recent excavations undertaken adjacent to the house. ✉ Rte. 42 ☎ 540/879–2280 ✉ Donation welcome ⊙ Mid-May–Oct., weekends 1–5.

Shopping

The **Dayton Farmers Market** (✉ Rte. 42, south of Dayton ☎ 540/879–9885), an 18,000-square-foot area, has homemade baked goods and fresh fruits and vegetables as well as butter churns and ceramic speckleware, made by the Mennonites who live in the area. It's one place to mingle with the craftspeople, as well as with students from James Madison University in nearby Harrisonburg. It's open Thursday–Sunday.

Staunton

⑪ 27 mi south of Dayton via I–81, 11 mi west of southern end of Skyline Dr. at Waynesboro off I–64.

Staunton (pronounced stan-ton) was once the seat of government of the vast Augusta County, which formed in 1738 and encompassed present-day West Virginia, Kentucky, Ohio, Illinois, Indiana, and the Pittsburgh area. After the state's General Assembly fled here from the British in 1781, Staunton was briefly the state's capital. Woodrow Wilson (1856–1924), the nation's 27th president and the eighth president from Virginia, is a native son.

★ ☾ The **Frontier Culture Museum,** an outdoor living museum, re-creates agrarian life in America. The four illustrative farmsteads, American, Scotch-Irish, German, and English, were painstakingly moved from their original sites and reassembled on the museum grounds. The livestock and plants here resemble the historic breeds and varieties as closely as possible. Special programs and activities, held throughout the year, include soap and broom making, cornhusking bees, and supper and barn dances. ✉ *1250 Richmond Rd., off I–81, Exit 222 to Rte. 250 W* ☎ *540/332–7850* ⊕ *www.frontiermuseum.org* 🖃 *$10* ☉ *Dec.–mid-Mar., daily 10–4; mid-Mar.–Nov., daily 9–5.*

Seven miles east of Staunton, the **P. Buckley Moss Museum** is a full-scale gallery of paintings and drawings by one of the Valley's most recognized artists. Moss, who moved to Waynesboro in 1964, was inspired by the quiet dignity and simplicity of the "plain people"—those in the Mennonite communities of the Shenandoah Valley—and has made these neighbors her subject matter. Don't miss the large-scale dollhouse built into a staircase. Her studio, a converted barn about 2 mi from the museum, opens a few times a year to the public. ✉ *2150 Rosser Ave., I–64, Exit 94, Waynesboro* ☎ *540/949–6473* ⊕ *www.pbuckleymoss.com* 🖃 *Free* ☉ *Mon.–Sat. 10–6, Sun. 12:30–5:30.*

The **Woodrow Wilson Presidential Library** has period antiques, items from Wilson's political career, and some original pieces from when this museum was the residence of Wilson's father, a Presbyterian minister. Wilson's presidential limousine, a 1919 Pierce-Arrow sedan, is on display in the garage. The site is being expanded to become a full presidential library, with space for scholarly research. The tentative completion date is 2008. ✉ *24 N. Coalter St.* ☎ *540/885–0897 or 888/496–6376* ⊕ *www.woodrowwilson.org* 🖃 *$8* ☉ *Mar.–Oct., Mon.–Sat. 9–5, Sun. noon–5; Nov.–Feb., Mon.–Sat. 10–4, Sun. noon–4.*

Where to Stay & Eat

★ $–$$ ✕ **Mrs. Rowe's Restaurant.** A homey restaurant with plenty of booths, Rowe's has been operated by the same family since 1947 and enjoys a rock-solid reputation for inexpensive and delicious Southern meals. The fried chicken—skillet-cooked to order—is a standout. A local breakfast favorite is oven-hot biscuits topped with gravy (your choice of sausage, tenderloin, or creamy chipped beef). For dessert, try the mince pie in the fall or the rhubarb cobbler in summer. ✉ *I–81, Exit 222* ☎ *540/886–1833* 🖃 *D, MC, V.*

$$$ ✕🖃 **Belle Grae Inn.** The sitting room and music room of this restored 1870 Victorian house have been converted into formal dining rooms, with brass wall sconces, Oriental rugs, and candles at the tables. The menu ($$$$), which changes weekly, has continental cuisine with a regional flair. Prime rib is a constant on the menu, and crab cakes are fre-

quently available. Accommodations are furnished with antique rocking chairs and canopied or brass beds; a complimentary snifter of brandy awaits in each one. ✉ *515 W. Frederick St., 24401* ☎ *540/886–5151 or 888/541–5151* 🖷 *540/886–6641* ⊕ *www.bellegrae.com* 🛏 *8 rooms, 7 suites, 2 cottages* ⚭ *Restaurant, some microwaves, Wi-Fi; no smoking* ▭ *AE, D, MC, V* ❙❍❙ *MAP.*

$–$$$ 🖭 **Frederick House.** Six restored town houses dating from 1810 make up this inn in the center of the historic district. All rooms are decorated with antiques, and some have fireplaces and private decks. A pub and a restaurant are adjacent. ✉ *28 N. New St., 24401* ☎ *540/885–4220 or 800/334–5575* 🖷 *540/885–5180* ⊕ *www.frederickhouse.com* 🛏 *11 rooms, 12 suites* ⚭ *Cable TV, meeting rooms; no smoking* ▭ *AE, D, DC, MC, V* ❙❍❙ *BP.*

Nightlife & the Arts

THEATER Experience Shakespeare's plays the way the Elizabethans did at ★ **Blackfriars Playhouse** (✉ 10 S. Market St. ☎ 540/885–5588), a near-duplicate of the Globe Theatre that has gained worldwide acclaim for its attention to detail. As in 17th-century London, most seating consists of benches (modern seat backs and cushions are available), and some stools are right on stage.

Shopping

At **Sheridan Sunspots Studios & Designs** (✉ 202 S. Lewis St. ☎ 540/885–8557), near downtown, you can see artisans at work, blowing glass and melding copper. Their exquisite items for the house and garden are available for purchase. In spring the studio hosts the Virginia Hot Glass Festival, which brings together hot-glass artists from across the region. **Virginia Made Shop** (✉ I–81, Exit 222 ☎ 540/886–7180) specializes in Virginia-made products, from pottery and wind chimes to peanuts and wine. At **Virginia Metalcrafters** (✉ 1010 E. Main St., I–64, Exit 94, Waynesboro ☎ 540/949–9400 or 800/368–1002) you can find a broad line of gifts and decorative accessories that are hand-cast in brass, iron, bronze, and pewter. All are made using the same techniques employed since the company was founded in 1890.

Lexington

⓬ *30 mi south of Staunton via I–81.*

Two deeply traditional Virginia colleges sit side by side in this town, each with a memorial to a soldier who was also a man of peace.

The inventor of the first mechanical wheat reaper is honored at the **Cyrus McCormick Museum,** which sits about a mile off I–81. Follow the signs to Walnut Grove farm; now a livestock research center, this mill farmstead is where McCormick did his work. In addition to the museum and family home, you can tour a blacksmith shop and gristmill. All are registered as national historic landmarks. ✉ *State Rte. 606, 5 mi north of Lexington* ☎ *540/377–2255* 🎟 *Free* ⊙ *Daily 8:30–5.*

The **George C. Marshall Museum** preserves the memory of the World War II army chief of staff. Exhibits trace his brilliant career, which began when he was aide-de-camp to John "Black Jack" Pershing in World War I and culminated when, as secretary of state, he devised the Marshall Plan, a strategy for reviving postwar Western Europe. Marshall's Nobel peace prize is on display; so is the Oscar won by his aide Frank McCarthy, who produced the Academy Award–winning Best Picture of 1970, *Patton*. An electronically narrated map tells the story of World War II. *VMI campus* ⊠ *Letcher Ave.* ☎ *540/463–7103* 💲 *$3* ◷ *Daily 9–5.*

Confederate general Jackson's private life is on display at the **Stonewall Jackson House,** where he is revealed as a dedicated Presbyterian who was devoted to physical fitness, careful with money, musically inclined, and fond of gardening. The general lived here only two years, while teaching physics and military tactics to the cadets, before leaving for his command in the Civil War. This is the only house he ever owned; it's furnished now with period pieces and some of his belongings. ⊠ *8 E. Washington St.* ☎ *540/463–2552* ⊕ *www.stonewalljackson.org* 💲 *$6* ◷ *Mon.–Sat. 9–5, Sun. 1–5.*

Adjacent to Washington and Lee University are the imposing Gothic buildings of the **Virginia Military Institute** (VMI), founded in 1839 and the nation's oldest state-supported military college. With an enrollment of about 1,300 cadets, the institute has admitted women since 1997. The **Virginia Military Institute Museum,** in the George C. Marshall Museum until renovations to Jackson Memorial Hall are completed in 2007, displays 15,000 artifacts, including Stonewall Jackson's stuffed and mounted horse, Little Sorrel, and the general's coat, pierced by the bullet that killed him at Chancellorsville. ⊠ *Letcher Ave.* ☎ *540/464–7232* ⊕ *www.vmi.edu* 💲 *$3* ◷ *Daily 9–5.*

Washington and Lee University, the ninth-oldest college in the United States, was founded in 1749 as Augusta Academy and later renamed Washington College in gratitude for a donation from George Washington. After Robert E. Lee's term as its president (1865–70), it received its current name. Today, with 2,000 students, the university occupies a campus of white-column, redbrick buildings around a central colonnade. Twentieth-century alumni include the late Supreme Court Justice Lewis Powell, newsman Roger Mudd, and novelist Tom Wolfe. The campus's **Lee Chapel and Museum** contains many relics of the Lee family. Edward Valentine's statue of the recumbent general, behind the altar, is especially moving: the pose is natural and the expression gentle, a striking contrast to most other monumental art. Here you can sense the affection and reverence that Lee inspired. ⊠ *Jefferson St., Rte. 11* ☎ *540/463–8768* ⊕ *www2.wlu.edu* 💲 *Free* ◷ *Chapel open Apr.–Oct., Mon.–Sat. 9–5, Sun. 1–5; Nov.–Mar., Mon.–Sat. 9–4, Sun. 1–4; campus tours Apr.–Oct., weekdays 10–4, Sat. 9:45–noon; Jan.–Mar., weekdays 10 and noon, Sat. 11.*

OFF THE BEATEN PATH

Fodor'sChoice ★

NATURAL BRIDGE OF VIRGINIA – About 20 mi south of Lexington, this impressive limestone arch (which supports Route 11) has been gradually carved out by Cedar Creek, which rushes through 215 feet below. The Monacan Native American tribe called it the Bridge of God. Surveying the structure for Lord Halifax, George Washington carved his own initials in the stone; Thomas Jefferson bought it (and more than 150 surrounding acres) from George III. The after-dark sound-and-light show may be overkill, but viewing and walking under the bridge itself and along the wooded pathway beyond are worth the price of admission. On the property are dizzying caverns that descend 34 stories, a wax museum, a toy museum, and an 18th-century village constructed by the Monacan Indian Nation. ⊠ *I–81 S, Exit 180, I–81 N, Exit 175* ☎ *540/291–2121 or 800/533–1410* ⊕ *www.naturalbridgeva.com* ⊡ *Bridge $12, all attractions $28* ⊙ *Mar.–Nov., daily 8 AM–dark.*

Where to Stay & Eat

$–$$ ✕ **The Palms.** Once a Victorian ice-cream parlor, this full-service restaurant in an 1890 building has indoor and outdoor dining. Wood booths line the walls of the plant-filled room; the pressed-metal ceiling is original. Specialties on the American menu include broccoli-cheese soup, charbroiled meats, and teriyaki chicken. ⊠ *101 W. Nelson St.* ☎ *540/463–7911* ⚖ *Reservations not accepted* ⊟ *AE, D, MC, V.*

$–$$ ✕▦ **Maple Hall.** For a taste of Southern history, spend a night at this country inn of 1850. Once a plantation house, it's on 56 acres 6 mi north of Lexington. All rooms have period antiques and modern amenities; most have gas log fireplaces as well. Dinner is served in three ground-floor rooms and on a glassed-in patio; the main dining room ($$–$$$) has a large decorative fireplace. Among notable entrées on the seasonal menu are beef fillet with green peppercorn sauce and chicken Chesapeake, a chicken breast stuffed with spinach and crabmeat. ⊠ *Rte. 11, 24450* ☎ *540/463–6693 or 877/283–9680* ⊟ *540/463–7262* ⊕ *www. lexingtonhistoricinns.com/maplehall.htm* ⇗ *17 rooms, 4 suites* ⚖ *Restaurant, tennis court, pool, fishing, hiking, meeting rooms* ⊟ *D, MC, V* ▯◎▯ *BP.*

¢–$ ▦ **Natural Bridge Hotel.** Within walking distance of the spectacular rock arch of the same name (there's also a shuttle bus), the Colonial-style brick hotel has a beautiful location as well as numerous recreational facilities. Long porches with rocking chairs allow leisurely appreciation of the Blue Ridge Mountains. Rooms are done in a Colonial Virginia style. ⊠ *Rte. 11, Box 57, Natural Bridge 24578* ☎ *540/291–2121 or 800/ 533–1410* ⊟ *540/291–1896* ⊕ *www.naturalbridgeva.com* ⇗ *180 rooms* ⚖ *Restaurant, snack bar, some microwaves, cable TV with movies and video games, miniature golf, 2 tennis courts, pool, hiking, bar, meeting rooms* ⊟ *AE, D, DC, MC, V.*

▌ EN ROUTE The drive to Bath County on the 35-mi stretch of Route 39 north and west from Lexington provides a scenic trip through 3-mi **Goshen Pass,** a dramatic gorge that follows the boulder-strewn Maury River through the Allegheny Mountains. Before the coming of railroads, it was the principal stagecoach route into Lexington. In May the scene becomes lush with rhododendrons and other flowering plants; in October, the colors of the rainbow paint the maples and oaks that fill the gorge. A day-use park enables picnickers to bask in this forest preserve, where the river allows for fishing, swimming, and tubing.

Bath County

⓭ *20 mi northwest of Lexington via Rte. 39.*

Bath County is where Virginia's rugged outdoors and refined elegance intermingle most delightfully. Amid its steep ridges and dense forests is the Homestead, a historic and elegant resort. The county's name is fitting: healing thermal springs were what originally brought visitors to town in the 1700s. Although they're less fashionable today, the sulfurous waters still flow at Warm Springs, Hot Springs, and Bolar Springs, their temperatures ranging from 77°F to 104°F.

Where to Stay & Eat

★ $$–$$$ ✕**Waterwheel Restaurant.** Part of a complex of five historic buildings, this restaurant is in a gristmill that dates from 1700. A walk-in wine cellar, set among the gears of the original waterwheel, has 100 wine selections; diners may step in and choose for themselves. The dining area is decorated with Currier & Ives and Audubon prints. Some menu favorites are fresh smoked trout and chicken Fantasio (breast of chicken stuffed with wild rice, sausage, apple, and pecans). Desserts include such Old Virginny recipes as a deep-dish apple pie baked with bourbon. On Sunday look for the hearty but affordable brunch. ✉ *Grist Mill Sq., Warm Springs* ☎ *540/839–2231* ▤ *D, MC, V* ⊙ *Closed Tues. Nov.–May.*

$$–$$$ 🏨**The Homestead.** An evening at the Homestead is like taking a cruise FodorsChoice ship through the mountains. Soothing orchestra music plays as guests ★ stroll the column-adorned hallways, sauntering into the ornately decorated dining room for a luxurious six-course meal of regional and continental cuisine. Daytime activities include far more than shuffleboard: there's three championship-grade 18-hole golf courses, 4 mi of streams stocked with rainbow trout, 100 mi of riding trails, skeet and trap shooting, and nine ski slopes (the Homestead was the site of the South's first downhill skiing in 1959). Host to a prestigious clientele since 1766, the Homestead has evolved from a country spa to a 15,000-acre resort and conference facility. Rooms in the sprawling redbrick building, built in 1891, have Georgian-style furnishings; some have fireplaces. ✉ *Rte. 220, Hot Springs 24445* ☎ *540/839–1766 or 800/838–1766* ▤ *540/839–7670* ⊕ *www.thehomestead.com* ➽ *429 rooms, 77 suites* ⟐ *6 restaurants, cable TV with movies and video games, 3 18-hole golf courses, 8 tennis courts, 2 pools (1 indoor), spa, bicycles, bowling, horseback riding, downhill skiing, ice-skating, cinema, video game room, Wi-Fi, meeting rooms, airport shuttle* ▤ *AE, D, DC, MC, V* ⦿*MAP.*

★ $–$$ 🏨**Inn at Gristmill Square.** Occupying five restored buildings at the same site as the Waterwheel Restaurant, the rooms of this state historical landmark inn are in a Colonial Virginia style. Four units are in the original miller's house; others occupy the former blacksmith's shop, hardware store, gristmill, and cottage. Some of the rooms have fireplaces and patios. ✉ *Rte. 645, Box 359, Warm Springs 24484* ☎ *540/839–2231* ▤ *540/839–5770* ⊕ *www.gristmillsquare.com* ➽ *12 rooms, 5 suites, 1 apartment* ⟐ *Restaurant, cable TV, 3 tennis courts, pool, sauna, bar, meeting rooms* ▤ *D, MC, V* ⦿*BP.*

$–$$ 🏨**Milton Hall.** This 1874 Gothic brick house, built as an elegant country retreat by English nobility, is on 44 acres. It's close to the George Washington National Forest and its abundant outdoor activities. The spacious rooms have Victorian furnishings and large beds. Box lunches can be ordered in advance. ✉ *207 Thorny La., I–64, Exit 10, at Callaghan, Covington 24426* ☎ *540/965–0196 or 877/764–5866*

⊕ *www.milton-hall.com* ➥ *6 rooms, 1 suite* ᗉ *Cable TV with movies, hiking; no smoking* ⊟ *D, MC, V* ⑩ *BP.*

¢ 🎫 **Roseloe Motel.** The modest and clean lodgings in this motel from the '50s are all homey and conventionally decorated. The Roseloe is halfway between Warm Springs and Hot Springs, where the fresh mountain air is bracing. ⊠ *Rte. 1, Box 590, Hot Springs 24445* ☎ *540/839–5373* ➥ *14 rooms* ᗉ *Some kitchenettes, refrigerators, cable TV* ⊟ *AE, D, MC, V.*

Nightlife & the Arts
Garth Newel Music Center (⊠ Rte. 220, Warm Springs ☎ 540/839–5018 or 877/558–1689) has weekend chamber-music performances in summer; you can make reservations and plan to picnic on the grounds.

Sports & the Outdoors
GOLF **The Homestead** has three excellent 18-hole golf courses. The par-70, 6,679-yard Cascades course, the site of USGA and Senior PGA events, has gently sloped fairways amid rugged terrain. The par-72, 6,752-yard Lower Cascades course, designed by Robert Trent Jones, has more wide-open fairways with many bunkers and breaks. The par-72, 6,211-yard Old Course is most famous for its first tee, established in 1892. It's the oldest tee still in continuous use in the United States.

HIKING & At **Douthat State Park** (⊠ Exit 27, 7 mi north of I–64 near Clifton Forge
MOUNTAIN ☎ 540/862–8100), there are more than 40 mi of well-signed, smoothly
BIKING groomed, and sometimes steep trails for hiking and biking. The trails pass by waterfalls and majestic overlooks. The Warm Springs Ranger District of the **George Washington and Jefferson National Forests** (☎ 540/839–2521) has information on hundreds of miles of local trails.

SOUTHWEST VIRGINIA

Southwest Virginia is a rugged region of alternating mountain ridges and deep valleys. Modern urban life is juxtaposed with spectacular scenery in the Roanoke and New River valleys. Other areas retain the quiet charm of yesteryear: they have many pleasant meadows, old country churches, and towns with just one stop sign. The gorge-incised Appalachian Plateau in far southwest Virginia is abundant in coal. Interstate 81 and Interstate 77 form a kind of "X" across the region, and the Blue Ridge Parkway roughly defines Southwest Virginia's eastern edge.

Roanoke

⓮ *49 mi south of Lexington (via I–81).*

They once called this city "Big Lick." But today Roanoke, with a population of 95,000, is Virginia's largest city west of Richmond, the largest city on the Blue Ridge Parkway, and in many ways, the capital of Southwest Virginia. The metropolitan area of 230,000 has enough city flavor to provide a degree of culture and elegance, but its location between the Blue Ridge Parkway and Appalachian Trail means that the wilds aren't too far away either; mountains dominate its horizons in all directions.

Market Square is the heart of Roanoke, with Virginia's oldest continuous farmer's market, a multiethnic food court inside the restored City Market Building, and several restaurants, shops, and bars. In a restored warehouse, **Center in the Square** (⊠ 1 Market Sq. SE ☎ 540/342–5700 ⊕ www.centerinthesquare.org) contains the Mill Mountain Theatre and regional museums covering science, history, and art. A combined $11 ticket grants access to the science museum, which has many interactive exhibits, as well as the MegaDome theater and Hopkins Planetarium.

Even in daylight, the Roanoke skyline is dominated by a star. The 100-foot-tall **Mill Mountain Star,** constructed in 1949, stands in a city park 1,000 feet above the Roanoke Valley. It is lighted in red, white, and blue each evening. From either of the park's two overlooks, Roanoke, the "Star City of the South," looks like a scale model of a city, framed by wave after wave of Appalachian ridgelines. ⊠ *Mill Mountain Park, follow Walnut St. south 2 mi from downtown Roanoke; or take Parkway Spur Rd. 3 mi north from Blue Ridge Pkwy. at milepost 120.3.*

Sharing the mountaintop with the star is the **Mill Mountain Zoo.** Asian animals are center stage here, including a rare Siberian tiger, snow leopards, and red pandas. ⊠ *Mill Mountain Park, follow Walnut St. south 2 mi from downtown Roanoke; or take Parkway Spur Rd. 3 mi north from Blue Ridge Pkwy. at milepost 120.3* ☎ 540/343–3241 ⊕ *www. mmzoo.org* ⊡ *$6.75* ☉ *Daily 10–5; gate closes at 4:30.*

★ You can relive the final days of steam trains at the **O. Winston Link Museum,** inside a renovated passenger train station. Link spent several years in the late 1950s and early 1960s photographing Norfolk & Western's last steam engines in the railroads of Southwest Virginia. The hundreds of stunning black and white photographs on display do much more than evoke nostalgia—they also capture day-to-day life: a horse-drawn carriage awaiting an oncoming train, a locomotive rocketing past lovers watching a drive-in movie. ⊠ *101 Shenandoah Ave.* ☎ *540/982–5465* ⊕ *www. linkmuseum.org* ⊡ *$5* ☉ *Mon.–Sat. 10–5, Sun. noon–5.*

Near Market Square, the **Virginia Museum of Transportation** has the largest collection of diesel and steam locomotives in the country—not surprising, considering Roanoke got its start as a railroad town and was once the headquarters of the Norfolk & Western railroad. The dozens of original train cars and engines, some of which can be boarded and many built here in town, include a massive Nickel Plate locomotive—just one of the many holdings that constitute an unabashed display of civic pride. The sprawling model train and miniature circus setups please young and old alike. ⊠ *303 Norfolk Ave.* ☎ *540/342–5670* ⊕ *www.vmt.org* ⊡ *$7.40* ☉ *Weekdays 11–4, Sat. 10–5, Sun. 1–5.*

OFF THE BEATEN PATH

NATIONAL D-DAY MEMORIAL – This site stirs the soul, bringing the sacrifice of D-Day home. When Allied forces landed at Normandy on June 6, 1944, in what would be the decisive military move of World War II, the small town of Bedford lost 19 of its young men, and four more in days to come. The memorial's focal point is a huge granite arch and flag plaza on a hill overlooking the town. There are also granite statues of soldiers in combat and a reflecting pool that periodically shoots up spurts of water, as if struck by bullets. Don't be surprised if you see some D-Day veterans sitting near the memorial. ✉ *U.S. 460, 27 mi east of Roanoke, Bedford* ☎ *540/587–3619* ⊕ *www.dday.org* 🎫 *$5* ☉ *Daily 10–5.*

BOOKER T. WASHINGTON NATIONAL MONUMENT – It would have been hard for Booker T. Washington to imagine the farm on which he was born into slavery hosting a national monument. But this restored tobacco farm 25 mi southeast of Roanoke and 21 mi south of Bedford is a fitting tribute to the humble origins of Washington (1856–1915), who broke through the yoke of oppression to become a remarkable educator and author, advising presidents McKinley, Roosevelt, and Taft and taking tea with Queen Victoria. More important, he started Tuskegee Institute in Alabama and inspired generations of African-Americans. Covering 224 acres, the farm's restored buildings; tools; crops; animals; and, in summer, interpreters in period costume all help show what life during slavery was like. ✉ *Rte. 122, 21 mi south of Bedford* ☎ *540/721–2094* ⊕ *www.nps.gov/bowa* 🎫 *Free* ☉ *Daily 9–5.*

NEED A BREAK?

At the **Homestead Creamery** (✉ Rte. 122, just east of intersection with Rte. 116, Burnt Chimney ☎ 540/721-5808), you can sample farm-fresh milk and ice cream. No plastic or paper cartons here—the milk is stored and sold in glass bottles, the way milkmen used to bring it. Gulping the chocolate milk is like drinking a chocolate cake. Unusual milk flavors such as mocha and orange cream are often available.

Where to Stay & Eat

$$-$$$ ✕**The Library.** This quiet, elegant restaurant in the Piccadilly Square shopping center is decorated with shelves of books. Its frequently changing menu specializes in seafood dishes. Expect dishes such as sautéed Dover sole with almonds, fillet of beef with béarnaise sauce, and lobster tail. ✉ *3117 Franklin Rd. SW* ☎ *540/985–0811* 🍴 *Reservations essential* ▤ *AE, DC, MC, V* ☉ *Closed Sun. and Mon. No lunch.*

★ **$-$$$** ✕**Carlos Brazilian International Cuisine.** High on a hill with a spectacular sunset view, this lively restaurant has French, Italian, Spanish, and Brazilian dishes. Try the *porco reacheado* (pork tenderloin stuffed with spinach and feta cheese) or the *moqueca mineira* (shrimp, clams, and whitefish in a Brazilian sauce). Brazilian radio often accompanies the meal. ✉ *4167 Electric Rd.* ☎ *540/345-7661* ▤ *AE, MC, V* ☉ *Closed Sun.*

$ ✕**The Homeplace.** Bring a big appetite with you on the drive up and over
Fodor'sChoice Catawba Mountain to get to the Homeplace. Famished Appalachian Trail
★ hikers in grimy shorts and suave diners in their Sunday best eat side by side in this farm home in a tiny country hamlet—come as you are. Old-fashioned cooking is dished up grandma style, with all-you-can-eat fried chicken, mashed potatoes and gravy, green beans, pinto beans, baked apples, hot biscuits, and an extra meat selection of your choice served to each table for $12 a person (throw in another dollar for yet another meat selection). No alcohol is served, but the lemonade is delicious. ✉ *7 mi west of Salem on Rte. 311 N, Exit 141 off I–81, Catawba* ☎ *540/384-7252* 🍴 *Reservations not accepted* ▤ *MC, V* ☉ *No lunch Thurs.–Sat., no dinner Sun.*

$ ✗ **Mac 'N' Bob's.** The enormous growth in seating since 1980, from 10 to 250, testifies to the popularity of this establishment in downtown Salem. Sports memorabilia line the walls of the attractive redbrick building near Roanoke College, and sporting events are likely to be on the many TVs near the bar. The menu runs from hamburgers to steak to seafood to pizza. If you have a big appetite, try a fully loaded calzone, which flops off the sides of your plate like a flounder. ✉ *316 E. Main St., Salem* ☎ *540/389–5999* ▤ *AE, D, MC, V.*

¢–$ ✗ **The Roanoker.** Fried chicken isn't on the menu every day, but when it is, it entices you from the parking lot. This local gathering place has been serving homestyle fare since 1941. A long list of lunch and dinner specials supplements the regular menu and includes an array of side dishes as part of reasonably priced, hearty meals. The choice between corn sticks, biscuits, or wheat rolls can be a tough one. ✉ *2522 Colonial Ave. SW, Roanoke* ☎ *540/344–7746, 540/772–4834 list of daily specials* ▤ *MC, V* ☻ *Closed Mon.*

$–$$$ ✗▥ **Hotel Roanoke and Conference Center.** This elegant Tudor revival building, listed on the National Register of Historic Places, was built in 1882 by the Norfolk & Western Railroad. The richly paneled lobby has Florentine marble floors and ceiling frescos. The formal restaurant serves regional Southern cuisine ($$–$$$); perennial favorites include peanut soup and steak Diane, prepared table-side. The Market Square Bridge, a glassed-in walkway, goes from the hotel to downtown attractions. ✉ *110 Shenandoah Ave., 24016* ☎ *540/985–5900* ▤ *540/345–2890* ⊕ *www.hotelroanoke.com* ↻ *313 rooms, 19 suites* ⚭ *2 restaurants, cable TV with movies and video games, pool, gym, bar, Wi-Fi, convention center, meeting rooms, airport shuttle* ▤ *AE, D, DC, MC, V.*

$$–$$$ ▥ **Bernard's Landing.** A resort set on Smith Mountain Lake 45 minutes southeast of Roanoke, Bernard's rents one- to three-bedroom condominiums with water views and two- to five-bedroom town houses (all waterfront) for periods of up to two weeks. Because the units are separately owned, the way they are furnished varies widely, but all have full kitchen facilities and private decks. Conferences are scheduled here year-round, and summer vacationers come for the many sports available. ✉ *775 Ashmeade Rd., Moneta 24121* ☎ *540/721–8870 or 800/ 572–2048* ▤ *540/721–8383* ⊕ *www.bernardslanding.com* ↻ *60 units* ⚭ *Restaurant, kitchens, microwaves, cable TV, 6 tennis courts, 2 pools, gym, sauna, boating, fishing, racquetball, playground, meeting rooms* ▤ *AE, D, MC, V.*

Nightlife & the Arts

BARS & CLUBS Roanoke's nightlife centers on the Market Square area of downtown, which is often bustling and lively on weekend nights. Near the Square, **Corned Beef and Co.** (✉ *107 Jefferson St.* ☎ *540/342–3354*) has live jazz and funk music on Friday and Saturday nights.

Sports & the Outdoors

HIKING The **Appalachian Trail** is north and west of Roanoke, crossing the valley at Troutville, 5 mi to the north. Two of the most photographed formations on the entire 2,000-mi route from Georgia to Maine, McAfee Knob and Dragon's Tooth, are accessible from trailheads on the Virginia 311 highway, west of the valley. The **Star Trail** (trailhead on Riverland Road, 2 mi southeast of downtown Roanoke) winds through a forest oasis amid the metropolitan area as it works its way up 1½ mi to the Mill Mountain Star. Other trails can be found along the Blue Ridge Parkway to the east and south and in the George Washington and Jefferson national forests to the north and west. For more information contact the national forests' **Supervisor's Office** (✉ 5162 Valleypointe Pkwy., Roanoke ☎ 540/265–5100 or 888/265–0019).

Blue Ridge Parkway

5 mi east of Roanoke.

The Blue Ridge Parkway takes up where Skyline Drive leaves off at Waynesboro, weaving south for 471 mi to Great Smoky Mountains National Park in North Carolina. The parkway goes up to higher elevations than the drive, up to 4,200 feet at Apple Orchard Mountain, and even higher in North Carolina. In Virginia the parkway is especially scenic between Waynesboro and Roanoke, winding through the George Washington National Forest, visiting numerous ridge-top overlooks that provide views of crumpled-looking mountains and patchwork valleys. Visit the **Blue Ridge Parkway Visitors Center,** open 9–5 daily year-round, 1 ½ mi north of milepost 115 near Roanoke, or call the National Park Service's office in Vinton (☎ 540/857–2490) for information on Virginia's section of the parkway.

Mabry Mill, north of Meadows of Dan and the Blue Ridge Parkway's junction with U.S. 58 at milepost 176, 55 mi south of Roanoke, is one of the parkway's most popular stops for photographers. The restored water-powered, weather-worn gristmill grinds cornmeal and buckwheat flour, which are for sale. ✉ *Blue Ridge Pkwy., milepost 176* ☎ *276/952–2947* 🎫 *Free* ☉ *May–Oct., daily 8–6.*

Peaks of Otter Recreation Area, 25 mi northeast of Roanoke, offers a close-up view of cone-shape Sharp Top Mountain, which no less an authority than Thomas Jefferson once called America's tallest peak. At 3,875 feet it's not even the tallest in the park—nearby Flat Top is 4,004 feet. You can hike to both peaks and to little brother Harkening Hill, as well as to Fallingwater Cascades, a thrilling multitier waterfall. For those not up to the climb, a bus heads most of the way up Sharp Top hourly throughout the day. The peaks rise about the shores of Abbott Lake, a bucolic picnic spot. A pleasant lakeside lodge and campground along the placid lake below are an ideal base for local trekking. ✉ *Blue Ridge Pkwy., mile marker 86* ☎ *540/586–4357* ⊕ *www.peaksofotter.com* 🎫 *Free.*

**OFF THE
BEATEN
PATH**

CRABTREE FALLS – A series of cascades falls a distance of 1,200 feet. Taken together, Virginia claims these cascades as the highest waterfall east of the Rockies, though no single waterfall within the series would qualify as such. Whatever the superlatives or qualifications, the falls are a wondrous sight. A trail winds up a steep mountainside all the way to the top, but the first overlook is an easy stroll 700 feet from the lower parking lot. The best time to see the waterfalls is winter through spring, when the water is high. ✉ *Rte. 56, 6 mi east of Blue Ridge Pkwy., or 19 mi* *from Wintergreen by following Rte. 151 south and then Rte. 56 west at Roseland.*

Where to Stay & Eat

¢–$ ✕▣ **Peaks of Otter Lodge.** This unpretentious, peaceful lodge is so popular that reservations are accepted beginning October 1 for the following year. Every room looks out on Abbott Lake from a private terrace or balcony, and their interiors have a folksy quality. The restaurant's big draw is the Friday night seafood buffet for $21.95. ✉ *Milepost 86, Rte. 664, Box 489, Bedford 24523* ☎ *540/586–1081 or 800/542–5927* ⊟ *540/586–4420* ⊕ *www.peaksofotter.com* ⊐ *63 rooms* ⚲ *Restaurant, fishing, hiking, bar, pub, meeting rooms; no a/c, no room phones, no room TVs* ⊟ *MC, V.*

New River Valley

41 mi southwest of Roanoke via I–81.

Despite its name, derived from being "new" to explorers when it was first discovered, the New River is actually one of the oldest rivers in the world: legend says only the Nile is older. The only river that flows from south to north completely through the Appalachian Mountains, the New River cuts a bluff-graced valley through its Virginia section for 60 mi from Galax near the North Carolina line to Pearisburg, just over the West Virginia line. Visitors will find cozy downtown areas in towns like Blacksburg, Christiansburg, Radford, and Pulaski, and many opportunities for outdoor recreation just outside the towns' limits.

Almost a century before Virginia Tech's founding in 1872, the **Historic Smithfield** plantation was built on what was then the frontier wilds. Aristocratic colonist and Revolutionary War patriot William Preston moved his family to the estate in 1774, a year before the war began. Among his descendants were three Virginia governors and four U.S. senators. Today, costumed interpreters, authentic period furniture, and Native American artifacts reveal how different life in the New River Valley was more than two centuries ago. ✉ *100 Smithfield Plantation Rd., Blacksburg* ☎ *540/231–3947* ⊕ *www.civic.bev.net/smithfield* ▣ *$5* ☉ *Mon., Tues., and Thurs.–Sat. 10–5, Sun. 1–5.*

With 26,000 students, **Virginia Tech** is Virginia's largest university. A small college just a few decades ago, Tech is now known for top-notch research programs and its Hokies football team, regularly ranked in the top 10. The focal point of the sprawling campus is the Drillfield, a vast green space surrounded by hefty neo-Gothic buildings built of what is known locally as "Hokie Stone" masonry. The **Virginia Museum of Natural History** (✉428 N. Main St. ☎ 540/231–3001) presents rotating exhibits on local and national wildlife; a separate geology museum in Deering Hall displays gems and minerals. ✉ *Blacksburg* ☎ *540/231–6000* ⊕ *www.vt.edu.*

What is now the **Wilderness Road Regional Museum** was once lodging for settlers making their way west on a Native American route that went from Pennsylvania through the Cumberland Gap. The man who founded the town of Newbern built this house in the same year, and the structure has since served as a private home, a tavern, a post office, and a store. Today the house contains antique dolls, swords and rifles, an old loom, and other artifacts of everyday life. A self-tour map of Newbern, the only Virginia town entirely within a National Register of Historic Places district, is available at the museum. ⊠ *I–81, Exit 98, Newbern* ☎ *540/674–4835* ⊕ *www.rootsweb.com/~vanrhs/wrrm* ☞ *$2* ⊙ *Mon.–Sat. 10–5, Sun. 1:30–4:30.*

Where to Stay & Eat

$–$$ ✕ **Boudreaux's Restaurant.** Ever eaten gator bites? Be sure and try them at Boudreaux's. What started as a project in business marketing for a pair of Virginia Tech students is now an established part of Blacksburg's downtown. The canopied rooftop is a particularly relaxing area to enjoy jambalaya or Cajun catfish. Live bands often perform in the evenings. ⊠ *205 N. Main St., Blacksburg* ☎ *540/961–2330* ⊟ *AE, D, MC, V.*

$ ✕ **The Cellar.** A gathering place and watering hole near the Virginia Tech campus, this storefront restaurant serves eclectic, inexpensive dishes. Try the Greek spaghetti with sautéed feta, garlic, and olives, or the "Mac Daddy": a single large meatball in marinara sauce and Parmesan. ⊠ *302 N. Main St., Blacksburg* ☎ *540/953–0651* ⊟ *MC, V.*

$$$ ⊡ **Mountain Lake.** Centered around the highest natural lake east of the Mississippi, this resort is a great place to cool off during a hot summer. Accommodations range from spartan cottages to plush suites in a majestic sandstone hotel from 1930 (the resort itself predates the Civil War). Atop 4,000-foot Salt Pond Mountain, outdoor activities abound: you can hike, mountain bike, ride horses, swim, and boat within the 2,500-acre Mountain Lake Wilderness, which surrounds the hotel. The adjacent Jefferson National Forest offers even more recreation, including a segment of the Appalachian Trail. ⊠ *115 Hotel Circle, 7 mi north of U.S. 460 on Rte. 700, Pembroke, 24136* ☎ *540/626–7121* ⊕ *www. mountainlakehotel.com* ☞ *28 cottages, 16 lodge rooms, 43 hotel rooms* ⚒ *Dining room, some microwaves, some refrigerators, pool, hot tub, bicycles, archery, hiking, video game room, shop, Wi-Fi, meeting rooms; no a/c, no room TVs* ⊟ *AE, D, MC, V* ❙◉❙ *MAP* ⊙ *Closed Dec.–Apr.*

$–$$ ⊡ **Holiday Inn University.** This hotel is across the street from Virginia Tech, with a golf course, movie theater, numerous restaurants and shopping areas, and even a beach volleyball court nearby. The rooms are modern and comfortable, with two phone lines in each one. ⊠ *900 Prices Fork Rd., Blacksburg 24060* ☎ *540/552–7001* ⊟ *540/552–0827* ☞ *148 rooms, 1 suite* ⚒ *Restaurant, dining room, cable TV with movies and video games, tennis court, 2 pools (1 indoor), lounge, recreation room, Wi-Fi, meeting rooms, airport shuttle* ⊟ *AE, D, DC, MC, V.*

Sports & the Outdoors

BIKING **Mountain Lake** (⊠ 115 Hotel Circle, 7 mi north of U.S. 460 on Rte. 700, Pembroke ☎ 540/626–7121) has more than 20 mi of mountain bike trails, with bicycles available at the hotel. The 52-mi **New River Trail**, Virginia's narrowest state park, runs from Pulaski to Galax following what was once a railroad bed. It parallels the river for 39 of those miles, passing through two tunnels. The trail is also open to hikers and horseback

CLOSE UP

Mountain Music

SOUTHWEST VIRGINIA'S HILLS AND VALLEYS have long reverberated with the sounds of fiddles, banjoes, mandolins, and acoustic guitars. Scotch-Irish settlers brought these sounds with them, and for the generations before radio and television, front-porch gatherings and community dances entertained local families isolated, geographically and culturally, from the rest of civilization.

Virginia has designated a 250-mi route snaking through the hills as "The Crooked Road: Virginia's Music Heritage Trail." What connects the communities and sites along this route is a passion for traditional mountain music—bluegrass, gospel, roots, and old-time country. Many people point to this region as the birthplace of the country-music industry. In 1927 talent scout Ralph Peer set up a makeshift recording studio in the Virginia-Tennessee border town of Bristol. From these sessions came such seminal acts as the Carter Family and Jimmie Rodgers. For more information, go to www.thecrookedroad.org. Sites are listed here from west to east.

Ralph Stanley Museum and Traditional Mountain Music Center (✉ Clintwood ☎ 276/926-5591 ⊕ www.ralphstanleymuseum.com). The Ralph Stanley Museum opened in 2004 to preserve traditional mountain music. Focusing on the life and career of local legend Ralph Stanley, the exhibits allow visitors to hear the music of Stanley and other artists.

Carter Family Fold (✉ U.S. 58/421, 19 mi west of Bristol, Hiltons ☎ 276/386-6054 or 276/386-9480 ⊕ www.

carterfamilyfold.org). At this 1,000-seat auditorium, live music is performed on Saturday night; a two-day festival is held each August. A museum in an adjacent building displays memorabilia from the Carter family; descendants often perform in the shows.

Old Fiddlers Convention (✉ Galax ☎ 276/236-8541 ⊕ www.oldfiddlersconvention.com). Hundreds of musicians and thousands of fans gather the second week of August for performances, contests, and jam sessions.

Rex Theatre (✉ 113 E. Grayson St., Galax ☎ 276/238-8130 or 276/236-0668 ⊕ www.rextheatregalax.com). Bluegrass, country, and gospel music is broadcast from here each Friday night on WBRF, FM-98.1.

Blue Ridge Music Center (✉ Blue Ridge Pkwy. milepost 213, near NC line ⊕ www.blueridgemusiccenter.net). The center's outdoor amphitheater is the site of an ambitious concert series of regional and national musicians that has included the likes of Ricky Skaggs and Doc Watson. Impromptu jam sessions often break out in the center's plaza area.

Floyd Country Store (✉ Floyd ☎ 540/745-4563 ⊕ www.floydcountrystore.com 🎟 $3). What were once just sessions have evolved into a Friday Night Jamboree attended by local folks and visitors from far off. In summer, music often breaks out all around the store as well. "Granny Rules" are in effect—"no smokin,' no cussin,' and no drinkin.' " But clogging on the dance floor is fine.

4

riders. The Jefferson National Forest's **Pandapas Pond Recreation Area,** on the edge of Blacksburg, is a popular place for mountain biking.

CANOEING & **FISHING** The **New River** is open to canoeing, kayaking, and fishing. For more information, or to rent or buy boats or fishing gear, contact the following local outfitters: **Back Country Ski & Sport** (✉ 3710 S. Main St., Blacksburg ☎ 540/552–6400); **Tangent Outfitters** (✉ 201 Cascade Dr., Pembroke ☎ 540/731–5202).

HIKING The **Appalachian Trail** crosses the New River Valley, visiting overlook sites such as Angel's Rest and Wind Rock. For more information on area hikes in the Jefferson National Forest, contact the **Blacksburg Ranger Station** (✉ 110 Southpark Dr., Blacksburg ☎ 540/552–4641). The 4-mi loop at **Cascades Recreation Area** (✉ Jefferson National Forest, off U.S. 460, 4 mi north of Pembroke on Rte. 623) passes a rushing stream and a 60-foot waterfall. This hike is popular locally and becomes crowded on weekends when the weather's good.

Abingdon

⑮ *135 mi southwest of Roanoke (via I–81).*

Abingdon, near the Tennessee border, is a cultural crossroads in the wilderness: the town of nearly 7,000 draws tens of thousands of people each year because of a fine theater company and exuberant local celebrations. By far the most popular event here is the **Virginia Highlands Festival** during the first two weeks of August: 200,000 people come to hear live music performances ranging from bluegrass to opera, to visit the exhibitions of mountain crafts, and to browse among the wares of more than 100 antiques dealers. This is followed by the **Burley Tobacco Festival,** held in September, during which country-music stars perform and prize farm animals are proudly displayed.

Regional artists exhibit their folk art and crafts at the **William King Regional Arts Center,** which also has an outdoor sculpture garden. ✉ *415 Academy Dr.* ☎*276/628–5005* ⊕*www.wkrac.org* ▧*Free* ☉ *Tues. 10–9, Wed.–Fri. 10–5, weekends 1–5.*

Where to Stay & Eat

$$–$$$$ ✗ **The Tavern.** Inside a building from 1779 is a cozy restaurant. The three dining rooms and cocktail lounge all have fireplaces, stone walls, and brick floors. In warm weather you can dine outdoors on a balcony overlooking historic Court House Hill or on a brick patio surrounded by trees and flowers. The menu includes rack of lamb and fresh seasonal seafood such as stuffed trout. ✉*222 E. Main St.* ☎*276/628–1118* ▭*AE, D, MC, V.*

$–$$ ✗ **The Starving Artist Cafe.** This eatery, which doubles as an art gallery, has many seafood and pasta dishes. The Friday and Saturday menu includes Cajun-style prime rib. ✉ *134 Wall St. NW* ☎ *276/628–8445* ▭ *AE, MC, V* ☉ *Closed Sun. No dinner Mon.*

★ $$–$$$$ ✗▣ **Camberley's Martha Washington Inn.** Constructed as a private house in 1832, turned into a college dormitory in 1860, and then used as a field hospital during the Civil War, the Martha Washington finally became an inn in 1935. Across from the Barter Theater, the inn has rooms furnished with Victorian antiques; some have fireplaces. The restaurant's contemporary American cuisine ($$$) includes roasted rainbow trout with crayfish, loin of lamb with hominy cheese grits, and—for dessert—Martha's marbled strawberry shortcake. There is complimentary afternoon tea on Friday and Saturday on the porch of the inn. ⊠ *150 W. Main St., 24210* ☎ *276/628–3161 or 800/555–8000* ᐸ *276/628–8885* ⊕ *www.marthawashingtoninn.com* ⤷ *51 rooms, 11 suites* ⟡ *Restaurant, bar, refrigerators, Wi-Fi, pool, health club, spa, meeting rooms, dry cleaning, laundry service, Internet room, airport shuttle* ⊟ *AE, D, DC, MC, V* ⟡⟡ *BP.*

¢ ⚏ **Alpine Motel.** The spacious, modern rooms of this clean motel have striking views of Virginia's highest mountain peaks: Mt. Rogers and Whitetop. The motel is far back from the road and is therefore popular with families, as well as traveling salespeople. The Barter Theatre is nearby. ⊠ *882 E. Main St., 24210* ☎ *276/628–3178* ᐸ *276/628–3179* ⤷ *19 rooms* ⟡ *Cable TV, microwaves, refrigerators, Wi-Fi* ⊟ *AE, D, MC, V.*

Nightlife & the Arts

From April through the Christmas season, audiences flock to the prestigious **Barter Theatre** (⊠ *133 W. Main St.* ☎ *276/628–3991*), America's longest-running professional repertory theater. Founded during the Depression by local actor Robert Porterfield, the theater got its name in the obvious way: early patrons who could not afford the 40¢ tickets could pay in produce. Kevin Spacey, Ned Beatty, and Gregory Peck are among the many stars who began their careers at the Barter, which today presents the classics of Shakespeare as well as works by contemporary playwrights such as David Mamet. Although times have changed since Noël Coward was given a Virginia ham for his contributions, the official policy still permits you to barter for your seat. But don't just show up at the box office with a bag of arugula—all trades must be approved by advance notice. Plays change every four weeks.

The Outdoors

HIKING Wild ponies on open grasslands studded with rocky knobs give the area around **Mt. Rogers** an appearance distinct from any other in Virginia. At 5,729 feet, Mt. Rogers is Virginia's highest point, but you don't need to hike all the way to its summit to experience the grandeur of Western-like terrain—a short walk of about a mile from **Grayson Highlands State Park** (⊠ *U.S. 58, 20 mi east of Damascus* ☎ *276/579 7092* ⛊ *$2*) into the adjacent **Mount Rogers Recreation Area** is all that's required. Through the 5,000-acre state park and 120,000-acre recreation area run an extensive network of riding and hiking trails; the Appalachian Trail passes through on its way to North Carolina and Tennessee, just to the south. ⊠ *Mount Rogers National Recreation Area, 3714 Hwy. 16, Marion 24354* ☎ *276/783–5196* ⛊ *Free.*

At the end of Abingdon's Main Street is the beginning of the 34-mi **Virginia Creeper Trail,** a former railbed of the Virginia-Carolina Railroad. You can hike it, bike it, or take to it on horseback. The trail has sharp curves, steep grades, and 100 trestles and bridges. It joins the Appalachian Trail at Damascus, a town known for its friendly attitude and the many businesses targeted toward hikers and cyclists. In May the town celebrates Trail Days, a festival celebrating hikers. ⊠ *Trailhead at end of Main St.* ☎ *540/676–2282 or 800/435–3440.*

CENTRAL & WESTERN VIRGINIA ESSENTIALS

To research prices, get advice from other travelers, and book travel arrangements, visit www.fodors.com.

Transportation

BY AIR

The region's three largest airports are small and relatively hassle-free. Regional carriers using small jets and turboprops are the norm, though larger jets sometimes serve Roanoke. The regional carriers primarily offer access to Washington, Charlotte, and Atlanta, but flights to and from Chicago, Pittsburgh, Cincinnati, New York, and Detroit are also available. Many travelers to western Virginia prefer to fly into international airports in the Washington-Baltimore area (Dulles, Reagan National, Baltimore-Washington International), Richmond, or Greensboro, North Carolina, then commute by rental car; all three areas are within two hours' drive of western Virginia destinations. Tri-City Regional Airport is just across the state line in Blountville, Tennessee, for easy access to the Abingdon area.

Van on the Go shuttles guests from the Charlottesville airport to hotels, downtown, and area tourist attractions. Reservations are required.

🛈 **Charlottesville-Albemarle Airport** ⊠ 8 mi north of Charlottesville at intersection of Rtes. 606/649 off Rte. 29 ☎ 434/973-8342 ⊕ www.gocho.com. **Lynchburg Regional Airport** ⊠ Rte. 29 S ☎ 434/455-6090. **Roanoke Regional Airport** ⊠ Off I-581 ☎ 540/362-1999 ⊕ www.roanokeairport.com. **Tri-Cities Regional Airport** ⊠ Blountville, TN ☎ 423/325-6000 ⊕ www.triflight.com. **Van on the Go** ⊠ Charlottesville-Albermarle Airport ☎ 434/975-8267 or 866/725-0200 ⊕ www.vanonthego.com.

BY CAR

The many pleasant highways and routes that snake through western Virginia's rolling countryside make driving a particularly good way to travel. The region's interstates (I–64, I–81, and I–77) are remarkably scenic, but the same mountainous terrain that contributes to their beauty can also make them treacherous. Dense valley fog banks, mountain-shrouding clouds, and gusty ridge-top winds are concerns at any time of the year, and winter brings ice and snow conditions that can change dramatically in a few miles when the elevation changes.

Charlottesville is where U.S. 29 (north–south) meets I–64. Lynchburg is the meeting point of U.S. 460 between Richmond and Roanoke and Route 29 south from Charlottesville. U.S. 460 meets I–81 at Roanoke.

Interstate 81 and U.S. 11 run north–south the length of the Shenandoah Valley and continue south into Tennessee. Interstate 66 west from Washington, D.C., which is 90 mi to the east, passes through Front Royal to meet I–81 and U.S. 11 at the northern end of the valley. Interstate 64 connects the same highways with Charlottesville, 30 mi to the east. Route

39 into Bath County connects with I–81 just north of Lexington. Interstate 77 cuts off the southwest tip of the state, running north–south and crossing I–81 at Wytheville. Interstate 77 crosses two major ridges and passes through two mountain tunnels in Virginia.

Travelers will rarely find bumper-to-bumper traffic jams in Charlottesville or any other city in the region. The major exception: autumn Saturdays when the University of Virginia has a home football game. Virginia Tech games can similarly snarl traffic in the Roanoke–New River Valley area, including on I–81.

BY TAXI
Taxis are generally ordered instead of hailed. If travel in the region takes you outside the city, a rental car is a better way to go.

🚖 Charlottesville Taxi Companies **AC Airport Cab & Wahoo Cab** ☎ 434/981-0585. **Quicksilver Taxi** ☎ 434/825-3499. **Taxinet** ☎ 434/245-8294.

🚖 Roanoke Taxi Companies **Liberty Cab** ☎ 540/344-1776. **Yellow Cab Services of Roanoke** ☎ 540/345-7711.

BY TRAIN
Amtrak has service three days a week to Charlottesville and Staunton, en route from New York and Chicago. The same train stops at Clifton Forge for the Homestead resort in Bath County. A complimentary shuttle bus on Sunday, Wednesday, and Friday connects Roanoke (Campbell Court and Roanoke Airport Sheraton) and Clifton Forge Rail Station. Amtrak's *Crescent* runs between New York City and New Orleans and stops daily in Lynchburg and Charlottesville.

🚆 **Amtrak** ☎ 800/872-7245 ⊕ www.amtrak.com. **Clifton Forge** ⊠ 400 Ridgeway St. **Kemper Street Station** ⊠ 825 Kemper St. , Lynchburg ☎ 434/847-8247. **Staunton** ⊠ 1 Middlebrook Ave. **Union Station** ⊠ 810 W. Main St., Charlottesville ☎ 434/296-4559.

Contacts & Resources

EMERGENCIES
Charlottesville is served by six locations of CVS. Pharmacies inside Kroger and Wal-Mart are also open 24 hours a day.

🏥 Doctors & Dentists **Martha Jefferson Hospital, Physician Referral Services** ☎ 434/982-8450.

🏥 Emergency Services **Albemarle County Office of Emergency Services** ☎ 434/971-1263. **Ambulance, Fire, Police** ☎ 911

🏥 Hospitals **Charlottesville: Martha Jefferson Hospital** ⊠ 459 Locust Ave. ☎ 434/982-7000. **University of Virginia Medical Center** ⊠ Lee St. ☎ 434/982-3865. **Roanoke: Carilion Roanoke Memorial Hospital** ⊠ Belleview Ave. and Jefferson St. ☎ 540/981-7000. **Lewis-Gale Medical Center** ⊠ 1900 Electric Rd., Salem ☎ 540/776-4000.

INTERNET, MAIL & SHIPPING
Charlottesville's main post office is on U.S. 29, north of downtown. The Jefferson-Madison Regional Library has computers with Internet access. Mudhouse Café, a cybercafé with Wi-Fi, is in the Downtown Mall.

In Roanoke, the Downtown Finance Station post office is three blocks from the Market Square. Wi-Fi is available in a downtown zone from Market Square to nearby Elmwood Park.

Post Office U.S. Post Office, Charlottesville ✉ 1155 Seminole Trail ☎ 434/978-7610. **U.S. Post Office, Downtown Finance Station, Roanoke** ✉ 101 West Church Ave. ☎ 540/343-3578

Internet Access Jefferson-Madison Regional Library ✉ 201 E. Market St., Charlottesville ☎ 434/979-7151. **Mudhouse Café** ✉ 213 W. Main St., Charlottesville ☎ 434/984-6833.

TOUR OPTIONS

For $16 the Lexington Carriage Company will take visitors around town in a horse-drawn carriage for 45–50 minutes, from April through October. Tours begin and end at the Lexington Visitor Center. A self-guided walking-tour brochure of the town is available from the Lexington Visitor Center. The Historic Staunton Foundation offers free one-hour walking tours Saturday morning at 10, Memorial Day through October, departing from the Woodrow Wilson Birthplace (24 North Coalter St.). A brochure for a self-guided tour is available from the Staunton/ Augusta County Travel Information Center.

Historic Staunton Foundation ✉ 1205 Augusta St. ☎ 540/885-7676. **Lexington Carriage Company** ☎ 540/463-5647 ⊕ www.lexcarriage.com. **Lexington Visitor Center** ✉ 106 E. Washington St. ☎ 540/463-3777. **Staunton-Augusta County Travel Information Center** ✉ 1290 Richmond Rd. ☎ 540/332-3972.

VISITOR INFORMATION

Tourist Information Abingdon Convention & Visitors Bureau ✉ 335 Cummings St., Abingdon 24210 ☎ 276/676-2282 ⊕ www.abingdon.com/tourism. **Charlottesville/ Albemarle Convention and Visitors Bureau** ✉ Rte. 20 S, Box 178, Charlottesville 22902 ☎ 434/293-6789 or 877/386-1102 ⊕ www.charlottesvilletourism.org. **Lynchburg Regional Convention and Visitors Bureau** ✉ 216 12th St., Lynchburg 24504 ☎ 434/847-1811 or 800/732-5821. **Roanoke Valley Convention and Visitors Bureau** ✉ 101 Shenandoah Ave. NE, Roanoke 24011 ☎ 540/342-6025 or 800/635-5535 ⊕ www.visitroanokeva.com. **Shenandoah Valley Travel Association** ✉ I-81, Exit 264 ☐ Box 1040, New Market 22844 ☎ 540/740-3132 or 800/847-4878 ⊕ www.shenandoah.org.

Richmond, Fredericksburg & the Northern Neck

WORD OF MOUTH

"We decided to take a day trip from the D.C. area and drove down to Fredricksburg. It is a wonderful town . . . We went on the trolley ride. It gives you a good overview of the history of the area and shows you the location of the sites . . . We felt it was very worthwhile. We brought a picnic lunch but there were a lot of cute places to eat on the main strip of town."

—suzanne97

Updated by
Norman
Renouf

A HOST OF PATRIOTS AND PRESIDENTS have lived and worked in the heart of the Old Dominion, an area that takes in Richmond, Fredericksburg, Petersburg, and the Northern Neck. The birthplaces, boyhood homes, or graves of notable figures such as George Washington, James Monroe, John Tyler, and Robert E. Lee can be found here, and the area has many associations with other leaders, including Patrick Henry and Thomas Jefferson. Serving as Virginia's capital since 1880, Richmond is also the former capital of the Confederacy. Besides numerous Revolutionary War and Civil War sites, the city also contains the Fan District, full of 19th-century homes, and the Virginia state capitol, designed by Thomas Jefferson.

A half hour south of Richmond, Petersburg is a delightful antebellum city with many historic attractions. Besieged by the Union Army in 1864, the townspeople bravely did their best to protect the Confederacy. Less than an hour north of Richmond sits the appealing city of Fredericksburg, a history buff's dream, with hundreds of impressive 18th- and 19th-century homes. The nearby Fredericksburg/Spotsylvania National Military Park presents the story of the area's role in the Civil War.

East of Fredericksburg, away from the blood-soaked and fought-over grounds, peace and quiet reign in a 90-mi-long peninsula Virginians call "The Northern Neck." This outdoorsman's escape was the birthplace of three presidents, including the Father of Our Country. Here, wide rivers and the briny Chesapeake Bay entice water lovers and sports anglers. Gazing across the peaceful property where Washington was born, it's easy to see why he longed for a life at Mount Vernon instead of serving two terms as our first president.

Top 5 Experiences for Richmond, Fredericksburg & the Northern Neck

- **Soak up art from around the world:** Richmond's Virginia Museum of Fine Arts, the most outstanding museum in the region, has among its treasures the Mellon collections of British sporting art and French impressionist and postimpressionist art—and those precious five Fabergé eggs.

- **Reflect at the somber Petersburg National Battlefield:** On the site where more than 60,000 Union and Confederate soldiers died during the siege of the city, today a 1,500-acre park is laced with several miles of earthworks and includes two forts.

- **Combine Revolutionary history with architecture appreciation:** Stratford Hill Plantation is the birthplace of the legendary Robert E. Lee, the only person to be a general in both the Confederate and Union armies. Built in the 1730s and the center of a 1,600-acre working plantation, it's one of the country's finest examples of Colonial architecture, and offers wonderful views of the Potomac River to boot.

- **Sail back in time to Tangier island:** In the middle of the Chesapeake Bay, this largely unspoiled fishing village with quaint, narrow streets also happens to be the soft crab capital of the nation.

- **Return to Colonial days at Fredericksburg's Kenmore:** The mansion was built in 1775 on a 1,300-acre plantation owned by Colonel Fielding Lewis, a patriot, merchant, and brother-in-law of George Washington. Among the gems here are the outstanding plaster moldings in the ceilings and over the fireplace in the dining room—even more ornate than those at Mount Vernon.

Exploring the Area

Richmond, 100 mi south of Washington, D.C., on the James River, is the state's historic capital. It's easy to get here on I–95. Midway between Washington and Richmond on I–95, Fredericksburg is a lovely place to relax and retrace 18th- and 19th-century history in homes and museums and on nearby battlefields. About 20 mi east of Fredericksburg, the Northern Neck begins. There's no public transportation to this rural area, but a car lets you wander at will among its many historic sites and water views. Petersburg, with its Civil War history, is a mere half hour south of Richmond.

About the Restaurants & Hotels

Keep in the mind that hotel rooms can be hard to come by during Richmond's NASCAR Nextel Cup races, held over two weekends in May and September.

WHAT IT COSTS					
	$$$$	$$$	$$	$	¢
RESTAURANTS	over $30	$22–$30	$14–$22	$7–$14	under $7
HOTELS	over $250	$175–$250	$130–$175	$80–$130	under $80

Restaurant prices are per person for a main course at dinner. Hotel prices are for a standard double room, excluding state and local taxes.

RICHMOND

Centered on the fall line of the James River, about 75 mi upriver from the Chesapeake Bay, Richmond completes the transition from Tidewater Virginia into the Piedmont, the central section of rolling plains that reaches toward the mountain barrier in the west. Not only is Richmond the capital of the Commonwealth, but it was also the capital of the Confederacy. As a result, the city is studded with historic sites.

At the start of the Civil War, Richmond was the most industrialized city in the South, and it remains an important city for national industries. After years of urban decay, Richmond transformed itself into a lively and sophisticated modern town, adding high technology to traditional economic bases that include shipping and banking.

> ### RICHMOND ART SCENE
>
> Richmond is one of the South's preeminent art cities, flourishing with avant-garde painting and sculpture in addition to artifacts and magnificent traditional works, such as the Fabergé eggs in the Virginia Museum of Fine Arts.

5

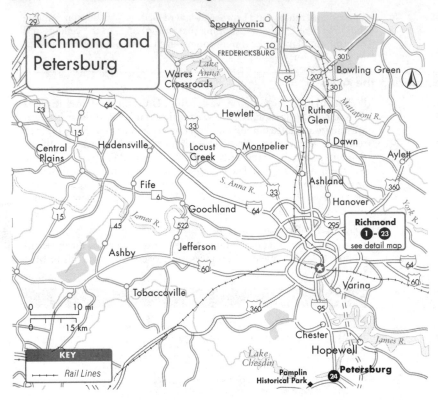

Richmond is also a great place for genealogy and history researchers. The following libraries or archives are interesting stops for the casual browser as well as for those in search of ancestors: the Library of Virginia, Virginia Historical Society Museum of Virginia History, Beth Ahabah Museum and Archives, and Black History Museum & Cultural Center of Virginia.

Downtown

Richmond's historic attractions lie north of the James River, which bisects the city with a sweeping curve. The heart of old Richmond is the Court End district downtown. This area, close to the capitol, contains seven National Historic Landmarks, three museums, and 11 additional buildings on the National Register of Historic Places—all within eight blocks.

Running west from the Court End district is Main Street, lined with banks; stores are concentrated along Grace Street, to the north. Cary Street, an east–west thoroughfare, becomes, between 12th and 15th streets, the cobblestone center of Shockoe Slip. This area (once the city's largest commercial trading district) and Shockoe Bottom (on land formerly occupied by a Native American trading post) are unique restored areas filled with trendy shops, restaurants, and nightlife. Shockoe

Bottom landmarks include the 17th Street Farmers' Market, operating since 1775, and Main Street Station, an elaborate Victorian structure capped by red tiles that was Richmond's first train station. To the east above the James River is Church Hill, which on the south side of Broad Street has become a fashionable neighborhood of restored 18th- and 19th-century homes and churches.

Drive west beyond the historic downtown to see a fascinating group of close-in, charming, and distinctive neighborhoods. Not far from the capitol is Jackson Ward, called the "Home of Black Capitalism," a cultural and entrepreneurial center after the Civil War.

Numbers in the text correspond to numbers in the margin and on the Richmond map.

Main Attractions

⑬ **Black History Museum & Cultural Center of Virginia.** The goal of this museum in the Jackson Ward is to gather visual, oral, and written records and artifacts that commemorate the lives and accomplishments of blacks in Virginia. On display are 5,000 documents, fine art objects, traditional African artifacts, textiles from ethnic groups throughout Africa, and artwork by Sam Gilllam, John Biggers, and P. H. Polk. ⌂ *00 Clay St., at Foushee St.* ☏ *804/780-9093* ⊕ *www.blackhistorymuseum.org* ⊡ *$5* ⊙ *Tues.–Sat. 10–5, Sun. 1–5.*

❸ **Edgar Allan Poe Museum.** Richmond's oldest residence, the Old Stone House in Shockoe Bottom, just west of Church Hill Historic District, now holds a museum honoring the famous writer. Poe grew up in Richmond, and although he never lived in this early- to mid-18th-century structure, his disciples have made it a monument with some of the writer's possessions on display. The Raven Room has illustrations inspired by his most famous poem. In the central garden, look for a shrine made of bricks salvaged from the magazine at which Poe worked while living in Richmond. ⌂ *1914 E. Main St.* ☏ *804/648-5523 or 888/213-2703* ⊕ *www. poemuseum.org* ⊡ *$6* ⊙ *Tues.–Sat. 10–5, Sun. 11–5. Guided tours on the hr; last tour departs at 4.*

❼ **John Marshall House.** John Marshall (1755–1835) was chief justice of the U.S. Supreme Court for 34 years—longer than any other. He built his red-brick Federal-style house with neoclassical motifs in 1790. Appointed to the court by President John Adams, Marshall also served as secretary of state and ambassador to France. The house, fully restored and furnished, has wood paneling and wainscoring, narrow arched passageways, and a mix of period pieces and heirlooms. The house has been a beautifully maintained museum since 1913. ⌂ *9th and Marshall Sts.* ☏ *804/648-7998* ⊕ *www.apva.org/marshall* ⊡ *$6* ⊙ *Tues.–Sat. 10–5, Sun. noon–5.*

Fodor's Choice
★

❺ **Museum and White House of the Confederacy.** These two buildings provide a look at a crucial period in the nation's history. The museum (a good place to start) has elaborate permanent exhibitions on the Civil War era. The "world's largest collection of Confederate memorabilia" includes such artifacts as the sword Robert E. Lee wore to the surrender at Appomattox. Next door, the "White House" has in fact always been painted gray.

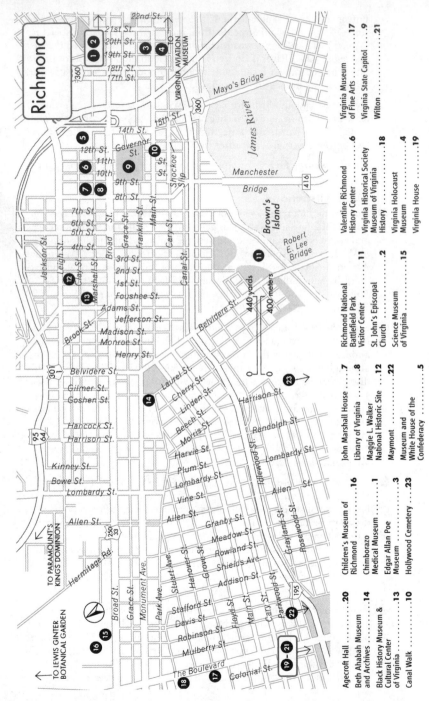

Richmond

22nd St.
21st St.
20th St.
19th St.
18th St.
17th St.
14th St.
15th St.
12th St.
11th
10th
9th St.
8th St.
7th St.
6th St.
5th St.
4th St.
3rd St.
2nd St.
1st St.
Broad St.
Grace St.
Franklin St.
Main St.
Cary St.
Canal St.

Governor St.
St.
St.
Shockoe Slip

Jackson St.
Leigh St.
Clay St.
Marshall St.
Clay St.
Foushee St.
Adams St.
Jefferson St.
Madison St.
Monroe St.
Henry St.
Brook St.

Belvidere St.
Gilmer St.
Goshen St.
Hancock St.
Harrison St.
Kinney St.
Bowe St.
Lombardy St.
Allen St.

VIRGINIA AVIATION MUSEUM

Mayo's Bridge

James River

Manchester Bridge

Brown's Island

Robert E. Lee Bridge

Belvidere St.

Laurel St.
Cherry St.
Linden St.
Beech St.
Morris St.
Harvie St.
Plum St.
Lombardy St.
Vine St.
Allen St.

Harrison St.
Randolph St.
Lombardy St.
Allen St.

Idlewood St.
Cherry St.

440 yards
400 meters

TO PARAMOUNT'S KINGS DOMINION

Hermitage Rd.

TO LEWIS GINTER BOTANICAL GARDEN

Broad St.
Grace St.
Monument Ave.
Park Ave.
Stuart Ave.
Hanover St.
Grove St.
Stafford St.
Davis St.
Robinson St.
Mulberry St.
The Boulevard

Granby St.
Meadow St.
Rowland St.
Shields Ave.
Addison St.
Floyd St.
Main St.
Cary St.
Colonial St.

Grayland St.
Rosewood St.
Parkwood St.

Allen St.

Made of brick in 1818, the building was stuccoed to give the appearance of large stone blocks. Preservationists have painstakingly re-created the interior as it was during the Civil War, when Jefferson Davis lived in the house. During the 45-minute guided tour, you see the entry hall's period 9-foot-tall French rococo mirrors and its floor cloth, painted to resemble ceramic tiles. You can park free in the adjacent hospital parking garage; the museum will validate tickets. ⊠ *1201 E. Clay St.* ☎ *804/649– 1861* ⊕ *www.moc.org* ⊞ *Combination ticket $10; museum only, $7; White House only, $7* ☉ *Mon.–Sat. 10–5, Sun. noon–5.*

OFF THE BEATEN PATH

PARAMOUNT'S KINGS DOMINION – This 400-acre theme park is home to more than 200 rides, shows, and attractions. It features one of the largest coaster collections on the East Coast—including the world's first air-launched coaster—two children's areas, and WaterWorks, a 19-acre waterpark. ⊠ *I–95, Doswell Exit 98* ☎ *804/876–5000* ⊕ *www. kingsdominion.com* ⊞ *$49.99 (includes free 2nd day admission), parking $10* ☉ *May and Sept., weekends; hrs vary, call ahead; June–Aug., daily 10 AM–10:30 PM.*

❷ **St. John's Episcopal Church.** For security reasons, the rebellious Second Virginia Convention met in Richmond instead of Williamsburg; it was in this 1741 church on March 23, 1775, that Patrick Henry delivered the speech in which he declared, "Give me liberty or give me death!" His argument persuaded the Second Virginia Convention to arm a Virginia militia. The speech is reenacted Memorial Day to Labor day on Sunday at 2 PM. The cemetery includes the graves of Edgar Allan Poe's mother, Elizabeth Arnold Poe, and many famous early Virginians, notably George Wythe, a signer of the Declaration of Independence. The visitor center, in a restored redbrick schoolhouse, has Colonial crafts and other items for sale. Guided tours are led on the half hour. ⊠ *2401 E. Broad St., at 24th St.* ☎ *804/648 5015* ⊕ *www.historicstjohnschurch. org* ⊞ *$6* ☉ *Mon.–Sat. 10–4, Sun. 1–4.*

Fodor's Choice ★

❻ **Valentine Richmond History Center.** For more than 100 years the Valentine Richmond History Center, established in 1898, has celebrated one of America's most historic cities. It has collected more than a million objects—one of the nation's largest collections focusing on a single city—including preserved photographs, textiles, and artifacts and interpreted 400 years of Richmond's history through items of everyday life. In various combinations, these are the basis for the ever-changing theme exhibits. The large collection is kept in the History Center Archives, and is available for study and research by appointment. **Wickham House** (1812), a part of the Valentine, is more rightly a mansion; it was designed by architect Alexander Parris, the creator of Boston's Faneuil Hall. John Wickham was Richmond's wealthiest citizen of the time, and Daniel Webster and Zachary Taylor were frequent guests. The house interiors are stunning, but not everything at the museum is opulent: the slave quarters, also meticulously restored, provide a chilling contrast to the mansion's splendor. ⊠ *1015 E. Clay St.* ☎ *804/649–0711* ⊕ *www. richmondhistorycenter.com* ⊞ *$10, includes John Marshall House and Wickham House* ☉ *Tues.–Sat. 10–5, Sun. noon–5; guided Wickham House tours Tues.–Sat. 11–4 and Sun. 1–4.*

5

OFF THE BEATEN PATH

VIRGINIA AVIATION MUSEUM – The legendary SR-71 Blackbird spy plane, once able to travel faster than three times the speed of sound and at an elevation of more than 85,000 feet (near the edge of the earth's atmosphere) sits proudly outside this museum. The U.S. Air Force's 32 Blackbirds were used on reconnaissance missions from 1964 to 1990. The museum also has Captain Dick Merrill's 1930s open cockpit mail plane; airworthy replicas of the Wright brothers' 1900, 1901, and 1902 gliders; a replica 1903 Flyer; and a World War I SPAD VII in mint condition. Virginia's Aviation Hall of Fame is also housed at this branch of the Science Museum of Virginia. To get here, take Exit 197 off I–64E and follow signs to the museum. ✉ *Richmond International Airport, 5701 Huntsman Rd.* ☎ *804/236–3622* ⊕ *www.vam.smv.org* 💲 *$6* ☉ *Mon.–Sat. 9:30–5, Sun. noon–5.*

★ ❹ **Virginia Holocaust Museum.** The city's newest, and most poignant, museum is housed in the former Climax Warehouse, which stored tobacco in Richmond's Shockoe Bottom. In keeping with the museum's aim to further "tolerance through education," the museum details the experiences of Holocaust survivors from across Virginia, who have recorded their stories and shared their memories. One permanent exhibit, the Ipson Saga, follows the life of a family who went from pre-war Lithuania to the Kovno ghetto concentration camp, as well as their escape and eventual resettlement in Virginia. After an introductory film in which six Richmond-based survivors tell their stories, visitors receive a book for a self-guided tour; a free audio tour (in English, Spanish, German, French, or Polish) is also available. The museum's auditorium, the Chore Shul, is a replica of the beautiful 18th-century interior of the only surviving synagogue in Lithuania. Because of the nature of the exhibits, the museum is not recommended for young children. ✉ *2000 E. Cary St.* ☎ *804/257–5400* ⊕ *www.va-holocaust.com* 💲 *Donations accepted* ☉ *Weekdays 9–5, weekends 11–5.*

★ ❾ **Virginia State Capitol.** Thomas Jefferson designed this grand edifice in 1785, modeling it on a Roman temple—the Maison Carrée—in Nîmes, France. Due to extensive renovations the interior of the Capitol is off limits until January 2007, and even the beautiful gardens are now being dug up so that a new visitor center can be constructed there. ✉ *Capitol Sq.* ☎ *804/698–1788.*

Also Worth Seeing

❿ **Canal Walk.** The 1¼-mi Canal Walk meanders through downtown Richmond along the Haxall Canal, the James River, and the Kanawha Canal, and can be enjoyed on foot or in boats. Along the way, look for history exhibits such as the Flood Wall Gallery, bronze medallions, and other exhibits placed on Brown's Island and Canal Walk by the Richmond Historical Riverfront Foundation. Many sights intersect with Canal Walk, including the Richmond National Battlefield Park Civil War Visitor Center, and 5th, 7th, Virginia, 14th, 15th, and 17th streets meet the water along it.

The James River–Kanawha Canal was proposed by George Washington to bring ships around the falls of the James River. Brown's Island hosts festivals and concerts in warmer months. **Richmond Canal Cruises**

(✉ 139 Virginia St. ☎ 804/649–2800) operates a 35-minute ride on the canal in a 38-seat open boat. Tours, which cost $5, depart from the Turning Basin near 14th and Virginia streets. Tours run from April through Thanksgiving; call for times. If you're in a car, try to find the site before parking. Lack of prominent signage makes it challenging to find, and parking lots are a few blocks away. ⊕ *www.richmondriverfront. com/canalwalk.shtml.*

❼ Chimborazo Medical Museum. This was once the Confederacy's largest and best-equipped hospital. Chimborazo opened in 1861 and treated more than 76,000 Confederate soldiers between 1862 and 1865. It could house more than 3,000 patients in its 100 wards. This site—once more than 40 acres—now contains a National Park Service visitor center and a small medical museum that tells the story of the patients, hospital, caregivers, and physicians through uniforms, documents, and other artifacts. ✉ *3215 E. Broad St.* ☎ *804/226–1981* ⊕ *www.nps.gov/ rich* ☎ *Free* ☉ *Daily 9–5.*

❽ Library of Virginia. As the official state archive, this library preserves and provides access to more than 99.5 million manuscript items documenting four centuries of Virginia history—fascinating to researchers and less so to everyone else. The library also houses and makes available to researchers more than 1½ million books, bound periodicals, microfilm reels, newspapers, and state and federal documents. Its collections include 240,000 photographs, prints, engravings, posters, and paintings. The building has free underground parking. ✉ *800 E. Broad St.* ☎ *804/692– 3500* ⊕ *www.lva.lib.va.us* ☎ *Free* ☉ *Mon.–Sat. 9–5.*

⓬ Maggie L. Walker National Historic Site. From 1904 to 1934, this restored 28-room brick building was the home of a pioneering African-American businesswoman and educator whose endeavors included banking, insurance, and a newspaper. You can take a 45-minute tour of the house and see a movie about her accomplishments. ✉ *Visitor center, 600 N. 2nd St.* ☎ *804/771–2017* ⊕ *www.nps.gov/malw* ☎ *Free* ☉ *Mon.–Sat. 9–5.*

⓫ Richmond National Battlefield Park Visitor Center. Inside what was once the Tredegar Iron Works, this is the best place to get maps and other materials on the Civil War battlefields and attractions in the Richmond area. A self-guided tour and optional tape tour for purchase covers the two major military threats to Richmond—the Peninsula Campaign of 1862 and the Overland Campaign of 1864—as well as the impact on Richmond's home front. Three floors of exhibits in the main building include unique artifacts on loan from other Civil War history institutions. Other original buildings on-site are a carpentry shop, gun foundry, office, and company store.

Built in 1837, the ironworks, along with smaller area iron foundries, made Richmond the center of iron manufacturing in the South. When the Civil War began in 1861, the ironworks geared up to make the artillery, ammunition, and other matériel that sustained the Confederate war machine. Its rolling mills provided the armor plating for warships, including the ironclad CSS *Virginia*. The works—saved from burning in 1865—went on to play an important role in rebuilding the devastated

South; it also produced munitions in both world wars. If you're lucky, you may still find free on-street parking; a pay lot is at the visitor center. ⊠ *5th and Tredegar Sts.* ☎ *804/771–2145* ⊕ *www.nps.gov/rich* ☜ *Free* ⊘ *Daily 9–5.*

The Fan District

To the west of downtown, Monument Avenue, 140 feet wide and divided by a verdant median, is lined with statues of Civil War heroes, as well as a newer one commemorating Arthur Ashe, and the stately homes of some of the first families of Virginia. A block south, a series of streets fanning out southwesterly from Park Avenue near Virginia Commonwealth University creates the Fan District, a treasury of restored turn-of-the-20th-century town houses that has become a popular neighborhood. Adjacent to it is Carytown, a restored area of shops and eateries along Cary Street.

Sights to See

⓮ Beth Ahabah Museum and Archives. This repository contains articles and documents related to the Richmond and southern Jewish experience, including the records of two congregations. ⊠ *1109 W. Franklin St.* ☎ *804/353–2668* ⊕ *www.bethahabah.org* ☜ *Free, $3 donation suggested* ⊘ *Sun.–Thurs. 10–3.*

★ ☾ **⓰ Children's Museum of Richmond.** A welcoming, hands-on complex for children and families, the museum is a place to climb, explore, experiment, and play until every surface area is smudged with fingerprints. Bright, colorful, and crowded, the museum's different sections focus on educational fun. How It Works lets children experiment with tools, materials, and their own endless energy. The Feeling Good Neighborhood has a functioning apple orchard as well as a monster-size digestive system. Our Great Outdoors houses the museum's most popular attraction, the Cave, where children explore a 40-foot replica of a Virginia limestone cave and are introduced to earth science, oceanography, and rock collecting. In the Art Studio, the paint gets on someone else's walls for a change. Specific exhibits include Children's Bank, Health and Safety, TV Studio, Super-Market, Computer Station, Art Studio, StagePlay, and In My Own Backyard (for toddlers). ⊠*2626 W. Broad St.* ☎*804/474–2667* ⊕*www.c-mor. org* ☜ *$7* ⊘ *Tues.–Sat. 9:30–5, Sun. noon–5.*

OFF THE BEATEN PATH

★ **LEWIS GINTER BOTANICAL GARDEN –** You'll find year-round beauty on this historic property with more than 40 acres of spectacular gardens, dining, and shopping. The classical domed conservatory is the only one of its kind in the Mid-Atlantic and houses ever-changing displays, tropical plants, and more than 200 orchids in bloom. A new Children's Garden offers a wheelchair-accessible tree house—fun for kids and adults—an Adventure Pathway, sand- and water-play areas, as well as an international village. More than a dozen theme gardens include a Healing Garden, Sunken Garden, Asian Valley, and Victorian Garden. The marvellous display of Christmas lights has become a Richmond tradition. Dining options include the Garden Café and the Tea House, and the shop offers an interesting selection of attractive gifts. ⊠ *1800 Lakeside Ave.* ☎ *804/262–9887* ⊕ *www.lewisginter.org* ☜ *$9* ⊘ *Daily 9–5.*

★ ☕ ⑮ **Science Museum of Virginia.** Aerospace, astronomy, electricity, physical sciences, computers, crystals, telecommunications, and the Foucault pendulum are among the subjects covered in exhibits here, many of which strongly appeal to children. The biggest spectacle is the Ethyl IMAX Dome and Planetarium, which draws the audience into the movie or astronomy show. The museum is in a former train station with a massive dome. ⊠ *2500 W. Broad St.* ☎ *804/367–1080* ⊕ *www.smv.org* ⊠ *Museum $8.50; IMAX $8.50; IMAX and planetarium $16* ⊘ *Mon.–Sat. 9:30–5, Sun. 11:30–5.*

⑱ **Virginia Historical Society Museum of Virginia History.** With 7 million manuscripts and 200,000 books, the library here is a key stop for researchers and genealogists. The visitor-friendly museum mounts regularly changing exhibits and has permanent exhibitions that include an 800-piece collection of Confederate weapons and equipment and "The Story of Virginia, an American Experience," which covers 16,000 years of history and has galleries on topics such as Becoming Confederates and Becoming Equal Virginians. ⊠ *428 North Blvd., at Kensington Ave.* ☎ *804/358–4901* ⊕ *www.vahistorical.org* ⊠ *$5* ⊘ *Mon.–Sat. 10–5, Sun., galleries only, 1–5. Research library closed Sun.*

⑰ **Virginia Museum of Fine Arts.** The panorama of world art here, spanning
Fodor'sChoice the ages from ancient times to the present, features such important
★ works as the Mellon collections of British Sporting Art and French impressionist and postimpressionist art—including nine original wax sculptures and seven bronzes by Edgar Degas; works by Goya, Renoir, and Monet; Classical and Egyptian art; Roman marble statues, and one of the world's leading collections of Indian, Nepalese, and Tibetan art. The museum's most beloved pieces are its five Fabergé eggs. Through 2008 the museum is undergoing a major expansion, which will double existing gallery space, create a sculpture garden, and enlarge parking. During this time some galleries and collections will be off view: call ahead for specific information. ⊠ *200 North Blvd.* ☎ *804/340–1400* ⊕ *www. vmfa.state.va.us* ⊠ *Free, $5 suggested donation* ⊘ *Wed.–Sun. 11–5.*

Richmond's Estates

Not far from downtown are mansions and country estates, two with buildings transported from England. Presidents and Confederate leaders are buried in Hollywood Cemetery.

Sights to See

⑳ **Agecroft Hall.** Built in Lancashire, England, in the 15th century during the reign of King Henry VIII, Agecroft Hall was transported here in 1926. It's one of the finest Tudor manor houses in the United States. Set amid gardens planted with specimens typical of 1580–1640, the house contains an extensive assortment of Tudor and early Stuart art and furniture (1485–1660) as well as collector's items from England and elsewhere in Europe. ⊠ *4305 Sulgrave Rd.* ☎ *804/353–4241* ⊕ *www.agecrofthall. com* ⊠ *$7* ⊘ *Tues.–Sat. 10–4, Sun. 12:30–5.*

㉓ **Hollywood Cemetery.** Many noted Virginians are buried here, including presidents John Tyler and James Monroe; Confederate president Jefferson Davis; generals Fitzhugh Lee, J. E. B. Stuart, and George E. Pickett; the statesman John Randolph; and Matthew Fontaine Maury, a naval scientist. ⊠ *Cherry and Albemarle Sts.* ☎804/648–8501 ☜*Free* ⊙ *Mon.–Sat. 7–5, Sun. 8–5.*

★ ☾ ㉒ **Maymont.** On this 100-acre Victorian estate is the lavish Maymont House museum, a carriage collection, and elaborate Italian and Japanese gardens. A true family attraction, Maymont's complex includes the Nature Visitor Center, native wildlife exhibits, and a children's farm. A café is open for lunch. ■ **TIP→ Tram tours and carriage rides are available.** ⊠ *2201 Shields Lake Dr.* ☎*804/358–7166* ⊕ *www.maymont. org* ☜*Donation welcome* ⊙ *Grounds Apr.–Oct., daily 10–7; Nov.–Mar., daily 10–5; mansion, nature center, and barn Tues.–Sun. noon–5.*

⑲ **Virginia House.** Alexander and Virginia Weddell had this 16th-century manor house, originally built on the site of a 12th-century English monastery, shipped across the Atlantic and up the James River in the 1920s. After three years of reconstruction and the planting of lush year-round gardens, the couple realized their dream of a re-created European estate. Alexander Weddell spent a lifetime in the diplomatic service in Mexico, Argentina, and Spain, and the house contains an extensive collection of Spanish and Latin American antiques. The estate (named after Mrs. Weddell, and not the state) passed to the Virginia Historical Society when the Weddells died in a New Year's Day train accident in 1948. ⊠ *4301 Sulgrave Rd.* ☎ *804/353–4251* ⊕ *www.vahistorical. org* ☜ *$5* ⊙ *Fri. and Sat. 10–4, Sun. 12:30–5; last tour begins 1 hr before closing.*

㉑ **Wilton.** William Randolph III built this elegant Georgian house in 1753 on what is now the only James River plantation in Richmond. Once 14 mi downriver, the home was moved brick by brick to its current site when industry encroached upon its former location. Wilton is the only house in Virginia with complete floor-to-ceiling panels in every room, and the pastel-painted panels and sunlit alcoves are a large part of its beauty. The home's 1815 period furnishings include the family's original desk bookcase and an original map of Virginia drawn by Thomas Jefferson's father. The Garden Club of Virginia landscaped the terraced lawns that overlook the James River. ⊠ *215 S. Wilton Rd., off Cary St.* ☎ *804/ 282–5936* ⊕ *www.wiltonhousemuseum.org* ☜ *$ 6* ⊙ *Mar.–Jan., Tues.–Fri. 1–4:30, Sat. 10–4:30, Sun. 1:30–4:30; Feb. by appt. only.*

Where to Eat

$$$$ ✕ **Old Original Bookbinder's.** Opened in 1865, the original branch of this restaurant has been a Philadelphia institution and has played host to the likes of astronauts, princesses, movie stars, and many other celebrities. Now the tradition continues in a beautifully renovated old tobacco

warehouse near the James River. Surrounded by exposed brick walls, a live lobster tank, and an open kitchen, you can enjoy meat and seafood dishes such as a grilled Bone in Pork chop, Sweet Crusted Mahi Mahi, Bookbinder's Signature Crab Cakes and Bookbinder's Steak. On nicer days eat on the open-air patio with a modern, cooling, nearby fountain. ⊠ *2306 E. Cary St.* ☎ *804/643–6900* 🖃 *AE, MC, V* ☯ *No lunch.*

$$$–$$$$ ✕ **Lemaire.** Named after Etienne Lemaire, Maître d'Hôtel to Thomas Jefferson from 1794 until the end of his presidency, this is the grandest restaurant in Richmond. Jefferson's tastes included adding light sauces and fresh herbs to dishes prepared with the region's more than abundant supply of ingredients. Today the menu follows the same theme with updated regional Southern cuisine that includes dashes of European classical and American contemporary influences. Typical dishes might include rack of venison, or crispy-skinned Chesapeake Bay rockfish. ⊠ *Jefferson Hotel, 101 W. Franklin St.* ☎ *804/788–8000* 🖃 *AE, D, DC, MC, V.*

$$$–$$$$ ✕ **Sensi.** In the up-and-coming Tobacco District, this low-key and pleasant restaurant sets the standard for modern Italian cuisine in Richmond. Modern art enhances the dining room, separated from a large, curved bar. Enjoy such delicacies as Seafood Quattro, an enticing combination of oysters, top-neck clam, tiger shrimp, and seared ahi tuna, and sautéed filet of Carolina line-caught black grouper with green Turkish peppercorns, Manakintowne basil, and "salsa" lobster crème. Or, if you fancy a bit of everything, try the Sensi Tasting Menu, which is priced daily. ⊠ *2222 East Cary St.* ☎ *804/648–3463* 🖃 *AE, D, MC, V* ☯ *No lunch.*

$$$ ✕ **The Dining Room.** This restaurant's rich mahogany paneling and impressionistic paintings create a feeling of warmth. The American cuisine here includes such dishes as a beef tenderloin served with oyster tempura, grilled asparagus, and béarnaise sauce. In addition to a tempting three-course prix-fixe menu, available at all times, there's a perennially popular champagne brunch on Sunday. ⊠ *Berkeley Hotel, 1200 E. Cary St.* ☎ *804/343–7300 or 888/343–7301* 🖃 *AE, D, DC, MC, V.*

★ $$–$$$ ✕ **Europa.** At this Mediterranean café and tapas bar, there are plenty of enticing main dishes, but many diners opt for making a meal from the extensive list of tapas priced in the single digits, including Spanish meats and cheeses, lamb meatballs, codfish fritters, and stewed squid. Housed in a former warehouse in Shockoe Bottom a few blocks from the capitol, the lively restaurant has a quarry-tile floor and original brick walls. Paella fanciers can choose from three versions: "La Valencia" (the traditional meats, fish, and shellfish); "La Marinera" (fish and shellfish); or "La Barcelonesa" (chicken, chorizo, and lamb). You can wash it all down with sangria made in-house. ⊠ *1409 E. Cary St.* ☎ *804/643–0911* 🖃 *AE, MC, V* ☯ *Closed Sun. No lunch Sat.*

$$–$$$ ✕ **La Grotta.** Leave modern Richmond behind and enter a brick-walled trattoria, strewn with Mediterranean artifacts, where an Italian chef cooks up authentic Italian cuisine. The house specialty is game, including *Bistecca di Bufalo* (sautéed buffalo rib eye); other options include *Quaglie Ripiene* (two roasted boneless quail stuffed with wild mushrooms, chestnuts, and sun-dried cranberries) and veal with fresh sage, toasted chestnuts, and natural pan juices. ⊠ *1218 E. Cary St.* ☎ *804/644–2466* 🖃 *AE, MC, V.*

$$–$$$ ✕ **The Hard Shell.** This fun and unpretentious restaurant has many fresh and local seafood dishes, and those with other tastes can choose from such options as filet mignon and prime rib; even vegetarians are well cared for. Raw Bar enthusiasts will be enticed, too, with choice being the only problem. The Sunday Brunch is especially attractive, as are the specialty drinks, particularly the martinis. ⊠ *1411 E. Cary St.* ☎ *804/ 643–2333* 🖃 *AE, D, DC, MC, V* ⊗ *No lunch weekends.*

$$–$$$ ✕ **The Iron Horse.** Twenty feet from this restaurant are the busiest train tracks on the East Coast, and the passing trains are certainly a novelty when dining here. The lunch menu includes tapas, pizzas, and sandwiches, and there are two major options for dinner. The more casual dinner menu, served in the Calvert Room and the lounge, includes sandwiches and entrées named after local celebrities. The à la carte menu, served in the Calvert Room only, changes seasonally and has more creative dishes, such as braised lamb shanks and roasted monkfish. ⊠ *100 S. Railroad Ave., Ashland* ☎ *804/752–6410* 🖃 *AE, D, DC, MC, V* ⊗ *No lunch weekends; no dinner Mon.*

$$–$$$ ✕ **Julep's.** In the River District, and in the city's oldest commercial building (1817), Julep's has a spiral staircase joining the upper and lower dining areas. The specialty here is new Southern cuisine, with seasonal lunch and dinner menus that include tempting dishes such as roasted game hen stuffed with a risotto of country ham, green peas, and mushrooms. The wine list is one to linger over. And try not to leave without sampling one of the restaurant's namesakes. ⊠ *1719–21 E. Franklin St.* ☎ *804/377–39* 🖃 *AE, MC, V* ⊗ *Closed Sun. No lunch Sat., no dinner Mon.*

$$–$$$ ✕ **Limani Fish Grill.** This is a serious seafood experience—it's one of the best seafood restaurants in the city—in an interesting minimalist dining room. Selecting only the freshest line-caught fish, Limani seasons them with sea salt, bastes them with oregano-infused olive oil, and then grills them over an open fire using oak and fruitwoods. Most dishes are priced by the half-pound. ⊠ *W. Cary St.* ☎ *804/353–5323* 🖃 *AE, MC, V* ⊗ *Closed Sun. No lunch.*

¢–$$ ✕ **Strawberry Street Café.** An unlimited salad bar ($5) in a claw-foot bathtub is this Fan District café's trademark. Homemade soups, unique sandwiches, and broiled crab cakes are among the offerings. Brunch is available on Sunday, and there's a Strawberry Street Market next door. ⊠ *421 Strawberry St.* ☎ *804/353–6860* 🖃 *AE, MC, V.*

¢–$ ✕ **3rd Street Diner.** Built on the site of a famous Confederate hospital, this friendly American diner has been serving great food, including breakfast dishes, sandwiches, and entrées like baked spaghetti and roast pork with stuffing, since 1926. The mix of booths and tables downstairs, and the tables upstairs, are surrounded by large prints of the era. The diner's open 24 hours a day. ⊠ *3rd and Main Sts.* ☎ *804/788–4750* 🖃 *MC, V.*

¢–$ ✕ **Penny Lane Pub & Restaurant.** The name and trademark Liver Bird (the symbol of Liverpool) at this 1976 Richmond institution give a clue that this is a little piece of that British city in Virginia. Host Terry O'Neill is a genuine scouser (Liverpudlian native). The menu is full of typical English favorites like cottage pie and fish-and-chips. ■ **TIP→ The selection of beers on tap here is the best in central Virginia.** Premiership soccer lovers will feel at home here, and there's also darts and pool available. ⊠ *421 E. Franklin St.* ☎ *804/780–1682* ⊟ *AE, D, MC* ⊙ *Closed Sun. No lunch Sat.*

Where to Stay

★ **$$$–$$$$** 🏨 **Jefferson Hotel.** The inspiration for this majestic hotel was Major Lewis Ginter, who wanted it to be one of the finest hotels in the country when it was opened in 1895. Reopened in 1907 after a fire, it hosted the famous and the rich until closing in 1980. Rebuilt again, it opened again in 1986. In this National Historic Landmark, there's a magnificent sweeping staircase reminiscent of the one in *Gone With the Wind,* embellished faux-marble columns, a 70-foot-high ceiling with a stained-glass skylight, rich tapestries, and replicas of traditional Victorian furniture. The rooms are done in a total of 57 different styles. ⊠ *101 W. Franklin St., at Adams St., 23220* ☎ *804/788–8000 or 800/424–8014* 🖷 *804/225–0334* ⊕ *www.jeffersonhotel.com* 🛏 *228 rooms, 36 suites* ♧ *2 restaurants, room service, indoor pool, health club, bar* ⊟ *AE, D, DC, MC, V.*

$$–$$$ 🏨 **Richmond Marriott.** The lobby of this luxury hotel near the 6th Street Marketplace has crystal chandeliers and marble flooring. Rooms are furnished in a contemporary style; a tanning salon keeps the beauty-conscious crowd content. ⊠ *500 E. Broad St., 23219* ☎ *804/643–3400 or 800/228–9290* 🖷 *804/788–1230* ⊕ *www.marriotthotels.com/ricdt* 🛏 *400 rooms* ♧ *2 restaurants, in-room broadband, indoor pool, health club, hot tub, lobby lounge, concierge* ⊟ *AE, D, DC, MC, V.*

$–$$$ 🏨 **Linden Row Inn.** Edgar Allan Poe played in the garden that became **Fodor'sChoice** the beautiful brick courtyards within this row of 1840s Greek Revival ★ town houses. The main building, completely renovated in 2004, is furnished in antiques and period reproductions, while the carriage-house garden quarters are decorated in Old English style and have European-style duvets. Mornings here begin with a free newspaper and deluxe continental breakfast. Enjoy the garden terrace, complimentary transportation to nearby historic attractions, and passes to the YMCA's health club. ⊠ *101 N. 1st St., at Franklin St., 23219* ☎ *804/783–7000 or 800/348–7424* 🖷 *804/648–7504* ⊕ *www.lindenrowinn.com* 🛏 *63 rooms, 7 suites* ♧ *In-room data ports, dry cleaning, laundry service, no-smoking rooms* ⊟ *AE, D, DC, MC, V* ⦿ *CP.*

★ **$$** 🏨 **Commonwealth Park Suites Hotel.** When it was the Rueger back in 1846, this hotel was a bootlegging saloon with rooms for its clientele. After a fire during the Civil War it fell into disrepair for 50 years. It was rebuilt in 1912, and after several renovations, it now has 59 luxurious rooms and suites. Because the Commonwealth is across from the Capitol, some senators and representatives make this their home when the state legislature is in session. The new Maxine's Café is now open for breakfast, lunch, and dinner. ⊠ *901 Bank St., 23219* ☎ *804/343–7300 or 888/343–7301* 🖷 *804/343–1025* 🛏 *10 rooms, 49 suites* ♧ *Restaurant, minibars, in-room broadband, dry cleaning, laundry service, meeting rooms, no-smoking rooms* ⊟ *AE, D, DC, MC, V.*

★ **$–$$** 🏨 **Berkeley Hotel.** Although built in the style of the century-old warehouses and buildings that surround it, this boutique hotel dates from

5

1988. Those seeking extra space and luxury should opt for the Governor's Suite, which has a luxurious king bed, a private terrace, and a living room with panoramic views over the historic Shockoe Slip area. Norman guest rooms have four-poster beds and traditional furnishings. Guests staying here get free entry to the YMCA health and fitness facilities. ✉ *1200 E. Cary St., 23219* ☎ *804/780–1300 or 888/780–4422* 🖶 *804/343–1885* ⊕ *www.berkeleyhotel.com* 🛏 *54 rooms, 1 suite* ⚐ *Restaurant, Wi-Fi, gym, lobby lounge, dry cleaning, laundry service, concierge, meeting rooms, parking (fee), no-smoking rooms* ⊟ *AE, D, DC, MC, V.*

$–$$ ▦ **Crowne Plaza Hotel.** Shaped like a piece of cheese, this is Richmond's most easily identifiable hotel. In the city's River District, the Crowne Plaza is close to the new Canal Walk and the James River. Club level floors include high-end amenities like fluffy bathrobes and access to the private Concierge Lounge with complimentary continental breakfast Tuesday to Friday and hors d'oeuvres and beverages weekday evenings. The rooms of choice are the two Bi-Level Point Suites with the floors connected by a spiral staircase, and classy extras like Oriental carpets and a wet bar. ✉ *555 E. Canal St., 23219* ☎ *804/788–0900 or 800/227–6963* 🖶 *804/788–7087* ⊕ *www.crowneplaza.com/ric-eastcanal* 🛏 *270 rooms, 29 suites* ⚐ *Restaurant, in-room broadband, pool, health club, sauna, bar, nightclub, concierge floor* ⊟ *AE, D, DC, MC, V.*

$–$$ ▦ **Henry Clay Inn.** Named after the local orator and statesman who was a three-time candidate for President in the early 1800s, this inn re-creates the Georgian Revival splendor of two inns that used to be nearby. Opened in 1992, the Henry Clay is furnished with reproductions of antiques as well as period pieces. The suites all have refrigerators, microwaves, and Jacuzzis. The Paramount Kings Dominion theme park is just to the north, and the Virginia Commons Center mall is to the south, between Ashland and Richmond. ✉ *114 N. Railroad Ave., Ashland 23005* ☎ *804/798–3100 or 800/343–4565* 🖶 *804/752–7555* ⊕ *www. henryclayinn.com* 🛏 *11 rooms, 3 suites* ⚐ *Restaurant, Wi-Fi, some in-room hot tubs, some microwaves, some refrigerators, cable TV, free parking; no smoking* ⊟ *AE, D, DC, MC, V.*

¢–$ ▦ **Comfort Inn Executive Center.** On the northwest side of Richmond, this three-building redbrick motel is near the University of Richmond and convenient to I–95 and I–64. From the street it looks attractive, but it also appears deceptively small; you see only the first of three buildings. The others stretch away from the street in a sort of private cul-de-sac. A deluxe continental breakfast is included. Thirty rooms have whirlpool bathtubs. ✉ *7201 W. Broad St., 23294* ☎ *804/672–1108* 🖶 *804/755–1625* ⊕ *www.comfortinn.com* 🛏 *123 rooms* ⚐ *Pool, gym, lobby lounge, laundry facilities* ⊟ *AE, D, DC, MC, V* ⫴ *CP.*

¢ ▦ **Days Inn.** This high-rise motel on the northwest side of Richmond is off West Broad Street, near several office buildings. A deluxe continental breakfast and in-room movies are free. Rooms are reached via secure interior corridors. "WorkZone" rooms with king-size beds are equipped for the business traveler. ✉ *2100 Dickens Rd., 23230* ☎ *804/282–3300 or 800/329–7466* 🖶 *804/288–2145* ⊕ *www.daysinn.com* 🛏 *180 rooms* ⚐ *Wi-Fi, pool, shop* ⊟ *AE, D, DC, MC, V* ⫴ *CP.*

Nightlife & the Arts

The **Richmond Coliseum** (✉ 601 E. Leigh St. ☎ 804/780–4956) has been a Richmond institution since the early 1970s. With 11,330 permanent seats, and nearly 2,000 more for concerts, it hosts top entertainers and artists, the Ringling Brothers circus, Richmond Riverdogs hockey team, wrestling, and other large events.

Bars

Among the delights at the martini bar and cocktail lounge **Tonic** (✉ 14 N. 18th St. ☎ 804/648–4300) is the "Strawberries and Champagne" cocktail. Tonic also serves a dinner menu of Mediterranean dishes; entrées are under $15.

Dance

The **Richmond Ballet** (✉ 407 E. Canal St. ☎ 804/344–0906), the city's professional classical ballet company, usually performs at the Carpenter Center and at the Theatre Virginia in the Virginia Museum of Fine Arts.

Music

The **Richmond Symphony** (☎ 804/788–1212), founded in 1957, often utilizes internationally known soloists at performances in the Carpenter Center. The Richmond Symphony All-Star Pops hosts popular guest artists.

Theater

Barksdale Theatre (✉ 1601 Willow Lawn Dr. ☎ 804/282–2620), the area's oldest not-for-profit theater, began in 1953. Performances ranging from classics to innovative new works are staged Thursday through Saturday evening and on Sunday afternoon. And, once again, productions are being staged at the historic Hanover Tavern.

Carpenter Center (✉ 600 E. Grace St. ☎ 804/225–9000), a restored 1928 motion-picture palace, is now a performing-arts center that mounts opera, traveling shows, symphonic music, and ballet.

Landmark Theatre (✉ 6 N. Laurel St. ☎ 804/646–4213) was built in an extremely elaborate style with towering minarets and desert murals: when it was built by the Shriners in 1926, it was called "the Mosque." Just west of downtown, the Landmark is known for its excellent acoustics and has the largest permanent proscenium stage on the East Coast. Many of America's most famous entertainers have performed here, and it continues to be used for the road versions of Broadway shows, symphony performances, ballet, children's theater, concerts, and fashion shows.

Sports & the Outdoors

Baseball

The Richmond Braves, a Triple-A farm team for Atlanta, play at the **Diamond** (✉ 3001 N. Blvd. ☎ 804/359–4444).

Car Racing

Richmond International Raceway (✉ Laburnum Ave. exit, off I–64 ☎ 804/345–7223 or 866/455–7223) holds two NASCAR Nextel Cup Series races, held on Saturday nights in May and September, as well as other races.

Tickets for the series cost $50–$110 and are extremely hard to come by, but tickets for all other events are readily available. Children under 12 are admitted free.

Golf

In Richmond aficionados tee off most of the year. The area has 24 golf courses open to the public—the **Virginia State Golf Association** (⊕ www.vsga.org) has a good handle on them all; its Web site even allows you to book tee times online.

Rafting

Richmond is the only city within the U.S. that has rafting within its city limits. **Richmond Raft** (☎ 804/222–7238 or 800/222–7238) conducts white-water rafting trips through the city on the James River (Class III and IV rapids), as well as float trips from March through November.

Shopping

Sixth Street Marketplace has specialty shops, chain stores, and eating places. **Shockoe Slip** (⊠ E. Cary St. between 12th and 15th Sts.), a neighborhood of tobacco warehouses during the 18th and 19th centuries, has some boutiques.

The open-air **Farmers' Market** (⊠ 17th and Main Sts.), beside the old Main Street Station, is surrounded by art galleries, boutiques, and antiques shops, many in converted warehouses and factories.

PETERSBURG

㉔ Historic **Petersburg,** 20 mi south of Richmond on I–95, lies along the Appomattox River. During the Civil War, the city was under siege by Union forces from June 1864 to April 1865—the so-called last stand of the Confederacy. A major railroad hub, the city was a crucial link in the supply chain for Lee's army, and its surrender brought about the evacuation of Richmond and the surrender at Appomattox. These days, like many other small Southern towns, it is struggling to overcome decades of depression, and this is readily apparent on the drive from I–95 to the downtown area. However, a great effort has been made in the area around the Petersburg Visitors Center, and there are many beautifully maintained houses in the historic residential area just to the west.

Centre Hill Mansion. This, the third home of the Bolling family, was originally built in 1823. Having been remodeled twice since then, it illustrates changing architectural styles; it was and is the grandest home in Petersburg. Inside are ornate woodwork, plaster motifs and period furnishings, and an 1840s service tunnel in the basement that once connected the work area of the house to the street below. ⊠ *1 Centre Hill Circle* ☎ *804/733–2401* ⊉ *$5* ⊙ *Daily 10–5.*

A parish church from the 18th century, **Old Blandford Church** is a memorial to the Southern soldiers who died during the Civil War. Some 30,000 Confederate soldiers are buried in the churchyard, which is surrounded by ornamental ironwork. The church's 15 spectacular stained-glass windows by Louis Comfort Tiffany are memorials donated by the

Confederate states. ■ TIP→ The Memorial Day tradition is said to have begun in this cemetery in June 1866. ⊠ *319 S. Crater Rd., 2 mi south of town* ☎ *804/733-2396* ⌨ *$5* ⊙ *Daily 10–5.*

★ On April 2, 1865, in what is now **Pamplin Historical Park,** Union troops successfully attacked General Robert E. Lee's formerly impenetrable defense line, forcing Lee to aban-

WORD OF MOUTH
"Pamplin Historical Park is awesome! Very moving. You get to pick a soldier and follow him (through his narration) through the war. At the end, you find out if he survived or was killed. They also have a reenactment area."   –lambyk

don Petersburg. Today you are greeted by the 300-foot-long facade of the Battlefield Center, a concrete representation of the Confederate battle lines. Besides the center, which focuses on the April 2 battle, there's a 2-mi battle trail with 2,100 feet of 8-foot-high earthen fortifications, reconstructed soldier huts, and original picket posts. Also on the grounds is Tudor Hall, an 1812 plantation home that served as the 1864 headquarters for Confederate general Samuel McGowan. Costumed interpreters bring the era to life, and reconstructed outbuildings have exhibits and displays. The **National Museum of the Civil War Soldier** on the grounds has interactive displays and nearly 1,000 artifacts. You can select an audio guide that includes the actual letters and diaries of a soldier. The park also has a café and a large store. Allow at least two hours to visit the park and museum. ⊠ *6125 Boydton Plank Rd., off U.S. 1, I–85S to Exit 63A* ☎ *804/861-2408 or 877/726-7546* ⊕ *www. pamplinpark.org* ⌨ *$13.50* ⊙ *Mid-Aug.–mid-June, daily 9–5; mid-June–mid-Aug, daily 9–6.*

Fodor'sChoice To walk **Petersburg National Battlefield** is to be where more than 60,000
★ Union and Confederate soldiers died during the siege of the city. A pronounced depression in the ground is the eroded remnant of the Crater, the result of a 4-ton gunpowder explosion set off by Union forces in one failed attack. The 1,500-acre park is laced with several miles of earthworks and includes two forts. In the visitor center, maps and models convey background information vital to the self-guided driving tour, during which you park at specified spots on the tour road and proceed on foot to nearby points of interest. ⊠ *Rte. 36, 2½ mi east of downtown* ☎ *804/732-3531* ⊕ *www.nps.gov/pete* ⌨ *$5 car, $3 cyclist or pedestrian* ⊙ *Park mid-June–Labor Day, daily 8:30–dusk; Labor Day–mid-June, daily 8–5. Visitor center daily 8:30–5:30.*

The **Petersburg Visitors Center** sells the Fort Henry Pass, which allows admission to the Siege Museum, Centre Hill Mansion, and Blandford Church for $11. The center also has information about Lee's Retreat Trail, a 26-stop driving tour around the area. Free parking is plentiful near the center. ⊠ *McIlwaine House, 425 Cockade Alley* ☎ *804/733-2400 or 800/368-3595* ⊕ *www.petersburg-va.org.*

★ The **Siege Museum,** inside a former commodities market from 1839, tells the story of how the city's lavish lifestyle gave way to a bitter struggle for survival during the Civil War: a single chicken could cost as much as $50 in Confederate currency. A 16-minute movie narrated by Petersburg-born actor Joseph Cotten dramatizes the upheaval. ⊠ *Exchange Bldg., 15 W. Bank St.* ☎ *804/733-2404* ☒ *$5* ⊙ *Daily 10–5.*

Where to Stay & Eat

$$–$$$ ✗ **Alexander's Fine Food.** White tablecloths flare from beneath glass tops at the tables of this Greek-American restaurant, which also has a bar. A souvlaki platter, leg of lamb, and Athenian-style chicken are specialties. ⊠ *101 W. Bank St.* ☎ *804/733-7134* ▤ *No credit cards* ⊙ *Closed Sun. No dinner Mon. and Tues.*

$–$$ ✗ **Andrades.** This bright restaurant also has a large outdoor terrace with tables covered by very colorful umbrellas. The cuisine has a southwestern and Mexican flair and includes such tempting dishes as *Zarzuela de Mariscos,* a seafood casserole, and *Masitas de Puerco,* Cuban-style pieces of pork marinated in criollo sauce and roasted in Sevilla's bitter oranges. ⊠ *7 Bollingbrook St.* ☎ *804/733-1515* ▤ *MC, V.*

$ ▥ **Ragland Mansion.** This stunningly attractive Italianate villa dates from the 1850s; it was the residence of General "Black Jack" Pershing during World War I. Inside are large formal rooms with crown moldings, French windows, 14-foot ceilings, mosaic parquet floors, and European and American artworks. The rooms and suite are furnished with antique furniture, claw-foot tubs, brass and iron beds, and paintings and engravings. It's a short walk from downtown and the Historic District. ⊠ *205 S. Sycamore St., 23803* ☎ *804/861-1932 or 800/861-8898* 🖷 *804/861-5943* ⊕ *www.raglandmansion.com* ◁⟩ *6 rooms, 3 suites* ⟨⟩ *free parking* ▤ *AE, MC, V.*

¢–$ ▥ **High Street Inn.** In the heart of the Historic District, this beautiful Queen Anne mansion dating from 1891 was built by J. A. Gill, a wealthy local merchant, of natural fired brick. Opened in late 2004, the public areas and rooms—all named after people or places that influenced Petersburg's history—are charmingly classical, and the intricacy of the woodwork on the king-size bed in the BollingBrook Room has to be seen to be believed. ⊠ *405 High St., 23803* ☎ *804/722-0800 or 888/474-1898* ◁⟩ *5 rooms* ⟨⟩ *Cable TV, Wi-Fi, free parking* ▤ *AE, D, DC, MC, V* ꙮ *CP.*

¢ ▥ **Best Western Steven Kent.** This pristine two-story motel has a home-style family restaurant, an Olympic-size swimming pool, and nearly 20 acres of recreational facilities. Local calls and newspapers are free, and rooms have a coffeemaker, hair dryer, iron, and ironing board. ⊠ *12205 S. Crater Rd., 23805* ☎ *804/733-0600 or 800/284-9393* ⊕ *www.bestwestern.com* 🖷 *804/862-4549* ◁⟩ *133 rooms* ⟨⟩ *Restaurant, microwaves, in-room broadband, putting green, 2 tennis courts, pool, basketball, horseshoes, bar, lounge, playground, laundry facilities, business services, meeting rooms* ▤ *AE, D, DC, MC, V* ꙮ *CP.*

FREDERICKSBURG

Halfway between Richmond and Washington near the falls of the Rappahannock River, Fredericksburg is a popular destination for history buffs. The town's 40-block National Historic District contains more than 350 original 18th- and 19th-century buildings, including the house George

Washington bought for his mother; the Rising Sun Tavern; and Kenmore, the magnificent 1752 plantation owned by George Washington's sister.

Although its site was visited by explorer Captain John Smith as early as 1608, Fredericksburg wasn't founded until 1728. It was named after England's crown prince at the time, Frederick Louis, the eldest

son of King George II. The streets still bear names of his family members: George, Caroline, Sophia, Princess Anne, William, and Amelia. Established as a frontier port to serve nearby tobacco farmers and iron miners, Fredericksburg was at one point the 10th largest port in the colonies.

George Washington knew Fredericksburg well, having grown up just across the Rappahannock on Ferry Farm, his residence from age 6 to 19. The myths about chopping down a cherry tree and throwing a coin (actually a rock) across the Rappahannock (later confused with the Potomac) refer to this period of his life. In later years Washington often visited his mother here on Charles Street.

Fredericksburg prospered in the decades after independence, benefiting from its location midway along the route between Washington and Richmond—an important intersection of railroad lines and waterways. When the Civil War broke out, it became the linchpin of the Confederate defense of Richmond and therefore the target of Union assaults. In December 1862, Union forces attacked the town in what was to be the first of four major battles fought in and around Fredericksburg. In the battle of Sunken Road, Confederate defenders sheltered by a stone wall at the base of Marye's Heights mowed down thousands of Union soldiers who charged across the fields.

At Chancellorsville in April 1863, General Robert E. Lee led 60,000 troops to a brilliant victory over a much larger Union force of 134,000, and this resulted in Lee's invasion of Pennsylvania. The following year, Grant's troops battled Lee's Confederates through the Wilderness, a region of dense thickets and overgrowth south of the Rapidan River, then fought them again at Spotsylvania. Although neither side was victorious, Grant continued heading his troops toward the Confederate capital of Richmond.

By the war's end, fighting in Fredericksburg and at the nearby Chancellorsville, Wilderness, and Spotsylvania Court House battlefields resulted in more than 100,000 dead or wounded. Fredericksburg's cemeteries hold the remains of 17,000 soldiers from both sides. Miraculously, despite heavy bombardment and house-to-house fighting, much of the city remained intact.

A few decades ago Fredericksburg was one of the numerous small Southern cities facing another battle for survival, but today the city is being overrun for a different reason. The charming, historic town appeals to commuters fleeing the Washington, D.C., area for kinder, less expensive environs. The railroad lines that were so crucial to transporting Civil War supplies now bring workers to and from the nation's capital an hour away, and the sacred Civil War battlegrounds share the area with legions of shopping centers. Tourists aren't scarce either, and not just to visit the historical sights. These days Fredericksburg has reinvented itself as a cute small town chock-a-block with boutiques and antiques and specialty stores, as well as a lively selection of small cafés and restaurants.

Numbers in the text correspond to numbers in the margin and on the Fredericksburg map.

Downtown Fredericksburg

Fredericksburg, a modern commercial town, includes a 40-block National Historic District with more than 350 original 18th- and 19th-century buildings. No play-acting here—residents live in the historic homes and work in the stores, many of which sell antiques. A walking tour through the town proper takes three to four hours; battlefield tours will take at least that long.

Main Attractions

❶ **Fredericksburg Visitor Center.** Beyond the usual booklets, pamphlets, and maps, this visitor center has passes that enable you to park for a whole day in what are usually two-hour zones as well as money-saving passes to city attractions ($29 for entry to nine sights; $19 for four sights— both a better than 35% discount over individual admission prices). Before beginning your tour, you may want to see the center's 10-minute orientation slide show. The center building itself was constructed in 1824 as a residence and confectionery; during the Civil War it was used as a prison. ■ TIP→ Before leaving, don't forget to get a pass for free all-day parking anywhere in the Old Town. ⊠ *706 Caroline St., Historic District* ☎ *540/373–1776 or 800/678–4748* ⊕ *www.visitfred.com* ⊘ *Daily 9–5; hrs extended in summer.*

NEED A BREAK?

Goolrick's Pharmacy (⊠ 901 Caroline St., Historic District ☎ 540/373–9878) opened in 1869 and has been in its present location since the late 1890s. In 1912 the soda fountain was installed, and it is now the oldest operating in the USA. In addition to malts and egg creams (made of seltzer and milk, but not egg or cream), Goolrick's serves light meals weekdays 8:30–7 and Saturday 8:30–6. Using only the freshest bread and produce, **Virginia Deli** (⊠ 101 William St., Historic District ☎ 540/371–2233 ⊘ Weekdays 8–4, Sat. 8–6) offers a tempting array of specialty and customized sandwiches as well as an enticing salad bar. For freshly made soups, sandwiches, and desserts, drop by **Olde Towne Wine and Cheese Deli** (⊠ 707 Caroline St., Historic District ☎ 540/373–7877 ⊘ Daily 11–4), in operation for more than a quarter century and directly opposite the Fredericksburg Tourism Center.

Fredericksburg, Virginia

🐾 **②** **Hugh Mercer Apothecary Shop.** Offering a close-up view of 18th- and 19th-century medical instruments and procedures, the apothecary was established in 1761, and demonstrates the work of Dr. Mercer, a Scotsman who served as a brigadier general of the Continental Army (he was killed at the Battle of Princeton). Dr. Mercer may have been more careful than other Colonial physicians, but his methods might still make you cringe. A costumed hostess explicitly describes amputations and cataract operations before the discovery of anesthetics. ■ **TIP→ You can also hear about therapeutic bleeding, see the gruesome devices used in Colonial dentistry, and watch a demonstration of leeching.** ✉ *1020 Caroline St., at Amelia St., Historic District* ☎ *540/373–3362* 💲 *$5* 🕑 *Mar.–Nov., Mon.–Sat. 9–5, Sun. 11–5; Dec.–Feb., Mon.–Sat. 10–4, Sun. noon–4.*

⑤ **Kenmore.** Named Kenmore by a later owner, this house was built in 1775 on a 1,300-acre plantation owned by Colonel Fielding Lewis, a patriot, merchant, and brother-in-law of George Washington. Lewis sacrificed his fortune to operate a gun factory and otherwise supply General Washington's forces during the Revolutionary War. As a result, his debts forced his widow to sell the home following his death. The outstanding plaster moldings in the ceilings and over the fireplace in the dining room are even more ornate than those at Mount Vernon. It's be-

Fodor's Choice
★

lieved that the artisan responsible for them worked frequently in both homes, though his name is unknown, possibly because he was an indentured servant. A major restoration is scheduled to be completed by late 2006, and at that time the lavish period furnishings (not original to the house) will be back in place. It is interesting to note that the walls vary in thickness: 36 inches in the basement, 24 inches on the ground floor, and 18 inches upstairs. Guided 45-minute architectural tours of the home are conducted by docents; the subterranean Crowningshield Museum on the grounds displays Kenmore's collection of fine Virginia-made furniture and family portraits as well as changing exhibits on Fredericksburg life. ⊠ *1201 Washington Ave., Historic District* ☎ *540/373–3381* ⊕ *www.kenmore.org* ⊠ *$8* ⊙ *Daily 10–5, last tour begins at 4:15.*

★ ❹ **Mary Washington House.** George purchased a three-room cottage for his mother in 1772 for £225, renovated it, and more than doubled its size with additions. She spent the last 17 years of her life here, tending the garden where her original boxwoods still flourish today, and where many a bride and groom now exchange their vows. The home has been a museum since 1930. Inside, displays include Mrs. Washington's "best dressing glass," a silver-over-tin mirror in a Chippendale frame; her teapot; Washington family dinnerware; and period furniture. The kitchen, in a rather lopsided wooden house in the pretty gardens, and its spit are original. Tours begin on the back porch with a history of the house. ⊠ *1200 Charles St., Historic District* ☎ *540/373–1569* ⊠ *$5* ⊙ *Mar.–Nov., Mon.–Sat. 9–5, Sun. 11–5; Dec.–Feb., Mon.–Sat. 10–4, Sun. noon–4.*

❸ **Rising Sun Tavern.** In 1760 George Washington's brother Charles built as his home what later became the Rising Sun Tavern, a watering hole for such patriots as the Lee brothers (the only siblings to sign the Declaration of Independence); Patrick Henry, the five-term governor of Virginia who said, "Give me liberty or give me death"; and future presidents Washington and Jefferson. Two male indentured servants and a "wench" in period costume lead a tour without stepping out of character. From them, you hear how travelers slept and what they ate and drank at this busy institution. ⊠ *1304 Caroline St., Historic District* ☎ *540/371–1494* ⊠ *$5* ⊙ *Mar.–Nov., Mon.–Sat. 9–5, Sun. 11–5; Dec.–Feb., Mon.–Sat. 10–4, Sun. noon–4.*

OFF THE BEATEN PATH   **BLUE & GRAY BREWING COMPANY –** To tour a home-grown brewery and have a free tasting, drive less than 2 mi southeast of the visitor center to the Blue & Gray Brewing Company, where the beers include Fred Red Ale, Falmouth American Pale Ale, and Blue & Gray Classic Lager.

✉ *Bowman Center Industrial Park, 3321 Dill Smith Dr.* ☏ *540/538–2379* ⊘ *Wed. 3–6, Fri. 4–8, Sat. 10–1.*

Also Worth Seeing

❼ Confederate Cemetery. This cemetery contains the remains of more than 2,000 soldiers (most of them unknown) as well as the graves of generals Dabney Maury, Seth Barton, Carter Stevenson, Daniel Ruggles, Henry Sibley, and Abner Perrin. ✉ *1100 Washington Ave., near Amelia St., Historic District* ⊘ *Daily dawn–dusk.*

❾ Fredericksburg Area Museum and Cultural Center. In an 1816 building once used as a market and town hall, this museum's six permanent exhibits tell the story of the area from prehistoric times through the Revolutionary and Civil wars to the present. The Civil War exhibits emphasize the civilian experience, although attention is also paid to the soldier. Military items on display include a Henry rifle, a sword with "CSA" carved into the basket, and a Confederate officer's coat. Most weapons and accessories were found on local battlefields. Other displays include dinosaur footprints from a nearby quarry, Native American artifacts, and an 18th-century plantation account book with an inventory of slaves. The first and third floors have changing exhibits. ✉ *907 Princess Anne St., Historic District* ☏ *540/371–3037* ⊕ *www.famcc.org* ✉ *$5* ⊘ *Mar.–Nov., Mon.–Sat. 10–5, Sun. 1–5; Dec.–Feb., Mon.–Sat. 10–4, Sun. 1–4.*

❽ James Monroe Museum and Memorial Library. This tiny one-story building—on the site where Monroe, who became the fifth president of the United States, practiced law from 1787 to 1789—contains many of Monroe's possessions, collected and preserved by his family until the present day. They include a mahogany dispatch box used during the negotiation of the Louisiana Purchase and the desk on which the Monroe Doctrine was signed. ✉ *908 Charles St., Historic District* ☏ *540/654–1043* ✉ *$5* ⊘ *Mar.–Nov., Mon.–Sat. 9–5, Sun. 1–5; Dec.–Feb., Mon.–Sat. 10–4, Sun. 1–4.*

❻ Mary Washington Grave and Monument. A 40-foot granite obelisk, dedicated by President Grover Cleveland in 1894, marks the final resting place of George's mother. It was laid at "Meditation Rock," a place on her daughter's property where Mrs. Washington liked to read.

❿ University of Mary Washington Galleries. On campus are two art galleries. The Ridderhof Martin Gallery hosts exhibitions of art from various cultures and historical periods. The duPont Gallery, in Melchers Hall, displays paintings, drawing, sculpture, photography, ceramics, and textiles by art faculty, students, and contemporary artists. Free gallery-visitor parking is available in the lot at the corner of College Avenue at Thornton Street. ✉ *1301 College Ave., Historic District* ☏ *540/654–1013* ✉ *Free* ⊘ *When college is in session, Mon., Wed., and Fri. 10–4, weekends 1–4.*

Around Fredericksburg

Surrounding the town of Fredericksburg are historic sites and gorgeous vistas where, in 1862, Union forces once stood. Today you see only the lively Rappahannock and beautiful homes on a lovely drive across the river.

Sights to See

⑫ Chatham. A fine example of Georgian architecture, Chatham was built between 1768 and 1771 by William Fitzhugh, a plantation owner, on a site overlooking the Rappahannock River and the town of Fredericksburg. Among Fitzhugh's guests were the likes of George Washington and Thomas Jefferson. During the Civil War, Union forces commandeered the house and converted it into a headquarters and hospital. President Abraham Lincoln conferred with his generals here, Clara Barton (founder of the American Red Cross) tended the wounded, and poet Walt Whitman visited for a few hours looking for his brother, who had been wounded in a battle. After the war, the house and gardens were restored by private owners and eventually donated to the National Park Service. The home itself is now a museum. Five of the 10 rooms in the 12,000-square-foot mansion house exhibits spanning several centuries and are open to the public. ☒ *120 Chatham La., Falmouth, VA* ☏ *540/370-0802* ⊕ *www.nps.gov/frsp* ☒ *Free* ☉ *Daily 9–4:30.*

⑭ Fredericksburg/Spotsylvania National Military Park. The 9,000-acre park
Fodor's Choice actually includes four battlefields and four historic buildings. At the Fred-
★ ericksburg and Chancellorsville visitor centers you can learn about the area's role in the Civil War by watching a 22-minute film ($2) and viewing displays of soldiers' art and battlefield relics. In season, park rangers lead walking tours. The centers offer tape-recorded tour cassettes ($4.95 rental, $7.50 purchase) and maps that show how to reach the battlefields, Chancellorsville (where General Stonewall Jackson was mistakenly shot by his own troops), and Spotsylvania Court House battlefields—all within 15 mi of Fredericksburg.

Just outside the Fredericksburg Battlefield Visitor Center is Sunken Road, where on December 13, 1862, the Confederates achieved a resounding victory over Union forces attacking across the Rappahannock (there were 18,000 casualties on both sides). Much of the stone wall that protected Lee's infantrymen is now a recreation, but 100 yards from the visitor center, part of the original wall overlooks the statue *The Angel of Marye's Heights,* by Felix de Weldon (sculptor of the famous *Marine Corps War Memorial* statue in Arlington). This memorial honors Sergeant Richard Kirkland, a South Carolinian who risked his life to bring water to wounded foes; he later died at the Battle of Chickamauga. ☒ *Fredericksburg Battlefield Visitor Center, 1013 Lafayette Blvd. and Sunken Rd., Historic District* ☏ *540/373–6122* ☒ *Chancellorsville Battlefield Visitor Center, Rte. 3 W, Plank Rd., Chancellorsville* ☏ *540/786–2880* ⊕ *www.nps.gov/frsp* ☒ *Free* ☉ *Visitor centers daily 9–5 with extended hrs in summer; walking tours on a seasonal basis dawn–dusk.*

⑬ Gari Melchers Home and Studio. The last owner of this 1790s Georgian-style house was American artist Gari Melchers, who chaired the Smithsonian Commission to establish the National Gallery of Art in Washington. His wife, Corinne, deeded the 27-acre estate and its collections to Virginia. Known as Belmont, the home is now a public museum and a Virginia National Historic Landmark administered by the University of Mary Washington. You can take a one-hour tour of the spacious house, which is furnished with a rich collection of the owners' antiques. Galleries in the stone studio, built by the Melchers in 1924, house the largest repository of the artist's work. An orientation movie is shown in the reception area, which was once the carriage house. ✉ *224 Washington St., Falmouth* ☎ *540/654–1015* ⊕ *www.garimelchers.org* ✉ *$7* ⊘ *Mar.–Nov., Mon.–Sat. 10–5, Sun. 1–5; Dec.–Feb., Mon.–Sat. 10–4, Sun. 1–4.*

⑪ **George Washington's Ferry Farm.** If it hadn't been for the outcries of historians and citizens, a Wal-Mart would have been built on this site, the boyhood home of our first president. The land was saved by the George Washington's Fredericksburg Foundation, and the discount store found a location farther out on the same road. Ferry Farm, which once consisted of 600 acres, is across the Rappahannock River from downtown Fredericksburg and was the site of a ferry crossing. Living here from ages 6 to 19, Washington received his formal education and taught himself surveying while *not* chopping a cherry tree or throwing a coin across the Rappahannock—legends concocted by Parson Weems. The mainly archaeological site also has an exhibit on "George Washington: Boy Before Legend." The ongoing excavations include a summer program for children and adults, "Digging for Young George." Ferry Farm became a major artillery base and river-crossing site for Union forces during the Battle of Fredericksburg. ✉ *Rte. 3 E, 268 Kings Hwy., at Ferry Rd., Fredericksburg 22405* ☎ *540/370–0732* ⊕ *www.kenmore. org* ✉ *$5* ⊘ *Daily 10–5; last tour begins at 4:15.*

⑮ **National Cemetery.** The National Cemetery is the final resting place of 15,000 Union dead, most of whom have not been identified. ✉ *Lafayette Blvd. and Sunken Rd., Historic District* ☎ *540/373–6122* ⊘ *Daily dawn–dusk.*

Where to Eat

$$$–$$$$ ✗**Chords.** Opened in 2005 in a historical building, this mulitifaceted restaurant has jazz- and blues-theme decor and a frequently changing menu that might include such delicacies as baby cod Wellington, gnocchi with sundried tomatoes and oyster mushrooms, and fruits de mer, and can also cater to those with food allergies. The Cellar Nightclub opens Tuesday through Saturday with daily specials and audience participation—karaoke anyone? ✉ *917 Caroline St., Historic District* ☎ *540/ 372-3434* ▤ *AE, D, DC, MC, V.*

$$–$$$$ ✗**Augustine's at Fredericksburg Square.** Named after Augustine Washington, George's father, who owned most of the property along Caroline Street, this is the place to go in Fredericksburg for AAA Four Diamond award-winning fare. In this very formal environment, the well-spaced tables are set in the traditional European style, including the use of gold charger plates. The creative and attractively presented dishes, prepared in a New American style, might include saffron-braised angler fish and ricotta gnocchi. The wine list is not only extensive in its selections but also creatively presented. ✉ *525 Caroline St.* ☎ *540/310– 0063* ▤ *AE, D, DC, MC, V* ⊘ *Closed Sun. and Mon. No lunch.*

$$–$$$ ✕ **Bistro Bethem.** In an 1833 storefront that served as a general store, buttermilk-color walls display local art. Copper chandeliers and original heart-of-pine floors lend a warm glow; when the weather's fine, tables are brought out onto the sidewalk for alfresco dining. The menu changes with the seasons and features modern American cuisine with a Southern accent, and the award-winning wine list features the most varietally diverse multicultural selections in the Fredericksburg region. ⊠ *309 William St.* ☎ *540/371–9999* ⊟ *AE, D, MC, V* ⊘ *Closed Mon. No dinner Sun.*

$$–$$$ ✕ **Brock's Riverside Grill.** On the edge of town, this restaurant has a large bar, various dining rooms, and a marvellous open-air terrace directly overlooking the river. The menu includes a wide range of starters and salads, along with steaks, chops, pasta, chicken, and burgers and sandwiches that appeal to all tastes. ⊠ *503 Sophia St., Historic District* ☎ *540/ 370–1820* ⊟ *AE, D, DC, MC, V.*

$$–$$$ ✕ **Claiborne's.** On the walls of this swank eatery in the 1910-era Fredericksburg train station are historic train photographs. The restaurant, decorated in dark green and navy with mahogany-and-brass bars, specializes in low-country Southern dishes, including crawfish, grits, and collard greens. Accompanying the steaks, chops, and seafood are ample vegetable side dishes served family style. On Sunday there's a lunch buffet. ⊠ *200 Lafayette Blvd., Historic District* ☎ *540/371–7080* ⊟ *AE, DC, MC, V.*

$$–$$$ ✕ **Ristorante Renato.** This family-owned restaurant, decorated with lace curtains, red carpeting, and walls covered with paintings, specializes in Italian cuisine, including veal, chicken, pasta, and seafood. Standouts include veal Florentine, fettuccine Alfredo, eggplant parmigiana, steamed mussels, and Italian desserts such as cannoli, spumoni, and tiramisu. ⊠ *422 William St., Historic District* ☎ *540/371–8228* ⊟ *AE, MC, V* ⊘ *No lunch weekends.*

$–$$$ ✕ **Merriman's Restaurant & Bar.** Inside an old brick storefront, Merriman's dining room is painted a bright yellow. On the eclectic menu are Mediterranean dishes such as linguine Mykonos, Greek salad, and Middle Eastern hummus, which jostle against classic Virginia meats and seafood. Desserts are made fresh daily. ⊠ *715 Caroline St., Historic District* ☎ *540/ 371–7723* ⊟ *AE, D, DC, MC, V.*

$–$$ ✕ **La Petite Auberge.** Housed in a pre–Civil War brick general store, this white-tablecloth restaurant actually has three dining rooms decorated like a French garden, with numerous paintings by local artists for sale. The interesting menu changes with the seasons, and the chef uses local produce and seafood. Specialties like house-cut beef, French onion soup, and seafood are all served with a continental accent. A fixed-price ($14) three-course dinner is served from 5:30 to 7 Monday through Thursday. ⊠ *311 William St., Historic District* ☎ *540/371–2727* ⊟ *AE, D, MC, V* ⊘ *Closed Sun.*

$–$$ ✕ **Smythe's Cottage & Tavern.** Entering this cozy dining room in a blacksmith's house built in the early 1800s is like taking a step back in time. The lunch and dinner menus are classic Virginia: seafood pie, quail, stuffed flounder, peanut soup, and Smithfield ham biscuits. ⊠ *303 Fauquier St., Historic District* ☎ *540/373–1645* ⊟ *MC, V* ⊘ *Closed Tues.*

¢–$$ ✕ **Sammy T's.** Vegetarian dishes, healthy foods, and homemade soups and breads share the menu with hamburgers and dinner platters at this unpretentious place. The bar is stocked with nearly 50 brands of beer. There's a separate no-smoking section around the corner, but a tin ceiling, high wooden booths, and wooden ceiling fans make the main dining room much chummier and more homey. ⊠ *801 Caroline St., Historic District* ☎ *540/371–2008* ▤ *AE, D, MC, V.*

Where to Stay

$–$$ ▦ **Kenmore Inn.** This 18th-century historic home is easily recognizable by its magnificent and inviting front porch. There are two types of rooms. The deluxe ones, in the original part of the house, have working fireplaces and canopy beds; the slightly smaller standard rooms have Colonial furnishings. The English pub, with its Mahogany Horseshoe Bar, serves lighter dishes and imported draft beer; it's open Tuesday to Sunday evenings. ⊠ *1200 Princess Anne St., Historic District, 22401* ☎ *540/371–7622* 🖷 *540/371–5480* ⊕ *www.kenmoreinn.com* 🛏 *9 rooms* ⚭ *Restaurant, some cable TV, Wi-Fi, pub; no TV in some rooms* ▤ *AE, D, DC, MC, V* ⦿l *CP.*

$–$$ ▦ **Richard Johnston Inn.** This elegant B&B was constructed in the late 1700s and served as the home of Richard Johnston, mayor of Fredericksburg from March 1809 to March 1810. Guest rooms are decorated with period antiques and reproductions. The aroma of freshly baked breads and muffins entices you to breakfast in the large Federal-style dining room, where the table's set with fine china, silver, and linens. The inn is just across from the visitor center and two blocks from the train station. Ample private parking is behind the inn. ⊠ *711 Caroline St., Historic District 22401* ☎ *540/899–7606 or 877/557–0770* ⊕ *www.therichardjohnstoninn.com* 🛏 *7 rooms, 2 suites* ⚭ *Cable TV, in-room VCRs, Wi-Fi, free parking; no smoking* ▤ *AE, MC, V* ⦿l *CP.*

$ ▦ **Wingate Inn.** Built in 2001 this four-story hotel has large rooms equipped for the business traveler. Guest rooms are decorated in a soothing cream and moss. Coffeemakers are standard in every room. The large lobby hosts the expanded continental breakfast and evening dessert and beverage pantry. There's a complimentary local shuttle. The Wingate is set back from U.S. Route 17 (Exit 133 off I–95, north toward Warrenton). Turn left at the first signal light west of I–95. ⊠ *20 Sanford Dr., 22406* ☎ *540/368–8000 or 800/228–1000* 🖷 *510/368–9252* ⊕ *www.wingateinns.com* 🛏 *83 rooms, 10 suites* ⚭ *Microwaves, refrigerators, in-room broadband, indoor pool, health club, spa, meeting rooms, free parking* ▤ *AE, MC, V* ⦿l *CP.*

$ ▦ **WyteStone Suites.** Near a small outlet mall, several restaurants, and the Spotsylvania County Tourism Office, this modern hotel is 2 mi from the historic area. Each suite has king or double beds with quilted bedspreads and a sofa bed in the living room. Rooms are entered from inside walkways around the six-story atrium. To get here, take Exit 126 off I–95, bear right onto U.S. 1 South, and turn left onto Southpoint Parkway; the hotel's on the right. ⊠ *4615 Southpoint Pkwy., 22407* ☎ *540/891–1112 or 800/794–5005* 🖷 *540/891–5465* ⊕ *www.wytestone.*

5

com ⇥ *85 suites* ⚭ *Microwaves, refrigerators, cable TV, in-room broadband, indoor pool, laundry facilities* ☰ *AE, D, DC, MC, V* ⃝ *BP.*

¢–$ ⊡ **Fredericksburg Colonial Inn.** This 1920s motel with moss green siding and forest green awnings has a beautifully decorated central staircase in the lobby. Rooms are furnished with antiques and appointments from the Civil War period, and the lobby has an old-time upright piano. Breakfast includes beverages, cereal, and coffee cake. ✉ *1707 Princess Anne St., Historic District, 22401* ☏ *540/371–5666* 🖷 *540/371–5884* ⊕ *www.fci1.com* ⇥ *27 rooms* ⚭ *Refrigerators, free parking; no smoking* ☰ *AE, MC, V* ⃝ *BP.*

THE NORTHERN NECK

Between Fredericksburg and the Chesapeake Bay is the "Northern Neck," an area attractive to nature lovers, anglers, and boaters. This 90-mi-long peninsula has a 1,200 mi total shoreline and is bathed on three sides by the Potomac and Rappahannock rivers, and the mighty Chesapeake Bay. Settled by Europeans more than 300 years ago, the Northern Neck is the birthplace of presidents George Washington, James Monroe, and James Madison as well as General Robert E. Lee and Washington's mother, Mary Ball.

The Northern Neck peninsula is as unspoiled today as when Captain John Smith first visited in 1608. Even at the peninsula's start, the area is forested and tranquil. You can find charming B&Bs; fresh-off-the-boat seafood; dozens of marinas; excursion boats to islands in the Chesapeake Bay; historic homes and museums; and places to commune with nature.

The sites below are listed in geographical order beginning at the intersection of routes 3 and 301. Though it's unusual that three presidents' birthplaces are in such proximity, that of James Madison and James Monroe are just markers off the highway, whereas Washington's is a national monument. A marker on Highway 301 in Port Conway, King George County, memorializes the onetime plantation where James Madison was born in 1751; an outline of the house and a marker in neighboring Westmoreland County identifies the birthplace of James Monroe, born in 1758, on Highway 205 between Oak Grove and Colonial Beach.

Numbers in the text correspond to numbers in the margin and on the Northern Neck map.

George Washington Birthplace National Monument

❶ *32 mi east of Fredericksburg on Rte. 3.*

After you pass the town of Oak Grove on Route 3, all signs point to the national park on the Potomac River. At Pope's Creek, **George Washington Birthplace National Monument** is a 550-acre park mirroring the peaceful rural life our first president preferred. The house in which Mary Ball Washington gave birth to George in 1732 burned in 1779, but native clay was used to make bricks for a representative 18th-century plantation home. Costumed interpreters lead tours through the house, which has items dating from the time of Washington's childhood. The grounds

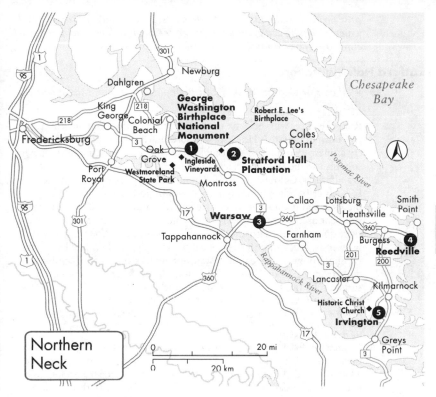

Northern
Neck

include a kitchen, garden, cemetery with 32 Washington family graves,
and the Colonial Living Farm, worked by methods employed in Colonial days. Picnic facilities are available year-round. ✉ *Rte. 3* ☎ *804/
224–1732* ⊕ *www.nps.gov/gewa* ✆ *$4* ☉ *Daily 9–5.*

Where to Stay

¢–$ 🏨 **Westmoreland State Park.** This 1,300-acre, full-service park is one of
Virginia's most beautiful campgrounds, with hiking trails winding
through marshlands, woods, meadows and along the Potomac River.
There are also places to fish, rent boats or kayaks, or simply picnic. The
comfortable, climate-controlled cabins have complete kitchens with mi-
crowave oven and toaster, dishes, silverware, and cooking utensils. Living rooms have a sofa, dining table, and working fireplace. The basic
furnishings include linens for four beds. From Memorial Weekend to
Labor Day Weekend there is a one-week minimum; at all other times
the minimum is two nights. Westmoreland also has 133 campsites available and six camping cabins that provide a shelter but few other amenities. ✉ *1650 State Park Rd., Rte. 1, Box 600, Montross 22520-9717*
☎ *804/493–8821 or 800/933–7275* ⊕ *www.dcr.state.va.us/parks/
westmore.htm* ⚷ *Cabins: Grocery, picnic area, kitchens, pool, boating,
fishing, hiking, laundry facilities; no room phones, no room TVs. Camp-*

sites: Grills, laundry facilities, flush toilets, partial hookups (electric and water), drinking water, showers, fire grates, picnic tables, electricity, general store ⌁ *27 cabins, 133 campsites* ▭ *AE, MC, V.*

Stratford Hall Plantation

❷ *8 mi east of George Washington Birthplace National Monument via Rte. 3.*

Robert E. Lee, who became the commander of the Confederate Army, was born in the Great House of **Stratford Hall Plantation,** one of the country's finest examples of Colonial architecture. Eight chimneys in two squares top the H-shape brick home, built in the 1730s by one of Lee's grandfathers, Colonial governor Thomas Lee. The house contains Robert E. Lee's crib, original family pieces, and period furnishings. The working Colonial plantation covers 1,600 acres and has gardens, a kitchen, smokehouse, laundry, orangery, springhouses, coach house, stables, slave quarters, and a gristmill that grinds from 11 to 2 on the first whole weekend of each month from April through September. The Plantation Dining Room, a log cabin restaurant, serves meals and sandwiches daily from 11:30 to 3 and a Plantation Buffet ($14.95) on weekends in summer. Its outdoor screened deck overlooks the woodlands. ⊠ *Rte. 3, Stratford* ☎ *804/493–8038 or 804/493–8371* ⊕ *www.stratfordhall. org* ▦ *$10* ☉ *Visitor center daily 9:30–4, house tours daily 10–4.*

Where to Stay

$ ⌂ **Stratford Hall.** Of the two guesthouses on the plantation property, Cheek, the larger one, has 15 rooms, which come with either two twin beds or a king-size bed. Astor, named after Lady Astor and made from a log cabin, is directly across from the Plantation Dining Room. Both guesthouses have a fully equipped kitchen, a living room with fireplace, and decks. ⊠ *485 Great House Rd., 22558* ☎ *804/493–8038 or 804/493–8371* 🖶 *804/493–0333* ⊕ *www.stratfordhall.org* ⌁ *20 rooms* ⚖ *Restaurant, free parking* ▭ *MC, V* ⎟⊙⎟ *CP.*

⚑ **Cole's Point Plantation.** This 110-acre wooded campground on the Potomac River has a boat ramp and a 120-slip full-service marina. The facility has four log cabins that can sleep 4–13 people. Reservations are essential. ⊠ *Rte. 612, north of Rte. 202* ⌕ *Rte. 728, Box 77, Coles Point 22442* ☎ *804/472–3955* 🖶 *804/472–4488* ⊕ *www.colespoint. com* ⚖ *Pool, flush toilets, full hookups, partial hookups (electric and water), swimming (river)* ⌁ *74 full hookups or tent sites, 35 partial hookups or tent sites, 1 tent-only site, 4 cabins* ▣ *Cabins $50, full hookups $30, partial hookups $21, tent sites $20* ▭ *AE, MC, V* ☉ *Open May–Oct.*

Warsaw

❸ *15 mi southeast of Stratford Hall via Rte. 3.*

The county seat of Richmond County, Warsaw is a pleasant town of 7,000 that's shaded by large oak trees. Near the U.S. 360 bridge over the Rappahannock, it's therefore closer to the city of Tappahannock (on the other side) than to its fellow towns on the Northern Neck.

Ingleside Vineyards is one of Virginia's oldest and largest wineries and has won the prestigious Virginia Governor's Cup more times than any other winery. It produces one of the few sparkling wines from Virginia. There are also white wines (viognier, sauvignon blanc, pinot gris, and chardonnay) and reds (sangiovese, cabernet franc, and sauvignon) as well as specially produced labels. The vineyards cover about 65 acres of gently rolling countryside whose climate and sandy loam soil is similar to that of Bordeaux, France. The winery has a tasting bar, a gift shop with grape-related gifts, a large outdoor patio with umbrella tables and a fountain, and a large indoor room for group tastings. The winery is about 40 minutes east of Fredericksburg and only a few miles from the Washington Birthplace National Monument. ⊠ *5872 Leedstown Rd., from Rte. 3, turn south on Rte. 638 at winery's signpost, Oak Grove* ☎ *804/ 224–8687* ⊕ *www.ipwine.com* ⊙ *Mon.–Sat. 10–5, Sun. noon–5 (summer daily until 6).*

A cruise 20 mi up the river to Ingleside Vineyards leaves from Tappahannock. **Rappahannock River Cruises** enlists its ship *Capt. Thomas* to take passengers on the narrated day cruise. A buffet lunch is served at the winery ($11), snacks are served on board, or you can bring your own. To reach the dock, take Highway 17 south from Tappahannock to Hoskins Creek. The cruise departs daily at 10, returning at 4:30. ⊠ *Hoskins Creek* ☎ *804/453–2628* ⊕ *www.tangiercruise.com* ⊠ *$25* ⊙ *May–Oct., daily at 10.*

Camping

¢–$ ▦ **Heritage Park Resort & Belle Mount Vineyards.** On Menokin Bay, this campground has panoramic views overlooking the Rappahannock River and scenic wildlife settings. The rustic, wooden, two-bedroom cottages are heated and air-conditioned so they can be rented year-round. Each has a living room with navy plaid chairs and sofa, a dining room, and a fully equipped kitchen. With its banquet facilities for 300, the resort is a good place for picnics, receptions, and family reunions. There are also 78 campsites, some of which have full hookups or partial hookups. Tours and tastings at the winery on the premises are available Wednesday through Sunday from mid-March to mid-December. This is a part of the Northern Neck Wine Trail. ⊠ *2570 Newland Rd., Rte. 624, 2½ mi west of U.S. 360, Warsaw 22572* ☎ *804/333–4038* 🖶 *804/333–4700* ⊕ *www.heritagepark.com* ⇆ *5 cottages, 78 campsites (20 with water and electric and 25 with water, electric, and sewer)* & *Kitchens, pool, boating; no smoking* ▱ *AE, D, MC, V.*

Reedville

❹ *31 mi from Warsaw via U.S. 360, 46 mi from Stratford Hall via Rtes. 202 and 360.*

This small town at the eastern tip of the Northern Neck was the home of wealthy fishermen and businessmen who made their fortunes from the menhaden fish abundant in the nearby Chesapeake Bay and Potomac waters.

The educational and activity-oriented **Reedville Fishermen's Museum** is housed in a restored fisherman's home and a larger building. Permanent and rotating exhibits document the area's fishing industry, and there are two fishing boats here, including a skipjack and a buy boat. ⊠ *Main St.* ☎ *804/453–6529* ⊕ *www.rfmuseum.org* ⊡ *$5* ☉ *Early Mar.–late Apr., weekends 10:30–4:30; May–Oct., daily 10:30–4:30; early Nov.–mid-Jan., Fri.–Mon. 10:30–4:30; mid-Jan.–early Mar. by appt. for groups.*

Popular cruises to quaint Smith Island in the Chesapeake Bay leave from Reedville. The 150-passenger ship *Captain Evans* and the 139-passenger air-conditioned *Spirit of Chesapeake* of **Smith Island and Chesapeake Bay Cruises** sail from the KOA Kampground at Smith Point on Route 802. The 13½-mi trip takes 1½ hours and passes a 5,000-acre waterfowl and wildlife refuge. Now a part of Maryland, Smith Island—a Methodist colony settled by British Colonists from Cornwall in the early 1700s—can also be reached from Crisfield, on Maryland's Eastern Shore. Lunch is available at several restaurants on the island. Cruise reservations are required. Due to the spiraling cost of oil and possible inclement weather, call ahead for the schedule and fare. ⊠ *382 Campground Rd., behind KOA Kampground* ☎ *804/453–3430* ⊕ *www. eaglesnest.net/smithislandcruise* ☉ *May–mid-Oct.*

Tangier is a Virginia island in the Chesapeake Bay named by Captain John Smith. This largely unspoiled fishing village with quaint, narrow streets also happens to be the soft crab capital of the nation. There's a small airport here for private planes and it also can be reached by the ship *Chesapeake Breeze* of **Tangier Island & Chesapeake Cruises** (ships also leave from Onacock, Virginia, and Crisfield, Maryland, on the Eastern Shore). The ship departs at 10 AM and returns at 3:30 PM daily, cruising 1½ hours each way. The island has several restaurants serving lunch. From the intersection of highways 360 and 646, drive 1½ mi; then turn left on Highway 656 (Buzzard's Point Road), which leads to the dock. Reservations are required. ⊠ *468 Buzzard's Point Rd.* ☎ *804/453–2628* ⊕ *www.tangiercruise.com* ⊡ *$25* ☉ *May–Oct., daily.*

Where to Stay

$$ 🏨 **Fleeton Fields.** Set amid beautifully manicured lawns and gardens, this lovely Colonial-style inn also overlooks a tidal pond on which you may be lucky enough to see ospreys, Great Blue Herons, and eagles. Inside the inn, you're greeted by fresh flowers and soothing music before being escorted to one of the three beautifully furnished suites. Cool evenings are warmed by inviting fireplaces, and each morning's breakfast is served using china, crystal, and silver. ⊠ *2783 Fleeton Rd., 22539* ☎ *804/453–5014 or 800/497–8215* 🖶 *804/453–5014* ⊕ *www. fleetonfields.com* ⇔ *3 suites* ⚲ *Minibars, cable TV* ⊟ *AE, D, DC, MC, V* ¶◎¶ *BP.*

$ 🏨 **The Gables.** A four-story redbrick Victorian mansion built in 1909, the Gables was built by Captain Albert Fisher, one of the founders of the local fishing industry. The house has been lovingly restored and has period antiques throughout. There are two guest rooms in the main house and four more in the adjacent carriage house. The Gables has its own deepwater dock on Cockrell's Creek with easy access to the Chesapeake

Bay. ⊠ *Main St., 22539* ☎ *804/453–5209* ⇌ *6 rooms* ⌂ *Dock; no kids under 13* ▤ *MC, V* ⟨◎⟩ *BP.*

EN ROUTE After leaving Reedville on Route 360, turn left on Route 200 and drive 13 mi to Kilmarnock. Turn right on Route 3 and drive to the little town of Lancaster, home of the **Mary Ball Washington Museum and Library.** This four-building complex honors George Washington's mother, who was born in Lancaster County. Lancaster House, built about 1798, contains Washington family memorabilia and historic items related to the county and the Northern Neck. The Steuart-Blakemore Building houses a genealogical library, and the Old Jail is a lending library and archives. ⊠ *8346 Mary Ball Rd., Lancaster* ☎ *804/462–7280* ⊕ *www.mbwm. org* ▱ *$2 museum house and grounds; $5 to work at library* ◎ *Tues.–Fri. 10–4; library Wed.–Sun. 10–4.*

Irvington

⑤ *5 mi from Kilmarnock.*

Although much older than the resort, the lovely town of Irvington has been associated with the Tides Inn for more than 50 years.

The **Historic Christ Church** was completed in 1735, when George Washington was three years old. The Georgian-style structure, on the National Register of Historic Places, was built by Robert "King" Carter and contains a rare "triple decker" pulpit made of native walnut. Bricks for the church were fired in a great kiln near the churchyard. A 12-minute video is screened in the museum. ⊠ *420 Christ Church Rd., from Irvington drive 1½ mi north on Rte. 200* ☎ *804/438–6855* ⊕ *www. christchurch1735.org* ▱ *Free* ◎ *Church daily; museum weekdays 8.30–4.30, Apr.–Nov., also Sat. 10–4 and Sun. 2–5.*

Where to Stay & Eat

¢ ✕ **White Stone Wine & Cheese.** This shop sells Mediterranean-style sandwiches, soups, and baked goods as well as wine and cheese. There are tables available to eat your picnic. ⊠ *101 William St.* ☎ *540/371–2233* ▤ *MC, V* ◎ *Closes at 5 daily.*

★ $$$$ ▥ **The Tides Inn.** Surrounded by manicured grounds overlooking Carters Creek, the Tides Inn, here since 1947, is sandwiched between the Potomac and Rappahannock rivers. Many of the rooms and suites, which are luxuriously decorated in a British Colonial style, have spectacular water views. The Golden Eagle Golf course is challenging, the par-3 course less so; the ponds are well-stocked with fish; and bird-watchers should take their binoculars. There's also a sailing school that's set up for all ages and experience levels, and you can take a cruise along the Rappahannock River on a 127-foot yacht. ⊠ *480 King Carter Dr., 22480* ☎ *804/ 438–5000 or 800/843–3746* ☎ *804/438–5222* ⊕ *www.tidesinn.com* ⇌ *84 rooms, 22 suites* ⌂ *4 restaurants, in-room DVDs, in-room data ports, 18-hole golf course, 9-hole golf course, 4 tennis courts, 3 pools, gym, spa, boating, marina, fishing, bicycles, croquet, horseshoes, shuffleboard, lounge, dance club, shops, babysitting, children's programs (ages 4–12), laundry facilities, airport shuttle, some pets allowed (fee)* ▤ *AE, D, DC, MC, V.*

$$ ⊡ **The Hope and Glory Inn.** This 1890 schoolhouse is now a pale-honey color Victorian B&B. The first-floor classrooms have been opened into an expansive, columned lobby with a painted checkerboard floor. The upstairs bedrooms and small cottages behind the inn are decorated in what might be called California romantic, with pastel painted floors and interesting (nonruffled) window treatments. ■ TIP→ **In the garden, surrounded by a tall wooden fence, there's a completely open-air bathroom that can be booked by adventurous couples.** In 2004 the inn built new cottages, called "tents," in an allusion to turn-of-the-20th-century Methodist tent communities. On wooded bluffs overlooking the headwaters of Carter's Creek, the tents each have three bedrooms and a kitchen, and there's a pool and dock for canoes and kayaks as well as the "Detention" wine bar. ⊠ *634 King Carter Dr., 22480* ☎ *804/438–6053 or 800/ 497–8228* 🖨 *804/438–6053* ⊕ *www.hopeandglory.com* ⇥ *7 rooms, 4 cottages* ⊟ *MC, V* ¶⊙¶ *BP.*

RICHMOND & ENVIRONS ESSENTIALS

To research prices, get advice from other travelers, and book travel arrangements, visit www.fodors.com.

Transportation

BY AIR

Richmond International Airport, 10 mi east of the city, Exit 197 off I–64, has scheduled flights by nine airlines. A taxi ride to downtown Richmond from the airport costs $20–$22.

🚪**Richmond International Airport** ⊠Airport Dr. ☎804/226-3000 ⊕www.flyrichmond. com.

BY BUS

Greyhound buses depart seven times a day from Washington to Fredericksburg and Richmond between 7 AM and 5 PM. A round-trip ticket is $25.50 to Fredericksburg and $44.50 to Richmond, but a ticket doesn't guarantee a seat, so arrive early and get in line to board. Fredericksburg buses stop at a station on Alternate Route 1, about 2 mi from the center of town; cabs and a cheap regional bus service are available there.

Greater Richmond Transit operates bus service in Richmond. Buses run daily, 5 AM–1 AM; fares are $1.25 (exact change required). Most buses are wheelchair accessible.

You can ride FRED, Fredericksburg's excellent little bus, for only 25¢. Six lines—red, yellow, blue, orange, green, and purple—serve the region and stop at all historic sites as well as shopping malls and other modern areas of the city from 7:30 AM to 8:30 PM.

There is no bus service within the Northern Neck.

🚪 **Bus Depots Fredericksburg Greyhound** ⊠ 1400 Jefferson Davis Hwy. ☎ 540/373-2103. **Richmond Greyhound** ⊠ 2910 N. Blvd. ☎ 804/254-5910.

🚪 **Bus Lines FRED** ☎ 540/372-1222 ⊕ www.fredericksburgva.gov. **Greater Richmond Transit** ☎ 804/358-4782 ⊕ www.ridegrtc.com. **Greyhound Lines** ☎ 800/231-3871 ⊕ www.greyhound.com.

BY CAR

Having a car is advisable in Richmond and Fredericksburg. It's essential for touring outlying attractions, including historic homes and battlefields, and the Northern Neck.

Richmond is at the intersection of Interstates 95 and 64, which run north–south and east–west, respectively. U.S. 1/301 also runs north–south past the city. To drive to Fredericksburg from Washington, D.C., take I–95 south to Route 3 (Exit 130-A), turn left, and follow the signs. The drive takes about an hour one-way; add 45 minutes during rush hour.

To reach the Northern Neck from Fredericksburg either take Route 3 South or U.S. 17 to Route 360, crossing the Rappahannock River at the Tappahannock Bridge. Driving north from Williamsburg and Hampton Roads, cross the river at Greys Point by driving north on Route 3. Access from Maryland and Washington, D.C., is over the Potomac River toll bridge on Route 301. If you cross here, you shortly come upon Virginia's Potomac Gateway Visitors Center in King George.

BY TAXI

Cabs are metered in Richmond; they charge $2.50 for the first mile and $1.50 for each additional mile.

🚖 Taxi Companies **Bumbreys Independent Cab Service** ⊠ 209 Lafayette Blvd., Fredericksburg ☎540/373–6111. **City Cab** ⊠ Fredericksburg ☎540/372–4484. **Groome Transportation** ⊠ Richmond Airport, Richmond ☎ 804/222-7222. **Metro Taxicab Service** ⊠ 2405 Westwood Ave., Richmond ☎ 804/353–5000. **Yellow Cab of Fredericksburg** ⊠ 2217 Princess Anne St., Fredericksburg ☎ 540/368–8120. **Yellow Cab Service Inc.** ⊠ 3203 Williamsburg Rd., Richmond ☎ 804/222–7300.

BY TRAIN

Amtrak trains operate between Washington's Union Station, Alexandria, Fredericksburg, Richmond, and a number of commuter stops several times daily. Richmond's train station is north of town. The unmanned Fredericksburg station is two blocks from the historic district.

A one-way ticket costs $25 between Fredericksburg and Washington and $33 between Washington and Richmond. Amtrak service between New York City and Newport News or Florida passes through Richmond daily.

The Virginia Rail Express, which uses the same tracks and station as Amtrak, provides workday commuter service between Fredericksburg and Washington's Union Station with additional stops near hotels in Crystal City, L'Enfant Plaza, and elsewhere. A round-trip ticket from Washington's Union Station to Fredericksburg costs $16.20.

There's no mass transit to the Northern Neck, but you can take the train to Fredericksburg and rent a car.

🚆 Train Stations **Fredericksburg station** ⊠ Caroline St. and Lafayette Blvd. **Richmond train station** ⊠ 7519 Staples Mill Rd. ☎ 804/553–2903.

🚆 Train Lines **Amtrak** ☎ 800/872–7245 ⊕ www.amtrak.com. **Virginia Rail Express (VRE)** ☎ 703/684–1001 or 800/743–3873 ⊕ www.vre.org.

Contacts & Resources

EMERGENCIES

Fredericksburg's Medic 1 Clinic is open weekdays 8 AM–9 PM, Saturday 9–7, and Sunday 9–3.

☎ **Ambulance, Fire, Police** ☎ 911.

☎ **Hospitals Medical College of Virginia Hospital** ✉ 401 N. 12th St., Richmond ☎ 804/828–9000. **Medic 1 Clinic** ✉ 3429 Jefferson Davis Hwy., Fredericksburg ☎ 540/371-1664.

☎ **24-Hour Pharmacies CVS Pharmacy** ✉ 2738 W. Broad St., Richmond ☎ 804/359–2497.

TOUR OPTIONS

Historic Richmond Tours, a service of the Valentine Richmond History Center, offers guided tours that cover such topics as the historic Hollywood Cemetery and the River District and Jackson Ward. You can take either a walking tour or travel throughout the city in your own vehicle with a "step-on guide" (one who rides with you).

> **WORD OF MOUTH**
>
> "Anyone coming to Virginia interested in the Civil War should contact the state tourism office in Richmond for the map 'Civil War Trails' which list battlefields and byways."
>
> –ronkala

Richmond Discoveries' excursions includes tours that highlight Civil War history, horseback tours, and customized trips for large groups or small families.

Trolley Tours of Fredericksburg runs a 75-minute narrated tour of Fredericksburg's most important sights. Tours cost $15 and leave from the visitor center.

The Living History Company of Fredericksburg can tailor walking tours to match what you want to see. In addition, the tour coordinator at the Fredericksburg Visitor Center can arrange a group walking tour of the city as well as of battlefields and other historic sites to which you can drive. Reservations are required. The Fredericksburg Department of Tourism (in the visitor center) publishes a booklet that includes a short history of Fredericksburg and a self-guided tour covering 29 sights.

Lee's Retreat is a 26-stop self-guided driving tour from Petersburg to Appomattox. For a route map and other information, contact the Petersburg Visitor Center (⇨ Visitor Information).

TOURS **Historic Richmond Tours** (☎ 804/649–0711 ⊕ www.richmondhistorycenter.com). **Living History Company of Fredericksburg** (☎ 540/899–1776 ⊕ www.historyexperiences.com). **Richmond Discoveries** (☎ 804/222–8595 ⊕ www.richmonddiscoveries.com). **Trolley Tours of Fredericksburg** (☎ 540/898–0737 ⊕ www.fredericksburgtrolley.com).

VISITOR INFORMATION

Richmond tourist brochures are available at the National Park Service's five Richmond area visitor centers (*see* Richmond National Battlefield Park Civil War Visitor Center *and* Chimborazo Medical Museum).

Northern Neck Visitor Information is available at the Potomac Gateway Visitor Center and other sites throughout the Northern Neck. There's no tourist bureau at Reedville, but tourist brochures are available in the Reedville Fishermen's Museum.

🛈 Tourist Information **Fredericksburg Visitor Center** ✉ 706 Caroline St., 22401 ☎ 540/373-1776 or 800/678-4748 🖷 540/372-6587 ⊕ www.visitfred.com. **Hanover Visitor Center** ✉ 112 N. Railroad Ave., I-95, Exit 92B, Ashland ☎ 804/752-6766 or 800/897-1479 ⊕ www.town.ashland.va.us. **Petersburg Visitor Center** ✉ 425 Cockade Alley ☎ 804/733-2400 or 800/368-3595 ⊕ www.petersburg-va.org ✉ Information by mail ✉ 15 Bank St., Petersburg 23803 ☎ 804/733-2402 🖷 804/861-0883. **Potomac Gateway Visitor Center** ✉ 3540 James Madison Pkwy., King George 22485 ☎ 540/663-3205 ⊕ www.northernneck.org. **Richmond Regional Visitor Center** ✉ 401 N. 3rd St., 23210 ☎ 800/370-9004 ⊕ www.visit.richmond.com. **Virginia Tourism Corporation** ✉ 901 E. Byrd St., Richmond ☎ 800/847-4882 ⊕ www.virginia.org ✉ Bell Tower at Capitol Sq., 9th and Franklin Sts., Richmond ☎ 800/545-5586 ✉ Information by mail ✉ 403 N. 3rd St., Richmond 23219. **Visitor Center at Richmond International Airport** ✉ 1 Richard E. Byrd Terminal Dr., 23210 ☎ 804/236-3260 ⊕ www.richmond.com/visitors.

Williamsburg & Hampton Roads

WORD OF MOUTH

"If you want a beautiful area to soak up some history along the way, Colonial Williamsburg would be a breath of fresh air. Fall is gorgeous . . . but Virginia is not to be missed any time of year."
—girlwilltravel

"There is a lot to do in Norfolk/VA Beach and across the tunnel in Newport News. The aquarium in VA Beach is one of the best I've seen . . . Nauticus in Norfolk would interest you if you like technology, science, and weather. Or you could go to the Air & Space Museum in Newport News. Newport News also has the beautiful Mariner's Museum, a must if you like boats, and the Virginia Living Museum has a new building filled with the flora and fauna of Virginia."   —Birdie

www.fodors.com/forums

Updated by
CiCi
Williamson

PERHAPS NO OTHER REGION IN VIRGINIA contains more variety and options for the traveler than its southeastern coastline. Colonial Williamsburg has evoked the days of America's forefathers since its restoration began during the 1920s. Jamestown and Yorktown make the area one of the most historically significant in the United States. When it's time for pure recreation, you can head to theme parks such as Busch Gardens Williamsburg and resort areas, including Virginia Beach.

At the end of the Virginia peninsula is the enormous Hampton Roads harbor, where the James, Elizabeth, and Nansemond rivers flow together into the Chesapeake Bay and then eastward into the Atlantic Ocean. Hampton Roads has also played a crucial role in the discovery and settlement of the nation, its struggle for independence, and the conflict that nearly dissolved the Union.

This entire area, known as the Tidewater, is land where water in rivers and streams is affected by tides. The cities in southeast Virginia take on different roles depending on their proximity to the Chesapeake Bay and the rivers that empty into it. Hampton contains the world's largest naval base, and enormous shipbuilding yards are in Norfolk and Newport News. The area is also committed to recreation and tourism: there are many resort hotels, a bustling beachfront, and boardwalk attractions. Virginia Beach, which in the 1950s claimed to have the world's longest public beach, has a showy boardwalk.

Linked to the Hampton Roads area by the unusual Chesapeake Bay Bridge-Tunnel is Virginia's "other coastline," the quiet, largely untrafficked Eastern Shore (*see* Chapter 10).

Top 5 Experiences for Williamsburg & Hampton Roads Area

- **Colonial Williamsburg:** Escape to the 18th century in the world's largest living-history museum. Virginia's capital from 1699 to 1780 and Britain's largest, wealthiest New World outpost was restored so "That the future may learn from the past."

- **Celebrate early American history:** 2007 marks the 400th birthday of Jamestown, the first permanent English settlement in the Americas. Washington's momentous 1781 Revolutionary War victory at Yorktown secured the country's independence.

- **Water, water, everywhere!** From the James River and Chesapeake Bay to the Atlantic Ocean, get in or on the waters of Tidewater Virginia. Surf the waves, steam past the world's largest naval station, sail on a schooner, or sup on a ship.

- **Immerse yourself in nautical and military history:** Don't miss the Mariners Museum, the MacArthur Memorial, the Virginia Air and Space Center, and the world's largest Naval base at Norfolk Naval Station.

- **Glimpse the gracious gentry life and the hard life of slaves:** Visit America's oldest plantations and historic homes, including one chartered in 1613 and continuously occupied by 11 generations, two homes of presidents, and one claiming to have celebrated the first Thanksgiving.

6

Exploring Williamsburg & Hampton Roads

The beginning of both Colonial America and of the United States of America should be required visiting, and this area is home to them both. To keep the chronology straight, visit Virginia's "historic triangle," in the order of Jamestown, Williamsburg, and then Yorktown. Although Jamestown is somewhat overshadowed by the much-larger Williamsburg, Jamestown Island was the first permanent English settlement (1607) in North America and is celebrating its momentous quadricentennial—400th anniversary—in 2007. Just a short drive along the tree-lined Colonial Parkway is Williamsburg, which subsequently grew into the political and economic center of the Virginia Colony. The 301 acres of modern-day Colonial Williamsburg contain re-created and restored structures peopled with costumed interpreters. Everything from momentous political events to blacksmithing is portrayed. Completing the "historic triangle," is Yorktown, 20 mi away, the site of the battle that ended the war for independence from England. Several 18th- and 19th-century plantations lie west of Williamsburg, along the James River. South of Yorktown are Newport News, the shipbuilding capital of Virginia, and Hampton. To see the rest of this waterfront area of Virginia, you can cross the James River at Hampton and visit Norfolk, Portsmouth, and, to the east, the Virginia Beach resort area.

> **A DATE TO NOTE**
>
> Those who want to mingle with—or avoid—the crowds attending the quadricentennial of the first permanent English settlement in America should make a note of May 13, 2007, four hundred years to the day in 1607 when settlers set foot on what they named "Jamestown." Most events will be free, open to the public, and without ticketing requirements. Monitor ⊕ www.jamestown2007.org for the latest information.

About the Restaurants & Hotels

Dining rooms within walking distance of Colonial Williamsburg's restored area are often crowded, and reservations (☎ 800/447–8679) are necessary. Many nationally known chain eateries line both sides of U.S. 60 on the east side of the city.

There are more than 200 hotel properties in Williamsburg. For a complete list, contact the **Williamsburg Area Convention and Visitors Bureau** (✉ 201 Penniman Rd., Box 3585, Williamsburg 23187-3585 ☎ 757/253–0192 or 800/368–6511).

BED & BREAKFASTS There are many bed-and-breakfasts in the Williamsburg area, especially near the James River Plantations off Route 10. Most are housed in historic properties with charming antiques. Rates usually include a full country breakfast.

Reservations at inns can be made through the Virginia Division of Tourism Reservation Service. Virginia Beach Reservations can make a reservation in your choice of about 75 hotels. Williamsburg Vacation

Reservations, representing more than 70 hostelries, provides free lodging reservation services.

HOME RENTALS Apartment and house rentals are not common in the Williamsburg area, but quite the thing to do at Virginia Beach. Rentals vary greatly in size, cost, and degree of luxury, so research possibilities thoroughly.

🏠 Local Agents **Long and Foster Real Estate** ✉ 317 30th St., Virginia Beach ☎ 757/428-4600 or 800/941-3333. **Siebert Realty** ✉ 601 Sandbridge Rd., Virginia Beach 23456 ☎ 757/426-6200 or 877/422-2200 ⊕ www.siebert-realty.com.

🏠 Reservation Services **Virginia Beach Reservations** ☎ 800/822-3224. **Virginia Division of Tourism Reservation Service** ☎ 800/934-9184. **Williamsburg Vacation Reservations** ☎ 800/446-9244.

WHAT IT COSTS					
	$$$$	$$$	$$	$	¢
RESTAURANTS	over $30	$22–$30	$14–$22	$7–$14	under $7
HOTELS	over $250	$175–$250	$130–$175	$80–$130	under $80

Restaurant prices are per person for a main course at dinner. Hotel prices are for a standard double room, excluding state and local taxes.

6

THE HISTORIC TRIANGLE

Virginia's number one tourist attraction has you pinching yourself to make sure you haven't entered a time machine. You'll believe you're in another century, and you really are. Colonial Williamsburg, a careful, on-the-spot restoration of the former Virginia capital, gives you the chance to walk into the 18th century and see how earlier Americans lived. The streets may be unrealistically clean for that era, and you can find hundreds of others exploring the buildings with you, but the rich detail of the re-creation and the sheer size of the city could hold your attention for days. A ticket or pass (price is based on the number of attractions and the duration of visit) admits the holder to sites in the restored area, but it costs nothing just to walk around and absorb the atmosphere.

Willamsburg anchors three elements of Colonial National Historical Park. The 23-mi Colonial Parkway links Williamsburg to Jamestown and Yorktown, two other significant historical sites on or near the peninsula bounded by the James and York rivers. Historic Jamestowne was the location of the first permanent English settlement in North America—celebrating its 400th anniversary in 2007—and it's an excellent place to begin a visit to the area; Yorktown was the site of the final major battle in the American Revolutionary War. The sites themselves as well as the parkway are maintained by the National Park Service. Close by are Jamestown Settlement and the excellent Yorktown Victory Center, both run by the Jamestown-Yorktown Foundation. Like Colonial Williamsburg, these two sights re-create the buildings and activities of the 18th century, using interpreters in period dress.

Numbers in the margin correspond to points of interest on the Williamsburg and Environs map.

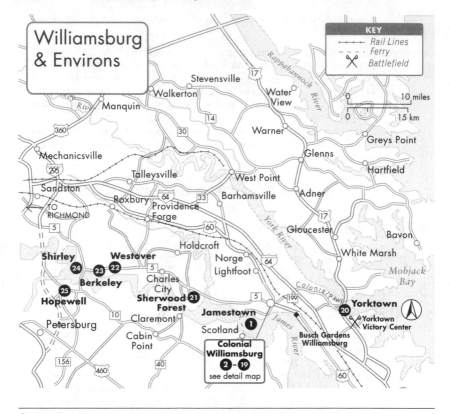

Jamestown

❶ *9 mi southwest of Colonial Williamsburg via Colonial Pkwy.*

The desperate strivings of Englishmen to stay alive and establish a foothold in the New World become evident when visiting Jamestown, the beginning of English settlement in this country. In this, the 400th anniversary, its two major sights are places to explore the early relationship between the English and Native Virginia Indians. From April to October, the Jamestown Area Shuttle provides loop service around the Jamestown area every 30 minutes between Historic Jamestowne, the Jamestown Settlement, and the Jamestown Glasshouse (part of Historic Jamestowne).

Historic Jamestowne, an island originally separated from the mainland by a narrow isthmus, was the site of the first permanent English settlement in North America (1607) and the capital of Virginia until 1699. May 13, 2007, marks the 400th anniversary of its founding. The first settlers' bitter struggle for survival here, on the now uninhabited land, makes for a visit that stirs the imagination. Redbrick foundation walls roughly outline the settlement, and artists' conceptions of the original buildings can be seen at several locations. The only standing structure

Fodor'sChoice
★

is the ruin of a church tower from the 1640s, now part of the Memorial Church built in 1907; the markers within indicate the original church's foundations. Other monuments around the site also date from the tercentenary celebration in 1907. Statues portray the founder of Jamestown, Captain John Smith, and his advocate, the Native American princess Pocahontas, whom Smith credited with saving him from being beheaded.

Near the entrance to the park, you can stop at the reconstructed Glasshouse to observe a demonstration of glassblowing, an unsuccessful business venture of the early colonists. The products of today are for sale in a gift shop. New in 2006, the Archaearium showcases the archaeological discoveries from the site. You can also observe digs on-site where archaeologists from the Association for the Preservation of Virginia Antiquities continue to dig up evidence of colonists' and Native Americans' ways of life, including the remains of the original 1607 fort.

A new visitor center near the main parking lot tells the history of Jamestown, and the Virginia Indians, Europeans, and African peoples who lived here. Ranger-guided tours, held daily, explore many different events in Jamestown's history. Living-history programs are presented daily in summer and on weekends in spring and autumn.

A 5 mi nature drive that rings the island is posted with informative signs and paintings. ⊠ *Off Colonial Pkwy.* ☎ *757/898–2410* ✉ *$8; combined entry to both Jamestowne and Yorktown, $10* ☉ *Daily 9–5; gates close at 4:30.*

Fodor'sChoice ★ Adjacent to but distinct from Historic Jamestowne is a mainland living-history museum called **Jamestown Settlement**. The site marries 40,000 square feet of indoor facilities (completed in 2006) with outdoor replicas of the early James Fort, the three ships that brought the founding colonists from England, and a Powhatan Indian village. The handsome new Tudor-style Great Hall borders extensive galleries arranged by decades from 1607 to 1699, when the capital was moved to Williamsburg, and leads to a 250-seat theater where the introductory film *1607: A Nation Takes Root* is shown. Within James Fort, interpreters in costume cook, forge metal, and describe what life was like living under thatch roofs and between walls of wattle and daub (stick framework covered with mud plaster). In the Powhatan Indian Village you can enter a *yehakin* (house) and see buckskin-costumed interpreters cultivate a garden and make tools. At the pier are full-scale reproductions of the ships in which the settlers arrived: *Godspeed, Discovery,* and *Susan Constant.* The new *Godspeed,* commissioned in 2006, sails to commemorative events along the East Coast; all the vessels are seaworthy. You may climb aboard the *Susan Constant* and find out more from the sailor-interpreters. Indoor exhibits examine the lives of the Powhatans and their English-born neighbors, their interaction, and world conditions that encouraged colonization. A riverfront discovery area that opened in 2004 provides information about 17th-century water travel, commerce, and cultural exchange, reflecting Powhatan Indian, European, and African traditions. Dugout-canoe making takes place in this area. Spring and fall bring lots

CLOSE UP

Jamestown & John Smith

YOU CAN'T BELIEVE EVERYTHING YOU READ in travel brochures: "Free land lush with hardwood trees! Food and water abundant! Gold for the taking! Fast side-trip to the Orient! Friendly welcoming committee!"

The real trip: 73 passengers will die. There's no gold. Fresh water and food are difficult to obtain. There is no way to sail to the Orient across North America. The land belongs to the natives, who are usually hostile and disease-carrying mosquitoes are omnipresent.

The men and boys who settled Jamestown in 1607 had little idea of what was in store for them. Most who sailed over were intent on finding riches and hadn't given much thought to how they would survive in Virginia. Almost immediately after landing, the colonists were under attack from the Algonquian natives and in a little over a month, the settlers built a wooden fort named for King James.

One man, Captain John Smith, a soldier and adventurer who had fought in Hungary and Transylvania, was familiar with challenges and worked toward the survival of Jamestown. "America's first hero" made contact with the native chief Powhatan, from whom the colonists obtained much of their food, and became leader of the colony. After being captured by Algonquians, he may or may not have been saved by the 11-year-old princess Pocahontas, but was returned to Jamestown.

Finding the colony languishing due to lack of supplies, a drought, laziness, and conflicts, Smith instituted a policy of rigid discipline and strengthened defenses. He encouraged farming with the admonishment: "He who does not work, will not eat." Because of his strong leadership, the settlement survived and grew during the next year. Unfortunately Smith was injured and returned to England for treatment in October 1609, never to set foot in Virginia again.

Nearly 300 years later, Jamestown was acquired by the Association for the Preservation of Virginia Antiquities (APVA) and the National Park Service. Early archaeologists concluded that James Fort lay completely under the James River. In 1994, however, in preparation for the 400th Anniversary of Jamestown, APVA initiated its own excavations to search for the original 1607 fort. They uncovered evidence that James Fort had not been washed into the river, as most had believed.

Excavation has since uncovered more than 150,000 artifacts dating to the first half of the 17th century. Nearly half date to the first years of English settlement (1607–10). These objects reflect trade between Europe and the New World, patterns of warfare, day-to-day survival, and status in the early colony. You can view a sampling of these artifacts at Historic Jamestowne, whose mission is "to preserve, protect and promote the original site of the first permanent English settlement in North America and to tell the story of the role of the three cultures—European, North American and African—that came together to lay the foundation for a uniquely American form of democratic government, language, free enterprise and society."

of school groups, so it's best to arrive after 2 PM. ⊠ *Rte. 31 off Colonial Pkwy.* ☎ *757/253–4838 or 888/593–4682* ⊕ *www.historyisfun.org* 🖾 *$13.50; combination ticket with Yorktown Victory Center $17.75* ☉ *June 15–Aug. 15, daily 9–6; Aug. 16–June 14, daily 9–5.*

Colonial Williamsburg

51 mi southeast of Richmond via I–64.

Fodor'sChoice
★

Williamsburg was the capital of Virginia from 1699 to 1780, after Jamestown and before Richmond. Williamsburg hasn't been politically important for a long time, but now that **Colonial Williamsburg** is there to represent it in its era of glory, it's a jewel of the commonwealth. Outside the restored area is a modern city with plenty of dining and lodging options and attractions, including outlet shops and a large water park.

All vehicular traffic is prohibited within Colonial Williamsburg to preserve the illusion. Shuttle buses run continuously from 9 AM to 10 PM to and from the visitor center.

Colonial Williamsburg sells a number of all-inclusive tickets that cost just a bit more than a $34 one-day pass. The Freedom Pass ($59) allows you to visit for one full year. The Independence Pass ($72), also valid for a year, includes all the benefits of the Freedom Pass as well as admission to all special events and special discounts.

> ### AUDIO TOURS OF HISTORIC WILLIAMSBURG
>
> Three self-guided audio tours of Colonial Williamsburg can be rented at the Colonial Williamsburg Visitor Center: "Highlights of the Historic Area," "Reading the Restoration Architecture," and "Voices of the Revolution." Wander at your own pace; when you stop in front of a numbered location, enter the number into the player and hear all about it. Each tape is about 45 minutes and costs $6 for ticketed guests or $15 for those without tickets. For more information, go to www.colonialwilliamsburg.org.

Numbers in the margin correspond to points of interest on the Colonial Williamsburg map.

Main Attractions

❶⑤ The lovely brick Episcopal **Bruton Parish Church** has served continuously as a house of worship since it was built in 1715. One of its 20th-century pastors, W. A. R. Goodwin, provided the impetus for Williamsburg's restoration. The church tower, topped by a beige wooden steeple, was added in 1769; during the Revolution its bell served as the local "liberty bell," rung to summon people for announcements. The white pews, tall and boxed in, are characteristic of the starkly graceful Colonial ecclesiastical architecture of the region. When sitting in a pew, listening to the history of the church, keep in mind that you could be sitting where Thomas Jefferson, Ben Franklin, or George Washington once listened to sermons. The stone baptismal font is believed to have come from an older Jamestown church. Many local eminences, including one royal governor, are interred in the graveyard. The fully operational church is open

Colonial Williamsburg Basics

THE RESTORATION PROJECT THAT GAVE BIRTH to Colonial Williamsburg began in 1926, inspired by a local pastor, W. A. R. Goodwin, and financed by John D. Rockefeller Jr. The work of the archaeologists and historians of the not-for-profit Colonial Williamsburg Foundation continues to this day. A total of 88 original 18th-century and early-19th-century structures have been meticulously restored, and another 500 have been reconstructed on their original sites. In all, approximately 225 period rooms have been re-created with the foundation's collection of more than 60,000 pieces of furniture, ceramics, glass, silver, pewter, textiles, tools, paintings, prints, maps, firearms, and carpets. Period authenticity also governs the landscaping of the 301 acres of gardens and public greens. The restored area is surrounded by a greenbelt controlled by the foundation, which guards against development that could mar the illusion of the Colonial city.

Despite its huge scale, Colonial Williamsburg can seem almost cozy. Nearly 1 million people come here annually, and all year hundreds of costumed interpreters, wearing bonnets or three-corner hats, rove and ride through the streets (you can even rent outfits for your children). Dozens of skilled craftspeople, also in costume, demonstrate and explain their trades inside their workshops. They include the shoemaker, the cooper (he makes barrels), the gunsmith, the blacksmith, the musical instrument maker, the silversmith, and the wig maker. Their wares are for sale nearby at the Prentis Store. Four taverns serve food and drink that approximate the fare of more than 220 years ago.

Colonial Williamsburg makes an effort to represent not just the lives of a privileged few, and not to gloss over disturbing aspects of history. Slavery, religious freedom, family life, commerce and trade, land acquisition, and the Revolution are portrayed in living-history demonstrations. In the two-hour "Revolutionary City Program," you can become an active citizen in everyday life against the backdrop of momentous, world-changing events. The vignettes that are staged throughout the day take place in the streets and in public buildings. These may include dramatic afternoon court trials or fascinating estate appraisals. Depending on the days you visit, you may see the House of Burgesses dissolve, its members charging out to make revolutionary plans at the Raleigh Tavern.

Because of the size of Colonial Williamsburg and the large crowds (especially in the warmer months), it's best to begin a tour early in the day, so it's a good idea to spend the night before in the area. The foundation suggests allowing three or four days to do Colonial Williamsburg justice, but that will depend on your own interest in the period—and that interest often increases on arrival. Museums, exhibits, and stores close at 5 PM, but walks and events take place in the evenings, usually ending by 10 PM. Some sites close in winter on a rotating basis.

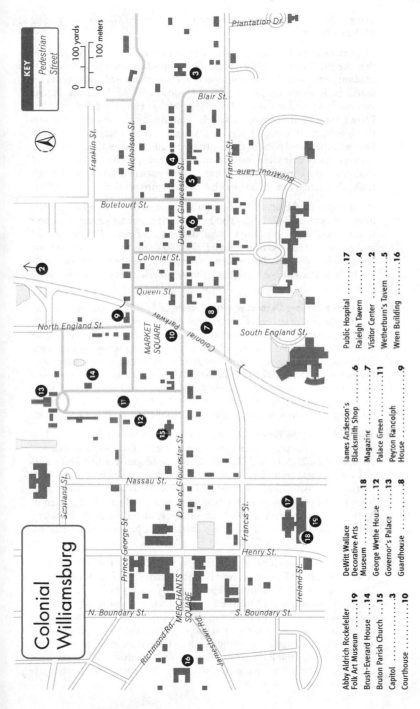

Colonial Williamsburg

Abby Aldrich Rockefeller
Folk Art Museum **19**
Brush-Everard House ...**14**
Bruton Parish Church **3**
Capitol **3**
Courthouse **10**

DeWitt Wallace
Decorative Arts
Museum **18**
George Wythe House ...**12**
Governor's Palace **13**
Guardhouse **8**

James Anderson's
Blacksmith Shop **6**
Magazine **7**
Palace Green **11**
Peyton Randolph
House **9**

Public Hospital **17**
Raleigh Tavern **4**
Visitor Center **2**
Wetherburn's Tavern **5**
Wren Building **16**

to the public; contributions are accepted. ⊠ *Duke of Gloucester St. west of Palace St.*

❸ The **Capitol** is the building that made this town so important. It was here that the pre-Revolutionary House of Burgesses (dominated by the ascendant gentry) challenged the royally appointed council (an almost medieval body made up of the bigger landowners). In 1765 the House eventually arrived at the resolutions, known as Henry's Resolves (after Patrick Henry), that amounted to rebellion. An informative tour explains the development, stage by stage, of American democracy from its English parliamentary roots. In the courtroom a guide recites the harsh Georgian sentences that were meted out: for instance, theft of more than 12 shillings was a capital crime. Occasional reenactments, including witch trials, dramatize the evolution of American jurisprudence.

What stands on the site today is a reproduction of the 1705 structure that burned down in 1747. Dark-wood wainscoting, pewter chandeliers, and towering ceilings contribute to a handsome impression. That an official building would have so ornate an interior was characteristic of aristocratic 18th-century Virginia. This was in telling contrast to the plain town meeting halls of Puritan New England, where other citizens were governing themselves at the same time. ⊠ *East end of Duke of Gloucester St.*

⑱ The **DeWitt Wallace Decorative Arts Museum** adds another cultural dimension that goes well beyond Colonial history. Grouped by medium are English and American furniture, textiles, prints, metals, and ceramics of the 17th to the early 19th century. If you're yawning at the thought of fancy tableware, stop: presentations here tend to be creative and surprising. Prizes among the 8,000 pieces in the collection are a full-length portrait of George Washington by Charles Willson Peale and a royally commissioned case clock surmounted by the detailed figure of a Native American. You enter the museum through the Public Hospital. ⊠ *Francis St.*

⑫ The **George Wythe House** was the residence of Thomas Jefferson's law professor; Wythe was also a signer of the Declaration of Independence. General Washington used the house as a headquarters just before his victory at Yorktown. The large brick structure, built in the mid-18th century, is conspicuously symmetrical: each side has a chimney, and each floor has two rooms on either side of a center hallway. The garden in back is similarly divided. The outbuildings, including a smokehouse, kitchen, laundry, outhouses, and a chicken coop, are reconstructions. ⊠ *West side of Palace Green.*

⑬ His Majesty's Governor Alexander Spotswood built the original **Governor's Palace** in 1720, and seven British viceroys, the last of them Lord Dunmore in 1775, lived in this appropriately showy mansion. The 540 weapons, including 230 muskets and pistols, arrayed on the walls of several rooms herald the power of the Crown. Some of the furnishings are original, and the rest are matched to an extraordinary inventory of 16,000 items. Lavishly appointed as it is, the palace is furnished to the time just before the Revolution. During the Revolution, it housed the commonwealth's first two governors, Patrick Henry and Thomas Jefferson. The original residence burned down in 1781, and today's reconstruction stands on the original foundation.

A costumed guide greets you at the door for a tour through the building, offering commentary and answering questions. Notable among the furnishings are several pieces made in Williamsburg and owned by Lord Dunmore. Social events are described on the walk through the great formal ballroom, where you might even hear the sounds of an 18th-century harp, clavichord, or piano. The supper room leads to the formal garden and the planted terraces beyond. ⊠ *Northern end of Palace Green.*

❾ The **Peyton Randolph House** was the home of a prominent colonist and revolutionary who served as attorney general under the British, then as Speaker of the House of Burgesses, and later as president of the first and second Continental Congresses. The oak-panel bedroom and Randolph family silver are remarkable. ⊠ *Nicholson St. at N. England St.*

❹ **Raleigh Tavern** was the scene of pre-Revolutionary revels and rallies that were often joined by Washington, Jefferson, Patrick Henry, and other major figures. The spare but elegant blue-and-white Apollo Room is said to have been the first meeting place of Phi Beta Kappa, the scholastic honorary society founded in 1776. The French general Marquis de Lafayette was feted here in 1824. In 1859 the original structure burned, and today's building is a reconstruction based on archaeological evidence and period descriptions and sketches of the building. ⊠ *Duke of Gloucester St., west of Capitol.*

❷ The **Visitor Center** is the logical first stop at Colonial Williamsburg. Here you can park free; buy tickets; see a 35-minute introductory movie, *Williamsburg—the Story of a Patriot*; and pick up *This Week,* which has a list of regular events and special programs and a map of the Historic Area. Tickets are also sold at the Lumber House in the Historic Area. ⊠ *102 Information Center Dr., off U.S. 60* ☎ *757/220-7645 or 800/447-8679* ⊕ *www.colonialwilliamsburg.com* ⌧ *$34–$72* ☉ *Daily 9–5.*

Also Worth Seeing

❶❾ The **Abby Aldrich Rockefeller Folk Art Museum,** within the DeWitt Wallace Decorative Arts Museum, showcases American "decorative usefulware"—toys, furniture, weather vanes, coffeepots, and quilts—within typical 19th-century domestic interiors. There are also folk paintings, rustic sculptures, and needlepoint pictures. Since the 1920s, the 2,000-piece collection has grown from the original 400 pieces acquired by the wife of Colonial Williamsburg's first and principal benefactor. ⊠ *Francis St.*

❶❹ The **Brush-Everard House** was built in 1717 by John Brush, a gunsmith, and later owned by Thomas Everard, who was twice mayor of Williamsburg. The wood-frame house contains remarkable, ornate carving work but is open only for special-focus tours. Temporary exhibits and vignettes on slaves' lives are held here in summer. ⊠ *Scotland St. and Palace Green.*

6

**⌐ NEED A
BREAK?**

At the west end of Duke of Gloucester Street, for a block on both sides, **Merchants Square** has more than 40 shops and restaurants, including an ice-cream parlor, coffee shop, cheese shop, chocolatier, peanut shop, and gourmet food store. Services also include three banks and a drugstore.

⑩ The original **Courthouse** of 1770 was used by municipal and county courts until 1932. Civil and minor criminal matters and cases involving slaves were adjudicated here; other trials were conducted at the Capitol. The stocks once used to punish misdemeanors are outside the building: they can make for a humorous photo opportunity. The courthouse's exterior has been restored to its original appearance. Visitors often participate in scheduled reenactments of court sessions. ⊠ *North side of Duke of Gloucester St., west of Queen St.*

> **WORD OF MOUTH**
>
> "The evening ghost walk sponsored by Colonial Williamsburg is really good. You move through Duke of Gloucester Street by lantern light."   —MelJ

The spine of Colonial Williamsburg's restored area is the broad 1-mi-long **Duke of Gloucester Street.** On Saturday at 1 PM from March to October, the Fifes and Drums Corp marches the length of the street and performs a stirring drill. Along this artery alone, or just off it, are two dozen attractions. Walking west on Duke of Gloucester Street from the Capitol, you can find a dozen 18th-century shops—including those of the apothecary, the wig maker, the silversmith, and the milliner.

❽ The **Guardhouse** once served in the defense of the Magazine's lethal inventory. Special interpretive programs about the military are scheduled here. ⊠ *Duke of Gloucester St. near Queen St.*

❻ At **James Anderson's Blacksmith Shop,** smiths forge the nails, tools, and other iron hardware used in construction throughout the town. The shop itself was reconstructed by carpenters using 18th-century tools and techniques. ⊠ *Between Botetourt and Colonial Sts., on south side of Duke of Gloucester St.*

❼ The original **Magazine** (1715), an octagonal brick warehouse, was used for storing arms and ammunition—at one time, 60,000 pounds of gunpowder and 3,000 muskets. It was used for this purpose by the British, then by the Continental army, and again by the Confederates during the Civil War. Today, 18th-century firearms are on display within the arsenal. ⊠ *West of Queen St., on south side of Duke of Gloucester St.*

In **Market Square,** an open green between Queen and Palace streets along Duke of Gloucester, cattle, seafood, dairy products, fruit, and vegetables were all sold—as were slaves. Both the market and slave auctions are sometimes reenacted.

⑪ The handsome **Palace Green** runs north from Duke of Gloucester Street up the center of Palace Street, with the Governor's Palace at the far end and notable historic houses on either side.

⓱ The **Public Hospital**, a reconstruction of a 1773 insane asylum, provides an informative, shocking look at the treatment of the mentally ill in the 18th and 19th centuries. It also serves as cover for a modern edifice that houses very different exhibitions; entrance to the DeWitt Wallace Decorative Arts Museum is through the hospital lobby. ✉ *Francis St.*

On the outskirts of the Historic Area is **Robertson's Windmill,** a Colonial mill for grinding grains. It's currently closed to the public. ✉ *N. England St.*

OFF THE BEATEN PATH

WILLIAMSBURG WINERY – Carrying on a Virginia tradition of wine making that began with early settlers, Virginia's largest winery produces 60,000 cases yearly. The winery offers guided tours, a well-stocked wine shop, a 17th-century tasting room, and a museum of wine-making artifacts. Be sure to give the cabernets and merlots a try. The Gabriel Archer Tavern serves a casual lunch daily and dinner Tuesday to Saturday (April–October only). Scheduled to open on the premises in 2007 is a 28-room country inn. The winery is off Route 199E. To get there, turn east on Brookwood Drive and left onto Lake Powell Road. ✉ *5800 Wessex Hundred, Williamsburg* ☎ *757/229–0999* ⊕ *www.williamsburgwinery.com* 🎫 *$7, includes tasting of 5–7 wines and a souvenir glass* ⊗ *Apr.–Oct., Mon.–Sat. 10–6, Sun. 11–6; Nov.–Mar., Mon.–Sat. 10–5, Sun. 11–5.*

6

⓹ **Wetherburn's Tavern,** which offered refreshment, entertainment, and lodging beginning in 1743, may be the most accurately furnished building in Colonial Williamsburg, with contents that conform to a room-by-room inventory taken in 1760. Excavations at this site have yielded more than 200,000 artifacts. The outbuildings include the original dairy and a reconstructed kitchen. Vegetables are still grown in the small garden. ✉ *Duke of Gloucester St., across from Raleigh Tavern.*

⓰ The **Wren Building** is part of the College of William and Mary, founded in 1693 and the second oldest college in the United States after Harvard University. The campus extends to the west; the Wren Building (1695) was based on the work of the celebrated London architect Sir Christopher Wren. Its redbrick outer walls are original, but fire gutted the interiors several times, and the current quarters are largely reconstructions of the 20th century. The faculty common room, with a table covered with green felt and an antique globe, suggests Oxford and Cambridge universities, the models for this New World institution. George Wythe became America's first law professor at the college and taught law to Thomas Jefferson, Henry Clay, James Monroe, and John Marshall. Tours, led by undergraduates, include the chapel where Colonial leader Peyton Randolph is buried. ✉ *West end of Duke of Gloucester St.*

Where to Eat

★ **$$–$$$$** ✕ **Regency Room.** This hotel restaurant is known for its elegance, attentive service, and quality cuisine. Among crystal chandeliers, Asian silk-screen prints, and full silver service, you can sample chateaubriand carved tableside, as well as rack of lamb, Dover Sole, lobster bisque, and house-smoked and -cured salmon. It may almost seem as if you're treated like royalty. A jacket and tie are required at dinner and optional at Sunday brunch. ⊠ *Williamsburg Inn, 136 E. Francis St.* ☏ *757/229–1000* ⚐ *Reservations essential* ▤ *AE, D, DC, MC, V.*

★ **$$–$$$$** ✕ **Le Yaca.** A mall of small boutiques is the unlikely location for this French-country restaurant. The dining room has soft pastel colors, hardwood floors, candlelight, and a central open fireplace. The menu is arranged in the French manner, with four prix-fixe menus and 10 entrées, including whole duck breast with peach and pepper sauce, leg of lamb with rosemary garlic sauce, Bouillabaisse, and fresh scallops and shrimp with champagne sauce. Le Yaca is on U.S. 60 East, near Busch Gardens. ⊠ *Village Shops at Kingsmill, 1915 Pocahontas Trail* ☏ *757/220–3616* ▤ *AE, D, DC, MC, V* ⊘ *Closed Sun. No lunch Sat.*

$$–$$$ ✕ **Aberdeen Barn.** Saws, pitchforks, oxen yokes, and the like hang on the barn walls, but the wood tables are lacquered, and the napkins are linen. Specialties include slow-roasted prime rib, baby-back Danish pork ribs barbecued with a sauce of peach preserves and Southern Comfort; and shrimp Dijon. An ample wine list offers a wide variety of domestic and imported choices. ⊠ *1601 Richmond Rd.* ☏ *757/229–6661* ▤ *AE, D, MC, V* ⊘ *No lunch.*

$$–$$$ ✕ **Berret's Restaurant and Taphouse Grill.** One of the most reliable seafood spots around, Berret's is in Merchants Square. Upscale but casual, the restaurant lights crackling fires during colder months and opens up its pleasant outdoor patio when it's warm. Entrées and appetizers employ fresh Chesapeake Bay seafood. It's usually a sure bet to try any of the nightly specials of fresh fish, which often include perfectly prepared flounder. The she-crab soup, a house favorite, blends crabmeat, cream, and crab roe with just a hint of sherry. Virginia wines and beers are featured. ⊠ *199 Boundary St.* ☏ *757/253–1847* ▤ *AE, D, DC, MC, V* ⊘ *Jan.–early Feb., closed Mon. Dining room: no lunch.*

$$–$$$ ✕ **The Trellis.** With vaulted ceilings and hardwood floors, the Trellis is an airy and pleasant place. The imaginative lunch and dinner menus change with the seasons. A good wine list complements such dishes as homemade tomato bisque, wild boar, and soft-shell crabs. The seafood entrées are particularly good, and many patrons wouldn't leave without ordering the rich Death by Chocolate, the restaurant's signature dessert. Prices on the outdoor terrace menu are lower than the indoor dining room. ⊠ *Merchants Sq., 403 Duke of Gloucester St.* ☏ *757/229–8610* ▤ *AE, MC, V.*

$–$$$ ✕ **The Whaling Company.** Fresh seafood is the drawing card at this large wooden building, which wouldn't look out of place in a New England fishing village. Despite its out-of-town look, the restaurant has an authenticity sometimes hard to find in touristy towns. Locals come in for the fresh Virginia scallops, shrimp, fish, and other seafood. Steaks and lemon herb chicken are available for the non–Whalers. The restaurant is off U.S. 60 near the Route 199 interchange. ⊠ *494 McLaws Circle* ☏ *757/229–0275* ▤ *AE, DC, MC, V* ⊘ *No lunch.*

$–$$ ✕ **Sal's Restaurant by Victor.** Locals love this family Italian restaurant and pizzeria. Victor Minichiello and his staff serve up pasta, fish, chicken, and veal dinners as well as subs and pizzas. The restaurant delivers free to nearby hotels. ⊠ *1242 Richmond Rd.* ☏ *757/220–2641* ▤ *AE, D, MC, V.*

¢–$ ✕ **College Delly.** It's easy to forget that this is a college town, but this cheerful dive keeps up the school spirit. The white-brick eatery with forest-green canvas awnings is dark and scruffy inside. Walls are hung with fraternity and sorority pictures, graduation snapshots, and sports-team photos. Booths and tables are in the William and Mary colors of green and gold. Deli sandwiches, subs, specialty pizzas, pasta, stromboli, and Greek dishes are all prepared with fresh ingredients and are all delicious, and there's a wide selection of beers on tap. The Delly delivers free to nearby hotels from 6 PM to 1 AM. ⊠ *336 Richmond Rd.* ☎ *757/229–6627* ▤ *MC, V.*

¢–$ ✕ **Old Chickahominy House.** Reminiscent of old-fashioned Virginia tearooms, this Colonial-style restaurant has delectable goodies served in an 18th-century dining room. For breakfast there's Virginia ham and eggs, made-from-scratch biscuits, country bacon, sausage, and grits. Lunch brings Brunswick stew, Virginia ham biscuits, fruit salad, and homemade pie. ⊠ *1211 Jamestown Rd.* ☎ *757/229–4689* ▤ *MC, V* ☯ *No dinner.*

COLONIAL
TAVERNS

For an authentic dining experience to match the historic setting, it's nearly a requirement to dine in one of the four reconstructed "taverns" in Colonial Williamsburg—essentially casual restaurants with beer and wine available. Colonial-style and modern American fare is served at lunch, dinner, and Sunday brunch. Although the food can be uneven (excellent one night and mediocre the next), a meal at any tavern is a good way to get into the spirit of the era.

No reservations are taken for lunch (or anytime at Chowning's Tavern), but make dinner reservations up to two or three weeks in advance. Hours also change according to season, so check by calling the reservations number (☎ 800/447–8679). Smoking is not permitted in any of the taverns. To see tavern menus, go to: www.history.org/visit/diningExperience/.

> ### WORD OF MOUTH
>
> "Have lunch at one of the Colonial Williamsburg taverns. It is pricey but lunch costs less than dinner. The food is OK, but nothing great—not worth the dinner prices."
> –MFNYC

$$$–$$$$ ✕ **Christiana Campbell's Tavern.** George Washington's favorite tavern is across the street from the Capitol. Concentrating on seafood, the menu includes Sherried Crab Stew, Pan Fried Stuffed Rainbow Trout, Grilled Sirloin of Beef, and tasty oyster fritters just the way the General liked them. The Mrs. Campbell's Waterman's Supp'r assortment comes with crab-stuffed shrimp, oyster stew, grilled salmon, seared scallops, and seasonal seafood. ⊠ *Waller St.* ▤ *AE, D, DC, MC, V.*

$–$$$$ ✕ **Kings Arms.** This 18th century–style chop house is where the finest gentry dined in Colonial days, and is still the best of the Historic Area's four Colonial taverns. The genteel surroundings imitate those experienced by Thomas Jefferson and Patrick Henry. Don't miss favorites such as peanut soup or Game Pye, made of venison, rabbit, duck, vegetables, and bacon in a wine sauce. Roast Prime Rib of Beef, tender pork, and lamb are on offer. Weather permitting, you can eat in the garden behind the tavern. ⊠ *Duke of Gloucester St.* ▤ *AE, D, DC, MC, V.*

¢–$$ ✕ **Chowning's Tavern.** A reconstructed 18th-century alehouse, Chowning's serves casual quick fare for lunch, including traditional pit-style BBQ, beef brisket sandwiches, and Smithfield ham and Gloucester cheese on a pretzel roll. You can eat either inside the tavern or under a grape arbor behind the tavern. After 5 PM, Chownings becomes a true Colonial tavern where Gambols (18th-century entertainment), a program presented for 25 years, operates throughout the evening.■ TIP➔ Costumed balladeers lead family sing-alongs, and costumed servers play popular games of the day. From 8 PM until closing, Chowning's caters to a more mature audience. ⊠ *Duke of Gloucester St.* ⊟ *AE, D, DC, MC, V.*

¢–$ ✕ **Shields Tavern.** The James Shields Tavern has returned to its roots as an 18th-century coffee house, with costumed interpreters engaging guests in "events of the day." The tavern's menu of light fare—gumbo soup, salads, wrap sandwiches, and pie—is served throughout the day. After 3, a part of the restaurant is given over to serving coffee, cider, and hot chocolate. ⊠ *Duke of Gloucester St.* ⊟ *AE, D, DC, MC, V.*

Where to Stay

★ $$$$ ⊞ **Williamsburg Inn.** This grand hotel from 1937 is owned and operated by Colonial Williamsburg. Rooms are beautifully and individually furnished with reproductions and antiques in the English Regency style, and genteel service and tradition reign. Rooms come with such perks as morning coffee and afternoon tea, a daily newspaper, turndown service, and bathrobes. The Providence Wings, adjacent to the inn, are less formal; rooms are in a contemporary style with Asian accents and overlook the tennis courts, a private pond, and a wooded area. ⊠ *136 E. Francis St., Box 1776, 23187-1776* ☎ *757/229–1000 or 800/447–8679* 🖶 *757/220–7096* ⊕ *www.colonialwilliamsburg.com* ⇌ *62 rooms, 14 suites* ⌂ *3 restaurants, room service, in-room VCRs, in-room data ports, 9-hole golf course, 2 18-hole golf courses, tennis court, pool, health club, spa, croquet, hiking, lawn bowling, lounge, piano, dry cleaning, laundry service, concierge, meeting rooms, no-smoking rooms* ⊟ *AE, D, DC, MC, V.*

$$$–$$$$ ⊞ **Liberty Rose.** Century-old beeches, oaks, and poplars surround this slate-roof, white-clapboard house on a hilltop-acre 1 mi from Colonial Williamsburg. The inn was constructed in the early 1920s; furnishings include European antiques and plenty of silk and damask. Most remarkable is that every room has windows on three sides. The large room on the first floor has a unique bathroom with a claw-foot tub, a red-marble shower, and antique mirrors. Breakfast is served on a sunporch. This two-story bed-and-breakfast does not have an elevator. ⊠ *1022 Jamestown Rd., 23185* ☎ *757/253–1260 or 800/545–1825* ⊕ *www. libertyrose.com* ⇌ *4 rooms* ⌂ *No smoking* ⊟ *AE, MC, V* ❙◯❙ *BP.*

$$$–$$$$ ⊞ **Williamsburg Lodge & Conference Center.** The total renovation of this classic hotel and the addition of a conference center were completed in 2006. Charmingly appointed with furnishings inspired by the collections of the Abby Aldrich Rockefeller Folk Art Museum, every room has a hair dryer, iron, ironing board, and clock radio. Rooms with fireplaces are available. ⊠ *310 S. England St., 23187-1776* ☎ *757/229–1000 or 800/447–8679* 🖶 *757/220–7799* ⊕ *www.colonialwilliamsburg.com* ⇌ *323 rooms* ⌂ *Room service, in-room data ports, in-room safes,*

room TVs *with movies, cable TV, in-room broadband, in-room data ports, some Wi-Fi, 9-hole golf course, 2 18-hole golf courses, pool, indoor pool, health club, bars, lobby lounge, laundry service, concierge, Internet room, business services, convention center, meeting rooms, travel services, free parking, no-smoking rooms* ▭ *AE, D, MC, V.*

★ **$$–$$$$** ▣ **Colonial Houses.** A stay here seems particularly moving at night, when the town's historic area is quiet and you have Williamsburg pretty much to yourself. Five of the 25 homes and three lodging taverns are 18th-century structures; the others have been rebuilt on their original foundations. Antiques and period reproductions furnish the rooms, and the costumed staff reinforces the historical air. Modern amenities include hair dryers, irons, ironing boards, coffeemakers, and a complimentary fruit basket and bottle of wine. The Colonial Houses share the facilities of the adjacent Williamsburg Inn and the Lodge. ☒ *136 E. Francis St., Box 1776, 23187-1776* ☎ *757/229–1000 or 800/447–8679* 🖷 *757/ 565–8444* ⊕ *www.colonialwilliamsburg.com* ⇨ *77 rooms* ⟁ *Room service, cable TV, dry cleaning; no smoking* ▭ *AE, D, DC, MC, V.*

★ **$$–$$$$** ▣ **Kingsmill Resort and Spa.** This manicured 2,900-acre resort on the James River owned by Anheuser-Busch is home to the largest golf resort in Virginia: it hosts the LPGA's Michelob ULTRA Open each May. You can play year-round on three championship courses, including the River Course, renovated in 2005. The 9-hole course is free if you stay here, and so is a shuttle bus to Busch Gardens, Water Country USA, and Colonial Williamsburg. The guest rooms have fireplaces and Colonial-style furniture. The inventive menu at the expensive Bray Bistro emphasizes seafood. Of note are the brunch and evening Chesapeake Seafood Buffet on Sundays. ☒ *1010 Kingsmill Rd., Williamsburg 23185* ☎ *757/ 253–1703 or 800/832–5665* ⊕ *www.kingsmill.com* ⇨ *235 rooms, 175 suites* ⟁ *6 restaurants, cable TV, in-room data ports, 9-hole golf course, 3 (18-hole) golf courses, putting green, 15 tennis courts, 2 pools (1 indoor), wading pool, health club, sauna, spa, steam room, beach, boating, marina, fishing, billiards, babysitting, dry cleaning, laundry service, concierge, business services, meeting rooms* ▭ *AE, D, DC, MC, V.*

¢**–$$$** ▣ **Woodlands Hotel and Suites.** An official Colonial Williamsburg property with contemporary furnishings, this 300-room hotel is adjacent to the HUZZAH! restaurant and the visitor center complex. You can enjoy the extensive free continental breakfast indoors or on the large patio— kids and adults enjoy making their own homemade waffles. There's gated free parking so you can abandon your car and walk to the free shuttle buses. ☒ *102 Visitor Center Dr., 23185* ☎ *757/229–1000 or 800/447– 8679 757/565–8797* ⊕ www.colonialwilliamsburg.com ⇨ 204 *rooms, 96 suites* ⟁ *Restaurant, microwaves, refrigerators, in-room broadband, pool, horseshoes, Ping-Pong, lobby lounge, playground, laundry service, business services, Internet room, meeting rooms, no-smoking rooms* ▭ AE, D, DC, MC, V ⎪◎⎪ *CP.*

$$ ▣ **The Fife and Drum Inn.** On the second floor of Merchant's Square and practically across the street from the historic district stands this family-run B&B (there's no elevator). Each room is stylishly decorated by the owner in a motif that spotlights an aspect of Williamsburg town history. Modern amenities include a hair dryer and in-room phones with voice mail. Rooms have either a shower or a combination tub–shower. Included in the rates are afternoon appetizers, homemade cookies, non-alcoholic beverages, and a full hot breakfast. ⊠ *441 Prince George St., 23185* ☎ *757/345–1776 or 888/838–1783* ᐁ *757/253–1675* ⊕ *www. fifeanddruminn.com* ➷ *7 rooms, 2 suites* ☾ *Cable TV, in-room VCRs, free parking* 🝙 *AE, D, DC, MC, V* ⧓ *BP.*

$$ 🎴 **Williamsburg Sampler Bed & Breakfast Inn.** Charming and hospitable, this redbrick inn near the historic district is modeled after a plantation-style house from the 1700s. Rooms have 18th- and 19th-century antiques, pewter pieces, four-poster beds, and pleasant views of the city. The suites are particularly inviting: each has a separate sitting room, French doors, and a porch overlooking gardens. There are no phones in the rooms, but local calls are free from the inn's foyer. ⊠ *922 Jamestown Rd., 23185* ☎ *757/253–0398 or 800/722–1169* ᐁ *757/253–2669* ⊕ *www. williamsburgsampler.com* ➷ *4 rooms, 2 suites* ☾ *Dining room, gym, sauna; no smoking* 🝙 *AE, D, DC, MC, V* ⧓ *BP.*

$ 🎴 **War Hill Inn.** This inn was designed by a Colonial Williamsburg architect to resemble a period structure: the two-story redbrick building at the center has a wood-frame wing. Appropriate antiques and reproductions decorate the interior. The War Hill is inside a 32-acre operating cattle farm, 4 mi from the Colonial Williamsburg information center. Those in search of privacy may want one of the cottages or the first-floor suite (other rooms open onto a common hallway). ⊠ *4560 Longhill Rd., 23188* ☎ *757/565–0248 or 800/743–0248* ⊕ *www.warhillinn. com* ➷ *4 rooms, 2 cottages* ☾ *Cable TV* 🝙 *MC, V* ⧓ *BP.*

¢–$ 🎴 **Quality Inn Lord Paget.** Tall white columns front this Colonial-style motel. Four rooms are accessed via stairs off the spacious lobby, which has Oriental carpets; others have parking at the front door, and some have canopy beds. Refrigerators and microwaves are available for a fee. The property has a 2½-acre lake and lovely gardens. Newspapers and local phone calls are free, and a full, hot breakfast is included. ⊠ *901 Capitol Landing Rd., 23185* ☎ *757/229–4444 or 800/537–2438* ➷ *94 rooms* ☾ *Coffee shop, lake, putting green, pool, dock, fishing, laundry service, no-smoking rooms* 🝙 *AE, D, DC, MC, V* ⧓ *BP.*

¢–$ 🎴 **Ramada Outlet Mall Willliamsburg.** Hard-core shoppers may wish to lodge directly across the street from the 200-acre Williamsburg Pottery Factory and near the numerous other outlets in the area. The contemporary building has two stories and exterior room entrances adjacent to parking. Rooms have quilted spreads, a desk, lounge chair, hair dryer, iron, ironing board and coffee maker. An extensive continental breakfast is included. ⊠ *6493 Richmond Rd., I–64 to Exit 234A Lightfoot Rd., to Rte. 60, 23188* ☎ *757/565–1111* ᐁ *757/564–3033* ⊕ *www. ramada.com* ➷ *128 rooms* ☾ *Coffee shop, refrigerators, cable TV with movies, in-room broadband, in-room data ports, pool, free parking, no pets, no-smoking rooms* 🝙 *AE, DC, MC, V* ⧓ *CP.*

¢–$ 🎴 **Williamsburg Hospitality House.** Across the street from the College of William and Mary and two blocks from the Historic Area, this hotel is a prime size for conferences and reunions, so you won't be the only one standing under the crystal chandelier in the lobby. Guest rooms are furnished in styles ranging from 18th century to art deco; all have hair dryers, irons, ironing boards, and in-room coffeemakers. The large poolside patio is very inviting after a day exploring the Historic Triangle. ✉ *415 Richmond Rd., 23185* ☎ *757/229–4020 or 800/932–9192* 🖷 *757/ 229–0731* ⊕ *www.williamsburghosphouse.com* ↩ *296 rooms, 17 suites* ♿ *2 restaurants, room service, cable TV with movies, in-room data ports, pool, exercise equipment, bar, shop, laundry service, concierge, business services, meeting rooms, free parking, no-smoking rooms, video game room, laundry facilities, concierge, business services* ☰ *AE, D, DC, MC, V* ♯ *CP.*

Nightlife & the Arts

Busch Gardens Williamsburg (✉ U.S. 60 ☎ 757/253–3350) hosts popular song-and-dance shows (country, gospel, opera, German folk) in several theaters; in the largest, the 5,000-seat Royal Palace, pop stars often perform. **Music Theatre of Williamsburg** (✉ 3012 Richmond Rd. ☎ 757/ 564–0200 or 888/687–4220) offers family-oriented live country music and comedy. Shows run Monday through Saturday beginning at 8 PM. Well-known artists on tour play at the 10,000-seat **Phi Beta Kappa Hall** (✉ Jamestown Rd. entrance to campus ☎ 757/221–3340) at the College of William and Mary.

Sports & the Outdoors

AMUSEMENT PARKS 🖑 **Busch Gardens Europe,** a 100-acre amusement park that has been voted the world's most beautiful theme park for 15 years, has more than 40 rides and six beautifully landscaped "countries" with recreations of French, German, English, Scottish, Irish, and Italian areas. In addition to roller coasters, bumper cars, and water rides, the park has eight mainstage shows and a magical children's area. Costumed actors add character to the theme areas while cable-car gondolas pass overhead. ✉ *U.S. 60, 3 mi east of Williamsburg* ☎ *757/253–3350 or 800/343–7946* 🎟 *$52, child $45; parking $10* ⊙ *Late Mar.–mid-May, weekends 10–8; mid-May–Labor Day, weekdays 10–9, weekends 10–10; early Sept.–Oct., Fri–Sun. 10–10; call for exact hrs.*

> **THEME "PARK"ING**
>
> What they don't tell you: even as expensive as they are, tickets don't include parking at either Busch Gardens or Water Country. You must pay $10 per car to enter and park ($15 for premium parking that's closer to the entrance). To avoid having to pay for parking, stay at a motel or hotel that offers free shuttle service to the parks.

JOGGING & WALKING The historic district as well as the College of William and Mary campus make for a splendid run. The best times for an amble along the sidewalks or cobblestone streets are early in the morning and at sundown. In the district is a 3-mi loop. Some of the nicest paths to run include the main thoroughfare of Duke of Gloucester Street, and the myriad side streets such as Botetourt and Blair streets. A 30-mi path starts at the college and runs all around the Colonial area.

Shopping

Merchants Square, on the west end of Duke of Gloucester Street, has both licensed Willliamsburg® shops and non-Colonial, upscale shops that include Laura Ashley, the Porcelain Collector of Williamsburg,

Williamsburg Outlet Shopping

YOU CAN FIND MANY OUTLET MALLS less than 10 minutes west of Colonial Williamsburg, in the tiny town of Lightfoot. If you're driving from Richmond to Williamsburg on I-64 take Exit 234 west to Lightfoot. When you reach U.S. 60 (Richmond Road), the outlets—both freestanding and in shopping centers—are on both sides of the road. Most outlet shops are open Monday–Saturday 10–9, Sunday 10–6. In January and February, some stores close weekdays at 6.

The **Williamsburg Pottery Factory** (✉ U.S. 60 W, Lightfoot ☎ 757/564–3326) is an attraction in itself, and the parking area is usually crammed with tour buses. Covering 200 acres, the enormous store sells luggage, clothing, furniture, food and wine, china, crystal, and—its original commodity—pottery. Individual stores such as Pfaltzgraff and Banister Shoes are within the compound.

The largest of the outlets, **Prime Outlets at Williamsburg** (✉ U.S. 60, Lightfoot ☎ 757/565–0702) has more than 85 stores. Liz Claiborne, Royal Doulton, L. L. Bean, Waterford-Wedgwood, Mikasa, Eddie Bauer, Tommy Hilfiger, Brooks Bros., Nike, Guess, Nautica, and Cole Haan are all here. It's also the country's only outlet for Lladro, known for its figurines.

The **Williamsburg Outlet Mall** (✉ U.S. 60 W, Lightfoot ☎ 888/746–7333) has more than 60 shops, including the Jockey Store, Linens 'n Things, Farberware, Levi's, and Bass.

Patriot Plaza (✉ 3032 Richmond Rd., Lightfoot ☎ 757/564–7570) has Lenox, Dansk, Prince Michel Wineshop, Villeroy & Boch, Polo Ralph Lauren, and other factory outlets.

and the J. Fenton Gallery. There's also Quilts Unlimited and the Campus Shop, which carries William and Mary gifts and clothing.

Three Colonial Williamsburg stores have individual offerings. **Williamsburg Celebrations** (☎ 757/565–8642) displays seasonal decorations and accessories. The **Williamsburg Craft House** (☎ 757/220–7747) sells a full line of Willliamsburg® dinnerware, flatware, glassware, pewter, giftware and jewelry. **Williamsburg at Home** (☎ 757/220–7749) features the full line of Willliamsburg® furniture, bedding, rugs, fixtures, and wallpapers.

Yorktown

⓴ *14 mi northeast of Colonial Williamsburg via Colonial Pkwy.*

It was at Yorktown that the combined American and French forces surrounded Lord Cornwallis's British troops in 1781; this was the end to the Revolutionary War and the beginning of our nation. In Yorktown today, as at Jamestown, two major attractions complement each other. Yorktown Battlefield, the historical site, is operated by the National Park Service; and Yorktown Victory Center, which has re-creations and informative exhibits, is operated by the state's Jamestown–Yorktown Foundation. From April through October, the Yorktown Trolley provides free service between the York-town Battlefield Visitor Center and the Yorktown Victory Center, as well as several stops between in the historic village. As well, a stately Watermen's Museum educates visitors about those who earn their living from the nearby waters.

New in 2005, Riverwalk Landing is a group of specialty shops, an upscale restaurant, and an outdoor performance venue on the shores of the York River. Two piers for medium cruise ships and personal watercraft are also along the waterfront. Yet Yorktown remains a small community of year-round residents. Route 238 leads into town, where along Main Street are preserved 18th-century buildings on a bluff overlooking the York River.

> ## COLONIAL PARKWAY
>
> For a beautiful drive along countryside that's nearly the same as land the Jamestown settlers trod, take the 23-mi scenic Colonial Parkway between Jamestown and Yorktown, a 40-minute drive one-way. The road between Yorktown and Williamsburg, which was aligned along the York River, was completed in 1937, but it wasn't until 1955, for the 350th anniversary of Jamestown, that the road was completed to America's first permanent English settlement. The limited access highway has broad sweeping curves, is meticulously landscaped, and is devoid of commercial development.

Settled in 1691, Yorktown had become a thriving tobacco port and a prosperous community of several hundred houses by the time of the Revolution. Nine buildings from that time still stand, some of them open to visitors. **Moore House,** where the terms of surrender were negotiated, and the elegant **Nelson House**, the residence of a Virginia governor (and a signer of the Declaration of Independence), are open for tours in summer and are included in the Yorktown Victory Center's entrance fee.

The **Swan Tavern,** a reconstruction of a 1722 structure, houses an antiques shop. **Grace Church,** built in 1697 and damaged in the War of 1812 and the Civil War, was rebuilt and has an active Episcopal congregation; its walls are made of native marl (a mixture of clay, sand, and limestone containing fragments of seashells). On Main Street, the **Somerwell House,** built before 1707, and the **Sessions House** (before 1699) are privately owned and closed to the public: they're the oldest houses in town. The latter was used as the Union's local headquarters during General George McClellan's Peninsula Campaign of the Civil War.

The **Watermen's Museum** is sited in a Colonial Revival manor house on Yorktown's waterfront that was floated across the York River on a barge in 1987. In it you can learn more about the generations of men who have wrested a living from the Chesapeake Bay and nearby waters. The five galleries house ship models, dioramas, and artifacts themed on Chesapeake watermen, bay boats, harvesting fish, aquaculture, tools, and treasures. Outdoor exhibits include an original three-log canoe, dredges, engines, and other equipment used by working watermen past and present. ⊠ *309 Water St.* ☎ *757/887–2641* ⊕ *www.watermens. org* ⊠ *$4* ☉ *Apr.–Thanksgiving, Tues.–Sat. 10–5, Sun. 1–5; Thanksgiving–Mar., Sat. 10–5; Sun. 1–5.*

☺ **Yorktown Battlefield** preserves the land where the British surrendered to
Fodor§Choice American and French forces in 1781. The museum in the visitor center
★ has on exhibit part of General George Washington's original field tent.
Dioramas, illuminated maps, and a film about the battle make the
sobering point that Washington's victory was hardly inevitable. A look
around from the roof's observation deck can help you visualize the events
of the campaign. Guided by an audio tour purchased from the gift
shop, you may explore the battlefield by car, stopping at the site of Washington's headquarters, a couple of crucial *redoubts* (breastworks dug
into the ground), the field where surrender took place, and the Moore
House where the surrender terms were negotiated. ⊠ *Rte. 238 off
Colonial Pkwy.* ☎ *757/898–2410* ⌨ *$5; combined entry fee to both
Jamestowne and Yorktown, $10* ☉ *Visitor center daily 9–5.*

☺ On the western edge of Yorktown Battlefield, the **Yorktown Victory Cen-**
Fodor§Choice **ter** has wonderful exhibits and demonstrations that bring to life the Amer-
★ ican Revolution. Textual and graphic displays along the open-air Road
to Revolution walkway cover the principal events and personalities. A
renovated *Declaration of Independence* entrance gallery and long-term
exhibition, *The Legacy of Yorktown: Virginia Beckons* debuted in 2006.
Life-size tableaux show 10 "witnesses," including an African-American
patriot, a loyalist, a Native American leader, two Continental Army soldiers, and the wife of a Virginia plantation owner. The exhibit galleries
contain more than 500 period artifacts, including many recovered during underwater excavations of "Yorktown's Sunken Fleet" (British ships
lost during the siege of 1781). Outdoors, visitors may participate in a
Continental Army drill at an encampment with interpreters costumed
as soldiers and female auxiliaries, who reenact and discuss daily camp
life. In another outdoor area, a re-created 1780s farm includes a dwelling,
kitchen, tobacco barn, crop fields, and kitchen garden, which show how
many Americans lived in the decade following the end of the Revolution. ⊠ *Rte. 238 off Colonial Pkwy.* ☎ *757/253–4838 or 888/593–4682*
⊕ *www.historyisfun.org* ⌨ *$8.25; combination ticket for Yorktown Vic-
tory Center and Jamestown Settlement, $17.75* ☉ *June 15–Aug. 15, daily
9–6; Aug. 16–June 14, daily 9–5.*

Where to Stay & Eat

$$–$$$ ✕ **Nick's Riverwalk Restaurant.** Whether you dine indoors or out, enjoy
the view of the York River, the Coleman Bridge, and Gloucester on the
opposite shore. Nick's Riverwalk offers casual meals of soups, salads,
and sandwiches at the Rivah Café and outdoor courtyard ($); the River-
walk Dining Room is more formal, with a menu featuring baked crabmeat imperial, sautéed fillets, and local oysters. ⊠ *323 Water St.* ☎ *757/
875–1522* ▭ *MC, V.*

¢–$$ ✕ **Waterstreet Landing.** The fare includes seafood, steaks, pizza, and
sandwiches at this cream-color brick café and bar across the street from
the York River. ⊠ *114 Water St.* ☎ *757/886–5890* ▭ *MC, V.*

$–$$ ▦ **Marl Inn.** Far from the crowds of Williamsburg and Jamestown, this
white picket-fenced inn is well known for its quiet, relaxing setting and
for the innkeepers' famous "crab-cake benedict" at breakfast. The inn
is steeped in history: it's on the grounds of the last battle of the Revolution. Antique and 18th-century reproduction furnishings are inside.

☒ *220 Church St., 23690* ☎ *757/898–3859 or 800/799–6207* ⊕ *www. marlinnbandb.com* ⤳ *1 room, 3 suites* ♿ *Cable TV, bicycles, some pets allowed* ▭ *AE, MC, V* ⭐ *BP.*

¢–$ ▣ **Duke of York Motel.** All rooms in this classic 1960s motel face the water and are only a few steps from a public beach. The furnishings include quilted bedspreads and Queen Anne–style reproduction wood furniture. The motel also has a swimming pool and a restaurant that serves breakfast and lunch daily and dinner Wednesday–Sunday. ☒ *508 Water St., 23690* ☎ *757/898–3232* ☏ *757/898–5922* ⊕ *www.dukeofyorkmotel. com* ⤳ *57 rooms* ♿ *Restaurant, cable TV with movies, in-room broadband, in-room data ports, pool, beach* ▭ *AE, D, DC, MC, V.*

Charles City County

35 mi northwest of Colonial Williamsburg via Rte. 5.

Colonists founded Charles City County in 1616. This tiny county is unique, being the only U.S. county to have a native president (William Harrison) and his vice president and successor (John Tyler) take office simultaneously, in 1841. Today you can get a taste of those early days by following Route 5 on its scenic way, parallel to the James River, past nine plantations—some of which are now bed-and-breakfasts. ■ TIP➔ **Make sure your gas tank is full and you may want to pack a picnic lunch. Service stations and restaurants are few.**

★ ㉓ Virginians say that the first Thanksgiving was celebrated at **Berkeley** in December 1619, not in Massachusetts in 1621. This plantation was the birthplace of Benjamin Harrison, a signer of the Declaration of Independence, and of William Henry Harrison, who became president in 1841. Throughout the Civil War, the Union general George McClellan used Berkeley as headquarters; during his tenure, his subordinate general Daniel Butterfield composed the melody for "Taps" while here in 1862 with 140,000 Union troops. An architectural gem, the original 1726 brick Georgian mansion has been carefully restored and furnished with 18th-century antiques. The gardens are in excellent condition, particularly the boxwood hedges. ☒ *Rte. 5, 12602 Harrison Landing Rd., Charles City* ☎ *804/829–6018 or 888/466–6018* ⊕ *www.berkeleyplantation. com* 🎫 *$11* ⊘ *Daily 9–5; last tour 4:30.*

㉑ **Sherwood Forest** (1720), at 300 feet said to be the longest wood-frame house in the United States, was the retirement home of John Tyler (1790–1862), 10th president of the United States. Tyler, who came into office in 1841 when William Henry Harrison died a month after inauguration, was a Whig who dissented from his party's abolitionist line in favor of the proslavery position of the Democrats. He died in 1862, having served briefly in the congress of the Confederate States of America. His house remains in the Tyler family and is furnished with heirloom antiques; it's surrounded by a dozen acres of grounds and the five outbuildings, including a tobacco barn. The house is only open to groups that have made a reservation in advance, but the grounds are open to the public. ☒ *Rte. 5, 14501 John Tyler Memorial Hwy., Charles City* ☎ *804/829–5377* ⊕ *www. sherwoodforest.org* 🎫 *Grounds $5* ⊘ *Grounds daily 9–5.*

㉔ **Shirley,** chartered in 1613 and the oldest plantation in Virginia, has been
Fodor'sChoice occupied by a single family, the Carters, for 11 generations. Their claim
★ to the land goes back to 1638, when it was settled by a relative, Edward
Hill. Robert E. Lee's mother was born here, and the Carters seem to be
related to every notable Virginia family from the Colonial and antebellum periods. The approach to the elegant 1723 Georgian manor is dramatic: the house stands at the end of a drive lined by towering Lombardy
poplars. Inside, the "Flying Staircase" rises for three stories with no visible support. Family silver is on display, ancestral portraits are hung
throughout, and rare books line the shelves. The family lives on the upper
floors, but the main floor, eight original Colonial outbuildings, and gardens of the working farm can be toured. ⊠ *501 Shirley Plantation Rd.,
Charles City* ☎ *804/829–5121* ⊕ *www.shirleyplantation.com* ☜ *$11*
⊙ *Daily 9–5; last tour 4:45.*

㉒ **Westover** was built in 1735 by Colonel William Byrd II (1674–1744),
an American aristocrat and founder of the city of Richmond who spent
much of his time and money in London. He was in Virginia frequently
enough to serve in both the upper and lower houses of the Colonial legislature at Williamsburg and to write one of the first travel books about
the region (as well as a notorious secret diary, a frank account of plantation life and Colonial politics). Byrd lived here with his beloved library
of 4,000 volumes. The house, celebrated for its moldings and carvings,
is open only during Garden Week in late April. However, it is worth the
short drive off Route 5 to walk on the grounds beside the peaceful James
River and smell the boxwoods. The grounds are arrayed with tulip
poplars at least 100 years old, and gardens of roses and other flowers
are well tended. Three wrought-iron gates, imported from England by
the colonel, are mounted on posts topped by figures of eagles with
spread wings. Byrd's grave is here, inscribed with the eloquent, immod-
est, lengthy, and apt epitaph he composed for himself. ⊠ *Rte. 5, 7000
Westover Rd., Charles City* ☎ *804/829–2882* ☜ *$2* ⊙ *Grounds daily
9–6, house daily in late Apr.; call for hrs.*

Where to Stay & Eat

$$–$$$ ✕**Indian Fields Tavern.** Because this restaurant is the best of only a few
places to dine in the area, you may encounter a wait to be seated and
served—especially at lunch when visitors touring the nearby plantations
descend. Housed in a restored farmhouse, the tavern specializes in southern dishes, especially regional specialties such as crab cakes and bread
pudding. Other main dishes include Tidewater shellfish in a tomato-and-
crab broth and a veal porterhouse chop. In season you can eat on the
screened porch overlooking gardens. There's brunch on Sunday. ⊠ *9220
John Tyler Memorial Hwy.* 804/829–5004 ☰ AE, D, MC, V.

$$ ☖**North Bend Plantation Bed & Breakfast.** The road to this historic home
winds past trailer homes and cottages before a gravel road turns to the
left between farm fields. As a working farm, it stands out from similar
B&Bs. The 1819 Greek Revival home was built for Sarah Harrison, sis-
ter of President William Henry Harrison, by her husband John Minge.
Inside, antebellum-era antiques, as well as Civil War maps and artifacts
decorate every room. Room amenities include robes and TVs. The

southern breakfast here might include buttermilk biscuits, Smithfield ham, apple butter, bacon, and grits, along with strong coffee. ⊠ *12200 Weyanoke Rd., Box 13A, Charles City 23030* ☎ *804/829–5176* 🖷 *804/ 829–6828* 🛏 *4 rooms, 1 suite* 🛠 *In-room VCR, pool, bicycles, croquet, horseshoes; no room phones* ☰ *MC, V* 🍽 *BP.*

Hopewell

㉕ *56 mi northwest of Colonial Williamsburg via Rte. 5 and 24 mi southeast of Richmond off I–295.*

City Point, the oldest part of Hopewell, was established in 1613 by Sir Thomas Dale. Across from Charles City County via the Route 106 Benjamin Harrison Bridge, Hopewell is worth a half-day exploration for its 19th-century buildings, nearby plantations, and 44 Sears Roebuck & Co. Catalog houses built from 1926 to 1937. Stop by the **Hopewell Visitor Center** (⊠ 4100 Oaklawn Blvd. [Rte. 36] ☎ 800/863–8687 or 804/541–2461) for maps to the Sears Catalog Homes in the Crescent Hills subdivision near downtown. The visitor center is just off I–295 at Exit 9A, and is open daily 9–5.

6

The history of **City Point** includes a Revolutionary War skirmish and 10 months as General Ulysses S. Grant's Union headquarters during the Civil War, from which he directed the Siege of Petersburg. It's free to take the open-air museum walking tour of 25 wayside exhibits; admission is charged to tour Grant's Headquarters ($4) and the City Point Early History Museum ($3), in a former U.S. Navy church, St. Dennis Chapel. ⊠ *Appamattox St. and Cedar La.* ☎ *804/541–2461 or 800/ 863–8687* 🎟 *Free; $7 combination ticket for Weston Manor and City Point Early History Museum* 🕑 *Daily dawn–dusk; buildings open Apr.–Oct., Mon.–Sat. 10–4:30, Sun. 1–4:30.*

Flowerdew Hundred was one of the earliest original land grants in Virginia, and played an important role in the Civil War for three days in 1864. Listed on the National Register of Historic Places, this working farm features a commemorative post windmill, a museum in a circa-1850 schoolhouse with exhibits on the plantation's history and its archaeological exploration, and a replicated 1820 detached kitchen housing exhibits on domestic slave life. You can also drive along 4 mi of riverfront, past archaeological sites, the site of Grant's Crossing, and Flowerdew's unique commemorative windmill. ⊠ *1617 Flowerdew Hundred Rd.* ☎ *804/541–8897* ⊕ *www.flowerdew.org* 🎟 *$8* 🕑 *Apr.–Nov., weekdays 10–4; last tour 3:30. Dec.–Mar. by appt.*

Weston Manor, built in 1789 by the Gilliam family, is a classic example of Virginia Georgian architecture, a formal five-bay manor with hipped roof. The family immigrated to Virginia in the 1600s as indentured servants, eventually acquiring several area plantations. Family members were descendants of Pocahontas, and a cousin married Thomas Jefferson's daughter Maria. The distinctive interior moldings, wainscoting, and chair rails are 85% original. A Jeffersonian dumb waiter is stowed in the dining room closet. ⊠ *Weston La. and 21st St.* ☎ *804/458–4682* 🎟 *$5* 🕑 *Apr.–Oct., Mon.–Sat. 10–4:30, Sun. 1–4:30; Nov.–Mar. by appt.*

Where to Eat

$–$$ ✕ **Dockside.** Broiled fresh seafood of a dozen kinds is the specialty at this casual, waterfront restaurant only a quick bridge-crossing from the James River Plantations. You could start with spiced shrimp on ice, and if you're really hungry, order the seafood platter. Other menu items include she-crab soup, Greek salads, and Italian main dishes. ✉ *700 Jordan Point Rd.* ☎ *804/541–2600* ▭ *AE, MC, V.*

HAMPTON ROADS AREA

The region known today as the Hampton Roads Area is made up of not only the large natural harbor, into which five rivers flow, but of the peninsula to the north that extends southeast from Williamsburg, and the Tidewater area between the mouth of the harbor and the Atlantic Ocean. On the peninsula are the cities of Newport News and Hampton; to the south and east are Norfolk, Portsmouth, Chesapeake, and Virginia Beach. These cities have been shaped by their proximity to the Chesapeake Bay and the rivers that empty into it, either as ports and shipbuilding centers or, in the case of Virginia Beach, as a hugely popular beach town. Hampton and Norfolk are the "old" cities of this area; recent development and revival efforts have made them worthy of a second look.

During the Civil War, the Union waged its thwarted 1862 Peninsula Campaign here. General George McClellan planned to land his troops on the peninsula in March of 1862 with the help of the navy, and then press westward to the Confederate capital of Richmond. Naval forces on the York and James rivers would protect the advancing army. However, beginning with the blockade that the ironclad CSS *Virginia* (formerly the USS *Merrimack*) held on the James until May, events and Confederates conspired to lengthen and foil the campaign.

Numbers in the margin correspond to points of interest on the Hampton Roads Area map.

Newport News

❷❻ *23 mi southeast of Williamsburg.*

Newport News stretches for almost 35 mi along the James River from near Williamsburg to Hampton Roads. Known mostly for its coal shipping and huge shipbuilding industry, the city is largely residential and is a suburb for both Williamsburg and the Norfolk area. Newport News has a number of Civil War battle sites and a splendid municipal park. The fabulous Mariners' Museum may be the best museum in the state. Close by, the Virginia Living Museum is a pleasant zoo experience for kids. The city's small, but busy, airport is convenient to both Williamsburg and the beach, making it a good base from which to visit both areas.

Newport News first appeared in the Virginia Company's records in 1619. It was probably named after Christopher Newport, captain of the *Susan Constant,* largest of the three ships in the company of Captain John Smith that landed at Jamestown in 1607. Newport News Shipbuilding is one

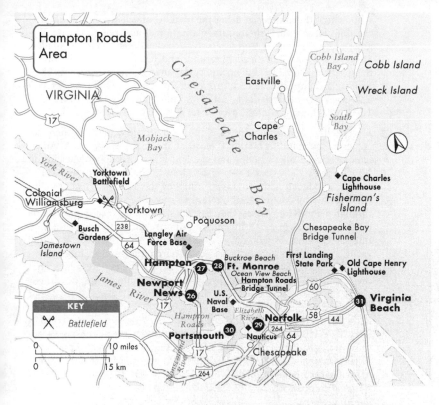

of the largest privately owned shipyards in the world, and with approximately 18,000 employees, probably the second-largest employer in Virginia. It's the only shipyard in the country capable of building nuclear-powered aircraft carriers.

Built in 1769 by William Harwood, the Georgian-style house known as **Endview Plantation** has witnessed momentous events in American history. Situated atop a knoll near a spring, Endview's land was traversed by Native Americans of the Powhatan Chiefdom a thousand years before the coming of the English. At the outbreak of the Civil War, Endview's owner, Dr. Humphrey Harwood Curtis, formed the Warwick Beauregards, which became Company H, 32nd Virginia Volunteer Infantry. During the subsequent Peninsula Campaign of 1862, Endview served as headquarters for Confederate generals Lafayette McLaws and Robert Toombs. Maintained today as a living-history museum, Endview offers a wide variety of programs; guided tours begin every 30 minutes. ⊠ *362 Yorktown Rd., Exit 247 off I-64, 23603* ☎ *757/887–1862* ⊕ *www.endview.org* ✉ *$6* ⊙ *Jan.–Mar., Mon. and Thurs.–Sat. 10–4, Sun. 1–5; Apr.–Dec., Mon. and Wed.–Sat. 10–4, Sun. 1–5.*

Lee Hall, an Italianate mansion constructed around 1859, was once home to one of Warwick County's leading landowners, Richard Decauter Lee, who achieved prominence using the method of scientific farming. It is the only large mid-19th-century plantation house remaining on Virginia's lower peninsula, and it served as the headquarters for Confederate generals John Bankhead Magruder and Joseph E. Johnston during the spring of 1862. Lee Hall now provides an in-depth review of the 1862 Peninsula Campaign. ⊠ *163 Yorktown Rd., Exit 247 off I–64* ☎ *757/ 888–3371* ⊕ *www.leehall.org* 🖃 *$6* ☉ *Jan.–Mar., Mon. and Thurs.–Sat. 10–4, Sun. 1–5; Apr.–Dec., Mon. and Wed.–Sat. 10–4, Sun. 1–5.*

Ⓒ A world history of seagoing vessels and the people who sailed them oc-
Fodor'sChoice cupies the outstanding **Mariners' Museum**, inside a 550-acre park. An al-
★ liance between the museum and the South Street Seaport Museum in New York City allows the two institutions to share collections, exhibitions, and educational programs. Many of the authentic scale models hand-carved by August Crabtree are so tiny that you must view them through magnifying glasses; they portray shipbuilding accomplishments from ancient Egypt to 19th-century Britain. Among the more than 50 full-size craft on display are a Native American bark canoe, a sailing yacht, a speedboat, a gondola, a Coast Guard cutter, and a Chinese sampan. In separate galleries you can often watch the progress of a boat under construction; view ornate and sometimes huge figureheads; examine the watermen's culture of the Chesapeake Bay; and learn about the history of the U.S. Navy. The museum also holds artifacts from the RMS *Titanic* and remains of the ironclad USS *Monitor,* which served in the 1862 Peninsula Campaign and was recovered from the coast of North Carolina. A 63,500-square-foot addition is under construction to house a major exhibition on the USS *Monitor,* set to open in March 2007. ⊠*100 Museum Dr., I–64, Exit 258A* ☎ *757/595–0368 or 800/581–7245* ⊕ *www.mariner.org* 🖃 *$12* ☉ *Daily 10–5.*

Ⓒ The **U.S. Army Transportation Museum,** at Fort Eustis, traces the history of army transportation by land, sea, and air, beginning with the Revolutionary War era. More than 90 vehicles, including experimental craft and numerous locomotives and trains dating to the 1800s, are on display. The museum's Korean War and World War II–era trucks can be toured inside and out. Be prepared to show a driver's license or other identification at the military checkpoint at the base entrance. ⊠ *Besson Hall, Bldg. 300, I–64, Exit 250A* ☎ *757/878–1115* 🖃 *Free* ☉ *Tues.–Sun. 9–4:30.*

Ⓒ At the **Virginia Living Museum,** visitors are transported to a steamy cypress swamp and cool mountain cove, the underwater world of the Chesapeake Bay and the underground realm of a limestone cave, all with living exhibits and hands-on activities. View the sun from the observatory and travel the universe in the planetarium theater. Outdoors, a ¾-mi boardwalk features animals native to Virginia in naturalized habitats and wildflower gardens. A special "Survivor: Jamestown" maze, coming in 2007, will challenge visitors with the conditions faced by Jamestown settlers, forcing them to make choices and find ways to survive the first year. ⊠ *524 J. Clyde Morris Blvd.* ☎ *757/595–1900* 🖃 *Museum $13, planetarium $3, combination ticket $15* ☉ *Memorial Day–Labor Day, daily 9–6; Labor Day–Memorial Day, Mon.–Sat. 9–5, Sun. noon–5.*

The **Virginia War Museum** houses more than 60,000 artifacts from all over the world. The collection includes a graffiti-covered section of the Berlin Wall, a Civil War blockade runner's uniform, weapons, uniforms, wartime posters, photographs, and other memorabilia. It traces military history from 1775 to the Gulf War and includes an outdoor exhibition of seven tanks and cannons, and the history of African-Americans and women in the military. Several war memorials are on the grounds of Huntington Park. ⊠ *9285 Warwick Blvd., Rte. 60* ☎ *757/247–8523* ⊕ *www. warmuseum.org* ▤ *$6* ⊙ *Mon.–Sat. 9–5, Sun. 1–5.*

Where to Stay & Eat

$ ✕ **Bill's Seafood House.** This reasonably priced seafood restaurant is a favorite with locals. The interior is simple—café curtains, tubular chairs, wood-grain Formica tables and nautical paintings. Seafood platters (broiled or fried) and other seafood dishes arrive with hush puppies and a choice of sides. For the landlubber, rib-eye steaks, chicken strips, and homemade pork barbecue are on the menu. No alcohol is served. ⊠ *10900 Warwick Blvd., U.S. Hwy. 60* ☎ *757/595–4320* ▤ *MC, V* ⊙ *Closed Sun. No lunch Sat.–Thurs.*

¢–$ ✕ **El Mariachi.** This very reasonably priced cantina and restaurant has a wide variety of lunch and dinner specials and combinations. Mexican food and cerveza on tap are the specialties. The building resembles a former chain take-out, but the interior is festive with Mexican-print vinyl tablecloths, cut-paper doilies hanging overhead, and two overhead TVs. ⊠ *660 J. Clyde Morris Blvd.* ☎ *757/596–4933* ▤ *D, MC, V.*

★ $ ✕▥ **Omni Newport News Hotel.** The burgundy, green, and gold color scheme of the lobby carries over to the guest rooms, which look out on the indoor pool below. Rooms have mahogany furnishings, granite vanities, desks, and sofas. Mitty's Ristorante and Piano Lounge ($–$$) serves regional Italian cuisine and local seafood, with exceptional homemade pasta and veal dishes. Specialties include ziti with broccoli and shrimp Capri (shrimp paired with spinach and fresh Italian herbs). To reach the hotel, take Exit 258A off I-64 and make the first right; turn right at the hotel sign. ⊠ *1000 Omni Blvd., 23606* ☎ *757/873–6664 or 800/873–6664* ▤ *757/873–1732* ⊕ *www.omnihotels.com* ⇨ *183 rooms, 4 suites* ⌂ *Restaurant, in-room data ports, in-room broadband, indoor pool, gym, sauna, bar, lobby lounge, nightclub, laundry facilities, business services, meeting rooms, no-smoking rooms* ▤ *AE, D, DC, MC, V.*

$ ▥ **Hilton Garden Inn Newport News.** New in 2004, this light and airy motel is within walking distance of a mall, restaurants, and movie theaters. Room amenities include free high-speed Internet access, a large work desk, irons, ironing boards, and coffeemakers. ⊠ *180 Regal Way, Exit 256B (Victory Blvd.)* ☎ *757/947–1080* ▤ *757/947–1081* ⊕ *http://hilton-gardeninn.hilton.com* ⇨ *122 rooms* ⌂ *Restaurant, microwaves, refrigerators, in-room broadband, indoor pool, gym, spa, dry cleaning, laundry service, business services, meeting rooms, no-smoking rooms* ▤ *AE, D, DC, MC, V.*

$ ▥ **Point Plaza.** This former Ramada has everything you could want in a hotel: reasonable rates and a location convenient to all the museums, plantation houses, and business centers of Newport News, plus Fort Lee, NASA

Langley, Colonial Williamsburg, Yorktown, and Busch Gardens. The rooms, decorated in paisley prints and mahogany furnishings, are loaded with every necessity and convenience, like refrigerators and microwaves. They'll even loan you a wireless card for your computer. Don't overlook the free shuttle for Newport News Williamsburg Airport, the Amtrak station, and Greyhound stop. ✉ *950 J. Clyde Morris Blvd., Exit 258 off I–64, 23601* ☎ *757/599–4460 or 800/841–1112* 🖷 *757/599–4336* ⊕ *www. pointplazasuites.com* ⇝ *78 rooms, 71 suites* ♿ *Restaurant, room service, BBQs, in-room data ports, in-room safes, microwaves, refrigerators, in-room DVD/VCRs, Wi-Fi, indoor-outdoor pool, gym, lounge, dry cleaning, laundry, concierge, business services, convention center, meeting rooms, airport shuttle, no-smoking rooms* ▤ *AE, D, DC, MC, V.*

Hampton

27 *5 mi north of Newport News, 16 mi northwest of Norfolk.*

Founded in 1610, Hampton is the oldest continuously existing English-speaking settlement in the United States. It also holds the country's first aviation research facility, NASA Langley Research Center. The center was headquarters for the first manned space program in the United States: astronauts for the *Mercury* and *Apollo* missions trained here.

Hampton was one of Virginia's major Colonial cities. In 1718 the pirate William Teach (better known as Blackbeard) was killed by Virginia sailors in a battle off North Carolina. As a warning to other pirates, the sailors brought his head back and mounted it on a pole at the entrance to the Hampton River (now Blackbeard Point, a residential area).

The city has been partially destroyed three times: by the British during the Revolution and again during the War of 1812, then by Confederates preempting Union invaders during the Civil War. Since the mid-1990s, Hampton has been undergoing a face-lift. It hosts many summer concerts and family festivals.

👐 The **Cousteau Society** operates a compact gallery displaying underwater photos, models of the research vessels *Calypso* and *Alcyone,* and diving equipment from the past and present. Artifacts from famed explorer-environmentalist Jacques-Yves Cousteau's expeditions are displayed, such as a pair of minisubs, one fully equipped and one reduced to its pressure sphere; a recompression chamber from the 1950s; and a clear plastic shark cage, along with the diver's journal describing his eye-to-eye experiences. Cousteau films from various expeditions run continuously. Free parking is available at the Radisson Hotel next door. ✉ *710 Settlers Landing Rd.* ☎ *757/722–9300* 🎫 *Free* ☉ *Nov.–Apr. 14, Wed.–Sat. 10–4, Sun. noon–3; Apr. 15–May 29 and Sept. 5–Oct. 31, Tues.–Sat. 10–4, Sun. noon–3; May 30–Sept. 4, daily 9:30–4.*

👐 Hampton's newest museum, the **Hampton History Museum** has 10 galleries of permanent and changing exhibits on Native Americans and the early colonists, the city's port, the infamous Blackbeard, contraband and the Civil War, the rise of Crabtown USA, and the development of NASA Langley Research Center. ✉ *120 Old Hampton La.* ☎ *757/727–1610* ⊕ *www. hampton.va.us/history_museum* 🎫 *$5* ☉ *Mon.–Sat. 10–5, Sun. 1–5.*

Hampton University was founded in 1868 as a freedmen's school, and ever since has had a distinguished history as an institution of higher education for African-Americans. Booker T. Washington was an early graduate. The **Hampton University Museum**, on the riverfront campus, is notable for its extensive and diverse collection, which includes more than 9,000 African, Native American, Pacific Island, and Asian art objects, as well as items related to the history of the university. Other valuable holdings include Harlem Renaissance paintings. ⊠ *Museum, Huntington Bldg., off Tyler St.; I–64, Exit 267, to campus* ☎ *757/727–5308* ⊕ *www.hamptonu.edu* ☒ *Free* ⊙ *Weekdays 8–5, Sat. noon–4.*

Little of early Hampton survived the shellings and conflicts of the past, but the brick walls of **St. John's Church** (1728) have. Today a stained-glass window honors Pocahontas, the Native American princess who is said to have saved the life of Captain John Smith in 1608. The communion silver on display, made in London in 1618, is the oldest such service still used in this country. The parish, founded in the same year as the city (1610), also claims to be the oldest Protestant church in continuous service in America. You may listen to a taped interpretation or take a guided tour (by arrangement) and visit a small museum in the parish house. ⊠ *100 W. Queens Way* ☎ *757/722–2567* ⊕ *www.stjohnshampton.org* ☒ *Free* ⊙ *Weekdays 9–3.*

6

Ⓒ The **Virginia Air and Space Center** traces the history of flight and space
Fodor'sChoice exploration. The nine-story, futuristic, $30 million center is the Visi-
★ tor Center for NASA Langley Research Center and Langley Air Force Base. Its space artifacts include a 3-billion-year-old moon rock, the *Apollo 12* command capsule, and a lunar lander. The center also holds a dozen full-size aircraft, a 3-D IMAX theater, a variety of flight simulators, and hands-on exhibits that let you see yourself as an astronaut or launch a rocket. ⊠ *Downtown Waterfront, 600 Settlers Landing Rd., I–64, Exit 267* ☎ *757/727–0800* ⊕ *www.vasc.org* ☒ *$8.75, IMAX movie $7.75, combination ticket $13.75* ⊙ *Memorial Day–Labor Day, Mon.–Wed. 10–5, Thurs.–Sun. 10–7; Labor Day–Memorial Day, Mon.–Sat. 10–5, Sun. noon–5.*

Where to Stay & Eat

$$$ ✕ **Captain George's.** Although you can order steaks off the à la carte menu, the main pull here is the 70-item, all-you-can-eat buffet of fried, steamed, and broiled seafood. Highlights are steamed Alaskan crab legs, steamed shrimp with Old Bay seasoning, steamed mussels, and she-crab soup. Among the desserts are baklava and fruit cobblers. A mural of the Chesapeake Bay dominates the largest of four dining rooms, which has tables with tops embedded with seashells. ⊠ *2710 W. Mercury Blvd., Exit 263 south off I–64* ☎ *757/826–1435* ☐ *AE, MC, V* ⊙ *No lunch Mon.–Sat.*

$$ ✕ **Pier 21.** Overlooking the Hampton marina inside the Radisson Hotel Hampton is this ship-shape restaurant serving three meals daily. The contemporary decor is carried out in forest green, brass, and natural woods. Main dishes at dinner include wahoo, snapper, flounder, steaks, and pasta. The all-you-can-eat soup and pasta bar at lunch is a good value at $6.95 (plus $1.50 for the salad bar, too). ⊠ *700 Settlers Landing Rd.* ☎ *757/727–9700* ☐ *AE, D, DC, MC, V.*

¢–$ ✕ **The Grey Goose Tearoom.** Beside the relocated Hampton History Museum, you're greeted by an enticing aroma and a gift shop with tea-related items when you enter this cozy room decorated with Victorian tea-party prints in gilded frames, antique teapots, and knickknacks. Brunswick stew, creamy Hampton blue-crab soup, and biscuits are permanent fixtures on the "everything-homemade" menu, and daily specials, such as chicken and dumplings, are posted on the wall. Desserts are especially good, but avoid the canned fruit salad on iceberg lettuce. The tearoom is open for lunch only. ⊠ *Old Hampton La. at History Museum Way* ☎ *757/723–7978* ▭ *AE, D, DC, MC, V* ⊘ *Closed Sun. No dinner.*

$–$$$ ▦ **Courtyard by Marriott.** The smell of homemade chocolate cookies greets you Monday through Thursday at the front desk of this modern hotel, where the chef refills a bottomless basket. As the naval items on the walls suggest, this Marriott takes in the local influence. The pool is set amid landscaped grounds. The restaurant serves breakfast only. ⊠ *1917 Coliseum Dr., 23666* ☎ *757/838–3300* 🖷 *757/838–6387* ⊕ *www.courtyard.com* ⬦ *146 rooms* ⌕ *Restaurant, cable TV, in-room broadband, pool, health club, dry cleaning, laundry service* ▭ *AE, D, DC, MC, V.*

★ $–$$$ ▦ **Radisson Hotel Hampton.** The nine-story Radisson has the premier location in town, right at a marina and a block away from the Virginia Air and Space Center. Most rooms look over the harbor or the handsome plaza in front of the space center. Guest rooms have an autumn color scheme with bleached wood furniture, a desk, and an easy chair. Amenities include hair dryers, irons, ironing boards, and coffeemakers. There's free wireless everywhere in the hotel, and free Internet via a lobby computer. ⊠ *700 Settlers Landing Rd., 23669* ☎ *757/727–9700 or 800/ 333–3333* 🖷 *757/722–4557* ⊕ *www.radisson.com* ⬦ *172 rooms* ⌕ *Restaurant, café, refrigerators, in-room data ports, Internet room, pool, gym, bar* ▭ *AE, D, DC, MC, V.*

¢–$$ ▦ **Holiday Inn Hampton.** Halfway between Colonial Williamsburg and Virginia Beach, this complex of buildings stands on 13 beautifully landscaped acres. About half the rooms have a pink-and-green color scheme; others have a darker look, with cherrywood dressers and tables. Many have sofas. Some rooms overlook the indoor pool in the atrium, and others have doors that open, motel-style, onto the parking lot. There's free wireless Internet, and it's free to borrow an Ethernet cord. ⊠ *1815 W. Mercury Blvd., 23666* ☎ *757/838–0200 or 800/842–9370* 🖷 *757/ 838–4964* ⊕ *www.sixcontinentshotels.com* ⬦ *314 rooms, 6 suites* ⌕ *Restaurant, 2 pools (1 indoor), gym, sauna, bar, convention center* ▭ *AE, D, DC, MC, V.*

Fort Monroe

🖑 ㉘   *Inside Phoebus, at the South end of Mellen St. and Mercury Blvd.*

The channel between Chesapeake Bay and Hampton Roads is the "mouth" of Hampton Roads. On the north side of this passage is Hampton's Fort Monroe, built in stages between 1819 and 1834. The largest stone fort in the country, it's also the only one still in operation to be enclosed by a moat. Robert E. Lee and Edgar Allan Poe served here in the antebellum years, and it remained a Union stronghold in Confederate territory throughout the Civil War. After the war, Confederate president Jefferson Davis was imprisoned for a time in one of the fort's casemates (a chamber in the wall); his cell and adjacent casemates now house the Casemate Museum. Exhibits of weapons, uniforms, models, drawings, and extensive Civil War relics retell the fort's history, depict coastal artillery activities, and describe the military lifestyle through the Civil War years and the 20th century. ⊠ *Mellen St., Phoebus* ☎ *757/788–3391* ☜ *Free* ⊙ *Daily 10:30–4:30.*

Norfolk

➋➒ *16 mi southeast of Hampton.*

Norfolk is reached from the peninsula by the Hampton Roads Bridge-Tunnel (I–64) as well as Route 460. There's plenty to see in this old Navy town, but the sites are spread out. Like many other old Southern towns, Norfolk has undergone a renaissance, one that's especially visible in the charming shops and cafés in the historic village of Ghent.

Main Attractions

★ By any standard the **Chrysler Museum of Art** downtown qualifies as one of America's major art museums. The permanent collection includes works by Rubens, Gainsborough, Renoir, Picasso, Cézanne, Matisse, Warhol, and Pollock, a list that suggests the breadth available here. Classical and pre-Columbian civilizations are also represented. The decorative-arts collection includes exquisite English porcelain and art nouveau furnishings. The Chrysler is home to one the most important glass collections in America, which includes glass objects from the 6th century BC to the present, with particularly strong holdings in Tiffany, French art glass, and English cameo, as well as artifacts from ancient Rome and the Near and Far East. ⊠ *245 W. Olney Rd.* ☎ *757/664–6200* ⊕ *www.chrysler.org* ☜ *$7; Wed. by voluntary contribution* ⊙ *Wed. 10–9, Thurs.–Sat. 10–5, Sun. 1–5.*

> **FREE EVENTS IN NORFOLK**
>
> Town Point Park, between Nauticus and Waterside Festival Marketplace, is the site of many free outdoor festivals and concerts, the annual Fleet Week and Harborfest, and a wine festival. Fun, food, and music are here most Fridays from May through October. Check for events at www.festeventsva.org or in the local newspapers.

The **MacArthur Memorial** is the burial place of one of America's most distinguished military officers. General Douglas MacArthur (1880–1964) agreed to this Navy town as the site for his monument because it was his mother's birthplace. In the rotunda of the old City Hall, converted according to MacArthur's design, is the mausoleum; 11 adjoining galleries house mementos of MacArthur's career, including his signature corncob pipe and the Japanese instruments of surrender that concluded World War II. However, this is a monument not only to General MacArthur but to all those who served in wars from the Civil to the Korean War. Its Historical Center holds 2 ½ million documents and more than 100,000 photographs, and assists scholars, students, and researchers from around the world. The general's staff car is on display in the gift shop, where a 24-minute biography is shown. ⊠ *Bank St. and City Hall Ave.* ☎ *757/441–2965* ⊕ *www.macarthurmemorial.org* ▱ *By donation* ⊘ *Mon.–Sat. 10–5, Sun. 11–5.*

★ ☾ A popular attraction on Norfolk's redeveloped waterfront is **Nauticus,** the National Maritime Center. With more than 70 high-tech exhibits on three "decks," the site places ancient shipbuilding exhibits next to interactive displays depicting the modern naval world. Weather satellites, underwater archaeology, and the Loch Ness Monster all come together here. The battleship USS *Wisconsin,* still maintained in a state of reduced readiness to allow reactivation, has found a home here. Most of its interior is off-limits, but its enormous gun turrets and conning tower are impressive up close. The *Wisconsin,* tied up just outside the museum, and the Hampton Roads Naval Museum, within Nauticus, are both operated by the U.S. Navy and can be toured without paying Nauticus's admission price. There are additional fees for the AEGIS Theater and Virtual Adventures. ⊠ *1 Waterside Dr.* ☎ *757/664–1000* ⊕ *www.nauticus.org, www.thenmc. org, www.hrnm.navy.mil* ▱ *$10* ⊘ *Memorial Day–Labor Day, daily 9–5; Labor Day–Memorial Day, Tues.–Sat. 10–5, Sun. noon–5.*

☾ The **Norfolk Naval Station,** on the northern edge of the city, is an impres-
Fodor'sChoice sive sight, home to more than 100 ships of the Atlantic Fleet. The base
★ was built on the site of the Jamestown Exposition of 1907: many of the original buildings survive and are still in use. Several large aircraft carriers, built at nearby Newport News, call Norfolk home port and can be seen from miles away, especially at the bridge-tunnel end of the base. You may see four or even more, each with a crew of up to 6,300, beside slightly smaller amphibious carriers that discharge marines in both helicopters and amphibious assault craft. The submarine piers, floating drydocks, supply center, and air station are all worth seeing. *The Victory Rover* and *Carrie B.* provide boat tours from downtown Norfolk to the naval station, and Hampton Roads Transit operates tour trolleys most of the year, departing from the naval-base tour office. Visitor access is by tour only, and photo ID is required to enter the base. ⊠ *9079 Hampton Blvd.* ☎ *757/ 444–7955* ⊕ *www.navstanorva.navy.mil/tour* ▱ *Tour $7.50* ⊘ *Tours Oct. 29–Mar. 18, Tues.–Sun. 1:30; Mar. 19–May 20, Tues.–Sun. 11–2 on the hr; May 21–Sept. 2, Tues.–Sun. 10–2 every ½ hr.*

Also Worth Seeing

The **Hermitage Foundation Museum,** an early-20th-century estate of the Sloane family, offers an outstanding presentation of architecture, art, and nature. The Sloanes, educated collectors with broad artistic interests, were among the founders of what is now the Chrysler Museum. Mr. Sloane was a wealthy New York businessman who moved to Virginia to operate textile mills. Docent-led tours are available on the hour. Visitors may also stroll the waterfront and 12-acre gardens and view contemporary art exhibitions. ⊠ *7637 N. Shore Rd.* ☎ *757/423–2052* ⊕ *www.thfm.org* ▱ *$5* ⊘ *Mon., Tues., and Thurs.–Sat. 10–5, Sun. 1–5.*

The federal redbrick **Moses Myers House,** built by its namesake between 1792 and 1796, is exceptional, and not just for its elegance. The furnishings, 70% of them original, include family portraits by Gilbert Stuart and Thomas Sully. A transplanted New Yorker as well as Norfolk's first Jewish resident, Myers made his fortune in Norfolk in shipping, then served as a diplomat and a customhouse officer. His grandson married James Madison's grandniece; his great-grandson served as mayor; and the family kept the house for five generations. ✉ *331 Bank St.* ☎ *757/333–1086* ⊕ *www.chrysler.org/houses.asp* 🎟 *Free* ☉ *Wed.–Sat. 10–4, Sun. 1–4.*

St. Paul's Church, constructed in 1739, was the only building in town to survive the bombardment and conflagration of New Year's Day 1776; a cannonball fired by the British fleet remains embedded in a wall. An earlier church had been built on this site in 1641, and the churchyard contains graves dating from the 17th century. Get a free visitor parking pass in the church office. ✉ *St. Paul's Blvd. and City Hall Ave.* ☎ *757/ 627–4353* 🎟 *By donation* ☉ *Tues.–Fri. 10–4.*

Where to Eat

★ **$$–$$$$** ✕ **La Galleria.** This restaurant has a favorable reputation in Norfolk. The interior is classic Mediterannean and includes Ionic columns and large urns imported from Italy. There's entertainment Friday and Saturday nights. Among the menu choices are *vongole al forno* (baked clams sprinkled with herbs, garlic, and bread crumbs) as an appetizer, and many excellent pastas and main courses, such as veal, chicken, steaks, and fish (for example, salmon sautéed in herbs, garlic, and white wine). ✉ *120 College Pl.* ☎ *757/623–3939* 🗐 *AE, DC, MC, V.*

$–$$$ ✕ **Freemason Abbey Restaurant and Tavern.** This former church near the historic business district has been drawing customers for a long time, and not without reason. It has 40-foot-high cathedral ceilings and large windows, making for an airy, and dramatic, dining experience. You can sit upstairs, in the large choir loft, or in the main part of the church downstairs. Beside the bar just inside the entrance is an informal sort of "diner" area, but with the whole menu to choose from. Regular appetizers include artichoke dip and Santa Fe shrimp. There's a dinner special every weeknight, such as lobster, prime rib, and wild game (wild boar or alligator, for example). ✉ *209 W. Freemason St.* ☎ *757/622– 3966* 🗐 *AE, D, DC, MC, V.*

$–$$ ✕ **Azars Natural Foods.** Lebanese specialties are featured at this casual restaurant in Ghent, which also has a Mediterranean food store. Indoor dining is on granite tables under a reproduction tin ceiling and exposed air ducts. Outdoors, the terra-cotta patio has umbrellas. A sampler Mashawee Platter includes *kibbi,* seasoned beef and bulghur patties; *kefta,* spiced lamb meatballs; and lamb kebab with grilled vegetables and side dishes. Vegan and vegetarian selections are noted on the menu, which includes appetizers, wraps, pizza, and kebabs. ✉ *2000 Colley Ave.* ☎ *757/664–7955* 🗐 *AE, MC, V.*

★ **¢–$$** ✕ **No Frill Bar and Grill.** This expansive café is in an antique building in the heart of Ghent. Beneath a tin ceiling and exposed ductwork, a central bar is surrounded by several dining spaces with cream-and-mustard walls and wooden tables. Signature items include its ribs; the Funky Chicken Sandwich, a grilled chicken breast with bacon, tomato, melted Swiss cheese, and Parmesan pepper dressing on rye; and the Spotswood Salad of baby spinach, Granny Smith apples, and blue cheese. ⊠ *806 Spotswood Ave., at Colley Ave.* ☎ *757/627–4262* ⊟ *AE, MC, V.*

¢ ✗ **Doumar's.** After he introduced the world to its first ice-cream cone at the 1904 World's Fair in St. Louis, Abe Doumar founded this drive-in institution in 1934. It's still operated by his family. Waitresses carry to your car the specialties of the house: barbecue, limeade, and ice cream in waffle cones made according to an original recipe. ⊠ *20th St. and Monticello Ave.* ☎ *757/627–4163* ⊟ *No credit cards* ☉ *Closed Sun.*

Where to Stay

$$–$$$$ ⊞ **Norfolk Waterside Marriott.** This hotel in the redeveloped downtown area is connected to the Waterside Festival Marketplace shopping area by a ramp and is close to Town Point Park, site of many festivals. The handsome lobby, with wood paneling, a central staircase, silk tapestries, and Federal-style furniture, sets a high standard that continues throughout the hotel. Rooms are somewhat small, but each has most everything the business traveler could ask for—including two telephones, voice mail, and Internet access. ⊠ *235 E. Main St., 23510* ☎ *757/627–4200 or 800/ 228–9290* ⎙ *757/628–6452* ⊕ *www.marriott.com* ⇗ *396 rooms, 8 suites* ⌂ *2 restaurants, in-room data ports, indoor pool, lobby lounge* ⊟ *AE, D, DC, MC, V.*

$–$$$ ⊞ **Sheraton Norfolk Waterside Hotel.** Modern is the word for this hotel's furnishings, from the bright, spacious lobby to the ample rooms and large suites. A ground-floor bar with dramatic 30-foot windows overlooks the Elizabeth—many rooms also have a beautiful view over the water. This property is convenient to the Waterside Festival Marketplace shopping area. ⊠ *777 Waterside Dr., 23510* ☎ *757/622–6664* ⎙ *757/625– 8271* ⊕ *www.sheraton.com* ⇗ *426 rooms, 20 suites* ⌂ *Restaurant, pool, lounge* ⊟ *AE, D, DC, MC, V.*

$$ ⊞ **Marriott Courtyard Downtown.** Built in 2005, this eight-story hotel is near everything visitors want to see and where business travelers need to be. It's next door to the MacArthur Memorial and near the MacArthur Center and Nauticus. A handsome, inviting lobby has a tailored look; the modern guest rooms have a large desk, comforters, hair dryers, coffeemakers, irons, ironing boards, and a free daily newspaper. ⊠ *520 Plume St., 23510* ☎ *757/963–6000 or 800/321–2211* ⎙ *757/963–6001* ⊕ *www.marriott.com* ⇗ *137 rooms, 3 suites* ⌂ *Restaurant, room service, in-room data ports, refrigerators, cable TV with movies, in-room broadband, indoor pool, wading pool, exercise equipment, shop, dry cleaning, laundry facilities, laundry service, business services, meeting rooms, parking (fee), no-smoking rooms* ⊟ *AE, D, DC, MC, V.*

$–$$ ⊞ **Holiday Inn Select Airport.** Surprisingly plush for a Holiday Inn property, this airport location welcomes business travelers with an elegant lobby bar and fireplace. Rooms are outfitted with two phone lines, high-speed DSL Internet access, and voice mail; the lobby has free wireless.

Behind the hotel is Lake Wright where guests may stroll or relax. ✉ *Lake Wright Executive Center, 1570 N. Military Hwy., 23502* ☎ *757/213–2231* 🖷 *757/213–2232* ⊕ *www.hiselect.com/norfolkva* 🛏 *147 rooms* 🍴 *Restaurant, microwaves, refrigerators, indoor pool, gym, hot tub, lobby lounge, laundry facilities, business services, meeting rooms, airport shuttle* ▭ *AE, D, DC, MC, V.*

Nightlife & the Arts

MUSIC The **Virginia Opera Company** (✉ 160 E. Virginia Beach Blvd. ☎ 757/623–1223) presents some of the best operatic talent in the nation during its season (September through April) at Norfolk's elegant Harrison Opera House, which is known for its excellent acoustics. Their schedule includes the most popular operas of Europe and the USA.

Shopping

An eclectic mix of chic shops, including antiques stores, bars, and eateries, line the streets of **Ghent,** a turn-of-the-20th-century neighborhood that runs from the Elizabeth River to York Street, to West Olney Road and Llewellyn Avenue. The intersection of Colley Avenue and 21st Street is the hub.

You can meet painters, sculptors, glassworkers, jewelers, photographers and other artists at work in their studios at the **d'Art Center** (✉ Selden Arcade, 208 E. Main St. ☎ 757/625–4211); the art is for sale.

In Ghent, the upscale clothing and shoe boutiques at the **Palace Shops** (✉21st St. and Llewellyn Ave.) are a good place to search out some finery.

Portsmouth

🔟 *6 mi southwest of Norfolk via I–264.*

Portsmouth, across the Elizabeth River from Norfolk, has a well-maintained historic area called Olde Towne, which has handsome buildings from the 18th and 19th centuries. A five-minute pedestrian ferry makes traveling between Portsmouth and Norfolk easy.

The **Children's Museum of Virginia,** the largest children's museum in the state, has more than 90 hands-on exhibits for kids of all ages, including an awesome toy train collection, a planetarium, and tons more. Here kids can learn engineering and scientific principles by playing with bubbles and blocks. ✉ *221 High St.* ☎ *757/393–5258* ⊕ *www.childrensmuseumva.com* 🎟 *$6* ⊙ *Tues.–Sat. 9–5, Sun. 11–5.*

The **Portsmouth Naval Shipyard Museum,** one block from the waterfront and about three blocks from the paddle wheel ferry landing, offers a history of Portsmouth, the Norfolk Naval Shipyard, and the armed forces in Hampton Roads. The museum gives visitors the opportunity to learn about this rich history through exhibited artifacts, uniforms, ship models, illustrations, and photographs. You can also explore the retired Coast Guard lightship *Portsmouth,* a floating lighthouse just outside the museum, whose quarters below deck have been authentically furnished. ✉*2 High St.* ☎ *757/393–8591 shipyard museum, 757/393–8741 lightship* ⊕*www.portsnavalmuseums.com* 🎟 *$3, free 1st Sun. of month* ⊙ *Memo-*

rial Day–Labor Day, Mon.–Sat. 10–5, Sun. 1–5; Labor Day–Memorial Day, Tues.–Sat. 10–5, Sun. 1–5.

Where to Stay

★ $ ▥ **Hawthorn Hotel & Suites at The Governor Dinwiddie.** The 1940s Governor Dinwiddie hotel in the center of Portsmouth's Olde Towne business district was beautifully restored in 2005. Guest rooms are furnished in reproduction Queen Anne with satin quilted spreads, ecru walls, and moss woodwork. Museums, restaurants, and the waterfront are within a few blocks. ⊠ *506 Dinwiddie, at High St., 23704* ☎ *757/392–1330 or 800/527–1133* 🖷 *757/399–1248* ⊕ *www.hawthornhotelandsuites.com* ☞ *45 rooms, 15 suites* ⚹ *Restaurant, in-room data ports, microwaves, refrigerators, cable TV with movies, fitness center, sauna, laundry service, Wi-Fi, lounge, business center, meeting rooms* ▤ *AE, MC, V.*

¢–$ ▥ **Holiday Inn Olde Towne.** With the Portsmouth waterfront just out the door, and Olde Towne's attractions so nearby, this hotel is very well situated. The undistinguished appearance of the building hides pleasant things inside: public and guest rooms vary in size, but all have a modern look. The bar and restaurant have long windows beside the Elizabeth River: it's the perfect spot for watching ships and boats and the Portsmouth and Norfolk waterfronts. High-speed Internet is being added to the guest rooms. ⊠ *8 Crawford Pkwy., 23704* ☎ *757/393–2573 or 800/465–4329* 🖷 *757/399–1248* ⊕ *www.sixcontinentshotels.com* ☞ *210 rooms, 5 suites* ⚹ *Restaurant, in-room data ports, pool, gym, lobby lounge, laundry facilities, laundry service, meeting rooms* ▤ *AE, D, DC, MC, V.*

Virginia Beach

③ *18 mi east of Norfolk via I–64 to Rte. 44.*

The heart of Virginia Beach—a stretch of the Atlantic shore from Cape Henry south to Rudee Inlet—has been a popular summertime destination for years. With 6 mi of public beach, high-rises, amusements, and a busy 40-block boardwalk, Virginia's most populated city is now a place for communion with nature. The Boardwalk and Atlantic Avenue have an oceanfront park; an old-fashioned fishing pier ($7.50) with shops, a restaurant, and a bar; and a 3-mi bike trail. Bikes (two- or four-wheel) can be rented at several shops and hotels along the beach for $4 to $20 per hour. The farther north you go, the more beach you find in proportion to bars, T-shirt parlors, and video arcades. Most activities and events in town are oriented to families.

Inland from the shore is the late-17th-century **Adam Thoroughgood House,** named for the prosperous plantation owner who held a land grant of 5,350 acres here in the early 1600s. This 45-by-22-foot brick house, probably constructed by a Thoroughgood grandson, recalls the English cottage architecture of the period, with a protruding chimney and a steeply pitched roof. The four-room early plantation home has a 17th-century garden with characteristic hedges. To get there, take I–264 Exit 17 (Independence Blvd.) 4 mi, turn right on Pleasure House Road, and right on Thoroughgood Drive. ⊠ *1636 Parish Rd., 23455* ☎ *757/460–7588* ⊕ *www.vbgov.com/dept/arts/* 🎟 *$4* ☉ *Tues.–Sat. 9–5, Sun. 11–5.*

☺ The **Naval Air Station, Oceana,** on the northern edge of the city, is an impressive sight, home to more than 200 Navy aircraft, including the F/A-18 Tomcat (the type of plane flown by the Blue Angels) and other planes assigned to the aircraft carriers of the Atlantic Fleet. From an observation park on Oceana Boulevard at the POW/MIA Flame of Hope Memorial Park, near the runways, you can watch aircraft take off and land. Non–Defense Department visitors can access the base only on the Hampton Roads Transit summer-only tours (photo ID required) or during the annual air show in September. Tours depart at 9:30 AM and 11:30 AM from the 24th Street transit kiosk on Atlantic Avenue in Virginia Beach and stop at an aviation historical park with 13 aircraft. ⊠ *Tomcat Blvd.* ☎ *757/433-3131* ⊕ *www.nasoceana.navy.mil/Visitors.htm* ☞ *Tour $7.50.*

At the northeastern tip of Virginia Beach, on the cape where the mouth of the bay meets the ocean, the historic **Old Cape Henry Lighthouse** is near the site where the English landed on their way to Jamestown in 1607. This lighthouse, however, didn't light anyone's way until 1792. You can climb to the top of the old lighthouse anytime except December 5 to January 4, when it's illuminated for Christmas. Across the street to seaward is the replacement to the old lighthouse, but it isn't open to visitors. Be prepared to show a photo ID at the military checkpoint at the Fort Story base entrance. ⊠ *U.S. 60* ☎ *757/422–9421* ☞ *$4* ☺ *Mid Mar.–Oct., daily 10–5; Nov.–mid-Mar., daily 10–4.*

Along the oceanfront, the **Old Coast Guard Station,** a 1903 Lifesaving Station, contains photographic exhibits, examples of lifesaving equipment, and a gallery that depicts German U-boat activity off the coast during World War II. ⊠ *24th St. and Atlantic Ave.* ☎ *757/422–1587* ☞ *$3* ☺ *Tues.–Sat. 10–5, Sun. noon–5.*

★ ☺ The sea is the subject at the popular **Virginia Aquarium and Marine Science Center,** a massive facility with more than 200 exhibits. This is no place for passive museumgoers; many exhibits require participation. You can use computers to

> **WORD OF MOUTH**
>
> "The Aquarium in Virginia Beach is awesome." –E

predict the weather and solve the pollution crisis, watch the birds in the salt marsh through telescopes on a deck, handle horseshoe crabs, take a simulated journey to the bottom of the sea in a submarine, and study fish up close in tanks that re-create underwater environments. The museum is almost 2 mi inland from Rudee Inlet at the southern end of Virginia Beach. ⊠ *717 General Booth Blvd.* ☎ *757/425-3474* ☞ *$12* ☺ *After Labor Day–before Memorial Day, daily 9–5; Memorial Day–Labor Day, daily 9–7.*

Where to Eat

$–$$ ✕ **Five 01 City Grill.** More than a grill in name only, this restaurant has an open-grill kitchen in the dining room. It can be noisy on the bar side when live bands play in the evening. Locals get comfortable in padded chairs and some booths as they quaff the $2 beer of the month or order from the extensive wine vault. The California-inspired fusion menu offers a variety of price ranges: excellent homemade pizza from wood-burning ovens, sandwiches, pasta, chicken, steaks, and seafood followed by sinful desserts such as Homemade Bourbon Chocolate Chip Pecan Pie. ⊠ *501 N. Birdneck Rd., 23451* ☎ *757/425–7195* ⊟ *AE, MC, V.*

$–$$ ✕ **Murphy's Irish Pub.** This combination Irish pub, sports bar, and restaurant has a large central dining room with an open fireplace in the middle, a bar on one side, and a smaller dining room at one end. The menu includes steaks and Irish, Italian, and seafood entrées as well as snacks and sandwiches. The Sunday brunch is reasonable, and so are the weekday dinner specials. A block from the boardwalk, Murphy's has plenty of easy parking. ⊠ *2914 Pacific Ave.* ☎ *757/417–7701* ⊟ *AE, D, DC, MC, V.*

$–$$ ✕ **Rockafeller's.** The Down East architecture of this local favorite with double-deck porches hints at the seafood that's available. The restaurant has a bar, a raw bar, and alfresco dining in good weather (in cool weather, the large window wall still gives you a water view). Seafood, pasta, chicken, and beef share the menu with salads and sandwiches. Rockafeller's (and several others) are on Rudee Inlet. To get here, go south on Pacific Avenue and turn right on Winston-Salem immediately before the Rudee Inlet bridge. The street ends at Mediterranean Avenue. ⊠ *308 Mediterranean Ave.* ☎ *757/422–5654* ⊟ *AE, D, DC, MC, V.*

★ $–$$ ✕ **Waterman's.** The last freestanding restaurant on the beach not inside a hotel, this aqua-painted clapboard building houses a family-owned seafood grill. Inside, the ochre walls heighten the sun rays penetrating the ceiling-to-floor windows. Awnings shade the outdoor patio where live musicians perform in season. A local menu favorite is the Crab Ripper, a crab-cake sandwich topped with mozzarella and crisp bacon. A fried seafood sampler, fish and steak platters, steamed fish, appetizers, salads, burgers, and other sandwiches fill out the menu. ⊠ *1423 N. Great Neck Rd.* ☎ *757/496–3333* ⊟ *AE, D, MC, V.*

Where to Stay

$$–$$$ ▦ **Crowne Plaza Virginia Beach.** This sparkling white, modern hotel is well situated, midway between Norfolk and the beach, and 15 mi from Norfolk International Airport. The skylighted lobby overlooks a glassed-in indoor pool. Rooms have a sitting area with desk; there are plush duvets and extra pillows on the beds. Every room has a hair dryer, iron, ironing board, and coffeemaker. ⊠ *4453 Bonney Rd., 23462* ☎ *757/ 473–1700 or 800/847–5202* ⊟ *757/552–0477* ⊅ *149 rooms* ⚘ *Restaurant, refrigerators, in-room data ports, pool, gym, hot tub, lobby lounge, dry cleaning, laundry service, meeting rooms, no-smoking rooms* ⊟ *AE, D, DC, MC, V.*

★ $$–$$$ ▦ **Ramada Plaza Resort Oceanfront.** With its 17-story tower, this Ramada is the tallest hotel in the city. Rooms that do not face the ocean directly have either a partial view or overlook the swimming pool. The modern lobby has a skylighted atrium. Each guest room has a coffeemaker, iron, ironing board, and hair dryer. Beds have quilted spreads and striped draperies. Gus' Mariner Restaurant's varied menu includes good seafood. An adjoining small pub serves soup and sandwiches after 4 PM. ⊠ *57th St. and Oceanfront, 23451* ☎ *757/428–7025 or 800/365–*

3032 🖶 *757/428–2921* ⊕ *www.ramadaplazavabeach.com* ⤶ *247 rooms* ♿ *Restaurant, in-room safes, microwaves, refrigerators, indoor-outdoor pool, hot tub, gym, sauna, bar, children's programs (ages 5–13), dry cleaning, laundry service, convention center, meeting rooms, no-smoking rooms* ▤ *AE, D, DC, MC, V.*

★ **$–$$$** 🏨 **Cavalier Hotels.** In the quieter north end of town, this 18-acre resort complex combines the original Cavalier Hotel of 1927, a seven-story redbrick building on a hill, with an oceanfront high-rise built across the street in 1973. The clientele is about evenly divided between conventioneers and families. F. Scott and Zelda Fitzgerald stayed regularly in the original hotel. If you stay on the hilltop, you can see the water—and get to it easily by shuttle van or a short walk. The newer building overlooks 600 feet of private beach. There's a fee for tennis, but the other athletic facilities are free. ⊠ *Atlantic Ave. and 42nd St., 23451* ☎ *757/ 425–8555 or 888/746–2327* 🖶 *757/425–0629* ⊕ *www.cavalierhotel. com* ⤶ *400 rooms* ♿ *5 restaurants, in-room broadband, in-room data ports, 2 clay tennis courts, 2 pools (1 indoor), wading pool, gym, beach, basketball, croquet, volleyball, babysitting, playground, no-smoking rooms* ▤ *AE, D, DC, MC, V.*

Nightlife

There's free nightly entertainment from April through Labor Day weekend at the 24th Street stage or 24th Street Park on the Boardwalk. **Murphy's Grand Irish Pub and Restaurant** (⊠ 2914 Pacific Ave. ☎ 757/417–7701) has entertainment every night in summer and Tuesday–Saturday during winter—there's typically an Irish musician or two. **Harpoon Larry's** (⊠ 24th and Pacific Sts. ☎ 757/422–6000) is a local watering hole with true character, not a tourist trap. Don't be surprised to see a great white shark staring back at you as you eat a juicy piece of that shark's cousin (mahimahi) stuffed with fresh Chesapeake Bay crabmeat, or enjoy raw oysters and a cold Corona.

Sports & the Outdoors

GOLF   There are several public golf courses in Virginia Beach, some with moderate fees. All charge more for nonresidents and have varying fees, depending upon the day of the week and start time. **Honey Bee Golf Club** (⊠ 2500 S. Independence Blvd. ☎ 757/471–2768) has greens fees of $27–$60 weekdays and $27–$69 weekends. **Kempsville Greens Municipal Golf Course** (⊠ 1810 Princess Anne Rd. ☎ 757/474–8441) is a municipal course and the least expensive: weekdays $18–$20, weekends $22–$24, not including cart.

WATER SPORTS   **Wild River Outfitters** (☎ 757/431–8566 or 877/431–8566) has guided kayak tours, moonlight paddles, river tours, dolphin tours, and more. **Lynnhaven Dive Center** (☎ 757/481–7949) leads dives and gives lessons. Their boats are at Rudee Inlet. **Chesapean Outdoors** (☎ 866/379–5188 or 757/961–0447) has kayak tours, dolphin tours, sunset paddles on the Chesapeake Bay, surfing lessons, and tours at First Landing State Park. **Back Bay Getaways** (⊠ Sandbridge, Virginia Beach ☎ 757/721–4484) has a variety of kayak rentals and tours, pontoon boats, surfboards, and Jet Skis in the Sandbridge area.

6

WILLIAMSBURG AREA ESSENTIALS

To research prices, get advice from other travelers, and book travel arrangements, visit www.fodors.com.

Transportation

BY AIR

The three major airports in the region are served by many national and international carriers. Ticket prices are often much less expensive to and from Norfolk and Newport News than nearby Richmond. All three airports are relatively small and easy to navigate.

Newport News/Williamsburg International Airport is served by Air Tran, America West, Delta, United, and US Airways. Norfolk International Airport, between Norfolk and Virginia Beach, is served by Continental, American, Northwest, US Airways, and Delta as well as smaller airlines. Richmond International Airport, 10 mi east of Richmond, off I–64 at Exit 197, is about 45 mi from Williamsburg.

🛈 Airport Information Newport News/Williamsburg International Airport ✉ 12525 Jefferson Ave., at I-64, Newport News ☎ 757/877-0221. Norfolk International Airport ✉ 2200 Norview Ave. ☎ 757/857-3351. Richmond International Airport ✉ Airport Dr. ☎ 804/226-3000.

BY BIKE

Biking around Colonial Williamsburg is a wonderful way to explore its 301 acres. Rental bikes are available for those staying at the Williamsburg Inn, Lodge, or Colonial Houses. Bikesmith, in Williamsburg, rents bikes and has especially reasonable multiday rental prices. Bikes Unlimited also rents bikes, close to the Williamsburg Transportation Center.

In Virginia Beach there are numerous locations along the boardwalk where you can rent bikes. Rental shops away from the boardwalk are more reasonable and have better bikes. Seashore Bikes & Fitness is near First Landing Park. Back Bay Getaways is on the other side of Virginia Beach in the Sandbridge area. They offer bikes and guided biking tours.

Hampton Roads Transit buses have bike racks, and their paddlewheel ferries across the Elizabeth River allow bikes, so cyclists can cover a lot of territory, from Newport News through Norfolk and on to Virginia Beach.

🛈 Bike Rentals Back Bay Getaways ✉ 3713 S. Sandpiper Rd., Virginia Beach ☎ 757/721-4484. Bikesmith ✉ 515 York St., Williamsburg ☎ 757/229-9858. Bikes Unlimited ✉ 759 Scotland St., Williamsburg ☎ 757/229-4620. Seashore Bikes & Fitness ✉ 2268 Seashore Shops, Virginia Beach ☎ 757/481-5191.

BY BOAT & FERRY

The **Elizabeth River Ferry** carries passengers (but no automobiles) between Waterside Festival Marketplace, in Norfolk, and Portsmouth's Olde Towne weekdays 7:15 AM–11:45 PM, weekends 10:15 AM–11:45 PM. Bikes and wheelchairs are allowed. Taking the ferry is more fun and normally faster than driving through the tunnel; it departs Norfolk 15 minutes before and after every hour and leaves Portsmouth on the hour and half hour.

The **Jamestown–Scotland Ferry** began providing service across the James River in 1925. ■ TIP➔ This is the best free ride in Virginia; it takes you back 400 years to when the colonists first spied the site where they founded Jamestown. The ferry leaves the Jamestown dock about every hour on the half-hour, leaving the opposite port, Scotland, on the hour 24 hours a day. Wait times vary from 15 to 30 minutes (sometimes longer in the summer). Cars, campers, trucks, and motorcycles are allowed on the ferry. Foot passengers may ride, but there's nowhere to park at the ferry landing.

🚢 Boat & Ferry Lines Jamestown–Scotland Ferry ✉ 2317 Jamestown Rd., Rte. 31 ☎ 757/222-6100 ⊕ www.virginiadot.org/comtravel/ferry-jamestown.asp. Elizabeth River Ferry ☎ 757/222-6100 💲 $1.

BY BUS

Greyhound Lines (or its cohort Carolina Trailways) typically has about six daily departures from Newport News, Hampton, Virginia Beach, and Williamsburg; Norfolk has a dozen or more; and Suffolk has two per day. Connections with the north require a transfer at Richmond, with no guarantee of a seat on the connecting bus. On the other hand, Hampton Roads Transit is everything you'd want in an integrated regional transit system, covering the cities of Chesapeake, Hampton, Newport News, Norfolk, Portsmouth, and Virginia Beach, including the paddle wheel ferry between Norfolk's Waterside and the Portsmouth waterfront and the "Wave" trolleys in Virginia Beach; the buses have bike racks. Bus fares are $1. ■ TIP➔ Norfolk's free shuttle, called NET, covers the downtown area.

🚌 Bus Depots Charles Carr/Hampton Depot ✉ 2 W. Pembroke Ave., Hampton ☎ 757/722-9861. Greyhound Norfolk Depot ✉ 701 Monticello Ave., Norfolk ☎ 757/625-7500. Greyhound Virginia Beach–Myles of Travel ✉ 1017 Laskin Rd., Virginia Beach ☎ 757/422-2998. Greyhound Suffolk–Newbreed Travel Center ✉ 812 W. Constance Rd., Suffolk ☎ 757/934-8068. Williamsburg Transportation Center ✉ 468 N. Boundary St., Williamsburg ☎ 757/229-1460 or 800/231-2222.

🚌 Bus Lines Greyhound Lines ☎ 800/231-2222 ⊕ www.greyhound.com. Hampton Roads Transit ☎ 757/222-6100 ⊕ www.hrtransit.org.

BY CAR

Williamsburg is west of I–64, 51 mi southeast of Richmond; the Colonial Parkway joins Williamsburg with Jamestown to the southwest and Yorktown to the east. I–664 forms the eastern part of a beltway through the Hampton Roads area and connects Newport News with Portsmouth. I–264 runs from I–664 to downtown Norfolk, and then extends all the way to Virginia Beach. I–64 runs from Hampton to Portsmouth around the west side of Norfolk to intersect I–664.

Parking near the Colonial Williamsburg historic area can be difficult during summer months and special events. It's best to park at the visitor center and ride the shuttle to the park. The parking lot behind the Merchants Square shopping area is a good bet if you're planning a short visit or going out to eat around the area.

Virginia Beach has no shortage of parking lots and spaces. The cost for a day of parking is about $5 to $7 at the central beach lots and $4 or $5 for the remote beach areas. Municipal lots/decks are at 4th Street (metered only), 9th Street and Pacific Avenue, 19th Street and Pacific Avenue, 25th Street and Pacific Avenue, 31st Street and Atlantic Avenue, and Croatan and Sandbridge beaches. Metered spaces have a three-hour limit.

The area is well served with expressways and interstate highways, but you have to share these routes with many local drivers. Because the ragged coastline is constantly interrupted by water, driving from one town to another usually means going through a tunnel or over a bridge, either one of which may create a traffic bottleneck. The entrance to the tunnel between Hampton and Norfolk can get very congested, especially on weekends, so listen to your car radio for updated traffic reports.

In the Tidewater area, with a long list of tunnels and bridges connecting myriad waterways, it's easy to find yourself headed in the wrong direction. Highways have adequate signs, but sometimes it may be too late to merge before entering a tunnel/bridge. Traffic is highly congested during rush hour and during peak summer months, when the beach traffic can grind everything to a halt. Tune in to your car radio for traffic reports, especially during rush hours.

In congested periods, use the less-traveled I–664. The 17½ mi Chesapeake Bay Bridge-Tunnel is the only connection between the southern part of Virginia and the Eastern Shore; U.S. 13 is the main route up the spine of the Eastern Shore peninsula into Maryland.

BY TAXI

There are a few taxi companies in Williamsburg, more in Norfolk and Virginia Beach. Unless you're at Newport News/Williamsburg International Airport or Norfolk International Airport, you must phone for a cab. Rates are metered and tipping is expected.

🚖 Taxi Companies Beach Taxi ✉ Virginia Beach ☎ 757/486-6585. Yellow Cab of Virginia Beach ✉ Virginia Beach ☎ 757/460-0605. Black and White Cabs ✉ Norfolk ☎ 757/855-4444. Yellow Cab ✉ Norfolk ☎ 757/857-8888. Yellow Cab ✉ Williamsburg ☎ 757/722-1111.

BY TRAIN

Amtrak trains stop in Williamsburg between Newport News and Richmond, Washington, D.C., and stations to the north. There are two trains daily in each direction. At Newport News, passengers ticketed to Norfolk or Virginia Beach board a chartered bus (James River Bus Lines) at the station. The Williamsburg station is centrally located, sharing a building with the bus station. The "stations" in Norfolk (Monticello and Virginia Beach Blvd.) and Virginia Beach (19th and Pacific Ave.) are really just bus stops. Service south of Richmond is slow, even for Amtrak. At Fredericksburg, Amtrak meets the Virginia Railway Express, which is cheaper, but only operates on workdays.

🚆 Train Lines Amtrak ☎ 800/872-7245.

🚆 Train Stations Newport News Amtrak Station ✉ 9304 Warwick Blvd. ☎ 757/245-3589. Williamsburg Transportation Center ✉ 468 N. Boundary St. ☎ 757/229-8750.

Contacts & Resources

EMERGENCIES
🛈 **Ambulance, Fire, Police** ☎ 911.

🛈 **Doctors & Dentists** Physicians Referral Services of Williamsburg ✉ Williamsburg ☎ 757/229-4636.

🛈 **Hospitals** Sentara Bayside Hospital ✉ 800 Independence Blvd., Virginia Beach ☎ 757/363-6100. **Sentara Norfolk General Hospital** ✉ 600 Gresham Dr. ☎ 757/668-3000. **Williamsburg Community Hospital** ✉ 301 Monticello Ave., Williamsburg ☎ 757/259-6000, 757/259-6005 emergency room.

🛈 **24-Hour Pharmacies** Rite Aid ✉ 525 W. 21st St., Norfolk ☎ 757/625-6073 ✉ 5795 Princess Ann Rd., Virginia Beach ☎ 757/490-0307.

Walgreens ✉ 810 W. 21st St., Norfolk ☎ 757/623-7213 ✉ 700 Frederick Blvd., Portsmouth ☎ 757/391-9123 ✉ 115 W. Little Creek Rd., Norfolk ☎ 757/489-5291.

INTERNET, MAIL & SHIPPING
Free Internet access is easy to find in Williamsburg and Hampton Roads. Besides the usual coffee shops, all the library systems have public terminals with free Internet access and most of the larger hotels provide free wireless access. For additional locations or operating hours, contact the libraries listed below.

The post office listings that follow are those with the most central location and the longest open hours. Hours are generally about 8–5 or 6.

🛈 **Internet Resources** Hampton Public Library ✉ 4207 Victoria Blvd. ☎ 757/727-1154 www.hampton.va.us/hpl/locations/index.html. **Newport News Public Library** ✉ 110 Main St. ☎ 757/247-8875 ⊕ www.nngov.com/library. **Norfolk Public Library** ✉ 301 E. City Hall Ave. ☎ 757/664-7337 ⊕ www.npl.lib.va.us. **Portsmouth Public Library** ✉ 601 Court St. ☎ 757/393-8501 ⊕ www.portsmouthpubliclibrary.org/pplmainhome.htm. **Norfolk Public Library** ✉ 301 E. City Hall Ave. ☎ 757/664-7337 ⊕ www.npl.lib.va.us. **Virginia Beach Library** ✉ 4100 Virginia Beach Blvd. ☎ 757/385-0150 ⊕ www.vbgov.com/dept/library/locations. **Williamsburg Regional Library** ✉ 515 Scotland St. ☎ 757/259-4040 ⊕ www.wrl.org/info.html.

🛈 **Post Offices** Hampton ✉ 1062 W Mercury Blvd. **Newport News** ✉ 359 Hiden Blvd. **Norfolk** ✉ 7712 Granby St. **Portsmouth** ✉ 933 Broad St. **Virginia Beach** ✉ 501 Viking Dr. **Williamsburg** ✉ 425 N Boundary St.

MEDIA
The main local newspaper in Williamsburg and Newport News is the *Newport News Daily Press*. The *Virginia Gazette* is published in Williamsburg. The *Virginian-Pilot* is the main paper for the entire Tidewater region.

TOUR OPTIONS
Hour-long guided walking tours of the historic area depart from the Greenhow Lumber House daily from 9 to 5. Reservations should be made on the day of the tour at the Lumber House and can be made only by those with tickets to Colonial Williamsburg. "The Original Ghosts of Williams-

burg" Candlelight Tour is based on the book of the same name by L. B. Taylor Jr. The tour is offered every evening at 8 (there's also an 8:45 tour June–August). The 1¼-hour, lantern-lighted guided tour through historic Williamsburg costs $8.50. Interpreters well versed in Williamsburg and Colonial history are available to lead groups on tours of the Historic Area. Carriage and wagon rides are available daily, weather permitting. General ticket holders may purchase tickets on the day of the ride at the Lumber House.

Lanthorn Tours take you on an evening walking tour of trade shops where jewelry and other products are made in 18th-century style. The separate ticket required for this program may be purchased at the visitor center or from the Greenhow Lumber House.

Boat tours aboard the 135-foot three-masted topsail schooner *American Rover* cruise Hampton Roads nautical historical landmarks. The *Victory Rover* and *Spirit of Norfolk* cruise the Elizabeth River to the Norfolk Naval Station. The *Spirit* has lunch, early dinner, dinner, and moonlight cruises. The *Carrie B.*, a scaled-down reproduction of a Mississippi riverboat, makes a variety of Hampton Roads cruises, including Naval Station, sunset, and moonlight cruises. All boats leave the Norfolk waterfront, the *Victory Rover* from beside Nauticus, and the others from beside Waterside. In addition, the *Carrie B.* stops at the Portsmouth waterfront to load passengers.

🚩 Boat Tours American Rover ☎ 757/627-7245. *Carrie B.* ☎ 757/393-4735. Spirit of Norfolk ☎ 757/625-3866. Victory Rover ☎ 757/627-7406.
🚩 Walking Tours Greenhow Lumber House ✉ Duke of Gloucester St. ☎ 757/220-7645 or 800/447-8679. Interpreters ☎ 800/228-8878. "The Original Ghosts of Williamsburg" Candlelight Tour ☎ 757/253-1058.

VISITOR INFORMATION

Visitor information centers throughout the area generally operate daily 9–5. Call ahead to get visitor packets from Colonial Williamsburg and Virginia Beach: they both include a wealth of information and great maps. The Virginia Beach packet also includes a useful coupon booklet.

🚩 Tourist Information Colonial National Historical Park ⌂ Box 210, Yorktown 23690 ☎ 757/898-3400 ⊕ www.apva.org. Colonial Williamsburg Dining and Lodging Reservations ☎ 800/447-8679. Colonial Williamsburg Visitor Center ⌂ Box 1776, Williamsburg 23187-1776 ☎ 800/246-2099 ⊕ www.history.org. Greater Williamsburg Chamber and Tourism Alliance ✉ 421 N. Boundary St., Box 3495, Williamsburg 23187-3495 ☎ 757/229-6511 or 800/368-6511 ⊕ www.visitwilliamsburg.com. Hampton Convention and Visitors Bureau ✉ 710 Settlers Landing Rd., Hampton 23669 ☎ 757/727-1102 or 800/800-2202 ⊕ www.hampton.va.us/. Newport News Tourism and Conference Bureau ✉ 2400 Washington Ave., Newport News 23607 ☎ 757/928-6843 or 888/493-7386 ⊕ www.newport-news.org. Newport News Visitor Information Center ✉ 13560 Jefferson Ave., I-64, Exit 250B, Newport News ☎ 757/886-7777 or 888/493-7386. Norfolk Convention and Visitors Bureau ✉ 232 E. Main St., Norfolk 23510 ☎ 757/664-6620 or 800/368-3097 ⊕ www.norfolkcvb.com. Portsmouth Convention and Visitors Bureau ✉ 6 Crawford Pkwy. Portsmouth 23704 ☎ 757/393-5111 ⊕ www.portsmouthva.gov/tourism/vstinfo.html. Virginia Beach Visitor Information Center ✉ 2100 Parks Ave., Virginia Beach 23451 ☎ 800/822-3224 ⊕ www.vbfun.com.

Baltimore

WORD OF MOUTH

"There's the fabulous Oriole Park at Camden Yard, and the Babe Ruth Museum. Even people who 'don't like baseball' enjoy going to games at Camden Yard. You can get seats standing in line before the game if you aren't picky about where you sit. The whole Inner Harbor area is lovely . . . the Aquarium is just extraordinary . . . The Baltimore Museum of Art is very fine, especially if you like furniture and glass."

–Diane

"If it's a nice day, definitely take the water taxi to Fort McHenry, which is very cool, and at the end of the day they have a flag lowering ceremony in which the kids can join that is quite moving."

–waxheimer

Updated by
Sam Sessa

BALTIMORE'S CHARM LIES IN ITS NEIGHBORHOODS. While stellar downtown attractions such as the National Aquarium and Camden Yards draw torrents of tourists each year, much of the city's character can be found outside the Inner Harbor. Scores of Baltimore's trademark narrow redbrick row houses with white marble steps line the city's east and west sides. Some neighborhood streets are still made of cobblestone, and grand churches and museums and towering, glassy high-rises fill out the growing skyline.

After World War II, as manufacturing jobs dried up and its populace moved to the suburbs, Baltimore declined. But in the 1970s, real estate development surged in some areas, and new arts and cultural events such as the city's ethnic festivals began to spring up. Homesteaders started moving into once-abandoned row houses, and city tourism grew dramatically when the National Aquarium opened in the early 1980s. Further development of the Inner Harbor, including Oriole Stadium at Camden Yards and M&T Bank Stadium, continued to fuel the city's resurgence.

Now the city's blue-collar past mixes with present urban professional revitalization. Industrial waterfront properties are giving way to high-end condos, and corner bars formerly dominated by National Bohemian beer—once made in the city—are adding microbrews to their beverage lists. And, with more and more retail stores replacing old, run-down buildings and parking lots, Baltimore is one of the nation's up-and-coming cities. Though Baltimore has seen a spike in development, signs of the city's pock-marked past still persist. Boarded up row houses sit just west of downtown, and abandoned factory shells still dot the landscape—signs of the troubles the city still faces.

Top 5 Experiences for Baltimore

- **See world-class art—free!** In 2006 two of the city's most prestigious museums, the Walters Museum and the Baltimore Museum of Art, started offering free admission. This chance to see works from world-renowned artists is one you won't want to pass up.

- **Cruise the Inner Harbor aboard a historic clipper ship.** The ships that once proliferated in Baltimore ports offer tours during warm months. From the water, you can see sights such as Fort McHenry and the city's newest development of the harbor.

- **The country's oldest cathedral is in top form.** After a recent sweeping renovation, the Basilica of the Assumption is an architectural landmark definitely worth visiting.

- **Head Down Under at Baltimore's treasured aquarium.** The National Aquarium is one of the city's gems. At its new exhibit, Animal Planet Australia: Wild Extremes, you can come face-to-face with creatures from the deep.

- **Crack 'em and eat 'em like a Baltimorean.** Baltimore loves crabs, especially at Bo Brooks in Canton—one of the city's best crab houses—.where you can crack into a piping hot crustacean year-round.

EXPLORING BALTIMORE

Visiting Baltimore without seeing the Inner Harbor is like touring New York City and skipping Manhattan. The harbor and surrounding area are home to a good number of the city's most popular sites: the National Aquarium in Baltimore, Camden Yards, M&T Bank Stadium, the Visionary Arts Museum and Science Center.

The neighborhoods themselves are fun to explore. Historic Federal Hill, just south of the Inner Harbor, is home to some of the oldest houses in the city. Fells Point and Canton, farther east, are lively waterfront communities. Mount Vernon and Charles Village have wide avenues lined with grand old row houses that were once home to Baltimore's wealthiest residents. Farther north are Roland Park (Frederick Law Olmsted Jr. contributed to its planning), Guilford, Homeland, and Mt. Washington, all leafy, residential neighborhoods with cottages, large Victorian houses, and redbrick Colonials. It's easy to tour the Inner Harbor and neighborhoods such as Mount Vernon, Federal Hill, Charles Village, and Fells Point by foot. To travel between areas or farther out, however, a car is more efficient. Most of the Inner Harbor's parking is in nearby garages, though meters can be found along Key Highway. In other neighborhoods, you can generally find meters and two-hour free parking on the street.

> ### WORD OF MOUTH
>
> "Make sure you walk up Federal Hill for the view. We always eat in Federal Hill, lots of restaurants. Bar hopping, dining is also good in Fells Point and Canton. Ft. McHenry is a nice quiet park—birthplace of the Star Spangled Banner. The American Visionary Art Museum is also downtown."
> –katiekb

Baltimore is not particularly known for its public transportation. The two main transit systems, buses and the light rail, don't reach every corner of the city and can be sluggish at times. A light rail train runs north–south along Howard Street from Baltimore Washington International Airport to Camden Yards and up into northern suburbs such as Hunt Valley. Cabs are your quickest option, though you will have to call for a pickup in most neighborhoods. You can also catch a water-taxi ride across the harbor.

Navigating Baltimore by bicycle is an uneasy proposition: bicycle lanes and bike racks are practically nonexistent. However, with caution and awareness, the compact core of the city can be negotiated and even enjoyed on two wheels.

Laid out in a more-or-less regular grid pattern, Baltimore is fairly easy to navigate. Pratt Street runs east along the Inner Harbor; from there the major northbound arteries are Charles Street and the Jones Falls Expressway (I–83). Cross street addresses are marked "East" or "West" according to which side of Charles Street they are on; similarly, Baltimore Street marks the dividing line between north and south. Residents refer to areas of the city by the direction of these major arteries: thus,

CLOSE UP

Baltimore Beginnings

THE COLONIAL GOVERNMENT ESTABLISHED BALTIMORE in 1729, at the end of the broad Patapsco River that empties into the Chesapeake Bay. Named for George Calvert, the first Lord Baltimore and the founder of Maryland, the town grew as a port and shipbuilding center and did booming business during the War of Independence.

A quantum leap came at the turn of the 19th century: from 6,700 in 1776, the population reached 45,000 by 1810. Because it was the home port for

U.S. Navy vessels and for the swift Baltimore clipper ships that often preyed on British shipping, the city was a natural target for the enemy during the War of 1812. After capturing and torching Washington, D.C., the British fleet sailed up the Patapsco River and bombarded Baltimore's Fort McHenry, but in vain. The 30- by 42-foot, 15-star, 15-stripe flag was still flying "by the dawn's early light," a spectacle that inspired "The Star-Spangled Banner."

South Baltimore, North Baltimore, East Baltimore, West Baltimore, Northeast Baltimore, Northwest Baltimore, etc. The major downtown north–south thoroughfares are Charles and Saint Paul (north of Baltimore Street) and Light Street (south of Baltimore). Downtown, east–west traffic depends heavily on Pratt and Lombard streets. The downtown area is bounded by Martin Luther King Boulevard on the west and by the Jones Falls Expressway (President Street) on the east.

The Baltimore Visitor Center offers the three-day Harbor Pass, which saves you on admission to local attractions and gives you discounts on parking, hotels, and tours.

Numerous Web sites offer discounted hotel rooms in Baltimore, but fewer sites do the same thing for dining. If you're willing to dine at off-peak hours to save up to 30% off your dinner bill, visit the Dinner Broker Web site, where you can see what restaurants participate and make free online reservations.

Mount Vernon

Baltimore's arts and cultural center, Mount Vernon is home to the Walters Museum of Art and the Peabody Institute—one of the country's top music schools—as well as some of the city's grandest architecture.

The Walters and nearby Mount Vernon Place, a wonderfully designed park, are two of the neighborhood's must-sees. A good plan is to visit the Walters first then rest for a while in Mount Vernon Place. You'll need a breather before and after climbing the Washington Monument, which sits in the middle of the park. After, there are plenty of restaurants on or near Charles Street, the neighborhood thoroughfare. From the Inner Harbor, you can walk up Charles Street into the heart of Mount Vernon in about 25–30 minutes. You can also drive or take the No. 3 bus.

The area was named for the nation's first significant monument to George Washington, erected at the neighborhood's center in Mount Vernon Place. In the 19th century Mount Vernon was home to some of Baltimore's wealthiest residents, including Enoch Pratt, a wealthy merchant who donated funds for the first public library; Robert Garrett, of the Baltimore & Ohio Railroad, and Henry and William Walters, who founded the art gallery that bears their names. Though some of the grand houses here remain single-family residences, many have been turned into apartments or offices.

Numbers in the text correspond to numbers in the margin and on the Baltimore map.

Main Attractions

② Basilica of the Assumption. Completed in 1821 the Catholic Basilica of the Assumption is the oldest cathedral in the United States. Designed by Benjamin Latrobe, architect of the U.S. Capitol, it stands as a paragon of neoclassicism, with a grand portico fronted by six Corinthian columns that suggest an ancient Greek temple. Two towers are surmounted by cupolas. The church, including 24 original skylights in the dome, which were covered over after World War II, is scheduled to be restored by November 2006, the bicentennial of the laying of the church's cornerstone. ⊠ *Mulberry St. at Cathedral St., Mount Vernon* ☎ *410/727–3564* ⊙ *Call for hrs.*

FodorsChoice ★

⑩ Contemporary Museum. Artists come from around the world to collaborate with local communities and institutions and produce artwork that is relevant to Baltimore. The museum's minimalistic interior shifts all of your focus to the unconventional art within. Works are shown both on-site and off, using traditional media and innovative approaches. ⊠ *100 W. Centre St., Mount Vernon* ☎ *410/783–5720* ⊕ *www. contemporary.org* ☞ *$5 suggested donation* ⊙ *Wed.–Sun. noon–5.*

⑨ Maryland Historical Society. More than 200,000 objects serve to celebrate Maryland's history and heritage at this museum. One major attraction is the original manuscript of "The Star-Spangled Banner." The first floor is devoted to an exhibit about Marylanders' pursuit of liberty, with a focus on religious freedom, voting rights, labor, and war. Featured on the second floor are portrait paintings by the Peale family and Joshua Johnson, America's first African-American portrait artist, as well as 18th- and 19th-century Maryland landscape paintings juxtaposed against present-day photographs of the same places. Furniture manufactured and designed in Maryland from the 18th century to the present is on the third floor. There's also a library with 7 million works that relate to the state's history. ⊠ *201 W. Monument St., Mount Vernon* ☎ *410/ 685–3750* ⊕ *www.mdhs.org* ☞ *$8* ⊙ *Museum: Wed.–Sun. 10–5; library: Wed.–Sat. 10–4:30.*

Ⓒ Maryland Zoo in Baltimore. The 150 acres of the Maryland Zoo in Baltimore—the third-oldest zoo in the country—are a natural stomping ground for little ones seeking out the spectacle of elephants, lions, giraffes, hippos, and penguins, among the 2,000 animals that make this their home. Don't miss the warthog exhibit, said to be the nation's only

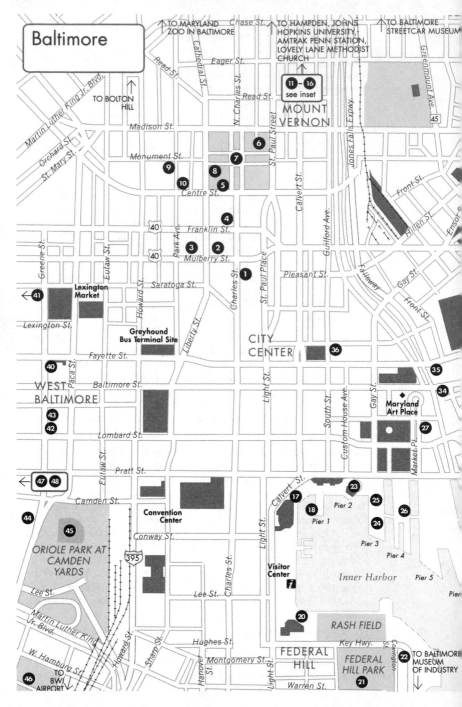

Baltimore

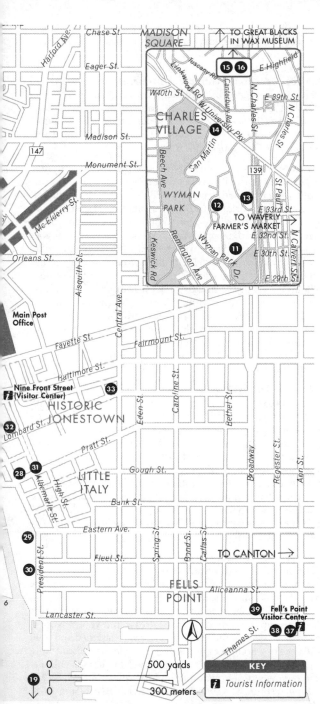

dedicated environment for the bumpy beasts. Favorite sights include a chimpanzee house and leopard lair, polar bears frolicking in an arctic pool, and a petting zoo with a recreated barnyard. If you make it all the way to the Africa exhibit and are too tired to walk back, you can hop on a tram that goes back to the entrance. Surrounding the zoo is Druid Hill Park, which was designed by Frederick Law Olmsted Jr.; the park has seen better days, but it's worth a drive through. ☒ *Druid Hill Lake Dr., Druid Hill* ☎ *410/366–5466* ⊕ *www.marylandzoo.org* ☞ *$15* ⊙ *Memorial Day–Labor Day, Sun.–Thurs. 10–4:30, Fri. and Sat. 10–6; Labor Day–Memorial Day, daily 10–4:30.*

★ ❻ **Mount Vernon Place.** One of the country's more beautifully designed public spaces, Mount Vernon Place is a prime spot for relaxing. It came into being when John Eager Howard donated the highest point in Baltimore as a site for a memorial to George Washington. With the monument as its center, the square is composed of four parks, each a block in length, that are arranged around Mount Vernon Place (which goes east–west) and Washington Place (north–south). Benches near are great for watching water calmly trickle from the fountains. The sculptures in the parks deserve a close look; of special note is a bronze lion by Antoine-Louis Barye in the middle of West Mount Vernon Place. Northeast of the monument is Mount Vernon Methodist Church, built in the mid-1850s on the site of Francis Scott Key's home and place of death. Take a moment to admire the brownstones along the north side of East Mount Vernon Place. They're excellent examples of the luxurious mansions built by 19th-century residents of Baltimore's most prestigious address.

❺ **Walters Art Museum.** The Walters' prodigious collection of more than
Fodor$Choice 30,000 artworks provides an organized overview of human history
★ over 5,500 years, from the 3rd millennium BC to the early 20th century.
■ **TIP➜ Thanks to a recent grant by the city, admission is free.** The original museum (1909) houses major collections of Renaissance and baroque paintings as well as a sculpture court. Two other buildings contain Egyptian, Greek and Roman, Byzantine, and Ethiopian art collections— among the best in the nation—along with many 19th-century paintings. There are also medieval armor and artifacts, jewelry and decorative works; Egyptology exhibits; a wonderful gift shop; and a café. ☒ *600 N. Charles St., Mount Vernon* ☎ *410/547–9000* ⊕ *www.thewalters.org* ☞ *Free* ⊙ *Wed.–Sun. 10–5.*

❼ **Washington Monument.** "If the stairs don't take your breath away, the view will." Overheard in a conversation at the top, that's Baltimore's Washington Monument in a nutshell. Completed on July 4, 1829, the monument was the first one dedicated to the nation's first president. An 18-foot statue depicting Washington caps the 160-foot white marble tower. Climb the 228 steps up the clammy spiral staircase and your reward is a stunning panoramic view of the city. The tower was designed and built by Robert Mills, the first architect born and educated in the United States; 19 years after completing Baltimore's Washington Monument, Mills designed and erected the national Washington Monument in D.C. ☒ *Mt. Vernon Pl., Mount Vernon* ☎ *410/396–1049* ☞ *$1* ⊙ *Wed.–Sun. 10–4.*

Also Worth Seeing

Baltimore Streetcar Museum. This often-overlooked museum lets you travel back to an era when streetcars dominated city thoroughfares. A film traces the vehicle's evolution, and there are beautifully restored streetcars to explore. ■ **TIP➜ Best of all, you can take unlimited rides on a working streetcar.** ⊠ *1901 Falls Rd., Midtown* ☎ *410/547–0264* ⊕ *www. baltimorestreetcar.org* ⊠ *$6* ⊙ *June–Oct., weekends noon–5; Nov.–May, Sun. noon–5.*

➌ Enoch Pratt Free Library. Donated to the city of Baltimore in 1882 by its namesake, a wealthy merchant, the Enoch Pratt Free Library was one of the country's first free-circulation public libraries; it remains one of the country's largest. The Pratt was remarkable for allowing any citizen to borrow books at a time when only the wealthy could afford to buy them. When the collection outgrew its original fortresslike rococo structure in 1933, Pratt's democratic ideals were incorporated into the new building's grand yet accessible design. Innovations such as a sidewalk-level entrance and department store–style exhibit windows set the standard for public libraries across the country. The building is still a treat to explore. A huge skylight illuminates the Central Hall's marble floors, gilded fixtures, mural panels depicting the history of printing and publishing, and oil portraits of the Lords Baltimore. The Children's Department, with a fish pond, puppet theater, and a large selection of books, is a real gem for little ones. An audio architecture tour of the museum is available at the circulation desk. ⊠ *400 Cathedral St., Mount Vernon* ☎ *410/396–5500* ⊕ *www.pratt.lib.md.us* ⊙ *June–Sept., Mon.–Wed. 11–7, Thurs. 10–5:30, Fri. and Sat. 10–5; Oct.–May, Mon.–Wed. 11–7, Thurs. 10–5:30, Fri. and Sat. 10–5, Sun. 1–5.*

➍ First Unitarian Church. Designed by Maximilian Godefroy in 1819, the church that year was the site for the sermon that definitively established Unitarianism as a denomination (the sermon was given by the church's founder, Dr. William Ellery Channing). ⊠ *At Charles and Franklin Sts., entrance at 1 W. Hamilton St., Mount Vernon* ☎ *410/685–2330* ⊙ *Weekdays 9–3.*

➑ Garrett-Jacobs Mansion. Originally built in 1893 by Stanford White for Robert Garrett, the president of the Baltimore & Ohio Railroad, this mansion was the largest and most expensive ever constructed in Baltimore (the neighbors objected to its size). After Garrett died in 1896, his widow, Mary, and her second husband, Dr. Henry Barton Jacobs, had John Russell Pope build an extension of equal size. ⊠ *11 W. Mt. Vernon Pl., Mount Vernon* ☎ *410/539–6914* ⊕ *www.garrettjacobsmansion. org* ⊠ *$3* ⊙ *Tours Mon. at 3 and by appt.; reservations required.*

NEED A BREAK?

Donna's (⊠ 800 N. Charles St. ☎ 410/385–0180) is a relaxing Mount Vernon spot for coffee; soups, salads, and sandwiches are also served. At artsy and elegant **Sascha's 527** (⊠ 527 N. Charles St. ☎ 410/539–8880) you can choose from a selection of salads and sandwiches.

➊ Woman's Industrial Exchange. This Baltimore institution was organized in the 1880s as a way for destitute women, many of them Civil War widows, to support themselves in a ladylike fashion through sewing and other domestic handiworks. To this day you can still purchase handmade quilts, embroidered baby clothes, sock monkeys, and many other crafts. But most come for lunch in the tearoom, where old-fashioned fare such as tomato aspic, chicken salad, yeast rolls, and homemade cakes are served. ⊠ *333 N. Charles St., Mount Vernon* ☎ *410/685–4388* ⊕ *www.womansindustrialexchange.org* ⊗ *Mon.–Sat. 10–4.*

OFF THE
BEATEN
PATH

GREAT BLACKS IN WAX MUSEUM – Though not as convincing as the likenesses at a Madame Tussaud's, the more than 100 wax figures on display here do a good job of recounting the triumphs and trials of Africans and African-Americans. The wax figures are accompanied by text and audio. Baltimoreans honored include Frederick Douglass, who as a youth lived and worked in Fells Point; singer Billie Holiday; and jazz composer Eubie Blake. To get here from Mount Vernon, take Charles north and turn left at North Avenue. ⊠ *1601 E. North Ave., East Baltimore* ☎ *410/563–3404* ⊕ *www.greatblacksinwax.org* ☒ *$9* ⊗ *Mid-Jan.–mid-Oct., Tues.–Sat. 9–6, Sun. noon–6; mid-Oct.–mid-Jan., Tues.–Sat. 9–5, Sun. noon–5. Closed Mon. except in Feb., July, Aug., and most federal holidays; holiday hrs 10–4.*

Charles Village

Though Johns Hopkins University anchors Charles Village, the Baltimore Museum of Art is the neighborhood's prime tourist draw—especially now that admission is free. Students, professors, writers, and artists are drawn to the area's intellectual environment. Row houses along Charles, St. Paul, and Calvert streets—some of them quite large—were built in the late 1890s and early 1900s for merchants, bankers, and other professionals. These early developments were constructed on old family estates, one of which became the basis for the present-day Johns Hopkins campus. Some of the old mansions are now museums, including Johns Hopkins's Homewood House and the Evergreen House, which also belongs to the university. On the eastern and northern sides of the Johns Hopkins campus are the neighborhoods of Tuscany-Canterbury and Roland Park. Farther to the north and east are Homeland and Guilford, tony areas worth exploring for their beautiful homes and lovely, tree-lined streets.

Main Attractions

⑪ **Baltimore Museum of Art.** Works by Matisse, Picasso, Cézanne, Gauguin, **Fodor'sChoice** van Gogh, and Monet are among the 90,000 paintings, sculptures, and ★ decorative arts on exhibit at this impressive museum, near Johns Hopkins University. Particular strengths include an encyclopedic collection of postimpressionist paintings donated to the museum by the Cone sisters, Baltimore natives who were pioneer collectors of early-20th-century art. The museum also owns the world's second-largest collection of Andy Warhol works, and many pieces of 18th- and 19th-century American painting and decorative arts. The museum's neoclassical main building was designed by John Russell Pope, the architect of the National Gallery in Washington; the modern aluminum and concrete wing houses the contemporary art collection. From Gertrude's, the museum restaurant, you can look out at 20th-century sculpture displayed in two landscaped gardens. ⊠ *10 Art Museum Dr., Charles Village* ☎ *410/396–7100* ⊕ *www.artbma.org* ⊒ *Free* ⊗ *Wed.–Fri. 11–5, weekends 11–6, 1st Thurs. of month 11–8.*

16 Evergreen House. Built in the 1850s, this 48-room Italianate mansion was the home of the 19th-century diplomat and collector John Work Garrett, whose father was president of the Baltimore & Ohio Railroad (the Garrett family continued to live here until the 1950s). Garrett bequeathed the house, its contents (an exquisite collection of books, paintings, and porcelain), and 26 acres of grounds to Johns Hopkins University. He required that the estate remain open to "lovers of music, art, and beautiful things." A tour of the mansion is a fascinating look at the luxury that surrounded a rich American family at the turn of the 20th century. ⊠ *4545 N. Charles St., Homeland* ☎ *410/516-0341* ⊒ *$6* ⊗ *Tues.–Fri. 11–4, weekends noon–4.*

13 Homewood House Museum. This elegant Federal-period mansion was once the home of Charles Carroll Jr., son of Charles Carroll of Carrollton, a signer of the Declaration of Independence. Deeded to Johns Hopkins University in 1902 along with 60 acres, the house served as faculty club and offices before being fully restored to its 1800 grandeur (it's one of the finest examples of the neoclassical architecture of the period). ⊠ *3400 N. Charles St., Charles Village* ☎ *410/516-5589* ⊒ *$6* ⊗ *Tues.–Fri. 11–4, weekends noon–4.*

12 Johns Hopkins University. The school was founded in 1876 with funds donated by Johns Hopkins, director of the Baltimore & Ohio Railroad. Much of the neo-Colonial architecture of the Homewood campus dates from the early 1900s, when the present-day campus was laid out. Dominating the school's main quad is Gilman Hall, which was built in 1904 and named for the university's first president, Daniel Coit Gilman. Pathways lead through campus; maps throughout can help you find your way. The medical school and hospital are in East Baltimore. ⊠ *3400 N. Charles St., Charles Village* ☎ *410/516-8000* ⊕ *www.jhu.edu.*

Also Worth Seeing

14 Lacrosse Museum and National Hall of Fame. Photos, objects, and videos tell the story of the history of lacrosse, a very popular sport in Maryland. One room is dedicated to outstanding players who have been honored by the U.S. Lacrosse Association since 1957. ⊠ *113 W. University Pkwy., Tuscany-Canterbury* ☎ *410/235-6882* ⊕ *www.uslacrosse.org* ⊒ *$3* ⊗ *June–Jan., weekdays 10–3; Feb.–May, Tues.–Sat. 10–3.*

Lovely Lane Methodist Church. Built in 1882, Lovely Lane Methodist Church is honored with the title "The Mother Church of American Methodism." Stanford White designed the Romanesque sanctuary after the basilicas of Ravenna, Italy; the stained-glass windows are excellent examples of Italian mosaic art. The buildings to the north that resemble the church are the original campus of the Women's College of Baltimore, now called Goucher College (the school moved to Towson in the 1950s). Dr. Goucher, the college's founder, was a pastor at Lovely Lane. Today, the building next to the church is occupied by the Baltimore Lab School. Tours of the church and the Methodist Historical Society are by appointment. ⊠ *2200 St. Paul St., North Charles* ☎ *410/ 889–1512* ⊕ *www.lovelylane.net* ☾ *Weekdays 9–3.*

⌐ **NEED A BREAK?**

With great vegetarian food, cocktails, and doors that stay open until 2 AM every day but Sunday, it's no surprise that students love the One World Cafe (⊠ 100 W. University Pkwy. ☎ 410/235–5777). In summer, take advantage of the café's sidewalk seating.

⑮ **Sherwood Gardens.** A popular spring destination for Baltimore families, this 6-acre park contains more than 80,000 tulips that bloom in late April. Azaleas peak in late April and the first half of May. The gardens are usually at their best around Mother's Day. ⊠ *Stratford Rd. and Greenway, east of St. Paul St., Guilford* ☎ *410/785–0444* ☒ *Free* ☾ *Daily dawn–dusk.*

Waverly Farmer's Market. Every Saturday morning locals gather to shop for fresh produce and baked goods at this popular farmer's market. You can get a cup of coffee and a muffin or a tasty grilled mushroom sandwich to snack on as you check out the scene. ⊠ *Parking lot at 33rd St. and Greenmount Ave., Waverly* ☎ *No phone* ☾ *Sat. 7–noon.*

Inner Harbor

The Inner Harbor has come a long way in the past 20-odd years. Before it was transformed into the city's biggest destination, the harbor consisted mostly of run-down warehouses. Now it includes the National Aquarium, Harborplace shopping centers, the Maryland Science Center, fountains, and high-rise offices. Oriole Park at Camden Yards and M&T Bank Stadium, where the NFL's Ravens play, are only a couple blocks away. The harbor is still a working port, and visitors can get on the water with sailboat tours, water taxis, and boat rentals. Just south of the Inner Harbor and best accessed by car or water taxi, Fort McHenry was bombarded by the British during the War of 1812. Despite a long night's siege by cannon and artillery the fort never fell, and the sight of the American flag flying above the its walls inspired Francis Scott Key to pen a poem that became the national anthem.

> **BEST VIEW OF THE INNER HARBOR**
>
> From the "Top of the World"–the observation level on the 27th floor of the World Trade Center–you can see for miles in any direction, or peer through binoculars for a closer look. The air-conditioning is a major bonus in the summertime. Best free view of the Inner Harbor: Federal Hill Park, across the water from the National Aquarium, offers a good vantage point for photos and picnics.

Main Attractions

② **American Visionary Art Museum.** The nation's primary museum and education center for self-taught or "outsider" art has won great acclaim by both museum experts and those who don't even consider themselves

Fodor'sChoice
★

art aficionados. Seven galleries exhibit the unusual creations—paintings, sculptures, relief works, and pieces that defy easy classification—of untrained "visionary" artists working outside the mainstream art world. In addition to the visual stimulation of amazingly intricate or refreshingly inventive works, reading the short bios of artists will give you insight to their often moving spiritual and expressive motivations. The museum's unusual, playful philosophy extends outside its walls, with large exhibits installed in a former whiskey warehouse and a 55-foot whirligig twirling in the museum's plaza. ⊠ *800 Key Hwy., Federal Hill* ☎ *410/244–1900* ⊕ *www.avam.org* 🖃 *$12* ⊙ *Tues.–Sun. 10–6.*

> ### WORD OF MOUTH
>
> "We just got back from a trip to Baltimore that was mostly focused on visiting friends and family. But we did do a little traveling, and discovered the American Visionary Arts Museum. Definitely a must-see, especially with kids! The art is so creative and unusual! To read about it, it sounds a little kitschy (their store definitely was!), but we thought the art was great and thought-provoking." –TravelinMom

☺ ㉕ **Baltimore Maritime Museum.** Consisting of three docked vessels and a restored lighthouse, this museum gives a good sense of Baltimore's maritime heritage as well as American naval power. On the west side of the pier, the submarine USS *Torsk,* the "Galloping Ghost of the Japanese Coast," is credited with sinking the last two Japanese warships in World War II. The lightship *Chesapeake,* built as a floating lighthouse in 1930 and now out of commission, remains fully operational. The *Taney* is a Coast Guard cutter that saw action at Pearl Harbor. Built in 1856 the Seven Foot Knoll Lighthouse marked the entrance to the Baltimore Harbor from the Chesapeake Bay for 133 years before its move to the museum. ⊠ *Pier 3, Inner Harbor* ☎ *410/396–3453* ⊕ *www.baltomaritimemuseum.org* 🖃 *$8* ⊙ *June–Aug., daily 10–5:30; Sept.–Nov. and Mar.–May, Sun.–Thurs. 10–5, Fri. and Sat. 10–6; Dec.–Feb., Fri.–Sun. 10–5.*

☺ **Baltimore Museum of Industry.** Housed in an 1865 oyster cannery, the fascinating and kid-friendly Baltimore Museum of Industry covers the city's industrial and labor history and is worth the ½-mi walk south of the Inner Harbor along Key Highway. Here you can watch and help operate the functional recreations of a machine shop circa 1900, a print shop, a cannery, and a garment workroom. A restored steam-driven tugboat that plied the waterfront for the first half of this century is docked outside. ⊠ *1415 Key Hwy., Federal Hill* ☎ *410/727–4808* ⊕ *www.thebmi.org* 🖃 *$10* ⊙ *Tues.–Sat. 10–4, Sun. 11–4.*

★ ㉑ **Federal Hill Park.** On the south side of Inner Harbor, Federal Hill Park was named in 1788 to commemorate Maryland's ratification of the U.S. Constitution. Later it was the site of Civil War fortifications, built by less-than-welcome Union troops under the command of Major General Benjamin "Spoonie" Butler. Until the early 1900s, a signal tower atop Federal Hill displayed the "house" flags of local shipping companies, notifying them of the arrival of their vessels. Some of the oldest homes in Baltimore surround the park, and its summit provides an excellent view of the Inner Harbor and the downtown skyline. The best vantage point for photographing Baltimore, the park is also a favorite spot for watching holiday fireworks. ⊠ *Battery Ave. and Key Hwy., Federal Hill.*

☼ ❿ **Fort McHenry.** This star-shape brick fort is forever associated with Fran-
Fodor'sChoice cis Scott Key and "The Star-Spangled Banner," which Key penned while
★ watching the British bombardment of Baltimore during the War of 1812. Key had been detained onboard a truce ship, where he had been negotiating the release of one Dr. William Beanes, when the bombard-ment began; Key knew too much about the attack plan to be released. Through the next day and night, as the battle raged, Key strained to be sure, through the smoke and haze, that the flag still flew above Fort McHenry—indicating that Baltimore's defenders held firm. "By the dawn's early light" of September 14, 1814, he saw the 30-foot by 42-foot "Star-Spangled Banner" still aloft and was inspired to pen the words to a poem (set to the tune of an old English drinking song). The flag that flew above Fort McHenry that day had 15 stars and 15 stripes, and was hand-sewn for the fort. A visit to the fort includes a 15-minute history film, guided tour, and frequent living history displays on sum-mer weekends. To see how the formidable fortifications might have ap-peared to the bombarding British, catch a water taxi from the Inner Harbor to the fort instead of driving. ⊠ *E. Fort Ave., Locust Point, , from Light St., take Key Hwy. for 1½ mi and follow signs* ☎ *410/962–4290* ⊕ *www. nps.gov/fomc* ⊠ *$5* ☉ *Memorial Day–Labor Day, daily 8–8; Labor Day–Memorial Day, daily 8–5.*

❶ **Harborplace and the Gallery.** Inside two glass-enclosed marketplaces are a plethora of shops and eateries: the Light Street Pavilion has two sto-ries of food courts and restaurants and the Pratt Street Pavilion is ded-icated mainly to retail stores. More than a dozen restaurants, including the Capitol City Brewing Company, Edo Sushi, Phillips and Tir Na Nog, offer waterfront dining, and such local specialty shops as Best of Baltimore and Maryland Bay Company carry interesting souvenirs. In summer, performers entertain at an outdoor amphitheater between the two pavilions, and paddleboats are available for rent south of the Pratt Street building. A skywalk from the Pratt Street Pavilion leads to **The Gallery,** an upscale four-story shopping mall with 70 more shops, including April Cornell, J. Crew, Coach, and Godiva Chocolatiers. ⊠ *100 Pratt St., Inner Harbor* ☎ *410/332–4191* ⊕ *www.harborplace. com* ☉ *Mon.–Sat. 10–9, Sun. 11–7. Harborplace and the Gallery have extended summer hrs; some restaurants open earlier for break-fast, and most close late.*

★ ☼ ⓴ **Maryland Science Center.** Originally known as the Maryland Academy of Sciences, this 200-year-old scientific institution is one of the oldest in the United States. Now housed in a contemporary building, the three floors of exhibits on the Chesapeake Bay, Earth science, physics, the body, dinosaurs, and outer space are an invitation to engage, experiment, and explore. The center has a planetarium, a simulated archaeological di-nosaur dig, an IMAX movie theater with a screen five stories high, and a playroom especially designed for young children. ⊠ *601 Light St., Inner Harbor* ☎ *410/685–5225* ⊕ *www.mdsci.org* ⊠ *$14.50, IMAX $8*

🕐 *Memorial Day–Labor Day, Thurs.–Sat. 10–8, Sun.–Wed. 10–6; Labor Day–Memorial Day, Tues.–Fri. 10–5, Sat. 10–6, Sun. 11–5.*

🕐 **24** **National Aquarium in Baltimore.** The most-visited attraction in Maryland
Fodor'sChoice has more than 10,000 fish, sharks, dolphins, and amphibians dwelling
★ in 2 million gallons of water. Animal Planet Australia: Wild Extremes, a new exhibit built to mimic a river running through a gorge, opened in 2006. It features lizards, crocodiles, turtles, bats and a black-headed python, among other animals from Down Under. The aquarium also features reptiles, birds, plants, and mammals in its rain-forest environment, inside a glass pyramid 64 feet high. The rain-forest ecosystem har-

> **WORD OF MOUTH**
>
> "The National Aquarium is a great place to spend a couple of hours. There are plenty of shops and restaurants with a view of the harbor." —mersingary

bors two-toed sloths in calabash trees, parrots in the palms, iguanas on the ground, and red-bellied piranhas in a pool (a sign next to it reads DO NOT PUT HANDS IN POOL). Each day in the Marine Mammal Pavilion, Atlantic bottlenose dolphins are part of several entertaining presentations that highlight their agility and intelligence. The aquarium's famed shark tank and Atlantic coral reef exhibits are spectacular; you can wind through an enormous glass enclosure on a spiral ramp while hammerheads and brightly hued tropical fish glide by. Hands-on exhibits include such docile sea creatures as horseshoe crabs and starfish. ■ TIP➜ **Arrive early to ensure admission, which is by timed intervals; by noon, the wait is often two or three hours.** ✉ *Pier 3, Inner Harbor* ☎ *410/576–3800* ⊕ *www.aqua.org* 💲 *$ 21.95* 🕐 *Nov.–Feb., Sat.–Thurs. 10–5, Fri. 10–8; Mar.–June, Sept., and Oct., Sat.–Thurs. 9–5, Fri. 9–8; July–Aug. 19, daily 9–8; Aug. 20–31, Sat.–Thurs. 9–6, Fri. 9–8; visitors may tour for up to 1½ hrs after closing. Timed tickets may be required on weekends and holidays; purchase these early in the day.*

🕐 **27** **Port Discovery—The Baltimore Children's Museum.** At this interactive museum, adults are encouraged to play every bit as much as children. A favorite attraction is the three-story KidWorks, a futuristic jungle gym on which the adventurous can climb, crawl, slide, and swing their way through stairs, slides, ropes, zip-lines, and tunnels, and even cross a narrow footbridge three stories up. In Miss Perception's Mystery House, youngsters help solve a mystery surrounding the disappearance of the Baffeld family by sifting through clues; some are written or visual, and others are gleaned by touching and listening. Changing interactive exhibits allow for even more play. ✉ *35 Market Pl., Inner Harbor* ☎ *410/ 727–8120* ⊕ *www.portdiscovery.com* 💲 *$11* 🕐 *Memorial Day–Labor Day, Mon.–Sat. 10–5, Sun. noon–5; Labor Day–Memorial Day, Tues.–Fri. 9:30–4:30, Sat. 10–5, Sun. noon–5.*

28 **Reginald F. Lewis Museum.** Named for the former CEO of TLC Beatrice International, the Reginald F. Lewis Museum is dedicated to the African-American experience in Maryland. The contemporary, predominantly red-and-black building holds exhibits on African-American history, art, and culture as told through the lives of such individuals as Frederick Douglass, Billie Holiday, and Kweisi Mfume. Facilities include an oral history recording and listening studio and an information resource center. ✉ *830 E. Pratt St., Inner Harbor* ☎ *443/263–1800* ⊕ *www. africanamericanculture.org* ✉ *$8* ⊙ *Tues.–Sat. 10–5, Sun. noon–5.*

⑱ USS Constellation. Launched in 1854, the USS *Constellation* was the last—and largest—all-sail ship built by the U.S. Navy. Before the Civil War, as part of the African Squadron, she saw service on antislavery patrol; during the war, she protected Union-sympathizing U.S. merchant ships from Confederate raiders. The warship eventually became a training ship for the navy before serving as the relief flagship for the Atlantic Fleet during World War II, finally arriving in Baltimore in 1955 for restoration to her original condition. You can tour the USS *Constellation* for a glimpse of life as a 19th-century navy sailor, and children can muster to become Civil War–era "powder monkeys." Recruits receive "basic training," try on replica period uniforms, participate in a gun drill, and learn a sea chantey or two before being discharged and paid off in Civil War money at the end of their "cruise." ✉ *Pratt and Light Sts., Inner Harbor* ☎ *410/539–6238* ⊕ *www.constellation.org* ✉ *$7.50* ⊙ *Apr.–Oct., daily 10–5:30; Nov.–Mar., daily 10–4:30.*

Visitor Center. Stop by the sweeping, all-glass center for information on the city, brochures, tickets, and hotel and restaurant reservations. ✉ *401 Light St., Inner Harbor* ☎ *877/225–8466* ⊕ *www.baltimore. org* ⊙ *Daily 9–6.*

★ **㉓ World Trade Center.** With 32 stories, this building, designed by I. M. Pei's firm, is the world's tallest pentagonal structure. The 27th-floor observation deck ("Top of the World") allows an unobstructed view of Baltimore and beyond from a height of 423 feet. ✉ *401 E. Pratt St., Inner Harbor* ☎ *410/837–8439* ⊕ *www.bop.org* ✉ *$5* ⊙ *Memorial Day–Labor Day, weekdays and Sun. 10–6, Sat. 10–8; Apr., May, Sept., and Oct., Wed.–Sun. 10–6.*

Also Worth Seeing

㊱ Baltimore City Hall. Built in 1875, Baltimore City Hall consists of mansard roofs and a gilt dome over a 110-foot rotunda, all supported by ironwork. Inside you can get tours of the chambers and view exhibits on Baltimore's history. Directly across the street is **City Hall Plaza,** on what was originally the site of the Holliday Street Theatre. The theater was owned and operated by the Ford brothers; they also operated Ford's Theatre in Washington, D.C., where President Lincoln was assassinated. "The Star-Spangled Banner" was first publicly sung here. ✉ *100 N. Holliday St., Downtown* ☎ *410/396–3100* ✉ *Free* ⊙ *Weekdays 8–4:30.*

㉚ Baltimore Civil War Museum-President Street Station. President Street Station offers a glimpse of the violence and divided loyalties that the war caused in Maryland, a state caught in the middle. Originally the Baltimore terminus of the Philadelphia, Wilmington & Baltimore Railroad, the relocated station, built in 1849, contains exhibits that depict the events that led to mob violence. It began when troops from the Sixth Massachusetts Regiment bound for Washington, D.C., walked from this station to the Camden Station (near Oriole Park). In what would be the first bloodshed of the Civil War, 4 soldiers and 12 civilians were killed; 36 soldiers and a number of civilians were wounded. The riot lasted for several hours and inspired the secessionist poem "Maryland, My Maryland," today the state song. Guided tours of the route of the Sixth Massachusetts are offered at 1 PM on weekends. ⊠ *601 President St., Inner Harbor East* ☎ *410/385–5188* ☜ *$3, guided tour $5* ⊘ *Daily 10–5.*

㉙ Baltimore Public Works Museum. A short walk east of the Inner Harbor, this museum is an unusual collection of artifacts displayed in an unusual location: the old Eastern Avenue Sewage Pumping Station, built in 1912. Here you can examine several generations of water pipe, including wood piping nearly 200 years old. Other exhibits tell the history of such city services as trash removal. Outdoors, a life-size model reveals what lies underneath Baltimore streets. Since the museum is still an operational sewage pumping station, it smells. ⊠ *844 E. Pratt St., Inner Harbor* ☎ *410/837–1793* ☜ *$3* ⊘ *Tues.–Sat. 10–4.*

㉜ Carroll Mansion. This was once the winter home of Charles Carroll, one of the signers of the Declaration of Independence. It's now a museum dedicated to the history of the city and the neighborhood, Historic Jonestown, as told by the various occupants of the house through the years. ⊠ *800 E. Lombard St., Historic Jonestown* ☎ *410/605–2964* ⊕ *www.carrollmuseums.org* ☜ *$5* ⊘ *Wed.–Sun. noon–4 or by appt.*

㉝ Jewish Museum of Maryland. Sandwiched between two 19th-century synagogues, the Jewish Museum of Maryland has changing exhibits of art, photography, and documents related to the Jewish experience in Maryland. The Lloyd Street Synagogue, to the left of the museum, was built in 1845 and was the first in Maryland and the third in the United States. The other, B'nai Israel, was built in 1876 in a uniquely Moorish style. Tours of both synagogues are available. ⊠ *15 Lloyd St., Historic Jonestown* ☎ *410/732–6400* ⊕ *www.jhsm.org* ☜ *$8* ⊘ *Tues.–Thurs. and Sun. noon–4 and by appt.*

Maryland Art Place. Surrounded by bars and restaurants in the Power Plant Live! complex, this cutting-edge gallery highlights works by contemporary local and regional artists. ⊠ *8 Market Pl., Suite 100, Inner Harbor* ☎ *410/962–8565* ⊕ *www.mdartplace.org* ☜ *Free* ⊘ *Tues.–Sat. 11–5.*

㉞ Nine Front Street. This cute two-story brick town house, built in 1790, was once the home of Mayor Thorowgood Smith, the second mayor of Baltimore. The Women's Civic League, which has its home here, gives tours of the house and of city hall; call for an appointment. ⊠ *9 Front St., Historic Jonestown* ☎ *410/837–5424* ⊘ *Tues.–Thurs. 9–2:30, Fri. 9–2; call ahead.*

㉟ Phoenix Shot Tower. The only remaining tower of three of this type that once existed in Baltimore, this brick structure was used to make shot pellets by pouring molten lead from the top. As the drops fell, they formed balls that turned solid in cold water at the bottom. In the summer months, the tower may close due to heat. ⊠ *801 E. Fayette St., His-*

toric Jonestown ☎ *410/605–2964* 🖂 *$1* 🕙 *May–Aug., Fri.–Sun. noon–4; Sept.–Apr., by appt.*

🦢 ㉖ **The Power Plant.** What actually was the city's former power plant is now a retail and dining complex that includes a Hard Rock Cafe, a Barnes & Noble, and a 35,000-square-foot ESPN Zone. Next door is the **Pier 4 Building**, which houses a Chipotle Mexican Grill and Blu Bamboo, a fast-casual Mongolian grill. 🖂 *Pier 5, 601 E. Pratt St., Inner Harbor* ☎ *No phone.*

> **WORD OF MOUTH**
>
> "Get some cannoli's at Vacarro's. YUM!"   −enjoylife

NEED A BREAK?

Espresso, cannolis, and other delicious Italian pastries can be found at **Vaccaro's** (🖂 222 Albermarle St., Little Italy ☎ 410/685–4905). **Whole Foods** (🖂 1001 Fleet St., Inner Harbor East ☎ 410/528–1640) has tables and chairs inside and outside for eating premade sandwiches, sushi, and salads.

㉛ **Star-Spangled Banner House.** Built in 1793, this Federal-style home was where Mary Pickersgill hand-sewed the 15-star, 15-stripe flag that survived the British bombardment of Fort McHenry in 1814 and inspired Francis Scott Key to write "The Star-Spangled Banner." The house contains Federal furniture and American art of the period, including pieces from the Pickersgill family. Outdoors, a map of the United States has been made of stones from the various states. A museum connected to the house tells the history of the War of 1812. 🖂 *844 E. Pratt St., Historic Jonestown* ☎ *410/837–1793* ⊕ *www.flaghouse.org* 🖂 *$7* 🕙 *Tues.–Sat. 10–4.*

Fells Point

Fells Point is a gathering ground for blue- and white-collar locals and tourists. Plenty of bars and small craft shops line Broadway, running north–south, and Thames (pronounced with a long "a" and thick "th"), running east–west along the water. Head here in the afternoon and tour the shops and two small museums; afterward stay for dinner and drinks at one of the neighborhood's many pubs—most of which host live local bands daily. From the Inner Harbor, it takes about five minutes to reach Fells Point by car. You can also opt for the water taxi, a much more fun way to get there.

Standing in the heart of Fells Point, you get the feeling little has changed since it was founded several hundred years ago. Englishman William Fell purchased the peninsula in 1726, seeing its potential for shipbuilding and shipping. Starting in 1763 his son Edward and his wife, Ann Bond Fell, divided and sold the land; docks, shipyards, warehouses, stores, homes, churches, and schools sprang up, and the area quickly grew into a bustling seaport. Fells Point was famed for its shipyards

> **WORD OF MOUTH**
>
> ". . . the inner harbor is great, but I really love the Fells Point area in the evening."   −brando

(the notoriously speedy clipper ships built here annoyed the British so much during the War of 1812 that they tried to capture the city, a move resulting in Fort McHenry's bombardment). Frederick Douglass worked at a shipyard at the end of Thames Street in the 1830s. Around the 1840s the shipbuilding industry started to decline, in large part because of the rise of steam ships, which were being constructed elsewhere.

Main Attractions

39 **Broadway Market.** Head to the market's two pavilions to grab a drink or light snack. You can also find pizza, sandwiches, and oysters at a raw bar. ⊠ *Broadway, between Fleet and Lancaster Sts., Fells Point.*

38 **Fells Point Maritime Museum.** For the history of the shipbuilding industry in Fells Point and the people involved in it, go to this small museum. You can find out about the speedy Baltimore clipper schooners, which once made this area famous; the cargoes they carried; and the shipbuilders, merchants, and sailors who sought their fortunes. ⊠ *1724 Thames St., Fells Point* ☎ *410/732–0278* ⊕ *www.mdhs.org* ⊠ *$4* ⊙ *Thurs.–Mon. 10–5.*

Fells Point Visitor Center. Be sure to take a neighborhood walking tour brochure from the gift shop. The tours depart from here on Friday evening and Saturday morning (April–October) and focus on topics such as ghosts, the War of 1812, maritime history, or slavery and Frederick Douglass's tenure in Fells Point. ⊠ *808 S. Ann St., Fells Point* ☎ *410/675–6750 Ext. 16* ⊕ *www.preservationsociety.com* ⊙ *Apr.–late Nov., Sun.–Thurs. 10–5, Fri. and Sat. 10–8; Nov. 26–Mar. 31, Tues.–Sun. noon–4.*

37 **Robert Long House Museum.** The city's oldest residence still standing, this small brick house was built in 1765 as both home and business office for Robert Long, a merchant and quartermaster for the Continental Navy who operated a wharf on the waterfront. Furnished with Revolutionary War–era pieces, the parlor, bedroom, and office seem as if Long himself just stepped away. A fragrant, flowering herb garden flourishes in warm months. ⊠ *812 S. Ann St., Fells Point* ☎ *410/675–6750* ⊕ *www. preservationsociety.com* ⊠ *$3* ⊙ *Tours daily Apr.–Nov. at 1 and 2:30.*

NEED A BREAK? The **Daily Grind** (⊠ 1720 Thames St., Fells Point ☎ 410/558–0399) is the neighborhood spot for coffee and Wi-Fi. A great place to sip tea is **Tea-volve** (⊠ 1705 Eastern Ave., Fells Point ☎ 410/327–4832).

West Baltimore

Though some sections are still dodgy, Baltimore's West Side is undergoing a much-needed transformation for the better. A multimillion dollar renovation recently turned the old Hippodrome movie house and its neighboring buildings into an elegant performing arts center. Up and down Eutaw and Howard streets, once-abandoned buildings are being converted into high-end loft apartments.

But the neighborhood's most popular draws are gems such as Oriole Park at Camden Yards and M&T Bank Stadium, where the Baltimore Ravens football team plays. West Baltimore is also home to birthplaces and former residences of historic figures such as Babe Ruth, Edgar Allan Poe, and Charles Carroll, a member of the Continental Congress. The University of Maryland medical campus, including the Dr. Samuel D. Harris National Museum of Dentistry, occupies a large swath of the neighborhood. A few blocks west of the school, the B&O Railroad Museum, with more than 100 trains on display, is captivating to most small children (and the inner kid in train-loving adults).

> **WEST BALTIMORE TIPS**
>
> Set aside several hours for a tour of West Baltimore, and at least a half hour for lunch at Lexington Market. Because the sights are scattered throughout the neighborhood and the streets are less safe than those in downtown Baltimore, parts of this area are best visited by car. It's safer to avoid walking through West Baltimore alone at night.

Main Attractions

🐚 **44** **Babe Ruth Birthplace and Museum.** This plain brick row house, three blocks from Oriole Park at Camden Yards, was the birthplace of "the Bambino." Although Ruth was born here in 1895, his family never lived here; they lived in a nearby apartment, above a tavern run by Ruth's father. The row house and the adjoining buildings make up a museum devoted to Ruth's life and to the local Orioles baseball club. Film clips and props, rare photos of Ruth, Yankees payroll checks, a score book from Ruth's first professional game, and many other artifacts can be found here. ⊠ *216 Emory St., West Baltimore* 🕾 *410/727–1539* ⊕ *www.baberuthmuseum.com* 🎫 *$6* ⊙ *Apr.–Oct., daily 10–6, until 7 before Oriole home games; Nov.–Mar., daily 10–5, until 8 before Ravens home games.*

★ 🐚 **48** **B&O Railroad Museum.** The famous Baltimore & Ohio Railroad was founded on the site that now houses this museum, which contains more than 120 full-size locomotives and a great collection of railroad memorabilia, from dining-car china and artwork to lanterns and signals. The 1884 roundhouse (240 feet in diameter and 120 feet high) adjoins one of the nation's first railroad stations. Train rides are available every day but Monday. The Iron Horse Café serves food and drinks. ⊠ *901 W. Pratt St., West Baltimore* 🕾 *410/752–2490* 🎫 *$14* ⊙ *Weekdays 10–4, Sat. 10–5, Sun. 11–4.*

46 **M&T Bank Stadium.** The Baltimore Ravens football team hosts home games in this state-of-the-art stadium from August to January. ⊠ *1101 Russell St., West Baltimore* 🕾 *410/261–7283.*

★ 🐚 **45** **Oriole Park at Camden Yards.** Home of the Baltimore Orioles, Camden Yards and the nearby area bustle on game days. Since it opened in 1992, this nostalgically designed baseball stadium has inspired other cities to emulate its neotraditional architecture and amenities. The Eutaw Street promenade, between the warehouse and the field, has a view of the stadium; look for the brass baseballs embedded in the sidewalk that mark where home runs have cleared the fence, or visit the Orioles Hall of Fame display and the monuments to retired Orioles. Daily 90-minute tours take you to nearly every section of the ballpark, from the massive JumboTron scoreboard to the dugout to the state-of-the-art beer delivery system. ✉ *333 W. Camden St., Downtown* ☎ *410/685–9800 general information, 410/547–6234 tour times, 888/848–2473 tickets to Orioles home games* ✉ *Eutaw St. promenade free; tour $7* ☉ *Eutaw St. promenade daily 10–3, otherwise during games and tours; tours Mar.–Sept., Mon.–Sat. 11, noon, 1, and 2; Oct., weekdays 11:30 and 1:30, Sat. 11, noon, 1, and 2, Sun. 12:30, 1, 2, and 3; Nov., Mon.–Sat. 11:30 and 1:30, Sun. 12:30 and 2:30.*

WORD OF MOUTH

"Babe Ruth's home is close to Camden Yards, where the Orioles play. The stadium is one of the nicest I've ever been to."   –emd

---

40 **Westminster Cemetery and Catacombs.** The city's oldest cemetery is the final resting place of Edgar Allan Poe and other famous Marylanders, including 15 generals from the American Revolution and the War of 1812. Dating from 1786, the cemetery was originally known as the Old Western Burying Grounds. In the early 1850s a city ordinance demanded that burial grounds be part of a church, so a building was constructed above the cemetery, creating catacombs beneath it. In the 1930s the schoolchildren of Baltimore collected pennies to raise the necessary funds for Poe's monument. Each year on Poe's birthday a mysterious stranger leaves three roses and a bottle of cognac on the writer's grave. ✉ *W. Fayette and Greene Sts., Downtown* ☎ *410/706–2072* ☉ *Daily 8–dusk.*

Also Worth Seeing

42 **Davidge Hall.** Built in 1812 for $35,000, this green-dome structure has been used for teaching medicine for nearly two centuries. Part of the downtown campus of the University of Maryland at Baltimore, Davidge Hall is a relic of the days when dissection was illegal; the acoustically perfect anatomy theater was lighted by skylights instead of windows so that passersby would not witness students working on cadavers. ✉ *522 W. Lombard St., West Baltimore* ☎ *410/706–7454* ✉ *Free* ☉ *Weekdays 8:30–4:30.*

43 **Dr. Samuel D. Harris National Museum of Dentistry.** This unusual museum, which has a set of George Washington's dentures, is on the Baltimore campus of the University of Maryland, the world's first dental school. Housed in a Renaissance Revival–style building, the museum has exhibits on the anatomy and physiology of human and animal teeth and the history of dentistry; you can also play a tune on the "Tooth Jukebox." One popular exhibit displays the dental instruments used in treating Queen Victoria in the mid-19th century. ✉ *31 S. Greene St., West Baltimore* ☎ *410/706–0600* ✉ *$4.50* ☉ *Wed.–Sat. 10–4, Sun. 1–4.*

47 **Mount Clare Museum House.** One of the oldest houses in Baltimore, this elegant mansion was begun in 1754. It was the home of Charles Carroll, author of the Maryland Declaration of Independence, member of the Continental Congress, and one of Maryland's major landowners. The state's first historic museum house has been carefully restored to its Georgian elegance; more than 80% of the 18th-century furniture and artifacts, including rare pieces of Chippendale and Hepplewhite silver, crystal, and Chinese export porcelain, were owned and used by the Carroll family. Washington, Lafayette, and John Adams were all guests here. The greenhouses are famous in their own right: they provided rare trees and plants for Mount Vernon. ⊠ *1500 Washington Blvd., Southwest Baltimore* ☎ *410/837-3262* ⊕ *www.mountclare.org* 🖾 *$6* ⊙ *Tues.–Sat. 10–4; tours every hr until 3.*

41 **Poe House.** Though the "Master of the Macabre" lived in this tiny row house only three years, he wrote "MS Found in a Bottle" and his first horror story, "Berenice," in the tiny garret chamber that's now furnished in an early-19th-century style. Besides visiting this room, you can view changing exhibits and a video presentation about Poe's short, tempestuous life. Because of the possibility of crime, it's best to visit this neighborhood during daylight hours as part of a group. ⊠ *203 N. Amity St., West Baltimore* ☎ *410/396-7932* ⊕ *www.eapoe.org/balt/poehse.htm* 🖾 *$3* ⊙ *Wed.–Sat. noon–3:45; call ahead.*

▌ **NEED A BREAK?** **Lexington Market** (⊠ Lexington St. between Paca and Eutaw Sts., West Baltimore ☎ 410/685-6169) is in a slightly sketchy area, but a trip there for Faidley's crab cakes and other famous food is definitely worth it. **Trinacria Foods** (⊠ 406 N. Paca. St., West Baltimore ☎ 410/685-7285) is an authentic Italian grocery store a few blocks away from Lexington Market that sells meat, cheese, fresh-baked bread, pastries, and wine. There's no better sandwich in the area.

WHERE TO EAT

Baltimore loves crabs. Soft- or hardshell crabs, crab cakes, crab dip—the city's passion for clawed crustaceans seems to have no end. Flag down a Baltimore native and ask them where the best crab joint is and you'll get a list of options. In addition to crabs and seafood, Baltimore's restaurant landscape also includes Afghan, Greek, American, tapas, and other cuisines. The city's dining choices may not compare to New York, or even Washington, but it does have some real standouts.

Since most of the Inner Harbor only has chain and hotel restaurants, you'll want to head north up Charles Street to Mount Vernon—the city's center for fine dining. Or, you can go south down Light Street to try Federal Hill's trendy pubs, sushi bars, and bistros. A few blocks east of the Inner Harbor, Little Italy has a host of Italian restaurants, most of which serve classic Southern Italian, spaghetti-with-garlic-bread fare. Yet father east, Fells Point has some renowned local restaurants. Charles Village, near Johns Hopkins University, and Hampden, just west, also have some funky casual options. Note that places generally stop serving by 10 PM, if not earlier.

WHAT IT COSTS				
$$$$	**$$$**	**$$**	**$**	**¢**
RESTAURANTS over $30	$22–$30	$14–$22	$7–$14	under $7

Restaurant prices are per person for a main course at dinner.

Mount Vernon

$$$-$$$$
Fodor'sChoice
★

✕ **Ixia.** From the food to the decor, Ixia sparkles. The walls are painted blue with gold trim, and large reflective chandeliers and thin white curtains hang from the ceiling. Service is top-notch, as are dishes such as tuna tartare, which features small, tender cubes of fish in an Asian chile vinaigrette and cucumber soup. Standards such as the juicy, well-spiced filet mignon are also mouth-watering. The list of more than a dozen inventive house martinis is a must-try. ✉ *518 N. Charles St., Mount Vernon* ☎ *410/727–1800* ▭ *AE, D, DC, MC, V* ⊘ *Closed Sun. and Mon.*

★ **$$-$$$$**
✕ **The Prime Rib.** Bustling and crowded, this luxuriously dark dining room is just north of Mount Vernon Square and five minutes from the Inner Harbor. Tables are set close together under a low ceiling, keeping things intimate for the bankers and lawyers who often eat here, as well as couples on expensive dates. The traditional menu is headed by a superb prime rib and an even better filet mignon; the jumbo lump crab cakes are also great. The surprisingly short wine list is predominantly Californian. ✉ *1101 N. Calvert St., Mount Vernon* ☎ *410/539–1804* ⌕ *Reservations essential* ⌂ *Jacket required* ▭ *AE, D, DC, MC, V.*

$$-$$$
✕ **The Brewer's Art.** Part brew pub, part restaurant, this spot in a redone mansion feels young but urbane, with an ambitious menu, a clever wine list, and the Belgian-style beers it brews itself: try the potent Resurrection ale. The upstairs dining room serves seasonal dishes with high-quality, locally available ingredients to create European-style country fare that is both hearty and sophisticated. Downstairs, the menu and decor are more casual. Made with rosemary and garlic, the classic steak frites are a best bet. ✉ *1106 N. Charles St., Mount Vernon* ☎ *410/547–6925* ▭ *AE, D, DC, MC, V* ⊘ *Closed Mon.*

$$-$$$
✕ **Tio Pepe.** Candles light up the whitewashed walls of these cellar dining rooms, where the menu covers all regions of Spain. The staple is *paella à la Valenciana* (chicken, sausage, shrimp, clams, and mussels with saffron rice); a less-well-known Basque preparation is red snapper with clams, mussels, asparagus, and boiled egg. Make dinner reservations well in advance; walk-in weekday lunch seating is usually available. ✉ *10 E. Franklin St., Mount Vernon* ☎ *410/539–4675* ⌕ *Reservations essential* ⌂ *Jacket and tie* ▭ *AE, D, DC, MC, V.*

★ **$$**
✕ **Abacrombie.** Across from Meyerhoff Symphony Hall, this elegant, clubby-feeling spot on the bottom floor of a B&B is popular for preconcert meals. But it's also worth coming at other times, when it's not as busy, for the creative, seasonal menu, which might include dishes such as roasted pork tenderloin with rutabaga puree or rock fish with smoked paprika sauce. Or try the three-course, prix-fixe dinner, which comes with matching wines for each course. ✉ *58 W. Biddle St., Mount Vernon* ☎ *410/837–3630* ⌕ *Reservations essential* ▭ *AE, D, DC, MC, V* ⊘ *Closed Mon. and Tues. No lunch.*

★ **$$**
✕ **The Brass Elephant.** The rooms of this grand antebellum house on Charles Street are filled with classical music and the chatter of diners (the Teak Room is the quietest, the Oak Room the noisiest). The northern Italian menu includes traditional piccatas and marinaras as well as updated versions of Italian classics, such as homemade cannelloni filled with duck

7

Where to Stay & Eat in Baltimore

Restaurants ▼	
Abacrombie	**2**
Afghan Kabob	**22**
Akbar	**15**
The Ambassador Dining Room	**8**
Amicci's	**32**
Attman's	**34**
b	**1**
Babalu Grill	**20**
The Bicycle	**24**
The Black Olive	**37**
Blue Agave	**27**
The Blue Moon Dining House	**38**
Blue Sea Grill	**21**
Bo Brooks	**41**
The Brass Elephant	**12**
The Brewer's Art	**4**
Charleston	**33**
Chiapparelli's	**31**
City Cafe	**3**
Corks	**26**
Donna's	**16**
Gertrude's	**10**
Golden West Cafe	**9**
Hamptons	**23**
The Helmand	**14**
Ixla	**18**
La Tavola	**30**
Louisiana	**39**
Matsuri	**25**
McCormick & Schmick's	**29**
Obrycki's Crab House	**35**
One World Cafe	**7**
Paper Moon Diner	**11**
Pazo	**36**
The Prime Rib	**6**
Red Maple	**13**
Rusty Scupper	**28**
Samos	**40**
Sascha's 527	**17**
Tapas Teatro	**5**
Tio Pepe	**19**

Hotels ▼	
Abacrombie	**1**
The Admiral Fell Inn	**19**
Baltimore Marriott Inner Harbor	**13**
Celie's Waterfront Bed & Breakfast	**20**
Courtyard by Marriott Baltimore Inner Harbor	**18**
Courtyard by Marriott Hunt Valley	**3**
Days Inn Inner Harbor	**12**
Hampton Inn and Suites	**11**
Hampton Inn Hunt Valley	**2**
Harbor Court	**15**
Hyatt Regency	**14**
Inn at 2920	**21**
Inn at Henderson's Wharf	**22**
Inn at the Colonnade	**5**
Marriott Baltimore Waterfront	**17**
Peabody Court	**6**
Radisson Hotel at Cross Keys	**4**
Radisson Plaza Lord Baltimore	**9**
Renaissance Harborplace Hotel	**16**
Tremont Park	**7**
Tremont Plaza Hotel	**8**
Wyndham Inner Harbor	**10**

confit, woodland mushrooms, and ricotta. Upstairs, the softly lighted Tusk Lounge is a comfortable, classy spot to meet for drinks. ⊠ *924 N. Charles St., Mount Vernon* ☎ *410/547–8480* ⊟ *AE, DC, MC, V.*

$–$$ ✕ **Akbar.** A few steps below street level, this small restaurant is usually crowded and always filled with pungent aromas and the sounds of Indian music. Among the vegetarian dishes, *alu gobi masala,* a potato-and-cauliflower creation, is prepared with onions, tomatoes, and spices. Tandoori chicken is marinated in yogurt, herbs, and strong spices, then barbecued in a charcoal-fired clay oven. Akbar also makes a good choice for Sunday brunch. ⊠ *823 N. Charles St., Mount Vernon* ☎ *410/ 539–0944* ⊟ *AE, D, DC, MC, V.*

$–$$ ✕ **City Cafe.** The lofty space and black-and-white tile floors give this casual spot a feeling of classic grandeur. Come here for basic American fare—sandwiches, salads, pasta, big brunches—and stick to that: the more creative ambitious attempts on the menu often fall short. In summer the frozen cappuccino is a sweet, creamy treat. ⊠ *1001 Cathedral St., Mount Vernon* ☎ *410/539–4252* ⊟ *AE, D, DC, MC, V.*

$–$$ ✕ **Donna's.** Basic black and light-wood are the backdrop for this casual American café and restaurant, part of a local chain (other locations are on St. Paul Street in Charles Village and in Cross Keys in Roland Park). For breakfast, bagels and muffins are served on weekdays and brunch is available Sunday; sandwiches, soups, and salads are the lunchtime offerings; dinner might include balsamic-glaze salmon, herb chicken breast with artichoke hearts, or a daily pasta dish. You can also just stop in for a cup of coffee any time of the day. ⊠ *800 N. Charles St., Mount Vernon* ☎ *410/385–0180* ⊟ *AE, D, MC, V.*

★ **$–$$** ✕ **The Helmand.** Owned by Hamid Kharzai's brother, Qayum Karzai, Helmand serves outstanding Afghan fare in a casual yet elegant space. Beautiful woven textiles and traditional dresses adorn the walls, adding color to the simple white table settings. Try one of the many outstanding lamb dishes such as *sabzy challow* (spinach sautéed with chunks of beef) or the vegetarian *aushak* (Afghan ravioli). For starters, *kaddo,* a sweet-and-pungent pumpkin dish, is unforgettable. ⊠ *806 N. Charles St., Mount Vernon* ☎ *410/752–0311* ⊟ *AE, DC, MC, V* ☉ *No lunch.*

$–$$ ✕ **Red Maple.** Theatrical, stylish Red Maple doesn't even have a sign out front. Instead, it's only marked with a small maple tree icon on the front door. Inside, the striking, minimalist space is warmed by a fireplace, candlelight, and sumptuous suede banquettes. The food is equally arresting: Asian-inspired tapas, artfully conceived and beautifully presented. Small plates such as wild mushroom and asparagus dumplings and shrimp and mango tapas are inexpensive, but it's easy to run up your tab because each is so compelling. ⊠ *930 N. Charles St., Mount Vernon* ☎ *410/547–0149* ⊟ *AE, DC, MC, V* ☉ *No lunch.*

$–$$ ✕ **Sascha's 527.** High ceilings, warm yellow walls hung with paintings, and a giant crystal chandelier add drama to this spacious, artsy spot near the Walters. Choose from an eclectic menu of "tastes" (appetizer-size plates), "grills" (chicken, lamb, or fish) served with a selection of unusual sauces, and other American fare with a twist. At lunch there's counter service only, with a choice of fancy sandwiches and inventive pizzas and salads on a rotating menu. On Thursday nights live jazz accompanies dinner. ⊠ *527 N. Charles St., Mount Vernon* ☎ *410/539–8880* ▤ *AE, DC, MC, V* ☺ *Closed Sun. No lunch Sat.*

$–$$ ✕ **Tapas Teatro.** Connected to the Charles Theater, the place for art and indie films in Baltimore, the Tapas Teatro is a popular pre- and post-movie spot. It's often a scene, especially in warm weather, when the glass front is open and tables spill onto the street. Tapas include marinated red peppers, spinach sautéed with crab, and lamb tenderloin. There's also an extensive list of wines by the glass. But be careful: it's so much fun to keep sampling that it's easy to run up a hefty bill. ⊠ *1711 N. Charles St., Station North Arts District* ☎ *410/332–0110* ▤ *AE, MC, V* ☺ *Closed Mon. No lunch.*

Bolton Hill

$–$$ ✕ **b.** In a residential neighborhood of lovely, large row houses, this casual corner bistro serves imaginative, Mediterranean-influenced fare. The seasonal menu includes such dishes as roasted vegetable ravioli in sage butter and sesame-encrusted salmon with honey horseradish crème fraîche. Or choose from one of the chalkboard specials, such as the risotto of the day or the "butcher's special." On Sunday, b is a popular spot for brunch. ⊠ *1501 Bolton St., Bolton Hill* ☎ *410/383–8600* ▤ *AE, D, MC, V* ☺ *Closed Mon. No lunch.*

Charles Village

$–$$$ ✕ **The Ambassador Dining Room.** A Tudor-style dining room in a 1930s apartment building is the setting for superb Indian fare. Go for the classics such as chicken *tikka masala* (grilled chicken in a sauce of red pepper, ginger, garlic, and yogurt) or *alu gobi* (spicy potatoes and cauliflower), or sample more creative options such as lamb tenderloin with fennel and chive sauce. In summer the lovely garden is a favorite spot for outdoor dining. The service does not disappoint. ⊠ *3811 Canterbury Rd., Tuscany-Canterbury* ☎ *410/366–1484* ▤ *AE, MC, V.*

$–$$$ ✕ **Gertrude's.** In the Baltimore Museum of Art, this casual yet classy spot cooks up creative Maryland cuisine. Crab cakes, served in many forms, are one option, as are cornmeal-encrusted catfish or one of the many daily specials. In warm weather the outdoor terrace overlooking the sculpture garden makes for very pleasant dining. On Tuesday nights, entrées are only $10. ⊠ *10 Art Museum Dr., Charles Village* ☎ *410/889–3399* ⚠ *Reservations essential* ▤ *AE, MC, V* ☺ *Closed Mon.*

¢–$ ✕ **One World Cafe.** A favorite of Johns Hopkins students, this low-key restaurant, café, and bar is open morning until night for tasty vegetarian fare. Settle onto a couch or one of the small tables for a portobello sandwich with caramelized onions and feta cheese, tofu baked with ginger and served with steamed vegetables, or One World's version of that Baltimore specialty: a crabless crab cake. Smoothies, espresso drinks, microbrews, and mixed drinks from the full bar fill out the menu. ⊠ *100 W. University Pkwy., Tuscany-Canterbury* ☎ *410/235–5777* ▤ *AE, DC, MC, V.*

¢–$ ✕ **Paper Moon Diner.** Everywhere you look in this funky, colorful diner are toys, and other objects glued to the ceilings and walls. People come

7

at all hours (it's open 24/7) for the overstuffed omelets, big stacks of pancakes, burgers, and other classic fare. The waiters have diner attitude—they don't always seem too interested in serving, and the food might take a while—but the place is always lively and entertaining. ⊠ 227 W. 29th St., Charles Village ☎ 410/889–4444 ☰ MC, V.

Hampden

★ ¢–$ ✕ **Golden West Cafe.** On "The Avenue," funky Hampden's main commercial street, Golden West is the go-to spot for breakfast, lunch, and dinner. The place is colorful and eclectic, and so is the menu of diner fare with a Tex-Mex and Asian twist. Try the cold Vietnamese salad with shrimp or the hefty huevos montuleños—fried eggs with yellow corn cakes covered in beans, feta, salsa, and a fried banana (and served at all hours). Large tables make it a good spot for groups, and the bar makes it good for pre- or post-dinner drinks. ⊠ 1105 W. 36th St., Hampden ☎ 410/889–8891 ☰ AE, D, MC, V ⊘ Closed Tues.

Inner Harbor

$$$$ ✕ **Hamptons.** A panoramic view of the Inner Harbor competes with the
Fodor'sChoice restaurant's elegant interior: tables set with bowls of flowers, are spaced
★ generously in a dining room decorated to resemble an English country house. Expect carefully composed seasonal cuisine at once contemporary and classic: roasted pheasant with butternut squash and mushroom risotto in Madeira demi-glace, for instance. The Sunday champagne brunch is a major draw. For a more casual meal, try the hotel's other restaurant, Brighton's. ⊠ Harbor Court Hotel, 550 Light St., Inner Harbor ☎ 410/347–9744 ⌂ Reservations essential ☰ AE, D, MC, V.

$$–$$$$ ✕ **Babalu Grill.** A prominent portrait of Desi Arnaz, conga drum bar stools, live salsa music on weekends: this place is all about fun. Many of the classic Cuban dishes on the menu come from owner Steve DeCastro's family recipes, such as savory ropa vieja (a stew of shredded beef) and seafood paella, brimming with shrimp, shellfish, and chorizo. The bar serves an impressive list of obscure rums and tequilas, and the wine list focuses on South American and Spanish vintages. ⊠ 32 Market Pl., Inner Harbor ☎ 410/234–9898 ☰ AE, D, DC, MC, V.

$$–$$$$ ✕ **Rusty Scupper.** A tourist favorite, the Rusty Scupper undoubtedly has the best view along the waterfront; sunset here is magical, with the sun sinking slowly into the harbor as lights twinkle on the city's skyscrapers. The interior is decorated with light wood and windows from floor to ceiling; the house specialty is seafood, particularly the jumbo lump crab cake, but the menu also includes beef, chicken, and pasta. Reservations are essential on Friday and Saturday, and service can be spotty. ⊠ 402 Key Hwy., Inner Harbor ☎ 410/727–3678 ☰ AE, D, DC, MC, V.

$$–$$$ ✕ **Blue Sea Grill.** Blue is the color, cool is the mood, and the ocean is the source for the fresh seafood served here in many forms. Start with a plate of raw oysters or a bowl of Maryland crab soup, then order from a selection of whole fishes—grilled, broiled, or panfried. The lobster macaroni and cheese is a favorite. ⊠ 614 Water St., Inner Harbor ☎ 410/837–7300 ☰ AE, D, DC, MC, V ⊘ Closed Sun. No lunch.

$$–$$$ ✕**McCormick & Schmick's.** It may be a chain restaurant, but it's a very good one. From its expansive location at the end of Pier 5, on the east side of the waterfront, there's a terrific harbor view; ask to be seated on the patio. More than two-dozen varieties of fish and seafood, available on a daily basis, are flown in from all over the world: the large menu changes daily. Choose from the more than half-dozen varieties of oysters on the half shell, or go for the signature cedar-plank wild Oregon king salmon. ✉ *711 Eastern Ave., Inner Harbor* ☏ *410/234–1300* 🖃 *AE, D, MC, V.*

$ ✕**Afghan Kabob.** A couple of blocks up from the Inner Harbor, this barebones spot serves simple, delicious Afghan fare. Order at the counter—start with the pumpkin appetizer, then try the lamb or beef kebab, which comes with salad, rice, and fresh pita bread, or a vegetarian plate that might include chickpeas, lentils, and okra—and grab a table. It's a good alternative to the pricier options by the water for lunch or an early dinner (it closes at 8 PM). ✉ *37 S. Charles St., City Center* ☏ *410/727–5511* 🖃 *AE, MC, V* ☯ *Closed Sun.*

★ ¢–$ ✕**Attman's.** Open since 1915, this authentic New York–style deli near the Jewish Museum is the king of Baltimore's "Corned Beef Row." Don't be put off by the long lines—they move fairly quickly, and the outstanding corned beef sandwiches are worth the wait, as are the pastrami, homemade chopped liver, and other oversize creations. Attman's closes at 6:30 PM daily. ✉ *1019 Lombard St., Historic Jonestown* ☏ *410/563–2666* 🖃 *AE, DC, MC, V.*

Federal Hill

★ $$$ ✕**Corks.** The creative American cuisine here is as stellar as the impressive wine list and the waitstaff are adept at pairing wines with dishes. Outstanding choices on the seasonal menu might include monkfish osso buco or braised veal breast with woodland mushrooms. It's so cozy in the dimly lighted, wood-panel dining room that you may never want to leave. ✉ *1026 S. Charles St., Federal Hill* ☏ *410/752–3810* ⌖ *Reservations essential* 🖃 *AE, D, MC, V* ☯ *No lunch.*

$$–$$$ ✕**The Bicycle.** Bright, energetic, and often noisy, Bicycle serves intelligent, creative cuisine. Caribbean, Asian, and Southwestern flavors influence the short but engaging menu, which is supplemented by specials that make use of the fresh seafood and local seasonal produce. Tables are close in this small bistro, but proximity enhances its liveliness. ✉ *1444 Light St., Federal Hill* ☏ *410/234–1900* ⌖ *Reservations essential* 🖃 *AE, D, MC, V* ☯ *Closed Sun. No lunch.*

$$–$$ ✕**Blue Agave.** At this authentic regional Mexican and American Southwestern restaurant, every sauce and salsa is made daily to create pure, concentrated flavors—the traditional mole sauces here are delicious. Dishes such as grilled quail served with both green and spicy yellow moles, or the more familiar chicken enchiladas with mole poblano, demonstrate the kitchen's command of this rich, complex concoction. More than 80 different kinds of tequila are available, and you would be hard-pressed to find a better margarita in the city. ✉ *1032 Light St., Federal Hill* ☏ *410/576–3938* 🖃 *AE, D, MC, V* ☯ *Closed Mon.*

7

★ **$–$$** ✕ **Matsuri.** Sit down at the counter or make your way to one of the tables as this small sushi place, a Federal Hill favorite. You can order by the roll, or opt for one of the bento boxes, udon soups, or tempura dishes like the signature crab and shrimp, wrapped in rice and seaweed and deep fried. ✉ *1105 S. Charles St., Federal Hill* ☎ *410/752–8561* ▤ *AE, D, MC, V* ◔ *No lunch weekends.*

Little Italy

$–$$$ ✕ **Chiapparelli's.** At this neighborhood favorite, families come to celebrate milestones—baptisms, communions, graduations, and such. Pictures of the Baltimore landscape adorn the redbrick walls, and some white-cloth tables overlook one of Little Italy's main streets. The reasonably priced pasta selections rely on standards, but there's also more upscale fare such as chicken Giuseppe: breaded chicken breast with spinach, crabmeat, and provolone in a lemon wine sauce. ✉ *237 S. High St., Little Italy* ☎ *410/837–0309* ▤ *AE, D, DC, MC, V.*

☾ **$–$$** ✕ **Amicci's.** At this self-proclaimed "very casual eatery," you don't have to spend a fortune to get a satisfying taste of Little Italy. Blue jean–clad diners and walls hung with movie posters make for a fun atmosphere. Service is friendly and usually speedy, and the food comes in large portions. Try the chicken Lorenzo: breaded chicken breast covered in a marsala wine sauce, red peppers, Prosciutto, and provolone. ✉ *231 S. High St., Little Italy* ☎ *410/528–1096* ▤ *AE, D, DC, MC, V.*

$–$$ ✕ **La Tavola.** Specializing in homemade, inventive pasta dishes, La Tavola is a cut above other Little Italy spaghetti houses. Don't miss the *mafalde alla fiorentina,* wide pasta with spinach, ricotta, pine nuts, and raisins in a nutmeg-flavor cream sauce. Veal cannelloni in béchamel tomato sauce is another standout. If you're still hungry after one of La Tavola's generous plates of pasta, the fresh fish is a good bet, as is the roasted veal chop. ✉ *248 Albemarle St., Little Italy* ☎ *410/685–1859* ▤ *AE, D, DC, MC, V.*

Fells Point

★ **$$$–$$$$** ✕ **The Black Olive.** One of the best Greek restaurants in the country, the Black Olive specializes in impeccably fresh seafood. Let the waiter give you a guided tour of the catch of the day, which reclines on a bed of ice in the kitchen case. You can have your selection simply grilled, lightly dressed, and filleted for you table-side, accompanied by a glass from the wine list's thoughtful selection of oft-neglected Greek vintages. For an appetizer be sure to try the *kakavia,* a spicy Greek bouillabaisse served with irresistible bread warm from the brick oven. ✉ *814 S. Bond St., at Shakespeare St., Fells Point* ☎ *410/276–7141* ⬧ *Reservations essential* ▤ *AE, D, MC, V* ◔ *Closed Mon. No lunch.*

★ **$$$–$$$$** ✕ **Charleston.** The kitchen here may have a South Carolina low-country accent, but it's also skilled in the fundamentals of French cooking. Inside the glowingly lighted dining room, such classics as she-crab soup, crisp cornmeal-crusted oysters, and spoon bread complement more elegant fare, such as squab roasted with apples. Best bets are Southern-inspired dishes such as shrimp sautéed with andouille and Cajun ham served over creamy grits. ✉ *1000 Lancaster St., Fells Point* ☎ *410/332–7373* ⬧ *Reservations essential* ▤ *AE, D, MC, V* ◔ *Closed Sun. No lunch.*

$$–$$$ ✕ **Louisiana.** Fells Point's most elegant dining room feels like a spacious, opulent antebellum parlor. The menu mixes creole and French with a touch of New American, and is accompanied by an expansive, thoughtful wine list. The lobster bisque, with a dollop of sherry added at the table by one of Louisiana's impeccable servers, is sublime, and crawfish étouffée is a worthy follow-up course. ✉ *1708 Aliceanna St., Fells Point* ☎ *410/327–2610* ▭ *AE, DC, MC, V* ☻ *No lunch.*

$$–$$$ ✕ **Obrycki's Crab House.** For 50 years Obrycki's has served steamed crabs with its unique black pepper seasoning. Go for the crabs: beyond that, the seafood menu is standard and the food just fair. ✉ *1727 E. Pratt St., Fells Point* ☎ *410/732–6399* ▭ *AE, D, DC, MC, V* ☻ *Closed mid-Dec.–early Mar.*

$–$$ ✕ **Samos.** East of Fells Point is Greektown (15 minutes by car from Inner Harbor hotels), home to Baltimore's Greek population. An informal restaurant, done in classic blue and white, Samos serves excellent Greek fare. Portions are generous, with lamb souvlaki and tender, juicy gyros leading the menu. ✉ *600 Oldham St., Greektown* ☎ *410/675–5292* ▭ *AE, D, DC, MC, V* ☻ *Closed Sun.*

¢–$ ✕ **Blue Moon Dining House.** A cozy café with a celestial motif appropriate to its name, the Blue Moon is a favorite for breakfast, served until 3 PM daily. Start with one of the enormous housemade cinnamon rolls, but save room for excellent brunch fare such as crab Benedict and sky-high French toast with fruit compote. On Friday and Saturday the Moon reopens at 11 PM and stays open all night, attracting revelers from Fells Point's many clubs and bars. On weekend mornings there's often a line, but it's well worth the wait. ✉ *1621 Aliceanna St., Fells Point* ☎ *410/522–3940* ≈ *Reservations not accepted* ▭ *AE, D, MC, V.*

¢–$ ✕ **Pazo.** An expansive 19th-century warehouse is now home to this fashionable, two-level restaurant serving Mediterranean-influenced fare. Enjoy tapas in the rich, red-hue setting lighted by giant wrought-iron chandeliers, or head upstairs to the mezzanine and watch the crowd below. Tasty tapas and warm, stylish decor make Pazo one of the city's better dinner destinations. ✉ *1425 Aliceanna St., Fells Point* ☎ *410/534–7296* ▭ *AE, DC, MC, V* ☻ *No lunch.*

Canton

★ **$–$$$**   ✕ **Bo Brooks.** Picking steamed crabs on Bo Brooks's waterfront deck with a pitcher of cold beer at hand as sailboats and tugs ply the harbor is a quintessential Baltimore pleasure. Brooks serves its famous crustaceans year-round, along with a menu of Chesapeake seafood classics. Locals know to stick to the Maryland crab soup, crab dip, jumbo lump crab cakes, and fried oysters. ✉ *2701 Boston St., Canton* ☎ *410/558–0202* ▭ *AE, D, MC, V.*

WHERE TO STAY

When booking a hotel or bed-and-breakfast in Baltimore, focus on the Inner Harbor, where you're likely to spend a good deal of time. The downside to staying in hotels near downtown is the noise level, which can rise early in the morning and stay up late into the night—especially if there's a baseball or football game. For quieter options, head to neighborhoods like Fells Point and Canton. All of the hotels listed are within a half-hour drive of the harbor. If you're coming to Baltimore in the summer or near Preakness (the third weekend in May), reserve your rooms well in advance. Hunt Valley, a suburb about a 25-minute drive north of Baltimore on I–83, has several convenient budget options.

WHAT IT COSTS					
	$$$$	$$$	$$	$	¢
HOTELS	over $250	$175–$250	$130–$175	$80–$130	under $80

Hotel prices are for a standard double room, excluding state (5% in Maryland) and Baltimore City tax (7.5%) for a total of 12.5% room tax.

Mount Vernon

$$$ 🏨 **Peabody Court.** Built as a luxury apartment house in 1924, this 13-story hotel faces the Washington Monument. The hotel retains its original distinguished lobby and other period touches such as marble bathrooms. Rooms have desks and two-line speakerphones with data ports; a lobby business center has a fax machine, copier, and computer station. Rooms with park views are the best choice. A courtesy shuttle will ferry you to destinations within a 2-mi radius. The hotel bistro, George's on Mount Vernon Square, serves American and Italian cuisine. ⊠ *612 Cathedral St., Mount Vernon, 21201* ☎ *410/727–7101* 🖶 *410/ 789–3312* ⊕ *www.peabodycourthotel.com* ⮢ *104 rooms* ⚭ *Restaurant, in-room safes, minibars, refrigerators, cable TV, gym, library, Wi-Fi, in-room broadband, business services, meeting rooms, parking (fee), no-smoking floors* ☰ *AE, D, DC, MC, V* ⒶⓄⓁ *CP.*

★ $ 🏨 **Abacrombie.** In a large, late-19th-century building, once a private house, this intimate inn has rooms furnished in Victorian style and an outstanding restaurant. It's across the street from the Meyerhoff Symphony Hall and in walking distance of MICA, the University of Baltimore, and Amtrak's Penn Station. Breakfast is served in the parlor room. The four-story inn has no elevator. ⊠ *58 W. Biddle St., Mount Vernon, 21201* ☎ *410/244–7227 or 888/922–3437* 🖶 *410/244–8415* ⊕ *www.badger-inn.com* ⮢ *12 rooms* ⚭ *Restaurant, cable TV, bar, free parking; no smoking* ☰ *AE, D, MC, V* ⒶⓄⓁ *CP.*

City Center

$$$ 🏨 **Hampton Inn and Suites.** The free breakfast and the logo may be the same, but this Hampton Inn tries to be more urban and chic than others in the chain. In an early-1900s office building that lay vacant for many years, the hotel follows the historical direction of the structure, but keeps things contemporary. Rooms, done in warm mauve and beige and dark wood, have a clubby, streamlined look. The biggest and most expensive rooms, on the top floor, are studio suites in the former executive offices. ⊠ *131 E. Redwood St., City Center, 21202* ☎ *410/539– 7888* 🖶 *410/539–7405* ⊕ *www.baltimorehamptoninn.com* ⮢ *116* *rooms, 10 studio suites* ♿ *Cable TV, indoor pool, gym, Wi-Fi, Internet room, business services, 2 meeting rooms, parking (fee), no-smoking floors* ▭ *AE, D, DC, MC, V.*

$$ 🏨 **Radisson Plaza Lord Baltimore.** Baltimore's historic landmark hotel, the Radisson extends its Jazz Age elegance to the guest rooms, which have been restored to their original style. Built in 1928, this 23-story hotel is distinguished by an elegantly gilded art deco lobby. Rooms on the south side have the best view, and from the top three floors you can see the harbor. The hotel is quiet and comfortable, and the location is central, three blocks from the Baltimore Convention Center or Harborplace. ✉ *20 W. Baltimore St., City Center, 21202* ☎ *410/539–8400* 🖷 *410/625–1060* ⊕ *www.radisson.com/lordbaltimore* ⇌ *440 rooms, 4 condos, 6 suites* ♿ *Restaurant, cable TV, gym, sauna, bar, Wi-Fi, Internet room, business services, meeting rooms, parking (fee), no-smoking floors* ▭ *AE, D, DC, MC, V.*

★ **$$** 🏨 **Tremont Park.** Built in the 1960s as an apartment house, the 13-story Tremont is now a European-style all-suites hotel that's elegant but still comfortable. The lobby and hotel restaurant, 8 East, are intimate and private—qualities attracting guests who might be easily recognized. The suites come in two sizes. The Tremont is near Mount Vernon and the Inner Harbor. The concierge will help arrange local transportation, which in most cases is free. ✉ *8 E. Pleasant St., City Center, 21202* ☎ *410/ 576–1200 or 800/873–6668* 🖷 *410/244–1154* ⊕ *www. tremontsuitehotels.com* ⇌ *60 suites* ♿ *Restaurant, kitchenettes, microwaves, cable TV, gym, bar, concierge, meeting rooms, parking (fee)* ▭ *AE, D, DC, MC, V.*

$$ 🏨 **Wyndham Inner Harbor.** One of Baltimore's largest, this hotel (four blocks from the harbor) divides its rooms between two towers and also houses the largest ballroom in the city, which makes it especially popular with conventioneers. Rooms, decorated in light colors, have a contemporary flair and marble-floor bathrooms. Amenities include in-room voice mail, Internet access, hair dryers, and ironing boards. The hotel restaurant is Don Shula's Steak House, where the menu is presented on an official NFL football autographed by Shula, a former coach for the Baltimore Colts. ✉ *101 W. Fayette St., City Center, 21201* ☎ *410/ 752–1100* 🖷 *410/752–0832* ⊕ *www.wyndham.com/hotels/BWIIH/ main.wnt* ⇌ *707 rooms, 21 suites* ♿ *2 restaurants, refrigerators, cable TV, pool, gym, bar, Wi-Fi, in-room broadband, Internet room, business services, convention center, meeting rooms, parking (fee), no-smoking rooms* ▭ *AE, D, DC, MC, V.*

★ **$–$$** 🏨 **Tremont Plaza Hotel.** This 37-story all-suites hotel, once an apartment building, is in the densest part of the business district. Its plain facade and minuscule brass-and-marble lobby belie the tasteful earth-tone guest rooms, which are a favorite of musicians and actors performing at local theaters. The suites come in six sizes. The best views of the city and the small park in the center of St. Paul Place are from rooms with numbers ending in 06. The restaurant, Tugs, has a nautical theme and a menu rich in seafood. ✉ *222 St. Paul Pl., City Center, 21202* ☎ *410/ 727–2222 or 800/873–6668* 🖷 *410/685–4215* ⊕ *www. tremontsuitehotels.com* ⇌ *253 suites* ♿ *Restaurant, kitchenettes, cable*

7

TV, pool, gym, sauna, bar, concierge, in-room broadband, meeting rooms, parking (fee) ☰ *AE, D, DC, MC, V.*

Inner Harbor

★ **$$$$** 🏨 **Harbor Court.** The entrance to the most prestigious hotel in Baltimore is set back from the street by a brick courtyard that provides an immediate sense of tranquillity. A grand spiral staircase dominates the lobby, which is decorated in English country opulence. All guest rooms include such deluxe touches as twice-daily maid service, plush bathrobes, and TVs in the bathrooms; upscale suite amenities also include 6-foot marble tubs, canopied four-poster beds, and CD players. Waterside rooms have a commanding view of the harbor, but courtyard rooms are quietest. ⊠ *550 Light St., Inner Harbor, 21202* 📞 *410/234–0550 or 800/ 824–0076* 🖷 *410/659–5925* 🌐 *www.harborcourt.com* 🛏 *195 rooms, 23 suites* 🍴 *2 restaurants, coffee shop, minibars, room TVs with movies and video games, tennis court, indoor pool, health club, sauna, racquetball, bar, library, concierge, Wi-Fi, in-room broadband, Internet room, business services, convention center, meeting rooms, parking (fee), no-smoking floors* ☰ *AE, D, DC, MC, V.*

$$$–$$$$ 🏨 **Baltimore Marriott Inner Harbor.** This 10-story hotel is a block away from Oriole Park at Camden Yards, Harborplace, and the convention center. The public areas are nondescript but surprisingly tranquil, as are the rooms, decorated in teal, mauve, and gray. The best views are from rooms facing the Inner Harbor and the ballpark. Rooms on the 10th floor come with concierge-level privileges. ⊠ *110 S. Eutaw St., Inner Harbor, 21201* 📞 *410/962–0202 or 800/228–9290* 🖷 *410/625–7832* 🌐 *www.marriott.com* 🛏 *524 rooms, 2 suites* 🍴 *2 restaurants, cable TV, indoor pool, gym, sauna, bar, concierge, in-room broadband, Internet room, business services, meeting rooms, parking (fee), no-smoking rooms* ☰ *AE, D, DC, MC, V.*

$$$–$$$$ 🏨 **Marriott Baltimore Waterfront.** The city's tallest hotel and the only one directly on the inner harbor itself, this upscale 31-story Marriott has a neoclassical interior that uses multihue marbles, rich jewel-tone walls, and photographs of Baltimore architectural landmarks. Although it's at the eastern end of the Inner Harbor, all downtown attractions are within walking distance; there's also a water taxi stop right by the front door. Most rooms offer unobstructed views of the city and harbor; ask for one that faces west toward downtown for a splendid panorama of the waterfront and skyscrapers. ⊠ *700 Aliceanna St., Inner Harbor East, 21202* 📞 *410/385–3000* 🖷 *410/895–1900* 🌐 *www.marriotthotels.com/BWIWF* 🛏 *751 rooms* 🍴 *Restaurant, coffee shop, in-room safes, minibars, indoor pool, health club, lounge, in-room broadband, business services, meeting rooms, parking (fee), no-smoking floors* ☰ *AE, D, DC, MC, V.*

$$$–$$$$ 🏨 **Renaissance Harborplace Hotel.** The most conveniently located of the Inner Harbor hotels—across the street from the shopping pavilions—the Renaissance Harborplace meets the needs of tourists, business travelers, and conventioneers. Guest rooms are light and cheerful, with amenities that include coffeemakers, terry robes, hair dryers, and ironing boards. Some rooms have a view of the harbor, the downtown landscape, or the indoor courtyard. The hotel adjoins the Gallery, a four-story shopping mall. ✉ *202 E. Pratt St., Inner Harbor, 21202* ☎ *410/547–1200 or 800/468–3571* 🖷 *410/539–5780* ⊕ *www.renaissancehotels.com/BWISH* 🛏 *562 rooms, 60 suites* ♨ *Restaurant, minibars, indoor pool, gym, sauna, bar, in-room broadband, Internet room, business services, convention center, meeting rooms, parking (fee), no-smoking rooms* ▭ *AE, D, DC, MC, V.*

$$–$$$$ 🏨 **Hyatt Regency.** This stretch of Light Street is practically a highway, but the unenclosed skyways allow ready pedestrian access to both Inner Harbor attractions and the convention center. Rooms have rich gold and black-purple prints and cherrywood furniture; most rooms have views of the harbor or the city. The lobby has glass elevators and the chain's trademark atrium. The 12th floor is the club level, with complimentary breakfast, evening hors d'oeuvres, and a private concierge available. Atop the hotel, the Pisces restaurant and lounge provides stunning city views, especially at night. ✉ *300 Light St., Inner Harbor, 21202* ☎ *410/528–1234 or 800/233–1234* 🖷 *410/685–3362* ⊕ *baltimore.hyatt.com* 🛏 *488 rooms, 26 suites* ♨ *2 restaurants, 3 tennis courts, pool, gym, sauna, 2 bars, Wi-Fi, Internet room, business services, parking (fee), no-smoking floors* ▭ *AE, D, DC, MC, V.*

$$–$$$ 🏨 **Days Inn Inner Harbor.** Less than three blocks from the Inner Harbor, this nine-story redbrick building provides reliable and relatively economical accommodations in the center of town. The utilitarian, pastel-hue guest rooms are sparsely furnished, but each has a small desk and phone with voice mail and Internet access. ✉ *100 Hopkins Pl., Inner Harbor East, 21201* ☎ *410/576–1000* 🖷 *410/576–9437* ⊕ *www.daysinnerharbor.com* 🛏 *250 rooms* ♨ *Restaurant, refrigerators, pool, bar, Wi-Fi, Internet room, business services, meeting rooms, parking (fee), no-smoking rooms* ▭ *AE, D, DC, MC, V.*

$–$$$ 🏨 **Courtyard by Marriott Baltimore Inner Harbor.** One block from the Inner Harbor waterfront and adjacent to Little Italy, this lodging is the farthest east of the Inner Harbor hotels. With sunny rooms in soothing neutral tones, the Courtyard Inner Harbor is a comfortable and attractive alternative to more central hotels with similar amenities and higher rates. Most downtown attractions are still within walking distance, though the stadiums and convention center are more comfortably reached by car or cab. ✉ *1000 Aliceanna St., Inner Harbor East, 21202* ☎ *443/923–4000* 🖷 *443/923–9970* ⊕ *www.marriott.com/BWIDT* 🛏 *205 rooms* ♨ *Restaurant, cable TV, pool, gym, business services, 4 meeting rooms, parking (fee), no-smoking floors* ▭ *AE, D, DC, MC, V.*

Fells Point

$$$–$$$$ 🏨 **Inn at Henderson's Wharf.** Built in the mid-1800s as a B&O Railroad tobacco warehouse, this richly decorated, warmly inviting B&B–style inn has harbor or garden views from all of its rooms. The inn is at the water's edge, on the very peninsula that gave Fells Point its name. Adjacent to the inn is a marina with slips to 150 feet; all possible amenities are available to visiting yachters. ✉ *1000 Fell St., Fells Point, 21231* ☎ *410/522–7777 or 800/522–2088* 🖷 *410/522–7087* ⊕ *www.hendersonswharf.com* 🛏 *37 rooms* ♨ *Gym, concierge, Wi-Fi, in-room* *broadband, Internet room, business services, meeting rooms, free parking; no smoking* ⊟ *AE, DC, MC, V* ⑩ *CP.*

$$$ ⊞ **The Admiral Fell Inn.** This inn is an upright anchor at the center of action in funky Fells Point. By joining together buildings constructed between the late 1770s and the 1920s, the owners created a structure that resembles a small, European-style hotel, with lots of character and quirks. The rooms, which vary in shape, all have four-poster canopy beds. Three suites and eight rooms have whirlpool baths. Some hallways have a few stairs, and some rooms face a quiet, interior courtyard: if steps or street noise bother you, let the reservation agent know. ⊠ *888 S. Broadway, Fells Point, 21231* ☎ *410/522–7377 or 800/292–4667* 🖷 *410/522–0707* ⊕ *www.admiralfell.com* ⇦ *80 rooms* ⚲ *Restaurant, cable TV, pub, some Wi-Fi, in-room broadband, Internet room, meeting rooms, free parking* ⊟ *AE, DC, MC, V* ⑩ *CP.*

$$–$$$ ⊞ **Celie's Waterfront Bed & Breakfast.** Proprietors Nancy and Kevin Kupec oversee every detail of this small inn in the heart of Fells Point. Guest rooms, all with private bath, are furnished in Early American style; two suites accommodate large groups. Upscale amenities include down comforters, terry robes, fireplaces, and whirlpool baths. Continental breakfast is served in the cozy dining room. The rooftop deck provides a wonderful view of Baltimore's skyline and harbor. ⊠ *1714 Thames St., Fells Point, 21231* ☎ *410/522–2323 or 800/432–0184* 🖷 *410/522–2324* ⊕ *www.celieswaterfront.com* ⇦ *7 rooms, 2 suites* ⚲ *Dining room, cable TV, Wi-Fi, parking (fee)* ⊟ *AE, D, MC, V* ⑩ *CP.*

Canton

$$–$$$ ⊞ **Inn at 2920.** In the heart of one of the city's liveliest neighborhoods, this stylish B&B is dedicated to tranquil, luxurious living. Low-allergen surroundings (natural fiber carpeting, low-chemical cleaning products, purified air) and high thread–count sheets are standard amenities, and each room has a Jacuzzi bathtub, satellite television with VCR, and CD player. Full-course breakfasts generally include fresh fruit salad, omelets, and waffles or pancakes, but different dietary needs can be accommodated. ⊠ *2920 Elliott St., 21224* ☎ *410/342–4450* 🖷 *410/342–6436* ⊕ *www.theinnat2920.com* ⇦ *4 rooms* ⚲ *Cable TV, in-room VCRs, Wi-Fi; no room phones, no kids under 13, no smoking, no pets* ⊟ *AE, MC, V* ⑩ *BP.*

Roland Park

$$–$$$$ ⊞ **Inn at the Colonnade.** Directly across the street from Johns Hopkins and within walking distance of the Baltimore Museum of Art, this hotel is also 10 minutes north of downtown. Rooms are welcoming, with rich, warm furnishings, and there are extras such as a glass-dome swimming pool and whirlpool baths. ⊠ *4 W. University Pkwy., Tuscany-Canterbury, 21218* ☎ *410/235–5400* 🖷 *410/235–5572* ⊕ *www.doubletree.com* ⇦ *125 rooms, 19 suites* ⚲ *Restaurant, cable TV, indoor pool, gym, hot tub, lobby lounge, Wi-Fi, business services, meeting rooms, parking (fee), no-smoking rooms* ⊟ *AE, D, DC, MC, V.*

$–$$$ ⊞ **Radisson Hotel at Cross Keys.** Ten minutes north of downtown, this secluded hotel is a respite from city bustle. Rooms come with high-speed

Internet access along with cheerful French country style. The health conscious will appreciate the wooded walking trails, tennis courts, and state-of-the-art exercise equipment. The hotel is adjacent to an outdoor mall with high-end boutique shopping. There's complimentary shuttle service to the Inner Harbor. ⊠ *5100 Falls Rd., Roland Park, 21210* 📞 *410/ 532–6900 or 800/756–7285* 📠 *410/532–2403* 🌐 *www.radisson.com* 🛏 *147 rooms, 10 suites* ✦ *Restaurant, cable TV, pool, gym, lounge, Wi-Fi, Internet room, business services, meeting rooms, free parking, no-smoking floors* 🖃 *AE, D, DC, MC, V.*

Northern Suburbs

$–$$ 🏨 **Courtyard by Marriott Hunt Valley.** About 25 minutes from downtown, in an affluent suburb that's a growing corporate center, this motel is comfortable and affordable. Guest rooms are as standardized as Courtyard's signature white-stucco exterior; coffeemakers, ironing boards, and hair dryers are added conveniences. The neighbors are office buildings, which means rooms are quiet at night but have uninteresting views. The nearby York and Shawan road corridors have many restaurants, and there's public transportation to downtown via the light-rail Hunt Valley stop. The restaurant serves breakfast only. ⊠ *221 International Circle, Hunt Valley, 21030* 📞 *410/584–7070* 📠 *410/ 584–8151* 🌐 *www.marriotthotels.com/BWIHU* 🛏 *134 rooms, 12 suites* ✦ *Restaurant, cable TV, indoor pool, gym, hot tub, bar, in-room broadband, Internet room, business services, free parking* 🖃 *AE, D, DC, MC, V.*

$ 🏨 **Hampton Inn Hunt Valley.** Guest rooms at this suburban hotel are brightly decorated with basic furnishings. The property is within walking distance of a light-rail station for transportation to downtown Baltimore; the city is an easy 25-minute drive directly down I–83. Although there's no restaurant in the hotel, a free breakfast bar is available every morning, and many restaurants are nearby. ⊠ *11200 York Rd., Hunt Valley, 21031* 📞 *410/527–1500* 📠 *410/771–0819* 🌐 *www.hamptoninn. com* 🛏 *125 rooms* ✦ *Refrigerators, cable TV, gym, Wi-Fi, Internet room, free parking* 🖃 *AE, D, DC, MC, V* 🍽 *CP.*

NIGHTLIFE & THE ARTS

The *City Paper* (www.citypaper.com), a free weekly distributed in shops and yellow street-corner boxes, has the most comprehensive and complete calendar for Baltimore events; it's published every Wednesday. Other event listings appear in the "Live" Thursday insert to the *Baltimore Sun* (www.baltimoresun.com/live) and the monthly *Baltimore* magazine.

Both Fells Point, just east of the Inner Harbor, and Federal Hill, due south, have hosts of bars, restaurants, and clubs draw a rowdy, largely collegiate, crowd. If you're seeking quieter surroundings, head for the upscale comforts of downtown or Mount Vernon clubs and watering holes.

Bars & Lounges

Upstairs at **The Brewer's Art** (⊠ 1106 N. Charles St., Mount Vernon 📞 410/ 547–6925) is an elegant bar and lounge with armchairs, marble pillars, and chandeliers, plus a dining room with terrific food; downstairs, the dark basement bar specializes in Belgian-style beers. With its stylized art deco surroundings, the funky **Club Charles** (⊠ 1724 N. Charles St., North Arts District ☎ 410/727–8815) is a favorite hangout for an artsy crowd, moviegoers coming from the Charles Theater across the street, and, reputation has it, John Waters. The patio at the waterside **DuClaw Brewery** (⊠ 901 S. Bond St., Fells Point ☎ 410/563–3400) is a great spot for an early-evening pint; the restaurant serves bar fare with a twist, but stick to the standards.

The well-heeled gather at the Harbor Court Hotel in the **Explorer's Lounge** (⊠ 550 Light St., Inner Harbor ☎ 410/234–0550), where there are antique elephant-tusk lamps and faux leopard-skin chairs. Enjoy a cigar and pick a single-malt scotch from the largest selection in town. A pianist performs every night, and on Friday and Saturday nights there's a jazz trio. **Red Maple** (⊠ 930 N. Charles St., Mount Vernon ☎ 410/547–0149) is one of the city's most stylish spots for drinks and tapas. The **Tusk Lounge** (⊠ 924 N. Charles St., Mount Vernon ☎ 410/547–8480), above the Brass Elephant restaurant, is a cozy, classy place for drinks.

At **Pickles Pub** (⊠ 520 Washington Blvd., Inner Harbor ☎ 410/752–1784), sports fans banter about trivia, dispute scores, and commiserate over scandals. This is a favorite postgame hangout for Orioles and Ravens fans. **McCafferty's** (⊠ 1501 Sulgrave Ave., Mt. Washington ☎ 410/664–2200), named for former Baltimore Colts coach Don McCafferty, is a haven for fans of both pigskin and beef.

Beer lovers should visit **Max's Taphouse** (⊠ 737 S. Broadway, Fells Point ☎ 410/675–6297), which has more than 70 brews on tap and about 300 more in bottles. The **Horse You Came In On** (⊠ 1626 Thames St., Fells Point ☎ 410/327–8111) is a dim, quiet neighborhood tavern during the day, and a raucous bar with live music almost every night. The **Thirsty Dog Pub** (⊠ 20 E. Cross St., Federal Hill ☎ 410/727–6077) has no TVs, so you focus more on conversation. About 10 beers are made from in-house recipes, and always served two at a time in 10-ounce glass mugs. At the top of the Belvedere Hotel, the **13th Floor** (⊠ 1 E. Chase St., Mount Vernon ☎ 410/347–0888) offers a great view, long martini list, and live dance music. **Club Hippo** (⊠ 1 W. Eager St., Mount Vernon ☎ 410/547–0069) is Baltimore's longest-reigning gay bar. **Gallagher's** (⊠ 940 S. Conkling St., Canton ☎ 410/327–3966) is the city's most popular lesbian bar. A dance club, martini bar, and pub have all helped make **Grand Central** (⊠ 1003 N. Charles St., Mount Vernon ☎ 410/752–7133) into a hip gay hotspot.

Classical Music

An die Musik (⊠ 409 N. Charles St., Mount Vernon ☎ 410/385–2638) is an intimate space for classical, jazz, and world music. **Meyerhoff Symphony Hall** (⊠ 1212 Cathedral St., Mount Vernon ☎ 410/783–8000) is the city's principal concert hall and home of the Baltimore Symphony Orchestra. **Friedberg Hall** (⊠ E. Mount Vernon Pl. and Charles St., Mount Vernon ☎ 410/659–8124), part of the Peabody Conservatory of Music, is the scene of recitals, concerts, and opera performances by students, faculty, and distinguished guests. At the outdoor **Pier Six Con-**

cert Pavilion (✉ Pier 6 at Pratt St., Inner Harbor ☎ 410/752–8632) there's both pavilion and lawn seating for concerts showcasing top national musicians and groups. Concerts run from June to September.

Comedy Clubs

The Comedy Factory (✉ 36 Light St., Inner Harbor ☎ 410/752–4189) is one of the best local spots to see live standup.

Film

The **Charles Theater** (✉ 1711 N. Charles St., Mount Vernon ☎ 410/727–3456) is Baltimore's preeminent venue for first-run, foreign, and art films. **Rotunda Cinematheque** (✉ 11 W. 40th St., Roland Park ☎ 410/235–4800) has two small theaters showing independent films. The **Senator Theatre** (✉ 5904 York Rd., Belvedere Square ☎ 410/435–8338) is the city's grande dame, a rare surviving example of a large neighborhood theater built during Hollywood's golden age.

Pop Music

The 8x10 Club (✉ 8–10 E. Cross St., Federal Hill ☎ 410/625–2000) is one of the city's premier spots for live music, from rock and reggae, to jazz, blues, and soul. The spring-loaded dance floor bounces under large crowds, and there is barely a bad place to stand inside. For some of the city's best and most authentic live blues and rockabilly, head to The **Full Moon Saloon** (✉ 1710 Aliceanna St., Fells Point ☎ 410/276–6388), which hosts live music every night. **The Ottobar** (✉ 2549 N. Howard St., Mount Vernon ☎ 410/662–0069) is the city's venue for live alternative music—a hipster magnet. **Sonar** (✉ 407 E. Saratoga St., Mount Vernon ☎ 410/327–8333) has three separate spaces: a warehouse with a large stage, a club room, and a smaller lounge. **Rams Head Live** (✉ 20 Market Place in Power Plant Live, Inner Harbor ☎ 410/244–8854) is one of the city's newest live music venues, regularly featuring international and local bands.

Theater

The **Baltimore Theatre Project** (✉ 45 W. Preston St., Mount Vernon ☎ 410/752–8558) is dedicated to showing original and experimental theater, music, and dance. **Center Stage** (✉ 700 N. Calvert St., Mount Vernon ☎ 410/332–0033) performs works by Shakespeare and Samuel Beckett as well as contemporary playwrights. The intimate **Fells Point Corner Theater** (✉ 251 S. Ann St., Fells Point ☎ 410/276–7837), an 85-seat venue focused on acting and directing workshops, stages eight off-Broadway productions a year, along with readings and poetry slams. A beautifully restored 1914 movie palace is home to the **France-Merrick Performing Arts Center at the Hippodrome** (✉ 12 N. Eutaw St., West Baltimore ☎ 410/837–7400), a stage for concerts, Broadway musicals, and other big productions.

Lyric Opera House (✉ 140 W. Mt. Royal Ave., Mount Vernon ☎ 410/685–5086) hosts plays and musicals in addition to opera productions. **Morris A. Mechanic Theatre** (✉ 25 Hopkins Plaza, at Baltimore and Charles Sts., City Center ☎ 410/625–4230) houses road productions of Broadway hits and serves as a testing ground for Broadway-bound productions. **Spotlighters Theater** (✉ 817 St. Paul St., Mount Vernon

☎ 410/752–1225) is a true community theater, staging locally produced (and cast) works that include original productions, Shakespeare, and musicals; there's one production a month, with performances on weekends. The **Vagabond Players** (✉ 806 S. Broadway, Fells Point ☎ 410/563–9135) hosts performances of recent Broadway hits and theater favorites every weekend.

SPORTS & THE OUTDOORS

Participant Sports

Bicycling

Baltimore lacks any kind of defined network of bicycling paths; exploring the city by bike means riding on the streets, a frequently hazardous experience. Or you could head to one of the city's parks or out of town to dedicated cycling trails. Bikes can be rented from **Light Street Cycles** (✉ 1015 Light St., Federal Hill ☎ 410/685–2234); ask for a map of local trails. Just south of the city is the **Baltimore and Annapolis Trail** (☎ 410/222–6244); to get on the trail near BWI airport, follow I–695 to I–97 south, take Exit 15 onto Dorsey Road, heading west away from the airport. Look for signs for Saw Mill Creek Park, which has 13 mi of paved trails, open space, bridges, and woodlands.

> **DUCKPIN BOWLING**
>
> Invented in Baltimore in 1900, duckpin bowling uses smaller balls and pins. For some fun and some real Baltimore character, head to the **Patterson Bowling Center** (✉ 2105 Eastern Ave., Fells Point ☎ 410/675–1011), the oldest duck pin bowling center in the country.

North of the city, the 21-mi **Northern Central Railroad Hike and Bike Trail** (☎ 410/592–2897) extends along the old Northern Central Railroad to the Maryland–Pennsylvania line. It begins at Ashland Road, just east of York Road in Hunt Valley, and heads north 20 mi to the Pennsylvania border. Parking is available at seven points along the way.

Golf

The *Baltimore Sun*'s **golf guide** (🌐 www.baltimoresun.com/golfguide) gives a detailed and thorough overview of local courses.

Public **Forest Park** (✉ 2900 Hillsdale Rd., North Baltimore ☎ 410/448–4653) has 18 challenging holes (par 71), with a tight, tree-lined front 9 and open back 9. Greens fees are $18 weekdays and $19 on weekends; reservations are accepted. Designed in 1936, **Mount Pleasant** (✉ 6001 Hillen Rd., North Baltimore ☎ 410/254–5100) was for many years the site of the Eastern Open. It has 18 holes of par-71 golf on bent grass. Greens fees are $23 on weekdays and $24 on weekends.

North of the city, **Pine Ridge** (✉ 2101 Dulaney Valley Rd., Lutherville ☎ 410/252–1408) is an attractive, well-maintained 18-hole, par-54 course with water in play; greens fees are $23 on weekdays and $24 on weekends.

Health & Fitness Clubs

A few clubs offer temporary membership to visitors. Your hotel may provide this as a courtesy, so ask the concierge. Among hotels, the **Harbor Court** has by far the best athletic facilities. At the **Downtown Athletic Club** (✉ 210 E. Centre St., Mount Vernon ☎ 410/332–0906), you can pay a daily fee of $20 to play squash and racquetball and to use the indoor pool and exercise equipment. **Gold's Gym** (✉ 601 E. Pratt St., Inner Harbor ☎ 410/576–7771) in the Power Plant charges $15 per day for use of its gym. The exercise facilities and squash courts at the **Meadow Mill Athletic Club** (✉ 3600 Clipper Mill Rd., Hampden ☎ 410/235–7000) are $11 per day.

Running

Scenic places to run around the Inner Harbor include the promenade around the water; Rash Field, on the south side, adjacent to the Science Center and Federal Hill Park; and the path at the water's edge at Fort McHenry. If you're staying in Mount Vernon, head north up Charles Street toward Charles Village and Johns Hopkins University.

Tennis

Courts can be found in the city's public parks, though if you're a serious player, you may be better off using hotel courts or tennis clubs.

Druid Hill Park (✉ Druid Hill Lake Dr., West Baltimore ☎ 410/396–6106) has 24 courts. **Patterson Park** (✉ Eastern Ave., East Baltimore ☎ 410/396–3774) has 10 courts.

Open year-round, the **Cross Keys Tennis Club** (✉ 5100 Falls Rd., Roland Park ☎ 410/433–1800) has courts available for $24–$30 per hour. The courts at the **Orchard Indoor Tennis Club** (✉ 8720 Loch Raven Blvd., Towson ☎ 410/821–6206) are available to nonmembers for $27–$37 per hour.

Spectator Sports

Baseball

The **Baltimore Orioles** (✉ Oriole Park at Camden Yards, 333 W. Camden St., West Baltimore ☎ 410/685–9800 general information, 410/481–7328 for tickets) play in their beautiful ballpark from early April until early October. Think twice about settling on a hot dog and Budweiser for your meal: the stadium also sells lump-meat crab cakes, former Orioles first baseman Boog Powell's barbecued pork loin and beef, and local microbrews, such as Clipper City's Ft. McHenry Lager.

Football

The **Baltimore Ravens** (✉ 1101 Russell St., West Baltimore ☎ 410/261–7283) play in state-of-the-art M&T stadium from August to January.

Horse Racing

On the third Saturday in May the prestigious Preakness Stakes, the second race in the Triple Crown, is run at Baltimore's **Pimlico Race Course** (✉ Hayward and Winner Aves., Northwest Baltimore ☎ 410/542–9400). The course has additional Thoroughbred racing. Call ahead for days and times.

Lacrosse

Lacrosse is serious business in Baltimore: outdoor high school and college lacrosse is very popular and fiercely played in spring, and there's even a professional team. The **Baltimore Bayhawks** (⊠ 2219 York Rd. ☎ 866/994–2957) play major league lacrosse from May through August at the Unitas Stadium at Towson University, which is about 20 minutes north of the Inner Harbor. The **Johns Hopkins University Blue Jays** (⊠ Homewood Field, Charles St. and University Pkwy., Charles Village ☎ 410/516–7490) are a perennial favorite. The **Loyola Greyhounds** (⊠ Charles St. and Cold Spring La., North Baltimore ☎ 410/617–5014), play on their college's campus.

Soccer

The **Blast** (⊠ Baltimore Arena, 201 W. Baltimore St., West Baltimore ☎ 410/732–5278 team, 410/347–2020 arena), a team in the Eastern Division of the Major Indoor Soccer League, plays from October to April.

SHOPPING

Baltimore isn't the biggest shopping town, but it does have some malls and good stores here and there. Hampden (the "p" is silent), a neighborhood west of Johns Hopkins University, has funky shops selling everything from housewares to housedresses along its main drag, 36th Street (better known as "The Avenue"). Some interesting shops can be found along Charles Street in Mount Vernon and along Thames Street in Fells Point. Federal Hill has a few fun shops, particularly for furnishings and vintage items.

Shopping Malls

About 7 mi north of downtown, at Northern Parkway and York Road, is **Belvedere Square** (⊠ E. Belvedere Ave. at York Rd. ☎ 410/464–9773), a small, open-air mall with shops for women's and children's clothing, furniture, and gifts as well as a number of gourmet food shops (the soup at Atwater's is delicious). At the Inner Harbor, the Pratt Street and Light Street pavilions of **Harborplace and the Gallery** (☎ 410/332–4191) contain almost 200 specialty shops that sell everything from business attire to children's toys. The Gallery has J. Crew, Banana Republic, and the Gap, among others. **Owings Mills Town Center** (⊠ Owings Mills exit from I–795, 20 minutes northwest of Inner Harbor, Owings Mills ☎ 410/363–1234) has Macy's and Hecht's department stores; specialty clothing stores; and shoe, toy, and bookstores as well as a multiplex cinema. The mall is at the northern terminus of the city's metro system. **Towson Town Center** (⊠ Dulaney Valley Rd. and Fairmount Ave., ½ mi south of I–695 at Exit 27A, Towson ☎ 410/494–8800) has nearly 200 shops, including Hecht's, Nordstrom, the Gap, and Anthropologie. **Village of Cross Keys** (⊠ 5100 Falls Rd., North Baltimore ☎ 410/323–1000), about 6 mi north of downtown, is an eclectic collection of 30 stores, including Talbot's, Chico's, Williams-Sonoma, Ann Taylor, and some small, high-end boutiques for women's clothing and gifts.

Department Stores

Merchandise at **Hecht's** includes men's, women's, and children's clothing along with housewares. There are five locations around Baltimore, including Owings Mills Town Center and Towson Town Center. Shop for top-name designer goods accompanied by courteous, service-oriented sales staff and live music from a grand piano at **Nordstrom** (⊠ Towson Town Center, 825 Dulaney Valley Rd., Towson ☎ 410/494–9111).

Food Markets

Baltimore's indoor food markets, all of which are at least 100 years old, are a mix of vendors selling fresh fish, meat, produce, and baked goods and a food court, with stands for street food such as crab cakes, sausages, fried chicken, and pizza. Lexington Market is the largest and most famous, and Broadway and Cross Street markets are close behind in terms of local, taste-tempting foods. City markets are generally open year-round, every day but Sunday, until 6.

Broadway Market (⊠ Broadway and Fleet St., Fells Point) has many stalls with fresh fruit, prepared foods, a raw bar, and baked goods that can be eaten at counters or taken outside for picnics along the waterfront. **Cross Street Market** (⊠ Light and Cross Sts., Federal Hill) has a terrific sushi bar along with stands selling produce, sandwiches, steamed crab, and baked items. Cross Street is open late on Friday and Saturday, when the market hosts one of the city's most popular happy hour scenes, attracting crowds of youngish professionals. The city's oldest and largest public market, **Lexington Market** (⊠ Lexington St. between Paca and Eutaw Sts., Downtown ☎ 410/685–6169) has more than 150 vendors selling meat, produce, seafood, baked goods, delicatessen items, poultry, and food products from around the world. Don't miss the world-famous crab cakes at Faidley's Seafood; other local specialties with market stalls are Rheb's chocolates, Polock Johnny's Polish sausages, and Berger's Bakery's chocolate-iced vanilla wafer cookies.

Specialty Stores

Antiques

Many of Baltimore's antiques shops can be found on historic Antique Row, which runs along the 700 and 800 blocks of North Howard Street. Shops include cluttered kitsch boutiques as well as elegant, high-end galleries of furniture and fine art. Fells Point shops are concentrated on Eastern, Fleet, and Aliceanna streets. Hampden shops are found primarily on 36th Street.

The **Antique Warehouse at 1300** (⊠ 1300 Jackson St., at Key Hwy., Federal Hill ☎ 410/659–0663) has 35 dealers under one roof. **Avenue Antiques** (⊠ 901 W. 36th St., Hampden ☎ 410/467–0329) is a collection of multiple dealers, selling antiques from Victorian to mid-century modern. At **Gaines McHale Antiques and Home** (⊠ 836 Leadenhall St., Federal Hill ☎ 410/625–1900) the owners build new pieces with old wood, turning antique armoires, for example, into entertainment centers.

There's also a large selection of unaltered, high-quality country and traditional antiques from England and France. **Second Chance** (✉ 1645 Warner St. Southwest Baltimore ☎ 410/385–1101) salvages unique architectural pieces from old buildings being renovated or destroyed; the store is open Thursday–Saturday 9–5. **The Turnover Shop** (✉ 3855 Roland Ave., Hampden ☎ 410/235–9585) is a consignment shop selling high-end antiques.

Books

Barnes & Noble (✉ 601 E. Pratt St., Inner Harbor ☎ 410/385–1709), in the Power Plant complex at the Inner Harbor, is the city's largest general-interest bookseller.

The **AIA/Baltimore Bookstore** (✉ 11 ½ W. Chase St., Mount Vernon ☎ 410/625–2585) carries all kinds of architecture books. **Atomic Books** (✉ 1100 W. 36th St., Hampden ☎ 410/662–4444) specializes in obscure titles and small-press publications, including independent comics and 'zines, along with videos. There's also a formidable selection of pop-culture toys such as lunch boxes, cookie jars, and stickers. **Book Thing** (✉ 3001 Vineyard La., Waverly ☎ 410/662–5631) takes donations and gives away free books—as many as you like, as long as you promise not to resell them; it's open weekends 9–6. **The Children's Bookstore** (✉ 737 Deepdene Rd., Roland Park ☎ 410/532–2000) is a cozy, well-stocked resource for current and classic children's literature. The **Kelmscott Bookshop** (✉ 32 W. 25th St., Charles Village ☎ 410/235–6810) is known for its enormous, well-preserved stock of old and rare volumes in every major category, especially art, architecture, American and English literature, and travel. **Lambda Rising** (✉ 241 W. Chase St., Mount Vernon ☎ 410/234–0069) is Baltimore's gay, lesbian, and bisexual bookstore. **Mystery Loves Company** (✉ 1730 Fleet St., Fells Point ☎ 410/276–6708) specializes in books and gifts for whodunit fans; the shop stocks an excellent selection of works by Baltimore native son (and inventor of the genre) Edgar Allan Poe.

Children's Clothing

Raw Sugar (✉ 524 E. Belvedere Ave., Belvedere Square ☎ 410/464–1240) carries clothing for the funky, fashionable six-and-under set as well as maternity wear and toys.

Gifts

Many of the city's museums have excellent shops, which are good sources for gifts. **Best of Baltimore** (✉ 301 S. Light St., Inner Harbor ☎ 410/332–4191) carries city-related souvenirs and local specialty products. For unique, truly local mementos of Baltimore, like crab-shape twinkle lights and a kit for cleaning row-house marble steps, **Hometown Girl** (✉ 1001 W. 36th St., Hampden ☎ 410/662–4438) is the place to go. It also stocks local history books and Baltimore guidebooks. The **Tomlinson Craft Collection** (✉ The Rotunda, 711 W. 40th St., Roland Park ☎ 410/338–1572) is a gallery of local artisan handiworks, from fine jewelry to ceramics and metalwork. The **Store Ltd.** (✉ Village of Cross Keys, Roland Park ☎ 410/323–2350) has an eclectic mix of top-quality (and pricey) jewelry, women's sportswear, glassware, and other high-design gifts.

Jewelry

Amaryllis (⊠ The Gallery, 200 E. Pratt St. ☎ 410/576–7622) specializes in handcrafted jewelry from more than 400 artists. Designers come from all over the world for the incredibly wide selection of beads at **Beadazzled** (⊠ 501 N. Charles St., Mount Vernon ☎ 410/837–2323); there's also a selection of already made jewelry.

Men's Clothing

Jos. A. Bank's Clothiers (⊠ 100 E. Pratt St., Inner Harbor ☎ 410/547–1700) is a century-old Baltimore source for men's tailored clothing and casual wear. **Samuel Parker Clothier** (⊠ Mt. Washington Mill, Mt. Washington ☎ 410/464–6180) carries a fine selection of updated traditional clothing by the likes of Ralph Lauren and Samuelson.

Women's Clothing

Jones & Jones (⊠ Village of Cross Keys, Roland Park ☎ 410/532–9645) carries stylish sportswear and business attire. **Ruth Shaw** (⊠ Village of Cross Keys, Roland Park ☎ 410/532–7886) sells the work of European designers like Gaultier and Paul Smith as well as chic evening wear. **Something Else** (⊠ 1611 Sulgrave Ave., Mt. Washington ☎ 410/542–0444) is the source for sophisticated hippie wear: Flax-brand clothes, flowing skirts, big scarves, and colorful sweaters.

Ma Petite Shoe (⊠ 832 W. 36th St., Hampden ☎ 410/235–3442) sells chocolates as well as funky, fabulous shoes. **Oh! Said Rose** (⊠ 840 W. 36th St., Hampden ☎ 410/235–5170) carries fun, feminine clothing with a vintage look. **The Shine Collective** (⊠ 3554 Roland Ave., Hampden ☎ 410/366–6100) carries hip accessories and clothing made by a group of local young designers.

7

SIDE TRIPS FROM BALTIMORE

Not far from Baltimore, Maryland's landscape is dotted with well-preserved 18th- and 19th-century towns. Harford County's Havre de Grace, at the top of the bay, and nearby Aberdeen, with a legacy of military history, make for an ideal day trip. Historic Ellicott City, southwest of Baltimore in Howard County, is a fun place to explore, have lunch, and shop.

Havre de Grace

40 mi northeast of Baltimore (via I–95).

On the site of one of Maryland's oldest settlements is the neatly laid-out town Havre de Grace, reputedly named by the Marquis de Lafayette. This "harbor of mercy," on the Chesapeake Bay at the mouth of the Susquehanna River, was shelled and torched by the British in the War of 1812, and few structures predate that period.

Havre de Grace is about a 40-minute drive from downtown Baltimore. From downtown, take I–395 to I–95; pick up I–95 north to New York and follow it to Harford County and Havre de Grace. Route 155 off Exit 89 leads to downtown Havre de Grace.

The conical **Concord Point Lighthouse** is the oldest continuously operated lighthouse on the Chesapeake Bay. Built in 1827, it was restored in 1980. You can climb up 30 feet for views of the bay, the river, and the town. ⊠ *Concord and Lafayette Sts. at Susquehanna River* ☏ *410/939–9040* ▦ *Free* ⊙ *Apr.–Oct., weekends 1–5.*

The **Havre de Grace Decoy Museum,** housed in a converted power plant, has 1,200 facsimiles of ducks, geese, and swans made from wood, iron, cork, papier-mâché, and plastic. Three classes—decorative, decorative floater, and working decoys—are represented. A festival during the first full weekend in May includes carving contests and demonstrations by retrievers. ⊠ *215 Giles St.* ☏ *410/939–3739* ⊕ *www.decoymuseum. com* ▦ *$6* ⊙ *Mon.–Sat. 10:30–4:30, Sun. noon–4.*

★ The **Ladew Topiary Gardens** displays the life's work of Harvey Smith Ladew. The trees and shrubs are sculpted into geometric forms and lifelike renditions of animals such as a fox and hounds, swans, and even a seahorse. The 15 formal gardens cover 22 acres. Besides the amazing topiary displays are rose, berry, and herb gardens, and a tranquil Japanese garden with pagoda, lily ponds, and lush flowers. In summer there are special events such as concerts and polo matches. The 18th-century manor house is filled with English antiques, paintings, photographs, and fox-hunting memorabilia. The café serves lunch and light snacks. ⊠ *3535 Jarrettsville Pike, 14 mi north of I–695, Monkton* ☏ *410/557–9466* ⊕ *www.ladewgardens.com* ▦ *House and gardens $12, gardens only $8* ⊙ *Mid-Apr.–Oct., weekdays 8–4, weekends 10:30–5.*

One of the few 18th-century structures in Havre de Grace, **Rodgers House** (⊠ 226 N. Washington St.) is a two-story redbrick Georgian town house topped by a dormered attic. The town's most historically significant building, it was the home of Admiral John Rodgers, who fired the first shot in the War of 1812. Like most of the other historic houses in Havre de Grace, it's closed to the public but still worth a drive past.

The **Steppingstone Museum** is a 10-acre complex of seven restored turn-of-the-20th-century farm buildings plus a replica of a canning house. Among the 12,000-plus artifacts in the collection are a horse-drawn tractor and an early gas-powered version, manual seeders and planters, and horse-drawn plows. A blacksmith, a weaver, a wood-carver, a cooper, a dairymaid, and a decoy artist regularly demonstrate their trades in the workshops. ⊠ *Susquehanna State Park, 461 Quaker Bottom Rd.* ☏ *410/ 939–2299* ▦ *$3* ⊙ *May–Sept., weekends 1–5.*

The **Susquehanna Museum,** at the southern terminal of the defunct Susquehanna and Tidewater Canal, tells the history of the canal and the people who lived and worked there. From 1839 until 1890 the canal ran 45 mi north to Wrightsville, Pennsylvania. It was a thoroughfare for mule-drawn barges loaded with iron ore, coal, and crops. The museum, in a lock tender's cottage built in 1840, is partially furnished with modest mid-century antiques that recall its period of service. ⊠ *Erie and Conesto Sts.* ☏ *410/939–5780* ⊕ *www.lockhousemuseum.org* ▦ *Donations accepted* ⊙ *Thurs.–Mon. 1–5.*

Susquehanna State Park, 6 mi upriver from Havre de Grace, sits on 2,500 acres. You can fish, bird-watch, hike, bike, and camp. A covered stone pavilion by the river is a good place for picnics. ⊠ *Rte. 155* ☎ *410/836–6735* 🎫 *Free* ☉ *Daily 9–sunset.*

Where to Stay & Eat

\$\$–\$\$\$ ✕ **Crazy Swede.** A nautical theme prevails in this restaurant on a tree-lined avenue. Windows and mirrors on all sides keep the dining room well lighted whether or not the sailboat lanterns on the tables are burning. On the menu, beef, seafood, and pasta dishes are all well represented. Veal Havre de Grace, served with shrimp and lump crabmeat in a Chablis cream sauce, is a specialty. ⊠ *400 N. Union Ave., Havre de Grace* ☎ *410/939–5440* 🍴 *AE, MC, V.*

\$\$–\$\$\$ ✕ **MacGregor's.** Behind the redbrick facade of a bank built in 1928, Mac-Gregor's occupies two dining rooms on two levels, with glass walls on three sides looking onto the Chesapeake Bay. The interior is adorned with carved duck decoys, mounted guns, and antique prints of the town; there's also outdoor dining on a deck with a gazebo. Seafood is the specialty, and the kitchen claims to have the best crab cakes on the bay. ⊠ *331 St. John's St., Havre de Grace* ☎ *410/939–3003* 🍴 *AE, D, DC, MC, V.*

\$–\$\$ 🏠 **Spencer-Silver Mansion.** This house was built in 1886 from gray granite quarried at nearby Port Deposit—the same kind of granite was used to build the Brooklyn Bridge. Characteristic Victorian details include stained-glass windows, a wraparound porch, and a turret. The carriage house is a lovely two-story stone cottage with loft bedroom, Jacuzzi, and fireplace; it sleeps up to four but is ideal for couples seeking a romantic hideaway. All rooms are furnished with period antiques supplemented by select reproductions. ⊠ *200 S. Union Ave., 21078* ☎ *410/939–1485 or 800/780–1485* ⊕ *www.spencersilvermansion.com* 🛏 *4 rooms, 1 suite* ♻ *Wi-Fi; no smoking* 🍴 *AE, MC, V* 🍽 *BP.*

\$–\$\$ 🏠 **Vandiver Inn.** This three-story wood house, built in 1886 and listed on the National Register of Historic Places, is 1½ blocks from the bay. Green with dark green trim on the outside, the inn has a Victorian look, with antique beds and other period pieces. A porch extends the width of the house front, and the gazebo in the backyard is as old as the house itself. ⊠ *301 S. Union Ave., 21078* ☎ *410/939–5200 or 800/245–1655* ⊕ *www.vandiverinn.com* 🛏 *17 rooms* ♻ *Cable TV, Wi-Fi, in-room broadband, meeting rooms; no smoking* 🍴 *AE, D, MC, V* 🍽 *BP.*

Aberdeen

30 mi northeast of Baltimore.

A site for artillery testing since 1917, Aberdeen celebrates its heritage every year on Armed Forces Day (the third Saturday in May) with tank parades and firing demonstrations. The town is also the birthplace of Cal Ripken Jr., who made baseball history in 1995 by breaking Lou Gehrig's record for most consecutive games played.

Cal Ripken Stadium (⊠ 873 Long Dr. ☎ 410/297–9292 ⊕ www. ripkenbaseball.com) brings Single-A baseball to town with the IronBirds, an Orioles minor-league affiliate team. Owned by Cal Ripken, the team plays short-season ball every June to September in Ripken Stadium, a 5,500-seat venue complete with skyboxes. The Ripken Museum and a hotel are slated to open at the stadium in late 2006.

Ellicott City

12 mi southwest of Baltimore.

Ellicott City was founded in 1772 by three Quaker brothers—John, Andrew, and Joseph Ellicott. By the 1860s, Ellicott City had become one of the most prominent milling and manufacturing towns in the east. Today the town retains its historical flavor and is a pleasant place to stroll and browse the many stores and antiques shops. The Howard County Office of Tourism (☎ 410/313–1900 or 800/288–8747) offers walking tours of the town.

Ellicott City was the B&O Railroad's first stop. The **Ellicott City B & O Railroad Station Museum,** built in 1831, is the oldest surviving railroad terminal in America. Exhibits focus on the history of the railroad and on its role in the Civil War. ⊠ *At Maryland Ave. and Main St.* ☎ *410/461–1945* ⊕ *www.ecbo.org* ⊠ *$5* ⊘ *Wed.–Sun. 11–4.*

The **Oella Mill** was once just that; today it houses antiques dealers and artisans under its large roof. ⊠ *840 Oella Ave.* ☎ *410/465–1313.*

BALTIMORE ESSENTIALS

To research prices, get advice from other travelers, and book travel arrangements, visit www.fodors.com.

Transportation

BY AIR

Travelling to Baltimore by air is fairly simple. The main airport is Baltimore-Washington International Airport (BWI), just south of town. BWI is easily reached by car, taxi, or light-rail; for most agencies, rental cars are returned to lots off the airport premises.

BWI Super Shuttle provides van service between the airport and downtown hotels, every half hour, 4 AM–midnight. Travel time is about 30 minutes; the fare is $20 for the first person, $5 per additional passenger. Hotel vans, which operate independently of the hotels, take 30 minutes on average.

Carey Limousines provides sedan service, which costs $80; make reservations 24 hours in advance. Private Car/RMA Worldwide Chauffeured Transportation has sedans, limos, and vans; the cost to the Inner Harbor is about $40 for a sedan.

Airport Taxis stand by to meet arriving flights. The ride into town on I–295 takes 20 minutes; a trip between the airport and downtown costs about $25. Airport Taxi service is available only *from* BWI; for transportation to the airport, consult a local cab company such as Jimmy's Cab Co. or Arrow Taxicab.

🔁 Airport Information **Baltimore-Washington International Airport (BWI)** ⊠ 10 mi south of Baltimore off Rte. 295/Baltimore-Washington Pkwy. ☎ 410/859-7111 for information and paging ⊕ www.bwiairport.com.

🔁 Airport Transfers **Airport Taxis** ☎ 410/859-1100 ⊕ www.bwiairporttaxi.com. **Arrow Taxicab** ☎ 410/358-9696. **Amtrak** ☎ 800/872-7245 ⊕ www.amtrak.com. **BWI Airport rail station** ☎ 410/672-6167 ⊕ www.mtamaryland.com. **BWI Super Shuttle** ☎ 800/258-3826 ⊕ www.supershuttle.com. **Carey Limousines** ☎ 410/880-0999 or 888/880-0999 ⊕ www.carey.com. **Jimmy's Cab Co.** ☎ 410/296-7200. **Maryland Area Rail Commuter (MARC)** ☎ 800/325-7245 or 410/539-5000 ⊕ www.mtamaryland.com. **Penn Station** ⊠ Charles St. and Mt. Royal Ave., Mount Vernon ☎ 410/291-4269. **Private Car/RMA Worldwide Chauffeured Transportation** ☎ 410/519-0000 or 800/878-7743 ⊕ www.rmalimo.com.

BY BUS

Buses provide an inexpensive way to see much of Baltimore, though you may have to transfer several times. The Maryland Transit Administration (MTA) has more than 70 bus routes and service between Baltimore and Annapolis.

Travel to Baltimore by bus is easy and convenient. Passengers can arrive at the downtown bus terminal or at the Baltimore Travel Plaza just off I–95; the plaza has long-term parking and local bus service to downtown and other destinations. Greyhound Lines has scheduled daily service to and from major cities in the United States and Canada. Peter Pan/Trailways Bus Lines offers slightly nicer travel to many destinations in the Northeast, including Washington, D.C., New York, and Boston.

Route and schedule information is available by contacting the Maryland Transit Administration. Bus and transit schedules are sometimes available inside the Charles Center metro station (Charles and Baltimore streets downtown). Fare is $1.60 (exact change is required). All-day passes are $3.50 and can be used with light-rail or metro travel. Some routes have service 24 hours daily.

🔁 **Baltimore Travel Plaza** ⊠ 5625 O'Donnell St., at I-95, East Baltimore ☎ 800/231-2222. **Downtown Bus Terminal** ⊠ 2110 Hanes St., at Russell St., City Center ☎ 410/752-7682.

Greyhound Lines ☎ 000/231 2222 ⊕ www.greyhound.com. **Maryland Transit Administration (MTA)** ☎ 800/325-7245 or 410/539-5000 ⊕ www.mtamaryland.com. **Peter Pan/Trailways Bus Lines** ☎ 800/237-8747 ⊕ www.peterpanbus.com.

BY CAR

From the northeast and south, I–95 cuts across the city's east side and the harbor; Route 295, the Baltimore–Washington Parkway, follows a similar route farther to the east and is the best route downtown from the airport. From the north, I–83, also called the Jones Falls Expressway, winds through Baltimore and ends at the Inner Harbor. I–395 serves as the primary access to downtown from I–95. From the west, I–70 merges with the Baltimore Beltway, I–695. Drivers headed downtown should use I–395.

Parking in downtown Baltimore tends to be difficult; on weekdays many garages fill up early with suburban commuters. When the Orioles or Ravens play a home game, parking around the Inner Harbor can be nearly impossible to find. Best bets for parking are hotel garages, which seem to often have spaces available. Attended parking lots are around the downtown periphery and cost less than garages.

It's hard to find a metered parking spot downtown, though in other areas it's much easier. Most meters in well-traveled areas charge 25¢ per 15-minute period and have a two-hour limit; around the Inner Harbor vicinity meters are in effect 24 hours a day.

BY SUBWAY

The Baltimore metro serves those coming into the city from the suburban northwest. Stops include Charles Center and Lexington Market, both within walking distance of the Inner Harbor. The single line runs from Owings Mills to Johns Hopkins Hospital, east of downtown. There's also a light-rail that runs between points north and south in the city (⇨ By Train below).

Fare is $1.60; day passes are $3.50. Trains run weekdays 5 AM–midnight, Saturday and Sunday 6 AM–midnight.

🚊 **Maryland Transit Administration** (MTA) ☎ 800/325-7245 or 410/539-5000 ⊕ www.mtamaryland.com.

BY TAXI

It can be hard to catch a cab on the street in Baltimore. The best places to flag one down are at Pratt and Light streets in the Inner Harbor, Cross and South Charles streets in Federal Hill, and at Broadway and Thames Street in Fells Point. Otherwise, your best option is to phone ahead and ask for a pickup, or ask your hotel concierge or doorman to summon one for you. Meters determine local fares, which average $7–$10, depending on how far you go.

Ed Kane's Water Taxis and the Seaport Taxi are fun and convenient ways to get around the Inner Harbor. They make stops at 16 points along the waterfront, including Fells Point, the National Aquarium, museums, restaurants, and Fort McHenry. All-day tickets for both services are $6. Look for stops, marked with signs, all along the waterfront; depending on season, boats arrive every 10–15 minutes in season or you can call to be picked up at a particular location.

🚊 **Arrow Taxicab** ☎ 410/358-9696. **Ed Kane's Water Taxis** ☎ 410/563-3901 ⊕ www.thewatertaxi.com. **Jimmy's Cab Co.** ☎ 410/296-7200. **Seaport Taxi** ☎ 410/675-2900.

BY TRAIN

All Amtrak trains on the northeast corridor between Boston and Washington stop at Baltimore's Penn Station. Maryland Area Rail Commuter (MARC) trains travel between Baltimore's Penn Station and Washington, D.C., Camden Station and Washington, and BWI Airport and Penn Station. The trip to Washington, D.C., takes about 1 hour and costs $7; the trip to BWI Airport from Penn Station takes about 20 minutes and costs $4. Trains run several times per hour, weekdays 4:45 AM–9:30 PM (note that MARC trains do not run on weekends).

Light-rail is an easy, comfortable (if slow) way to reach downtown from the northern and southern suburbs. Stops near downtown include Oriole Park at Camden Yards, Howard Street, and Centre Street near Mount Vernon. The city's cultural center can be reached by the Cathedral Street stop. Light-rail extends to Hunt Valley, BWI Airport, and Glen Burnie. The fare is $1.60 (exact change is required); day passes are $3.50.
🚆 **Amtrak** ☎ 800/872-7245 ⊕ www.amtrak.com. **Amtrak Penn Station** ⊠ Charles St. and Mt. Royal Ave., Mount Vernon ☎ 410/291-4269. **Maryland Area Rail Commuter (MARC)** ☎ 800/325-7245 or 410/539-5000. **Maryland Transit Administration (MTA)** ☎ 800/325-7245 or 410/539-5000 ⊕ www.mtamaryland.com.

Contacts & Resources

EMERGENCIES
To report non-life-threatening situations that are nonetheless of concern, the Baltimore City Police Department operates an alternative phone line, **311**, which connects directly to a police operator. For emergencies, call 911.

Mercy Medical Center has set up a "Dial a Downtown Doctor" hotline for physician referrals and appointments. The service is available around the clock, seven days a week. Also downtown, the University of Maryland Medical Center operates a similar service from 7 AM to 7 PM daily, and can provide access to dentists as well as medical doctors.
🚑 **Ambulance, fire, police** ☎ 911.
🏥 **Doctors & Dentists Dial a Downtown Doctor** ☎ 800/636-3729 ⊕ www.mdmercy.com. **University of Maryland Physicians Referral** ☎ 800/492-5538 ⊕ www.umm.edu.
🏥 Hospitals **Johns Hopkins Hospital** ⊠ 600 N. Wolfe St., East Baltimore ☎ 410/955-2280. **Mercy Medical Center** ⊠ 301 St. Paul Pl., City Center ☎ 410/332-9000. **Sinai Hospital** ⊠ 2401 Belvedere Ave., Mt. Washington ☎ 410/601-8800. **University of Maryland University Hospital** ⊠ 22 S. Greene St., West Baltimore ☎ 410/328-8667.
🏥 24-Hour Pharmacies **CVS** ⊠ 4625 Falls Rd., Roland Park ☎ 410/662-1670. **Rite Aid** ⊠ 250 W. Chase St., Mount Vernon ☎ 410/752-4473 ⊠ Rotunda shopping center, 711 W. 40th St., Charles Village ☎ 410/467-3343.

INTERNET, MAIL & SHIPPING
Baltimore's main post office is convenient to downtown and open 24 hours.

Free public Internet access is available at the Enoch Pratt Free Library (just ask the librarian for a temporary library card). Baltimore is not big on Internet cafés, though most coffeehouses have free Wi-Fi access. Between the Inner Harbor and Fells Point, Bluehouse has a Wi-Fi server. Red Emma's, in Mount Vernon, has a couple of free Internet terminals.
🚩 **Bluehouse** ⊠ 1407 Fleet St., Fells Point ☎ 410/276-1180. **Enoch Pratt Free Library** ⊠ 400 Cathedral St., Mount Vernon ☎ 410/396-5500. **Main Post Office** ⊠ 900 E. Fayette St., Inner Harbor East ☎ 410/347-4425. **Red Emma's** ⊠ 800 St. Paul St., Mount Vernon ☎ 410/230-0450.

MEDIA
Baltimore's two daily papers are the *Baltimore Sun* and *The Baltimore Examiner*. On weekdays, you can pick up copies of the *Baltimore Sun*

at newsstands throughout the city for $.50; the Sunday paper is $1. The *Sun* has longer, more in-depth news, sports and feature stories, is generally regarded as the more prestigious of the two daily papers. The *Examiner,* a tabloid that began publishing in 2006, is distributed free to doorsteps and newsstands Monday–Saturday. It provides news, sports and entertainment in short, succinct stories, often half the length of those in the *Baltimore Sun.* The *City Paper,* which comes out Wednesday in yellow newsstands, is free, and has the widest selection of entertainment listings of any Baltimore paper.

Baltimore Magazine, a monthly lifestyle and entertainment magazine, caters to an affluent crowd. You can pick up a copy at most grocery and bookstores around town. *Urbanite,* a free monthly, targets city architectural and societal trends, and also publishes local literary pieces. Grab an *Urbanite* at cafés, corner bars, and bookstores.

TOUR OPTIONS

Tours of Baltimore, on foot or four wheels, run from traditional surveys of historic buildings and sites to quirkier explorations such as the Fells Point Ghost Tour. The Baltimore Shuttle offers a 90-minute narrated trolley tour of the city; tours are $18 and depart daily at 11 and 2 from the visitor center at the Inner Harbor.

For a general overview of Baltimore, energetic, irrepressible Zippy Larson offers many different walking tours with historic, cultural, and architectural themes. Zippy's witty, well-researched tours start at $60 per person (which includes a restaurant meal) and take you outside the tourist bubble.

A particularly fascinating experience is local historian Wayne Schaumburg's guided tour to Greenmount Cemetery. Baltimore's largest and most prestigious burial ground is the final resting place of John Wilkes Booth, Johns Hopkins, and other native sons and daughters. Tours take place Saturday mornings in May and October and are $10 per person.

The Fells Point Ghost Tour interweaves narrative about the maritime neighborhood's colorful past with tales of its spectral inhabitants. Tours, which are suitable for children, run every Friday and Saturday evening at 7 PM from July to October, and Saturday only March to June and November; the cost is $12 per adult; reservations are recommended. The Fells Point Visitors Center also offers a Fells Point Ghost Walk as well as tours focusing on such topics as maritime history and immigration.

For building buffs, the Baltimore Architectural Foundation sponsors walking tours of the historic and architecturally significant neighborhood of Mount Vernon; reservations are required and the cost is $10. The Mount Vernon Cultural District also organizes tours of Mount Vernon and other nearby neighborhoods.

Most cruise and tour boats depart from docks in the Inner Harbor. The tall ship *Clipper City* offers excursions around the harbor aboard a 158-foot replica of an 1850s topsail schooner. The two-hour tours depart twice a day from May to October from the pier in front of Harbor place's Light Street Pavilion. Harbor Cruises, Ltd. and Pintail Yachts present lunch, dinner, and evening cruises around the harbor. Ride the Ducks of Baltimore provides a tour of the city by both land and water.

🛈 Trolley Tours **The Baltimore Shuttle** ☎ 410/732-5098.

🛈 Walking Tours **Baltimore Architectural Foundation** ☎ 410/962-0241 ⊕ www. baltimorearchitecture.org. **Fells Point Ghost Walk** ☎ 410/522-7400 ⊕ www. fellspointghost.com. **Fells Point Visitors Center Tours** ☎ 410/675-6750 ⊕ www. preservationsociety.com. **Greenmount Cemetery Tours** ☎ 410/256-2180 ⊕ home. earthlink.net/~wschaumburg. **Mount Vernon Cultural District** ✉ 217 N. Charles St., Mount Vernon ☎ 410/605-0462 ⊕ www.mvcd.org. **Zippy Larson's Shoe Leather Safaris** ☎ 410/817-4141 ⊕ www.bcpl.net/~zipbooks.

🛈 Water Tours **Clipper City** ✉ 800 Light St., Inner Harbor ☎ 410/837-6700 ⊕ www. sailingship.com. **Harbor Cruises, Ltd.** ☎ 410/727-3113 or 800/695-2628 ⊕ www. harborcruises.com. **Pintail Yachts** ✉ Pier 5, Inner Harbor ☎ 410/539-3485. **Ride the Ducks of Baltimore** ✉ 25 Light St., Inner Harbor ☎ 410/727-3825.

VISITOR INFORMATION

Contact the Baltimore Visitor Center for information on the city. A live operator can answer your questions weekdays 9–5:30; otherwise an automated system is in place. The Web site is also full of information about the city. The drop-in Visitor Center is open Monday through Thursday and Sunday 9–6, and Friday and Saturday 9–7:30. A parking lot is behind it; the first 45 minutes are free.

The Baltimore Office of Promotion's Web site has the most detailed information on city events such as New Year's Eve, the Waterfront Festival, the Book Festival, Hampdenfest, and the Thanksgiving Parade (the Saturday before Thanksgiving).

The Fell's Point Visitor Center has information particular to the neighborhood, including a handout that covers many buildings' histories and architecture.

For more information on Havre de Grace and Aberdeen, contact the Harford County Tourism Council or the local visitor centers. For more information on Ellicott City, contact the Howard County Tourism Council.

🛈 **Baltimore Convention Center** ✉ 100 W. Pratt St., Inner Harbor ☎ 410/649-7000 ⊕ www.bccenter.org. **Baltimore Office of Promotion** ☎ 410/752-8632 ⊕ www.bop. org. **Baltimore Visitor Center** ✉ 401 Light St., Inner Harbor ☎ 877/225-8466 ⊕ www. baltimore.org. **Fell's Point Visitor Center** ✉ 808 S. Ann St., Fells Point ☎ 410/675-6750 ⊕ www.preservationsociety.com. **Harford County Tourism Council** ✉ 211 W. Belair Rd., Aberdeen ☎ 410/272-2325 or 800/597-2649 ⊕ www.harfordmd.com. **Havre de Grace Visitor Center** ✉ 450 Pennington Ave., Havre de Grace ☎ 410/939-2100. **Howard County Office of Tourism** ✉ 8267 Main St., Ellicott City ☎ 410/313-1900 or 800/288-8747 ⊕ www.visithowardcounty.com.

Frederick & Western Maryland

WORD OF MOUTH

"I would encourage a trip to Antietam. For me, the area that gave me the greatest impact was at Antietam at the site of "Bloody Lane." To me, the air was almost palpable with the ghosts of the dead. So moving."

—jersey

"Antietam is an easy one for a day, it is a wonderful experience, and you could perhaps even combine it with a short trip to Harpers Ferry."

—dan_woodlief

Updated by
Loretta
Chilcoat

MARYLAND'S MOUNTAINSIDE used to be known to few people beyond the locals. But the secret's out now. Stretching from the Piedmont region's rolling farmland to the remote mountaintops of Garrett County and the heights of the Appalachians, the area is a land where white-tail deer, wild turkey, and even black bear roam among its miles of oaks, hickories, and maples. Seeking a temporary escape from the bustle of urban and suburban life, travelers head here to camp under light pollution–free skies, hike along waterfall trails in lush state parks, and sink into plush, goose-down beds in bed-and-breakfasts.

The past is alive (and often reenacted) here in its historic towns and Civil War battlefields. You're virtually guaranteed to hit a friendly festival celebrating anything from the intense colors of fall to the snowy peaks of Wisp Mountain.

In the early 1700s Germans and other immigrants came to farm the fertile valleys of Frederick and Washington counties, where large dairy farms still dot the pastoral landscape. The Irish and Scots arrived in the first half of the 19th century to help build railroads, the National Road, and the Chesapeake & Ohio (C&O) Canal. Western Maryland was an important transportation gateway for the nation's first pioneers. The Historical National Road, the nation's first federally funded road, paved the way for future settlers, and today travelers can still journey on the twisty road that parallels Interstate 70. The dream of the C&O Canal revolutionizing the way goods would be transported was short lived, as the railroad came into the region at the same time. However, remnants of this nearly 185-mi-long waterway, paralleling the meandering Potomac River from Washington's Georgetown to Cumberland, remain, and today the canal's towpath is a popular hiking and biking trail. The railroad was big business in Hagerstown and Cumberland, providing jobs and a speedy link to Baltimore and Washington, D.C.

Because of its proximity to Baltimore and Washington, Frederick, the region's largest city, became a staging area for many important events in American history. Ben Franklin helped plan aspects of the French and Indian War from Braddock Heights, a mountain on Frederick's western edge. Meriwether Lewis stopped by before meeting up with William Clark on their trek westward. During the Civil War, Confederate and Union troops clashed on the streets of Frederick, on their way to the battles of South Mountain and Antietam.

A surprising number of American presidents have visited Frederick. George Washington slept and ate his way through here. Abraham Lincoln passed through after the Battle of Antietam, which was fought on the other side of the green mountains that border Frederick on the western horizon. Franklin Roosevelt showed British prime minister Winston Churchill the town before moving on to Camp David.

The region's other big towns, Hagerstown and Cumberland, were transportation hubs in earlier centuries. Though the railroad plays a much less important role in both cities today, its past is used to lure visitors. Hagerstown is known for its Roundhouse Museum, which has an extensive collection of railroad memorabilia, history books, and a miniature railroad layout. Cumberland is in the midst of turning the western terminus of the Chesapeake & Ohio Canal into a heritage and recreational area. A new visitor center has already opened at the C&O Canal National Historical Park. The city's Victorian-era train station has been restored and is the starting point of a popular excursion up the mountains. Eventually, a stretch of the canal will be restored for tours on replicas of the original canal boats.

The region's mountains, forests, and world-famous rivers are an equally important draw. Kayakers and white-water rafters rave about the rapids on the Savage River and the north-flowing Youghiogheny River, and hikers, bicyclists, and campers flock to state parks throughout the region. Deep Creek Lake, the state's largest, is frequented by boaters and anglers.

Disagreement lingers on just where western Maryland begins. For Baltimoreans, more familiar with the Eastern Shore and Ocean City, anything west of their beltway is western Maryland. Washingtonians, on the other hand, tend to lump Frederick and points west together as a distinct region. For the people who live in the hills of Allegany and Garrett counties, western Maryland begins just west of a man-made cut in a mountain called Sideling Hill. This unusual geological formation has become an attraction among motorists tooling along Interstate 68. Passing rock formations several million years old, the highway opens to sweeping views of mountain ridges, shaded blue in the fading sunset. These are the Alleghenies, Maryland's mountainside.

Top 5 Experiences for Frederick & Western Maryland

- **Contact the "Other Side":** Stroll the shadowy, cobblestone streets of historic Frederick on a chilling candlelight ghost tour and see if you can feel the presence of the town's former citizens.

- **Honor the Fallen:** Stand on hallowed ground from the bloodiest one-day battle of the Civil War and pay homage to the Blue and Grey heroes at Antietam National Battlefield.

- **Go Jump in the Lake:** Spend a long weekend at Maryland's largest man-made body of water, Deep Creek Lake, and enjoy all-season activities from summer swimming to winter skiing.

- **Get Your Peanuts and Crackerjacks:** Take a break from expensive sporting events and treat the kids to a casual, family-friendly Frederick Keys minor-league baseball game.

- **Enjoy the Silence:** Cool temperatures, serene vistas and a vibrant explosion of red, orange, and yellow leaves make fall the most perfect time for a romantic B&B excursion.

Exploring Frederick & Western Maryland

Frederick, Maryland's second-largest city, is surrounded by rolling farmlands and rugged mountains, where outdoor activities beckon. In Washington County, northwest of Frederick, Hagerstown is the county seat and a great base for excursions to the C&O Canal, various state parks, and the Appalachian Trail. Farther west, the rugged mountains of Allegany County are crossed by the Old National Highway: today the site of a scenic railroad excursion, this is the same route that westward pioneers traveled in covered wagons. Maryland's westernmost county, Garrett County, was once the vacation destination of railroad barons and Washington's high society; today it's a big destination for boaters, fishermen, and outdoors enthusiasts.

About the Restaurants & Hotels

WHAT IT COSTS					
	$$$$	$$$	$$	$	¢
RESTAURANTS	over $30	$22–$30	$14–$22	$7–$14	under $7
HOTELS	over $250	$175–$250	$130–$175	$80–$130	under $80

Restaurant prices are per person for a main course at dinner. Hotel prices are for a standard double room, excluding state tax.

FREDERICK

Frederick has one of the best-preserved historic districts in Maryland, perhaps second only to Annapolis. Within the 50-block district, tree-shaded streets are lined with buildings from the 18th and 19th centuries, and brick walks connect lovely courtyards. Eclectic shops, museums, antiques stores, and fine restaurants attract crowds of weekend visitors.

Numbers in the text correspond to numbers in the margin and on the Frederick map.

Main Attractions

8

★ **Barbara Fritchie House and Museum.** After you visit this modest brick cottage, a reproduction of the original, it's easy to imagine Dame Fritchie sticking her white-capped head out of a second-floor window and waving a Union flag at Confederate troops. Poet John Greenleaf Whittier made her famous; his poem "Barbara Fritchie" appeared in the *Atlantic Monthly* a year after Confederate troops passed through Frederick. His stirring account of Fritchie defiantly waving the flag at the invading Confederates stirred patriotism and made the 95-year-old woman a heroine. Her unusual life, at least as told by Whittier, has fascinated history enthusiasts around the world. Even British prime minister Winston Churchill visited the house; on his way to Camp David with President Franklin Roosevelt, he stood outside and recited Whittier's poem: "Shoot if you must, this old gray head, but spare your country's flag. . . ." A tea set Fritchie used to serve George Washington is on display. ⊠ *154 W. Patrick St.* ☎ *301/698–8992* ☞ *$2* ⊙ *Call for hrs.*

Frederick Visitor's Center. At the center you can pick up brochures of historic sites and maps for a self-guided tour or join a guided 90-minute walking tour. Tours begin at 1:30 PM and are offered on holidays and weekends May through October. ⊠ *19 E. Church St.* ☎ *301/228–2888 or 800/999–3613* ⊕ *www.fredericktourism.org* ☞ *Tour $7* ⊙ *Daily 9–5.*

National Museum of Civil War Medicine. The only museum devoted to the study and interpretation of Civil War medicine is also rumored to be haunted. No wonder: the museum is inside what was once a furniture

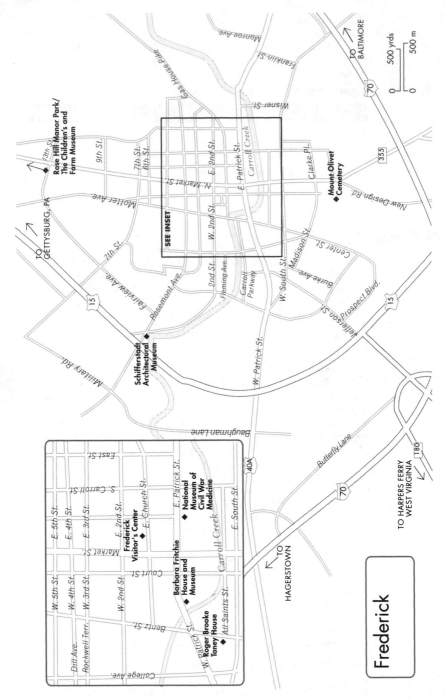

Frederick

SEE INSET

TO GETTYSBURG, PA

Rose Hill Manor Park/
The Children's and
Farm Museum

13th St.

9th St.

7th St.

6th St.

N. Market St.

E. 2nd St.

E. Patrick St.

Carroll Creek

Mottler Ave.

W. 2nd St.

Gas House Pike

Monroe Ave.

Franklin St.

Wisner St.

Wisner St.

Mount Olivet
Cemetery

Clarke Pl.

New Design Rd.

355

TO BALTIMORE

70

500 yrds
500 m

Schifferstadt
Architectural
Museum

7th St.

Fairview Ave.

Rosemont Ave.

2nd St.

Fleming Ave.

Carroll
Parkway

Madison St.

Center St.

Burke Ave.

W. South St.

Jefferson St.

W. Prospect Blvd.

15

Military Rd.

15

W. Patrick St.

Baughman Lane

Butterfly Lane

70

180

TO HARPERS FERRY
WEST VIRGINIA

40A

TO
HAGERSTOWN

Inset:

East St.

E. 5th St.

E. 4th St.

E. 3rd St.

E. 2nd St.

S. Carroll St.

E. Church St.

E. Patrick St.

National
Museum of
Civil War
Medicine

Frederick
Visitor's Center

Market St.

Court St.

Barbara Fritchie
House and
Museum

Carroll Creek

E. South St.

W. 5th St.

W. 4th St.

W. 3rd St.

W. 2nd St.

Bentz St.

W. Patrick St.

Roger Brooke
Taney House

All Saints St.

College Ave.

Dill Ave.

Rockwell Terr.

store in 1830 and then a funeral home until 1978: the dead from the Battle of Antietam (1862) were taken here for embalming. Exhibits at the museum cover "Recruitment," "Camp Life," "Medical Evacuation," and "Veterinary Medicine." More than 3,000 artifacts are on display, including a Civil War ambulance and the only known surviving Civil War surgeon's tent. Photographs and a video help explain the state of the healing arts during this period. ✉ *48 E. Patrick St.* ☎ *301/695–1864* ⊕ *www.civilwarmed.org* ✉ *$6.50* ✹ *Mon.–Sat. 10–5, Sun. 11–5.*

Roger Brooke Taney House. A two-story Federal-style house contains a museum dedicated to Taney (1777–1864) and his brother-in-law Francis Scott Key, author of the "Star-Spangled Banner." History remembers Supreme Court Justice Taney as the author of the 1857 Dred Scott Decision, which stated that blacks had no constitutional rights. Taney and Key practiced law together in Frederick; their office still stands across from City Hall. Personal belongings of both men are on display at the Taney House. Behind the home is the former slave quarters, one of the few such surviving structures in the region. ✉ *121 S. Bentz St.* ☎ *301/663–1188* ✉ *$3* ✹ *Mid-Apr.–Dec., Sat. 10–4, Sun. 1–4.*

Also Worth Seeing

Community Bridge Mural. Confusing birds since it was built in 2000, this life-size optical illusion transforms an ordinary bridge into a public work of art. Detailed stonework, an archangel that seems to jump out at you, and ivy so real you can almost smell it are just a few delights of the mural, which is also a popular gathering place for summer festivals. ✉ *Carroll Street Bridge, between E. Patrick and E. All Saints Sts.* ☎ *301/228–2888* ⊕ *http://bridge.skyline.net.*

Mount Olivet Cemetery. Some of Frederick's most famous sons and daughters rest here, including Francis Scott Key and Barbara Fritchie. The cemetery also shelters the graves of more than 800 Confederate and Union soldiers killed during the battles of Antietam and Monocacy. ✉ *515 S. Market St.* ☎ *301/662–1164* ⊕ *www.mountolivetcemeteryinc.com* ✹ *Daily.*

♻ **Rose Hill Manor Park/The Children's and Farm Museum.** Although this lovely Georgian manor is intended as a place for elementary-school children to study local and regional history, it's more than just this. Maryland's first governor, Thomas Johnson, lived here from 1798 to 1819. Guided tours of the gracious home focus on the early 19th century, covering the manor's owners and their lifestyles. During the tour, children can card wool, weave on a table loom, play with reproductions of old toys, and dress in period costumes. Also open are several outbuildings, including a log cabin, ice house, smokehouse, blacksmith shop, and large shed housing a carriage collection. You can also wander through herb, vegetable, and rose gardens. ✉ *1611 N. Market St.* ☎ *301/694–1646* ⊕ *www.rosehillmuseum.com* ✉ *$5* ✹ *Apr.–Oct., Mon.–Sat. 10–4, Sun. 1–4; Nov., Sat. 10–4, Sun. 1–4.*

Schifferstadt Architectural Museum. Believed to be the oldest house in Frederick, this unusual stone structure was built in 1756 by German immigrants. Spared from the wrecking ball two decades ago by preservation-minded citizens, the house is considered one of the finest examples of German architecture in Colonial America. Because the rooms are empty, it's easy to observe structural details such as the sandstone walls, which are 2½ feet thick. ⊠ *1110 Rosemont Ave.* ☎ *301/663–3885* 🖃 *$3* ⊙ *Wed.–Sun. noon–4.*

WHERE TO STAY & EAT

$$–$$$$ ✕ **The Red Horse.** A local institution and landmark—note the red horse on the roof—the Red Horse is primarily a steak house. The rustic dining room has a stone fireplace, rafters, and large wagon-wheel chandelier. The service is first-rate; you can watch your steak being grilled from behind a window. A lower-level cigar parlor serves cognac, ports, sherries, and bourbons. ⊠ *996 W. Patrick St.* ☎ *301/663–3030* 🖃 *AE, D, DC, MC, V.*

$–$$$ ✕ **Cafe Kyoko.** This sushi and Thai restaurant sets itself apart from the standard eateries in downtown. The sparsely decorated dining room is still inviting, with wooden booths along the window front, exposed rafters, and ceiling fans. In addition to the fresh and inventive sushi choices, pad thai is excellent and one of the more popular dishes. There's also chicken teriyaki, steak, and seafood entrées, and a vegetarian menu. The wine and beer selection is limited. ⊠ *10 E. Patrick St.* ☎ *301/695–9656* 🖃 *AE, D, MC, V.*

$–$$$ ✕ **Firestone's.** In a 1920s-era building that in earlier incarnations was a bank, a sporting goods store, and an Irish pub, Firestone's is a casual, slightly upscale place for good American fare. At first glance, it seems more like a local pub, with a wooden bar dominating the main floor. Look more closely, and you can see the white linens covering the tables. Steak and seafood are plentiful on the menu, which also offers a few surprises, including marinated and roasted portobello mushrooms stacked with onions, peppers, eggplant, and zucchini. Desserts are made in-house. ⊠ *105 N. Market St.* ☎ *301/663–0330* 🖃 *AE, D, MC, V* ⊙ *Closed Mon.*

$–$$$ ✕ **Isabella's.** Consistently at the top of locals' and visitors' "must eat" list, this Spanish eatery brings some flair to downtown Frederick's predominantly American restaurant scene. Most people head here for the tapas—appetizers that originated in the Andalusia region of Spain. Isabella's tapas may include lamb, beef, chicken, and seafood with various spices, herbs, and wonderful sauces. The spinach and eggplant omelet, and the shrimp wrapped in sweet serrano ham are favorites. Three should make a satisfying meal. ⊠ *44 N. Market St.* ☎ *301/698–8922* 🖃 *AE, D, DC, MC, V* ⊙ *Closed Mon. except for happy hr 4–6:30.*

$–$$$ ✕ **John Hagan's Tavern.** Yes, George Washington ate here, and the tavern enjoys a bit of fame as the one-time headquarters for the Blue as well as the Gray during the Civil War: some say ghostly soldiers still pace the tavern. Built in 1785, the fieldstone structure served as a stopping point between Baltimore and Cumberland. Staff wear period dress, and all desserts and breads are made on the premises. The regional food on the menu has an Early American influence: specialties include housesmoked salmon, duck, and quail; Maryland-style roast chicken with lump-crabmeat sauce; and twin grilled duck breasts in a pear–orange confit. ✉ *5018 Old National Pike, Braddock Heights* ☎ *301/371–9189* ▤ *AE, D, DC, MC, V* ☺ *Closed Mon.*

$–$$$ ✕ **Tauraso's.** The mouthwatering smell of pizza baked in a wood oven greets diners approaching the reservations desk of this wood-panel, white-tablecloth trattoria. Other specialties include pasta dishes, poultry, steaks, and seafood. A favorite appetizer is Tauraso's own homemade seafood sausage. The restaurant has a bar, separate dining room, and a garden patio open seasonally. ✉ *6 East St.* ☎ *301/663–6000* ▤ *AE, D, DC, MC, V.*

$–$$ ✕ **Bentz Street Sports Bar.** Frederick's answer to the bar from *Cheers,* this comfy hangout is the place to go for quick pub food, a friendly game of pool, and a professional sports game on satellite television. Loaded burgers, stuffed chicken breasts, and Maryland crab cakes are joined by surprises like fried catfish, grilled tuna steak, and a creative veggie plate. Weekends bring in live, local rock bands; laugh it up during Comedy Night every Wednesday. ✉ *6 S. Bentz St.* ☎ *301/620–2222* ▤ *AE, MC, V.*

$–$$ ✕ **Brewer's Alley.** Frederick's first brewpub is still going strong, with an international selection of sweet to hoppy beers that'll satisfy the palates of tailgaters to beer connoisseurs. The eatery is clean and bright, with copper brewing pots gleaming next to the bar and the wooden tables. Be prepared to head south for inventive dishes like crawfish and sausage spring rolls, buttermilk-battered redfish and chips, and banana-pecan crusted salmon. Several kinds of beer are made on the premises. ✉ *124 N. Market St.* ☎ *301/631–0089* ▤ *AE, DC, MC, V.*

★ $$–$$$$ ✕▥ **Antrim 1844.** Once part of a 2,500-acre plantation, this pre–Civil War mansion, less than 10 mi from Gettysburg, is an elegant retreat. The owners have re-created the genteel spirit of a 19th-century estate. The nine mansion guest rooms are furnished with period antiques, working fireplaces, canopy feather beds, and marble baths or whirlpools. Other guest rooms are in a restored 19th-century carriage house, and buildings that were once an ice house and a plantation office. Don't miss the prix-fixe, six-course dinner ($62), an evening-long event. The menu includes seafood, beef, and poultry, all served with exquisite sauces. ✉ *30 Trevanion Rd., Taneytown 21787* ☎ *410/756–6812 or 800/858–1844* ▤ *410/756–2744* ⊕ *www.antrim1844.com* ⇋ *38 rooms* ☖ *Restaurant, putting green, tennis court, pool, croquet, lawn bowling, bar; no room phones, no TV in some rooms, no kids under 12, no smoking* ▤ *AE, MC, V* ❧ *BP.*

$$–$$$ ✕▥ **Catoctin Inn Resort & Spa.** A taste of Colonial Williamsburg in Frederick, this historic venue is a modern oasis of quiet, just a few miles south of Frederick. Antiques, books, family pictures, and heirlooms decorate the large Manor House from 1790. Its adjacent three buildings—the smokehouse, kitchen, and owner's cottage—are now intimate hideaways with king-size beds and double whirlpool tubs. The on-site restaurant, Quills ($$–$$$), is open to the public, and offers savory mains like chicken peanut pye, Cumberland duck, and Smithfield pork medallions; Friday and Saturday evenings offer surf-and-turf and prime rib specials. The on-site Serenity Spa, in the Manor House, pampers with

8

a small selection of massages and body treatments, some inside your own room. The Catoctin is no-smoking with the exception of one room (Baker 8). ⊠ *3619 Buckeystown Pike, Buckeystown 21717* ☎ *301/874–5555 or 800/730–5550* 🖷 *301/874–2026* ⊕ *www.catoctininn.com* ⇆ *12 rooms, 3 cottages* ☼ *Wi-Fi, refrigerators, cable TV, in-room VCRs, outdoor hot tub, business services, meeting rooms, airport shuttle, no-smoking rooms, some pets allowed (fee)* ☰ *AE, D, DC, MC, V.*

$–$$ 🏨 **Inn at Buckeystown.** An inviting wraparound porch fronts this B&B, an 1897 mansion in a village with pre–Revolutionary War roots, near the Civil War battlefield. The small but cozy rooms are furnished with Victorian accents that include lace bedspreads; heavy, floral curtains; and reproduction pieces. One room has a fireplace. A fixed-price five-course dinner is available for an additional $40; high tea is available most days. You don't have to stay here to eat in the restaurant, but you do need a reservation. ⊠ *3521 Buckeystown Pike, Buckeystown 21717* ☎ *301/874–5755 or 800/272–1190* 🖷 *301/831–1355* ⊕ *www.innatbuckeystown.com* ⇆ *9 rooms, 5 with private bath* ☼ *Restaurant, some cable TV, bar* ☰ *D, MC, V* ⦿| *BP.*

$ 🏨 **Hollerstown Hill B&B.** Sprinkled with chintz and a pale-pink color scheme, this B&B is full of Victorian touches right down to the marble claw-foot tubs and pull-chain toilets. You can have a drink on the wraparound porch or a lively game of billiards in the game room. The Hollerstown is right across the street from a park and within walking distance of most of Frederick's restaurants and attractions. ⊠ *4 Clarke Pl., Frederick 21701* ☎ *301/228–3630* ⊕ *www.hollerstownhill.com* ⇆ *4 rooms* ☼ *Wi-Fi; no kids under 15, no smoking* ☰ *AE, MC, V.*

Nightlife & the Arts

Drop by the **Frederick Coffee Company** (⊠ Shab Row–Everedy Sq., 100 East St. ☎ 301/698–0039 or 800/822–0806) for pastries, soup, sandwiches, quiche, dessert, and—of course—exotic and traditional coffees and other beverages. As you walk in the door of this former 1930s gas station, you can smell the heady fragrance of beans roasting in front of you. The Frederick Coffee Company is open 7–9 weekdays and 9–9 weekends; folk and jazz musicians perform Saturday night.

The **Weinberg Center for the Arts** (⊠ 20 W. Patrick St. ☎ 301/228–2828) was a movie house in the 1920s. Now the theater offers plays, musicals, and concerts throughout the year.

Sports & the Outdoors

Hiking

The famed **Appalachian Trail** crosses the spine of South Mountain just west of Frederick, from the Potomac River to the Pennsylvania line. Several well-known viewpoints can be found along Maryland's 40-mi stretch, including Annapolis Rocks and Weverton Cliffs. The best access points that have parking available are Gathland State Park, Washington Monument State Park, and Greenbrier State Park. For more information, contact the **Appalachian Trail Conference** (⊠ 799 Washington St., Harpers Ferry, WV 25425 ☎ 304/535–6331).

Shopping

In downtown Frederick, **Everedy Square & Shab Row** was once a complex of buildings that manufactured kitchen utensils and wares; now it's a center for retail shops, restaurants, and boutiques. At the family-owned **Candy Kitchen** (✉ 52 N. Market St. ☎ 301/698–0442) you can get hand-dipped chocolates.

The area's best outdoor store, the **Trail House** (✉ 17 S. Market St. ☎ 301/694–8448) sells and rents quality hiking, backpacking, camping, and cross-country skiing equipment. The store also stocks a good selection of maps and books. The **Museum Shop** (✉ 20 N. Market St. ☎ 301/695–0424) sells museum-quality ceramics, sculpture, hand-crafted jewelry, Whistler etchings, and Japanese woodcuts.

Away from downtown, **Wonder Book & Video** (✉ 1306 W. Patrick St. ☎ 301/694–5955) stocks more than 600,000 new and used books, videos, and compact discs.

SIDE TRIPS FROM FREDERICK

Not only is Frederick within easy driving distance of Baltimore and Washington, D.C., but it's also surrounded by other areas of interest, including historic towns, scenic parks, and national battlefields.

Numbers in the margin correspond to points of interest on the Side Trips from Frederick map.

8

Monocacy National Battlefield

2 mi south of Frederick via Rte. 355.

Monocacy National Battlefield was the site of a little-known, hugely mismatched confrontation between 18,000 Confederates and 5,800 Union troops on July 9, 1864; many historians believe the Union victory thwarted a Confederate invasion of Washington, D.C. Although the Union troops were outnumbered, they delayed the Rebels by burning a bridge along the Monocacy. This tactic, along with some intensive fighting in the river, delayed the Confederates' approach to Washington, allowing the federal government time to bolster its forts. The farmland surrounding the battlefield remains largely unchanged. An electronic map in the visitor center explains the battle. ✉ 4801 Urbana Pike ☎ 301/662–3515 ⊕ *www.nps.gov/mono* 🎟 *Free* ⊘ *Daily 8–4:30, until 5:30 Memorial Day–Labor Day.*

New Market

8 mi east of Frederick via Rte. 70.

The self-proclaimed antiques capital of Maryland, New Market is a 200-year-old village surrounded by farmland. Though some things have remained the same for the past two centuries, a new addition to town is the throngs of tourists walking Main Street in search of furnishings and knickknacks.

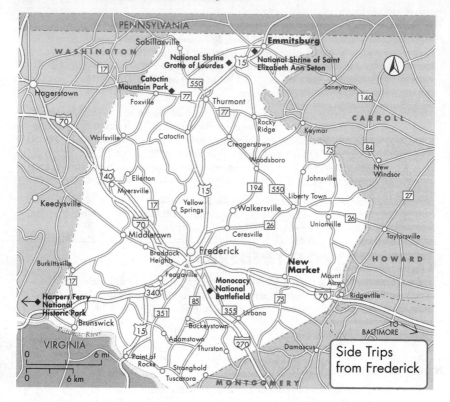

Side Trips from Frederick

Where to Eat

$–$$$ ✕ **Mealey's.** Once a store and hotel on the National Pike, Mealey's today is a busy restaurant in the heart of New Market, appropriately decorated with antiques. A large stone fireplace dominates the spacious main dining room, which is often filled to capacity on weekend evenings and Sunday afternoons; smaller dining rooms offer more privacy. Beef and Chesapeake Bay seafood are the specialties. Desserts are worth saving room for—especially the bread pudding, served with a bourbon vanilla sauce. ✉ *8 Main St.* ☎ *301/865–5488* 🖃 *AE, D, DC, MC, V.*

Harpers Ferry National Historical Park

24 mi southwest of Frederick via Rte. 340.

Less than a mile from both Maryland's and Virginia's state lines is Harpers Ferry National Historic Park in West Virginia. Thomas Jefferson described the area that makes up the park best: "On your right comes up the Shenandoah, having ranged along the foot of the mountains a hundred miles to seek a vent. On your left approaches the Potomac, in quest of a passage also. In the moment of their junction they rush together against the mountain, rend it asunder, and pass off to the sea. . . . This scene is worth a voyage across the Atlantic." The spot where these rivers converge so dramatically is also where, on October 16, 1859, the radical abolitionist John Brown led his 21-man assault on the Harpers Ferry arsenal. Today, much of Harpers Ferry has been restored as it was during the time of John Brown's raid, and historic markers and exhibits tell the story of that infamous event and the town's tumultuous involvement in the Civil War.

The township of **Harpers Ferry** grew around a U.S. armory built in 1740, and many buildings have been preserved. Meriweather Lewis (of Lewis and Clark fame) stopped here in 1803 to outfit his expedition with rifles from the armory and arsenal. Lining the cobblestone streets are shops and museums in which park employees in period costume demonstrate Early American skills and interpret the evolution of American firearms. A portion of the Appalachian Trail winds along the Potomac River and climbs uphill through the town. On the second Saturday in October the park service stages Election Day 1860, when the presidential candidates on the slate in the region (Stephen Douglas, John Bell, and John Breckinridge—Abraham Lincoln was not on this ballot) again debate the hot topic of their day: states' rights versus a strong federal union. Parking is tricky and scarce in Harpers Ferry; most visitors park at the Cavalier Heights Visitor Center and take a free shuttle into the town. The visitor center has exhibits on John Brown and the Civil War as well as the wetlands in the area. ⊠ *Parking lot 1 mi past Shenandoah bridge on Rte. 340, Harpers Ferry, WV* ☎ *304/ 535–6298* ⊕ *www.nps.gov/hafe* ⌨ *$6 per vehicle, $4 per person arriving by other means* ⊙ *Memorial Day–Labor Day, daily 8–6; Labor Day–Memorial Day, daily 8–5.*

Above the park on High Street is the small, somewhat creepy **John Brown Wax Museum,** which depicts the abolitionist's raid on the town and the highlights of his life. ⊠ *High St.* ☎ *304/535–6342* ⌨ *$4.50* ⊙ *Mid Mar.–mid-Dec., daily 9–5.*

Catoctin Mountain Park

15 mi north of Frederick via Rte. 15.

Hidden within this park is Camp David, the presidential retreat that was the site of the famous peace accords between Egypt and Israel. You won't see the camp, which has been used by presidents since Franklin D. Roosevelt, and even if you come close, you can run into security officers. What you will find are 6,000 acres of rocky outcrops and thick forests traversed by 20 mi of moderate to strenuous hiking trails, the most popular of which have scenic overlooks. A small visitor center has exhibits on the area's wildlife. Across Route 77 is **Cunningham Falls State Park,** the site of a cascading 78-foot waterfall and a man-made lake. Both parks have camping facilities. ⊠ *Rte. 77, west of Rte. 15, Thurmont* ☎ *301/ 663–9388* ⊕ *www.nps.gov/cato* ⌨ *Free* ⊙ *Visitor center: Mon.–Thurs. 10–4:30, Fri. 10–5, weekends 8:30–5. Park: daily dawn–dusk.*

Catoctin Wildlife Preserve & Zoo, 6 mi from the park, holds more than 350 animals on 30 acres. The zoo is easily navigable by children, and the tall trees and winding paths make for comfortable walking. Exotic animals here include tigers, macaws, monkeys, and boas. A petting zoo allows children to mingle with goats and other small animals. Throughout summer there are interactive shows, when children can touch snakes, talk to tigers, and learn about grizzlies. ⊠ *13019 Catoctin Furnace Rd., Thurmont* ☎ *301/271–3180* ⊕ *www.cwpzoo.com* ⬚ *$12.95* ⊙ *Mar., weekends 10–4; Apr. and Oct., daily 10–5; early to late May and early to late Sept., daily 9–5; Memorial Day–Labor Day, daily 9–6.*

Where to Eat

$–$$ ✕ **Cozy Restaurant.** A local institution, the Cozy Restaurant became internationally famous during the 1979 Camp David Accords, when hordes of reporters stayed at the adjacent inn to cover the Israeli-Egyptian peace talks. Photographs, newspaper clippings, and memorabilia from that era are on display in the restaurant's entrance halls. The 750-seat restaurant is best known these days for its all-you-can-eat buffets ($10–$15), which include seafood, steaks, fried chicken, and a belt-loosening brunch. Like spice? Don't miss the "Wall of Fire," a collection of 200 mouth-burning hot sauces; some are so hot that diners sign waivers before trying them. ⊠ *103 Frederick Rd., Thurmont* ☎ *301/271–4301* ▤ *AE, MC, V.*

▌ **EN ROUTE**   Two of Frederick County's three covered bridges span creeks near Thurmont, and make a lovely detour, especially in the fall. The **Loy's Station Covered Bridge,** originally built in 1848 and reconstructed after a fire, is east of Thurmont off Route 77. Look closely at the rooftop shingles and you'll see the signatures of the people who helped pay for the restoration. An adjacent park with playground makes a nice lunch stop if you're traveling with kids. **Roddy Road Covered Bridge,** built in 1856, is north of Thurmont, just off Route 15. The smallest of the covered bridges, it's surrounded by a cooling canopy of trees on either side and a small picnic area to enjoy.

Emmitsburg

24 mi north of Frederick via Rte. 15.

By the foothills of the Catoctin Mountains, Emmitsburg, founded in 1757, was the site of the first parochial school in the United States and the final home of the first American saint. Its Main Street remains a showcase of fine examples of Federal, Georgian, and Victorian architecture; many of the buildings are still in use as homes and businesses.

The **National Shrine Grotto of Lourdes** reproduces the famous grotto in France where a peasant girl saw visions of the Virgin Mary. The grotto, tucked into a mountain overlooking Mount Saint Mary's College, draws hundreds of thousands of people a year, and a sunrise Easter service attracts a crowd. Beautifully landscaped paths lead to the grotto and a small chapel. ⊠ *U.S. Rte. 15* ☎ *301/447–5318* ⊕ *www.msmary.edu/grotto* ⬚ *Free* ⊙ *Daily dawn–dusk.*

The **National Shrine of St. Elizabeth Ann Seton** contains the home of the first American-born saint, who came to the Maryland mountains to establish the Sisters of Charity and the nation's first parochial school. Born to wealth in New York City, Elizabeth Ann Seton (1774–1821) was widowed with five children before her experiences in Italy led her to convert to Catholicism. A short film and exhibits tell her story, and a class-room contains authentic furnishings. She is buried in a small graveyard on the well-maintained and shaded grounds. She was canonized in Rome in 1975; Pope John Paul II designated the chapel of her shrine a minor basilica in 1991. ⊠ *333 S. Seton Ave.* ☎ *301/447–6606* ⊕ *www.setonshrine.org* ✉ *Donations requested* ☉ *Tues.–Sun. 10–4:30.*

WESTERN MARYLAND

The South Mountains that divide Frederick and Washington counties once sheltered Confederates, who formed a defensive line against advancing Union soldiers just before the Battle of Antietam. Monuments and interpretive signs now tell their story at the South Mountain State Battlefield. Hikers and cyclists come to travel the South Mountains' section of the Appalachian Trail and marvel at panoramic views of the Potomac River and the valley that surrounds Hagerstown to the west.

Numbers in the margin correspond to points of interest on the Western Maryland map.

Hagerstown

❶ *25 mi west of Frederick via I–70, 75 mi west of Baltimore via I–70.*

Once a prosperous railroad hub and manufacturing center, Hagerstown is striving to redefine itself, spending millions refurbishing downtown buildings for offices and retail stores. Chic restaurants have opened along the Public Square, and plans call for the creation of an arts-and-entertainment district around the venerable Maryland Theatre, home of the Maryland Symphony Orchestra. Downtown Hagerstown has the Discovery Station, a new museum with hands-on exhibits exploring science, technology, and history. One entire floor of the museum is dedicated to the history of transportation in Washington County and features the Hagerstown Aviation Museum. The investment seems to be paying off: in 2004 *Money* magazine named Hagerstown one of its "Cities to Watch."

Hagerstown is considered the Crossroads of the Civil War. With its strategic location at the border between the North and the South, it became a principal staging area and supply center for four major campaigns in the east during the Civil War. In 1861, General Robert Patterson's troops used the town as a springboard to attack Virginia Rebels in the Shenandoah Valley Campaign. Confederates skirmished with Union forces at nearby Fort Frederick and in Hancock in December 1861. During the Maryland Campaign of 1862, General Longstreet's command occupied the town en route to the Battle of South Mountain and Antietam. In 1863 Hagerstown was the site of several military incursions and engagements as General Lee's army invaded and retreated at the Gettysburg Campaign. During the Maryland/Shenandoah Campaign of 1864, the town was occupied several times by Confederate troops and ransomed for $20,000 during General Jubal Early's invasion of Maryland.

☾ The **Hager House and Museum** is the original home of the town's founder, Jonathan Hager, who built the home in 1739 over two springs to give

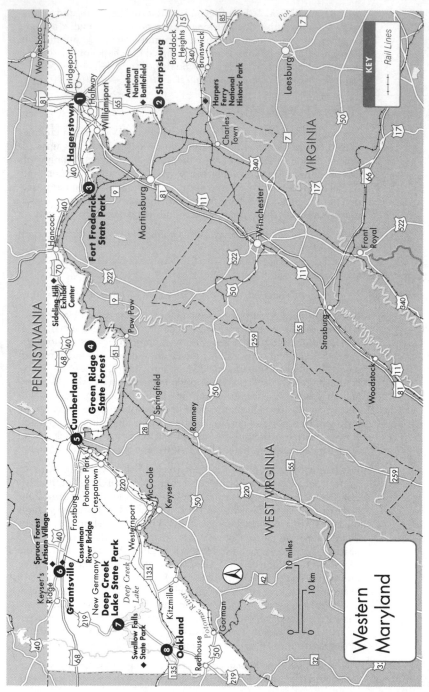

his family a protected water supply and an indoor springhouse (used to refrigerate food). Built of uncut fieldstones, the house has 22-inch-thick walls and 18th-century furnishings. Colonial-style flower and herb gardens surround it. A small museum next to the house contains an extensive collection of 18th- and 19th-century coins, forks, combs made of bone, pottery, buttons, and ironwork. The items were excavated during the house's 1953 restoration. ☒ *110 Key St.* ☎ *301/739–8393* ⊕ *www. hagerhouse.org* ☒ *$3* ⊙ *Apr.–Dec., Tues.–Sat. 10–4, Sun. 2–5.*

☾ **Hagerstown Roundhouse Museum.** Although the city's 89-year-old roundhouse was demolished in 1999, photographs, artifacts, and memorabilia from Hagerstown's railroading heyday can be found in this two-story museum, inside a former office of the Western Maryland Railway. Lights, lanterns, bells, and whistles are among the artifacts, and model railroad layouts add to the fun. ☒ *300 S. Burhans Blvd.* ☎ *301/739– 4665* ⊕ *www.roundhouse.org* ☒ *$3.50* ⊙ *Fri.–Sun. 1–5.*

★ The **Washington County Museum of Fine Arts** has an impressive collection of American paintings, drawings, prints, and sculpture from the 18th century to the present. The museum's holdings include the work of Benjamin West, James McNeill Whistler, and Norman Rockwell, as well as two portraits by Joshua Johnson, believed to be the first African-American portrait artist. The building is inside Hagerstown's beautiful **City Park,** a 27-acre wooded and landscaped haven with two small, manmade lakes—they're filled with ducks, geese, and swans in spring and fall. ☒ *91 Key St.* ☎ *301/739–5727* ⊕ *www.washcomuseum.org* ☒ *Free* ⊙ *Tues.–Fri. 9–5, Sat. 9–4, Sun. 1–5.*

Where to Stay & Eat

$–$$$ ✕ **Roccoco.** From the terrazzo floor to the crisp black-and-white photos of glamorous old movie stars, this downtown restaurant is a glitzy spot for a special evening. The selections here go beyond the usual, including crispy duck spring rolls, white pizza, potato gnocchi, and avocado pizza. Entrée standouts include a shrimp and sweet-corn risotto and sweet-pea raviolini with fried leeks and sweet cream. The wine list is extensive, impressive, and expensive (Thursday is half-price night); pastries and desserts are made on the premises. ☒ *20 W. Washington St.* ☎ *301/790–3331* ▭ *AE, D, MC, V* ⊙ *Closed Sun. and Mon.*

$$ ▣ **Wingrove Manor Bed & Breakfast.** The large, inviting front porch on this Victorian house on the north side of town has a brick stairway leading up to it, adding to the general grandeur. The three guest rooms are stately and dignified, and they also include TVs and VCRs (there's a large video library) for unwinding; some include electric fireplaces. Breakfast is served in the main dining room. ☒ *635 Oak Hill Ave., Hagerstown 21740* ☎ *301/733–6328* ▤ *301/733–5523* ⊕ *www.wingrovemanor. com* ⇋ *3 rooms* ♻ *Cable TV, Wi-Fi* ▭ *AE, DC, MC, V* ⎟◎⎟ *BP.*

¢–$ ▣ **Four Points Sheraton Hotel.** Of the plethora of chain hotels in the area, this is one of the nicest, especially after a complete overhaul of all facilities in 2006. Moving past the shocking plaid bedding, the rooms are big and surprisingly soundproof, and all are just a short walk to the indoor pool. It's also convenient to the downtown attractions and

8

neighboring Antietam National Battlefield. ⊠ *900 Dual Hwy., Hagerstown 21740* ☎ *301/790–3010* 🖨 *301/733–4559* ⊕ *www.fourpointshagerstown.com* ⇝ *108 rooms* ⟳ *Restaurant, room service, in-room data ports, pool, gym, sports bar, business services, meeting rooms* ⊟ *AE, D, DC, MC, V.*

Shopping

Prime Outlets (⊠ 495 Prime Outlets Blvd. ☎ 888/883–6288), open daily, is a cornucopia of more than 100 designer and specialty outlet stores like Polo Ralph Lauren, Coach, Banana Republic, Harry and David, Le Creuset, Nautica, and L. L. Bean.

Sharpsburg

❷ *10 mi south of Hagerstown via Rte. 65, 20 mi west of Frederick via Alt. Rte. 40 to Rte. 34.*

Fodor'sChoice
★ Among the cornfields and woods that surround Sharpsburg is the **Antietam National Battlefield,** where Union and Confederate troops clashed on September 17, 1862. It was the single bloodiest one-day battle of the war: more than 23,000 men were killed or wounded. Landmarks on the largely undisturbed battlefield include the Burnside Bridge, Dunkard Church, and Bloody Lane. The Union's victory at Sharpsburg gave President Abraham Lincoln the momentum to announce on September 22 that unless the Confederacy stopped fighting and rejoined the Union, an "Emancipation Proclamation" would be issued on January 1 that would free all slaves in Confederate states. At the visitor center are Civil War artifacts, a short film about Lincoln's visit, an hour-long documentary about the battle (shown at noon daily), and rental cassettes for narrated driving tours. An overlook provides a panoramic view of the battlefield and the countryside. ⊠ *Rte. 65, Sharpsburg Pike* ☎ *301/432–5124* ⊕ *www.nps.gov/anti* ⊠ *$4* ⊘ *Battlefield: daily dawn–dusk; visitor center: Labor Day–Memorial Day, daily 8:30–5; Memorial Day–Labor Day, daily 8:30–6.*

> ### WORD OF MOUTH
>
> "Antietam is a well-preserved battle site in a rather pretty section of Maryland. It might especially be a beautiful place to visit in October when the leaves begin to turn."
>
> –Shane

★ The modest house that holds the **Boonsborough Museum of History** is jam-packed floor-to-ceiling with unique and just plain wacky artifacts that the owner, Doug Bast, has collected. Standout exhibits include Geronimo's walking stick, a Civil War cannonball lodged in a piece of wood, and a marble piece of the original White House. There's also a mummified hand, a re-created General Store with old-timey signage, and myriad Civil War scraps, from bullets to bibles, that were collected from the area's battlefields. The museum is a must-see if you want to see something out of the ordinary. ⊠ *113 Main St., Boonsboro* ☎ *301/432–6969* 🖨 *Donations accepted* ⊘ *May–Sept., Sun. 1–5 and by appt.*

Where to Stay & Eat

$$–$$$ ✕ **Old South Mountain Inn.** Built in 1732, the South Mountain Inn was a trading post in its early days. Now a restaurant, the 18th-century stone structure is atop South Mountain along the National Pike (now Route 40). In addition to an indoor dining room, there's also an enclosed garden patio with white-wicker furniture and plants as well as a garden patio. Highlights on the continental menu include Rockfish Chesapeake, a fillet smothered in cream sauce dotted with lump crab and country ham, and Brace of Quail, quail stuffed with sausage (made in-house) and then braised in a wild mushroom and red wine sauce. ☒ *6132 Old National Pike, Boonsboro* ☎ *301/432–6155 or 301/371–5400* 🖷 *301/432–2211* 🖃 *AE, DC, MC, V* ☺ *Closed Mon.*

$–$$$ 🏨 **Inn at Antietam.** Built in 1908, this Victorian home sits on 8 acres. The site was once the campgrounds of Gen. George Pickett during the Battle of Antietam, and now it's next door to the Antietam National Cemetery. Common areas at the inn include a solarium, parlor, and wraparound porch. The country-lodgelike Gen. Burnside Smokehouse Suite has a very low-ceiling sleeping loft and an enormous Colonial kitchen brick fireplace that takes up half the room. Breakfast, with a menu that changes daily, often includes favorites like blueberry pancakes, eggs Benedict, and Belgian waffles. ☒ *220 E. Main St., Sharpsburg 21782* ☎ *301/432–6601 or 877/835–6011* 🖷 *301/432–5981* ⊕ *www.innatantietam. com* 🛏 *4 suites, 1 penthouse* ♿ *Library; no room phones, no TV in some rooms, no kids under 6, no smoking* 🖃 *AE, MC, V* ☺ *Closed Jan.*

$–$$ 🏨 **Jacob Rohrbach Inn.** The ornate Federal facade is so well preserved, you half expect a Civil War soldier to step out from behind the unusual pink-color front door. This inn served as a Civil War hospital, and some guests have reported hearing footsteps when no one was there. But the past is what draws people to the inn, which is near Antietam Battlefield, and other historic sites like the C&O Canal and Harpers Ferry. Guests can rent bikes ($6 per hour) and tour the battlefield at their leisure. ☒ *138 W. Main St., Sharpsburg 21782* ☎ *301/432–5079 or 877/839–4242* ⊕ *www.jacob-rohrbach-inn.com* 🛏 *4 rooms* ♿ *Library, Wi-Fi, massage; no room phones, no TV in some rooms, no kids under 10, no smoking* 🖃 *AE, D, MC, V.*

Fort Frederick State Park

❸ *17 mi west of Hagerstown via I-70, 40 mi west of Frederick via I-70.*

Along the Potomac River stands the only remaining stone fort from the French and Indian War, built in 1756. This was the first state park to be established in Maryland; the barracks were reconstructed in the 1930s by the Civilian Conservation Corps, to which a small museum here is dedicated. A visitor center displays artifacts from the French and Indian War and the Colonial era. ☒ *11100 Fort Frederick Rd., Big Pool* ☎ *301/842–2155* 🎟 *$3* ☺ *Apr.–Oct., daily 8 AM–dusk; Nov.–Mar., weekdays 8 AM–dusk, weekends 10 AM–dusk.*

EN ROUTE Interstate 68 cuts through Sideling Hill—the mountain that separates Washington and Allegany counties—thus exposing nearly 850 vertical feet of sedimentary rock formed 350 million years ago. At the top of the mountain is the **Sideling Hill Exhibit Center,** which seeks to explain one of the best rock exposures in the eastern United States. The four-story visitor center also has interpretive exhibits of animals native to western Maryland. Forty-minute tours that cover the center and the mountain's geology are given at 11, 1, and 3 daily. Picnic areas overlook the stunning valleys. ⊠ *I–68, 5 mi west of Hancock* ☎ *301/678–5442* 🖭 *Free* ☉ *Daily 9–5.*

Green Ridge State Forest

❹ *23 mi west of Ft. Frederick State Park via I–70 to I–68, 62 mi west of Frederick via I–70 to I–68.*

At nearly 40,000 acres, Maryland's second-largest forest stretches across most of eastern Allegany County. Its vast stands of oak, maple, hickory, and pine attract those from Baltimore, who come here to hunt, bike, and camp in fall and spring. Beneath the forest growth, decaying tombstones and crumbling stone foundations are remnants of the lives of the immigrants who worked on the C&O Canal and the railroad. Within the forest is a Potomac River overlook, where Union soldiers once stood on the lookout for Confederate saboteurs. A *Baltimore Sun* columnist called one of the park's overlooks, just off the interstate, "the best deck in Maryland" because of its phenomenal view of heavily wooded mountains. ⊠ *28700 Headquarters Dr. NE, Flintstone* ☎ *301/478–3124* 🖭 *Free* ☉ *Park office daily 8–4.*

Cumberland

❺ *17 mi west of Green Ridge State Park via I–68, 89 mi west of Frederick via I–70 to I–68, 142 mi west of Baltimore via I–70 to I–68.*

Cradled in the Allegheny Mountains, Cumberland was once America's gateway to the west. Pioneers, and later, trains and motorists, took advantage of a 1-mi-long natural pass in the mountains—the Narrows—to make their way west. The National Pike, the first federally funded highway, appropriated by Congress in 1806; the Chesapeake & Ohio Canal; and the Baltimore & Ohio Railroad all converged here in the mid-19th century. When the B&O Railroad beat the canal to Cumberland, it doomed the waterway as the future transportation route.

Today, Cumberland is revisiting its transportation heritage to help its economy and attract tourists. A two-lane highway and an excursion train now cross through the 900-foot-deep Narrows, whose exposed red shale and sandstone cliffs above make for a scenic ride. In addition, millions of dollars are being spent to restore a stretch of the canal and offer mule-drawn barge rides to visitors. The city's historic train station has been restored, and by 2007, the entire complex, known as Canal Place, will be finished to include recreational areas, pedestrian bridges, and other amenities.

In the mid- to late 19th century, Cumberland's leading politicians, doctors, lawyers, and businessmen lived in the **Washington Street Historic District,** which stretches along Washington Street from Wills Creek to Allegany Street and from Greene Street to Fayette Street. The six-block district, on the National Register of Historic Places, still reflects the architecture of the period, with prominent Federal, Greek Revival, Italianate, Queen Anne, and Georgian revival homes. Of particular interest is the **Emmanuel Episcopal Church and Parish Hall** (⊠ 16 Washington St.). It was built in 1849–50 on the site of the former Fort Cumberland, a frontier outpost during the French and Indian War. The Gothic revival church is built of native sandstone and contains three large Tiffany windows.

The only surviving structure from Fort Cumberland, **George Washington's Headquarters** (⊠ Washington and Greene Sts. ☎ 301/777–5132 ⌨ Free ⊙ By appt.) was used by the future president and military hero when he was an aide to General Braddock. The one-room cabin, built in 1754–55, stands at Prospect Square in Riverside Park, downhill from where Fort Cumberland once stood.

The Second Empire–style **Gordon-Roberts House** was built in 1867 by Josiah Gordon, president of the C&O Canal, on fashionable Washington Street. Today it's the home of the Allegany County Historical Society, and a repository for hundreds of items of local and national significance, including furniture, clothing, hats, accessories, and toys. *⊠ 218 Washington St. ☎ 301/777–8678 ⊕ www.historyhouse.allconet.org ⌨ $5 ⊙ Tues.–Sat. 10–5.*

★ ☺ The **Western Maryland Scenic Railroad** allows riders to relive the glory days of trains in Cumberland. A 1916 Baldwin locomotive, once used in Michigan's Upper Peninsula, carries you uphill through the Narrows and up scenic mountains on a 32-mi (3½-hour) round-trip to Frostburg. A 90-minute layover in Frostburg allows time for lunch at one of the many restaurants on the city's main street, just up the hill. A diesel engine typically runs on weekdays, with the more popular steam engine saved for weekends. Some rides have themes, such as murder mysteries or a train transformed into the North Pole Express. Also in Frostburg, the **Thrasher Carriage Collection Museum** (⊠ 19 Depot St. ☎ 301/689–3380 ⊕ www.thrashercarriagemuseum.com ⌨ $4 ⊙ Mar.–Dec., Wed.–Sun. 10–3; Jan. and Feb. by appt.) contains almost every style of horse-drawn vehicle, including carriages, milk wagons, sleighs, and funeral wagons. These vehicles from another era were collected by James R. Thrasher, a local blacksmith's son who became a successful businessman. Museum admission is included in the train fare. *⊠ 13 Canal St. ☎ 301/759–4400 or 800/872–4650 ⊕ www.wmsr.com ⌨ $23 ⊙ Departures at 11:30 AM: May–Sept., Wed.–Sun; Oct., daily; Nov.–mid-Dec., weekends.*

8

The **C&O Canal National Historical Park** explains Cumberland's role as the western terminus of the C&O Canal. Interactive exhibits relate to boatbuilding at the Cumberland boatyards and the regional coal industry, which used the canal to transport coal to D.C. You can walk through a re-created Paw Paw Tunnel, one of the landmarks along the nearly 185-mi canal. *⊠ Western Maryland Railway Station, 13 Canal St. ☎ 301/722–8226 ⊕ www.canalplace.org ⌨ Free ⊙ Daily 9–5.*

Where to Stay & Eat

$$–$$$ ✕ **J. B.'s Steak Cellar.** A blazing fireplace, dark paneling, and cushioned chairs keep this basement-level restaurant cozy in winter, when skiers returning home from the Wisp Ski Area in neighboring Garrett County stop by. Cuts of beef and fresh seafood are displayed in a glass case in one of the two small dining rooms, and steaks are grilled in front of diners. The menu, predominantly beef, chicken, and seafood, also includes pasta dishes such as seafood Alfredo and portobello mushroom linguine. Prime rib remains a favorite. ⊠ *12801 Ali Ghan Rd. NE, Exit 46, I–68, 1 mi east of Cumberland, Cumberland* ☎ *301/722–6155* ▤ *AE, D, DC, MC, V.*

$–$$$ ✕ **Au Petit Paris.** Murals of Paris street scenes welcome diners to this restaurant, where the three intimate dining rooms are decorated with pictures of the City of Light. Duckling, lamb, veal, and seafood are the specialties here. Signature dishes include ostrich medallions served in a wine sauce with mushroom caps, and baked shrimp stuffed with crab. The chateaubriand steak ($60) serves two and must be ordered 24 hours in advance. Desserts include bananas Foster and cherries jubilee. ⊠ *86 E. Main St., Frostburg* ☎ *301/689–8946* ⚖ *Reservations essential* ▤ *AE, D, DC, MC, V* ☉ *Closed Sun. and Mon.*

$–$$$ ✕ **City Lights.** This casual restaurant, inside a two-story building, has wooden booths and tables covered in white linens. Seafood, hand-cut steaks, and pasta dishes are the dinner staples here. The lasagna Florentine, an eye-popping 32-layer spinach lasagna, attracts attention most evenings. Housemade New York–style cheesecakes are among the desserts. ⊠ *59 Baltimore St.* ☎ *301/722–9800* ▤ *AE, D, DC, MC, V* ☉ *Closed Sun.*

¢–$$ ✕ **When Pigs Fly.** It's a virtual pig explosion inside this local favorite. All creatures pink and pudgy grace the walls and the ceiling. Known for their sweet ribs (of course), there's also a comprehensive selection of all meats served BBQ-style. ⊠ *18 Valley St.* ☎ *301/722–7447* ▤ *AE, MC, V.*

★ $$$ ✕▥ **Savage River Lodge.** Halfway between Grantsville and Frostburg, the Lodge is hidden in Maryland's largest state forest. This rustic retreat on a plot of 45 acres has 18 cozy, two-level cabins, a first-rate restaurant, and a lovable dog mascot. The handsome three-story lodge, with a towering stone fireplace that splits the room, is a short walk from the cabins. The cabins contain oversize furniture, queen-size beds in a loft, and gas log fireplaces and ceiling fans. Muffins and orange juice are delivered to your room every morning. The restaurant, open Thursday through Sunday, uses only the freshest local meats, dairy products and seasonal vegetables. The cornish hen with sausage and cornbread stuffing and the seared duck breast are particular favorites. Reservations are required. ⊠ *1600 Mount Aetna Rd., 5.2 mi off I–68, Exit 29, Frostburg 21532* ☎ *301/689–3200* ⬚ *301/689–2746* ⊕ *www. savageriverlodge.com* ↬ *18 cabins* ⚖ *Restaurant, fishing, mountain bikes, hiking, cross-country skiing, bar, library, business services, meeting rooms, some pets allowed (fee); no room TVs* ▤ *AE, D, MC, V.*

$$ ▥ **Rocky Gap Lodge and Golf Resort.** With Evitts Mountain and Lake Habeeb as a backdrop, this resort is in one of the state's most idyllic spots. The lobby, dining room, and lounge overlook a 243-acre man-made lake. In keeping with the nature outside, greens and browns are used throughout the six-story hotel. Rooms, larger than usual, are appointed with Shaker-style furniture, and most have views of a breathtaking ridge of mountains. If traveling with your pet, request a special "V.I.P." room, which greets your furry one with a special treat basket. Suites include a gas fireplace and sitting area. Try a spa treatment, 18 holes on the golf course, a hike along the park's trails, or boating, fishing, and swimming. ⊠ *Rocky Gap State Park, 16701 Lakeview Rd., Box 1199, Flintstone 21530* ☎ *301/784–8400 or 800/724–0828* 🖶 *301/784–8408* ⊕ *www.rockygapresort.com* ➯ *203 rooms, 15 suites* ♿ *2 restaurants, 18-hole golf course, 3 tennis courts, indoor-outdoor pool, lake, gym, spa, beach, boating, fishing, hiking, bar, business services, meeting rooms, some pets allowed (fee)* ⊟ *AE, D, DC, MC, V.*

¢–$ 🏨 **Holiday Inn-Downtown.** Cumberland's only downtown hotel is within walking distance of the downtown mall, historic sites, and the C&O Canal. The hotel caters to many business travelers and includes the usual Holiday Inn amenities: in-room coffeemaker, hair dryer, iron, and ironing board. Rooms on the west side of the six-story hotel come with a panoramic view of the mountains. Passing night trains can sometimes bother those sleeping on the opposite side. ⊠ *100 S. George St., 21502* ☎ *301/724–4001* 🖶 *301/724–4001* ⊕ *www.cumberland-dtn.holidayinn.com* ➯ *130 rooms* ♿ *Restaurant, room service, in-room data ports, pool, gym, bar, business services, meeting rooms, airport shuttle, some pets allowed (fee)* ⊟ *AE, MC, V.*

☾ $–$$ 🏨 **Inn at Walnut Bottom.** Within two 19th-century row houses connected by a modern addition, this charming country inn is within walking distance of Cumberland's historic district. Antiques and reproductions of 19th-century country furniture are standard in each of the guest rooms. Lemonade, apple cider, and homemade sweets are served every afternoon in an upstairs sitting room that's filled with games, puzzles, books, and magazines. You can rent bicycles for a ride along the flat towpath of the C&O Canal, and then unwind with a Danish massage treatment called Afspaending, which means "unbuckling." ⊠ *120 E. Greene St., 21502* ☎ *301/777–0003 or 800/286–9718* 🖶 *301/777–8288* ⊕ *www.iwbinfo.com* ➯ *12 rooms* ♿ *Massage, bicycles; no smoking* ⊟ *AE, D, MC, V* ⊙ *BP.*

Sports & the Outdoors
Allegany Expeditions Inc. (⊠ 10310 Columbus Ave. NE, Cumberland ☎ 301/722–5170) offers guided backpacking, caving, canoeing, fishing, and kayaking tours. The company also rents out camping equipment.

EN ROUTE Along the Old National Road out of Cumberland stands the only remaining tollhouse in Maryland. Built in 1836, the **LaVale Toll Gate House** is a four-room building that housed the gatekeepers who collected tolls until the early 1900s. ⊠ *Historic National Rd., Rte. 40, LaVale* ☎ *301/729–3047* ⊙ *May–mid-Oct., weekends 1:30–4:30.*

8

350 < Frederick & Western Maryland

Grantsville

6 *21 mi west of Cumberland via I–68.*

Two miles south of the Mason-Dixon Line, Grantsville is a village amid some of the most productive farmland in the region. It is also in the heart of the county's Amish and Mennonite communities. To the west and south is Maryland's largest forest, the 53,000-acre Savage River State Forest. Mostly undeveloped, it's used by hikers, campers, anglers, and, in winter, cross-country skiers. Also nearby is New Germany State Park, which has hiking trails, campsites, and cabins.

By the time you see the **Casselman River Bridge** (⊠ Rte. 40), you're almost in Grantsville. This single-span stone arch bridge ½ mi east of town was built in 1813; at the time it was the largest of its kind. Though the bridge is no longer in use, it serves as the backdrop for a small state park and picnic area.

The history and craftsmanship of Upper Appalachia are exhibited at the rustic **Spruce Forest Artisan Village and Penn Alps,** a museum village where spinners, weavers, potters, stained-glass workers, wood sculptors, and bird carvers demonstrate their skills. The Winterberg House, a log stagecoach stop, is the last remaining log tavern along the Old National Pike. It's now used as a crafts store and restaurant. ⊠ *177 Casselman Rte., at Rte. 40* ☎ *301/895–3332* ⊕ *www.spruceforest.org* ⊠ *Free* ⊙ *Mon.–Sat. 10–5.*

In the northern end of Savage River State Forest, the much smaller **New Germany State Park** (400 acres) contains stands of hemlocks and pines planted in the late 1950s. In winter this popular hiking spot's 8 mi of trails are groomed for cross-country skiing. A 13-acre man-made lake is available for swimming, fishing, and boating. The park also has picnic shelters, 39 campsites, and 11 rental cabins, fully equipped for year-round use. ⊠ *349 Headquarters La., 25 mi southwest of Cumberland via I–68 and Lower New Germany Rd., Exit 24* ☎ *301/895–5453* ⊕ *www.dnr.state.md.us* ⊠ *$2 Memorial Day–Labor Day; $3 during ski season* ⊙ *Daily dawn–dusk.*

Shopping
Yoder Country Market (⊠ Rte. 669 ☎ 301/895–5148), open Monday through Saturday, began as a butcher shop on a Mennonite family farm in 1947. Today, the market sells breads, cookies, pies, and pastries baked on the premises. There's also a nice selection of bulk groceries, local food products, meats, and homemade jams and jellies. A Mennonite kitchen serves a limited menu.

Deep Creek Lake

21 mi southwest of Grantsville via I–68 and Rte. 219.

Garrett County's greatest asset, the 3,900-acre Deep Creek Lake was created in the 1920s as a water source for a hydroelectric plant on the Youghiogheny (pronounced "Yok-a-gainy") River—a favorite among kayakers and white-water rafters. Though much of Deep Creek Lake's

65-mi shoreline is inaccessible to the public, it's visible from Route 219 and from numerous restaurants and motels, many of which have private docks.

★ ❼ For best public access, visit **Deep Creek Lake State Park** (✉ 898 State Park Rd. ☎ 301/387–4111 ⊕ www.dnr.state.md.us). The 1,818-acre park hugs the eastern shore of the lake and has a public boat launch, small beach, and picnic and camping sites. At the park's Discovery Center are hands-on educational activities for children, a

> ### WORD OF MOUTH
>
> "In August Deep Creek Lake in Western Maryland is a great place to escape the heat and humidity . You could rent a cabin on the lake and fish, swim or canoe."   –larry

freshwater aquarium, native animals on display, and a small gift shop. The center is also a staging area for organized outdoor activities, including lake boat tours.

Ⓒ The two biggest attractions in the area are the lake and Marsh Mountain. And the **Wisp Resort** takes advantage of both. Not only does the resort boast Maryland's only alpine ski slopes, but it's a virtual amusement park with water and snow tubing, a skatepark, paintball course, climbing wall, white-water rafting and waterskiing, mountainbiking, and even summer skiing to name a few activities. Called "the Wisp" by locals, the mountain has a humble history: its eastern face was once a cow pasture. Today it's one of the area's most popular destinations.

Where to Stay & Eat

The area's most popular lodging choice is the ski resort. You can also rent a private house through **Railey Mtn. Lake Vacations** (☎ 800/846–7368 or 301/387–2124 ⊕ rentals.deepcreek.com). Year-round options include lakefront chalets as well as log cabins inside the woods. Many of the rentals have amenities like outdoor hot tubs, double balconies, game rooms, stone fireplaces, whirlpool tubs, and private piers.

$–$$ ✕ **Deep Creek Brewing Co.** You know it's not your typical brew pub when the menu includes Wild Stew—venison, elk, and ostrich cooked in beer. (There are also more traditional entrées like fish-and-chips, paninis, and a unique crab Caesar salad.) Just off Route 219 above Deep Creek Lake, the pub pours four handcrafted beers—golden and pale ales and stouts—as well as seasonal selections. No alcohol is served Sunday. ✉ 75 Visitor Center Dr., McHenry ☎ 301/387–2182 ☰ AE, D, MC, V.

¢–$$ ✕ **Bumble Q's.** The Texas flavor of the barbecue here may seem out of place in Appalachia, but owner and Garrett County native Vivian Padgett spent some time cooking on a Texas ranch. Taste her pulled pork sandwich or BBQ ribs and you'll know why the unassuming joint is a local favorite. Her chili contains three types of beans and chopped roast beef. The homemade desserts are great. ✉ 145 Bumble Bee Rd., just off Rte. 219 ☎ 301/387–7667 ☰ No credit cards ☉ No dinner Sun.–Tues.

¢–$ ✕ **Canoe on the Run.** This casual coffee bar and café near Deep Creek Lake serves a health-conscious menu. The food is freshly prepared and includes a selection of green salads as well as turkey, cheese, mushroom, and seafood sandwiches. Appetizers include red chili and a smoked gouda

8

and chicken quesadilla; there are jumbo cookies, muffins, scones, and mini–bundt cakes for dessert. A short walk uphill from the lake, the café opens at 8 AM. ✉ *2622 Deep Creek Dr., McHenry* ☎ *301/387–5933* ▤ *AE, D, DC, MC, V.*

$$$ 🏨 **Lake Pointe Inn.** This restored 1890 stone farmhouse sits on a cove 13 feet from Deep Creek Lake. A wraparound porch has rocking chairs in which you can pass the afternoon gazing out at the water. A stone fireplace dominates the inn's great room, where guests can relax by a blazing fire, or opt for a rejuvenating massage from the small spa menu. The floor and paneling on the first floor are original chestnut. All rooms have lake or ski slope views, and seven have fireplaces and spa tubs. Hors d'oeuvres are served in the great room in the evenings. ✉ *174 Lake Pointe Dr., McHenry 21541* ☎ *301/387–0111 or 800/523–5253* ☎ *301/387–0190* ⊕ *www.deepcreekinns.com* ⇨ *9 rooms, 1 suite* ☐ *Cable TV, in-room VCRs, Wi-Fi, tennis court, lake, outdoor hot tub, dock, boating, bicycles; no smoking* ▤ *D, MC, V* ⏐◯⏐ *BP.*

$–$$ 🏨 **Savage River Inn.** Way off the beaten path within the Savage River State Forest, this inn began as a farmhouse in 1934. Additions since have created a modern, four-story structure. The great room has a large stone fireplace and splendid views of mountain scenery. Outside, enjoy a landscaped garden, pool, and hot tub. Rooms are decorated with country furnishings, and two have sitting areas and fireplaces. ✉ *Rte. 495 S to Dry Run Rd., Box 147, McHenry 21541* ☎ *301/245–4440* ⊕ *www.savageriverbandb.com* ⇨ *4 rooms* ☐ *Pool, hot tub, bicycles, hiking; no room TVs* ▤ *MC, V* ⏐◯⏐ *BP.*

🌣 **$–$$** 🏨 **Wisp Resort Hotel.** This is the big gun of Western Maryland, with activities that run the gamut from skiing, fly-fishing, an on-site spa, skatepark, and paintball arena. Some of the rooms here are ski-in ski-out, and they all include modern appliances, fluffy comforters, and comfortable lodge furniture to sink into after a long day on the slopes, the water, or on your derriere. Parents can take advantage of the Club Wisp Kids' Night Out program as they skip out to the spa or for a round of golf. All activities are arranged through the hotel. ✉ *290 Marsh Hill Rd., McHenry 21541* ☎ *800/462–9477 or 301/387–5581* ☎ *301/387–8634* ⊕ *www.wispresort.com* ⇨ *102 suites, 67 rooms* ☐ *2 restaurants, food court, some kitchenettes, refrigerators, spa, bar, shop, some pets allowed (fee)* ▤ *AE, D, DC, MC, V.*

Sports & the Outdoors

BICYCLING **High Mountain Sports** (✉ 21327 Garrett Hwy., McHenry ☎ 301/387–4199) rents mountain bikes, snow and water skis, kayaks, and snowboards and sells outdoor gear and equipment. Kayak, mountain bike, and other outdoor tours are available as well.

BOATING At the docks at Deep Creek Lake State Park, **Nature Lake Tours** (✉ 898 State Park Rd. ☎ 301/746–8782) runs sunrise, nature, dinner, and family-oriented tours of the lake daily from April through October.

SKIING **Wisp Resort** has 94 acres of trails ranging from beginner to difficult; most are open for night skiing. A "Savage Super Pipe" and two terrain parks challenge snowboarders and extreme skiers. The Bear Claw Tubing Park has nine 800-foot-long tubing lanes. Peak season lift rates (mid-

Dec. through early Mar.) are $28/$23 adult/junior for ½ day on weekdays, $39/$31 on weekends; prices go up about $3–$4 on holidays. Ski/snowboard rentals are $32/$36 respectively. Tubing sessions run in two-hour blocks; rates are $15/$19 per person weekdays–weekends and holidays. ⊠ *290 Marsh Hill Rd., McHenry* ☎ *800/462–9477 or 301/387–4911* ☰ *AE, D, MC, V* ⊘ *Closed Apr.–mid-Dec.*

Oakland

8 *11 mi southwest of Deep Creek Lake State Park via Rte. 219.*

Though it's the Garrett County seat, the town of Oakland keeps a low profile. Tucked away in Maryland's extreme southwestern corner, the town sits atop a mountain plateau, 2,650 feet above sea level. Oakland prospered during the last half of the 19th century, when the famous Baltimore & Ohio Railroad reached town, bringing summer vacationers. Trains no longer bring tourists, but Oakland survives as the government and commercial center of the county.

At **Swallow Falls State Park,** paths wind along the Youghiogheny River, past shaded rocky gorges and rippling rapids, to a 63-foot waterfall. The park is also known for its stand of 300-year-old hemlocks and for its excellent camping, hiking, and fishing facilities. ⊠ *222 Herrington La., off Rte. 219, Oakland* ☎ *301/334–9180* ⊕ *www.dnr.state.md.us* ⊠ *$2 Memorial Day–Labor Day; $1 Labor Day–Memorial Day* ⊘ *Daily dawn–dusk.*

Where to Stay & Eat

$$–$$$ ✕ **Cornish Manor.** Built in 1868 this ornate Victorian house was once the home of a Washington, D.C., judge. Today the 7-acre grounds and expansive home have been turned into one of the area's best-known restaurants. Seafood dishes reflect U.S. states, including Floridian grilled tuna and Alaskan wild salmon. Perhaps the most decadent entrée is the chicken breast imperial, stuffed with jumbo lump crab and topped with a sweet béchamel sauce. The thick, butcher-block steaks and lobster ravioli aren't too shabby, either. Don't forget to pick up airy croissants, stacked muffins and dense fruit tarts at the on-site bakery. ⊠ *Memorial Dr.* ☎ *301/334–6499* ⚲ *Reservations essential* ☰ *AE, D, MC, V* ⊘ *Closed Sun. and Mon.*

$$–$$$ ✕ **Deer Park Inn.** French-born chef and owner Pascal Fontaine uses locally grown produce in many of his dishes at this French country restaurant. His favorite dish is confit of duck, which he marinates in its own juices after curing it overnight. Beef, seafood, chicken, and lamb round out the entrée choices. Dessert highlights include crêpes and a strawberry and rhubarb tart with crème fraîche. The restored Victorian mansion lies between Deep Creek Lake and Oakland. During the area's off-season months, the restaurant may be closed Monday–Wednesday, so call ahead. And if the name reminds you of that bottled water you're drinking, it's because this area contains one of the springs used to bottle the drink. ⊠ *65 Hotel Rd., Deer Park* ☎ *301/334–2308* ☰ *AE, D, MC, V* ⊘ *Closed Sun. No lunch.*

★ $$–$$$ ⊡ **Carmel Cove Inn.** This former monastery retreat sits on a ridge above a Deep Creek Lake cove. The chapel has been converted into an English-style great room, where you can play billiards or board games, watch movies, listen to music, or browse through magazines. Guests have free use of on-site sporting equipment, and a communal refrigerator is stocked with wine and beer. Breakfast can be taken in the small, bright dining room, in your room, or on the deck, weather permitting. Some rooms have private decks and fireplaces. ⊠ *290 Marsh Hill Rd., Oakland 21550* ☎ *301/387–0067* 🖷 *301/387–4127* ⊕ *www.carmelcoveinn.com* ⇔ *10 rooms* ♨ *Room service, in-room DVDs, tennis court, lake, outdoor hot tub, dock, boating, fishing, bicycles, billiards, cross-country skiing; no kids under 12, no smoking* ▤ *D, MC, V* ⚹⊙⚹ *BP.*

Sports & the Outdoors

Ten minutes from Deep Creek Lake, **Precision Rafting** (⊠ Main St., Friendsville ☎ 301/746–5290) provides kayaking instruction and guided white-water rafting trips on the Upper Youghiogheny, Savage, Gauley, and Cheat rivers. Serious river rats can get decked out at **Upper Yough Whitewater Expeditions** (⊠ Macadam Rd., Friendsville ☎ 301/746–5808 or 800/248–1893), which specializes in white-water rafting.

WESTERN MARYLAND ESSENTIALS

To research prices, get advice from other travelers, and book travel arrangements, visit www.fodors.com.

Transportation

BY AIR

Travelers to western Maryland fly into international airports in the Washington-Baltimore area (Dulles, Reagan National, Baltimore-Washington International) and then commute by rental car; all three are within two hours' drive of western Maryland destinations.

🚩 **Baltimore/Washington International-Thurgood Marshall Airport** ☎ 410/859–7100 ⊕ www.bwiairport.com. **Dulles International Airport** ☎ 703/572–2700 ⊕ www.metwashairports.com/Dulles. **Ronald Reagan Washington National Airport** ☎ 703/417–8000 ⊕ www.metwashairports.com/National.

BY BUS

Greyhound Lines provides daily transportation to Frederick, Hagerstown, Cumberland, and Keysers Ridge in Garrett County, from Baltimore; Washington, D.C.; and Pittsburgh, Pennsylvania. Frederick, Hagerstown, and Cumberland all operate municipal bus lines.

Frederick Transit provides bus service within Frederick and to outlying towns, including Thurmont, Emmitsburg, Jefferson, and Walkersville. Shuttle buses transport commuters to the Washington Metro at Shady Grove and Maryland's commuter train at Point of Rocks. The shuttle fare is $1.10; children under 3 feet tall ride free.

🚩 **Bus Depots Frederick Train Station** ⊠ 100 S. East St., Frederick ☎ 301/663–3311. 🚩 **Bus Lines Frederick TransIT** ☎ 301/694–2065. **Greyhound Lines** ☎ 800/229–9424 ⊕ www.greyhound.com.

BY CAR

The best way to see western Maryland is by car. Interstate 70 links Frederick to Hagerstown and intersects with Route 15 and I–270, the main highway to Washington, D.C. West of Hagerstown, I–68—the main road through western Maryland—passes through some of the most scenic stretches of the state. Follow Route 219 off I–68 to reach Deep Creek Lake and the more remote areas of Garrett County.

BY TAXI

You won't find many taxis on the streets anywhere in Western Maryland. It's best to call one of the local companies to ensure a ride.
🚹 Taxis **Antietam Cab Assn.** ✉ Hagerstown ☎ 301/393–8811. **City Cab Co.** ✉ Hagerstown ☎ 301/662–2250. **Deep Creek Lake Taxi Cab** ✉ Deep Creek ☎ 301/616–7407.

BY TRAIN

The Maryland Area Rail Commuter line runs from Frederick southwest to Point of Rocks on the Potomac River and then onto Washington, D.C. Amtrak service is available from Washington, D.C., to Cumberland.
🚹 Train Lines **Maryland Area Rail Commuter** (MARC) ☎ 866/743–3682. **Amtrak** ☎ 800/872–7245.
🚹 Train Stations **Cumberland Station** ✉ E. Harrison St. and Queen City Dr., Cumberland. **Frederick Train Station** ✉ 100 S. East St., Frederick ☎ 301/694–2065. **Point of Rocks Station** ✉ Clay St.

Contacts & Resources

EMERGENCIES
🚹 Emergency Services **Ambulance, fire, police** ☎ 911.
🚹 Hospitals **Frederick Memorial Hospital** ✉ 400 W. 7th St., Frederick ☎ 240/556–3300 ⊕ www.fmh.org. **Garrett County Memorial Hospital** ✉ 251 N. 4th St., Oakland ☎ 301/533–4000 ⊕ www.gcmh.com. **Memorial Hospital** ✉ 600 Memorial Ave., Cumberland ☎ 301/723–4000. **Sacred Heart Hospital** ✉ 900 Seton Dr., Cumberland ☎ 301/723–4200 ⊕ www.wmhs.com.

INTERNET, MAIL & SHIPPING

The mountains in this region make it hard to maintain cell phone service, let alone grab a strong Wi-Fi signal for checking your e-mail. Your best bet is your hotel room or lobby, or the handful of Internet cafés in the major cities.
🚹 Internet **Barley & Hops Grill and Microbrewery** ✉ 5473 Urbana Pike, Frederick ☎ 301/668–4444 ⊕ www.barleyandhops.net. **Port City Java** ✉ 1551 Potomac Ave., Hagerstown ☎ 301/790–5040 ⊕ www.portcityjava.com. **Trader's Coffee House** ✉ 21311 Garrett Hwy., Oakland ☎ 301/387–9246 ⊕ www.brendaspizzeria.com/coffeehouse/index.html. **Wild Mountain Cafe** ✉ 17 Howard St., Cumberland ☎ 301/759–9453 ⊕ www.wildmountaincafe.com.
🚹 Post Offices **Cumberland Post Office** ✉ 215 Park St. ☎ 301/722–8190. **Frederick Post Office** ✉ 201 E. Patrick St. ☎ 301/662–2131. **Hagerstown Post Office** ✉ 44 W. Franklin St. Hwy. ☎ 301/797–8100. **Oakland Post Office** ✉ 11 S. 2nd St. ☎ 301/334–3151.
🚹 Overnight Shipping **FedEx Kinkos** ✉ 1046 W. Patrick St., Frederick ☎ 301/631–0789. **Frederick Post Office** ✉ 201 E. Patrick St. ☎ 301/662–2131.

TOUR OPTIONS

Heritage Koaches provides horse-drawn trolley, carriage, and stage-coach tours of Cumberland. Mountain Getaway Tours offers guided bus tours of the mountains and historic sites in Allegany and Garrett counties and West Virginia and Pennsylvania. Westmar Tours conducts group bus tours of the Allegheny Mountain region and the Shenandoah Valley, led by guides in Colonial and 19th-century garb.

In Frederick, guides lead walking tours ($7) that focus on the town's 250 years of history by day. By night, visitors see the haunted side on the Candelight Ghost Tour ($8), weaving a spooky trail through the city's most notorious and gruesome sites. Tours start at the visitor center, which also has brochures that outline a self-guided tour.

🚌 Bus Tours **Heritage Koaches** ⊠ 13 Canal St., Cumberland ☎ 301/777-0293 ⊕ www.wstmr.com. **Mountain Getaway Tours** ☎ 800/459-0510. **Westmar Tours** ⊠ 13 Canal St., Cumberland ☎ 301/777-0293 ⊕ www.wstmr.com.

VISITOR INFORMATION

Travelers can pick up information at the official tourism offices in each major town. However, since those towns are quite a distance apart, pamphlets and brochures can be found in many regional hotel and restaurant lobbies, and posted at attractions. There are a few official Maryland Welcome Centers (open daily 9 AM–5 PM) along I–70 and I–68, which are staffed with volunteers who can book accommodations on the spot before you reach your next destination.

🚪 Tourism Offices **Allegany County Tourism Department** ⊠ Western Maryland Station, 13 Canal St., Cumberland 21502 ☎ 301/777-5132 or 800/425-2067 ⊕ www.mdmountainside.com. **Garrett County Chamber of Commerce** ⊠ 15 Visitors Center Dr., McHenry 21541 ☎ 301/387-4386 ⊕ www.garrettchamber.com. The **Tourism Council of Frederick County** Visitor center ⊠ 19 E. Church St., Frederick 21701 ☎ 301/228-2888 or 800/999-3613 ⊕ www.fredericktourism.org. **Hagerstown/Washington County Convention & Visitor's Bureau** ⊠ Elizabeth Hager Center, 16 Public Sq., Hagerstown 21740 ☎ 301/791-3246 ⊕ www.marylandmemories.org.

🚪 Welcome Centers **I-70 East and West** ⊠ I-70 at South Mountain, between Frederick and Hagerstown ☎ 301/293-4161 East, 301/293-2526 West. **Youghiogheny Overlook** ⊠ I-68 eastbound, 1.5 mi east of Friendsville in Garrett County ☎ 301/746-5979. **Sideline Hill Interpretive Center** ⊠ I-68 10 mi west of Hancock in Washington County ☎ 301/678-5442 ⊕ www.dnr.state.md.us/publiclands/western/sidelinghill.html.

Annapolis & Southern Maryland

WORD OF MOUTH

"The Naval Academy was one of those delightful finds . . . I am not really that interested in the military, but found the Academy tour absolutely fascinating and beautiful."

—MikeT

"Yes, the U.S. Naval Academy is a wonderful place to visit! Try to time it so you're there around lunchtime; you'll see the "Plebes" line up and march in formation into the dining hall. VERY cool and moving! Definitely spend time roaming the historic town, too, as there are many nice shops and seafood restaurants on the waterfront. Annapolis is a treasure!"

—ellen_griswold

Updated by
Norman
Renouf

THE PAST IS NEVER FAR AWAY from the present among the coves, rivers, and creeks of the Chesapeake Bay's lesser known *western* shore. In the lively port of Annapolis, Colonial Maryland continues to assert itself. Today, "Crabtown," as the state capital is sometimes called, has one of the highest concentrations of 18th-century buildings in the nation, including more than 50 that predate the Revolutionary War.

The region south of Annapolis and D.C. is a peninsula broken in two by the Patuxent River, a 110-mi-long tributary to the Bay. The counties of Anne Arundel, Calvert, Charles, and St. Mary's, which make up the area, have all been supported since their founding in the 1600s through tobacco fields and fishing fleets. More recently, the northern parts of the counties have emerged as prime residential satellites for the Annapolis-Baltimore-D.C., metro triangle—but despite the subdivisions and concomitant shopping centers, southern Maryland retains much of its rural character. With the exception of the fair-weather getaway enclave Solomons Island, and the archaeological site-in-progress, Historic St. Mary's City, the region remains largely undiscovered. All the better for travelers who do come to enjoy stunning water vistas, miles of scenic roads, dozens of historic sites, and a plethora of inns and bed-and-breakfasts on the water, in tiny towns, and in the fields and woodlands of its unspoiled countryside.

Top 5 Experiences for Annapolis & Southern Maryland

- **Experience much Colonial history:** The Maryland State House is both the oldest State House in continuous legislative use and also the only one in which the U.S. Congress has sat. General George Washington resigned as commander in chief of the Continental Army and the Treaty of Paris was ratified here, ending the Revolutionary War.

- **Salute the navy at Annapolis (an absolute must-see):** The United States Naval Academy is the most important site in town. Don't miss its centerpiece, the bright copper-clad dome of the interdenominational U.S. Naval Academy Chapel, beneath which lies the crypt of the Revolutionary War naval officer John Paul Jones.

- **Return to the golden age of the railroad:** At the Chesapeake Bay Railway Museum, housed in the railroad's 1898 trackside terminus, check out a glass-enclosed model of the town of Chesapeake Beach and a gleaming, black Ford Model T that once carried guests from the station to their hotels.

- **Dive in to local maritime history:** Discover life-size examples of historically significant types of working and pleasure boats and 17 tanks of local marine life at the Calvert Marine Museum.

- **Visit a 17th-century British settlement:** At Historic St. Mary's, the fourth permanent settlement in British North America and eventually the first (albeit short-lived) capital of Maryland, you can view ongoing restoration work in this much smaller, and less refined, version of Williamsburg, Virginia.

About the Restaurants & Hotels

In the beginning, there was crab: crab cakes, crab soup, whole crabs to crack. These days, most likely because of overfishing and habitat changes, crabs from the Bay are pretty scarce. Maryland's favorite crustacean is still found in abundance on menus, but most arrive from out of state. In addition, Annapolis has broadened its horizons to include eateries—many in the Historic District—that offer many sorts of cuisines. Ask for a restaurant guide at the visitor center.

Dinner reservations in Annapolis are recommended throughout the summer and at times of Naval Academy events.

There are many places to stay near the heart of Annapolis, as well as at area B&Bs and chain motels a few miles outside town (some of which offer free transportation to the downtown historic area). A unique "Crabtown" option is Boat & Breakfasts, in which you sleep, eat, and cruise on a yacht or schooner; book ahead. Contact the visitor center for information.

Hotel reservations are necessary, even a year in advance, during the sailboat and powerboat shows in the spring and fall and Naval Academy commencement in May.

Two reservation services operate in Annapolis. **Annapolis Accommodations** (✉ 41 Maryland Ave. ☎ 410/280–0900 or 800/715–1000 ⊕ www.stayannapolis.com) specializes in long-term rentals. The office is open 9–5 weekdays. **Annapolis Bed & Breakfast Association** (☎ 410/295–5200 ⊕ www.annapolisbandb.com) books lodging in the old section of town, which has many restaurants and shops as well as the Maryland State House and the City Dock. The U.S. Naval Academy and St. John's College serve as the northern and western boundaries of the territory.

9

WHAT IT COSTS					
	$$$$	**$$$**	**$$**	**$**	**¢**
RESTAURANTS	over $30	$22–$30	$14–$22	$7–$14	under $7
HOTELS	over $250	$175–$250	$130–$175	$80–$130	under $80

Restaurant prices are per person for a main course at dinner. Hotel prices are for a standard double room, excluding state and local taxes.

Exploring Annapolis & Southern Maryland

Annapolis and southern Maryland encompass the western shore of the Chesapeake Bay, an area within easy driving distance of Baltimore and Washington, D.C. Annapolis, on a peninsula bounded by the Severn and South rivers and the Chesapeake Bay, is a Mid-Atlantic sailing capital and the gateway to southern Maryland. Calvert County, just south of Annapolis, promises compelling Bayside scenery that includes the imposing Calvert Cliffs and several miles of bay beaches. Beyond the Patuxent River, across the 1⅓-mi Thomas Johnson Bridge, lies St. Mary's

County, a peninsula that protrudes farther into the Chesapeake, with the Patuxent and the Potomac rivers on either side of it.

ANNAPOLIS

In 1649 a group of Puritan settlers moved from Virginia to a spot at the mouth of the Severn River, where they established a community called Providence. Lord Baltimore, who held the royal charter to settle Maryland, named the area around this town Anne Arundel County, after his wife; in 1684 Anne Arundel Town was established across from Providence on the Severn's south side. Ten years later, Anne Arundel Town became the capital of Maryland and was renamed Annapolis after Princess Anne, who later became queen. It received its city charter in 1708 and became a major port, particularly for the export of tobacco. In 1774 patriots here matched their Boston counterparts (who had thrown their famous tea party the previous year) by burning the *Peggy Stewart,* a ship loaded with taxed tea. Annapolis later served as the nation's first peacetime capital (1783–84).

The city's considerable Colonial and early republican heritage is largely intact and, because it's all within walking distance, highly accessible.

■ TIP➔ Although it has long since been overtaken by Baltimore as the major Maryland port, Annapolis is still a popular pleasure-boating destination. On warm sunny days, the waters off City Dock become center stage for an amateur show of powerboaters maneuvering through the heavy traffic. Annapolis's enduring nautical reputation derives largely from the presence of the U.S. Naval Academy, whose strikingly uniformed midshipmen throng the city streets in crisp white uniforms during the summer and navy blue in winter.

Numbers in the text correspond to numbers in the margin and on the Annapolis map.

Main Attractions

★ ☾ ❸ **Banneker-Douglass Museum.** Named for abolitionist Frederick Douglass and scientist Benjamin Banneker, this former church and its next-door neighbor make up a museum that tells the stories of African-Americans in Maryland through programming, art, and interactive historic exhibits. The church hosts performances, lectures, and educational programs, while the four-floor addition houses changing exhibits and permanent shows. Audio and visual presentations and hands-on exhibits make the museum engaging for kids, while also bringing home the hardships of slave life. ⊠ *84 Franklin St.* ☎ *410/216–6180* ⊕ *www.bdmuseum.com* ⊠ *Free* ☾ *Tues.–Fri. 10–3.*

★ ❽ **Hammond-Harwood House.** This is the only Colonial home in America built to a design of the famous Italian architect Andrea Palladio. The Anglo-Palladian residence was based on a plate of the Villa Pisani in Montagnana, Italy, by William Buckland, one of America's best-known Colonial architects. Built in 1774, on the cusp of the American Revolution, it is considered America's greatest Colonial high-style residence. This architectural "Jewel of Annapolis" was greatly admired by Thomas

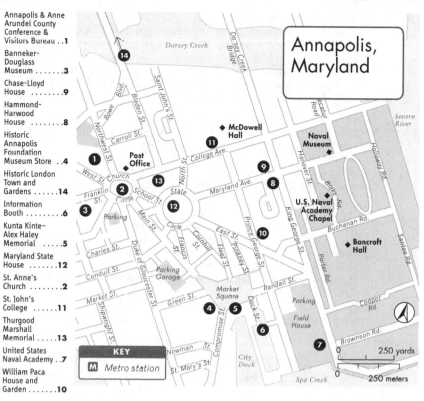

Annapolis,
Maryland

Jefferson when he sketched the house in 1783. The woodcarvings surrounding the front door and enriching the dining room are some of the best surviving of their kind in America. Today the house museum exhibits famous Colonial art by Charles Willson Peale, Rembrandt Peale, James Peale, John Trumbull, John Hesselius, Jeremiah Theus, and John Beale Bordley. The museum also exhibits the world's largest collection of inspired Colonial cabinetwork by the Annapolis native John Shaw. The Hammond-Harwood House decorative arts collection is extensive and covers everything from Chinese export porcelain to Georgian period silver. The Colonial Revival garden is by noted landscape architect Alden Hopkins from Colonial Williamsburg. Tours leave on the hour; the last begins at 4. ⊠ *19 Maryland Ave.* ☎ *410/263–4683* ⊕ *www. hammondharwoodhouse.org* 🖼 *$6* ⊙ *Late Mar.–late Oct., Tues.–Sun. noon–5; early Nov–late Mar., by appointment only.*

★ ⑭ **Historic London Town and Gardens.** This National Historic Landmark is on the South River, a short car ride from Annapolis. The three-story waterfront brick house, built by William Brown between 1758 and 1764, and with a dramatic view of the river, is one of two remaining original Colonial structures. The 17th-century tobacco port of London, made up of 40 dwellings, shops, and taverns, disappeared in the 18th century, its buildings abandoned and left to decay. The excavation of the town is underway, and some buildings have been restored. Docents conduct 30- to 45-minute house tours; allow more time to wander the grounds. From March 15 to December, house tours leave on the hour (the last is at 3). ⊠ *839 Londontown Rd., Edgewater 21037* ☎ *410/222–1919* ⊕ *www.historiclondontown.com* ≥ *$7* ⊙ *Mid-Mar.–Dec., Tues.–Sat. 10–3, Sun. noon–3.*

⓬ **Maryland State House.** Completed in 1780, the State House is the old-
Fodor'sChoice est state capitol in continuous legislative use; it's also the only one in
★ which the U.S. Congress has sat (1783–84). It was here that General George Washington resigned as commander in chief of the Continental Army and where the Treaty of Paris was ratified, ending the Revolutionary War. Both events took place in the Old Senate Chamber, which is filled with intricate woodwork (attributed to Colonial architect William Buckland) featuring the ubiquitous tobacco motif. Also decorating this room is Charles Willson Peale's painting *Washington at the Battle of Yorktown,* a masterpiece of the Revolutionary War period's finest portrait artist. The Maryland Senate and House now hold their sessions in two other chambers in the building. Also on the grounds is the oldest public building in Maryland, the tiny redbrick Treasury, built in 1735. Note that you must have a photo ID to enter the State House. ⊠ *State Circle* ☎ *410/974–3400* ≥ *Free* ⊙ *Welcome center open weekdays 8:30–5, weekends 10–4; ½-hr tour daily at 11 and 3.*

▌ NEED A BREAK? **Chick and Ruth's Delly** (⊠ **165 Main St.** ☎ **410/269–6737) is a longtime counter-and-table institution where the waitstaff is friendly and the deli sandwiches are named after local state politicos. Burgers, subs, milk shakes, and other ice-cream concoctions are also on offer. Built in 1901, it's been run by Baltimoreans Chick and Ruth Levitt since 1965.**

⓫ **St. John's College.** Students at St. John's, home to the Great Books curriculum, all follow the same four-year, liberal arts curriculum, which includes philosophy, mathematics, music, science, Greek, and French. Students are immersed in the classics, through small classes conducted as discussions rather than lectures. Start a visit here by climbing the gradual slope of the long, brick-paved path to the cupola of **McDowell Hall.** The Annapolis campus of St. John's, the third-oldest college in the country (after Harvard and William and Mary), once held the last Liberty Tree, under which the Sons of Liberty convened to hear patriots plan the Revolution. Damaged in a 1999 hurricane, the 400-year-old tree was removed; its progeny stands to the left of McDowell Hall. The **Elizabeth Myers Mitchell Art Gallery** (☎ 410/626–2556), on the east side of Mellon Hall, presents world-class exhibits and special programs that relate to the fine arts. Down King George Street toward the water is the **Carroll-Barrister House,** now the college admissions office. Once home to Charles Carroll (not the signer of the Declaration but his cousin), the house was built in 1722 at Main and Conduit streets and moved onto campus in 1955. ⊠ *60 College Ave., at St. John's St.* ☎ *410/263–2371* ⊕ *www.sjca.edu.*

⑦ United States Naval Academy. Probably the most interesting and impor-
FodorsChoice tant site in Annapolis, the Naval Academy runs along the Severn River
★ and abuts downtown Annapolis. Men and women enter from every part
of the United States and foreign countries to undergo rigorous study in
subjects that include literature, navigation, and nuclear engineering. The
academy, established in 1845 on the site of a U.S. Army fort, occupies
329 waterfront acres. The centerpiece of the campus is the bright copper-clad dome of the interdenominational **U.S. Naval Academy Chapel.**
Beneath it lies the crypt of the Revolutionary War naval officer John Paul
Jones, who, in a historic naval battle with a British ship, uttered the in-
spirational words, "I have not yet begun to fight!"

Near the chapel in Preble Hall is the **U.S. Naval Academy Museum &
Gallery of Ships** (⊠ 118 Maryland Ave. ☎ 410/293–2108), which tells
the story of the U.S. Navy through displays of model ships and memorabilia from naval heroes and fighting vessels. The U.S. Naval Institute
and Bookstore is also in this building. Admission for the museum, institute, and bookstore is free; hours are Monday through Saturday from
9 to 5 and Sunday from 11 to 5.

On the grounds, midshipmen (the term used for women as well as men)
go to classes, conduct military drills, and practice or compete in inter-
collegiate and intramural sports. **Bancroft Hall,** closed to the public, is
one of the largest dormitories in the world—it houses the entire 4,200-
member Brigade of Midshipmen. The **Statue of Tecumseh,** in front of
Bancroft Hall, is a bronze replica of the USS *Delaware*'s wooden fig-
urehead, "Tamanend." It's decorated by midshipmen for athletics events;
and for good luck during exams, students pitch pennies into his quiver
of arrows. ■ TIP➔ If you're there at noon weekdays in fair weather, you can
see midshipmen form up outside Bancroft Hall and parade to lunch accompanied by the Drum and Bugle Corps.

Adjoining Halsey Field House is the **USNA Armel-Leftwich Visitor
Center** (⊠ 52 King George St. ☎ 410/263–6933), which has exhibits
on life as a midshipman, including a mockup of a midshipman's room,
and the Freedom 7 space capsule flown by astronaut Alan Shepard, an
Academy graduate. Don't miss the award-winning film "To Serve and
to Lead." Walking tours of the Naval Academy led by licensed guides
leave from the center. You must have a photo ID to be admitted through
the Academy's gates, and only cars used for official Department of Defense business may enter the grounds. ⊕ *www.navyonline.com*
🎫 *Grounds tour $7.50* ☉ *USNA Armel-Leftwich Visitor Center.
Mar.–Dec., daily 9–5; Jan. and Feb., daily 9–4. Guided walking tours
generally leave Mon.–Sat. 10–3 on the hr and Sun. 12:30–3 on the ½
hr; call ahead to confirm and for Jan. and Feb. tour times.*

⑩ William Paca House and Garden. A signer of the Declaration of Independence, Paca (pronounced "PAY-cuh") was a Maryland governor from
1782 to 1785. His house was built in 1765, and its original garden was
finished in 1772. Inside, the main floor (furnished with 18th-century
antiques) retains its original Prussian blue and soft gray color scheme.
The second floor contains 18th-century pieces. The adjacent 2-acre gar-

den provides a longer perspective on the back of the house, plus worthwhile sights of its own: upper terraces, a Chinese Chippendale bridge, a pond, a wilderness area, and formal arrangements. An inn, Carvel Hall, once stood on the gardens. After the inn was demolished in 1965, it took eight years to rebuild the gardens, which are planted with 18th-century perennials. You can take a self-guided tour of the garden, but to see the house you must go on the docent-led tour, which leaves every hour at half past. The last tour leaves 1½ hours before closing. ⊠ *186 Prince George St.* ☎ *410/263–5553* ⊕ *www.annapolis.org* ⛋ *House and garden $8, house only $5, garden only $5* ⊙ *House and garden mid-Mar.–Dec., Mon.–Sat. 10–5, Sun. noon–5; Jan.–mid-Mar., Fri. and Sat. 10–4, Sun. noon–4.*

Also Worth Seeing

❶ Annapolis & Anne Arundel County Conference & Visitors Bureau. Start your visit at Annapolis's main visitor center. Here you can pick up maps and brochures or begin a guided tour. ⊠ *26 West St., West Side* ☎ *410/280–0445* ⊙ *Daily 9–5.*

❾ Chase-Lloyd House. Built by the prominent Colonial architect William Buckland, the Chase-Lloyd House was begun in 1769 by Samuel Chase, a signer of the Declaration of Independence and future Supreme Court justice. Five years later the tobacco planter and revolutionary Edward Lloyd IV completed the work. The first floor is open to the public and contains some impressive examples of Buckland's handiwork, including a parlor mantelpiece with tobacco leaves carved into the marble. (Buckland was famous for his interior woodwork; you can see more of it in the Hammond-Harwood House across the street and in George Mason's Gunston Hall in Lorton, Virginia.) The house, furnished with a mixture of 18th-, 19th-, and 20th-century pieces, has a staircase that parts dramatically around an arched triple window. For more than 100 years the house has served as a home for older women, who live upstairs. ⊠ *22 Maryland Ave.* ☎ *410/263–2723* ⛋ *$2* ⊙ *Mar.–Dec., Mon., Tues., Thurs., and Fri. 2–4.*

❹ Historic Annapolis Foundation Museum Store. In a redbrick building at the base of Main Street, the store occupies the site of a warehouse that held supplies for the Continental Army during the Revolutionary War. Today it's filled with maps, Maryland history books, ceramics, and nautical knickknacks. You can rent taped narrations here for 90-minute walking tours. ⊠ *77 Main St.* ☎ *410/268–5576* ⊕ *www.annapolis.org* ⛋ *Free* ⊙ *Mon.–Thurs. 10–8, Fri. and Sat. 10–9, Sun. 10–7; fewer hrs in winter.*

❻ Information Booth. From April to October the information booth on City Dock, adjacent to the harbormaster's office, is open and stocked with maps and brochures. ⊠ *Dock St. parking lot* ☎ *410/280–0445.*

❺ Kunta Kinte–Alex Haley Memorial. A series of plaques along the waterfront recounting the story of African-Americans in Maryland lead to a sculpture group depicting the famed author reading to a group of children. On the other side of the street, a three-sided obelisk and plaque commemorates the 1767 arrival of the African slave immortalized in Alex Haley's *Roots.* ⊠ *Market Sq.* ⊕ *www.kintehaley.org.*

② **St. Anne's Church.** Residing in the center of one of the historic area's busy circles, this brick building is one of the city's most prominent places of worship. King William III donated the Communion silver when the parish was founded in 1692, but the first St. Anne's Church wasn't completed until 1704. The second church burned in 1858, but parts of its walls survived and were incorporated into the present structure, built the following year. The churchyard contains the grave of the last Colonial governor, Sir Robert Eden. ☒ *Church Circle* ☎ *410/267–9333* ☑ *Free* ⊙ *Weekdays 6–6, Sat. 6–2; services on Sun.*

⑬ **Thurgood Marshall Memorial.** Born in Baltimore, Thurgood Marshall (1908–93) was the first African-American Supreme Court Justice and was one of the 20th century's foremost leaders in the struggle for equal rights under the law. Marshall won the decision in 1954's *Brown v. Board of Education,* in which the Supreme Court overturned the doctrine of "separate but equal." Marshall was appointed as U.S. Solicitor General in 1965 and to the Supreme Court in 1967 by President Lyndon B. Johnson. The 8-foot statue depicts Marshall as a young lawyer. ☒ *State House Sq., bordered by Bladen St., School St., and College Ave.*

Where to Eat

$$$–$$$$ ✕ **aqua terra.** This funky restaurant gives history-minded Annapolis an alternative to the Colonial flavor found at most other downtown eateries. Inside are blond-wood furniture, an open kitchen, and a handsome granite counter under a row of blue teardrop-shape lamps. The menu features ingredients from the water (aqua) and the earth (terra), with additional small plates, soups, and salads. Offerings change with the season but include seafood, beef, and pasta as regular features. ☒ *164 Main St.* ☎ *410/263–1985* ☐ *AE, MC, V* ⊙ *Closed Mon. No lunch.*

☾ $$–$$$$ ✕ **Buddy's Crabs & Ribs.** With a great location overlooking Main Street and City Dock, this fun and informal restaurant features all kinds of seafood and shellfish, including their famous "Big Buddy" crab cakes and all-you-can-eat buffets. With each full-price entrée, one child 10 and under can eat free from the kids' menu. ☒ *100 Main St.* ☎ *410/626–1100* ☐ *AE, D, DC, MC, V.*

★ $$–$$$$ ✕ **Harry Browne's.** In the shadow of the State House, this understated establishment has a reputation for quality food and attentive service that ensures bustle year-round, especially during the busy days of the legislative session (early January into early April) and special weekend events at the Naval Academy. The menu clearly reflects the city's maritime culture, but also has seasonal specialties such as rack of lamb and wild mushroom ravioli. ■ **TIP➔** Live Irish music is performed in the lounge every Monday night. The sidewalk café is open, weather permitting, April through October. ☒ *66 State Circle* ☎ *410/263–4332* ☐ *AE, D, DC, MC, V.*

$$–$$$$ ✕ **Phillips Annapolis Harbor.** Overlooking the dock and water, this popular restaurant is the destination of choice for serious seafood lovers. This small chain has been a tradition since 1956. Besides their extraordinary crab cakes, the shrimp and various combination platters are mouthwateringly enticing, and don't overlook the mahimahi, rockfish, and flounder dishes. ☒ *12 Dock St.* ☎ *410/990–9888* ☐ *AE, D, DC, MC, V.*

9

$$–$$$ ✕ **Café Normandie.** Ladder-back chairs, wood beams, skylights, and a four-sided fireplace make this French restaurant homey. Out of the open kitchen comes an astonishingly good French onion soup, made daily from scratch. Bouillabaisse, puffy omelets, crêpes, and seafood dishes are other specialties. The restaurant's breakfast, served only on weekends, includes poached eggs in ratatouille, eggs Benedict, seafood omelets, and crêpes, waffles, and croissants. ⊠ *185 Main St.* ☎ *410/263–3382* 🖃 *AE, D, DC, MC, V.*

$$–$$$ ✕ **Carrol's Creek.** You can walk, catch a water taxi from City Dock, or drive over the Spa Creek drawbridge to this local favorite in Eastport. Whether you dine indoors or out, the view of historic Annapolis and its harbor is spectacular. The all-you-can-eat Sunday brunch ($21.95) is worth checking out, as are the seafood specialties. Any of the entrées, including the herb-encrusted rockfish or Muscovy duck breast, can be turned into a four-course meal with the addition of soup, salad, and dessert for $12 more. ⊠ *410 Severn Ave., Eastport* ☎ *410/263–8102* 🖃 *AE, D, DC, MC, V.*

$$–$$$ ✕ **Middleton Tavern.** Horatio Middleton began operating this "inn for seafaring men" in 1750; Washington, Jefferson, and Franklin were among his guests. Today, two fireplaces, wood floors, paneled walls, and a nautical theme make it cozy. Seafood tops the menu; the Maryland crab soup and pan-seared rockfish are standouts. Try the tavern's own Middleton Pale Ale, perhaps during happy hour or during a weekend blues session in the upstairs piano bar. Brunch is served on weekends, and you can dine outdoors in good weather. ⊠ *City Dock at Randall St.* ☎ *410/263–3323* 🖃 *AE, D, DC, MC, V.*

$–$$$ ✕ **Cantler's Riverside Inn.** Opened in 1974, this local institution was founded by Jimmy Cantler, a native Marylander who worked as a waterman on the Chesapeake Bay. The no-nonsense interior has wooden blinds and floors and nautical items laminated beneath tabletops. Food is served on disposable dinnerware; if you order steamed crabs, they'll come served atop a "tablecloth" of brown paper. Waterview outdoor dining is available seasonally. Boat owners can tie up at the dock; free parking spaces are rare during the busy summer season. Specialties include steamed mussels, clams, and shrimp as well as Maryland vegetable crab soup, seafood sandwiches, oysters, crab cakes, and numerous finfish. This place is easiest to find by boat, so if you're coming by car, call for directions. ⊠ *458 Forest Beach Rd.* ☎ *410/757–1311* 🖃 *AE, D, DC, MC, V.*

★ $$ ✕ **Rams Head Tavern.** A traditional English-style pub also houses the Fordham Brewing Company, which you can tour. The Rams Head serves better-than-usual tavern fare, including spicy shrimp salad, crab cakes, beer-battered shrimp, and daily specials, as well as more than 100 beers— 15 on tap—including six Fordham's beers and others from around the world. Brunch is served on Sunday. The nightclublike Rams Head Tavern On Stage brings in nationally known folk, rock, jazz, country, and bluegrass artists. Dinner-show specials are available; the menu has light fare. ⊠ *33 West St.* ☎ *410/268–4545* 🖃 *AE, D, DC, MC, V.*

$–$$ ✕ **El Toro Bravo.** A local favorite, this authentic Mexican restaurant is family-owned. The wooden Colonial exterior conceals colorful, south-of-the-border scenes hand painted on the interior walls, hanging plants, and padded aqua booths. There's often a line, but takeout is available. Lunch and dinner specials include a variety of enchiladas, fish tacos, grilled shrimp, and steak. The guacamole is made on the premises. ⊠ *50 West St., 1 block from visitor center* ☎ *410/267–5949* ⊟ *AE, D, DC, MC, V.*

$–$$ ✕ **49 West Coffeehouse and Gallery.** In what was once a hardware store, this eclectic, casual eatery has one interior wall of exposed brick and another of exposed plaster; both are used to hang art for sale by local artists. Daily specials are chalked on a blackboard. Menu staples include a large cheese and pâté plate, deli sandwiches, and soups and salads. There's free Wi-Fi, and live music every night but Sunday. ⊠ *49 West St.* ☎ *410/626–9796* ⊟ *AE, D, DC, MC, V.*

¢–$$ ✕ **McGarvey's Saloon and Oyster Bar.** An Annapolis institution since 1975, this dockside eatery and watering hole is full of good cheer, great drink, and grand food. A heritage of seasonal shell- and finfish dishes, the finest burgers and steaks, as well as unstinting appetizers, make McGarvey's menu one of the most popular in the area. The full menu is available daily until 11 PM. ⊠ *8 Market Space* ☎ *410/263–5700* ⊟ *AE, DC, MC, V.*

Where to Stay

$$$$ ▦ **The Annapolis Inn.** An extraordinarily elegant B&B, this circa-1770 house has richly colored rooms decorated in the formal style of the home's original era. The master suite has a sitting room and two fireplaces. Each suite has a king-size bed with luxury linens and a bathroom with hand showers, bidets, and heated towel holders and marble floors. From the third-floor suite's sundeck there's a close-up view of the domes of the Naval Academy Chapel and the state capitol and the harbor. Breakfast is a sumptuous three-course event served in the stately dining room. TVs are placed in the rooms on request. ⊠ *144 Prince George St., 21401* ☎ *410/295–5200* ☐ *410/295–5201* ⊕ *www.annapolisinn.com* ⬐ *3 suites ₰ Dining room, in-room data ports, free parking; no kids, no smoking* ⊟ *AE, MC, V* ⭘ *BP.*

$$$$ ▦ **Annapolis Marriott Waterfront.** You can practically fish from your room at the city's only waterfront hotel. Rooms have either balconies over the water or large windows with views of the harbor or the historic district. The outdoor bar by the harbor's edge is popular in nice weather. ⊠ *80 Compromise St., 21401* ☎ *410/268–7555 or 800/336–0072* ☐ *410/269–5864* ⊕ *www.annapolismarriott.com* ⬐ *150 rooms ₰ Restaurant, cable TV, in-room data ports, gym, boating, 2 bars, shop, laundry service, concierge, business services, meeting rooms, parking (fee), no-smoking rooms* ⊟ *AE, D, DC, MC, V.*

$$$–$$$$ ▦ **Loews Annapolis Hotel.** Although its redbrick exterior blends with the city's 1700s architecture, the interior is airy, spacious, and modern in this AAA 4-Diamond hotel. Guest rooms, decorated in a sailing theme, include coffeemakers and terry robes. A free hotel shuttle bus takes you anywhere you want to go in Annapolis, and a complimentary breakfast is served in the Breeze restaurant for concierge-level guests. ⊠ *126 West St., 21401* ☎ *410/263–7777 or 800/235–6397* ☐ *410/263–0084* ⊕ *www.loewsannapolis.com* ⬐ *210 rooms, 7 suites ₰ 2 restaurants,*

9

room service, minibars, cable TV with movies, in-room data ports, gym, hair salon, bar, laundry service, concierge, concierge floor, business services, meeting rooms, airport shuttle, parking (fee), no-smoking floors ⊟ *AE, D, DC, MC, V.*

$$$–$$$$ ⊞ **O'Callaghan Hotel.** When this Irish-owned and -operated hotel opened in 2002, it was the city's first new downtown hotel in more than two decades. Floor-length drapes and the lush, blue carpets flecked in gold colors were custom-made in Ireland (much of the attentive staff is from the Emerald Isle as well). Meeting rooms are named after counties in Ireland, and maps and pictures of the Old Country adorn the elegant guest rooms. The first-floor restaurant and bar overlooks West Street and carries a limited but fine selection of entrées. ⊠ *174 West St., 21401* ☎ *410/263–7700* 🖷 *410/990–1400* ⊕ *www.ocallaghanhotels-us.com* ⇋ *120 rooms, 2 suites* ⏶ *Restaurant, cable TV with movies and video games, Wi-Fi, health club, bar, laundry service, concierge, Internet room, business services, meeting rooms, parking (fee)* ⊟ *AE, D, DC, MC, V.*

$–$$$$ ⊞ **Sheraton Annapolis Hotel.** Next to Westfield Shoppingtown, and near numerous chain restaurants, this large Sheraton has a free hourly shuttle bus to and from downtown Annapolis. (Traffic and parking there can be difficult.) The lobby is outfitted with marble floors, fresh flowers and ferns, and two sitting areas among marble columns. The café is adjacent to the lobby. Rooms are furnished with blond woods, geometric carpeting, and burgundy-print bedspreads. ⊠ *173 Jennifer Rd. 21401* ☎ *410/266–3131 or 888/627–8980* 🖷 *410/266–6247* ⊕ *www.starwoodhotels.com/sheraton* ⇋ *196 rooms* ⏶ *Café, room service, cable TV, in-room broadband, indoor pool, gym, lobby lounge, business services, meeting rooms, free parking, no-smoking rooms* ⊟ *AE, D, DC, MC, V.*

★ $$$ ⊞ **Historic Inns of Annapolis.** Three 18th-century properties in the historic district are now grouped as one inn with registration for all three at the **Governor Calvert House.** Built in 1727, Calvert House is steps from the capitol building. Also on State Circle, **Robert Johnson House** was built for the Annapolis barber in 1772. The **Maryland Inn,** on nearby Church Circle, has some rooms that date back to the Revolutionary era. The Treaty of Paris Restaurant and two pubs serve all three inns. Guest rooms are individually decorated with antiques and reproductions; all have coffeemakers and hair dryers, and some have kitchenettes, sitting suites, or whirlpools. ⊠ *58 State Circle, 21401* ☎ *410/263–2641 or 800/847–8882* 🖷 *410/268–3613* ⊕ *www.annapolisinns.com* ⇋ *110 rooms, 10 suites* ⏶ *Restaurant, some kitchenettes, in-room data ports, health club, bar, 2 pubs, laundry service, concierge, business services, meeting rooms, parking (fee), no-smoking rooms* ⊟ *AE, D, DC, MC, V.*

$$$ ⊞ **William Page Inn.** Built in 1908, this dark-brown, cedar-shingle, wood-frame structure was the local Democratic party clubhouse for 50 years. Today its wraparound porch is furnished with Adirondack chairs. The third-floor suite, with dormer windows and a sloped ceiling, includes an Italian-marble bathroom with whirlpool. Breakfast is served in the common room. There's a two-night minimum for weekend stays. ⊠ *8 Martin St., 21401* ☎ *410/626–1506 or 800/364–4160* ⊕ *www.*

williampageinn.com ⇔ *4 rooms, 2 with shared bath, 1 suite* ♿ *Free parking, no-smoking rooms; no TV in some rooms* ⊟ *MC, V* ⊺⃝ *BP.*

$$–$$$ ⊞ **Gibson's Lodgings.** Three detached houses from three decades— 1780, 1890, and 1980—are operated together as a single inn. One of the houses' hallways is strikingly lined with mirrors. Guest rooms are furnished with pre-1900 antiques. One first-floor room, which has a private bath and porch, is designed for universal access. Free parking in the courtyards is a big advantage in the heart of this small Colonial-era city (the houses are opposite the U.S. Naval Academy). Continental breakfast is served in the formal dining room of the 18th-century Patterson House. Some rooms have free Wi-Fi. ✉ *110–114 Prince George St., 21401* ☎ *410/268–5555 or 877/330–0057* 🖷 *410/268–2775* ⊕ *www. gibsonlodgings.com* ⇔ *21 rooms, 4 with shared bath* ♿ *Meeting rooms, free parking* ⊟ *AE, MC, V* ⊺⃝ *CP.*

$–$$ ⊞ **Country Inn & Suites.** True to its name, a cozy, country mood, as well as the gentle aroma of potpourri, permeates this suburban hotel. Rooms all have standard chain-hotel decor, but a large fireplace, wooden floors, and overstuffed sofas make the lobby an inviting place to linger. Exterior windows, trimmed with shutters and latticework, look out at a wooded area or a shopping plaza. Within walking distance of Annapolis's largest mall, the hotel also has a free shuttle that can take you to the historic district and to business parks. Four rooms have whirlpool tubs and two have fireplaces. ✉ *2600 Housely Rd., 21401* ☎ *410/571–6700 or 800/456–4000* 🖷 *410/571–6777* ⊕ *www.countryinns.com* ⇔ *100 rooms* ♿ *Microwaves, refrigerators, cable TV, Wi-Fi, indoor pool, gym, laundry facilities, meeting rooms* ⊟ *AE, D, DC, MC, V* ⊺⃝ *CP.*

$–$$ ⊞ **Hampton Inn and Suites.** A two-sided fireplace separates the check-in area from the lobby's bright and airy breakfast space. Just off I–97, this hotel is minutes from historic Annapolis. Guest rooms are traditional, but the spacious apartment-style suites have fully equipped kitchens. ✉ *124 Womack Dr., 21401* ☎ *410/571–0200 or 800/426–7866* 🖷 *410/571–0333* ⊕ *www.hamptoninn.com* ⇔ *86 rooms, 31 suites* ♿ *In-room data ports, pool, exercise equipment, billiards, shop, laundry facilities, laundry service, business services, meeting rooms* ⊟ *AE, D, DC, MC, V* ⊺⃝ *BP.*

$–$$ ⊞ **Scotlaur Inn.** On the two floors above Chick and Ruth's Delly, rooms in this family-owned B&B are papered in pastel Colonial prints. The high beds are topped with fluffy comforters and lots of pillows. Chandeliers in each room and marble floors in the private bathrooms bring this place a long way from its first days as a boardinghouse with only two bathrooms. Check-in as well as breakfast are done in the famous deli downstairs. ✉ *165 Main St., 21401* ☎ *410/268–5665* 🖷 *410/269–6738* ⊕ *www.scotlaurinn.com* ⇔ *10 rooms with bath* ♿ *Restaurant, cable TV, Wi-Fi, in-room VCRs* ⊟ *MC, V* ⊺⃝ *CP.*

Nightlife & the Arts

Bars & Clubs

The lounge at **Harry Browne's** (✉ 66 State Circle ☎ 410/263–4332) gives people something fun to do on Tuesday night: listen to live Irish music.

Middleton Tavern (✉ City Dock ☎ 410/263–3323) presents local and regional acoustic musicians nightly at its Oyster Bar lounge. The Oyster Shooter—raw oysters served in a shot glass with vodka and cocktail sauce and washed down with beer—supposedly originated here. The upstairs piano bar is open on Friday and Saturday nights.

The **Rams Head Tavern on the Stage** (✉ 33 West St. ☎ 410/268–4545) hosts nationally known folk, rock, jazz, country, and bluegrass groups. Past performers include Lyle Lovett, Ralph Stanley, and Linda Thompson. Dinner combinations are available; the tavern is no-smoking.

Music & Theater

Annapolis Summer Garden Theater (✉ 143 Compromise St., at Main St. ☎ 410/268–9212) stages a mix of musicals and plays outdoors (May–September), including occasional works by local playwrights. The **Colonial Players** (✉ 108 East St. ☎ 410/268–7373), active since the 1940s, is the city's principal theater troupe.

Entertainment at the **Naval Academy** (☎ 410/293–2439 for schedules, 800/874–6289 for tickets) includes the Distinguished Artists Series, the Masqueraders (the Academy's theatrical club), chamber music recitals, and Glee Club concerts. **Naval Academy Band** (☎ 410/293–0263) concerts, many held outside during fair weather, are free.

Sports & the Outdoors

☾ **Sandy Point State Park** (✉ 1100 E. College Pkwy., Rte. 50, 12 mi east of Annapolis ☎ 410/974–2149) has beaches for fishing and swimming, 22 launching ramps for boats, rock jetties extending into the bay, and a fishing pier. Admission is about $5 per person or $3 a vehicle (depending on the season and day of the week) from April to October; from November to March admission is $3 per vehicle.

Participant Sports

BIKING The **Baltimore and Annapolis (B&A) Trail** (✉ Boulters Way, Arnold ☎ 410/222–6244) runs through 13 mi of farmland and forests as well as urban and suburban neighborhoods, from Annapolis to Glen Burnie. It follows the old Baltimore and Annapolis Railroad and is linked directly to the 12½-mi trail encircling Baltimore-Washington International Airport. The trail is open sunrise to sunset to hikers, bikers, runners, and rollerbladers. Access to the northern end of the trail is via Dorsey Road off I–97 Exit 15 near Friendship Park. Parking is free but limited.

Pedal Pushers Bike Shop (✉ 546 Baltimore and Annapolis Blvd., Rte. 648, Severna Park ☎ 410/544–2323) rents bikes for the B&A Trail.

FISHING **Anglers** (✉ 1456 Whitehall Rd. ☎ 410/757–3442) sells equipment for archery and hunting as well as for fresh- and saltwater fishing. Anglers is also a full-service Orvis fly-fishing dealer.

SAILING **Annapolis Sailing School** (✉ 601 6th St. ☎ 800/638–9192 or 410/267–7205) bills itself as America's oldest and largest sailing school. The inexperienced can take a two-hour basic lesson. In addition, live-aboard, cruising, and advanced-sailing programs are available, as are boat rentals.

Womanship (✉ 137 Conduit St. ☎ 410/267–6661 or 800/342–9295) is a sailing school with programs for women, for mother–daughter partners, and couples. Classes can be custom-designed for special needs or desires. Men are welcome to take classes as half of a couple or as part of a group.

Spectator Sports

The teams of the **United States Naval Academy Athletic Association (NAAA)** (☎ 800/874–6289 ticket office) compete in about 20 varsity sports, most notably football. The team plays home games in the fall at the Navy–Marine Corps Stadium on Rowe Boulevard in Annapolis.

BOAT RACES **Annapolis Yacht Club** (☎ 410/263–9279) sponsors sailboat races at 6 PM each Wednesday from mid-May through early September in Annapolis Harbor, starting at the Eastport bridge.

JOUSTING For more than 40 years the **Amateur Jousting Club of Maryland** (⊕ ajc. psyberia.com) has been providing details on the state sport's tournaments and events, which take place from April through November in rural areas like southern Maryland.

Shopping

Along Maryland Avenue as well as on Main Street in downtown Annapolis you'll find antiques and fine art, fashions, arts and crafts, home furnishing, and gifts and souvenirs as well as nautical clothing and other necessities for seasoned salts and would-be sailors alike.

A destination in itself, the **Arundel Mills** (✉ 7000 Arundel Mills Circle, Hanover ☎ 410/540–5100) shopping mall holds more than 200 well-known retailers and eateries, including Ann Taylor Loft, Kenneth Cole, Bass Pro Shops, and T. J. Maxx. Many of the shops are outlets with great bargains, making the 40-minute trip from Annapolis well worth it.

Art & Antiques

Dealers in fine antiques and art abound along Annapolis's "other main street," Maryland Avenue. At the **Annapolis Pottery** (✉ 40 State Circle ☎ 410/268–6153) you can actually watch the potters at work as you browse the store filled with their wares. Other shops are in West Annapolis. **2009 West Antiques** (✉ 2009 West St. ☎ 410/266–0635) is a consortium of 35 dealers with an inventory that includes Victorian and art deco pieces. **Ron Snyder Antiques** (✉ 2011 West St. ☎ 410/266–5452) specializes in 18th- and 19th-century American furniture displayed in seven tastefully decorated rooms.

Clothing

Inside the Annapolis Marriott Waterfront, **Pussers Company Store** (✉ 80 Compromise St. ☎ 410/268–7555) is part of a small chain originating in another big sailing destination, the British Virgin Islands. The store peddles Pussers Rum merchandise as well as seasonal chutneys, nautical knickknacks, purses, and sundries, but the main product here is nautical clothing—raffia hats, khaki shorts, and pin-stripe shirts with collars—that will have you looking the part of a sailor.

9

CALVERT COUNTY

The long, narrow peninsula between the Patuxent River and the Chesapeake Bay is Calvert County, an area that has not yet been completely overrun by tourism. Two principal routes—Route 2 from Annapolis and Route 4 from Washington, D.C.—merge near Sunderland and continue on together to the county's southern tip. Exploring the bayside and riverside communities to either side of the highway, as well as the inland sites and attractions, will immerse you quickly in the tangible history and heritage of agriculture and fishing.

North Beach

31 mi south of Annapolis, via Rte. 2, Rte. 260, and Rte. 261.

In some ways a quieter, more residential extension of Chesapeake Beach, North Beach has a fishing pier and a quiet boardwalk. When it was founded in 1900, it was a resort for family summer vacations, and amusement centers, bingo halls, theaters, and bathhouses defined the town until the Great Depression. Then, in 1933, a hurricane ravaged the beach and destroyed many of its buildings. Post–World War II programs sponsored by the Veterans Administration facilitated a building boom, turning North Beach into a year-round community.

Where to Eat

$-$$ ✕ **Neptune's.** Modest Neptune's claims of preparing "the world's best mussels" rings true with many, making the trip to this tiny town just north of Chesapeake Beach worthwhile. Attached to the small bar, a glass-enclosed dining room with a brick floor is a friendly, informal spot to dig in to its signature dish. Also on the menu are seafood pastas, burgers, and cuts of Angus beef. ⊠ *8800 Chesapeake Ave., at 1st St.* ☎ *410/257-7899* 🖃 *AE, D, MC, V.*

Chesapeake Beach

⓯ *1 mi south of North Beach, via Rte. 261, 32 mi south of Annapolis, via Rte. 2, Rte. 260, and Rte. 261.*

This charming little town beside the Bay was founded at the close of the 19th century as a resort to rival those along the French Riviera. It was served by steamboats from Baltimore and by a railroad from Washington, D.C. Steamboat service diminished over time and the railroad failed in 1935, but the town survived as private automobiles became more readily available. It boomed again in 1948 with the legalization of slot machines, although they lasted only 20 years. Today Chesapeake Beach is once again staging a tourism comeback with the addition of a water park and a new waterfront hotel.

Ⓒ The **Chesapeake Bay Railway Museum,** housed in the railroad's 1898
Fodor'sChoice trackside terminus, provides memorable glimpses of the onetime re-
★ sort's turn-of-the-20th-century glory days. Among its exhibits are a glass-enclosed model of the town of Chesapeake Beach, a gleaming,

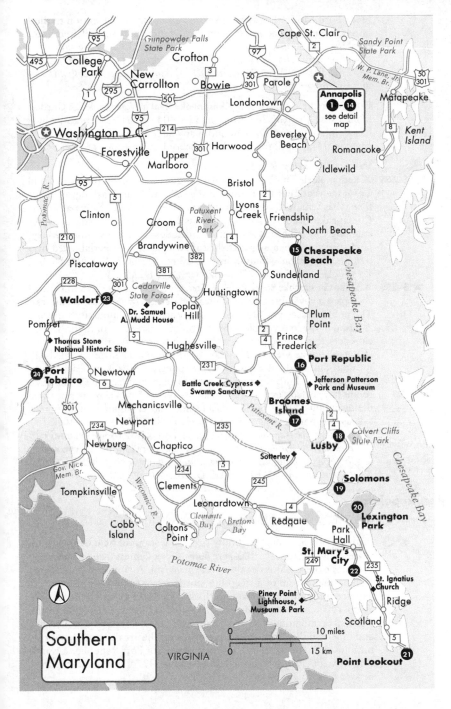

Southern Maryland

VIRGINIA

black Ford Model T that once carried guests from the station to their hotels, a hand-carved horse from the magnificent carousel, and a slot machine as well as photos of early vacationers. One of the railroad's passenger cars rests nearby. ⊠ *4155 Mears Ave., Rte. 261* ☎ *410/257–3892* ⊞ *Free* ○ *May–Sept., daily 1–4; Apr. and Oct., weekends 1–4 and by appt.*

☺ Families make a day of it at **Chesapeake Beach Water Park** (⊠ Gordon Stinnett Ave., at Rte. 261 ☎ 410/257–1404 or 301/855–3803), which has a children's pool, beach, and many slides. The park is open from Memorial Day until the first day of school. Admission is $16–$18.

Where to Stay & Eat

$$–$$$ ✗ **Rod 'n' Reel.** This family-owned restaurant opened optimistically in 1936, the year after the demise of the railroad from Washington. Since then it has remained synonymous with superb seafood. Now part of the Chesapeake Beach Resort & Spa, its bayside location still provides stunning views. The extensive menu includes succulent southern Maryland specialties such as rockfish stuffed with crab imperial, fried oysters, and the region's ubiquitous crab cakes. ⊠ *Rte. 261 and Mears Ave.* ☎ *410/257–2735 or 877/763–6733* ⊟ *AE, D, MC, V.*

★ $–$$$ ✗⊡ **The Chesapeake Beach Resort & Spa.** Opened in 2004 this luxury hotel and spa is a key part of the revitalization of the town's tourism business. The public spaces pay homage to the beachfront community's history. A mural in the lobby depicts the old roller coaster that once thrilled vacationers, and framed photographs line the corridors, tracing the town's changes from its Victorian heyday to the present. The whitewashed oak furniture and sand-color walls give the rooms an elegant yet beachy style. The resort was built right on the water's edge, and its suites and deluxe rooms have balconies that seem to hang over the bay. There are also three dining options, a boardwalk, and a fishing charter company at the hotel's full-service marina. ⊠ *4165 Mears Ave.* ☎ *410/257–5596 or 301/855–0096* ⊕ *www.chesapeakebeachresortspa.com* ⟳ *72 rooms, 6 suites* ♨ *3 restaurants, café, cable TV, in-room broadband, indoor pool, gym, sauna, spa, boating, fishing, video game room, shop, business services, meeting room, free parking* ⎮⚆⎮ *BP* ⊟ *AE, D, DC, MC, V.*

Port Republic

⑯ *17 mi south of Chesapeake Beach.*

★ ☺ With the northernmost naturally occurring stand of bald cypress trees in the United States, the 100-acre **Battle Creek Cypress Swamp Sanctuary** provides close-up looks at the forest primeval. A ¼-mi elevated boardwalk at the bottom of a steep but sturdy set of steps gives you a good vantage point to see the swamp, thick with 100-foot-tall trees that are 75 to 100 years old. Guides at the nature center can alert you to the seasonal permutations of the vegetation and the doings of squirrels, owls, and other wildlife. Indoor exhibits focus on the area's natural and cultural history. The swamp is about 5 mi west of Port Republic. ⊠ *Sixes Rd., Rte. 506, Prince Frederick* ☎ *410/535–5327* ⊕ *www.calvertparks.org* ⊞ *Free* ○ *Tues.–Sat. 10–4:30, Sun. 1–4:30.*

Christ Church traces its origins to 1672, when a log-cabin church stood at the site. Its 1772 brick replacement, coated with plaster, is notable for its biblical garden, planted with species mentioned in the scriptures. Port Republic School No. 7 is on the church's property. ■ TIP→ **Since immediately after the Civil War the grounds have been a venue for jousting (Maryland's state sport) on the last Saturday in August.** ⊠ *3100 Broomes Island Rd., Rte. 264* ☎ *410/586–0565* ⊠ *Free* ☉ *Daily dawn–dusk.*

Port Republic School No. 7, a classic one-room schoolhouse built in the 1880s, looks for all the world as if today's lesson could begin any minute. Here, you can find a restored classroom with archetypal desks, inkwells, and a school bell. Until 1932 a single teacher taught children in seven grades here. ⊠ *3100 Broomes Island Rd., Rte. 264* ☎ *410/586–0482* ⊠ *Free* ☉ *Memorial Day–Labor Day, Sun. 2–4 and by appt.*

EN ROUTE Behind 2½ mi of scenic Patuxent riverfront stretch 544 acres of woods and farmland. The 70-odd archaeological sites have yielded evidence of 9,000 years of human habitation—from prehistory on through to Colonial times. At the **Jefferson Patterson Park and Museum** you can follow an archaeology trail to inspect artifacts of the successive hunter-gatherer, early agricultural, and plantation societies that once roamed and settled this land. Displays include primitive knives and axes, fragments of Native American pottery, and Colonial glassware. Stroll along the nature trails to take a look at wildlife, antique agricultural equipment, and fields of crops. The park is 2 mi south of Port Republic. ⊠ *10115 Mackall Rd., Rte. 265, St. Leonard* ☎ *410/586–8501* ⊕ *www.jefpat. org* ⊠ *Free* ☉ *Mid-Apr.–mid-Oct., Wed.–Sun. 10–5.*

Broomes Island

⑰ *7 mi south of Port Republic, via Rte. 264.*

An area without specific boundaries, Broomes is not even an island per se, except during a very high tide or in a strong storm. It's made up of little more than a few houses and stores, a post office, and a church. This little area at the mouth of Island Creek is a portrait of a water-dependent community amid change: weather-beaten structures of its past now mingle with new, expensive waterfront homes.

Where to Eat

★ $–$$ ✕ **Stoney's Seafood House.** Popular with boaters who tie right up to the dock, this restaurant overlooking Island Creek has one dining room that actually juts out over the water and another on higher ground with great views from its floor-to-ceiling windows. There's also ample seating—and a tiki bar—outside. Stoney's hefty crab cakes are made with plenty of back fin meat and little filler. Oyster sandwiches and Stoney's Steamer—handpicked selections of fresh seafood—are also good choices. The intense, house-made desserts, such as the strawberry shortcake and the Snickers pie, are not for the faint of heart. ⊠ *Oyster House Rd.* ☎ *410/586–1888* ⊟ *AE, D, MC, V* ☉ *Closed Nov.–early Mar.*

Lusby

⑱ *12 mi southeast of Broomes Island.*

☾ Like its better known neighbor Calvert Cliffs State Park, **Flag Ponds Nature Park** has spectacular views of the cliffs, but with just a short stroll to the beach, this county park is the more accessible of the two. Until the 1950s the area was a busy fishery, and some of the buildings from that era still stand. Today it beckons with bathhouses, a fishing pier, 3 mi of gently graded hiking trails, observation decks at two ponds, a boardwalk through wetlands, and indoor wildlife exhibits. Soaring cliffs, flat marshland, and wildflowers (including the Blue Flag Iris, for which the park is named) provide stunning contrasts. ■ TIP→ A shark's tooth dating back 10–20 million years ago is the big prize in a fossil hunt on the beach, one of the park's most popular activities. ⊠ *Rte. 2/4* ☏ *410/586–1477* ⊕ *www.calvertparks.org* ✉ *$6 per vehicle Apr.–Oct., $3 per vehicle Nov.–Mar.* ☉ *Memorial Day–Labor Day, weekdays 9–6, weekends 9–8; Labor Day–Memorial Day, weekends 9–5.*

Nightlife & the Arts

For a taste of the tropics *and* the South Pacific along St. Leonard's Creek, wet your lips with an umbrella-topped cocktail at **Vera's White Sands** (⊠ Rte. 4, Lusby ☏ 410/586–1182 ☉ Closed Nov.–Apr.). ■ TIP→ With an exotic environment and fantastic location with open-air decks overlooking a deepwater marina and delightful river views—not to mention a swimming pool—it's well worth a visit, despite its difficult-to-find location west off Route 2/4. Vera has sold the place now, but the new owners promise great dining.

Solomons

⑲ *8 mi south of Lusby.*

On the tip of the peninsula, Solomons is where the Patuxent empties into the Chesapeake. The town has become a popular getaway for sailors, boaters, and affluent professionals. But it's still a laid-back waterfront town—at least when compared with, say, Annapolis or St. Michaels. Several excellent boatyards and marinas cater to powerboaters and sailors, with nautical services from the simplest to the most sophisticated. There are several antiques, book, gift, and specialty shops and galleries side by side, parallel to the boardwalk. Wherever you go, stunning views surround you at nearly every turn.

A world-class sculpture and botanical venue, **Annmarie Garden on St. John** is a 30-acre property on the St. John Creek. The sculptural art is by artists both local and from around the world. One of the more intriguing installations is a series of 13 "Talking Benches." Each tells an ecological story by depicting a plant

> **WORD OF MOUTH**
>
> "Walking, biking, or boating around Solomons Island is my favorite, where the Patuxent river meets the Chesapeake. The Calvert Marine Museum is a gem, and there is a great selection for unique dining choices. And the sunsets . . ."   —miller20621

that grows in southern Maryland, including dogwood, loblolly pines, papaw trees, and tobacco. Smooth, user-friendly pathways curve through the grounds. Little here is off-limits, and picnickers are welcome to settle in virtually anywhere. Be sure to visit the mosaic-filled restrooms. ✉ *Dowell Rd.* ☎ *410/326–4640* ⊕ *www.annmariegarden.org* 🎫 *Free* ☉ *Daily 9–5.*

🅒 **FodorsChoice** ★ The **Calvert Marine Museum** is concerned with the history of both the river and the Bay. The bright, spacious exhibition hall contains models and life-size examples of historically significant types of working and pleasure boats. A grouping of 17 tanks holds examples of marine life; the river otters here are often at play. The jaws of a white shark open above an exhibit on fossils, and children can sift through sharks' teeth and other specimens and examine them under microscopes. Outside, small craft of different periods are on display in a waterside shed, and on many summer afternoons you can take a cruise aboard a converted 1899 bugeye sailboat, the *William B. Tennison.* There's also a restored hexagonal lighthouse from 1883 that's perched like an insect on six slender legs. The **J. C. Lore & Sons Oyster House** (☉ June–Aug., daily 1–4:30, May and Sept., weekends 1–4:30), operated by the museum, is a processing plant built in 1934 that's now a museum of the local seafood industries. This National Historic Landmark displays the tools used by oystermen, crabbers, and fishermen. ✉ *Rte. 2 at Solomons Island Rd.* ☎ *410/326–2042, 410/326–8217 weekends* ⊕ *www.calvertmarinemuseum.com* 🎫 *$7* ☉ *Daily 10–5.*

Where to Stay & Eat

$$–$$$ ✕ **DiGiovanni's Dock of the Bay.** It's rare to be able to enjoy elegant waterside dining and professional service at budget prices. The chef creates succulent Italian dishes using fresh herbs and spices. The *cacciucco* (seafood soup) alone is worth a special trip, as is the homemade crab-stuffed ravioli. A folk singer entertains on Wednesday. ✉ *14556 Solomons Island Rd.* ☎ *410/394–6400* ▤ *AE, D, MC, V* ☉ *Closed Sun. Jan.–May. No lunch.*

★ **$–$$$** 🏨 **Back Creek Inn.** Built for a waterman in 1880, this blue wood-frame house sits in a residential neighborhood on well-tended grounds at the edge of Back Creek. You can soak in the open-air hot tub or lounge on the deck next to a beautiful perennial garden. Three rooms have water views, and one opens onto the garden. Breakfast is served in the dining room or by the lily pond. ✉ *Calvert and Alexander Sts., 20688* ☎ *410/326–2022* ▤ *410/326–2946* ⊕ *www.bbonline.com/md/backcreek* ➥ *4 rooms, 2 suites, 1 cottage* ⚇ *Dining room, cable TV, outdoor hot tub, bicycles, Wi-Fi, no-smoking rooms; no kids under 12* ▤ *MC, V* ☉ *Closed mid-Dec.–early Jan.* ⅩⅠ *BP.*

$–$$$ 🏨 **Solomons Victorian Inn.** On the Back Creek side of narrow Solomons Island this three-story, yellow frame house was built in 1906 by the foremost shipbuilder on the Chesapeake Bay. Six rooms look onto Solomons Harbor and two have garden views. All are furnished with period antiques and reproductions, and every room has an ornate armoire. Afternoon refreshments and breakfast are served on an enclosed porch. ✉ *125 Charles St., 20688* ☎ *410/326–4811* ▤ *410/326–0133* ⊕ *www.*

solomonsvictorianinn.com 🛏 *8 rooms* 🛁 *In-room data ports; no smoking* ☰ *AE, MC, V* ⑩ *BP.*

ST. MARY'S COUNTY

"Just at the mouth of the river, we observed the natives in arms. That night, fires blazed through the whole country and since they had never seen such a large ship, messengers were sent in all directions, who reported that a 'canoe' like an island had come with as many as there were trees in the woods."—Father Andrew White, recounting the arrival of the *Ark* and the *Dove* in 1634.

Father White arrived in the New World in 1634 as a member of Lord Baltimore's contingent of 140 colonists. The two "canoes" the Native Americans spotted were the tiny sailing vessels that had just crossed the Atlantic to reach the southernmost tip of Maryland's western shore, where the Potomac River meets the Chesapeake Bay. The peninsula between the Potomac and the Patuxent rivers is today St. Mary's County, easily one of the state's most beautiful regions, and gradually attracting development because of its easy access to Washington, D.C., to the north.

Like so much of Maryland south of Annapolis and Washington, many scenic drives throughout St. Mary's County bring together charming inland and waterside towns and historic sites. Hearty food and homey places to stay are easy to find.

■ TIP→ St. Mary's County also boasts another curiosity: its numerous liquor stores sell popular brands of U.S. beer in rare 8-oz. and 10.-oz cans.

Lexington Park

⑳ *9 mi southeast of Solomons, 68 mi south of Annapolis, via Rte. 2/4 to Rte. 235.*

The Patuxent River Naval Air Station covers 25 mi of the shoreline at the mouth of the eponymous river, and it assists naval aviation operations by its research, development, and testing of aircraft and things associated with them. Its facilities are also utilized by private industry, academic institutions, and foreign governments. The ☾ **Patuxent River Naval Air Museum** houses items from the research, development, test, and evaluation of naval aircraft. Nineteen vintage aircraft are displayed outside. Inside, you can climb into a cockpit trainer and view some of the more improbable creations that failed to pass muster, such as the Goodyear "Inflatoplane." ✉ *Patuxent River Naval Air Station, Rte. 235, 3 Notch Rd.* ☎ *301/863–7418* ⊕ *www.paxmuseum.com* ✉ *Free* ⊙ *Tues.–Sun. 10–5.*

The St. Mary's River, which once powered **Historic Cecil's Old Mill**, is just a trickle in this area now, so the water wheel now runs on electricity. Today, the building, which dates to 1900, contains an artist co-op as well as a small display of artifacts and photographs of the mill. In keeping with the setting, most of the arts and crafts on sale are quaint and rustic: rural scenes painted on circular saw blades or lighthouses on driftwood, crocheted placemats, and colorful quilts. The mill is a few miles west of the naval station and quite difficult to find—there are no sign posts. ⊠ *Indian Bridge Rd. off Rte. 5, Great Mills* ☎ *301/994–1510* ⊗ *Mar.–Oct., Thurs.–Sat. 10–5, Sun. 11–5; Nov. and Dec., Mon.–Sat. 10–5, Sun. 11–5.*

**OFF THE
BEATEN
PATH**

SOTTERLEY – The distinguished house on the grounds of this 18th-century plantation is the earliest known (1717) post-in-ground structure in the United States: in place of a foundation, cedar timbers driven straight into the ground support it. The house is a sampler of architectural styles and interior design from the last two centuries. On the grounds of this National Historic Landmark are other buildings from the 18th through early 20th centuries, including a Colonial customs warehouse, a smoke-house, a "necessary" (an outhouse), and a restored slave cabin. ⊠ *Rte. 245 near Hollywood, 12 mi north of Lexington Park via Rte. 235 and Rte. 245* ☎ *301/373–2280* ⊕ *www.sotterley.com* 🖾 *$7* ⊗ *May–Oct., Tues.–Sat. 10–4, Sun. noon–4. Grounds open year-round.*

Where to Eat

$$–$$$$ ✕ **The Roost.** Like the place itself, food at the Roost is homey but still elegant. A large fireplace dominates the spacious dining room, which is accented by green floral wallpaper, Depression-era chandeliers, and lad-der-back chairs. The adjacent bar holds a collection of Navy memora-bilia. Oyster stew (in season), grilled lamb chops, and broiled rainbow trout are on the regular menu, but around the holidays look for the re-gion's signature dish, stuffed ham. Steaming apple dumplings topped with a dollop of ice cream are a treat year-round. ⊠ *21736 Great Mills Rd.* ☎ *301/863–5051* 🖃 *AE, MC, V.*

Point Lookout

㉑ *20 mi south of Lexington Park, 88 mi south of Annapolis, via Rte. 2/ 4 and Rte. 235 to Rte. 5.*

When Father Andrew White came to Point Lookout and saw the Po-tomac at its side, he mused that the Thames was a mere rivulet in com-parison. But instead of being overwhelmed by the wildness of the New World, he observed that "fine groves of trees appear . . . growing in in-tervals as if planted by the hand of man."

On the approach to **Point Lookout State Park,** two memorial obelisks re-mind travelers of the dark history of this starkly alluring point of land. Beginning in 1863 a Union prison stood at the farthest tip of the penin-sula, just across the Potomac from Confederate Virginia. During those last two years of the conflict, nearly 4,000 of the 52,000 Confederate soldiers here died because of disease and poor conditions. All that re-mains of the prison are some earthen fortifications, partially rebuilt and known as Fort Lincoln, with markers noting the sites of hospitals and other buildings. A small museum supplies some of the details. The 500-acre state park has boating facilities, nature trails, and a beach for swimming. The RV campground, with hookups, is open year-round; tent camping facilities close from early November through late March. ⊠ *Rte. 5* ☎ *301/872–5688* ⊕ *www.dnr.state.md.us* 🖾 *Weekends and*

9

holidays May–Sept. $5 per person, all other times $3 per vehicle ⊘ *Year-round, daily 6 AM–sunset.*

ST. IGNATIUS CHURCH – Built in 1758, St. Ignatius is all that survives of the pre-Revolutionary plantation of St. Inigoes. A church dating from the 1630s had stood where this church, named for the founder of the Jesuits, stands now; the graveyard is one of the oldest in the United States. Several veterans of the Revolution are buried here, alongside Jesuit priests who served here. To see inside the church, ask for the key at the sentry box of the naval installation next door. ⊠ *Villa Rd. off Rte. 5, St. Inigoes* ☎ *301/872–5590* ⊯ *Free.*

> OFF THE
> BEATEN
> PATH

Where to Stay & Eat

¢–$ ▣ **St. Michael's Manor & Vineyard.** Joe and Nancy Dick have run their B&B on Long Neck Creek since the early 1980s—and they've harvested grapes from their 3 acres of vines nearly as long as that. Rooms, which overlook the water, are decorated with antiques and family heirlooms, the beds covered with hand-sewn quilts. There's a working fireplace at each end of the public space in the Federal-style main building. Nancy's eggs Benedict are always popular, and her airy Austrian puff pancakes over fresh apples or peaches are delicious. Upon arrival guests are invited to sample wine from the vineyards. ⊠ *50200 St. Michael's Manor Way, Scotland 20687* ☎ *301/872–4025* ⊕ *www. stmichaels-manor.com* ⇆ *4 rooms, 3 with shared bath* ⟳ *Pool, bicycles; no room TVs, no smoking* ⊟ *No credit cards* ⊘ *Closed Nov.–mid Feb.* ⦿ *BP.*

Sports & the Outdoors

Scheibel's (⊠ Wynne Rd., Ridge ☎ 301/872–5185) will arrange fishing charters.

St. Mary's City

㉒ *73 mi south of Annapolis, via Rte. 2/4 to Rte. 5 North.*

An intrepid group of 140 English settlers sailed the *Ark* and the *Dove* up the Potomac and into one of its tributaries, the St. Mary's River. About halfway up, on an east bank, they founded St. Mary's City, the fourth permanent settlement in British North America and eventually the first (albeit short-lived) capital of Maryland.

Long before a Constitution or a Bill of Rights, the first law of religious tolerance in the New World was enacted in St. Mary's City, guaranteeing the freedom to practice whatever religion one chose. Here, too, almost three centuries before American women achieved suffrage, Mistress Margaret Brent challenged the status quo and requested the right to vote (she didn't get it). The settlement served as Maryland's capital city until 1695, when the legislature moved to Annapolis and the county seat moved to Leonardtown. St. Mary's City virtually vanished, its existence acknowledged only in historical novels and textbooks. Today the city is home to a living-history park and a small liberal arts college that share its name. St. Mary's College of Maryland, which dates to 1840, functions as the cultural center for the surrounding community.

In 1934 a first step in the rebirth of St. Mary's was taken. In commemoration of the 300th anniversary of Maryland, the Colony's imposing State House, originally built in 1676, was reconstructed. In the early 1970s a vast archaeological-reconstruction program began in earnest, a project that has revealed nearly 200 individual sites. The entire 800-plus acres have become a living-history museum and archaeological park called **Historic St. Mary's City.** The historic complex includes several notable reconstructions and reproductions of buildings. The **State House of 1676,** like its larger and grander counterpart in Williamsburg, has an upper and a lower chamber for the Council and General Assembly. This 1934 reproduction is based on court documents from the period; the original was dismantled in 1829, with many of the bricks used for Trinity Church nearby. The square-rigged ship *Maryland Dove,* docked behind the State House, represents the smaller of the two vessels that conveyed the original settlers from England.

Godiah Spray Tobacco Plantation depicts life on a 17th-century tobacco farm in the Maryland wilderness. ■ TIP→ **Interpreters portray the Spray family—the real family lived about 20 mi away—and its indentured servants, enlisting visitors in such household chores as cooking and gardening or in working the tobacco field.** The buildings, including the main dwelling house and outbuildings, were built with period tools and techniques.

Throughout Historic St. Mary's City, you're encouraged to explore other sites and exhibits-in-progress, including the town center, the location of the first Catholic church in the English Colonies, a "victualing" and lodging house, and the Woodland Indian Hamlet. Historic interpreters in costume—some in character—add realism to the experience. ⊠ *Rte. 5* ☎ *240/895–4990 or 800/762–1634* ⊕ *www.stmaryscity. org* ⊠ *$7.50* ☉ *Call for exhibit hrs.*

OFF THE BEATEN PATH

PINEY POINT LIGHTHOUSE, MUSEUM & PARK – The first permanent lighthouse constructed on the Potomac River is now the center of a small, 6-acre park. The grounds, which are free, have a boardwalk, pier, and picnic tables. ⊠ *Lighthouse Rd., Piney Point* ☎ *301/769–2222* ⊕ *www. co.saint-marys.md.us/recreate/museums* ⊠ *$3* ☉ *Mid-May–Oct., Fri.–Mon. noon–5.*

Where to Stay & Eat

★ **$-$$$** ✕⊡ **Brome-Howard Inn.** Set on 30 acres of farmland, this 19th-century farmhouse provides a trip through time to life on a tobacco plantation. Rooms are decorated with original family furnishings. Relax on one of the big outdoor porches or patios and watch the lazy St. Mary's River nearby. In the evening there are two candlelight dining rooms—the foyer or the formal parlor. Five miles of hiking trails lead to St. Mary's City, and the inn has bikes for the use of guests. The restaurant ($$-$$$) specializes in seafood and occasionally serves such exotic items as bison, ostrich, or shark. ⊠ *18281 Rosecroft Rd., 20686* ☎ *301/866–0656* ☎ *301/866–9660* ⊕ *www.bromehowardinn.com* ➴ *3 rooms, 1 suite* ⚫ *Restaurant, bicycles, hiking, library* ☰ *AE, MC, V* ⨉ *BP.*

9

CHARLES COUNTY

To the north of St. Mary's County and about 35 mi southwest of Annapolis, relatively rural Charles County is flanked on its west by the Potomac River's big bend as it flows south from Washington, D.C. In what used to be tobacco country, less-traveled county and state roads crisscross the pristine countryside dotted with depot towns, riverfront ports-of-call, wildlife preservation centers, and unsung historical sites.

Waldorf

㉔ *40 mi south of Annapolis on Rte. 301.*

The **American Indian Cultural Center and Piscataway Indian Museum** strives to be a source for information on the art and culture of the Piscataway Native Americans; the museum emphasizes the life of Maryland's indigenous people prior to the 17th century. Artifacts, tools, and weapons are on display, and there's a full-scale reproduction of a traditional longhouse. ⊠ *16816 Country La.* ☎ *301/782–2224* ⊕ *www.piscatawayindians. org* ⌸ *$3* ☉ *Sun. 11–4; other times by appt. only.*

The **Dr. Samuel A. Mudd House** is where John Wilkes Booth ended up at 4 AM on Good Friday, 1865, his leg broken after having leaped from the presidential box at Ford's Theater. Most likely, the 32-year-old Dr. Mudd had no idea his patient was wanted for the assassination of Abraham Lincoln. Nonetheless, Mudd was convicted of aiding a fugitive and sentenced to life in prison. (President Andrew Jackson pardoned him in 1869.) Today the two-story house, set on 10 rolling acres, looks as if the doctor is still in. The dark purple couch where Mudd examined Booth remains in the downstairs parlor, 18th-century family pieces fill the rooms, and the doctor's crude instruments are displayed. There's a 30-minute guided tour of the house, an exhibit building, and Mudd's original tombstone. ⊠ *14940 Hoffman Rd.* ☎ *301/645–6870* ⊕ *www.somd.lib.md.us/MUSEUMS/ Mudd.htm* ⌸ *$4* ☉ *Late Mar.–late Nov., Wed. and weekends 11–4.*

Port Tobacco

㉕ *11 mi southwest of Waldorf via Rte. 301 and Rte. 6.*

One of the oldest communities in the East, Port Tobacco first existed as the Native American settlement of "Potopaco." (The similarity between this Native American name—meaning "the jutting of water inland"— and the name for the plant that was to become a cornerstone of the region's economy is purely coincidental.) Potopaco was colonized by the English in 1634, and later in the century emerged as the major seaport of Port Tobacco. The Historic District includes the reconstructed early-19th-century courthouse; Catslide House, one of the area's four surviving 18th-century homes; and a restored one-room schoolhouse, dating to 1876 and used as such until 1953.

★ **Thomas Stone National Historic Site,** built in the 1770s, was the Charles County home of Thomas Stone, one of four Maryland signers of the Declaration of Independence. It has been painstakingly rebuilt after a devastating fire left it a shell in the late 1970s. The restoration re-created the distinctive five-part Georgian house inside and out. The two-story main plantation house is linked to the two wings and adjoining hallways in an arc rather than a straight line. All the rooms have exquisite details, such as built-in cabinets, elaborate moldings, a table set in fine china, gilded mirrors, and a harpsichord. The house and family grave site are just a short stroll from the parking lot and visitor center, where you can examine a model of the house or watch a video about Stone. ⊠ *6655 Rose Hill Rd., between Rtes. 6 and 225, 4 mi west of La Plata* ☎ *301/392–1776* ⊕ *www.nps.gov/thst* ⊠ *Free* ☉ *Mid-June–Aug. daily 9–5; Sept.–mid-June, Wed.–Sun. 9–5.*

SOUTHERN MARYLAND ESSENTIALS

To research prices, get advice from other travelers, and book travel arrangements, visit www.fodors.com.

Transportation

BY AIR

Baltimore-Washington International Airport (BWI) is convenient to Annapolis and attractions in southern Maryland.

The most convenient way to get to Annapolis is by car or taxi (the fare is roughly $50). From BWI, follow airport exit signs and then take I–97 south to Route 50 east. Take Exit 24 onto Rowe Boulevard and follow signs to the Annapolis visitor center.

You can also reach Annapolis by bus or shuttle. The Sky Blue Bus Route runs from the International Terminal Bus Stop to Annapolis. You can transfer from the Spa Road stop to other routes, several of which stop near the visitor center.

BWI Ground Transportation has information on Super Shuttle and Airport Vans.

⛴ **Baltimore-Washington International Airport (BWI)** ⊠ Exit 2 off Baltimore Washington Pkwy. ☎ 410/859-7111 ⊕ www.bwiairport.com. **BWI Ground Transportation** ☎ 800/435-9294. **Sky Blue Bus Route (Dept. of Public Transportation)** ☎ 410/263-7964.

BY BUS

Maryland's Mass Transit Administration offers regularly scheduled bus service from Baltimore to Annapolis (it's about one hour and 20 minutes one-way from downtown Annapolis). The fare is $4.25.

Bus service between Washington, D.C., and Annapolis is geared to commuters rather than vacationers. Weekday mornings and afternoons, MTA buses arrive at and depart from the Navy–Marine Corps Stadium parking lot, from College Avenue by the state buildings, and also from St. John's College. The one-way fare is $4.25. On weekends Greyhound makes one trip daily, arriving at and departing from the stadium.

⛴ **Greyhound** ☎ 800/231-2222 ⊕ www.greyhound.com. **Mass Transit Administration (MTA)** ☎ 410/539-5000 ⊕ www.mtamaryland.com.

BY CAR

Annapolis is normally 35–45 minutes by car from Washington, D.C., on U.S. 50 (Rowe Boulevard exit). During rush hour (weekdays 3:30–6:30 PM), however, it takes about twice as long. From Baltimore, following routes 3 and 97 to U.S. 50, travel time is about the same. To tour southern Maryland, follow Route 2 south from Annapolis, and Route 4, which continues through Calvert County.

Parking spots on Annapolis's historic downtown streets are scarce, but you can pay $5 to park at the Navy–Marine Corps Stadium (to the right of Rowe Boulevard as you enter town from Route 50) and ride a free shuttle bus downtown. Parking garages on Main Street and Gott's Court (adjacent to the visitor center) are free for the first hour and $1 an hour thereafter with an $8 maximum but are often full on weekdays. On weekends these garages cost $4 a day. Street parking in the Historic Area is metered (in effect 10–7:30 daily) or limited to two hours for those without a residential parking permit.

Contacts & Resources

EMERGENCIES

🚺 **Ambulance, Fire, Police** ☎ 911.

🚺 **Hospitals Anne Arundel Medical Center** ✉ 2001 Medical Pkwy., off Jennifer Rd., Annapolis ☎ 443/481-1000 ⊕ www.aahs.org. **Calvert Memorial Hospital** ✉ 100 Hospital Rd., Prince Frederick ☎ 410/535-4000 ⊕ www.calverthospital.com. **St. Mary's Hospital** ✉ 25500 Point Lookout Rd., Rte. 5, Leonardtown ☎ 301/475-8981 ⊕ www.smhwecare.com.

INTERNET, MAIL & SHIPPING

🚺 **Annapolis Main Post Office** ✉ 1 Church Circle, 21401 ☎ 410/263-9291, 877/877-7833 TTY.

TOUR OPTIONS

Discover Annapolis Tours leads one-hour narrated minibus tours ($15) that introduce you to the history and architecture of Annapolis. Tours leave from the visitor center daily April through November and most weekends December through March.

Walking tours are a great way to see Annapolis's Historic District. The Historic Annapolis Museum Store rents two self-guided (with audiotapes and maps) walking tours: "Historic Annapolis Walk with Walter Cronkite" and "Historic Annapolis African-American Heritage Audio Walking Tour." The cost for each is $5.

Guides from Three Centuries Tours wear Colonial-style dress and take you to the state house, St. John's College, and the Naval Academy. The cost is $13. Tours depart daily April through October at 10:30 from the visitor center and at 1:30 from the information booth, City Dock. From November through March one tour a week leaves on Saturday at 1:30 from the information booth.

The *Schooner Woodwind* and the *Schooner Woodwind II* are twin 74-foot boats that make two to four trips Tuesday through Sunday between

April and October, with some overnight trips. Two-hour sails are $31 to $34.

When the weather's good, Watermark Cruises runs boat tours that last from 40 minutes to 7½ hours and go as far as St. Michaels on the Eastern Shore, where there's a maritime museum, yachts, dining, and boutiques. Prices range from $10 to $60.

Discover Annapolis Tours ⊠ 31 Decatur Ave., Historic District ☎ 410/626-6000 ⊕ www.discover-annapolis.com. **Historic Annapolis Foundation Walking Tours** ⊠ 18 Pinkney St., Historic District ☎ 410/267-7619 or 800/603-4020 ⊕ www.annapolis.org. *Schooner Woodwind* and *Schooner Woodwind II* ⊠ Annapolis Marriott Hotel dock, City Dock ☎ 410/263-7837 ⊕ www.schooner-woodwind.com. **Three Centuries Tours** ⊠ 48 Maryland Ave., Historic District ☎ 410/263-5401 ⊞ 410/263-1901 ⊕ www. annapolis-tours.com. **Watermark Cruises** ⊠ City Dock, Historic District ☎ 410/268-7600 or 410/268-7601 ⊕ www.watermarkcruises.com.

VISITOR INFORMATION

Crain Memorial Welcome Center is a good place to pick up information if you're traveling north from Virginia.

Tourist Information Annapolis-Anne Arundel County Conference and Visitors Bureau ⊠ 26 West St., Annapolis 21401 ☎ 888/302-2852 ⊕ www.visit-annapolis.org. **Calvert County Dept. of Economic Development & Tourism** ⊠ County Courthouse, Prince Frederick 20678 ☎ 410/535-4583 or 800/331-9771 ⊕ www.co.cal.md.us. **Charles County Office of Tourism** ⊠ 8190 Port Tobacco Rd., Port Tobacco 20677 ☎ 800/766-3386. **Crain Memorial Welcome Center** ⊠ U.S. Rte. 301, 12480 Crain Hwy., near Newburg, 1 mi north of Governor Nice bridge over the Potomac River ☎ 301/259-2500. **St. Mary's County Tourism** ⊠ 23115 Leonard Hall Dr., Leonardtown 20650 ☎ 800/327-9023 ⊕ www.co. saint-marys.md.us.

9

The Eastern Shore

WORD OF MOUTH

"If you are looking for a quiet, peaceful place, then Virginia's Eastern Shore is the place for you . . . It's a great balance of fields, forests and quaint little villages."   —hansman

"The interesting part is the back streets—wonderful old restored houses and interesting little gardens. Chestertown is another fine colonial town on the Eastern Shore, more out of the way than Easton and St. Michaels. It has an even more splendid historic area."   —poss

"For a working waterman's town, you might try Tilghman Island, fifteen miles down the road from touristy St. Michaels. For dining, Harrison's Chesapeake Inn has good food."

—GeorgeW

www.fodors.com/forums

Updated by
Loretta
Chilcoat

SAILING THE CHESAPEAKE BAY nearly four centuries ago in search of new territory for his English king, Captain John Smith wrote that "heaven and earth never agreed better to frame a place for man's habitation." Today the counties of Maryland and Virginia on the eastern side of the Bay retain an enchanting culture and landscape of calm despite their proximity to Baltimore and Washington, D.C.

The Eastern Shore's first permanent English settlement—indeed, the first in Maryland and one of the earliest along the Atlantic—took root on Kent Island, now Queen Anne's County, in 1631. The region's long heritage is recorded in architecture and on paper and canvas, and many Eastern Shore families have been here for many generations; residents of Smith Island still retain a peculiar Elizabethan lilt in their speech.

A thorough visit to the Shore might consist of exploring hospitable communities and historic sites, strolling through wildlife parks and refuges, pausing at a few of the myriad shops, dining at third-generation-owned waterfront restaurants, and overnighting at inns and bed-and-breakfasts. One of the region's most popular summertime destinations is Ocean City, which clings to a narrow barrier island off the southeastern edge of Maryland's Eastern Shore. Its ocean-side culture differs dramatically from that of the Chesapeake, lacking as it does the early-American aura that pervades the rest of the peninsula.

To understand the Eastern Shore, look to the Bay. The Chesapeake is 195 mi long and the nation's largest estuary (a semi-enclosed body of water with free connection to the open sea). Freshwater tributaries large and small flow south and west into the Bay, ensuring the agricultural wealth of the peninsula as well as the bounty of the Bay ("Chesapeake" is an Algonquian word meaning "great shellfish"). At day's end look west across Chesapeake Bay and you can see the sun set over water—a rare sight for any East Coast resident.

Top 5 Experiences for the Eastern Shore

- **Glide on a majestic skipjack:** Though they once dominated the Chesapeake Bay waterways, these traditional boats today are nearly extinct. Fortunately you can still experience a bit of history by taking an afternoon or sunset cruise aboard one from the Tilghman Island area.

- **Tuck into Maryland's trademark crustacean:** Don't leave the Eastern Shore without sampling the slightly sweet taste of the beloved blue crab, or even better, find a down-home crab feast and crack those shells with your own wooden mallet.

- **Get back to nature:** Escape to the Blackwater National Wildlife Refuge, where you can paddle the tidal marsh pathways and try to catch a glimpse of the beautiful American bald eagles that call this place home.

- **Indulge in a little pampering at one of the region's finest spas:** Inspired by calm-inducing natural beauty and wildlife along the shore, head to the Five Gables Inn in St. Michaels, among the top spas in the Mid-Atlantic.

- **Need the perfect family getaway?** Consider spending a few days at family-friendly Ocean City, where frolicking along the wide beaches and

10

strolling the boardwalk against a backdrop of flashing lights and amusement rides keeps everyone young at heart.

Exploring the Eastern Shore

The Eastern Shore takes up most of the Delmarva (for Delaware-Maryland-Virginia) Peninsula, which reaches down from Pennsylvania and stretches some 200 mi to its tip just above Norfolk and Virginia Beach, Virginia. Only two bridges connect the Eastern Shore to the western and southern mainland. To the north, the William Preston Lane Jr. Bridge, or "the Bay Bridge," crosses just above Annapolis, its dual spans stretching 4½ mi across. To the south, the impressive, 17½-mi Chesapeake Bay Bridge-Tunnel connects Norfolk, Virginia Beach, and other Tidewater-area towns with the peninsula.

Whether you choose road, air, or water, it's easy to get around on the Eastern Shore. The rural roads make for pleasant driving and easy cycling, the airports allow for regional air service, and the dozens of marinas have many years' experience with almost every vessel type.

For glimpses into the past, stop by towns with deep roots, including Chestertown, Easton, Oxford, and St. Michaels. The life of the waterman—as Bay fishermen are traditionally known—still reigns in Crisfield, on Smith Island, and on Tilghman Island. A visit to Virginia's Eastern Shore, the slim peninsula running from the Maryland line to the Chesapeake Bay Bridge-Tunnel, calls for getting off U.S. 13 to take in the 300-year-old port town of Onancock, secluded Tangier Island, popular Chincoteague Island, and the Chincoteague National Wildlife Refuge.

About the Restaurants & Hotels

Outside of Cambridge and Ocean City, the great majority of accommodations throughout Maryland's and Virginia's Eastern Shore are B&Bs, inns, and budget chain hotels. Many, if not most, of the B&Bs and small inns throughout both Maryland's and Virginia's Eastern Shore require two-night minimum stays on weekends in summer as well as in late spring and early fall. This policy often applies during special events such as fairs and festivals. Long-term rentals are available year-round in Ocean City, and many B&Bs welcome long-term stays.

Like larger hotels and motels, many smaller inns have teamed up with other businesses to create packages that include boat tours, golf, tennis, galleries, and museums. Some offer incentives for longer stays.

WHAT IT COSTS				
$$$$	$$$	$$	$	¢
RESTAURANTS over $30	$22–$30	$14–$22	$7–$14	under $7
HOTELS over $250	$175–$250	$130–$175	$80–$130	under $80

Restaurant prices are per person for a main course at dinner. Hotel prices are for a standard double room, excluding state tax.

QUEEN ANNE'S COUNTY

The eastern landfall of the Bay Bridge, which carries U.S. 50/301, is Kent Island, home to historic Stevensville and a thriving hub of seafood restaurants and bars surrounding the slim Kent Narrows channel. This island gateway is 5 mi wide where U.S. 50/301 crosses it, and 14 mi long. William Claiborne established Maryland's first permanent settlement here in 1631 as part of Virginia. Today the small towns in this one-time trading post all have their share of churches and homes that recall the region's past, and it also makes a popular leg-stretching pit stop for eastbound travelers on their way to the beach.

Numbers in the margin correspond to points of interest on the Maryland's Eastern Shore map.

Stevensville

❶ *10 mi east of Annapolis via U.S. 50/301.*

Stevensville, just north of the Bay Bridge's eastern landfall, is a popular stop for its seafood restaurants and local artisans and craftspeople. Its galleries and studios sell original pottery, stained glass, and painted furniture as well as antiques and fine art. Its historic center has been on the National Register since 1986.

Completed in 1809 the **Cray House** is a glimpse into middle-class life of the early 19th century. The two-story cottage, furnished with period pieces, sits in a little yard surrounded by a picket fence. Also on the site, the restored **Stevensville Train Depot,** from the early 1900s, was the western terminus of the old Queen Anne's Railroad Company system. ✉ *Cockey's La.* ☏ *410/643–5969* ⬛ *Donations accepted* ☉ *May–Oct., 1st Sat. of month and by appt.*

In the 17th century Kent Island was the site of the earliest Anglican settlement in the colony. Built in 1880 the **Old Christ Church** served as the sanctuary for Maryland's Anglican church. The current congregation moved to another site in 1995, but the church is still used for religious purposes. The curious Queen Anne structure is mostly wood, but bricks from a church that stood on nearby Broad Creek in 1652 form the chimney, and its peaks and eaves make it seem medieval. ✉ *Rte. 8, 117 E. Main St.* ☏ *410/758–0835* ☉ *May–Oct., 1st Sat. of month and by appt.*

The **Old Stevensville Post Office,** now owned by the Kent Island Heritage Society, is a small building from the late 1800s. On a narrow lot, the structure stands with its side facing the street. ✉ *408 Love Point Rd.* ☏ *410/643–5969* ⬛ *Donations accepted* ☉ *May–Oct., 1st Sat. of month and by appt.*

Guitar aficionados will understand what PRS stands for, and might be surprised to know that the **Paul Reed Smith Guitars factory** is not in New York or Chicago, but right here in Stevensville. Visitors can take tours of this revered name in music and admire the intricate woodworkings of each instrument. Tours happen Monday–Wednesday at 4 PM the first

10

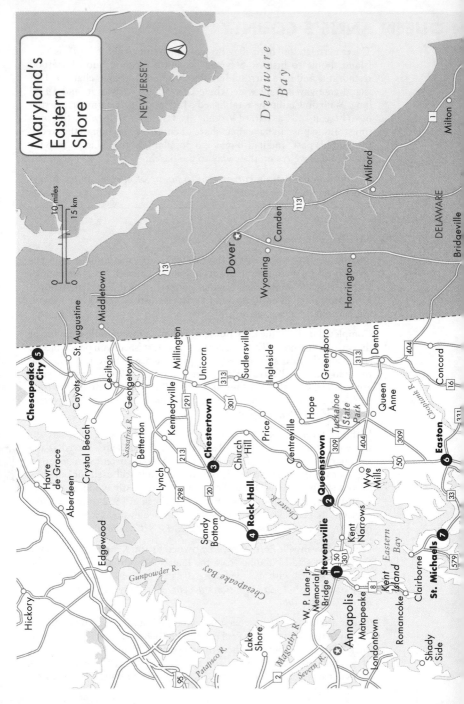

Maryland's Eastern Shore

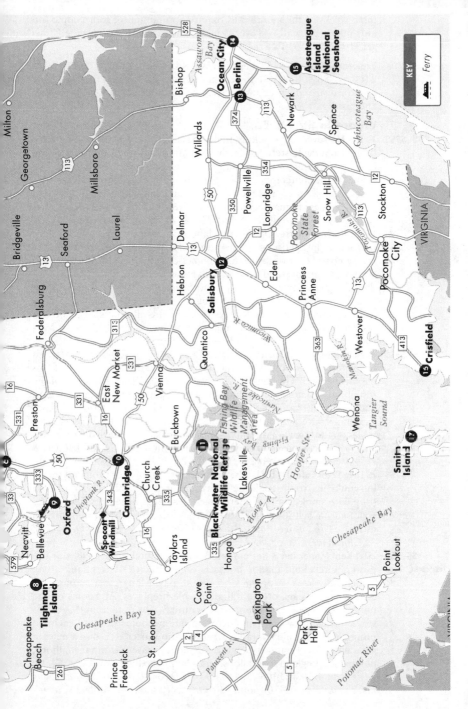

KEY

⛴ Ferry

three weeks of the month and require a minimum of four people (no kids under 12); call 4–8 weeks in advance. ⊠ *380 Log Canoe Circle* ☎ *410/643–9970* ⬚ *Free.*

Exploration Hall (⊠ 425 Piney Narrows Rd., Chester 21619 ☎ 410/604–2100 or 888/400–7787), the county's visitor center, is at the Kent Narrows bridge, and has an interactive exhibit on Chesapeake Bay ecology and history.

Where to Stay & Eat

$$$–$$$$ ✕ **The Narrows.** Overlooking the namesake waterway separating Kent Island from the Eastern Shore, this restaurant has views that include the home port of one of the region's largest commercial fishing fleets. The atrium of the contemporary dining room, with a skylight and large windows, is airy. Specialties include a Caesar salad with fried oysters and grilled peppered tuna, served over sautéed spinach. ⊠ *3023 Kent Narrows Way S, Grasonville* ☎ *410/827–8113* ⬚ *AE, D, DC, MC, V.*

★
☉ $$–$$$$ ✕ **Harris Crab House.** On the mainland side of Kent Narrows, this family-friendly institution provides ample docking space for diners arriving by boat. Some of the seafood comes directly from local watermen. Cream-of-crab soup and back-fin crab cakes are among the best around—the cakes are spicy enough to promote plenty of beer drinking. A nautical theme prevails in the large dining room; oyster cans and other relics from an adjacent abandoned oyster house are all on display. You can get expansive water views from a table on the deck. ⊠ *433 Kent Narrows Hwy., Grasonville* ☎ *410/827–9500* ⬚ *MC, V.*

$–$$$$ ✕ **Hemingway's.** A broad veranda and an upper-level section indoors both have great views west across the Bay, at its narrowest here, and of Annapolis beyond. The sunsets can rival those off Key West, home of the restaurant's namesake. This long-popular restaurant serves tapas, soups, and salads; entrées include Atlantic salmon and coconut sesame shrimp. In summer a very informal bar and grill opens on the lower level, with tables on the lawn adjacent to its private dock. Live music on weekends enhances its simple soup and sandwich menu. ⊠ *Pier 1 Rd. off Rte. 8* ☎ *410/643–2722* ⬚ *AE, D, MC, V.*

$–$$ ✕ **Love Point Cafe.** Don't let the unassuming exterior fool you into thinking you're in a traditional café—it's more than that. Silky cream-of-crab soup with smoky hints of sherry, meltaway eggs Benedict Chesapeake-style, and a belt-loosening stuffed rockfish are all standouts on the menu. ⊠ *401 Love Point Rd.* ☎ *410/604–0910* ⬚ *AE, D, MC, V* ☉ *Closed weekdays Jan.–Mar.*

$$–$$$ ✕⊞ **Kent Manor Inn & Restaurant.** A summer hotel since 1898, this imposing antebellum manor house is on 226 acres of farmland along Thompson Creek, near the Chesapeake Bay. Many guest rooms have cozy window seats, others Italian marble fireplaces. All rooms on the upper floors open onto semiprivate verandas. The restaurant ($$–$$$$) serves meals in two elegant Victorian dining rooms or in an enclosed porch. You can follow a tangy Crab Cosmo starter served in a martini glass with Chef Kent's Trio, which includes beef tenderloin medallions, plump New England sea scallops, and a fat jumbo lump crab cake. ⊠ *500 Kent Manor Dr., 21666* ☎ *410/643–7716 or 800/820–4511* ⊕ *www. kentmanor.com* ⬎ *20 rooms, 4 suites* ♿ *Restaurant, cable TV, tennis*

Fodor$Choice
★

court, pool, dock, boating, croquet, volleyball, bar, meeting rooms; no smoking ▭ *AE, D, MC, V* ⊙ *Restaurant closed Mon. and Tues., except for guest breakfast* 🍽 *BP.*

Nightlife

In addition to having live music and a seafood menu, the **Crab Deck at the Fisherman's Inn** (✉ 3116 Main St., Grasonville ☎ 410/827–6666) also has a duck pond to amuse the kids. The deck is closed in winter.

Like other aspects of Kent Island, its nightlife revolves around the water. Most of the bars here are attached to restaurants. One exception is **Gravity Lounge** (✉ 51 Piney Narrows Rd., Grasonville ☎ 410/604–6955). This steadfast waterman's community is an odd location for a groovy martini and sushi bar, but it works. Dress like you didn't just step off a fishing boat and order the whopping "Best of the Bite" sushi platter to share with friends. The full sushi menu here comes with stellar waterfront views of Piney Cree.

With its blinding hot green and yellow colors the **Jetty** (✉ 201 Wells Cove Rd., Grasonville ☎ 410/827–4959) helps re-create a slice of the tropics among its very laid-back crowd, especially when it's karaoke night or when there's live music on weekends.

The raucous, open-air **Red Eye's Dock Bar** (✉ 428 Kent Narrows Way North, Grasonville ☎ 410/827–3937) is a hopping, good place to grab a brew—as long as you don't have a problem with the wildly popular bikini contests here.

Sports & the Outdoors

You can stroll or roll along the **Cross Island Trail** between Kent Narrows on the western edge of Kent Island—5½ mi wide here—and Bay beachfront on its eastern side. Here the smoothly paved or hard-packed trail joins the **Terrapin Nature Area,** 279 flat, lush acres that hug the Chesapeake Bay. The area, made up of five identifiable habitats—wetlands, woodlands, wildflower meadows, tidal ponds, and sandy beaches—has ample parking at both ends.

10

BOATING Queen Anne's County has 18 public landings for boats of all sizes. Of these, nine have trailer launching ramps, but the others are "unimproved" and can be used only for canoes, kayaks, and other small boats that can be carried to the water. A seasonal or daily permit is required to launch a boat from public landing ramps and for parking at these sites. For locations where permits may be purchased, contact **Parks and Recreation** (☎ 410/758–0835).

C & C Charters (✉ Mears Point Marina, 506 Kent Narrows Way N ☎ 410/827–7888 or 800/733–7245 🖷 410/827–5341 🌐 www.cccharters.com) has an extensive fleet of power- and sailboats over 30 feet. It's one of the northern Bay's most experienced and hospitable boat firms. **Island Boat Rentals** (✉ 201 Wells Cove Rd., Exit 42 off Rte. 50 ☎ 410/827–4777) provides small skiffs or pontoon boats for use on the Chester River and the eastern Bay. All necessary equipment is provided for short- or long-term rentals. **Tuna the Tide Charter Service** (✉ 404 Greenwood Creek La. ☎ 410/827–5635 or 410/827–6188 🖷 410/827–9331

⊕ www.exploredelmarva.com) has two boats for light tackle and fly-fishing expeditions as well as for crabbing or sightseeing.

Join Captain Michael Hayden as part of the crew of **Nellie L. Byrde** (☎410/886–2906), part of the Bay's historic skipjack fleet.

Shopping

Eastern Bay Trading is a barn of a building packed with a near-random gathering of castoffs and antiques. It's a great place for rummaging. ✉*4917 Main St., Rte. 18, Grasonville* ☎ *410/827–9286* ☉ *Thurs.–Mon. 11–5.*

Old Stevensville's popular art gallery, the **Kent Island Federation of Art** (✉ 405 Main St. ☎ 410/643–7424), showcases local artists.

Ye Olde Church House (✉ 426 Love Point Rd. ☎ 410/643–6227) in old Stevensville is just that, but now it's a shop filled with crafts and hand-spun yarn, hand-dipped candles, old-fashioned soap and candy, and the occasional antique. With sheep grazing in the pasture next door, it's hard to miss and worth seeking out.

Queenstown

❷ *11 mi east of Stevensville, 21 mi east of Annapolis via U.S. 50/301.*

The cove of Queenstown's harbor is protected by a bend of the mouth of the Chester River. Established in 1707 as "Queen Anne's Town," it became an important enough port to be attacked by the British during the War of 1812. A pleasantly sleepy little community, it's worth a short visit.

Where to Stay

$$$ ▣ **Lands End Manor on the Bay.** On 17 secluded acres on Eastern and Prospect bays, a 10-minute drive east of Queenstown, this stunningly decorated former hunting lodge has see-forever views from its three spacious rooms, which all have king-size beds. The cozy common areas include a great room, gun room, and solarium. When evening arrives, homemade cookies and sherry are set out. Deep-draft docking is available for guests. ✉ *232 Prospect Bay Dr., Grasonville 21638* ☎ *410/827–6284* ⊕ *www.bbonline.com/md/landsend* ⟿ *3 rooms* ᗜ *Cable TV, refrigerators, pool, dock, boating, canoes, bicycles; no smoking* ☉ *Closed Nov. 15–Mar. 15* ▤ *AE, D, MC, V* ⑩*BP.*

Sports & the Outdoors

Queenstown is home to a pair of the finest golf courses in the region, both of which are part of **Queenstown Harbor Golf Links** (✉ 32 Links La., off Rte. 301 ☎ 410/827–6611 or 800/827–5257). The River Course and the adjacent Lakes Course, par 71 and par 72 respectively, have 36 holes beside the place where the Chester River flows into the bay. Fees range from $39–$49 for 9 holes on weekdays to $84–$109 for 18 holes on weekends.

Operated by the Wildfowl Trust of North America, the 500 acres of the **Chesapeake Bay Environmental Center** will open your eyes, ears, and mind to the wildfowl and waterscapes that characterize Maryland's Eastern Shore. The aviary and waterfowl ponds are full of ducks, geese, swans, and birds of prey. Pause a moment in a secluded blind and explore native woodlands, marshes, and meadows along 4 mi of trails. A visitor center and picnic facilities are on the grounds. ⋈ *600 Discovery La., Grasonville* ☎ *410/827–6694* ⌨ *$5* ⊙ *Daily 9–5.*

Shopping

A major layover between the western shore and the beaches, the completely remodeled **Prime Outlets at Queenstown** (⋈ 441 Outlet Center Dr., at intersection of U.S. 50/301 ☎ 410/827–8699 ⊙ Mon.–Sat. 10–9, Sun. 11–8), just 10 mi east of the Bay Bridge, has upscale factory outlet stores including Coach, Banana Republic, Tommy Hilfiger, Calvin Klein, Eddie Bauer, and L. L. Bean.

KENT COUNTY

The communities on the upper reaches of Maryland's Eastern Shore are steeped in history and determined to preserve it. Those in Kent County, whose idyllic location between the Chester and Sassafras rivers is enhanced by a long, ragged Chesapeake Bay shoreline, are among the most fiercely protective. Hidden hamlets untouched by time savor their quiet anonymity; others struggle to balance acceptance of their recent renown with a heritage of 300 years.

Chestertown

❸ *47 mi northeast of Annapolis via U.S. 50/301 to Rte. 213, 24 mi north of Wye Mills via U.S. 50 to Rte. 213.*

Second only to Annapolis in its concentration of 18th-century houses, Chestertown was a major international port in Colonial days: a tall, brick customhouse continues to dominate the High Street waterfront. Still the home of families whose local roots go back many generations, the town has its share of newer residents, many of them retirees. Today, inns and good restaurants, fine art galleries and antiques shops line the brick pavements of High Street, Chestertown's broad, tree-lined main street. To walk along its narrow streets, some of them cobbled, is to commune quietly with some of the country's oldest history. At the northern edge of Chestertown is **Washington College,** one of the nation's oldest liberal-arts institutions. George Washington helped found the college in 1782 through a gift of 50 guineas.

10

Geddes-Piper House, home of the Historical Society of Kent County, is a splendid Federal-style home containing 18th-century furniture and an impressive teapot collection, a historical library, and shop. It's a good place to begin a visit to Chestertown. ⋈ *Church Alley* ☎ *410/778–3499* ⌨ *$4* ⊙ *Wed.–Fri. 10–4.*

The *Sultana,* a reproduction of a 1768 Colonial schooner by the same name, was launched in 2001. With a length of 97 feet, the original *Sultana* was the smallest schooner ever registered on the Royal Navy Lists. The mission of this "Schoolship of the Chesapeake" is to provide unique, hands-on educational experiences in Colonial history and environmental science. Several two-hour public sails ($30) are available each month from April through November. Daylong and multiday public sails are also scheduled regularly. The *Sultana* can be seen close-up when she is anchored in the Chester River, at the end of Cannon Street. ✉ *105 S. Cross St.* ☎ *410/778–5954.*

OFF THE BEATEN PATH

★

Looking for that pink flamingo piñata? You're almost guaranteed to find one at **DIXON'S FURNITURE AUCTION** (✉ 2017 Dudley Corner Rd., at intersection of Rtes. 290 and 544, Crumpton ☎ 410/928–3006) – , which is much more than furniture. At this rite-of-passage for antiques (and flea market) bargain hunters, you browse among acres of objects, from genuine antiques to everyday "other people's treasures," then bid against amateurs and pros alike. Want to bid low? Start at the $5 field—the loot is divided into sections, and minimum bids increase by $5 increments. Some of the food and beverage concessions here are run by members of the local Amish community. The auction takes place every Wednesday from 9 AM and ends when the last pink flamingo piñata is sold.

Where to Stay & Eat

$$–$$$ ✗ **Kennedyville Inn.** In a little town 8 mi north of Chestertown, the Kennedyville is known for its legendary pit barbecue and microbrews as well as daily seafood specials and light fare. The polished service and personal attention are as fine as the food, and the wine and spirits selection has been carefully chosen. It's not open long hours: seating is Wednesday and Thursday 5–8, Friday and Saturday 5–9, and Sunday 3–6:30. ✉ *Rte. 213, east side, Kennedyville* ☎ *410/348–2400* ⊕ *www. kennedyvilleinn.com* ▤ *D, MC, V* ⊘ *Closed Mon. and Tues.*

¢–$ ✗ **Feast of Reason.** Head to this lunch spot for extraordinary sandwiches with uncommon ingredients, including roast beef with pesto mayonnaise on French bread, or tomatoes, spinach, zucchini, and sprouts in a garlic herb wrap. For dessert, have a cookie, brownie, granola bar, or "fuslbous." "Fuslbous"? Ask the proprietor for the story of how this delicious item got its name. ✉ *203 High St.* ☎ *410/778–3828* ▤ *No credit cards* ⊘ *Closed Sun. No dinner.*

$$–$$$$ ⌂ **Brampton Bed & Breakfast Inn.** On 35 landscaped acres between the Chester River and the Chesapeake Bay, 1 mi south of downtown Chestertown, this mid-19th-century inn still resembles the plantation house it once was. The brick building's entrance has a 3½-story walnut-and-ash staircase, pine floors, and plaster ceiling medallions. Most of the large guest rooms have fireplaces, and five have hot tubs. Classic videos, available from the innkeepers' private collection, can be viewed in the library, which also has an extensive supply of books. Rates include afternoon tea with homemade pastries. ✉ *25227 Chestertown Rd., Rte. 20 W, 21620* ☎ *410/778–1860* 🖷 *410/778–1805* ⊕ *www. bramptoninn.com* ➥ *10 rooms* ⌂ *Library, pets allowed in 1 room; no room phones, no TV in some rooms, no kids under 12, no smoking* ▤ *AE, D, MC, V* ⦿❙ *BP.*

★ $$–$$$ ⌂ **White Swan Tavern.** Step back in time at this inn, restored to its appearance circa 1790. Built as a home in 1733, it was a tavern, then a general store; it may be the town's oldest building. Brick fireplaces and deep window seats, an old writing desk, and pewter candleholders are all in keeping with its Colonial past. The original kitchen, shaded by a giant elm, is the inn's most requested guest room. Its rough ceiling beams, brick floor, and large fireplace attest to its antiquity. Afternoon tea is served in the dining room, on the rear stone patio, or in guest rooms ($5). ⊠ *231 High St., 21620* ☎ *410/778–2300* 🖷 *410/778–4543* ⊕ *www.whiteswantavern.com* ↯ *4 rooms, 2 suites, 2 apartments* ₰ *Meeting room, cable TV, Wi-Fi; no room phones, no room TVs, no smoking* ▭ *MC, V* ┦◎ *CP.*

$–$$ 🔳 **The Inn at Mitchell House.** The long history of this 1743 manor house includes the tale of a War of 1812 British commander who died of his wounds here in 1814: his body left for England preserved in a barrel of rum. The inn sits on 10 serene acres surrounded by woods about 10 mi from downtown Chestertown. Nature enthusiasts are as much at home here as the songbirds, migrating geese, white-tailed deer, and eagles. With access to Tolchester Marina and its private beach, it's convenient to boating, fishing, crabbing, and swimming, as well as to biking, hiking, hunting, sporting clays, golf, and tennis. Four guest rooms have working fireplaces. ⊠ *8796 Maryland Pkwy., 21620* ☎ *410/778–6500* ⊕ *www. innatmitchellhouse.com* ↯ *6 rooms* ₰ *Lounge, meeting room; no room phones, no room TVs, no smoking* ▭ *MC, V* ┦◎ *BP.*

Sports & the Outdoors

At the mouth of the Sassafras River, about 12 mi north of Chestertown, **Betterton Beach**, the bay's only jellyfish-free beach, has a bathhouse, boardwalk, picnic pavilion, and boat ramp. To help fully enjoy this tiny community, bike, boat, and kayak rentals are available in and around Chestertown.

Rock Hall

❹ *13 mi southwest of Chestertown via Rte. 291 to Rte. 20.*

No longer just a side trip, Rock Hall, its hardy maritime character intact, has emerged as a viable destination in its own right, to be reached either by road or by boat. It reveres its heritage, despite the pleasure boats anchored in its waters and moored at its docks—which far outnumber actual working fishing boats.

10

At the tip of the Eastern Neck peninsula, at the mouth of the Chester River, is the superb **Eastern Neck National Wildlife Refuge.** This 2,285-acre park, 8 mi south of Rock Hall, is a prime place to spot migratory waterfowl, wild turkey, Delmarva fox squirrels, and southern bald eagles, undeterred by the experimental power-generating solar panels and wind turbines installed nearby. Nearly 6 mi of roads and trails and an observation tower provide excellent vantage points. ⊠ *1730 Eastern Neck Rd.* ☎ *410/639–7056* ◷ *Daily dawn–dusk.*

The **Waterman's Museum** profiles the hard life on the Bay in absorbing detail, celebrating a Chesapeake way of life that in many ways is dying out. On display are exhibits on oystering and crabbing that include historical photos and local carvings, as well as preserved examples of the watermen's all-important boats and a reproduction of a waterborne shanty. ⊠ *20880 Rock Hall Ave.* ☎ *410/778–6697* ⋈ *Free* ◷ *May–Sept., daily 8–5; Oct.–Apr., weekdays 8–5, Sat. 9–5, Sun. 10–4.*

Where to Stay & Eat

$–$$$ ✕ **Waterman's Crabhouse.** This casual dockside restaurant looking out toward the Chesapeake Bay Bridge has lots of local color. The menu includes ribs, steaks, and fried oysters, but its crab dishes are legendary, as are its homemade cheesecake and key lime pie. Warm summer weekends mean live entertainment and seating on the 40-foot deck. There's a deep-draft dock for diners arriving by boat. ⊠ *21055 Sharp St.* ☎ *410/639–2261* ☰ *AE, D, MC, V* ☉ *Closed Jan. and Feb.*

$$–$$$ ✕🛏 **The Inn at Osprey Point.** On 30 lush acres along Swan Creek, this stately Colonial-style building has brick fireplaces and exposed beams. It's worth staying here for the views alone. Rooms have four-poster, canopied beds; the spacious two-room Escapade suite has French doors and a marble bath with a whirlpool hot tub. At the inn's restaurant ($$–$$$; closed Tuesday and Wednesday), regional fare is served. The cream-of-crab soup with sherry is a favorite among regulars, as are entrées such as Maryland jumbo lump crab cakes and pan-seared duck breast. ⊠ *20786 Rock Hall Ave., 21661* ☎ *410/639–2194* ⊕ *www.ospreypoint.com* ⇆ *6 rooms, 1 suite* ☖ *Restaurant, picnic area, cable TV, pool, marina, meeting rooms; no room phones, no kids, no smoking* ☰ *D, MC, V* ❏ *CP.*

Sports & the Outdoors

Canoeing and kayaking on quiet creeks and rivers throughout the Eastern Shore's ragged western shorelines are popular pastimes here. Two firms in Kent County provide rentals, tours, and lessons for the area: they're also good sources for waterside camping advice. Gear up at **Kayak-Canoe** (⊠ Swan Creek Rd., 4 mi north of Rock Hall ☎ 410/639–9000). The folks at **Chester River Kayak Adventures** (⊠ 5758 Main St., Rock Hall ☎ 410/639–2001) also operate two B&Bs.

CECIL COUNTY

Cecil County includes the northern extremities of Chesapeake Bay. Its western boundary with Harford County, the Susquehanna River, is the Bay's principal northern tributary. Its southern boundary with Kent County is another tributary, the Sassafras River. The all-important Chesapeake and Delaware (C&D) Canal is cut between Cecil's third major river, the Elk, and the Delaware River, a major shipping route that connects Chesapeake Bay with Delaware Bay and the Atlantic Ocean. Some 12,000 acres of public parks and forests in addition to a wildlife management area help preserve connections with nature and the outdoors.

Chesapeake City

❺ *31 mi north of Chestertown via Rte. 213.*

A town split dramatically in two by the Chesapeake and Delaware (C&D) Canal, Chesapeake City homes and businesses face each other across the busy waterway. Those sitting at the restaurants and taverns next to the canal often marvel at the giant oceangoing vessels that slide by—seemingly within arm's reach. Chesapeake City's own well-protected harbor cove welcomes visiting pleasure craft virtually year-round.

NEED A BREAK? The **Canal Creamery** (⊠ 9 Bohemia Ave. ☎ 410/885–3314) dishes out some of the richest ice-cream scoops around, including Happy Days (peanut butter, fudge, and miniature peanut butter cups) and Bananas Foster (bananas, caramel, and rum flavoring). You can enjoy a cup or a cone (some made from chocolate chip cookies) at an umbrella-covered table outside. The creamery is open daily from May through October.

Where to Stay & Eat

★ **$$–$$$** ✕ **The Bayard House.** One of the few restaurants in Chesapeake City, the Bayard House boasts cuisine and service that would stand out almost anywhere. Patrons in the know travel to this canal-shop eatery for dishes such as grilled breast of duck; tournedos Baltimore, twin fillets of beef topped with crab and lobster; and the de rigueur Maryland crab cakes. The Maryland crab soup is even more widely renowned. ⊠ *11 Bohemia Ave.* ☎ *410/885–5040* ▤ *AE, D, MC, V.*

$–$$$ ▣ **Ship Watch Inn.** Three levels of broad decks mean that every room has a place from which to relax and watch international watercraft sail in and out of the C&D Canal just yards away. (A canal-side hot tub offers an even closer view.) Built as a residence in 1920, this elegant, waterfront B&B blends eclectic furnishings with modern amenities. The decades-old black-and-white photos hanging in the public areas reveal much about the roles the owner-innkeepers' families played in the history of Chesapeake City. ⊠ *401 1st St., 21915* ☎ *410/885–5300* ⊕ *www.shipwatchinn.com* ⋥ *8 rooms, 2 suites* ⟨ *Cable TV, meeting rooms, hot tub; no smoking* ▤ *AE, MC, V* ⦿ *BP.*

North East

12 mi northwest of Chesapeake City via Rte. 213 and Rte. 40.

Uncommon neighborliness along a main street of antiques and collectibles shops and homey eateries gives Cecil's riverside county seat its welcoming charm.

The **Day Basket Factory** has been crafting oak baskets by hand since 1876. Skilled craftspeople and weavers use techniques passed down through the generations; you can often watch them as they work. ⊠ *714 S. Main St.* ☎ *410/287–6100* ⊙ *Wed.–Fri. 10:30–5, Sat. 10–5, Sun. 1–5; until 6 PM on Sat. in summer.*

About 6 mi south of the town of North East, **Elk Neck State Park** juts into the headwaters of the Chesapeake Bay to its west, with the Elk River flowing along its eastern flank. You can drive almost the length of the peninsula and then walk about a mile through pleasant woodlands to the cliffs on its tip. There you can find the sparkling-white Turkey Point Lighthouse. No longer in use, it's maintained by volunteers. The 270-plus-degree view from Turkey Point is stunning. Camp sites are available here, as are some charming 1950s-era wooden cabins that are admirably well maintained. Elk Neck is a prime location for picnicking as well as for fishing and swimming off sandy beaches. ⊠ *Rte. 272 south of North East* ☎ *410/287–5333 or 888/432–2267.*

10

You could spend a weekend in the **5&10 Antique Market.** Originally the Hotel Cecil, it became Cramer's 5&10, an old-fashioned variety store with hard-to-find items, penny candy jars, and a pair of proprietors who themselves became historic treasures. The building's enterprising current owner created an antiques mart but fully restored the building's exterior and retained its well-worn wood flooring, candy jars, and display counters. ⊠ *111 S. Main St.* ☎ *410/287–8318.*

The two spacious buildings of the **Upper Bay Museum** at the head of the North East River preserve the rich heritage of both the commercial and recreational hunter. This unusual museum houses an extensive collection of boating, fishing, and hunting artifacts native to the Upper Chesapeake Bay: sleek sculling oars, rare working decoys, and the outlawed "punt" gun and "gunning" rigs. ⊠ *Walnut St. at Rte. 272* ☎ *410/ 287–2675* ⊙ *Sat. 10–3, Sun. 10–4.*

Where to Stay & Eat

⏲ **$–$$**   ✕ **Woody's Crab House.** You can get the crabs here, of course, and have them served any number of imaginative ways. But slurp one of the thick homemade soups, or down the famous Carolina shrimp burger, to understand why this funky little eatery is so popular. The kids' menu is a thoughtful extra. But go easy on the real food: Woody's ice-cream parlor, next door, includes seasonal favorite flavors such as apple, pumpkin, and Fourth of July (a celebration of red, white, and blue ice creams). ⊠ *29 S. Main St.* ☎ *410/287–3541* ♢ *Reservations not accepted* ▭ *D, MC, V.*

★ **$–$$**   ▦ **Elk Forge B&B Inn and Retreat.** An easy hour's drive from either Baltimore or Philadelphia, Elk Forge is an appealing destination unto itself. On 5 acres of woods and gardens, the inn is along the Big Elk Creek. Each of the 12 guest rooms is uniquely decorated and well appointed. A daily afternoon tea includes the innkeepers' own herbal blends; services at the Spa in the Garden include Swedish massage and aromatherapy facials. ⊠ *807 Elk Mills Rd., Rte. 316, Elk Mills 21920* ☎ *410/ 392–9007 or 877/355–3674* ⊕ *www.elkforge.com* ➷ *7 rooms, 5 suites* ♿ *Cable TV, in-room VCRs, in-room data ports, outdoor hot tub, massage, spa, badminton, croquet, meeting rooms; no smoking* ▭ *AE, MC, V* ❙⊙❙ *BP.*

TALBOT COUNTY

Water defines the landscape of Talbot County, which has some of the region's most vibrant little towns, including Easton, Oxford, and St. Michaels. The Chesapeake Bay forms its western border, and the meandering Choptank River slices through the Delmarva Peninsula to form its southern and eastern borders. Waterfront hamlets that started as fishing villages now include comfortable inns and downtown B&Bs. Fine waterside restaurants and folksy main-street taverns are also part of this comfortably refined region.

Easton

★ ❻   *79 mi south of North East and 36 mi south of Chestertown via Rte. 213 and U.S. 50, 36 mi southeast of Annapolis via U.S. 50/301 to U.S. 50.*

Well-preserved buildings dating from Colonial through Victorian times still grace the downtown of this affluent, genteel town. Fine art galleries, high-quality antiques shops, and gift boutiques sit side by side along North Harrison Street and others that make up the small midtown mall called Talbottown.

★ In its 1820s-era schoolhouse, the **Academy Art Museum** houses a permanent collection of fine art by such American artists as James McNeil Whistler, Grant Wood, Lichtenstein, and Rauschenberg, as well as Chagall and Dürer. ■ TIP➔ **Special exhibitions often cover Eastern Shore artists, and the juried art show the museum holds in early October is one of the finest in the region.** ⊠ *106 South St.* ☎ *410/822–2787 or 410/822–0455* 🖶 *410/822–5997* 🎫 *$2* ☽ *Mon. and Sat. 10–4, Tues.–Thurs. 10–8.*

A three-story Federal brick house, restored by a Quaker cabinetmaker in 1810, houses the **Historical Society of Talbot County,** which maintains a small museum of local history and manages Tharpe Antiques. The society also operates Three Centuries Tours, a one-hour overview of authentically furnished homes of the 17th through 19th centuries. ⊠ *25 S. Washington St.* ☎ *410/822–0773* 🎫 *$5* ☽ *Mon.–Sat. 10–4. Guided house tours Tues.–Sat. 11:30 and 1:30.*

Rebellious citizens gathered at the **Talbot County Courthouse** to protest the Stamp Act in 1765 and to adopt the Talbot Resolves, a forerunner of the Declaration of Independence. Today, the courthouse, built in 1712 and expanded in 1794, along with two wings added in the late 1950s, is still in use. The two-tier cupola is topped by a weather vane. ⊠ *11 N. Washington St.* ☎ *410/770–8001* ☽ *Weekdays 8–5.*

Where to Stay & Eat

$$$$ ✕ **Restaurant Columbia.** A newcomer on the Easton dining scene, this upscale restaurant offers creative entrées, which change every three weeks, from Chef Stephen Mangasarian's whimsical repertoire. The vibrant Victorian porch leads into a tony city townhome with crisp, white tables set in every room, ready for an elegant affair. Grilled gulf shrimp as thick as lobster claws topped with red chili pepper–peanut sauce, and a delicate balsamic glaze–covered pan-seared Copper River salmon are highlights. An extensive wine cellar caps the fine dining experience. ⊠ *28 S. Washington St.* ☎ *410/770–5172* 🖃 *AE, D, MC, V* ☽ *Closed Sun. and Mon.*

★ $$$–$$$$ ✕ **Mason's.** A family-run landmark for more than 30 years, Mason's uses fresh ingredients from its own garden. The chef brings bold flavors like pan-seared crab cakes topped with a corn and soybean succotash, crispy-skin red snapper surrounded by braised artichokes, and gentle rockfish stuffed with lump crab meat, a local delicacy. Sip a classic martini in the swanky lounge while waiting for a table—make sure to ask for one on the porch in warm weather. Next door is a coffee bar and a food store that sells hard-to-find cheeses and meats, wonderful hand-crafted chocolates, and all manner of esoteric edibles. ⊠ *42 E. Dover St.* ☎ *410/822–3204* ⊕ *www.masonsgourmet.com* 🖃 *AE, D, MC, V* ☽ *Closed Sun.*

$$–$$$ ✕ **Out of the Fire.** A spare, modern interior sets this neighborhood bistro apart from its Colonial neighbors. Of note is the owner's insistence that

10

all equipment and furnishings—including a trompe l'oeil mural, faux-finish walls, and pottery—be obtained locally. One of the more interesting entrées is Caribbean spiced pork with ginger mango chutney. Breads are baked in a stone-hearth oven; desserts are produced on-site. Enjoy one of more than 100 labels at the wine bar or in the overstuffed seating off to one side of the open kitchen. ⊠ *22 Goldsborough St.* ☎ *410/770–4777* ☲ *AE, D, MC, V* ☉ *Closed Sun.*

$–$$$
Fodor'sChoice
★

✕ **General Tanuki's.** A most unusual and exciting blend of Pacific Rim, California surf, and grandma's kitchen await adventurous tastebuds in this intimate venue. A *tanuki* is akin to a Japanese leprechaun, and the creative flavors here play tricks on traditional dishes. Imagine a restaurant serving buttery sushi and sashimi, lamb lettuce wraps, Thai mussels simmered in Woodpecker cider, and a classic Hawaiian pizza under one roof? Run, don't walk, to this place, and make sure to check out happy hour (4–6 PM) at the U-shape bar. ⊠ *25 Goldsborough St.* ☎ *410/819–0707* ☲ *MC, V.*

★ **$$$–$$$$**

✕▥ **Inn at Easton.** This B&B operates one of the finest restaurants ($$$–$$$$) in the country. Delightfully imaginative creations include green Thai bouillabaisse, but the signature dish is roasted lamb sirloin with a Dijon herb crust. With a colorful interior that's full of antiques and gracious touches, this circa-1790 Federal mansion is a bit like a boutique hotel (the 2006 movie *Wedding Crashers* filmed a reception scene there). Original paintings by the Russian impressionist Nikolai Timkov are hung in the common areas. Upstairs, the seven rooms and suites skillfully combine old-time charm with modern amenities. ⊠ *28 S. Harrison St., 21601* ☎ *410/822–4910 or 888/800–8091* ☲ *410/820–6961* ⊕ *www.theinnateaston.com* ⤶ *3 rooms, 4 suites* ⚇ *Restaurant; no room TVs, no kids under 9, no smoking* ☲ *AE, D, MC, V* ☉ *No lunch* ⏀▯ *BP.*

$–$$$

▥ **The Tidewater Inn & Conference Center.** This stately four-story brick hotel was built in 1949. Beyond its first-story archways, a Colonial theme pervades its spacious common areas, where there are hurricane lamps, huge fireplaces, and paintings of old Easton. Mahogany reproduction furniture fills the charming rooms, done in greens and golds. In the hotel's full-service dining room, a "hunting breakfast" is available early every morning in season. A small on-site spa takes care of manicures and massages. ⊠ *101 E. Dover St., 21601* ☎ *410/822–1300 or 800/237–8775* ⊕ *www.tidewaterinn.com* ⤶ *114 rooms, 7 suites* ⚇ *Restaurant, spa, cable TV, pool, bar, business services, meeting rooms, kennel, no-smoking floors* ☲ *AE, D, MC, V.*

Nightlife & the Arts

Avalon Theatre (⊠ 40 E. Dover St. ☎ 410/822–0345), a former vaudeville house built in 1921, has been restored as a venue for the Talbot Chamber Orchestra and the Eastern Shore Chamber Music Festival, as well as films and other performances.

With a name like **Chez Lafitte** (⊠ 13 S. Washington St. ☎ 410/770–8868), you might think that this bar is going to ooze pretentiousness. But no. The owners, a New York actress and her husband, named this intimate yet welcoming piano jazz bar after their Great Dane. The rich furnishings, including giant gilded mirrors and crushed velvet drapes, evoke Parisian bistros.

St. Michaels

❼ *9 mi west of Easton via Rte. 33, 49 mi southeast of Annapolis.*

St. Michaels, once a shipbuilding center, is today one of the region's major leisure-time destinations. Its ever-growing popularity has brought more and more shops, cafés, waterfront restaurants, and inns. In warmer months, tourists and boaters crowd its narrow streets and snug harbor.

★ ☺ The **Chesapeake Bay Maritime Museum**, one of the region's finest, chronicles the Bay's rich history of boatbuilding, commercial fishing, navigating, and hunting in compelling detail. Exhibits among nine buildings on the 18-acre waterfront site include two of the Bay's unique skipjacks among its more than 80 historic regional boats. There's also the restored 1879 Hooper Strait Lighthouse, a working boatyard, and a "waterman's wharf" with shanties and tools of oystering and crabbing. In the Bay Building, you can see a dugout canoe hewn by Native Americans and a crabbing skiff.

> ### WORD OF MOUTH
>
> "If you want to relax, St. Michaels is a great place—especially when you add in trips to nearby Easton and Oxford, I think you can find enough activities to keep it interesting but leave enough time to kick back and relax." –Iolfn

The Waterfowl Building contains carved decoys and stuffed birds, including wood ducks, mallards, and swans. ✉ *Mill St. at Navy Point* ☎ *410/745–2916* 💲 *$10* ☺ *June–Sept., daily 10–6; Oct., Nov., and Mar.–May, daily 10–5; Dec.–Feb., daily 10–4.*

Where to Stay & Eat

★ **$$$–$$$$** ✕ **208 Talbot.** Unobtrusively situated on St. Michaels' busy main street, 208 Talbot has several intimate dining rooms with exposed brick walls and brick floors. Specialties include such original starters as little-neck clams and pork sausage in a tomato coulis, and sweet ruby red beets with Humboldt Fog goat cheese. Entrées, all served with tossed salad, include a variety of traditional seafood dishes accompanied by innovative sides like stone-ground grits, bread salad, and truffled flageolets. Small plates ($6–$12) are available for lighter bites, and on Saturday, there's a prix-fixe menu ($55). ✉ *208 N. Talbot St.* ☎ *410/745–3838* ▭ *D, MC, V* ☺ *Closed Mon. and Tues.*

$$$ ✕ **Town Dock Restaurant.** Every seat in this vast restaurant overlooks the water, and every window frames its own scene; the deck is also open. Fresh seafood dishes such as local red snapper and rockfish and Atlantic salmon are favorites. Or if you just can't decide, try the Land and Sea Buffet. For a finale, sample some strawberries hand-dipped in chocolate. ✉ *125 Mulberry St.* ☎ *410/745–5577* ▭ *AE, D, DC, MC, V* ☺ *Closed Tues. and Wed. Nov.–Mar.*

$–$$ ✕ **Crab Claw Restaurant.** Owned and operated by the same family since 1965, this St. Michaels landmark started as a clam- and oyster-shuck-

10

ing house for watermen long before that. Diners at both indoor and outdoor tables have panoramic views over the harbor to the river beyond, but eat dockside if you can. As the name suggests, this is *the* down-home place for fresh steamed and seasoned blue crabs. But the extensive menu also includes sandwiches and other light fare as well as other seafood and meat dishes. Children's platters are available, too. ⊠ *End of Mill St., at Harbor* ☎ *410/745–2900 or 410/745–9366* ▭ *No credit cards* ⊘ *Closed Dec.–early Mar.*

★ $$$$ ✕🏨 **Inn at Perry Cabin.** On 25 acres beside the Miles River, this luxury inn employs a nautical theme throughout to elegant effect. Each guest room has unique charm and elegant appointments; standard amenities include heated towel racks, fresh flowers in all rooms, and afternoon tea. Above all, staying here means finding impeccable service. Dining at the inn's restaurant with its flawless cuisine and stellar wine selection is an event. The signature crab spring roll with pink grapefruit, avocado, and toasted almonds, and the lamb shank glazed with honey and tarragon are both exquisite. ⊠ *308 Watkins La., 21663* ☎ *410/745–2200 or 800/722–2949* 🖷 *410/745–3348* ⊕ *www.perrycabin.com* ⇌ *54 rooms, 27 suites* ⌂ *Restaurant, in-room data ports, pool, pond, exercise equipment, massage, sauna, steam room, dock, bar, library, concierge, meeting rooms, helipad; no smoking* ▭ *AE, DC, MC, V.*

★ $$$ 🏨 **Five Gables Inn & Spa.** Three circa-1860 houses have been turned into an elegant and comfortable getaway. All rooms have a private porch or balcony, and all are decorated with antique furnishings, fine linens and towels, and down comforters. The hot stone massage and invigorating rosemary mint body wrap are treatments in the spa. Refreshments are served daily at 3. ⊠ *209 N. Talbot St., 21663* ☎ *410/745–0100 or 877/466–0100* 🖷 *410/745–2903* ⊕ *www.fivegables.com* ⇌ *11 rooms, 3 suites* ⌂ *Dining room, in-room hot tubs, cable TV, in-room VCRs, pool, sauna, spa, steam room, bicycles, shops, some pets allowed (fee); no phones in some rooms, no smoking* ▭ *AE, MC, V* ¶⊙¶ *CP.*

$$–$$$ 🏨 **The Oaks, a Country Inn.** Antebellum grace defines this 1748 mansion on 17 acres along the banks of Oak Creek, 3 mi from St. Michaels. The antiques-filled inn has a stunning black-and-white tile foyer; its best rooms have fireplaces, private porches, and hot tubs. The day starts with a full country breakfast served in the sunny yellow-and-red dining room. After that, you might want to go fishing off the pier, or head no farther than one of the rockers in the screened porch overlooking the water. ⊠ *Rte. 329 at 329 Acorn La., Royal Oak 21662* ☎ *410/745–5053* ⊕ *www.the-oaks.com* ⇌ *22 rooms, 1 cottage* ⌂ *Dining room, cable TV, putting green, pool, dock, boating, fishing, bicycles, shuffleboard, volleyball, meeting rooms; no kids (Memorial–Labor Day only), no smoking* ▭ *MC, V* ¶⊙¶ *BP.*

$$–$$$ 🏨 **Victoriana Inn.** Adirondack chairs line a sloping expanse of lawn leading to the formal gardens of what was once a Civil War army officer's home. Set on the town's harbor and across a footbridge from the Maritime Museum, this inn is a relaxing haven. All rooms include queen-size beds; two have fireplaces and three overlook the water. The suite has a private water-view deck and a fireplace as well as a TV. There's a nightly happy hour that includes wine, beer, and light hors d'oeuvres. No kids under 13 on weekends. ⊠ *205 Cherry St., 21663* ☎ *410/745–3368*

⊕ *www.victorianainn.com* ⮥ *6 rooms, 1 suite* ⚲ *Bicycles, some fireplaces; no room phones, no TV in some rooms, no smoking* ⊟ *MC, V* ⦿ *BP.*

★ **$$-$$$** ⊡ **Wades Point Inn on the Bay.** Combining the serenity of the country and the splendor of the Chesapeake Bay, this complex of three brick and Colonial wood-frame Victorian buildings is on 120 acres of fields and woodland. The two sun-bright corner rooms in one wing are closest to the water, but each carefully decorated period room has a private porch or balcony. Cows and goats grazing along a 1-mi trail through the property welcome hikers, joggers, and bird-watchers. All are welcome with an unusual stipulation—fishermen, hunters, and children under 14 need to stay on the first floor of one of the buildings. ⊠ *Wades Point Rd., Rte. 33, Box 7, 21663* ☎ *410/745–2500 or 888/923–3466* ⊕ *www. wadespoint.com* ⮥ *23 rooms, 1 farmhouse* ⚲ *Some kitchenettes, pond, dock, hiking, meeting rooms; no a/c in some rooms, no room phones, no room TVs, no kids under 1, no smoking* ⊟ *MC, V* ⦿ *CP.*

Sports & the Outdoors

Town Dock Marina (⊠ 305 Mulberry St. ☎ 410/745–2400 or 800/678–8980) rents bicycles as well as surrey-top electric boats and small powerboats. *The Patriot* (⊠ Docked near Crab Claw Restaurant and Chesapeake Bay Maritime Museum, St. Michaels ☎ 410/745–3100), a 65-foot steel-hull yacht, departs four times daily, from March through September, for one-hour cruises on the Miles River. The tour covers the ecology and history of the area as it passes along the tranquil riverfront landscape. For a true taste of the old way of life on the water, consider taking a skipjack cruise. The *H. M. Krentz* (⊠ Docked at the Crab Claw Restaurant, St. Michaels ☎ 410/745–6080) can carry 32 passengers. Built in 1886, the *Rebecca T. Ruark* (⊠ docked in Dogwood Harbor at 21308 Phillips Rd., Tilghman Island ☎ 410/829–3976 or 410/886–2176) is the oldest working skipjack on the Bay.

Shopping

Talbot Street, the main street in St. Michaels, is lined with restaurants, galleries, and all manner of shops, including a hardware store that doubles as a retro gift shop. Stroll between Mill Street, the lane to the Chesapeake Bay Maritime Museum, and Willow Street, or head just beyond to Canton Alley.

Tilghman Island

❽ *13 mi southwest of St. Michaels via Rte. 33.*

A visit to Tilghman Island provides intriguing insight into the Eastern Shore's remarkable character. Leave your car and explore by bike or kayak. A handful of B&Bs and intimate inns provide excellent accommodations here. A small fleet of working fishing boats, including a few of the region's remaining skipjacks, call Dogwood Harbor "home port."

Where to Stay & Eat

$$-$$$$ ✕⊡ **Tilghman Island Inn.** Warm, welcoming conviviality and casual elegance define this compact, modern resort overlooking the Chesapeake Bay (there are also views of a neighboring waterfowl marsh). Five deluxe

10

The Venerable Skipjacks of the Chesapeake Bay

SETTLEMENT ALONG THE FERTILE shores of the Chesapeake Bay was an obvious choice for 17th-century English immigrants, who soon farmed the cash crop of tobacco and plucked plentiful blue crabs and plump oysters from its bottom. Among the reminders of the Bay's fishing culture, which endures, are its dwindling fleet of native skipjacks: broad, flat-bottom wooden sailing vessels for dredging oysters. Economical to build, skipjacks had the shallowest draft—the distance from the waterline to the lowest point of the keel—of any boat in the Chesapeake Bay. This made them excellent for cruising above the grassy shoals favored by oysters.

At first, oyster harvesters would stand in small boats and use simple, long-handle tongs, like a pair of scissored rakes, to grasp clumps of oysters from the bottom and bring them aboard. It was tiresome, difficult work. In the early 1800s, sturdy Yankee schooners, having left the depleted waters of New England, entered the Chesapeake Bay with dredges, ungainly iron contraptions that dragged up oysters along the bottom. With their first large harvest, Chesapeake's fishing industry changed forever.

Dredging was initially banned as being exploitive and intrusive, first by Virginia and later by Maryland, but after the Civil War drained the region's economy, Maryland changed legalized the practice, allowing it under certain conditions for boats powered only by sails. By 1875, more than 690 dredging licenses were issued. Soon, more sophisticated dredgers emerged; all were loosely called *bateaux*, French for "boats."

The oyster bounty was not to last. After peaking in 1884 with 15 million bushels, less than a third of that amount was caught in 1891. Despite the growing use of steam and gasoline power on land and water, "only under sail" laws prevailed in the Bay. As the 19th century drew to a close, boat builders were forced to experiment with boat designs that were cheap to build yet had sails that would provide enough power for dredging and transporting the harvests. In 1901 one of these new bateaux appeared in Baltimore's harbor. She caught the eye of a *Baltimore Sun* newspaper reporter, who wrote that their "quickness to go about may have earned for them the name of skipjack." The name stuck.

Oysters—and the Chesapeake's renowned blue crab—are still harvested by a dwindling number of watermen, their fleets concentrated in locales such as Crisfield and Kent Narrows, and Smith Island but only a dozen sail-powered skipjacks are still working. Taking a ride on one of them (generally from early April through October, when they're not dredging) is an exhilarating way to fully experience the culture and history of the Chesapeake. The region's second-largest working skipjack, the *Nellie L. Byrde*, is docked in front of Explorer Hall beside Kent Narrows. The *Nathan of Dorchester* is berthed in Cambridge. The *Herman M. Krentz*, built in 1955, and the 80-foot *Rebecca T. Ruark*, originally built in 1886, both sail from Tilghman Island or nearby St. Michaels.

waterside rooms have hot tubs, fireplaces, and spacious decks. Dishes served at the Gallery Restaurant ($$–$$$) include the unusual black-eyed pea cake and Oysters Choptank. The 5-acre complex includes a 20-slip transient marina and a small fleet of tandem and single kayaks available for rent. ⊠ *Coopertown Rd., Box B, 21671* ☎ *410/886–2141 or 800/866–2141* ⊕ *www.tilghmanislandinn.com* ⟳ *15 rooms, 5 suites* ⚭ *Restaurant, cable TV, in-room data ports, tennis court, pool, dock, marina, croquet, 2 bars, meeting rooms, some pets allowed; no smoking* ▤ *AE, D, DC, MC, V* ⎮◯⎮ *CP.*

$$–$$$ 🏨 **Chesapeake Wood Duck Inn.** Once a bordello as well as a house for a respectable waterman's family, this waterfront 1890 boardinghouse has been impeccably restored with original artworks. A first-floor fireplace, screened porch, and sunporch make the inn suitable for all seasons. In the elegant dining room, your hosts—one of whom is an experienced professional chef—present wonderful breakfasts that may include crêpes, maple-braised sausage and apples, and eggs whipped with white truffles and served with an Asiago cheese sauce. A prix-fixe dinner with wine is available for 4 to 12 guests by prior arrangement. ⌂ *Box 202, Gibsontown Rd., 21671* ☎ *410/886–2070 or 800/956–2070* 🖷 *410/677–7256* ⊕ *www.woodduckinn.com* ⟳ *7 rooms, 1 cottage* ⚭ *Dining room, Wi-Fi; no room TVs (cottage has TV), no kids under 14, no smoking* ▤ *MC, V* ⎮◯⎮ *BP.*

$$–$$$ 🏨 **Lazyjack Inn on Dogwood Harbor.** Although this beautiful island inn was severely damaged during a 2003 hurricane, it has since resurfaced with aplomb, now sitting 6 feet higher than its original 1855 foundation. The impeccable rooms are equipped with down comforters and candles in the windows. Guests are welcomed with fresh flowers and a tray of sherry on the bureau. Both suites include a fireplace and an oversize hot tub. You can reserve a sail on the innkeepers' restored 1935 45-foot boat, the *Lady Patty.* ⊠ *5907 Tilghman Island Rd., 21671* ☎ *410/886–2215 or 800/690–5080* ⊕ *www.lazyjackinn.com* ⟳ *2 rooms, 2 suites* ⚭ *Boating; no room phones, no room TVs, no kids under 12, no smoking* ▤ *AE, MC, V* ⎮◯⎮ *BP.*

★ $ 🏨 **Sinclair House.** Built in the 1920s as a fishermen's inn, Sinclair House eventually became Tilghman's first B&B. Today, the innkeepers' former lives in international relations are tastefully reflected here. Each guest room is decorated with crafts and artwork from a different culture: baskets and tapestries from southern Africa; rattan furniture and puppets from Indonesia; hand-painted headboards and antique mirrors from Morocco; textiles and *retablos* (small devotional paintings) from Peru. American, European, or Latin specialties are served at breakfast. The common room has satellite TV, along with a VCR and a group of classic films. ⊠ *5718 Black Walnut Point Rd., 21671* ☎ *410/886–2147 or 888/859–2147* ⊕ *www.sinclairhouse.biz* ⟳ *4 rooms* ⚭ *Library; no room TVs* ▤ *AE, D, MC, V* ⎮◯⎮ *BP.*

Sports & the Outdoors

Tilghman Island's tiny Dogwood Harbor is the home port of two of the region's revered skipjacks. They are available for tours between early April and late October. A two-hour tour on the 32-passenger *H. M. Krentz* (⊠ Dogwood Harbor, Tilghman Island ☎ 410/745–6080) costs

10

$30. The *Rebecca T. Ruark* (✉ Dogwood Harbor, Tilghman Island ☎ 410/886–2176 or 410/829–3976 💻 2-hr hands-on learning cruise $30) holds 49 passengers.

EN ROUTE The **Oxford-Bellevue Ferry,** begun in 1683, may be the oldest privately owned ferry in continuous operation in the United States. It crosses the Tred Avon River between Bellevue, 7 mi south of St. Michaels via Routes 33 and 329, and Oxford. ✉ *N. Morris St. at Strand, Oxford* ☎ *410/745–9023* 💻 *Ferry: $7 car and driver one-way, $2 pedestrian, $3 bicycle, $4 motorcycle* ☉ *Mar.–Memorial Day and Labor Day–Nov., weekdays 7 AM–sunset, weekends 9 AM–sunset; Memorial Day–Labor Day, weekdays 7 AM–9 PM, weekends 9–9.*

Oxford

⑨ *7 mi southeast of St. Michaels via Rte. 33 and Rte. 333.*

Tracing its roots to 1683, Oxford remains secluded and untrammeled. Robert Morris, a merchant from Liverpool, lived here with his son, Robert Morris Jr., a signer of the Declaration of Independence. The younger Morris helped finance the Revolution but ended up in debtor's prison after losing at land speculation.

The **Oxford Museum** displays models and pictures of sailboats. Some boats were built in Oxford, site of one of the first Chesapeake regattas (1860). Check out the full-scale racing boat by the door. Other artifacts include the lamp from a lighthouse on nearby Benoni Point, a sailmaker's bench, and an oyster-shucking stall. Docents elaborate on the exhibits, which set the context for a walking tour of nearby blocks. ✉ *Morris and Market Sts.* ☎ *410/226–5122* 💻 *Free* ☉ *Apr.–Oct., Fri.–Sun. 2–5.*

Where to Stay & Eat

$–$$$$ ✕▣ **Robert Morris Inn.** In the early 1700s, this building on the banks of the Tred Avon River was crafted as a home by ships' carpenters using ship nails, hand-hewn beams, and pegged paneling. In 1738 it was bought by an English trading company as a house for its Oxford representative, Robert Morris. Four guest rooms have handmade wall paneling and fireplaces built of English bricks used as boat ballast. Other buildings in the complex include a newer manor house on a private beach. Circa 18th-century murals of river scenes adorn the walls of the main room in the inn's restaurant ($$–$$$$), known for its meticulous preparation of the Chesapeake Bay's bounty. ✉ *314 N. Morris St., 21654* ☎ *410/226–5111* 🖷 *410/226–5744* ⊕ *www.robertmorrisinn.com* ⮑ *35 rooms* ⚌ *Restaurant, beach, taproom, Wi-Fi, meeting rooms; no room phones, no TV in some rooms, no smoking* ⊟ *AE, MC, V.*

★ $$$$ ▣ **Combsberry.** This 1730 brick house, together with a carriage house and cottage and a formal garden, is amid magnolias and willows on the banks of Island Creek. Inside are five arched fireplaces, floral chintz fabrics, and polished wood floors. All the rooms and suites of this luxurious B&B have water views and are furnished with English manor–style antiques, including four-poster and canopy beds. Some also have hot tubs and working fireplaces; the two-bedroom Carriage House has a kitchen. ✉ *4837 Evergreen Rd., 21654* ☎ *410/226–5353* ⊕ *www.*

combsberry.net ⌨ 2 *rooms, 2 suites, 1-bedroom cottage, 2-bedroom carriage house* & *Dining room, library, some pets allowed; no room phones, no room TVs, no kids under 12* ▭ *AE, MC, V* ⬤ *BP.*

DORCHESTER COUNTY

One of the larger, yet sparsely populated counties on Maryland's Eastern Shore, Dorchester retains bits of early America in its picture-postcard towns and waterfront fishing villages. Gunslinger Annie Oakley and Underground Railroad activist Harriet Tubman are among the county's most famous past residents. The expansive Choptank River, its northern boundary, and the rambling 28,000-acre Blackwater National Wildlife Refuge are idyllic locales for biking and boating, hiking and camping, and hunting and fishing (including crabbing).

Cambridge

❿ *15 mi southeast of Oxford via U.S. 50, 55 mi southeast of Annapolis via U.S. 50/301 to U.S. 50.*

In this county seat Annie Oakley used to aim at waterfowl from the ledge of her waterfront home. Graceful Georgian, Queen Anne, and Colonial Revival buildings abound: with an art gallery here and a museum there, a night or two in Cambridge can be very refreshing.

The **La Grange Plantation** is headquarters to the Dorchester County Historical Society, and houses two historic homes on its property. The three-story, 18th-century Georgian **Meredith House** is rich with Chippendale, Hepplewhite, and Sheraton period antiques, and the Children's Room holds an impressive doll collection, cradles, miniature china, and baby carriages. Portraits and effects of seven former Maryland governors from Dorchester County adorn the Governor's Room. In the **Neild Museum** are agricultural, maritime and Native American artifacts. There's also a restored smokehouse, blacksmith's shop, and medicinal herb garden on the grounds. Fall is ablaze with vibrant leaves and many family activities. ✉ *902 La Grange Ave.* ☎ *410/228-7953* 🎟 *Free* ☉ *Weekdays 10–3, and by appt.*

The small **Harriet Tubman Learning Center & Museum** is dedicated to the former slave who helped lead more than 300 other slaves to freedom along the Underground Railroad. Tubman was born and raised in and around Cambridge. At the museum, artifacts and documents about her life are on display. ✉ *424 Race St.* ☎ *410/228-0401* 🎟 *Donations accepted* ☉ *Fri. 10–3, Sat. noon–4.*

The **Richardson Maritime Museum** in downtown Cambridge celebrates and chronicles Chesapeake boatbuilding with impressive, scaled-down versions of boats peculiar to the Chesapeake Bay, such as bugeyes, pungies, skipjacks, and log canoes—and the tools used to build them. Photos, a film, and a model boatbuilding workroom complement the models. ✉ *401 High St.* ☎ *410/221-1871* 🎟 *Free* ☉ *Wed. and Sun 1–4, Sat. 10–4, and by appt.*

10

OFF THE
BEATEN
PATH

OLD TRINITY CHURCH – Seven miles southwest of Cambridge stands tiny Old Trinity Church. Built around 1675 and extensively altered in the 1800s, the church has been restored to its 17th-century appearance. In the churchyard are the graves of four governors of Maryland and several members of the distinguished political and clerical Carroll family. Services are still held here every Sunday at 11. ⊠ *Rte. 16 near Church Creek* ☎ *410/228–2940* ☉ *Tours by appt.*

Where to Stay & Eat

$–$$$ ✕ **Snappers Waterfront Cafe.** Join regulars at this casual waterside restaurant and bar on the edge of town. Choose from an extensive menu of dishes with a Southwestern flavor, healthy portions of steak, and such entrées as baked stuffed shrimp. ⊠ *112 Commerce St.* ☎ *410/228–0112* ▤ *AE, D, MC, V.*

$$$$ ▥ **Hyatt Regency Chesapeake Bay Golf Resort, Spa and Marina.** This 370-acre complex is the Eastern Shore's first full-service, year-round resort, and one that takes full advantage of the soothing natural light and spectacular views of the Choptank River. The resort includes an 18-acre Blue Heron rookery, an 18,000-square-foot spa, and a golf course designed by Keith Foster. All rooms and suites have a private balcony; those on the upper level have raised ceilings. The resort's restaurants include the self-service Bay Country Market and the Blue Point Provision Company for seafood. Two outdoor sandstone fireplaces make perfect s'more hubs, and a 30-foot-high wall of windows welcomes you to Michener's Library. ⊠ *100 Heron Blvd., 21613* ☎ *410/901–1234* 🖷 *410/901–6301* ⊕ *chesapeakebay.hyatt.com* ⇝ *384 rooms, 16 suites* ♺ *5 restaurants, snack bar, room service, in-room safes, refrigerators, cable TV, in-room data ports, 18-hole golf course, 4 tennis courts, indoor-outdoor pool, health club, spa, beach, marina, bar, lounge, shops, concierge, Wi-Fi, business services, convention center, meeting rooms* ▤ *AE, D, MC, V.*

$$ ▥ **Lodgecliffe on the Choptank.** This home was the first bed-and-breakfast in the county and remains one of the most charming. Don't sleep through breakfast or you might miss blueberry blintzes and crab quiches freshly made and hot from the oven. ⊠ *103 Choptank Terr., 21613* ☎ *866/273–3830* ⊕ *www.lodgecliffeonthechoptankbandb.com* ⇝ *3 rooms* ♺ *Dining room, sun porch, breakfast, Wi-Fi; no smoking, no pets* ▤ *AE, D, MC, V.*

Sports & the Outdoors

All of the land of the **Fishing Bay Wildlife Management Area,** bordering Blackwater National Wildlife Refuge, is along **Fishing Bay** at the southern end of Dorchester County. Here you can take a pair of "water trails" through some scenic rivers and streams—it's reminiscent of Florida's Everglades. A short canoeing or kayaking trek down one of these water trails—recommended only for paddlers with some experience—is an exceptional way to experience a salt marsh and the wildlife that lives in one. Contact the Dorchester County Department of Tourism (410/228–1000) for more information, as well as a waterproof map.

Rent kayaks and bikes at **Blackwater Paddle & Pedal Adventures,** which also provides guided instruction in and around the wildlife refuge. ⊠ *4303 Bucktown Rd.* ☎ *410/901–9255.*

The **Nathan of Dorchester,** a skipjack replica, cruises the Choptank River from Long Wharf at the foot of High Street in Cambridge. In summer the 28-passenger *Nathan* sets sail on most Saturday evenings and Sunday afternoons. Two-hour cruises cost $20. ⊠ *Long Wharf, 526 Poplar St.* ☎ *410/228–7141.*

Blackwater National Wildlife Refuge

⑪ *8 mi south of Cambridge via Rte. 16 to Rte. 335, 63 mi southeast of Annapolis.*

The largest nesting bald eagle population north of Florida makes Blackwater its home. You can often see the birds perching on the lifeless tree trunks that poke from the wetlands here, part of nearly 28,000 acres of woods, open water, marsh, and farmland. In fall and spring some 35,000 Canada and snow geese pass through in their familiar V formations to and from their winter home, joining more than 15,000 ducks. The rest of the year, residents include endangered species such as peregrine falcons and silver-hair Delmarva fox squirrels. Great blue heron stand like sentinels while ospreys dive for meals, birds sing, and tundra swans preen endlessly. By car or bike, you can follow a 5-mi road through several habitats or follow a network of trails on foot. Exhibits and films in the visitor center provide background and insight. ⊠ *2145 Key Wallace Dr., at Rte. 335* ☎ *410/228–2677* 🖃 *$3 car, $1 pedestrian or cyclist* ☉ *Wildlife drive, daily dawn–dusk. Visitor center, weekdays 8–4, weekends 9–5* ♧ *No pets allowed.*

THE LOWER EASTERN SHORE

The three counties of Maryland's lower Eastern Shore—Wicomico, Worcester, and Somerset—contain the contrasting cultures of the Chesapeake Bay and the Atlantic coast but still share a common history.

From the north the Nanticoke River flows out of southern Delaware across fertile farmland into the Chesapeake Bay near the Blackwater National Wildlife Refuge. To the east the Atlantic alternately caresses and pounds sturdy shorelines and fragile barrier islands stretching from the Delaware Bay to easternmost Virginia. In the Eastern Shore's southwestern corner a few towns cling to the shoreline of Tangier Sound among vast Wildlife Management Areas.

The small towns throughout the region sometimes seem a century away from the oceanfront's summertime bustle. Main Street shops, Early-American inns, and unsung restaurants are a far cry from the boutiques and galleries, the high-rise hotels and condos, and the eateries of nearby Ocean City, which clings to a narrow, sandy strip.

10

Salisbury

⑫ *32 mi southeast of Cambridge via U.S. 50, 87 mi southeast of Annapolis via U.S. 50/301 to U.S. 50.*

Barges still ply the slow-moving Wicomico River between the Bay and Salisbury, the Eastern Shore's second-largest port after Baltimore. The tree-shaded waterfront is a popular draw for hiking, biking, boating, fishing, and shopping. Antiques shops and galleries, along with some exemplary Victorian architecture, fill the six blocks that make up downtown.

Ⓒ Stretch your legs at **Pemberton Historic Park** with more than 5 mi of riverfront hiking trails. ⊠ *Pemberton Dr.* ☎ *410/860–2447* ⊙ *Daily dusk–dawn.*

★ Ⓒ Operated in partnership with Salisbury University, the **Ward Museum of Wildfowl Art** presents realistic marshland and wildfowl displays. Two brothers from Crisfield, Lem and Steve Ward, helped transform decoy making from just a utilitarian pursuit to an art form; their re-created studio is a must-see exhibit. Besides the premier collection of wildfowl art, the 30,000-square-foot museum has some 2,000 other artifacts as well as a gift shop and library. ⊠ *909 S. Schumaker Dr.* ☎ *410/742–4988* ▧ *$7* ⊙ *Mon.–Sat. 10–5, Sun. noon–5.*

Where to Eat

$–$$$ ✕ **The Red Roost.** Inside a former chicken barn, inverted bushel baskets now serve as light fixtures at this down-home crab house, where hammering mallets rival the beat of piano and banjo sing-alongs. The Red Roost gets rave reviews for its seafood specialties and ribs, as well as its meaty steamed crabs. ⊠ *Rte. 352 and Rte. 362, Whitehaven* ☎ *410/546–5443 or 800/953–5443* ▤ *AE, MC, V* ⊙ *Closed Nov.–Mar. and Mon. and Tues., Labor Day–Memorial Day. No lunch.*

Berlin

⓭ *15 mi northeast of Snow Hill via Rte. 113, 22 mi east of Salisbury via U.S. 50; 7 mi west of Ocean City via U.S. 50.*

Berlin is a short drive from Ocean City but is far less strident and loud in temperament. Magnolias, sycamores, and ginkgo trees line streets filled with predominantly Federal- and Victorian-style buildings (47 are on the National Register of Historic Places). By the way, the name comes not from the German city but from Burleigh Inn, a Colonial way station.

Where to Stay & Eat

★ **$–$$** ✕▥ **Atlantic Hotel.** This fully restored 1895 inn blends the taste of grand living with modern conveniences. Guest rooms are spacious and have four-poster beds on hardwood floors. Beneath chandeliers, the hotel's formal dining room ($$–$$$) serves scrumptious entrées that may include a pistachio duck dish or rockfish topped with oysters, ham, and crabmeat. In the tavern a very talented waiter periodically joins the pianist and sings. The second-floor parlor, done in bold red-and-green hues with ornate furnishings, is a perfect place to relax. ⊠ *2 N. Main St., 21811* ☎ *410/641–3589 or 800/814–7672* ▤ *410/641–4928* ⊕ *www.atlantichotel.com* ⮌ *17 rooms* ↻ *Restaurant, café, cable TV, library, meeting rooms; no smoking* ▤ *AE, MC, V.*

$–$$ ▥ **Merry Sherwood Plantation.** A wealthy Philadelphian built this striking, three-story Italianate mansion with its white, lacelike trim for his future bride in 1859, and its aristocratic flavor remains. Inside are a mahogany staircase and railing, a dining room with carved rosewood furniture once owned by the Vanderbilts, a rosewood chair made for Queen

Victoria, and antiques-filled guest rooms. Surrounding a broad wrap-around porch is an impeccably landscaped 18-acre parcel of topiary, rose, and perennial gardens, viewed also from a sprawling enclosed sunroom. ⊠ *8909 Worcester Hwy., 21811* ☎ *410/641–2112 or 800/660–0358* ⊕ *www.merrysherwood.com* ☞ *7 rooms, 5 with bath; 1 suite* ⚲ *Library; no room phones, no room TVs, no smoking* ▭ *MC, V* ⫶◉⫶ *BP.*

Ocean City

⓮ *7 mi east of Berlin and 29 mi east of Salisbury via U.S. 50.*

Stretching some 10 mi along a narrow barrier island off Maryland's Atlantic coast, Worcester County's Ocean City draws millions annually to its broad beaches and the innumerable activities and amenities that cling to them, as well as to the quiet bayside.

On the older, southern end of the island, where the 3-mi Boardwalk begins, is a restored 19th-century carousel as well as traditional stomach-churning amusement park rides and a fishing pier. The north–south roads, as well as the Boardwalk itself, are crowded with shops selling the prerequisites of resort destinations everywhere, from artwork to T-shirts to snack food to beer. Beyond the northern end of the Boardwalk (27th Street), high-rise condos prevail, and the beaches are less congested.

Lodging options include modern high-rises, sleepy motels, two B&Bs, and older hotels with oceanfront porches filled with wooden chaise longues and rocking chairs. Cuisine here includes Thrasher's renowned "Boardwalk" fries, available from three outlets throughout Ocean City, as well as fine restaurant fare accompanied by impressive wine lists. Fresh seafood abounds.

> **WORD OF MOUTH**
>
> "The beaches at Ocean City are not as soft as the west coast of FL but extremely clean and you can stay on the beach all day b/c it never gets too hot. There is so much to do and great nightlife too!"
>
> –travelingirl

10

A year-round destination, Ocean City is particularly appealing in the fall and early winter, then again in late winter and early spring, when the weather is mild. Most hotels and better restaurants remain open year-round, although the latter may operate on fewer days and/or shorter schedules. Furthermore, many festivals and other special events are scheduled for the off-season.

Jacob Fussell began a wholesale ice-cream business in Baltimore in 1851, the first in the United States. Today, privately owned and operated ice-cream parlors abound along Maryland's Eastern Shore, but **Dumser's Dairyland,** created from the ground up in 2002, takes ice cream to new heights.

★ ⚘ On the southernmost tip of the island, the **Ocean City Life Saving Station Museum** traces the resort to its days as a tiny fishing village in the late 1800s. Housed in an 1891 building that once held the U.S. Lifesaving Service and the Coast Guard, the museum's exhibits include models of the grand old hotels, artifacts from shipwrecks, boat models, five salt-water aquariums, an exhibit of sands from around the world, and even itchy wool swimsuits and an old mechanical laughing lady from the Boardwalk. Press the button, and you can be laughing with her. ⊠ *Boardwalk at Inlet* ☎ *410/289–4991* ⊠ *$3* ⊙ *June–Sept., daily 11–10; May and Oct., daily 11–4; Nov.–Apr., weekends 10–4.*

🐣 **Trimper's Amusement Park,** at the south end of the Boardwalk, has a "boomerang" roller coaster; the rickety and terrifying "Zipper"; and the Hirschell Spellman Carousel, from 1902. The park has been owned by the Trimper family since it opened in 1890. ⊠ *Boardwalk and S. 1st St.* ☎ *410/289–8617* ⊠ *Pay per ride or attraction* ⊙ *Memorial Day–Labor Day, weekdays 1 PM–midnight; weekends noon–midnight. Labor Day–Memorial Day indoor portion only, weekends noon–midnight.*

Where to Eat

★ **$$–$$$$** ✕ **Fager's Island.** This bayside restaurant gives you white-linen treatment and views of soothing wetlands and the bay, and stunning sunsets through its large windows. White stucco walls and white columns contrast with red-tile floors and brass chandeliers. Entrées include prime rib, fresh mahimahi, and salmon. There's an outside deck for more informal dining and a raw bar with lighter fare. ⊠ *60th St. at Bay* ☎ *410/524–5500* ⚓ *Reservations essential* ⊟ *AE, D, DC, MC, V.*

> **A NOTE ABOUT FAGER'S ISLAND**
>
> On a whimsical note: Tchaikovsky's *1812* Overture is played every evening, with the tumultuous finale timed to coincide with the setting of the sun.

$$–$$$$ ✕ **Galaxy 66 Bar & Grill.** This unusual watering hole is a welcome breeze of creative cuisine. Appetizers are light and delicate, like seared foie gras and asparagus shrimp risotto. Equally innovative mains include homemade manchego cheese gnocchi, seared duck with sun-dried cherries, and a pistachio-encrusted rockfish that is, pardon the pun, out of this world! The second and third floors open up to outdoor seating and views of the bay. The cosmic Star Bar is becoming quite the hot spot for local celebs and those looking for a dark hideaway for specialty martinis, and they serve tapas until midnight. ⊠ *66th St. Bayside* ☎ *410/723–6272* ⊟ *AE, D, DC, MC, V.*

$$–$$$$ ✕ **Phillips Crab House & Seafood Buffet.** Feast on crab cakes, crab imperial, or stuffed and fried shrimp at the original 1956 home of a restaurant that has since become a chain. The dark-panel dining room has decorative stone floors, hanging Tiffany-style lamps, stained-glass windows, and funky wall art. Its wildly popular buffet is served in an upstairs dining room. ⊠ *21st St. and Philadelphia Ave.* ☎ *410/289–6821 or 800/549–2722* ⊟ *AE, D, MC, V.*

🐣 **$–$$$** ✕ **Fish Tales Bar and Grill.** When the kids need a break from the standard Boardwalk fare, take 'em to this incredibly family-friendly restaurant where children are part of the action. Antsy kids can play on an awesome pirate ship or on the soft beach with the Frisbee that comes with their meals. The food is as easy-going as the atmosphere, with Maryland-style shrimp salad, a stuffed seafood burrito, and a creative shrimp and artichoke ravioli. At night, a bit of a rowdy (yet civilized), older bar crowd likes to congregate on the waterfront benches. ⊠ *Bayside, between 21st and 22nd Sts.* ☎ *410/289–7438* ⊟ *AE, D, DC, MC, V.*

$–$$$ ✕ **The Shark.** A restaurant you shouldn't be afraid of at the beach, this upscale place takes advantage of every bay view, including from the sweeping rooftop bar. The namesake dish can be prepared any way you like. Other dishes experiment with unusual flavors like the tuna with wasabi cream sauce and pineapple meringue, and the plank-grilled salmon with raspberry-chipotle BBQ sauce. Go for the Eggplant Tower stuffed with layers of shrimp, lump crab, and wild mushrooms with fresh-shaved Parmesan. Entrées are $5 3–5 PM, and a live jazz band plays on Thursday nights. ⊠ *46th St. Bayside, behind Sunsations* ☎ *410/723–1221* ⊟ *AE, D, DC, MC, V.*

Where to Stay

The narrow island means that no lodging is far from either the ocean or the bay. Rates vary dramatically through the year, with the lowest typically between mid-November and mid-March, and the highest during July and August. An ocean view will usually raise the rate.

★ **$$$$** ▦ **The Edge.** In this boutique hotel, the accommodations exude quality and style. Each room is uniquely furnished to evoke such locales as Bali or the Caribbean, the French Riviera or southern Italy, and even the *Orient Express.* From queen- and king-size feather beds to gas-fed fireplaces, no amenity is amiss. Windows that take up the entire west-facing room walls allow for panoramic views at sunset. ⊠ *56th St. at Bay, 21842* ☎ *410/524–5400 or 888/371–5400* 🖶 *410/524–3928* ⊕ *www.fagers.com* ⇄ *10 rooms, 2 suites, 1 penthouse* ♿ *In-room hot tubs, minibars, refrigerators, pool* ⊟ *AE, D, DC, MC, V.*

☾ **$$–$$$$** ▦ **Park Place.** Filling a need for more affordable, family- and child-friendly accommodations, this small, multistory, family-owned and -operated hotel is on the Boardwalk. All rooms are efficiencies with fully equipped kitchenettes and sofa beds. Some have extra-long beds and hot tubs. ⊠ *2nd and 3rd Sts. at Boardwalk, 21842* ☎ *410/289–6440 or 888/212–7275* 🖶 *410/289–3389* ⊕ *www.ocparkplacehotel.com* ⇄ *89 rooms* ♿ *Restaurant, TVs, kitchenettes, microwaves, refrigerators, some in-room data ports, some Wi-Fi, pool, bar, free parking* ⊟ *AE, D, MC, V.*

★ **$–$$$$** ▦ **Lighthouse Club Hotel.** This elegant all-suites hotel is a Chesapeake Bay "screwpile" lighthouse look-alike of uncommonly quiet luxury, just blocks from the busy Coastal Highway. Its airy, contemporary suites have high ceilings and views of sand dunes that slope to the Assawoman Bay. Rooms have white-cushion rattan furniture and marble bathrooms with two-person hot tubs and the convenience of coffeemakers and plush terry robes. Sliding glass doors lead to private decks with steamer chairs. ⊠ *60th St. at Bay, 21842* ☎ *410/524–5400 or 888/371–5400* ⊕ *www.fagers.com* ⇄ *23 suites* ♿ *Minibars, refrigerators, hot tubs* ⊟ *AE, D, DC, MC, V.*

☾ **$–$$$** ▦ **Castle in the Sand Hotel.** This compound of castles is a popular family destination for its sheer amount of kid-friendly amenities. "Castle Kid" activities include tales of pirates and ghosts of Assateague Island

10

weaved by Captain J. one night a week in the summers, and Lady Sunshine is on hand to pamper young princesses. All rooms are basic, with pastel walls and random, motel-esque furniture. But all are oceanfront, looking onto a wide swath of beach, with some overlooking the largest pool in Ocean City. Two off-site cottages a block away provide a cozy home-away-from-home atmosphere. ⊠ *3701 Atlantic Ave., 21842* ☎ *410/289–6846 or 800/552-7263* ⊕ *www.castleinthesand.com* ⟿ *rooms, efficiencies, suites, apartments ⚹ Restaurant, cable TV, in-room VCRs, some kitchens, some kitchenettes, microwaves, refrigerators, indoor-outdoor pool, game room, bar, free parking ⊟ AE, D, DC, MC, V.*

$–$$ 🏨 **Atlantic Hotel.** Family-owned and -operated, the three-story, H-shape frame hotel—Ocean City's oldest—is a replacement of the original Victorian hotel that burned in 1922. Rooms are plainly furnished and decorated just as they were originally, but now with modern comforts, such as air-conditioning. This is oceanside vacationing as it was in a calmer era. ⊠ *Boardwalk and Wicomico St., 21843* ☎ *800/328–5268 or 410/289–9111* 🖷 *410/289–2221* ⊕ *www.atlantichotelocmd.com* ⟿ *90 rooms ⚹ Cable TV ⊟ MC, V ⊙ Closed Oct.–Apr.*

¢–$$ 🏨 **The Lankford Hotel & Apartments.** Opened in 1924, the Lankford is still owned by the family of the original owners. Many combinations of rooms in the hotel and the adjacent lodge are available for small groups of friends and families. Bicycle storage and Ocean City Golf Course privileges are included in the rate. Lazing in a rickety rocking chair on the front porch off the small (unair-conditioned) lobby, cooled by overhead fans, is a true throwback to quieter times. (All guest rooms are air-conditioned.) ⊠ *8th St. at Boardwalk, 21842* ☎ *410/289–4041 or 800/282–9709 late May–Sept., 410/289–4667 Oct.–late May* 🖷 *410/289–4809* ⊕ *www.ocean-city.com* ⟿ *23 rooms, 28 suites ⚹ Laundry facilities, free parking ⊟ No credit cards ⊙ Closed Columbus Day–Apr.*

Nightlife & the Arts

In summer Ocean City provides enough entertainment for everyone, ranging from refined to rowdy. Some bars and clubs close in midwinter, but most of those with live music remain open.

BARS   Open since 1976, the large sports saloon known as the **Greene Turtle** (⊠ Coastal Hwy. at 116th St. ☎ 410/723–2120) is a beach landmark and a must for casual drinks to soothe the afterburn.

The waterside **Seacrets Bar and Grill** (⊠ 49th St. at Bay ☎ 410/524–4900) often presents four live bands at four different entertainment venues. The crowds run in age from those in their early twenties on through baby boomers, proving that you're never too old to sip a piña colada on an inner tube.

DANCE CLUBS   One of the most versatile complexes for twenty-one-plus-somethings, the **Party Block** (⊠ Coastal Hwy. at 17th St. ☎ 410/289–6331) encompasses a handful of somewhat raunchy, yet crazy popular nightclub venues. **Big Kahuna** is a DJ-driven "party place"; others include the **Paddock**, pumping out heart-thumping recorded and live music with a bit more volume and flash; and **Rush,** a Miami-style dance club for a well-dressed clientele.

The huge **Bonfire Restaurant & Nightclub** (⊠ 71st St. and Ocean Hwy.
☎410/524–7171) serves an all-you-can-eat buffet and an à la carte menu.
It caters to thirties-and-over diners enjoying the live Top 40 music
played by local groups. It's closed Monday–Thursday, mid-October–mid-
March.

Sports & the Outdoors

Although Ocean City is mainly a summertime resort, there are also lots
of outdoor things to do once you feel like getting up off your beach towel.
Besides fishing of many kinds, power boating, and sailing, you can also
kiteboard, parasail, and jet ski. For the less adventurous, kayaks and
canoes glide through the gentle bay wetlands. Back on land there's biking, tennis, volleyball, and (especially) golf.

BICYCLING A portion of Coastal Highway has been designated for bus and bicycle
traffic. Bicycle riding is allowed on the Ocean City Boardwalk from 5
AM to 10 AM in summer and 5 AM to 4 PM the rest of the year. The bike
route from Ocean City to Assateague Island (U.S. 50 to Rte. 611) is a
9-mi trek, and Assateague itself is crisscrossed by a number of clearly
marked, paved trails.

Bike rentals are available throughout Ocean City, "every three blocks"
according to some. One of the oldest bike rental, sales, and service en-
terprises is the highly respected **Mike's Bikes** (⊠ N. Division St. and Baltimore Ave. ☎ 410/289–5404 ⊠ N. 1st St. at Boardwalk ☎ 410/289–
4637). Rates are $5 for the first hour, $3 for every hour thereafter for
regular adult bikes up to $20 an hour for a six-passenger-and-two-tod-
dler surrey.

BOATING Assawoman Bay, between the Ocean City barrier island and the mainland, is where you can go deep-sea fishing, sailing, jet skiing, and
paragliding. **Sailing, Etc.** (⊠ 5305 Coastal Hwy. ☎ 410/723–1144) rents
sailboats, catamarans, kayaks, and Windsurfers and teaches sailing and
windsurfing.

FISHING No fishing licenses are required in Ocean City. Public fishing piers on
the Assawoman Bay and Isle of Wight Bay are at (south to north) 3rd,
9th, 40th, and 125th streets and at the inlet in Ocean City. Other fishing and crabbing areas include the U.S. 50 bridge, Oceanic Pier, and Ocean
City Pier, at Wicomico Street and the Boardwalk. Crabbing is especially
good at Northside Park.

Bahia Marina (⊠ 21st St. and Bay ☎ 410/289–7438 or 888/575–3625)
is a great venue for sportfishing enthusiasts. It has spotless charterboats,
live bait and tackle, and opportunities for bottom fishing.

Ocean City Fishing Center (⊠ U.S. 50 and Shantytown Rd., West Ocean
City ☎ 410/213–1121) is Ocean City's largest deep-sea charter boat marina with some 30 vessels and Coast Guard–licensed professional captains. In addition to catering to preformed groups, the Fishing Center
will form fishing groups of individuals who are on their own.

GOLF Now rivaling premier golfing destinations around the United States, Ocean
City is within easy driving distance of more than 21 golf courses. For a
complete listing, contact the Worcester County Tourism office or Ocean

10

City Visitor Center. The Web site **Ocean City Golf Getaway** (⊕ www.
oceancitygolf.com) is full of good information about courses.

Shopping

Ocean City's 3-mi-long boardwalk is lined with retail outlets for food,
gifts, and souvenirs, as well as several specialty stores. Side streets are
rife with still more. Shopping malls are along the length of the island
on Coastal Highway. Factory outlets are just across the U.S. 50 bridge.

The Kite Loft (✉ 5th St. at Boardwalk ☎ 410/289–6852 ✉ 45th St. Village ☎ 410/524–0800 ✉ Coastal Hwy. at 131st St. ☎ 410/250–4970)
has a dazzling line of kites as well as banners, flags, and wind socks,
hammocks and sky chairs, whirligigs and wind chimes.

South Moon Under (✉ 8019 Coastal Hwy. ☎ 410/524–4567) is a boutique-type shop that epitomizes life at the beach with earth-tone linen
clothing, shell and sand-inspired jewelry, and evocative wall plaques that'll
keep that ocean feeling going after your visit. The standard selection of
hats, mugs, and souvenirs is also on hand, only with a touch of class.

Assateague Island National Seashore

15 *11 mi south of Ocean City.*

Fodor'sChoice
★

The Assateague Island National Seashore occupies the northern two-thirds of the 37-mi-long barrier island: a small portion of the seashore
is operated as Assateague State Park. ("Assateague" means "a marshy
place across.") The southern third
of the island is the Chincoteague
National Wildlife Refuge, in Virginia. Although most famous for the
small, shaggy, sturdy wild horses
(adamantly called "ponies" by the
public) that roam freely along the
beaches and roads, the National
Seashore is also worth getting to
know for its wildland, wildlife (including the beautiful Sika deer),
and opportunities for having fun
outdoors. In summer the seashore's
mild surf is where you can find
shorebirds tracing the lapping waves
back down the beach. Behind the

> **WORD OF MOUTH**
>
> "Assateague Island has wild (sort
> of) ponies living on it. Lots of
> birds. Nice paths to walk in search
> of ponies and scenery. The kayaking is very nice. You can sometimes see ponies from the kayaks
> as well. There's a couple of places
> there to rent boats. April would be
> a nice time to visit. You would be
> there before the mosquitos." –AIJ

dunes, the island's forests and bayside marshes are well worth exploring, and there are three self-guided nature trail walks that let you do
just that.

Swimming, biking, hiking, surf fishing, picnicking, and camping are all
available on the island. The visitor center at the entrance to the park
has aquariums and hands-on exhibits about the seashore's birds and ocean
creatures as well as the famous ponies. ✉ *7206 National Seashore La.,
Rte. 611* ☎ *410/641–1441* 🎟 *7-day pass Maryland/Virginia section
$3/$10 per vehicle; $2 per person for bicycles and pedestrians* ☉ *Visitor center daily 9–5, park daily 24 hrs.*

Crisfield

⑯ *33 mi southwest of Salisbury via U.S. 13 to Rte. 113.*

In William W. Warner's study of the Chesapeake Bay, *Beautiful Swimmers,* Crisfield was described as a "town built upon oyster shells, millions of tons of it. A town created by and for the blue crab, Cradle of the Chesapeake seafood industries, where everything was tried first." Unfortunately, visitors can see the creeping hand of development changing the face of this charming, end-of-the-road town with the sprawling condominium complex at the end of Main Street. The many bustling seafood processing plants here—where workers still pick crabs and shuck oysters as they have for more than a century, by hand—have dwindled to just three from more than 150, but you can still marvel at the craft and listen to workers singing hymns as they work.

Sports & the Outdoors

Eco-Tours on the *Learn-It* (⊠ Crisfield City Dock, 1021 W. Main St. ☎ 410/ 968–9870) depart daily at 10 and 1:30 from the Captain's Galley restaurant. Learn about the wildfowl and water creatures of the Chesapeake Bay, find out why bay grasses are important, explore the effects of shoreline erosion, and visit an experienced waterman—as bay fishermen are known— at work, all while aboard the comfortable 40-foot bay workboat.

Shopping

The Ice Cream Gallery (⊠ 5 Goodsell Alley ☎ 410/968–0809) is a sweets emporium that doubles as a crafts outlet for local artisans. From here there's a spectacular view out over the bay. **Tropical Chesapeake** (⊠ 712 Broadway ☎ 410/968–3622) prepares oven-baked deli sandwiches and sells gifts and clothing.

Smith Island

⑰ *12 mi west of Crisfield by boat.*

For more than three centuries, Smith Islanders have made their living coaxing creatures from the Chesapeake Bay. Today, the tiny island's three villages (Tylerton, Ewell, and Rhodes Point), made up of simple homes, churches, and a few stores, remain reachable only by boat, fiercely independent, and fairly remote (cable TV didn't arrive here until 1994). Listen for the residents' distinct accents, which echo that of their 17th-century English ancestors. A midday visit by passenger ferry allows ample time for a stroll around the island and a leisurely meal overlooking watermen's shanties and workboats. Stop by **Ruke's,** a venerable general store that serves excellent fresh seafood.

Air-conditioned **Smith Island Cruises** leave Crisfield's Somers Cove Marina for the 60-minute trip to Smith Island at 12:30 PM daily from Memorial Day to mid-October. ⊠ *Somers Cove Marina, Crisfield* ☎ *410/425–2771* ⊠ *$22.*

Another way to get to Smith Island is via the mail boat, *Island Belle* (☎ 410/ 968–1118). There are two departures daily (12:30 and 5 PM) and the cost is $22 round-trip.

10

Two freight boats, **Captain Jason I** and **Captain Jason II** (☎ 410/425–4471), also take passengers to Smith Island for $22 round-trip. All three boats (including the above-mentioned *Island Belle*) depart daily at 12:30 PM and return to Crisfield at 5:15 PM, year-round, weather permitting. You can ride back to Smith Island later in the evening; both captains live on the island.

Started in 1996 by 12 gutsy Smith Island women, **Smith Island Crabmeat Co-op** produces the finest, shell-less quality crabmeat, with all proceeds going straight back to the women and their families. Visitors can drop by and see the lightning-fast pickers at work. Don't forget to pick up a pound before you leave, and ask Janice (the founder and president) about her secret crab cake ingredient. ⊠ *3019 Union Church Rd., Tylerton* ☎ *410/968–1344.*

Where to Stay
An overnight on Smith Island gives new meaning to the term "getaway." Your neighbors include more egrets, heron, osprey, and pelicans than people.

$ ☷ **Inn of Silent Music.** Part of a town that's separated by water from the other two villages on Smith Island, this remote English cottage–style inn takes its soothing name from a phrase in a poem by the mystic St. John of the Cross, a Carmelite monk. The rooms are small with antique linens and big windows. Tylerton has no restaurants, but the eclectic innkeepers will cook a fresh seafood dinner for guests for an extra charge. ⊠ *Tylerton 21866* ☎ *410/425–3541* ⊕ *www.innofsilentmusic.com* ➵ *3 rooms* ⚒ *Dining room, dock, bicycles; no room phones, no room TVs, no kids under 12, no smoking* ⊟ *No credit cards* ⊙ *Closed mid-Nov.–early Mar.* ⦿│ *BP.*

¢–$ ☷ **Ewell Tide Inn and B&B.** On the northern tip of Smith Island, downhome hospitality is heartily extended by a licensed ferry- and charterboat captain and his wife. Dinner is available, but must be ordered in advance. Open year-round, the inn welcomes children, as well as pets, on weekdays, and complimentary drinks and snacks are served throughout the day. This couple also operates Ewell's Driftwood General Store as well as the adjacent marina, a separate operation. ⊠ *Ewell 21824* ☎ *410/425–2141 or 888/699–2141* ⊕ *www.smithisland.net* ➵ *4 rooms, 2 without bath* ⚒ *Dining room, cable TV, in-room data ports, dock, bicycles, pub, meeting rooms, some pets allowed; no room phones, no smoking* ⊟ *MC, V* ⦿│ *BP.*

VIRGINIA'S EASTERN SHORE

A narrow 70-mi-long peninsula between the Chesapeake Bay and the Atlantic Ocean, Virginia's Eastern Shore has one main artery bisecting its full length. U.S. 13's occasional gentle curves interrupt an otherwise straight, flat route through unremarkable landscape. It's the wild ponies, a small slice of NASA, gloriously uncrowded beaches, and waterfront views in every direction that draw thousands of snowbirds here every summer. Tiny hamlets remain scattered among farms and protected wildlife habitats, and along the shore watermen still struggle for their living.

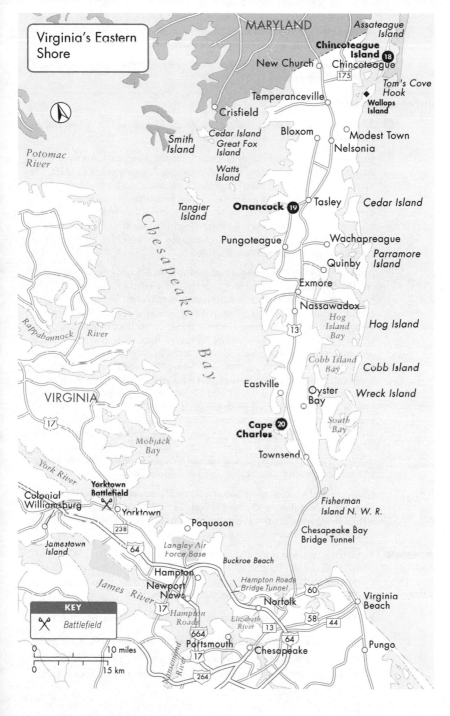

Virginia's Eastern Shore

At its southernmost tip, the extraordinary Chesapeake Bay Bridge-Tunnel sweeps 17½ mi across the Chesapeake Bay to connect with the Virginia Tidewater towns of Hampton Roads, Norfolk, and Virginia Beach.

Numbers in the margin correspond to points of interest on the Virginia's Eastern Shore map.

Chincoteague Island

⑱ *27 mi southeast of Snow Hill, MD via U.S. 13 to Rte. 175, 43 mi southeast of Salisbury, MD via U.S. 13 to Rte. 175.*

Just south of the Maryland-Virginia line, the Virginia Eastern Shore's island resort town (Chincoteague, meaning "large stream or inlet," is pronounced "**shin**-coh-teeg") exudes a pleasant aura of seclusion, despite the renown it has gained since the publication of the 1947 children's book *Misty of Chincoteague*, the story of one of the wild ponies that are auctioned off every summer. Chincoteague Island's inns, restaurants, and shops are eminently reachable by walking; relatively uncrowded beaches stretch out nearby.

Most of Virginia's **Chincoteague National Wildlife Refuge** occupies the southern third of Assateague Island, directly off Chincoteague Island. (The northern two-thirds, part of Maryland, is taken up by the Assateague Island National Seashore.) Created in 1943 as a resting and breeding area for the imperiled greater snow goose as well as other birds, this refuge's location makes it a prime "flyover" habitat. It also protects native and migratory nonavian wildlife, including the small Sika deer that inhabit its interior pine forests. A 3.2-mi self-guided wildlife loop is a great introduction to the refuge. Bike or walk it; it's open to vehicles only between 3 PM and dusk. The Chincoteague ponies occupy a section of the refuge isolated from the public, but they may still be viewed readily from a number of spots. ✉ *Herbert H. Bateman Educational and Administrative Center and entrance: 8231 Beach Rd.* ☎ *757/336–6122* 💲 *$10 per car, valid for 7 days* 🕐 *Refuge hrs: May–Sept., daily 5 AM–10 PM; Oct. and Apr., daily 6 AM–8 PM; Nov.–Mar., daily 6–6. Visitor center hrs vary seasonally; call for information.*

Islanders and visitors alike savor one of the shore's specialties during October's **Chincoteague Oyster Festival** (✉ 6733 Maddox Blvd. ☎ 757/336–6161), which can sell out months in advance. The Chincoteague Chamber of Commerce sells tickets.

OFF THE BEATEN PATH

From the street, **sea star café gourmet carryout** (✉ 4121 Main St. ☎ 757/336–5442) doesn't look very gourmet, but the shacklike exterior of this take-out place belies the delectable salads, sandwiches, and roll-ups, much of it vegetarian, inside. Most items are less than $5.

Each of the three ice-cream parlors on the island has its own personality:

The Island Creamery (✉ **6243 Maddox Blvd.** ☎ **757/336–6236), more than a quarter century in business, sells ice cream as well as sorbets, sherbets, and frozen yogurt. Consider a Round Up: five scoops of ice cream, three toppings,**

nuts, whipped cream, and a cherry. If you manage to finish it by yourself, your picture goes up on the Creamery's bulletin board.

On a warm summer's night, visit **Muller's Old Fashioned Ice Cream Parlour** (✉ 4034 Main St. ☎ 757/336–5894) for soda fountain treats on the candle-light porch. Roll back in time with malted milk shakes, root beer, and warm Belgian waffles served with ice cream, fresh fruit, and homemade whipped cream.

Soft-serve shop **Mr. Whippy** (✉ 6201 Maddox Blvd. ☎ 757/336–5122) is a local favorite.

The **Oyster and Maritime Museum** chronicles the local oyster trade with displays of mostly homemade tools; elaborate, hand-carved decoys; marine specimens; a diorama; and audio recordings based on museum records. ✉ *7125 Maddox Blvd.* ☎ *757/336–6117* ✆ *$3* ◷ *June–Sept., daily 10–5; Mar.–May, Sat. 10–5, Sun. noon–4.*

Where to Stay & Eat

♨ **$–$$** ✕ **Etta's Channel Side Restaurant.** On the eastern side of the island, along the Assateague Channel, this meticulously maintained family-friendly restaurant has a vista as soothing as its food. Its dishes include pastas and popular meat dishes as well as typical fish and shellfish creations. Its signature dish is flounder stuffed with crab imperial. ✉ *7452 East Side Dr.* ☎ *757/336–5644* ⊟ *D, MC, V* ◷ *Closed Jan. and Feb. No lunch Mon.–Thurs.*

★ **¢–$$** ✕ **Shucking House Café.** This relaxed eatery is just the place to unwind after a day on the water. Featuring oyster, crab, and fish sandwiches along with fish-and-chips, this café is a pleasant change from fancy restaurants or fast-food franchises. Be sure to try the rich New England or Manhattan clam chowders, both prepared with local mollusks. A sister property, **Landmark Crabhouse** (☎ 757/336–3745), is a bit more upscale, with the same fresh, locally harvested seafood dishes and peaceful waterfront views. ✉ *6162 Landmark Pl.* ☎ *757/336–5145* ⊟ *MC, V.*

★ **$–$$$** 🏨 **Channel Bass Inn.** This three-story, beige clapboard house just off Chincoteague Bay was built in the 1870s, then expanded and converted to an inn 50 years later. Its luxurious rooms all have comfortable sitting areas, and outside is a lovely Japanese garden with delicate waterfalls. In addition to its full breakfast, the inn serves afternoon tea daily in the public tearoom. Delicacies such as *apfel kuchen* (German apple cake), butterscotch pecan tarts, and firm ginger scones, all homemade, are served on Wedgwood china. ✉ *6228 Church St., 23336* ☎ *757/336–6148 or 800/249–0818* ⊕ *www.channelbass-inn.com* ⇴ *8 rooms, 1 suite* ⚭ *Shop, some pets allowed (fee); no room phones, no room TVs, no kids under 6, no smoking* ⊟ *AE, D, MC, V* ⦿ *BP.*

★ **$–$$$** 🏨 **The Garden and the Sea Inn.** Victorian charm imbues every room of this three-building inn on a quiet lane a mile south of the Maryland line and 11 mi west of Chincoteague. Rooms are furnished with canopy or sleigh beds, Oriental rugs, and cozy sitting areas with antique and period pieces, and most have hot tubs. The Victorian main house was built in 1802 as a tavern and later enlarged. When it's time for the grand break-

10

fasts here, keep an eye out for French toast with cream cheese and orange marmalade. On Saturday, between early March and late November, dinner is available for guests by advance reservation. ⊠ *4188 Nelson Rd., Box 275, turn west off U.S. 13 at Rte. 710 and go ¼ mi, New Church 23415* ☎ *800/824–0672* 🖨 *757/824–5605* ⊕ *www. gardenandseainn.com* 🛏 *8 rooms* ⚄ *Cable TV, exercise equipment, boating, some pets allowed; no room phones, no smoking* ⊟ *AE, D, MC, V* ¶◯ *BP.*

$–$$ 🏨 **Miss Molly's.** Operated by the same innkeepers as the Channel Bass Inn, this unassuming 1886 Victorian inn claims fame as the temporary home of author Marguerite Henry, who wrote *Misty of Chincoteague.* Here, in 1946, she spent two of her six weeks in Chincoteague preparing the background for her renowned children's novel. Miss Molly, the daughter of the home's builder, spent most of her life here. Guests have their pick of five bay-front porches loaded with comfy rocking chairs, and traditional English high tea is served every afternoon (for an additional fee). ⊠ *4141 Main St., 23336* ☎ *757/336–6686 or 800/221–5620* 🖨 *757/336–0600* ⊕ *www.missmollys-inn.com* 🛏 *7 rooms* ⚄ *Bicycles; no room phones, no room TVs, no kids under 6, no smoking* ⊟ *AE, D, MC, V.*

★ $–$$ 🏨 **The 1848 Island Manor House.** The unusual design of the Island Manor House was a result of splitting the home in two, providing adequate privacy for the original owners, who were brothers, and their wives, who were sisters. Most rooms have water views of the channel and an intimate brick patio, with a multitier fountain, makes a nice summer gathering place. ⊠ *4160 Main St., 23336* ☎ *757/336–5436 or 800/852–1505* 🖨 *757/336–1333* ⊕ *www.islandmanor.com* 🛏 *8 rooms, 2 with shared bath* ⚄ *No room phones, no room TVs, no kids under 10, no smoking* ⊟ *MC, V* ¶◯ *BP* ⊘ *Closed Jan.*

$–$$ 🏨 **The Inn at Poplar Corner and the Watson House.** These two stately structures across the street from each other both look Victorian. But whereas the Watson House is from the 1890s, the Inn at Poplar Corner was built a century later. Both contain impressive Victorian furniture. All four of the Poplar Corner rooms have hot tubs and private showers. Rates include breakfast, served at the Poplar Corner's antique dining table or on the inviting side porch. For visits to the National Wildlife Refuge, you can borrow beach chairs and binoculars. ⊠ *4240 Main St., Box 905, 23336* ☎ *757/336–1564 or 800/336–6787* 🖨 *757/336–5776* ⊕ *www.watsonhouse.com* 🛏 *10 rooms* ⚄ *Bicycles; no room phones, no room TVs, no kids under 10, no smoking* ⊟ *MC, V* ⊘ *Closed Dec.–Mar.* ¶◯ *BP.*

OFF THE BEATEN PATH

☾

WALLOPS ISLAND – NASA's Wallops Flight Facility Visitors Center fires the imagination with full-scale rockets, films on space and aeronautics, and displays on NASA projects. Although this was the site of early rocket launchings and NASA occasionally sends up satellites here, the facility now focuses primarily on atmospheric research. ⊠ *Rte. 175, 20 mi southwest of Chincoteague* ☎ *757/824–2298 or 757/824–1344* 🖃 *Free* ⊘ *July and Aug., daily 10–4; Sept.–Nov. and Feb.–June, Thurs.–Mon. 10–4.*

Onancock

⑲ *30 mi southwest of Chincoteague via Rte. 175 to U.S. 13.*

Four miles from the Chesapeake Bay at the mouth of Onancock Creek, Onancock, pronounced Oh-NAN-cock and which means "foggy place," was once the home of a handful of Algonquin families. It was established as a port in 1690 and later emerged as an important ferry link with the burgeoning waterside cities of Maryland and Virginia. Today, this quiet community of 1,600, the second-largest town on Virginia's Eastern Shore, is worth a short visit for a flavor of its past as a transfer point between water and land.

Where to Stay & Eat

$–$$ ✕ **Hopkins & Bros. General Store & Eastern Shore Steamboat Co. Restaurant.** Beside the wharf, inside a general store (circa 1842) on the National Register of Historic Places, you can imagine yourself waiting for a steamer to Baltimore. At the charming eatery adjacent to the store, there's fresh baked grouper with locally picked crabmeat stuffing as well as prime meats that are hand cut to order. ⊠ *2 Market St.* ☎ *757/787–3100* ▭ *MC, V* ☉ *Closed Sun. No lunch.*

$$ ✕☷ **Inn and Garden Cafe.** This 1880s house is now an intimate inn and creative restaurant ($$) with stunning waterfront views. A wall of windows encloses the dining room. The inn has four guest suites decorated in beachy pastel greens and yellows, with comfy patchwork quilts. ⊠ *145 Market St., 23417* ☎ *757/787–8850* ⊕ *www.theinnandgardencafe.com* ⇩ *4 suites* ▭ *MC, V* ☉ *Restaurant closed Sun.–Tues. No lunch.*

Tangier Island

Crab traps stacked 10 feet high, watermen's shanties on the water, and a landscape virtually devoid of excessive commercialization await those who come to this Virginia fishing community in the Chesapeake Bay. You can't bring a car, but you can join a guided tour near the boat dock, rent a golf cart to roam the few narrow roads, or simply soak in the timelessness on foot. Stop by the Waterfront Sandwich Shop or head to the Islander Seafood

WORD OF MOUTH
"Tangier Island is a relatively quiet almost sleepy village." –rb traveler

10

Restaurant. As on Maryland's Smith Island, you can hear the distinct accents that reveal the English origins of the residents' 17th-century ancestors. Note that Tangier Island is "dry"; you may bring your own alcohol for personal use, but you must use discretion.

Narrated trips from Onancock to the island are available on **Tangier-Onancock Cruises** (☎ 757/891–2240) at 10 AM daily Memorial Day–October 15. The return trip leaves Tangier at 2 PM, allowing ample time to explore.

Where to Stay

$ 🏨 **Bay View Inn.** This is pretty much your only lodging choice, but this fanciful complex of Gingerbread-style cottages is an enchanting and relaxing place to experience the bay. Breakfast is served on 100-year-old china, and dinner consists of—what else—crab served up in cakes, soup, or imperial-style. An overnight on Tangier Island is an uncommon experience. ✉ *16408 West Ridge Rd., 23440* ☎ *757/891–2396* ⊕ *www.tangierisland.net* ☜ *9 cottages* ♦ *Refrigerators, cable TV, ceiling fans, beach; no room phones, no smoking* ⊟ *No credit cards.*

Cape Charles

⑳ *30 mi south of Onancock via U.S. 13.*

Cape Charles, established in the early 1880s as a railroad-ferry junction, quieted down considerably after its heyday, but in the past few years its very isolation has begun to attract people from farther and farther away. The town holds one of the largest concentrations of late-Victorian and turn-of-the-20th-century buildings in the region. Clean, uncrowded public beaches beckon, as do a marina, renowned golf course, and the Eastern Shore of Virginia National Wildlife Refuge.

Where to Stay

$–$$ 🏨 **Chesapeake Charm.** Two blocks from the beach, this B&B feels like a summer beach house. It's also one of the few family-friendly B&Bs in Virginia. Golfing packages for play at the Arnold Palmer Signature Course at Bay Creek are also available. ✉ *202 Madison Ave., 23310* ☎ *757/331–2676* ⊕ *www.chesapeakecharmbnb.com* ☜ *4 rooms* ♦ *Golf privileges, boating, fishing, bicycles; no TV in some rooms, no smoking* ⊟ *D, MC, V.*

$–$$ 🏨 **Pickett's Harbor.** Clinging to the southernmost tip of the peninsula, this land parcel is part of a 17th-century grant to the owner's family. The current clapboard B&B was built in 1976 according to a Colonial-era design, with floors, doors, and cupboards from several 200-year-old James River farms reinstalled here. All guest rooms overlook small sand dunes and the Chesapeake; the backyard is actually 27 acres of private beach. Runners and bikers are likely to find the area's long country lanes and untrafficked paved roads a delight. ✉ *28288 Nottingham Ridge La., Cape Charles 23310* ☎ *757/331–2212* ⊕ *www.pickettsharbor.com* ☜ *6 rooms, 4 with bath* ♦ *Beach, bicycles, some pets allowed (fee); no room phones, no room TVs, no smoking* ⊟ *No credit cards* ⏐◎⏐ *BP.*

National Wildlife Refuges

13 mi south of Cape Charles.

At the southernmost tip of the Delmarva Peninsula, the unique Eastern Shore of Virginia and the Fisherman Island National Wildlife Refuges—including nearby Skidmore Island—were established in 1984. Their maritime forest, myrtle and bayberry thickets, grasslands, and croplands, as well as ponds are used by such species as bald eagles and peregrine falcons. Each fall, between late August and early November, migrating birds "stage," or gather in large groups, on refuge lands until favorable winds and weather conditions allow for easy crossing of the Chesapeake Bay. ⊠ *Southern extremity of Rte. 13* ☎ *757/331–2760* ☜ *Free.*

THE EASTERN SHORE ESSENTIALS

To research prices, get advice from other travelers, and book travel arrangements, visit www.fodors.com.

Transportation

BY AIR

There are a handful of small regional airports on the Eastern Shore, but none have commercial flights. Most travelers will fly into BWI, Regan National, or Washington Dulles, and then drive to the Eastern Shore.

🔢 **Baltimore/Washington International-Thurgood Marshall Airport** ☎ 410/859-7100 ⊕ www.bwiairport.com. **Dulles International Airport** ☎ 703/572-2700 ⊕ www.metwashairports.com/Dulles. **Ronald Reagan Washington National Airport** ☎ 703/417-8000 ⊕ www.metwashairports.com/National.

BY BIKE

Flat and friendly, the Eastern Shore is a great region to go biking. The most popular places are in Kent Island along the Cross Island Trail, St. Michaels, Oxford, Chestertown, Wicomico County's 100-mi Viewtrail 100 loop, and Ocean City's Boardwalk in the mornings. Call Maryland's Department of Transportation for a state bicycle map and for more information.

Bicycles are available for rent at Stevensville's Happy Trails Bike Repair, which also hosts escorted group rides of 15 to 30 mi Sunday at 9 AM. Chestertown's Bikework Bicycle Shop rents bikes for adults and children. A group, open to those just visiting, rides up to 60 mi every Sunday at 8 AM.

You can also bike inn to inn with **InnTours** (☎ 410/632–2722 ⊕ www.inntours.com), which maps out a relatively flat route between Berlin in Maryland and New Church, Virginia near Chincoteague. Prices start at $350 per couple per day and includes inn accommodation, luggage transportation, and all meals.

Viewtrail 100, a marked 100-mi biking circuit, runs along less-traveled secondary roads between Berlin and Pocomoke City. For a brochure and map, contact the Worcester County Tourism Office.

BY BOAT & FERRY

Two ferries operate on the Eastern Shore—between Reedville, VA, and Tangier Island, and between Crisfield and Smith Island—both with very limited service.

🔢 **Tangier Island–Reedville, VA** ☎ 804/453-2628. **Crisfield–Smith Island** *Captain Jason* ☎ 410/425-4471. *Island Belle* ☎ 410/968-1118

10

BY BUS

Carolina Trailways makes several round-trip runs daily between Baltimore or Washington and Easton, Cambridge, Salisbury, and Ocean City.

Greyhound Lines leaves regularly from Norfolk and Virginia Beach for destinations on the Eastern Shore.

When you're in Ocean City, you can avoid the aggravation of driving in slow-moving traffic by taking the **Bus**, which travels 10-mi-long Coastal Highway 24 hours a day, in its own lane. Service is about every 10 minutes from bus stops every other block. A $2 ticket is good for 24 hours.

A park-and-ride facility on the mainland—on Route 50 just west of Ocean City—has free parking for some 700 vehicles. It's on the Bus's route.
🚌 Bus Depots **Cambridge** ☒ 2903 Ocean Gateway Dr., at Rte. 50 ☎ 410/228-5825. **Easton** ☒ FastStop Convenience Store, U.S. 50, 2 mi north of town, opposite airport ☎ 410/822-3333. **Ocean City** ☒ 2nd St. and Philadelphia Ave., at U.S. 50 bridge ☎ 410/289-9307. **Salisbury** ☒ 350 Cypress St. ☎ 410/749-4121.
🚌 Bus Lines **The Bus** ☎ 410/723-1607. **Carolina Trailways** ☎ 800/231-2222. **Greyhound Lines** ☎ 800/231-2222.

BY CAR

A car is indispensable for touring the region. To reach the Eastern Shore from Baltimore or Washington, D.C., travel east on U.S. 50/301 and cross the 4½-mi Chesapeake Bay Bridge (toll collected eastbound only, $2.50) northeast of Annapolis.

The extraordinary 17½-mi Chesapeake Bay Bridge-Tunnel is the only connection between Virginia's Eastern Shore and Norfolk, Virginia Beach, and other Tidewater-area towns. There's a toll of $12 in either direction.

The bridge-and-tunnel complex comprises 12 mi of trestled roadway, two tunnels, two bridges, almost 2 mi of causeway, and four man-made islands. U.S. 13 is the main route up the spine of the peninsula into Maryland.

In summer, Friday afternoon eastbound (beach-bound) traffic can be very heavy; conversely, Sunday and sometimes Saturday afternoon westbound traffic (from the beaches toward Baltimore and Washington, D.C.) can be equally congested.
🚗 Traffic info: **Chesapeake Bay Bridge-Tunnel** ☎ 757/331-2960 in Maryland, 410/974-0341 in Virginia ⊕ www.cbbt.com.

BY TAXI

This is a driving and walking region—you arrive by car and either walk or bike around your destination. Cabs are a rarity, but a handful exist.
🚕 **Kent Island Coach & Courier** ☒ Stevensville ☎ 410/604-0486. **Light Up Your Night** ☒ Ocean City ☎ 410/289-9700. **Scotty's Taxi & Courier Service** ☒ Easton ☎ 410/822-1475. **Sunshine Cab** ☒ Ocean City ☎ 410/208-2828. **Yellow Cab** ☒ Salisbury ☎ 410/749-3500.

BY TRAIN

Amtrak runs from Salisbury to Baltimore and Wilmington, DE, at least twice per day.

🚆 **Amtrak station** ⊠ 350 Cypress St. Salisbury ☎ 800/872-7245

Contacts & Resources

EMERGENCIES

🚑 **Ambulance, Fire, Police** ☎ 911.

🏥 **Hospitals Atlantic General Hospital** ⊠ 9733 Healthway Dr., Berlin, MD ☎ 410/641-1100. **Dorchester General Hospital** ⊠ 300 Byrn St., Cambridge, MD ☎ 410/228-5511. **Memorial Hospital at Easton** ⊠ 219 S. Washington St., Easton, MD ☎ 410/822-1000. **Chester River Hospital Center** ⊠ 100 Brown St., Chestertown, MD ☎ 410/778-3300. **Shore Memorial Hospital** ⊠ 9507 Hospital Ave., Nassawadox, VA ☎ 757/414-8000. **Peninsula Regional Medical Center** ⊠ 100 E. Carroll St., Salisbury, MD ☎ 410/546-6400.

INTERNET, MAIL & SHIPPING

Wi-Fi access is limited on the Eastern Shore except in major areas like Stevensville, Easton/St. Michaels, Cambridge, and Salisbury. Ocean City has free Wi-Fi access along Somerset Avenue in downtown, as do all county public libraries.

📶 Internet Access **Wicomico County Free Library** ⊠ 122 S. Division St., Salisbury ☎ 410/749-3612 ⊕ www.wicomicolibrary.org. **Talbot County Free Library** ⊠ 100 W. Dover St., Easton ☎ 410/822-1626.

📮 Post Offices **Easton Post Office** ⊠ 116 E. Dover St. ☎ 410/822-0491. **Ocean City Post Office** ⊠ 408 N. Philadelphia Ave. ☎ 410/524-7611. **Stevensville Post Office** ⊠ 366 Thompson Creek Mall ☎ 410/643-5640.

Tours

Besides any number of tours by boat from several of the waterside towns on Maryland's and Virginia's Eastern Shore, there are day-trip tours into the region from Annapolis and Baltimore. Larger towns, including Annapolis as well as St. Michaels, are home port for diesel- or gasoline-powered tour boats and yachts. As part of its Day on the Bay Cruise series, the Annapolis-based Watermark Cruises operates between there and St. Michaels on Saturday, May through September, and also on Monday in summer, a thoroughly enjoyable way to visit one town while staying in the other. It costs $55 per adult. Chesapeake Bay Lighthouse Tours ($35–$120) offer a rare chance to see the Bay's lighthouses up close by boat. Passengers on the all-day Great Circle Route visit 12 lighthouses, and those on the Passage, a half-day tour, visit five. There's also a "two light" sunset cruise. Bring your camera. A full day costs $120 for an adult, a half day $60, and two hours costs $35. Board the *Cambridge Lady* to explore the Choptank River and its tributaries. In addition to Cambridge, some departures are available from Denton and Oxford; tours ($20) are available May to October.

Rock Hall Trolleys, with 35 stops, is the way to explore this burgeoning Bayside community (adults, $2; children, $1)—and to travel between here and Chestertown ($5 per person, round-trip). It runs Friday–Sunday.

10

A self-guided walking tour of downtown Salisbury is available from the chamber of commerce. Pick up a walking map of Ocean City's historic sites at its Visitor Information Center. Historic Chestertown and Kent County Tours schedules guided, narrated walking tours (by appointment only) that focus on history and architecture. Guided tours of Crisfield are run by the J. Millard Tawes Historical Museum. From May through October, the tours include a visit to a crab processing plant.

Chesapeake Horse Country Tours allow you to roll through Cecil's stunning acres of emerald grassland. The tours head to horse farms that have produced such notable racing legends as Northern Dancer and Kelso.

⚓ Boat Tours *Cambridge Lady* ☎ 410/221-0776 ⊕ www.cambridgelady.com. **Chesapeake Bay Lighthouse Tours** ☎ 410/886-2215 or 800/690-5080 ⊕ www.chesapeakelights.com. **Watermark Cruises** ☎ 410/268-7601 Ext. 104 ⊕ www.watermarkcruises.com.

⚓ Trolley Tours Rock Hall Trolleys ☎ 410/639-7996 or 866/748-7658 ⊕ www.rockhalltrolleys.com.

⚓ Walking Tours Chesapeake Horse Country Tours ☎ 410/885-2797 or 800/466-1402 ⊕ www.ccmagazine.org/visitcecil/tours.htm. **Historic Chestertown and Kent County Tours** ☎ 410/778-2829. **The Port of Crisfield Tour and Crisfield Heritage Tour** ✉]. Millard Tawes Historical Museum at Somers Cove Marina ☎ 410/968-2501.

VISITOR INFORMATION

⚓ Tourist Information in Maryland Bay Country Welcome Center ✉ 1000 Welcome Center Dr., Centreville ☎ 410/758-6803. **Cecil County Tourism** ✉ 1 Seahawk Dr., Suite 114, North East 21901 ☎ 410/996-6290 or 800/232-4595 🖷 410/996-6279 ⊕ www.seececil.org. **Chesapeake House Welcome Center** ✉ Chesapeake House Service Area, I-95, between exits 93 and 100, near Perryville ☎ 410/287-2313. **Dorchester County Tourism Department** ✉ 2 Rose Hill Pl., Cambridge 21613 ☎ 410/228-1000 or 800/522-8687 🖷 410/221-6545 ⊕ www.tourdorchester.org. **Kent County Tourism Development Office** ✉ 400 High St., Chestertown 21620 ☎ 410/778-0416 🖷 410/778-2746 ⊕ www.kentcounty.com. **Ocean City Department of Tourism** ✉ 4001 Coastal Hwy., at 41st St., Ocean City 21842 ☎ 410/289-2800 or 800/626-2326 🖷 410/289-0058 ⊕ www.ococean.com. **Queen Anne's County Office of Tourism** ✉ 425 Piney Narrows Rd., Chester 21619 ☎ 410/604-2100 or 888/400-7787 🖷 410/604-2101 ⊕ www.qac.org. **Salisbury Chamber of Commerce** ✉ 114 E. Main St. ☎ 410/749-0144. **Somerset County Tourism Office and Visitors Center** ✉ 11440 Ocean Hwy., Princess Anne 21853 ☎ 410/651-2968 or 800/521-9189 🖷 410/651-3917 ⊕ www.visitsomerset.com. **Talbot County Office of Tourism** ✉ 11 S. Harrison St., Easton 21601 ☎ 410/770-8000 🖷 410/770-8057 ⊕ www.tourtalbot.org. **U.S. 13 Welcome Center** ✉ 144 Ocean Hwy., Rte. 13, 15 mi south of Snow Hill, Pocomoke City ☎ 410/957-2484. **Wicomico County Convention & Visitors Bureau** ✉ 8480 Ocean Hwy., Delmar 21875 ☎ 410/548-4914 or 800/332-8687 🖷 410/341-4996 ⊕ www.wicomicotourism.org. **Worcester County Tourism Office** ✉ 104 W. Market St., Snow Hill 21863 ☎ 410/632-3110 or 800/852-0335 🖷 410/632-3158 ⊕ www.visitworcester.org.

⚓ Tourist Information in Virginia Chincoteague Chamber of Commerce ✉ 6733 Maddox Blvd., Box 258, Chincoteague 23336 ☎ 757/336-6161 ⊕ www.chincoteaguechamber.com. **Eastern Shore of Virginia Tourism** ✉ Rte. 13, Box 460, Melfa 23410 ☎ 757/787-2460 ⊕ www.esvachamber.org.

Virginia & Maryland Essentials

PLANNING TOOLS, EXPERT INSIGHT, GREAT CONTACTS

There are planners, and there are those who fly by the seat of their pants. We happily place ourselves among the planners. Our writers and editors try to anticipate all the issues you may face before and during any journey, and then they do their research. This section is the product of their efforts. Use it to get excited about your trip to Virginia and Maryland, to inform your travel planning, or to guide you on the road should the seat of your pants start to feel threadbare.

GETTING STARTED

We're really proud of our Web site: Fodors. com is a great place to begin any journey. Scan Travel Wire for suggested itineraries, travel deals, restaurant and hotel openings, and other up-to-the-minute info. Check out Booking to research prices and book plane tickets, hotel rooms, rental cars, and vacation packages. Head to Talk for on-the-ground pointers from travelers who frequent our message boards. You can also link to loads of other travel-related resources.

▌RESOURCES

ONLINE TRAVEL TOOLS

For Civil War buffs, ⊕ www. civilwartraveler.com has information on battlefields and war-related sites and events. Wine enthusiasts can learn the basics of Maryland and Virginia wines (including winery locations) at ⊕ www. marylandwine.com and ⊕ www. virginiawines.org, respectively.

Find arts and entertainment listings online for Baltimore at the *Baltimore Sun,* for Richmond at the *Richmond Times-Dispatch,* and for D.C. at the *Washington Post.* For D.C. gay bars and clubs, click on the Web site for the gay newspaper *Washington Blade* or the bar guide *Metro Weekly.*

All About Virginia & Maryland Baltimore Sun ⊕ www.baltimoresun.com. **Metro Weekly** ⊕ www.metroweekly.com. **Richmond Times-Dispatch** ⊕ www.timesdispatch.com. **Washington Blade** ⊕ www.washblade.com. **Washington Post** ⊕ www.washingtonpost. com.

Weather Accuweather.com ⊕ www. accuweather.com is an independent weather-forecasting service with especially good coverage of hurricanes. **Weather.com** ⊕ www. weather.com is the Web site for the Weather Channel.

VISITOR INFORMATION

For city and local tourism offices, *see* Visitor Information *in* the Essentials sections at the end of each chapter.
State Tourism Offices Maryland Office of Tourism Development ☎ 410/767-3400 or 800/634-7386 ⊕ www.mdisfun.org. **Virginia Tourism Corporation** ☎ 804/786-2051 or 800/847-4882 ⊕ www.virginia.org.
National Park Service The National Park Service ☎ 202/619-7222 ⊕ www.nps.gov/parks.html.

▌THINGS TO CONSIDER

GEAR

If you're visiting the mountains and the caverns of Virginia, prepare for colder-than-average temperatures. Hiking along the Appalachian Trail, even in spring and fall, frequently requires a coat.

Where dress is concerned, Washington, Baltimore, and Richmond are relatively conservative. In the more expensive restaurants, men are expected to wear a jacket and tie.

At the bay and ocean resorts, "formal" means long trousers and a collared shirt for men, and shoes for everybody. A tie might never get tied during a stay in these areas.

TRIP INSURANCE

What kind of coverage do you honestly need? Do you even need trip insurance at all? Take a deep breath and read on.

We believe that comprehensive trip insurance is especially valuable if you're booking a very expensive or complicated trip (particularly to an isolated region) or if you're booking far in advance. Who knows what could happen six months down the road? But whether or not you get insurance has more to do with how comfortable you are assuming all that risk yourself.

PACKING 101

Why do some people travel with a convoy of huge suitcases yet never have a thing to wear? How do others pack a duffle with a week's worth of outfits *and* supplies for every contingency? We realize that packing is a matter of style, but there's a lot to be said for traveling light. These tips help fight the battle of the bulging bag.

MAKE A LIST. In a recent Fodor's survey, 29% of respondents said they make lists (and often pack) a week before a trip. You can use your list to pack and to repack at the end of your trip. It can also serve as a record of the contents of your suitcase—in case it disappears in transit.

THINK IT THROUGH. What's the weather like? Is this a business trip? A cruise? Going abroad? In some places dress may be more or less conservative than you're used to. As you create your itinerary, note outfits next to each activity (don't forget accessories).

EDIT YOUR WARDROBE. Plan to wear everything twice (better yet, thrice) and to do laundry along the way. Stick to one basic look—urban chic, sporty casual, etc. Build around one or two neutrals and an accent (e.g., black, white, and olive green). Women can freshen looks by changing scarves or jewelry. For a week's trip, you can look smashing with three bottoms, four or five tops, a sweater, and a jacket.

BE PRACTICAL. Put comfortable shoes atop your list. (Did we need to say this?) Pack lightweight, wrinkle resistant, compact, washable items. (Or this?) Stack and roll clothes, so they'll wrinkle less. Unless you're on a guided tour or a cruise, select luggage you can readily carry. Porters, like good butlers, are hard to find these days.

CHECK WEIGHT & SIZE LIMITATIONS. In the United States you may be charged extra for checked bags weighing more than 50 pounds. Abroad some airlines don't allow you to check bags over 60 to 70 pounds, or

they charge outrageous fees for every excess pound—or bag. Carry-on size limitations can be stringent, too.

CHECK CARRY-ON RESTRICTIONS. Research restrictions with the TSA. Rules vary abroad, so check them with your airline if you're traveling overseas on a foreign carrier. Consider packing all but essentials (travel documents, prescription meds, wallet) in checked luggage. This leads to a "pack only what you can afford to lose" approach that might help you streamline.

RETHINK VALUABLES. On U.S. flights, airlines are liable for only about $2,800 per person for bags. On international flights, the liability limit is around $635 per bag. But items like computers, cameras, and jewelry aren't covered, and as gadgetry can go on and off the list of carry-on no-no's, you can't count on keeping things safe by keeping them close. Although comprehensive travel policies may cover luggage, the liability limit is often a pittance. Your home-owner's policy may cover you sufficiently when you travel—or not.

LOCK IT UP. If you must pack valuables, use TSA-approved locks (about $10) that can be unlocked by all U.S. security personnel.

TAG IT. Always tag your luggage; use your business address if you don't want people to know your home address. Put the same information (and a copy of your itinerary) inside your luggage, too.

REPORT PROBLEMS IMMEDIATELY. If your bags—or things in them—are damaged or go astray, file a written claim with your airline *before leaving the airport*. If the airline is at fault, it may give you money for essentials until your luggage arrives. Most lost bags are found within 48 hours, so alert the airline to your whereabouts for two or three days. If your bag was opened for security reasons in the States and something is missing, file a claim with the TSA.

Trip Insurance Resources

INSURANCE COMPARISON SITES		
Insure My Trip.com		www.insuremytrip.com.
Square Mouth.com		www.quotetravelinsurance.com.
COMPREHENSIVE TRAVEL INSURERS		
Access America	866/807-3982	www.accessamerica.com.
CSA Travel Protection	800/873-9855	www.csatravelprotection.com.
HTH Worldwide	610/254-8700 or 888/243-2358	www.hthworldwide.com.
Travelex Insurance	888/457-4602	www.travelex-insurance.com.
Travel Guard International	715/345-0505 or 800/826-4919	www.travelguard.com.
Travel Insured International	800/243-3174	www.travelinsured.com.
MEDICAL-ONLY INSURERS		
International Medical Group	800/628-4664	www.imglobal.com.
International SOS	215/942-8000 or 713/521-7611	www.internationalsos.com.
Wallach & Company	800/237-6615 or 504/687-3166	www.wallach.com.

Comprehensive travel policies typically cover trip-cancellation and interruption, letting you cancel or cut your trip short because of a personal emergency, illness, or, in some cases, acts of terrorism in your destination. Such policies also cover evacuation and medical care. Some also cover you for trip delays because of bad weather or mechanical problems as well as for lost or delayed baggage. Another type of coverage to look for is financial default—that is, when your trip is disrupted because a tour operator, airline, or cruise line goes out of business. Generally you must buy this when you book your trip or shortly thereafter, and it's only available to you if your operator isn't on a list of excluded companies.

Expect comprehensive travel insurance policies to cost about 4% to 7% of the total price of your trip (it's more like 12% if you're over age 70). A medical-only policy may or may not be cheaper than a comprehensive policy. Always read the fine print of your policy to make sure that you are covered for the risks that are of most concern to you. Compare several policies to make sure you're getting the best price and range of coverage available.

■ TIP→ If you travel frequently, look into the TSA's Registered Traveler program. The program, which is still being tested in several U.S. airports, is designed to cut down on gridlock at security checkpoints by allowing pre-screened travelers to pass quickly through kiosks that scan an iris and/or a fingerprint. How sci-fi is that?

BOOKING YOUR TRIP

Unless your cousin is a travel agent, you're probably among the millions of people who make most of their travel arrangements online. But have you ever wondered just what the differences are between an online travel agent (a Web site through which you make reservations instead of going directly to the airline, hotel, or car-rental company), a discounter (a firm that does a high volume of business with a hotel chain or airline and accordingly gets good prices), a wholesaler (one that makes cheap reservations in bulk and then resells them to people like you), and an aggregator (one that compares all the offerings so you don't have to)? Is it truly better to book directly on an airline or hotel Web site? And when does a real live travel agent come in handy?

ONLINE

You really have to shop around. A travel wholesaler such as Hotels.com or Hotel-Club.net can be a source of good rates, as can discounters such as Hotwire or Priceline, particularly if you can bid for your hotel room or airfare. Indeed, such sites sometimes have deals that are unavailable elsewhere. They do, however, tend to work only with hotel chains (which makes them just plain useless for getting hotel reservations outside of major cities) or big airlines (so that often leaves out upstarts like jetBlue and some foreign carriers like Air India). Also, with discounters and wholesalers you must generally prepay, and everything is nonrefundable. And before you fork over the dough, be sure to check the terms and conditions, so you know what a given company will do for you if there's a problem and what you'll have to deal with on your own.

■ TIP→ To be absolutely sure everything was processed correctly, confirm reservations made through online travel agents, discounters, and wholesalers directly with your hotel before leaving home.

Booking engines like Expedia, Travelocity, and Orbitz are actually travel agents, albeit high-volume, online ones. And airline travel packagers like American Airlines Vacations and Virgin Vacations—well, they're travel agents, too. But they may still not work with all the world's hotels.

An aggregator site will search many sites and pull the best prices for airfares, hotels, and rental cars from them. Most aggregators compare the major travel-booking sites such as Expedia, Travelocity, and Orbitz; some also look at airline Web sites, though rarely the sites of smaller budget airlines. Some aggregators also compare other travel products, including complex packages—a good thing, as you can sometimes get the best overall deal by booking an air-and-hotel package.

WITH A TRAVEL AGENT

If you use an agent—brick-and-mortar or virtual—you'll pay a fee for the service. And know that the service you get from some online agents isn't comprehensive. For example Expedia and Travelocity don't search for prices on budget airlines like jetBlue, Southwest, or small foreign carriers. That said, some agents (online or not) do have access to fares that are difficult to find otherwise, and the savings can more than make up for any surcharge.

■ TIP→ Remember that Expedia, Travelocity, and Orbitz are travel agents, not just booking engines. To resolve any problems with a reservation made through these companies, contact them first.

A knowledgeable brick-and-mortar travel agent can be a godsend if you're booking a cruise, a package trip that's not available to you directly, an air pass, or a complicated itinerary including several overseas flights. What's more, travel agents that specialize in a destination may have exclusive access to certain deals and insider information on things such as charter flights. Agents who specialize in types of

Online Booking Resources

AGGREGATORS

Kayak	www.kayak.com	also looks at cruises and vacation packages.
Mobissimo	www.mobissimo.com.	
Qixo	www.qixo.com	also compares cruises, vacation packages, and even travel insurance.
Sidestep	www.sidestep.com	also compares vacation packages and lists travel deals.
Travelgrove	www.travelgrove.com	also compares cruises and vacation packages.

BOOKING ENGINES

Cheap Tickets	www.cheaptickets.com	is a discounter.
Expedia	www.expedia.com	is a large online agency that charges a booking fee for airline tickets.
Hotwire	www.hotwire.com	is a discounter.
lastminute.com	www.lastminute.com	specializes in last-minute travel; the main site is for the U.K., but it has a link to a U.S. site.
Luxury Link	www.luxurylink.com	has auctions (surprisingly good deals) as well as offers on the high-end side of travel.
Onetravel.com	www.onetravel.com	is a discounter for hotels, car rentals, airfares, and packages.
Orbitz	www.orbitz.com	charges a booking fee for airline tickets, but gives a clear breakdown of fees and taxes before you book.
Priceline.com	www.priceline.com	is a discounter that also allows bidding.
Travel.com	www.travel.com	allows you to compare its rates with those of other booking engines.
Travelocity	www.travelocity.com	charges a booking fee for airline tickets, but promises good problem resolution.

ONLINE ACCOMMODATIONS

Hotelbook.com	www.hotelbook.com	focuses on independent hotels worldwide.
Hotel Club	www.hotelclub.net	is good for major cities worldwide.
Hotels.com	www.hotels.com	is a big Expedia-owned wholesaler that offers rooms in hotels all over the world.
Quikbook	www.quikbook.com	offers "pay when you stay" reservations that allow you to settle your bill when you check out, not when you book.

OTHER RESOURCES

Bidding For Travel	www.biddingfortravel.com	is a good place to figure out what you can get and for how much before you start bidding on, say, Priceline.

travelers (senior citizens, gays and lesbians, naturists) or types of trips (cruises, luxury travel, safaris) can also be invaluable. Travelers with access to the Internet or telephone service don't need a travel agent for a visit to Virginia and Maryland. There are toll-free telephone numbers in this guide for the state tourism agencies, and they are only too happy to provide information and other resources.

Agent Resources American Society of Travel Agents ☎ 703/739-2782 ⊕ www.travelsense. org.

▌ ACCOMMODATIONS

The lodgings we list are the cream of the crop in each price category. We always list the facilities that are available, but we don't specify whether they cost extra; when pricing accommodations, always ask what's included and what costs extra.

Properties are assigned price categories based on the range between their least and most expensive standard double rooms at high season (excluding holidays). Properties marked ✕🔄 are lodging establishments whose restaurants warrant a special trip.

Most hotels and other lodgings require you to give your credit-card details before they will confirm your reservation. If you don't feel comfortable e-mailing this information, ask if you can fax it (some places even prefer faxes). However you book, get confirmation in writing and have a copy of it handy when you check in. If you book through an online travel agent, discounter, or wholesaler, you might even want to confirm your reservation with the hotel before leaving home—just to be sure everything was processed correctly.

▌ TIP→ **Assume that hotels operate on the European Plan (EP, no meals) unless we specify that they use the Breakfast Plan (BP, with full breakfast), Continental Plan (CP, continental breakfast), Full American Plan (FAP, all meals), Modified American Plan (MAP, breakfast and dinner) or are all-inclusive (AI, all meals and most activities).**

10 WAYS TO SAVE 🏨

1. Join "frequent guest" programs. You may get preferential treatment in room choice and/or upgrades in your favorite chains.

2. Call direct. You can sometimes get a better price if you call a hotel's local toll-free number (if available) rather than a central reservations number.

3. Check online. Check hotel Web sites, as not all chains are represented on all travel sites.

4. Look for specials. Always inquire about packages and corporate rates.

5. Look for price guarantees. For overseas trips, look for guaranteed rates. With your rate locked in you won't pay more, even if the price goes up in the local currency.

6. Look for weekend deals at business hotels. High-end chains catering to business travelers are often busy only on weekdays; to fill rooms they often drop rates dramatically on weekends.

7. Ask about taxes. Verify whether local hotel taxes are included in quoted rates. In some places taxes can add 20% or more to your bill.

8. Read the fine print. Watch for add-ons, including resort fees, energy surcharges, and "convenience" fees for such things as unlimited local phone service you won't use or a free newspaper in a language you can't read.

9. Know when to go. If your destination's high season is December through April and you're trying to book, say, in late April, you might save money by changing your dates by a week or two. Ask when rates go down, though: if your dates straddle peak and non-peak seasons, a property may still charge peak-season rates for the entire stay.

10. Weigh your options (we can't say this enough). Weigh transportation times and costs against the savings of staying in a hotel that's cheaper because it's out of the way.

Online Booking Resources

CONTACTS

Atkinson Realty	757/428-4441	www.atkinsonrealty.com.
Bud Church Coldwell Banker	800/851-7326 com.	www.coldwellbankerbudchurch.
Coldwell Banker	301/387-6187	www.deepcreekrealty.com.
Interhome	954/791-8282 or 800/882-6864	www.interhome.us.
Railey Mountain Lake Vacations	800/846-7368	http://realty.railey.com/.
Vacation Home Rentals Worldwide	201/767-9393 or 800/633-3284	www.vhrww.com.
Villas International	415/499-9490 or 800/221-2260	www.villasintl.com.

RENTAL LISTINGS

Hideaways International	603/430-4433 or 800/843-4433.
Property Rentals International	804/378-6054.

Be sure you understand the hotel's cancellation policy. Some places allow you to cancel without any kind of penalty—even if you prepaid to secure a discounted rate—if you cancel at least 24 hours in advance. Others require you to cancel a week in advance or penalize you the cost of one night. Small inns and B&Bs are most likely to require you to cancel far in advance. Most hotels allow children under a certain age to stay in their parents' room at no extra charge, but others charge for them as extra adults; find out the cutoff age for discounts.

APARTMENT & HOUSE RENTALS

At shoreline resorts, as well as Deep Creek Lake in western Maryland, real estate agents generally handle apartment, condo, and town house rentals. For rentals in Deep Creek Lake, contact Railey Mountain Lake Vacations or Coldwell Banker. Call Atkinson Realty for Virginia Beach and Bud Church Coldwell Banker for Ocean City. Seashore homes usually rent by the week.

BED & BREAKFASTS

Houses in this region make it a natural area for bed-and-breakfast accommodations. The majority of B&Bs in Virginia and Maryland are Victorian structures with fewer than 10 rental units; a full or a continental breakfast is typically included in the lodging rate, and rooms rarely have their own TV. Most rooms, however, have private bathrooms.

Reservation Services Bed & Breakfast.com ☎ 512/322-2710 or 800/462-2632 ⊕ www.bedandbreakfast.com also sends out an online newsletter. **Bed & Breakfast Accommodations Ltd. of Washington, DC** ☎ 202/328-3510. **Bed & Breakfast Association of Maryland** ☎ 301/432-5079. **Bed & Breakfast Inns Online** ☎ 615/868-1946 or 800/215-7365 ⊕ www.bbonline.com. **BnB Finder.com** ☎ 212/432-7693 or 888/547-8226 ⊕ www.bnbfinder.com. **Maryland Office of Tourism** ☎ 410/767-3400 or 800/634-7386 ⊕ www.mdisfun.org. **Virginia Tourism Corporation** ☎ 804/786-2051 or 800/847-4882 ⊕ www.virginia.org.

CAMPING

Camping is popular in the Shenandoah and Blue Ridge mountains—particularly on the Appalachian Trail, which crosses Virginia and Maryland—and at state forests and parks in western Maryland. The Maryland Department of Natural Resources sells trail guides online. You can reserve sites at Virginia state parks online or by phone.

Assateague Island State Park in Maryland, the Assateague Island National Seashore (in Maryland and Virginia), and the state park at Cape Henry in Virginia are popular campgrounds. State-maintained sites include primitive and full-service sites (with showers, bathrooms, and hookups). Private campgrounds offer more amenities.

There are 30 free National Park Service campsites along the C&O Canal towpath in Maryland with water, chemical toilets, and grills. Bike camping is a very practical way to travel the towpath, and five drive-in campsites rent for $10.

C&O National Historical Park ⊕ www.nps. gov/choh/Recreation/Camping.html. **Go Camping America** ⊕ www. gocampingamerica.com. **Maryland Department of Natural Resources** ☎ 410/260-8100 ⊕ www.dnr.state.md.us, trail guides www. easycart.net/ MarylandDepartmentofNaturalResources/ Western_Maryland_Trail_Guides.html. **Virginia Department of Conservation and Recreation** ☎ 804/786-1712 ⊕ www.dcr.state.va.us, reservations www.dcr.state.va.us/parks/ reserve.htm.

HOME EXCHANGES

With a direct home exchange you stay in someone else's home while they stay in yours. Some outfits also deal with vacation homes, so you're not actually staying in someone's full-time residence, just their vacant weekend place.

Exchange Clubs Home Exchange.com ☎ 800/877-8723 ⊕ www.homeexchange. com; $59.95 for a 1-year online listing. **HomeLink International** ☎ 800/638-3841 ⊕ www. homelink.org; $80 yearly for Web-only membership; $125 includes Web access and two catalogs. **Intervac U.S.** ☎ 800/756-4663 ⊕ www.intervacus.com; $78.88 for Web-only membership; $126 includes Web access and a catalog.

HOSTELS

Hostels offer bare-bones lodging at low, low prices—often in shared dorm rooms

with shared baths—to people of all ages, though the primary market is young travelers, especially students. Most hostels serve breakfast; dinner and/or shared cooking facilities may also be available. In some hostels you aren't allowed to be in your room during the day, and there may be a curfew at night. Nevertheless, hostels provide a sense of community, with public rooms where travelers often gather to share stories. Many hostels are affiliated with Hostelling International (HI), an umbrella group of hostel associations with some 4,500 member properties in more than 70 countries. Other hostels are completely independent and may be nothing more than a really cheap hotel.

Membership in any HI association, open to travelers of all ages, allows you to stay in HI-affiliated hostels at member rates. One-year membership is about $28 for adults; hostels charge about $10–$30 per night. Members have priority if the hostel is full; they're also eligible for discounts around the world, even on rail and bus travel in some countries.

With few exceptions, hostels in Virginia and Maryland are near popular outdoor spots or resort communities. In Maryland, the HI-Harpers Ferry is near the Appalachian Trail in Knoxville, across the Potomac River from Harpers Ferry. Virginia's Bears Den Lodge is near the Appalachian Trail in Bluemont, HI-Galax is near the Blue Ridge Parkway, and HI-Angie's Guest Cottage is in Virginia Beach. **HI-Angie's Guest Cottage Hostel** ☎ 757/ 428-4690 ⊕ www.angiescottage.com. **Bears Den Lodge** ☎ 540/554-8708 ⊕ www. bearsdencenter.org/. **HI-Galax** ☎ 276/236-

4962. **HI-Harpers Ferry** ☏ 310/834-7652 ⊕ www.harpersferryhostel.org. **Hostelling International-USA** ☏ 301/495-1240 ⊕ www. hiusa.org.

HOTELS

The large hotels of Baltimore, Richmond, Norfolk, and the Virginia suburbs of Washington, D.C., are in competitive markets for business travelers: standards and prices are high. The beach and mountain resorts in the region are among the oldest and largest in the country, and on the expensive side. Accommodations at beach resorts in Maryland and Virginia can be difficult to find during summer holiday weekends—be sure to make reservations. Off season, rates often go down in both metropolitan areas and resorts.

All hotels listed have private bath unless otherwise noted.

■ AIRLINE TICKETS

Most domestic airline tickets are electronic; international tickets may be either electronic or paper. With an e-ticket the only thing you receive is an e-mailed receipt citing your itinerary and reservation and ticket numbers. The greatest advantage of an e-ticket is that if you lose your receipt, you can simply print out another copy or ask the airline to do it for you at check-in. You usually pay a surcharge (up to $50) to get a paper ticket, if you can get one at all. The sole advantage of a

---

WORD OF MOUTH

Did the resort look as good in real life as it did in the photos? Did you sleep like a baby, or were the walls paper thin? Did you get your money's worth? Rate hotels and write your own reviews in Travel Ratings or start a discussion about your favorite places in Travel Talk on www.fodors. com. Your comments might even appear in our books. Yes, you, too, can be a correspondent!

---

paper ticket is that it may be easier to endorse over to another airline if your flight is canceled and the airline with which you booked can't accommodate you on another flight.

■ TIP→ Discount air passes that let you travel economically in a country or region must often be purchased before you leave home. In some cases you can only get them through a travel agent.

Flying into BWI Airport could save money; airlines, including Southwest, often have good deals to this airport. Good sales can sometimes be found to Dulles and occasionally to Reagan National. Fares into Richmond International are sometimes more expensive.

■ RENTAL CARS

When you reserve a car, ask about cancellation penalties, taxes, drop-off charges (if you're planning to pick up the car in one city and leave it in another), and surcharges (for being under or over a certain age, for additional drivers, or for driving across state or country borders or beyond a specific distance from your point of rental). All these things can add substantially to your costs. Request car seats and extras such as GPS when you book.

■ TIP→ Make sure that a confirmed reservation guarantees you a car. Agencies sometimes overbook, particularly for busy weekends and holiday periods.

Rates are sometimes—but not always—better if you book in advance or reserve through a rental agency's Web site. There are other reasons to book ahead, though: for popular destinations, during busy times of the year, or to ensure that you get certain types of cars (vans, SUVs, exotic sports cars).

CAR-RENTAL INSURANCE

Everyone who rents a car wonders whether the insurance that the rental companies offer is worth the expense. No one—including us—has a simple answer. It all depends on how much regular insurance

Car Rental Resources

AUTOMOBILE ASSOCIATIONS		
U.S.: American Automobile Association (AAA)	315/797-5000	www.aaa.com; most contact with the organization is through state and regional members.
National Automobile Club	650/294-7000	www.thenac.com; membership is open to California residents only.
MAJOR AGENCIES		
Alamo	800/462-5266	www.alamo.com.
Avis	800/230-4898	www.avis.com.
Budget	800/527-0700	www.budget.com.
Hertz	800/654-3131	www.hertz.com.
National Car Rental	800/227-7368	www.nationalcar.com.

you have, how comfortable you are with risk, and whether or not money is an issue.

If you own a car and carry comprehensive car insurance for both collision and liability, your personal auto insurance will probably cover a rental, but read your policy's fine print to be sure. If you don't have auto insurance, then you should probably buy the collision- or loss-damage waiver (CDW or LDW) from the rental company. This eliminates your liability for damage to the car. Some credit cards offer CDW coverage, but it's usually supplemental to your own insurance and rarely covers SUVs, minivans, luxury models, and the like. If your coverage is secondary, you may still be liable for loss-of-use costs from the car-rental company (again, read the fine print). But no credit-card insurance is valid unless you use that card for *all* transactions, from reserving to paying the final bill.

■ **TIP→** Diners Club offers primary CDW coverage on all rentals reserved and paid for with the card. This means that Diners Club's company—not your own car insurance—pays in case of an accident. It *doesn't* mean that your car-insurance company won't raise your rates once it discovers you had an accident.

You may also be offered supplemental liability coverage; the car-rental company is required to carry a minimal level of liability coverage insuring all renters, but it's rarely enough to cover claims in a really serious accident if you're at fault. Your own auto-insurance policy will protect you if you own a car; if you don't, you have to decide whether you are willing to take the risk.

U.S. rental companies sell CDWs and LDWs for about $15 to $25 a day; supplemental liability is usually more than $10 a day. The car-rental company may offer you all sorts of other policies, but they're rarely worth the cost. Personal accident insurance, which is basic hospitalization coverage, is an especially egregious rip-off if you already have health insurance.

■ **TIP→** You can decline the insurance from the rental company and purchase it through a third-party provider such as Travel Guard (www.travelguard.com)—$9 per day for $35,000 of coverage. That's sometimes just under half the price of the CDW offered by some car-rental companies.

In Maryland the cr-rental agency's insurance is primary; therefore, the company must pay for damage to third parties up to a preset legal limit, beyond which the renter becomes liable.

Virginia and Maryland car rental agencies normally don't rent to drivers younger than 21.

TRANSPORTATION

■ BY AIR

Flying time to Baltimore-Washington International Airport is just over one hour from New York; approximately two hours from Chicago; and five hours from Los Angeles. Flying time to Richmond International Airport is approximately 1½ hours from New York, two hours from Chicago, and seven to nine hours from Los Angeles (because there are no nonstop flights). A flight to D.C. is a little more than an hour from New York, about two hours from Chicago, and five hours from San Francisco. Those flying from London can expect a trip of about six hours. A trip from Sydney takes about 20 hours.

Airlines & Airports Airline and Airport Links.com ⊕ www.airlineandairportlinks.com has links to many of the world's airlines and airports.

Airline Security Issues Transportation Security Administration ⊕ www.tsa.gov has answers for almost every question that might come up.

AIRPORTS

Virginia has Richmond International Airport (RIC), 10 mi east of Richmond; the busy Ronald Reagan Washington National Airport (DCA), 3 mi south of downtown Washington; and Washington Dulles International Airport (IAD), 26 mi northwest of Washington. There is considerable service nationwide into and out of Norfolk (ORF) and even Newport News (aka Patrick Henry, PHF). Maryland's Baltimore-Washington Thurgood Marshall International Airport (BWI) is about 25 mi northeast of Washington and 10 mi south of Baltimore. Amtrak and commuter trains stop at BWI.

Most travelers fly to the nearest major airport and rent a car to get to areas covered by smaller regional airports. Many smaller airports have flights or connections to Washington, Baltimore, Richmond, Norfolk, and Philadelphia, especially on

US Airways. Hagerstown Regional Airport has US Airways flights to Pittsburgh and other Pennsylvania airports (but not to Washington or Baltimore). Salisbury-Ocean City-Wicomico Regional Airport serves the lower Eastern Shore with US Airways service to Philadelphia. Airports at Staunton, Charlottesville, Lynchburg, and Roanoke have scheduled service.

■ TIP→ Long layovers don't have to be only about sitting around or shopping. These days they can be about burning off vacation calories. Check out www.airportgyms.com for lists of health clubs that are in or near many U.S. and Canadian airports.

Airport Information Newport News/ Williamsburg International Airport (PHF) ☎ 757/877-0221 ⊕ www.nnwairport.com. **Richmond International Airport** (RIC) ☎ 804/226-3000 ⊕ www.flyrichmond.com. **Ronald Reagan Washington National Airport** (DCA) ☎ 703/417-8000 ⊕ www. metwashairports.com/National. **Thurgood Marshall Baltimore-Washington International Airport** (BWI) ☎ 410/859-7111 or 800/ 435-9294 ⊕ www.bwiairport.com. **Washington Dulles International Airport** (IAD) ☎ 703/572-2700 ⊕ www.metwashairports. com/dulles.

Secondary Airports Charlottesville Albemarle County (CHO) ☎ 434/973-8342. **Hagerstown Regional** (HGR) ☎ 240/313- 2777. **Lynchburg Regional** (LYH) ☎ 434/455- 6090. **Roanoke Regional Airport** (ROA) ☎ 540/362-1999. **Salisbury-Ocean City-Wicomico Regional** (SBY) ☎ 540/548-4827. **Shenandoah Valley Regional** (SHD) ☎ 540/ 234-8304.

GROUND TRANSPORTATION

Reagan National, Dulles, and BWI airports are served by SuperShuttle, which takes passengers to a hotel or residence. Buy tickets and request service at the SuperShuttle counter.

The most reasonable way to BWI is by Maryland Transit Administration (MTA)

train, MTA light rail, Washington Metropolitan Transit Authority (WMATA) bus, or a combination thereof. All northbound Amtrak and MTA Penn Line trains from Washington's Union Station or southbound from Baltimore Penn Station make a BWI stop, where there's a free shuttle bus to the terminal. MTA costs about a third of the Amtrak fare, but only operates on workdays. MTA light trains run from BWI to downtown Baltimore and the suburbs daily. WMATA has an express bus (B30) to BWI every 40 minutes from its Greenbelt, MD, Metrorail station.

Taxi fare to Baltimore's Inner Harbor is about $25.

Dulles is served by Washington Flyer bus and WMATA's Metrobus. Washington Flyer operates between Dulles and the West Falls Church Metrorail station every half hour from 5:45 AM (7:45 on weekends) until 10:15 PM for $9. WMATA Metrobuses and trains operate from the Metrorail station. ■ TIP➜ The little-known express Metrobus, route 5A, runs between Dulles and L'Enfant Plaza Metrorail station in downtown Washington and costs only $3.

Taxi fares from Dulles to downtown Washington range from $51 to $58; drivers accept major credit cards.

Reagan National has its own Metrorail station just outside the main terminal. There is virtually no bus service to the airport. Taxi drivers must accept credit card payment, and they charge a $1.75 airport-access fee. Fare to the U.S. Capitol is about $10.

TRANSFERS BETWEEN AIRPORTS

Taxi service is by far the most expensive option between airports; sample fares are $70 between BWI and National, $100 between BWI and Dulles, and $55 between Dulles and National.

Travel between BWI and National for $6.85: Take WMATA's express bus from BWI to the Greenbelt Metrorail station, then switch to the Metrorail and transfer at Gallery Place. Between BWI and Dulles, take WMATA's express bus, then the

10 WAYS TO SAVE 🚗

1. Beware of cheap rates. Those great rates aren't so great when you add in taxes, surcharges, and insurance. Such extras can double or triple the initial quote.

2. Rent weekly. Weekly rates are usually better than daily ones. Even if you only want to rent for five or six days, ask for the weekly rate; it may very well be cheaper than the daily rate for that period of time.

3. Don't forget the locals. Price local companies as well as the majors.

4. Airport rentals can cost more. Airports often add surcharges, which you can sometimes avoid by renting from an agency whose office is just off airport property.

5. Wholesalers can help. Investigate wholesalers, which don't own fleets but rent in bulk from firms that do, and which frequently offer better rates (note that you must usually pay for such rentals before leaving home).

6. Look for rate guarantees. With your rate locked in, you won't pay more, even if the price goes up in the local currency.

7. Fill up farther away. Avoid hefty refueling fees by filling the tank at a station well away from where you plan to turn in the car.

8. Pump it yourself. Don't buy the tank of gas that's in the car when you rent it unless you plan to do a lot of driving.

9. Get all your discounts. Find out whether a credit card you carry or organization or frequent-renter program to which you belong has a discount program. And confirm that such discounts really are a deal. You can often do better with special weekend or weekly rates offered by a rental agency.

10. Check out package rates. Adding a car rental onto your air/hotel vacation package may be cheaper than renting a car separately on your own.

10 WAYS TO SAVE ✈

1. Nonrefundable is best. If saving money is more important than flexibility, then non-refundable tickets work. Just remember that you'll pay dearly (as much as $100) if you change your plans.

2. Comparison shop. Web sites and travel agents can have different arrangements with the airlines and offer different prices for exactly the same flights.

3. Beware those prices. Many airline Web sites—and most ads—show prices *without* taxes and surcharges. Don't buy until you know the full price.

4. Stay loyal. Stick with one or two frequent-flier programs. You'll rack up free trips faster and you'll accumulate more quickly the perks that make trips easier. On some airlines these include a special reservations number, early boarding, access to upgrades, and more roomy economy-class seating.

5. Watch those ticketing fees. Surcharges are usually added when you buy your ticket anywhere but on an airline Web site. (That includes by phone—even if you call the airline directly—and paper tickets regardless of how you book.)

6. Check early and often. Look for cheap fares up to a year in advance, and keep looking till you see something you like.

7. Don't work alone. Some Web sites have tracking features that will e-mail you immediately when good deals are posted.

8. Jump on the good deals. Waiting even a few minutes might mean paying more.

9. Be flexible. Look for departures on Tuesday, Wednesday, and Thursday, typically the cheapest travel days. Check on prices for departures at different times and to and from alternative airports.

10. Weigh your options. A cheaper flight might have a long layover rather than being nonstop, or it might land at a secondary airport, where your ground transportation costs are higher.

Metrorail to L'Enfant Plaza, then switch to the 5A express bus; total fare is $8.30.

For a little more comfort on weekdays, take the MTA train to or from BWI and transfer to the Metrorail at New Carrolton or Union Station. It adds about $2.50 to the fare.

Maryland Transportation Administration ☎ 410/539-5000 ⊕ www.mtamaryland.com/. **SuperShuttle** ☎ 800/258-3826 ⊕ www.supershuttle.com/. **Washington Flyer** ☎ 888/927-4359 ⊕ www.washfly.com. **WMATA** ☎ 202/637-7000 ⊕ www.wmata.com.

FLIGHTS

Airline Contacts Alaska Airlines ☎ 800/252-7522 or 206/433-3100 ⊕ www.alaskaair.com. **American Airlines** ☎ 800/433-7300 ⊕ www.aa.com. **ATA** ☎ 800/435-9282 or 317/282-8308 ⊕ www.ata.com. **Continental Airlines** ☎ 800/523-3273 for U.S. and Mexico reservations, 800/231-0856 for international reservations ⊕ www.continental.com. **Delta Airlines** ☎ 800/221-1212 for U.S. reservations, 800/241-4141 for international reservations ⊕ www.delta.com. **jetBlue** ☎ 800/538-2583 ⊕ www.jetblue.com. **Northwest Airlines** ☎ 800/225-2525 ⊕ www.nwa.com. **Southwest Airlines** ☎ 800/435-9792 ⊕ www.southwest.com. **Spirit Airlines** ☎ 800/772-7117 or 586/791-7300 ⊕ www.spiritair.com. **United Airlines** ☎ 800/864-8331 for U.S. reservations, 800/538-2929 for international reservations ⊕ www.united.com. **US Airways** ☎ 800/428-4322 for U.S. and Canada reservations, 800/622-1015 for international reservations ⊕ www.usairways.com.

Smaller Airlines AirTran Airways ☎ 800/247-8726 ⊕ www.airtran.com.

FLYING 101

Flying may not be as carefree as it once was, but there are some things you can do to make your trip smoother.

MINIMIZE THE TIME SPENT STANDING IN LINE. Buy an e-ticket, check in at an electronic kiosk, or—even better—check in on your airline's Web site before leaving home. Pack light and limit carry-on items to only the essentials.

ARRIVE WHEN YOU NEED TO. Research your airline's policy. It's usually at least an hour before domestic flights and two to three hours before international flights. But airlines at some busy airports have more stringent requirements. Check the TSA Web site for estimated security waiting times at major airports.

GET TO THE GATE. If you aren't at the gate at least 10 minutes before your flight is scheduled to take off (sometimes earlier), you won't be allowed to board.

DOUBLE-CHECK YOUR FLIGHT TIMES. Do this especially if you reserved far in advance. Schedules change, and alerts may not reach you.

DON'T GO HUNGRY. Ask whether your airline offers anything to eat; even when it does, be prepared to pay.

GET THE SEAT YOU WANT. Often, you can pick a seat when you buy your ticket on an airline Web site. But it's not guaranteed; the airline could change the plane after you book, so double-check. You can also select a seat if you check in electronically. Avoid seats on the aisle directly across from the lavatories. Frequent fliers say those are even worse than back-row seats that don't recline.

GOT KIDS? Get info. Ask the airline about its children's menus, activities, and fares. Sometimes infants and toddlers fly free if they sit on a parent's lap, and older children fly for half price in their own seats. Also inquire about policies involving car seats; having one may limit seating options. Also ask about seat-belt extenders for car seats.

CHECK YOUR SCHEDULING. Don't buy a ticket if there's less than an hour between connecting flights. Although schedules are padded, if anything goes wrong you might miss your connection. If you're traveling to an important function, depart a day early.

BRING PAPER. Even when using an e-ticket, always carry a hard copy of your receipt; you may need it to get your boarding pass, which most airports require this.

COMPLAIN AT THE AIRPORT. If your baggage goes astray or your flight goes awry, complain before leaving the airport. Most carriers require that you file a claim immediately.

BEWARE OF OVERBOOKED FLIGHTS. If a flight is oversold, the gate agent will usually ask for volunteers and offer some sort of compensation for taking a different flight. If you're bumped from a flight *involuntarily*, the airline must give you some kind of compensation if an alternate flight can't be found within one hour.

KNOW YOUR RIGHTS. If your flight is delayed because of something within the airline's control (bad weather doesn't count), the airline must get you to your destination on the same day, even if they have to book you on another airline and in an upgraded class. Read the Contract of Carriage, which is usually buried on the airline's Web site.

BE PREPARED. The Boy Scout motto is especially important if you're traveling during a stormy season. To quickly adjust your plans, program a few numbers into your cell: your airline, an airport hotel or two, your destination hotel, your car service, and/or your travel agent.

■ BY BOAT

Water sports and activities are popular recreational pursuits in Virginia and Maryland, which share the expansive Chesapeake Bay and the Potomac River. Harbor and river cruises are offered in Baltimore, St. Michaels, Annapolis, Washington, D.C. (along the Potomac), Hampton, and Norfolk, to name a few starting points. Sailboats and other pleasure craft can be chartered for trips on the Chesapeake Bay or inland rivers. Popular ports include Rock Hall, Havre de Grace, and Solomons in Maryland, and Newport News and Chincoteague in Virginia.

For a complete list of ferries operating in Virginia, including commercial ferries and those operating to the Maryland shore, see ⊕ www.vdot.virginia.gov/comtravel/ferry. asp.

■ **TIP→** If you're over 60, chances are you qualify for greatly discounted transit fares in Virginia and Maryland. If you're over 60 in the Norfolk area, they almost pay you to ride their excellent system of buses and ferries. And if you're over 65 Maryland and WMATA let you ride their trains, buses, and subways at half price.

All state-operated ferries in Virginia are free. The Elizabeth River ferry between Portsmouth and Norfolk costs $1. Ferries to Tangier and Smith islands cost about $25 round trip.
Hampton Roads Transit ☎ 757/222-6100 ⊕ www.hrtransit.org/ferryservice.html. **Smith Island Cruises** ☎ 410/425-2771 ⊕ www. smithislandcruises.com. **Tangier Island Cruises** ☎ 800/863-2338 or 410/968-2338 ⊕ tangierislandcruises.com. **Virginia Department of Transportation** ☎ 804/786-2801 ⊕ www.vdot.virginia.gov/comtravel/ferry.asp.

■ BY BUS

A bus is a very practical way to get to a one-stop resort destination such as Ocean City or Virginia Beach, but many of Maryland's and Virginia's more scenic attractions lie outside the cities served by bus routes. Municipal buses do provide point-to-point transportation in Baltimore, Richmond, the Hampton Roads area, and metropolitan Washington, D.C.

Greyhound Lines has extensive service to Virginia and Maryland, supplemented by Peter Pan from Washington to points north to Massachusetts. Unfortunately, there is no system for reserving or assigning seats, so even ticket holders may not get a seat or may lose their seat during stops to change buses. Buses in Virginia and Maryland tend to be quite crowded, so competition is fierce for seats.

A low-cost alternative is the system of "Chinatown" buses, which operate primarily between little travel agencies in northeastern cities. Reservations can be made in person or online, and the price is about half the equivalent Greyhound ticket or less. Chinatown Bus Lines has information for some (but by no means all) "Chinatown" bus companies on the East Coast.
Bus Information Chinatown Bus Lines ⊕ www.staticleap.com/chinatownbus. **Greyhound Lines** ☎ 800/231-2222 ⊕ www. greyhound.com. **Peter Pan Trailways** ☎ 800/343-9999 ⊕ www.peterpanbus.com.

■ BY CAR

A car is by far the most convenient means of travel throughout Maryland and Virginia, and in many areas it's the only practical way to get around. (Where it exists, public transportation is clean, reasonable, and comfortable, but too often it bypasses or falls short of travel high points.)

HIGHWAYS
Interstate 95 runs north–south through Maryland and Virginia, carrying traffic to and from New England and Florida and intermediate points. U.S. 50 links I-95 with Annapolis and Maryland's Eastern Shore. U.S. 97 links Baltimore with Annapolis. I-695 forms a beltway around Baltimore, and I-495 and I-95 form a

beltway around Washington. The Baltimore-Washington Parkway is an old four-lane road that parallels I–95 between the two beltways. I–64 intersects I–95 at Richmond and runs east–west. At Staunton, I–64 intersects I–81, which runs north–south. Interstate 70 runs west from Baltimore's Beltway, I–695, to Hancock in western Maryland. I–68 connects Hancock to Cumberland and Garrett County. U.S. 40—the National Pike—travels east and west, the entire length of Maryland. I–83 journeys south from Pennsylvania to the top of I–695, the Baltimore Beltway.

ROAD MAPS

The state tourist offices of Maryland and Virginia (⇨ Visitor Information) publish official state road maps (and special interest maps like bike maps and scenic highway maps), free for the asking, that contain directories and other useful information. For the excellent, free *Maryland Scenic Byways* guide, call 877/632–9929 or look for one at a state welcome center.

RULES OF THE ROAD

The maximum speed limit is 65 mph on stretches of major highways in both states. Radar detectors are legal in Maryland, but are not permitted in D.C. or Virginia. Front-seat passengers in all jurisdictions must wear seat belts.

In Virginia, D.C., and Maryland, you may usually turn right at a red light after stopping if there's no oncoming traffic and no pedestrians present. Watch the signs.

In both states, HOV lanes are restricted to a minimum of two (three in some places) people during rush hour. Look for the diamond on the highway and on signs telling you when the restrictions are in effect.

Talking on cell phones while driving is not allowed in D.C.

Children must be in approved child restraints if they are under six in Maryland and Virginia (or under 40 lbs at any age in Maryland). In D.C. they must be in an infant, toddler, or booster seat up to age eight.

▌ BY TRAIN

Amtrak trains run out of Baltimore, Maryland, north toward Boston and south toward Washington, D.C., along the busy "northeast corridor." A rail station at Baltimore-Washington International Airport serves both Baltimore (about 15 mi to the north) and Washington, D.C. (about 30 mi to the south). Some trains running between New York and Chicago stop at Charlottesville, Virginia, and at two locations in western Virginia. Trains run between Newport News, Virginia, and New York City, stopping in northern Virginia, Richmond, and Williamsburg in between. Stops in Richmond and northern Virginia are also made on runs between New York City and Florida.

The Maryland State Railroad Administration operates commuter trains (on weekdays only) between Baltimore's Penn Station and D.C.'s Union Station. It also operates trains from Baltimore's downtown Camden Station and from Union Station in Washington, D.C. There's free bus transportation between the Baltimore-Washington International Airport Rail Station and the airport passenger terminal.

Virginia Railway Express, or VRE, provides workday commuter service between Union Station in Washington and Fredericksburg and Manassas, with additional stops near hotels in Crystal City, Alexandria, and elsewhere.

Amtrak ☎ 800/872-7245 ⊕ www.amtrak. com. **Maryland Transit Administration** (MTA) ☎ 800/325-7245 ⊕ www.mtamaryland.com. **Virginia Railway Express** (VRE) ☎ 800/743-3873 ⊕ www.vre.org.

ON THE GROUND

■ COMMUNICATIONS

INTERNET

Local internet cafes are listed in the Essentials of each chapter. **Cybercafes** ⊕ www.cybercafes.com lists more than 4,000 Internet cafés worldwide.

■ EATING OUT

The restaurants listed are the cream of the crop in each price category. Properties indicated by an ✗⊡ are lodging establishments whose restaurant warrants a special trip.

The treasure of the Chesapeake Bay is the blue crab. In Maryland and Virginia, the locals like crabs steamed in the shells, seasoned by the bushel, and dumped on brown-paper-covered tables in spartan crab houses. Diners use wooden mallets to crack the shells, and nimble fingers to reach the meat. Crab cakes, soft-shell crab, crab imperial (enriched crabmeat stuffed back into shells), crab soup, and a host of other such dishes can be found throughout the region. Rockfish (striped bass) is another seafood delicacy, harvested in summer and fall.

In Virginia, country ham, biscuits, collard greens, and fried chicken—Southern staples—are popular Sunday meals. Grits (often served for breakfast) and pecan and sweet-potato pies are other popular Southern foods.

MEALS & MEALTIMES

Unless otherwise noted, the restaurants listed in this guide are open daily for lunch and dinner.

PAYING

For guidelines on tipping *see* Tipping *below.*

RESERVATIONS & DRESS

Regardless of where you are, it's a good idea to make a reservation if you can. In some places (Hong Kong, for example), it's expected. We only mention them specifically when reservations are essential (there's no other way you'll ever get a table) or when they are not accepted. For popular restaurants, book as far ahead as you can (often 30 days), and reconfirm as soon as you arrive. (Large parties should always call ahead to check the reservations policy.) We mention dress only when men are required to wear a jacket or a jacket and tie.

Online reservation services make it easy to book a table before you even leave home. OpenTable covers most states, including 20 major cities, and has limited listings in Canada, Mexico, the United Kingdom, and elsewhere. DinnerBroker has restaurants throughout the United States as well as a few in Canada. **OpenTable** ⊕ www.opentable.com. **Dinner-Broker** ⊕ www.dinnerbroker.com.

WINES, BEER & SPIRITS

In Maryland and Virginia, restaurants and bars can serve wine, beer, and spirits seven days a week.

■ **TIP→** In Virginia, the state-run ABC liquor stores are open daily. In Maryland, liquor stores don't sell on Sunday, but some restaurants and bars package alcohol to go, even on Sunday. Beer and wine are sold throughout the region in convenience stores, markets, drug stores, and even gas stations every day.

■ HOURS OF OPERATION

The business week runs from 9 to 5 weekdays, and in some instances, on Saturday in the metropolitan regions of Virginia and Maryland. Stores, restaurants, and other services maintain longer hours. Hours vary in small towns and resort areas, especially those dependent on seasonal visitors. In rural areas, many retail establishments close on Sunday.

Most businesses in the area close for many religious holidays and all holidays that are celebrated on a Monday. However, shopping malls and plazas, as well as restaurants, remain open.

Sunday liquor sales in D.C., Virginia, and Maryland are limited to wine and beer.

Most art and historical museums in the region are open from 10 or 11 to 5 or 6, Monday through Saturday, and noon to 5 on Sunday. Some museums are closed on Monday and/or Tuesday. Many parks and historical homes tend to have later closing hours in the summer, and some close during the winter months. In this book's sight reviews, open hours are denoted by a clock icon.

In the metropolitan areas, retail stores and shopping malls are open 10–9, Monday through Saturday, and 11–6 on Sunday. In suburban Baltimore, Washington, and Richmond, grocery stores and superstores often are open 24 hours. Retailers in small towns and in the downtown office districts close earlier and are often not open on Sunday.

■ MONEY

Generally, lodging, restaurants, and attractions are most expensive in Washington, D.C., Baltimore, Richmond, suburban Washington, and resort areas, especially Ocean City and Virginia Beach. Gas prices tend to be higher in the mountainous regions. Lodging and restaurant costs are considerably less expensive in the western Maryland mountains and rural Virginia.

Coupons for hotel discounts and services in Maryland and Virginia can be printed at www.travelcoupons.com.

Prices throughout this guide are given for adults. Substantially reduced fees are almost always available for children, students, and senior citizens.

CON OR CONCIERGE?

Good hotel concierges are invaluable—for arranging transportation, getting reservations at the hottest restaurant, and scoring tickets for a sold-out show or entree to an exclusive nightclub. They're in the know and well connected. That said, sometimes you have to take their advice with a grain of salt.

It's not uncommon for restaurants to ply concierges with free food and drink in exchange for steering diners their way. Indeed, European concierges often receive referral *fees*. Hotel chains usually have guidelines about what their concierges can accept. The best concierges, however, are above reproach. This is particularly true of those who belong to the prestigious international society of Les Clefs d'Or.

What can you expect of a concierge? At a typical tourist-class hotel you can expect him or her to give you the basics: to show you something on a map, make a standard restaurant reservation (particularly if you don't speak the language), or help you book a tour or airport transportation. In Asia concierges perform the vital service of writing out the name or address of your destination for you to give to a cab driver.

Savvy concierges at the finest hotels and resorts can arrange for just about any good or service imaginable—and do so quickly. You should compensate them appropriately. A $10 tip is enough to show appreciation for a table at a hot restaurant. But the reward should really be much greater for tickets to that U2 concert that's been sold out for months or for those last-minute sixth-row-center seats for *The Lion King*.

FOR INTERNATIONAL TRAVELERS

CURRENCY
The dollar is the basic unit of U.S. currency. It has 100 cents. Coins are the penny (1¢); the nickel (5¢), dime (10¢), quarter (25¢), half-dollar (50¢), and the very rare golden $1 coin and even rarer silver $1. Bills are denominated $1, $5, $10, $20, $50, and $100, all mostly green and identical in size; designs and background tints vary. You may come across a $2 bill, but the chances are slim.

CUSTOMS
U.S. Customs and Border Protection ⊕ www. cbp.gov.

DRIVING
Driving in the United States is on the right. Speed limits are posted in miles per hour (usually between 55 mph and 70 mph). Watch for lower limits in small towns and on back roads (usually 30 mph to 40 mph). Most states require front-seat passengers to wear seat belts; many states require children to sit in the back seat and to wear seat belts. In major cities rush hour is between 7 and 10 AM; afternoon rush hour is between 4 and 7 PM. To encourage carpooling, some freeways have special lanes, ordinarily marked with a diamond, for high-occupancy vehicles (HOV)—cars carrying two people or more.

Highways are well paved. Interstates—limited-access, multilane highways designated with an "I-" before the number—are fastest. Interstates with three-digit numbers circle urban areas, which may also have other limited-access expressways, freeways, and parkways. Tolls may be levied on limited-access highways. U.S. and state highways aren't necessarily limited-access, but may have several lanes.

Gas stations are plentiful. Most stay open late (24 hours along major highways and in big cities) except in rural areas, where Sunday hours are limited and where you may drive for long stretches without a refueling opportunity. Along larger highways, roadside stops with restrooms, fast-food restaurants, and sundries stores are well spaced. State police and tow trucks patrol major highways. If your car breaks down on an interstate, pull onto the shoulder and wait for help, or have your passengers wait while you walk to an emergency phone (available in most states). If you carry a cell phone, dial *55, noting your location on the small green roadside mileage marker.

ELECTRICITY
The U.S. standard is AC, 110 volts/60 cycles. Plugs have two flat pins set parallel to each other.

EMBASSIES
Australia ☎ 202/797-3000 ⊕ www.austemb. org. **Canada** ☎ 202/682-1740 ⊕ www. canadianembassy.org. **United Kingdom** ☎ 202/588-7800 ⊕ www.britainusa.com.

EMERGENCIES
For police, fire, or ambulance, dial 911 (0 in rural areas).

HOLIDAYS
New Year's Day (Jan. 1); Martin Luther King Jr. Day (3rd Mon. in Jan.); Presidents' Day (3rd Mon. in Feb.); Memorial Day (last Mon. in May); Independence Day (July 4); Labor Day (1st Mon. in Sept.); Columbus Day (2nd Mon. in Oct.); Thanksgiving Day (4th Thurs. in Nov.); Christmas Eve and Christmas Day (Dec. 24 and 25); and New Year's Eve (Dec. 31).

MAIL
You can buy stamps and aerograms and send letters and parcels in post offices. Stamp-dispensing machines can occasionally be found in airports, bus and train stations, office buildings, drugstores, and convenience stores. U.S. mail boxes are stout, dark blue steel bins; pickup schedules are posted inside the bin (pull down the handle to see them). Parcels weighing more

than a pound must be mailed at a post office or at a private mailing center.

Within the United States a first-class letter weighing 1 ounce or less costs 39¢; each additional ounce costs 24¢. Postcards cost 24¢. A 1-ounce airmail letter to most countries costs 84¢, an airmail postcard costs 75¢; a 1-ounce letter to Canada or Mexico costs 63¢, a postcard 55¢.

To receive mail on the road, have it sent c/o General Delivery at your destination's main post office (use the correct five-digit ZIP code). You must pick up mail in person within 30 days, with a driver's license or passport for identification.
DHL ☎ 800/225-5345 ⊕ www.dhl.com. **Federal Express** ☎ 800/463-3339 ⊕ www.fedex.com. **Mail Boxes, Etc./The UPS Store** ☎ 800/789-4623 ⊕ www.mbe.com. **United States Postal Service** ⊕ www.usps.com.

PASSPORTS & VISAS
Visitor visas aren't necessary for citizens of Australia, Canada, the United Kingdom, or most citizens of European Union countries coming for tourism and staying for fewer than 90 days. If you require a visa, the cost is $100, and waiting time can be substantial, depending on where you live. Apply for a visa at the U.S. consulate in your place of residence; check the U.S. State Department's special Visa Web site for further information. **Visa Information Destination USA** ⊕ www.unitedstatesvisas.gov.

PHONES
Numbers consist of a three-digit area code and a seven-digit local number. Within many local calling areas you dial only the seven digits; in others you dial "1" first and all 10 digits—just as you would for calls between area-code regions. The same is true for calls to numbers prefixed by "800," "888," "866," and "877"—all toll free. For calls to numbers prefixed by "900" you must pay—usually dearly.

For international calls, dial "011" followed by the country code and the local number. For help, dial "0" and ask for an overseas operator. Most phone books list country codes and U.S. area codes. The country code for Australia is 61, for New Zealand 64, for the United Kingdom 44. Calling Canada is the same as calling within the United States, whose country code, by the way, is 1.

For operator assistance, dial "0." For directory assistance, call 555-1212 or occasionally 411 (free at many public phones). You can reverse long-distance charges by calling "collect"; dial "0" instead of "1" before the 10-digit number.

Instructions are generally posted on pay phones. Usually you insert coins in a slot (usually 25¢-50¢ for local calls) and wait for a steady tone before dialing. On long-distance calls the operator tells you how much to insert; prepaid phone cards, widely available in various denominations, can be used from any phone. Follow the directions to activate the card (there's usually an access number, then an activation code), then dial your number.

CELL PHONES
The United States has several GSM (Global System for Mobile Communications) networks, so multiband mobiles from most countries (except for Japan) work here. Unfortunately, it's almost impossible to buy a pay-as-you-go mobile SIM card in the U.S.—which allows you to avoid roaming charges—without also buying a phone. That said, cell phones with pay as you go plans are available for well under $100. The cheapest ones with decent national coverage are the GoPhone from Cingular and Virgin Mobile, which only offers pay-as-you-go service.
Cingular ☎ 888/333-6651 ⊕ www.cingular.com. **Virgin Mobile** ☎ No phone ⊕ www.virginmobileusa.com.

CREDIT CARDS

Throughout this guide, the following abbreviations are used: **AE**, American Express; **D**, Discover; **DC**, Diners Club; **MC**, MasterCard; and **V**, Visa.

It's a good idea to inform your credit-card company before you travel. Otherwise, the credit-card company might put a hold on your card owing to unusual activity—not a good thing halfway through your trip. Record all your credit-card numbers—as well as the phone numbers to call if your cards are lost or stolen—in a safe place, so you're prepared should something go wrong. Both MasterCard and Visa have general numbers you can call if your card is lost, but you're better off calling the number of your issuing bank, since MasterCard and Visa usually just transfer you to your bank; your bank's number is usually printed on your card.

Reporting Lost Cards American Express ☎ 800/992-3404 in U.S. ⊕ www.americanexpress.com. **Diners Club** ☎ 800/234-6377 in U.S. ⊕ www.dinersclub.com. **Discover** ☎ 800/347-2683 in U.S. ⊕ www.discovercard.com. **MasterCard** ☎ 800/622-7747 in U.S. ⊕ www.mastercard.com. **Visa** ☎ 800/847-2911 in U.S. ⊕ www.visa.com.

WORST-CASE SCENARIO

All your money and credit cards have just been stolen. In these days of real-time transactions, this isn't a predicament that should destroy your vacation. First, report the theft of the credit cards. Then get any

---

WORD OF MOUTH

Was the service stellar or not up to snuff? Did the food give you shivers of delight or leave you cold? Did the prices and portions make you happy or sad? Rate restaurants and write your own reviews in Travel Ratings or start a discussion about your favorite places in Travel Talk on www.fodors.com. Your comments might even appear in our books. Yes, you, too, can be a correspondent!

---

traveler's checks you were carrying replaced. This can usually be done almost immediately, provided that you kept a record of the serial numbers separate from the checks themselves. If you bank at a large international bank like Citibank or HSBC, go to the closest branch; if you know your account number, chances are you can get a new ATM card and withdraw money right away. **Western Union** (☎ 800/325-6000 ⊕ www.westernunion.com) sends money almost anywhere. Have someone back home order a transfer online, over the phone, or at one of the company's offices, which is the cheapest option.

TRAVELER'S CHECKS & CARDS

Some consider this the currency of the cave man, and it's true that fewer establishments accept traveler's checks these days. Nevertheless, they're a cheap and secure way to carry extra money, particularly on trips to urban areas. Both Citibank (under the Visa brand) and American Express issue traveler's checks in the United States, but Amex is better known and more widely accepted; you can also avoid hefty surcharges by cashing Amex checks at Amex offices. Whatever you do, keep track of all the serial numbers in case the checks are lost or stolen.

American Express now offers a stored-value card called a Travelers Cheque Card, which you can use wherever American Express credit cards are accepted, including ATMs. The card can carry a minimum of $300 and a maximum of $2,700, and it's a very safe way to carry your funds. Although you can get replacement funds in 24 hours if your card is lost or stolen, it doesn't really strike us as a very good deal with its high initial cost ($14.95 to set up the card, plus $5 each time you "reload") and an ATM transaction fee of $2.50. Add it all up and it can be considerably more than you would pay for simply using your own ATM card. Regular traveler's checks are just as secure and cost less.

American Express ☎ 888/412-6945 in U.S. ⊕ www.americanexpress.com.

▌TAXES

Sales tax is 5.75% in D.C., 5% in Maryland, and 4.5% in Virginia. The hotel tax varies because a local tax is added to the state tax. The result in Maryland varies from 5% to 12.5% and in Virginia from 6.5% to 12.5%; in D.C. it's 13%.

▌TIME

Maryland and Virginia are in the eastern time zone. Daylight saving time is in effect from early April through late October; eastern standard time, the rest of the year. The area is 3 hours ahead of Los Angeles, 1 hour ahead of Chicago, 5 hours behind London, and 14 hours behind Sydney.

▌TIPPING

Tipping is expected in restaurants and bars. Waiters receive 15%–20% of the total bill, depending on the level of service; for groups of six or more, a 15%–20% gratuity may be tacked onto the bill (if gratuity is covered, additional tips aren't necessary). Bartenders get $1–$2 or more, depending on the number of drinks and the number of people in the party. Taxi drivers are generally tipped 10%–15% of the total price of the ride; more if they have been particularly helpful. Doormen carrying bags to the registration desk and porters carrying bags between the lobby and the room are usually tipped $1 per bag, as are Red Caps at the airport or the train station. Chambermaids are generally tipped $1 to $3 a night for inexpensive-to-average hotels and up to $5 a night per guest for high-end properties. Barbers, hairdressers, and masseuses are usually tipped 10%–20% of the total cost of the service, depending on the place and the amount of time spent.

Tipping Guidelines for Virginia and Maryland

Bartender	$1 to $5 per round of drinks, depending on the number of drinks
Bellhop	$1 to $5 per bag, depending on the level of the hotel
Hotel Concierge	$5 or more, if he or she performs a service for you
Hotel Doorman	$1–$2 if he helps you get a cab
Hotel Maid	1$–$3 a day (either daily or at the end of your stay, in cash)
Hotel Room-Service Waiter	$1 to $2 per delivery, even if a service charge has been added
Porter at Airport or Train Station	$1 per bag
Skycap at Airport	$1 to $3 per bag checked
Taxi Driver	15%–20%, but round up the fare to the next dollar amount
Tour Guide	10% of the cost of the tour
Valet Parking Attendant	$1–$2, but only when you get your car
Waiter	15%–20%, with 20% being the norm at high-end restaurants; nothing additional if a service charge is added to the bill.and a few others
Restroom attendants	in more expensive restaurants expect some small change or $1. Tip coat-check personnel at least $1–$2 per item checked unless there is a fee, then nothing.

EFFECTIVE COMPLAINING

Things don't always go right when you're traveling, and when you encounter a problem or service that isn't up to snuff, you should complain. But there are good and bad ways to do so.

TAKE A DEEP BREATH. This is always a good strategy, especially when you are aggravated about something. Just inhale, and exhale, and remember that you're on vacation. We know it's hard for Type A people to leave it all behind, but for your own peace of mind, it's worth a try.

COMPLAIN IN PERSON WHEN IT'S SERIOUS. In a hotel, serious problems are usually better dealt with in person, at the front desk; if it's something quick, you can phone.

COMPLAIN EARLY RATHER THAN LATE. Whenever you don't get what you paid for (the type of hotel room you booked or the airline seat you pre-reserved) or when it's something timely (the people next door are making too much noise), try to resolve the problem sooner rather than later. It's always going to be harder to deal with a problem or get something taken off your bill after the fact.

BE WILLING TO ESCALATE, BUT DON'T BE HASTY. Try to deal with the person at the front desk of your hotel or with your waiter in a restaurant before asking to speak to a supervisor or manager. Not only is this polite, but when the person directly serving you can fix the problem, you'll more likely get what you want quicker.

SAY WHAT YOU WANT, AND BE REASONABLE. When things fall apart, be clear about what kind of compensation you expect. Don't leave it to the hotel or restaurant or airline to suggest what they're willing to do for you. That said, the compensation you request must be in line with the problem. You're unlikely to get a free meal because your steak was undercooked or a free hotel stay if your bathroom was dirty.

CHOOSE YOUR BATTLES. You're more likely to get what you want if you limit your complaints to one or two specific things that really matter rather than a litany of wrongs.

DON'T BE OBNOXIOUS. There's nothing that will stop your progress dead in its tracks as readily as an insistent "Don't you know who I am?" or "So what are you going to do about it?" Raising your voice will rarely get a better result.

NICE COUNTS. This doesn't mean you shouldn't be clear that you are displeased. Passive isn't good, either. When it comes right down to it, though, you'll attract more flies with sugar than with vinegar.

DO IT IN WRITING. If you discover a billing error or some other problem after the fact, write a concise letter to the appropriate customer-service representative. Keep it to one page, and as with any complaint, state clearly and reasonably what you want them to do about the problem. Don't give a detailed trip report or list a litany of problems.

INDEX

PHOTO CREDITS

NOTES

NOTES

NOTES

NOTES

NOTES

NOTES

NOTES

NOTES

NOTES

ABOUT OUR WRITERS

The updater for Western Maryland and the Eastern Shore, **Loretta Chilcoat** grew up among Maryland's cornfields. She also worked many hot summers in those very fields, stretching from Queenstown to Salisbury. As a former writer and editor at the Maryland Office of Tourism, she has insider knowledge of the state's most popular and hidden attractions—Maryland's mountain region is one of her favorite haunts. Now a freelance travel writer, Loretta has 11 guidebooks and many articles under her belt. Although it's tough at times, she enjoys traveling with her 2½-year-old daughter in search of Maryland's newest hot spots.

Matthew Cordell is a freelance writer who has also contributed to *Fodor's Boston* and *Fodor's Washinton, D.C.*

Raised in Hawaii and educated in Maryland, California, and Virginia, **John Kelly** traveled extensively as a marine, merchant mariner, and writer. For various reasons, he has visited or lived in 85 countries and speaks French and Urdu. With his wife and collaborator CiCi Williamson, his wandering continues from near Washington, D.C.

Kevin and Erica Myatt have enjoyed living in the scenic environs of Southwest Virginia for 7 and 13 years, respectively. Kevin, a copy editor at the *Roanoke Times*, writes a twice-weekly weather column for the newspaper and keeps an accompanying blog on Roanoke.com. He became familiar with Western Virginia on his many hiking trips, and ventures to many other parts of the country while chasing storms. Erica works for the *Roanoke Times* as a copy editor and edits the feature and community sections of the paper. A New York native, she grew up on the East Coast before turning to the mountains to gain degrees in history and creative writing at Hollins College in Roanoke. Kevin and Erica married in 2005 and began their honeymoon at the Homestead, featured in the Central & Western Virginia chapter.

Norman Renouf, the updater for the Richmond, Fredericksburg & the Northern Neck chapter, was born in London and educated at Charlton Secondary School, Greenwich. He started writing travel guides, articles, and newspaper essays in the early 1990s and has covered destinations throughout Europe. Norman lived in Richmond, Virginia, from the mid-90s until 2006 and wrote several guidebooks about Washington, D.C., and the mid-Atlantic region. He now makes his home in southern Spain.

Sam Sessa writes nightlife, food, and human interest features for the *Baltimore Sun* and hosts a weekly local music show for 89.7-FM WTMD. A native Marylander, he lives in a Federal Hill row house and eats crabs as often as possible.

Food and travel writer **CiCi Williamson** updated our chapter on Williamsburg and the Hampton Roads area. The author of more than 1,500 articles in newspapers and magazines and 6 cookbooks, her latest book is *The Best of Virginia Farms* travel guide and cookbook. She is also the host of a PBS series based on the book. Before turning to book writing full time, she wrote a syndicated weekly food column for 22 years in 160 newspapers across the country. She has been an updater for Fodor's for 10 years.